Psychology of Love

Edited by Lisa Diamond

cognella
San Diego, CA

First published in the United States of America in 2011 by Cognella, a division of University Readers, Inc.

15 14 13 12 11 1 2 3 4 5

Printed in the United States of America

ISBN: 978-1-60927-774-1

cognella™

www.cognella.com 800.200.3908

Contents

ORIGINS AND DEVELOPMENT OF AFFECTIONAL BONDING: ATTACHMENT

A Secure Base from Which to Explore Close Relationships

By Everett Waters and E. Mark Cummings

The theory of attachment as a secure-base relationship integrates insights about affect, cognition, and behavior in close relationships across age and culture. Empirical successes based on this theory include important discoveries about the nature of infant-caregiver and adult-adult close relationships, the importance of early experience, and about stability and change in individual differences. The task now is to preserve these insights and successes and build on them. To accomplish this, we need to continually examine the logic and coherence of attachment theory and redress errors of emphasis and analysis. Views on attachment development, attachment representation, and attachment in family and cross-cultural perspective need to be updated in light of empirical research and advances in developmental theory, behavioral biology, and cognitive psychology. We also need to challenge the theory by formulating and testing hypotheses which, if not confirmed, would require significant changes to the theory. If we can accomplish these tasks, prospects for important developments in attachment theory and research are greater than ever, as are the prospects for integration with other disciplines.

Everett Waters, E. Mark Cummings, "A Secure Base from Which to Explore Close Relationships," from *Child Development*, Vol. 71, No. 1; January/February 2000, Pp. 164–172.

For attachment theorists and researchers, the first year of this new century also marks the first year of attachment study without John Bowlby and Mary Ainsworth. Of course, we are not entirely without them. The Bowlby-Ainsworth attachment theory is a valuable legacy, and can continue to serve as a secure base from which to explore close relationships. This reflects: (1) the value of Freud's insights about the nature and importance of early relationships; (2) Bowlby's wisdom in reconceptualizing the infant-mother tie as a secure-base relationship; (3) the health and progress of control systems theory, evolutionary theory, and cognitive psychology, the sciences that underpin attachment theory; and (4) the lasting value of Ainsworth's initial ethological studies of infant attachment in Uganda and Baltimore. The task now is to enrich this legacy by rigorous theoretical and empirical analysis.

The state of the art. Advances in attachment theory have introduced productive new ideas about early relationship experience (e.g., Bretherton & Munholland, 1999; Cummings & Davies, 1996). Building on these ideas, advances in assessment (e.g., Crowell & Treboux, 1995; Davies & Cummings, 1998; Waters, 1997) have led to an explosion of research on attachment beyond infancy (e.g., Cassidy & Shaver, 1999; Greenberg, Cicchetti, & Cummings, 1990). Infants whose attachment security was assessed in the late 1970s are becoming young adults, a circumstance which offers the first opportunities to test key hypotheses about relations between infant attachment and adult love relationships (e.g., Waters, Hamilton, & Weinfield, in press).

Maintaining the coherence and empirical underpinnings of attachment theory is a continuous process of updating key ideas in light of advances in theory, data, and other areas of psychology, and subjecting the theory to severe tests, tests which, if not passed, would require us to reject the theory or at least to make significant revisions, thereby influencing subsequent research (viz., Mayo, 1996; Meehl, 1978; Smedslund, 1994).

For attachment theory, a significant challenge is to assimilate so many advances and remain coherent. The greatest risk is resting on the laurels of past successes-foregoing Bowlby's commitment to rigorous theoretical and empirical analysis-and settling for research that can at best confirm what we already know. Accordingly, this essay proposes: (1) keeping the underlying logic of Bowlby's theory and the secure-base concept at center stage in attachment theory and research, (2) updating traditional views of attachment development, function, and working models, and, (3) looking to family, life span, and cross-cultural contexts to test key postulates of attachment theory.

A secure base from which to explore. Like a secure attachment, a well-formed scientific theory encourages exploration, organizes experience, and helps one work effectively under uncertainty. In an era dominated by domain specific theory, the Bowlby-Ainsworth tradition is a rare example of a more general or "grand theory" that makes predictions about behavior and emotion across multiple domains of psychological functioning and across the life span. Accordingly, the historical origins and underlying logic of attachment theory, which are rarely considered, merit examination.

Bowlby (1958) realized sooner than many that a paradigm shift was sweeping psychoanalytic theory from the mainstream of scientific psychology. He also realized that we might, in the process, discard genuine insights about infant-mother and adult-adult relationships. Thus, a primary goal in developing modern attachment theory was to preserve the kernels of truth in Freud's insights about close relationships by replacing his image of a needy, dependent infant motivated by drive reduction with one of a sophisticated, competence-motivated infant using the primary caregiver as a secure base from which to explore and, when necessary, as a haven of safety and a source of comfort.1 Within this framework, the child's tie to his or her mother reflects the operating characteristics of an underlying control system that collates information about the infant's state, the state of the environment, and past and current access to the caregiver. Bowlby introduced the term attachment to refer specifically to this secure-base formulation of infant-adult and adult-adult ties and to distinguish it from psychodynamic and learning theory perspectives (viz., Ainsworth, 1969). It is not a generic term for relationships in general. Nor is the secure base component the only facet of relationships worth studying.

Devoted to rigorous analysis, Bowlby realized that replacing Freud's drive theory with an attachment control-system could amount to little more than replacing one kind of magic with another unless he could explain the origin and nature of behavioral control-systems. For this, he turned to evolutionary theory, arguing from many examples that such control systems reflect species-specific biases in learning abilities that can be shaped by evolution. The attachment control system is constructed during development through interaction between biases in our learning abilities and experience with caregivers and environments. These biases in our learning abilities are part of our primate heritage and are available to every human infant. Attachment control-systems are constructed through experience, not prewired, and are thought to play a role in the organization of behavior and emotion in close relationships throughout the life span.

The secure base concept is central to the logic and coherence of attachment theory and to its status as an organizational construct (Sroufe & Waters, 1977). For both Bowlby and Ainsworth, to be attached is to use someone preferentially as a secure base from which to explore. The term secure attachment refers both to* Referred to hereafter as the prototype hypothesis. Skillful secure-base use over time and contexts in naturalistic settings and to confidence in a caregiver's availability and responsiveness. Within this framework, naturalistic observations of secure-base behavior are the gold standard against which attachment measures are validated and against which they must be revalidated for use in different age groups, research populations, and cultures (Ainsworth, Blehar, Waters, & Wall, 1978; Waters, Kondo-Ikemura, Posada, & Richters, 1991).

* Referred to hereafter as the prototype hypothesis.

It is surprising, therefore, to find the secure-base concept increasingly removed from center stage in current theory and research, displaced by cognitive constructs such as *working models* and psychometric constructs such as *anxiety* and *avoidance.* Clearly, for Bowlby the working models concept represented an insight into the mental representation of appraisal and set goal components of the secure-base control system, not a new formulation to replace them. In fact, ideas about the representation of early experience play an important role in applying the secure-base concept to attachment relationships after infancy. Without the constraints imposed by the secure-base control systems framework, however, the working models concept and constructs such as anxiety and avoidance become too loosely defined and offer to explain more than they should.

It is also surprising that the secure-base concept is often overlooked as a criterion against which to validate new or traditional attachment measures when they are to be used in new age groups, at-risk samples, or across cultures. Over time, this can erode the coherence of attachment theory and research.

Insights into the nature of attachment representations and advances in measurement are always welcome. But it is important to clearly define their links to the secure-base concept. This concept is central to the logic of key insights about early experience and close relationships. Unless we want to discard these insights or develop alternative explanations, logic requires that we keep the secure-base concept at center stage in attachment theory and research.

SECURING KEY CONCEPTS

Attachment development. A detailed developmental analysis is integral to attachment theory. Bowlby's (1969/1982) developmental outline included four phases: undiscriminating social responsiveness (0–3 months), preferential social responsiveness (3–6 months), emergence of secure-base behavior (6–24 months), and goal corrected partnership (24–30+ months). Although this outline has served well, it was not meant to be the last word. In particular, it provided much more detail about the origins and onset of attachment behavior than about the fate of such behavior after infancy. In part, this was because the data at hand provided better coverage of early infancy. In addition, Bowlby emphasized the early phases because accounting for the onset and organization of attachment behavior was critical to explaining his new theory.

Unfortunately, Bowlby's emphasis on the early phase of attachment development has been a source of misunderstanding and missed opportunity misunderstanding because it suggests that secure-base behavior emerges rather quickly (which implies to some that learning and socialization play little part in his model), and missed opportunity because it doesn't direct attention to the maintaining and shaping influence of caregiver behavior or developmental changes in secure-base use beyond infancy, much less in the course of adult-adult relationships. Missed opportunities can be remedied, however. Developments in secure-base use after infancy are readily accessible to direct observation, as are corresponding changes in caregiver behavior. Figure 1 highlights key steps in the development of secure-base behavior and representations from infancy through adolescence. The contexts and patterns of caregiver support that organize developing secure-base use are on the left side of the table. These range from sensitive and cooperative interaction and explicit secure-base teaching in infancy, to a supervision partnership beginning in early childhood, to service as an experienced listener and testing ground for emerging beliefs about self, others, and relationships beginning in middle childhood and early adolescence.

Key developments in secure-base use and representation are listed on the right. These begin with mere familiarity and preference leading into an extended period of acquiring and consolidating secure-base skills in infancy and toddlerhood. This period is followed by a similarly extended period of formulating and consolidating representations of secure-base experience, expectations, and skills through adolescence. The outline also incorporates the notion that experience with peers and early romantic partners plays a significant role in this development.

Extending the time frame for attachment development and highlighting corresponding changes in care-giver behavior clarifies a number of points on which attachment theory is often misunderstood, particularly regarding openness to developmental change after infancy. It also highlights the strengths of the secure-base concept as an organizational construct. Traditionally, attachment theory has been a theory of infancy and of adult relationships, with a great deal of what lies in between left to the imagination. Completing this picture is essential to understanding the effects of early experience, the mechanisms underlying stability and change, and the relevance of ordinary socialization processes in attachment development (viz., Waters et al., 1991). In particular, more emphasis should be placed on learning-related mechanisms, especially from the second year of life onward.

Extending the time frame for attachment development also has important implications for longitudinal research. Specifically, it highlights the importance of including concurrent assessments of caregiver behavior in causal models of infant attachment and later development. Building severe tests of the mediating and moderating effects of caregiving and family dynamics into prospective, longitudinal designs is useful insurance against unstated premises and magical mechanisms slipping unnoticed into attachment theory.

Attachment in emergency and ordinary circumstances. The image of an infant fleeing to the safety of its mother's arms is one of the most evocative in human experience. Unfortunately, Bowlby's emphasis on protection from predators as *the* evolutionary function of attachment has led current theorists and researchers to focus almost exclusively on attachment as an emergency response system.* This issue is also a continuing source of

---

* In practice, the evolutionary function of a behavior is not open to empirical verification. The evolution of attachment reflects the evolution of a control system that integrates specific behaviors into a useful

Relationship Contexts and Caregiver Support	Secure-Base Behavior and Representations
Sensitive, cooperative interaction.	Infant acquires familiarity, preference, and anticipation of caregiver behavior.
Caregiver monitors infant activities, retrieves, provides explicit secure-base instruction.	Onset of secure-base use.
Infant's exploration, practice, operant learning, improved locomotion, experience.	Secure-base use consolidated.
Caregiver encourages independence, continued supervision.	Secure-base representation becomes portable, supervision partnership.
Caregiver explicitly summarizes secure-base experience; early co-construction of attachment representations.	Script-like representation of secure-base experience.
Caregiver as experienced interlocutor; peers as ad hoc secure-base figures; peer demands for secure-base support.	Applying representations of past experience to organize secure-base use and service in romantic relationships; elaboration and consolidation of attachment representations.
Caregiver's reactions to relationship decisions; caregivers' and peers' relationships as models.	Discovery of implicit expectations, preferences, and sensitivities; reflection on successes and failures.

Figure 1 The secure-base phenomenon from infancy to adolescence.

misunderstanding and missed opportunities for assessment, hypothesis testing, and new directions in attachment research.

For Bowlby and Ainsworth, the ability to use an attachment Figure as a secure base affords a child a haven of safety and also provides the confidence necessary to explore and master ordinary environments. As currently formulated, attachment theory implies that a single control system appraises access to the caregiver and maintains a balance between proximity and exploration across both ordinary and emergency situations. This is supported by the fact that both emergency behavior in the Strange Situation and affect regulation in response to stressful attachment-related stories are closely related to nonemergency attachment behavior at home (Ainsworth et al., 1978; Lay, Waters, Posada, & Ridgeway, 1995; Vaughn & Waters, 1990). In addition, mothers' representations of attachment experiences in both ordinary and emergency situations strongly predict their ability to serve as a secure base for their children in ordinary free-play situations (e.g., Gao & Waters, 1999; Posada, Waters, Crowell, & Lay, 1995).

Attachment in ordinary and emergency situations deserves high priority in both developmental and cross-cultural research. Evidence that they are consistently related would be strong support for Bowlby's notion of an underlying attachment control system. It would also open up a wide range of new possibilities for attachment assessment and new research on the effects of early experience. Evidence to the contrary would affect how we frame and test hypotheses about early experience. It might even require significant changes in current attachment theory.

behavioral system; it does not reflect the evolution of those specific behaviors themselves. Although predator avoidance may have played a role in the evolution of specific behaviors, that is far too narrow a construction to place on the secure-base phenomenon.

The child's construction of security. As mentioned above, the attachment control system emerges from extended interplay of biases in human learning abilities with sensitive, cooperative care and secure-base support. In infancy, experience with a particular caregiver can only be retained in the form of sensorimotor and sensori-affective representations. These forms of representation reflect only the behavioral possibilities and affective responses associated in experience with a particular person in a particular affective-behavioral context. They cannot be accessed voluntarily or in situations very different from the ones they reflect (viz., Sroufe, 1996). True symbolic representations of experience do not emerge until after infancy.

Bowlby was keenly aware that cognitive and conceptual development had implications for attachment after infancy. Even as he was detailing his ideas about attachment onset and development in infancy, he marked these issues for future study by including the goal corrected partnership in his developmental outline.

Acquiring the capacity for symbolic representation has significant implications for (1) what defines a "secure base" and (2) the kinds of information that shape secure-base expectations. The speech and behavior of toddlers and young children suggest that they (at least implicitly) construe "my parents," "my family," and perhaps even broader reference groups as sources of security. Better understanding these implications has become critical to developing the secure-base concept for use beyond infancy and early childhood. The task is made easier and the prospects brighter by the successes of social cognition theory and research in developmental, social, and clinical psychology.

After infancy, social (observational) learning also emerges as an important influence on secure-base expectations. The onset of social learning greatly expands the child's store of attachment-related information beyond what can be learned by direct interaction. On the positive side, noting skillful and consistent support of other family members can broaden a child's sense that the primary caregiver will be willing and able to serve as a secure base in any and all situations. On the negative side, unresolved family conflict and other evidence of adult's limitations can diminish a child's confidence in a caregiver's power or availability to provide support in difficult situations (viz., Cummings & Davies, 1996).

Cognitive development also has important implications for understanding (1) the child's view of the family as a source of security, and (2) how, by early adolescence, friends, teachers, and other people with whom the child is close may be used selectively as secure-base Figures of convenience in specific contexts. Close attention to links between cognitive development and representations of secure-base experience can play an important role in clarifying both the content and organization of attachment *working models.*

These are important issues. Unless we can define the content and organization of attachment working models rigorously, they soon take on properties as needed, push aside more parsimonious explanations, and ultimately attempt to explain too much (Hinde,

1988). Fortunately, as Bowlby had hoped, cognitive psychology today offers concepts and methods that can help us formulate and test a wide variety of hypotheses about the representation of early experience. Significant collaboration among cognitive and social psychologists is long overdue and would be a valuable contribution to the next phase of attachment theory and research.

Security in family context. One of the cornerstones of modern developmental theory is the notion that dyadic relationships are nested within broader contexts (Bronfenbrenner, 1979). The family is one of the most influential of these contexts. Bowlby (1949) was one of the first to point out the need to consider the family in understanding children's distress and security. Applying secure-base and control system concepts to the family context can be a fertile source of new insights about relationships and development. For example, Cummings and Davies (1994) pointed out that infants and older children respond very differently to resolved versus unresolved family conflict. Even when both parents are readily accessible, children become distressed about and often intervene in the unresolved conflicts, which suggests that secure-base access and coherent family relations are distinct sources of emotion regulation and security.

Consistent with this study and others on children's reactions to family stresses, Cummings and Davies (1996) proposed a control system model for children's security as a function of multiple family relationships and events. Within this model, a wide range of emotional, behavioral, and representational processes are organized by the overarching goal of preserving emotional security. Davies and Cummings (1998) provided direct support for this model by demonstrating that children's emotional security about marital conflict mediates relations between marital conflict and child outcomes. This explicit theoretical model and emphasis on rigorous operationalization of constructs afford strong tests of the notion that security mediates links between family-wide functioning and child outcomes.

Byng-Hall (1995, 1999) has also proposed an extension of the secure-base notion to the family as a whole. Based on a clinical perspective, he has stressed the importance to children's well-being of a reliable family network and a *secure family base*, with a shared awareness among family members that attachments should be protected and not undermined (see also Marvin & Stewart, 1990). Explorations of attachment in family context and the extension of the secure-base construct to family-wide models is an important challenge for attachment theory. It is also an essential step toward realizing Bowlby's goal of significant clinical applications.

Secure-base use and secure-base support in adult relationships. As mentioned above, the notion that across the life span close relationships are similar in kind was one of Freud's most daring speculations. Although rarely explicitly stated in current theory or research, it is reflected in the notion that attachment theory is relevant across the life span and in the notion that early relationship experience influences later development. The first step in testing this hypothesis is to apply Ainsworth's conceptualizations of secure-base use and secure-base support in infancy to adult's close relationships. Successfully measuring

Relationship Contexts and Partner Support	Secure-Base Behavior and Representations
Partner supports exploration and personal goals; partner requires secure-base support.	Commitment in adult partnership; secure-base support of friends and junior partners (mentoring).
Transition to parenthood.	Close coordination with partner; balancing parenthood with other goals; drawing upon secure-base experience to organize and motivate secure-base support for partner and child.
Children require extended secure-base support.	Serving as secure base for children; effectively requesting and using partner's (and parents') support in parenthood.
Emergencies; aging parents and partner.	Secure-base service outside of parenting.
Aging; increased need for secure-base support in ordinary activities.	Requesting and accepting secure-base support from partner, children, and others.

Figure 2 The secure-base phenomenon in adulthood.

secure-base use and support in adults would lend considerable support to attachment theory, provide a criterion against which to validate measures of adult attachment security, and help clarify the origins and functioning of close relationships in adulthood. Failure to find secure base behavior in adults would undermine the notion that attachment theory is relevant across the life span, rendering it, perhaps, little more than a domain-specific theory of infant-caregiver relationships.

Crowell, Gao, Pan, & Waters (1997) have taken first steps in this direction by developing scales for assessing adults' skill at serving as and using the partner as a secure base during 15-minute discussions of marital disagreements. Serving as a secure base is assessed in terms of criteria derived from Ainsworth et al.'s (1978) conceptualization of maternal sensitivity. It entails detecting the partner's implied or explicit requests for secure-base support, correctly interpreting the request, and responding appropriately and in a timely manner. Secure-base use is assessed in terms of criteria derived from Ainsworth et al.'s conceptualization of secure response in the Strange Situation. Key features include clearly signaling the need for secure-base support, maintaining signals until they are detected, openness to the partner's response, and finding appropriate response comforting.

Preliminary results (Gao & Waters, 1998) indicate that secure-base use and support are indeed evident in couples' interactions. Moreover, as predicted from the notion that both are organized by the same secure base control system, they are significantly correlated. They are also significantly correlated with the coherence of attachment representations derived from the couples' experience with their own parents and the relationships to each other.* These results provide preliminary support for the notion that close adult-adult relationships have significant secure-base components.

Secure-base use and support are not limited to the early phases of adult relationships or to early adulthood. New demands for secure-base use and opportunities to serve as a secure base arise throughout life. Figure 2 outlines a typical course of secure-base use and

* Social psychologists interested in adult attachment have also begun to examine relations between attachment security and secure-base behavior in adults (viz., Crowell, Fraley, & Shaver, 1999).

support across the span of adulthood. As in Figure 1, the contexts and patterns of support that organize secure-base use in adulthood are on the left side of the Figure and patterns of secure-base use are on the right. This extended developmental outline opens up many new opportunities to study the influences of early experience on later attachment behavior. Particularly important is the opportunity to examine relations between early attachment experience and *both* secure-base use and secure-base support skills later in life, and to examine them across contexts such as marriage, parenting, caring for adult parents, and requesting care from others. As currently formulated, attachment theory suggests that these are all organized by the same attachment control system and that skills would be correlated across these domains. Empirical evidence on this point could either provide strong support for this formulation or suggest a more differentiated view of attachment representations.

The task of better assessing secure-base use and support throughout adulthood deserves high priority in attachment research. Traditional views of close adult relationships focus primarily on processes in play when relationships are in distress. But just as peace is not merely the absence of war, the best close relationships offer adults more than well-regulated or benign conflicts. A secure-base perspective on close relationships in adulthood offers a rich framework for conceptualizing and studying both troubled and successful relationships. The possibilities here are exciting and suggest new directions in research on adult development and marriage. They also suggest that attachment theory and research can serve as a useful organizational framework for prevention, intervention, and outcome research, and eventually for clinical practice.

Attachment across cultures. Cross-cultural research on key issues in attachment theory is one of the most exciting prospects for the next generation of attachment research. At the present time, however, the implications of attachment theory for attachment across cultures are widely misunderstood. Some of the misunderstanding can be traced to Bowlby's use of concepts and examples from classical ethology to support the notion that the kinds of learning biases necessary to account for an attachment control system can be shaped by natural selection. Bowlby's references to (1) attachment as part of our primate heritage, (2) imprinting and critical periods, (3) the importance of early care in the onset of attachment, (4) the relatively quick onset of attachment behavior in infancy, and (5) the enduring impact of early experience have led some to misconstrue and sometimes caricature his perspective as a modern instinct theory with strong assumptions about universality across cultures. These include the notion that the distribution of Strange Situation classifications should be similar across cultures.

In fact, close reading of Attachment and Loss (Bowlby, 1969) supports a more sophisticated view. For Bowlby, the function of secure-base relationships is always to support competence development and promote safety. This function is enhanced by access to (and confidence in) a sensitive and responsive secure-base figure. Attachment theory *does* assume that sensitivity to infant signals, cooperative interaction, availability, and responsiveness play a role in attachment development. It *does not* assume that these are equally prevalent in every culture or community, or that the distribution of Strange Situation classifications would be similar across cultures.

Moreover, the logic of modern attachment theory easily accommodates: (1) the fact that the Strange Situation is not valid in every culture, (2) the use of multiple caregivers, (3) cultural influences, especially after infancy, on how caregiver availability and responsiveness are communicated, (4) communities or cultures in which attachment relationships are not the most salient factors in socialization and social adjustment, and (5) the fact that circumstances and social systems do not always give free rein to humans' capacity to form and maintain secure-base relationships.

Thus, data on the distribution of Strange Situation classifications *per se* say little about the relevance of attachment theory across cultures. In contrast, studies examining the cross-cultural generality of (1) secure-base behavior and (2) the relation of caregiver behavior to the organization of secure-base behavior afford very useful tests of key attachment theory postulates. In the only study that has directly addressed the generality of secure-base behavior, Posada et al. (1995) found evidence of secure-base organization in all seven of the cultures they studied. In addition, Posada, Jacobs, Carbonell, Alzate, Bustamante, and Arenas (1999) have recently reported strong correlations (.45-.60) between maternal sensitivity and infant secure-base behavior in samples of Colombian infants observed in home and hospital settings. These studies are models of cross-cultural research that closely track the logic of modern attachment theory and thus afford severe tests of key postulates. This is one of the most exciting directions in recent attachment theory and research, and promises to bring cross-cultural perspectives back into the mainstream of attachment study.

Attachment and human security. As we enter this new era, attachment theorists seem more comfortable than ever exploring new directions. If we are mindful of the central role of the secure-base concept and the control systems model, and put well-formed hypotheses to severe tests, the theory can continue to evolve without losing its coherence or overreaching. Pushing the secure-base and control system concepts to their limits is part of fully understanding them and provides a source of new insights about relationships and development. It can also be a source of insights into the place of attachment in the grand scheme of things.

Although attachment theory captures important features of security provision across the life span, it doesn't exhaust them. Clearly there are many other assets and circumstances that can also contribute the sense of security (broadly construed). Although a responsive, available caregiver may be the primary source of security in infancy, by middle childhood social relationships, athletic and academic competence, physical assets, and traits such as patience, bravery, or common sense can also be important sources of security. By adulthood, the list has expanded to include social alliances, status, and a broad array of assets that are important across cultures (e.g., good health, experience, wealth) and

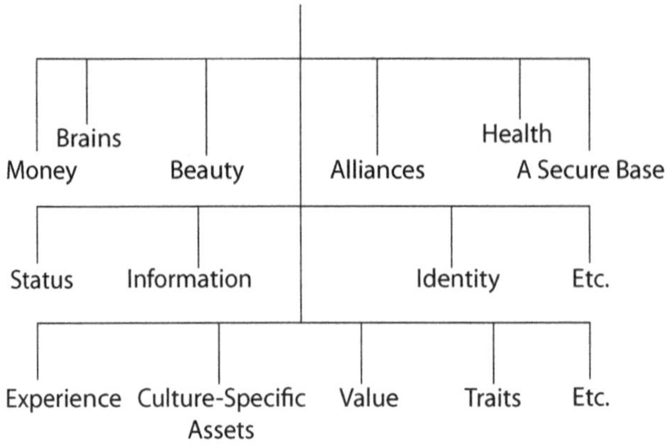

Figure 3 Some sources of human security.

culture-specific assets (e.g., religious values, rank, and socially valued traits). Figure 3 outlines some of the sources of human security. The common thread among them is that in one way or another each reduces uncertainty about the risks involved in exploration or in novel (including emergency) situations. The role of attachment Figures in children's acquiring, conceptualizing, and learning to effectively use such assets deserves high priority in research on socialization and personality development.

That attachment relationships may be integral to many sources of human security does not imply that the Bowlby-Ainsworth perspective promises a general theory of human security. As we have mentioned, Bowlby's attachment concept refers to a very specific range of phenomena. It is about secure-base use and secure-base support in the context of close relationships that involve significant emotional bonds. It is too much to expect it to serve as a general framework for understanding human security or personality. Instead, the challenge is to find a scientific framework within which we can understand the many sources of human security, their interplay, and the roles of security in social development, personality, relationships, and adjustment. Although Bowlby's integrative approach to theory building can serve as a model for first steps in this direction, the answer lies in placing attachment theory in the context of broader perspectives such as developmental psychopathology or cognitive self theory.

CONCLUSION

These are interesting times in attachment theory and research. For some, the issues we have raised are overdue; others may disagree. We have tried to keep to issues that can be addressed by explicating theoretical differences and putting them to empirical tests. This was a strength of Bowlby's and Ainsworth's approach to preserving Freud's insights about early experience and close relationships. It can serve equally well as we try to do for Bowlby and Ainsworth what they did for Freud-identify key insights, redress errors of analysis and emphasis, and enrich their legacy.

Psychology's grand theories rarely survive to celebrate a silver anniversary. In this era of specialization and domain-specific theory, many have concluded that grand theory is unattainable or even discredited as a way of organizing and guiding empirical research (viz., McKinney, 1976). Nonetheless, its promise remains attractive (e.g., Berscheid, 1995; Toews, 1985).

Measured from Bowlby's (1958) paper, "The nature of the child's tie to its mother," modern attachment theory is entering its fifth decade. With continued commitment to rigorous theoretical and empirical analysis, it promises to reach its silver anniversary more coherent and productive than ever, a fine legacy from John Bowlby and Mary Ainsworth that reflects well on developmental psychology and on the tradition of grand theory in the behavioral sciences.

ACKNOWLEDGMENTS

The authors would like to thank Judith Crowell, Melanie Elliot, Dominique Treboux, Brian Vaughn, Polly Vittorini, and Harriet Waters for valuable editorial comments. Preparation of this paper was supported in part by grants from the National Institute of Mental Health (MH 44935) to Everett Waters and Judith Crowell and from the National Institute of Child Health and Human Development (HD 36261) to Mark Cummings.

ADDRESSES AND AFFILIATIONS

Corresponding author: Everett Waters, Department of Psychology, SUNY, Stony Brook, NY 11794–2500; e-mail: everett.waters@sunysb.edu. E. Mark Cummings is at Notre Dame University, Notre Dame, IN.

REFERENCES

Ainsworth, M. D. S. (1969). Object relations, dependency, and attachment: A theoretical review of the infant-mother relationship. *Child Development, 40*, 969–1025.

Ainsworth, M., Blehar, M., Waters, E., & Wall, S. (1978). *Patterns of attachment.* Hillsdale, NJ: Erlbaum.

Berscheid, E. (1995). Help wanted: A grand theorist of interpersonal relationships, sociologist or anthropologist preferred. *Journal of Social and Personal Relationships, 12*, 529- 533.

Bowlby, J. (1949). The study and reduction of group tensions in the family. *Human Relations, 2*, 123–128.

Bowlby, J. (1958). The nature of the child's tie to its mother. *International Journal of Psycho-analysis, 39*, 350–373.

Bowlby, J. (1982). *Attachment and loss: Vol. 1. Attachment.* London: Hogarth Press. (Original work published in 1969)

Bretherton, I., & Munholland, K. (1999). Internal working models in attachment relationships: A construct revisited. In J. Cassidy & P. Shaver (Eds.), *Handbook of attachment: Theory, research, & clinical applications* (pp. 89–111). New York: Guilford Press.

Bronfenbrenner, U. (1979). *The ecology of human development.* Cambridge: Harvard University Press.

Byng-Hall, J. (1995). Creating a secure family base: Some implications of attachment theory for family therapy. *Family Process, 34*, 45–58.

Byng-Hall, J. (1999). Family and couple therapy. In J. Cassidy & P. Shaver (Eds.), *Handbook of attachment: Theory, research, and clinical applications* (pp. 625–645). New York: Guilford Press.

Cassidy, J., & Shaver, P. (Eds.). (1999). *Handbook of attachment: Theory, research, and clinical applications.* New York: Guilford Press.

Crowell, J., Fraley, R. C., & Shaver, P. (1999). Measurement of individual differences in adolescent and adult attachment. In J. Cassidy & P. Shaver (Eds.), *Handbook of attachment: Theory, research, and clinical applications* (pp. 434- 465). New York: Guilford Press.

Crowell, J., Gao, Y., Pan, H., & Waters, E. (1997). *The Secure-Base Scoring System for adults (SBSS).* Unpublished measure. SUNY, Stony Brook, NY.

Crowell, J., & Treboux, D. (1995). A review of adult attachment measures: Implications for theory and research. *Social Development, 4*, 294–327.

Cummings, E. M., & Davies, P. (1994). *Children and marital conflict: The impact of family dispute and resolution.* New York and London: Guilford Press.

Cummings, E. M., & Davies, P. (1996). Emotional security as a regulatory process in normal development and the development of psychopathology. *Development and Psycho-pathology, 8*, 123–139.

Davies, P., & Cummings, E. M. (1998). Exploring children's emotional security as a mediator of the link between marital relations and child adjustment. *Child Development*, 69, 124–139.

Gao, Y., & Waters, E. (1998, June). *Secure base behavior and attachment security in engaged couples.* Paper presented at the meeting of the International Society for the Study of Personal Relationships, Saratoga Springs, NY.

Greenberg, M., Cicchetti, D., & Cummings, M. (Eds.). (1990). *Attachment in the preschool years: Theory, research, and intervention.* Chicago: University of Chicago Press.

Hinde, R. (1988). Continuities and discontinuities. In M. Rutter (Ed.), *Studies of psychosocial risk: The power of longitudinal data* (pp. 367–384). Cambridge, UK: Cambridge University Press.

Lay, K., Waters, E., Posada, G., & Ridgeway, D. (1995). Attachment security, affect regulation, and defensive responses to mood induction. In E. Waters, B. Vaughn, G. Posada, & K.

Kondo-Ikemura (Eds.), *Caregiving, cultural, and cognitive perspectives on secure-base behavior and working models: New growing points of attachment theory and research. Monographs of the Society for Research in Child Development, 60*(2–3, Serial No. 244), 179–196.

Marvin, R., & Stewart, R. B., (1990). A family systems framework for the study of attachment. In M. Greenberg, D. Cicchetti, & M. Cummings (Eds.), *Attachment in the preschool years: Theory, research, and intervention* (pp. 51–86). Chicago: University of Chicago Press.

Mayo, D. (1996). *Error and the growth of experimental knowledge.* Chicago: University of Chicago Press.

McKinney, F. (1976). Fifty years of psychology. *American Psychologist, 31*, 834–842.

Meehl, P. E. (1978). Theoretical risks and tabular asterisks: Sir Karl, Sir Ronald, and the slow progress of soft psychology. *Journal of Consulting and Clinical Psychology, 46*(4), 806–834.

Posada, G., Jacobs, A., Carbonell, O., Alzate, G., Bustamante, M., & Arenas, A. (1999). Maternal care and attachment security in ordinary and emergency contexts. *Developmental Psychology, 35*, 1379–1388.

Posada, G., Gao, Y., Wu, F., Posada, R., Tascon, M., Schöel-merich, A., Sagi, A., Kondo-Ikemura, K., Haaland, W., & Synnevaag, B. (1995). The secure base phenomenon across cultures: Children's behavior, mothers' preferences, and experts' concepts. In E. Waters, B. Vaughn, G. Posada, & K. Kondo-Ikemura (Eds.), *Caregiving, cultural, and cognitive perspectives on secure-base behavior and working models: New growing points of attachment theory and research. Monographs of the Society for Research in Child Development, 60*(2–3, Serial No. 244), 27–48.

Posada, G., Waters, E., Crowell, J., & Lay, K. L. (1995). Is it easier to use a secure mother as a secure base: Attachment Q-sort correlates of the Berkeley Adult Attachment Interview. In E. Waters, B. Vaughn, G. Posada, & K. Kondo-Ikemura (Eds.), *Caregiving, cultural, and cognitive perspectives on secure-base behavior and working models: New growing points of attachment theory and research. Monographs of the Society for Research in Child Development, 60*(2–3, Serial No. 244), 133–145.

Smedslund, J. (1994). What kind of propositions are set forth in developmental research? Five case studies. *Human Development, 37*, 280–292.

Sroufe, L. A. (1996). Emotional Development: The organization of emotional life in the early years. *Cambridge Studies in Social and Emotional Development.* New York: Cambridge University Press.

Sroufe, L. A., & Waters, E. (1977). Attachment as an organizational construct. *Child Development, 48*, 1184–1199.

Toews, J. E. (1985). The return of grand theory in the human sciences. *The American Historical Review, 92*, 879–907.

Vaughn, B., & Waters, E. (1990). Attachment behavior at home and in the laboratory: Q-sort observations and Strange Situation classifications of one-year-olds. *Child Development, 61*, 1965–1973.

Waters, E. (1997). *The attachment Q-set advisor* [Online]. Available: http://www.psychology.sunysb.edu/ewaters/ measures/aqs.htm.

Waters, E., Hamilton, C., & WeinFIeld, N. (in press). The stability of attachment security from infancy to adolescence and early adulthood: General introduction. *Child Development.*

Waters, E., Kondo-Ikemura, K., Posada, G., & Richters, J. (1991). Learning to love: Mechanisms and milestones. In M. Gunner & A. Sroufe (Eds.), *Minnesota Symposia on Child Psychology: Vol. 23. Self processes and development.* (pp. 217–255). Hillsdale, NJ: Erlbaum. [Available online: www.psychology.psy.sunysb.edu/ewaters]

Sex and The Psychological Tether

By Cindy Hazan and Debra Zeifman

The scientific study of relationships is a relatively new but rapidly growing field that crosses several disciplines (Duck, 1988; Perlman & Jones, 1993). A review of this now voluminous empirical literature indicates that sexual aspects of relationships have not been the focus of much research. Yet sex is a very important ingredient of some relationships, most notably romantic ones. Sex researchers (e.g., Kinsey, Masters & Johnson) have emphasized the physical more than the psychological aspects of sex, and have focused on *individual* sexual behavior and response rather than on sexual *relationships* between individuals. Relationship researchers have virtually ignored the sexual aspects of relationships, especially relative to such phenomena as intimacy, trust, jealousy, equity, communication, and commitment (McKinney & Sprecher, 1991). As Berscheid (1988) says, this omission is like leaving the tiger out of a recipe for tiger soup.

Within attachment theory (Bowlby, 1969/1982, 1973, 1980, 1988), sex is viewed as an integral part of adult romantic relationships. Nevertheless, issues concerning the multiple functions of sex within a relationship and its changing nature and importance over the course of a developing relationship have not been systematically addressed within attachment theory or research. These issues will be explored in this chapter.

In the first part of the chapter, we present results from two recent studies which indicate that, beyond infancy, attachments are formed almost exclusively with sexual partners. In

Cindy Hazan, Debra Zeifman; K. Bartholomew, D. Perlman, eds., "Sex and the Psychological Tether," from *Advancements in Personal Relationships: A Research Annual*, Vol. 5, Pp. 151–177. Copyright © 1994 by Jessica Kingsley Publishers . Permission to reprint granted by the publisher.

the second part, we draw upon empirical findings from diverse sources and disciplines to derive a conceptualization of the role of sexual interest and sexual behavior in adolescent and adult attachment relationships.

ATTACHMENT FORMATION AND TRANSFER

Ethological attachment theory (Bowlby, 1969/1982, 1973, 1980) grew out of the observation that infants and young children behave in ways that maintain a degree of physical proximity to their primary caregivers and are distressed by separations from them. On the basis of his observations and the well-documented similarity of behavior in nonhuman primates (Harlow, 1958), Bowlby postulated the existence of an inborn behavioral system that evolved to protect infants from danger and maximize safe exploration by regulating proximity to a caregiver. According to this control-systems model, the infant has a 'set-goal' for caregiver proximity; a discrepancy between the set-goal and actual proximity activates the system. Once sufficient proximity is restored, the attachment system becomes quiescent, potentiating the activation of other behavioral systems such as exploration or affiliation. Bowlby argued that these various inborn behavioral systems, which help ensure that important needs are met, developed as a result of selection pressures over the course of human evolution. Like other species whose young are born relatively immature and require a long period of care and protection if they are to survive, humans are innately predisposed to form attachment bonds (Bowlby, 1969/1982).

Defining Attachment

Attachments are defined in terms of four components: proximity seeking, separation protest, safe haven, and secure base (Ainsworth, Blehar, Waters & Wall, 1978; Bowlby, 1988). The components are most readily observable in the behavior of infants in relation to their caregivers. Infants tend to *seek and maintain proximity* to an attachment figure and *resist separations.* In the presence of the attachment figure, they usually show interest in exploring the physical environment. Movement away from the attachment figure for exploratory purposes is referred to as the *secure base* function of attachment. If a threat is perceived, infants will typically cease exploratory activity and retreat to their attachment figures for comfort and reassurance - referred to as the *safe haven* function. (The components are represented in Figure 1.)

A basic assumption of Bowlby's theory is that attachment behavior characterizes humans across the life span, from 'the cradle to the grave' (Bowlby, 1979). Until recently, researchers have focused almost exclusively on attachment during infancy and childhood. In the last several years, however, adult relationship researchers have begun to test the life span developmental implications of attachment theory (e.g.,

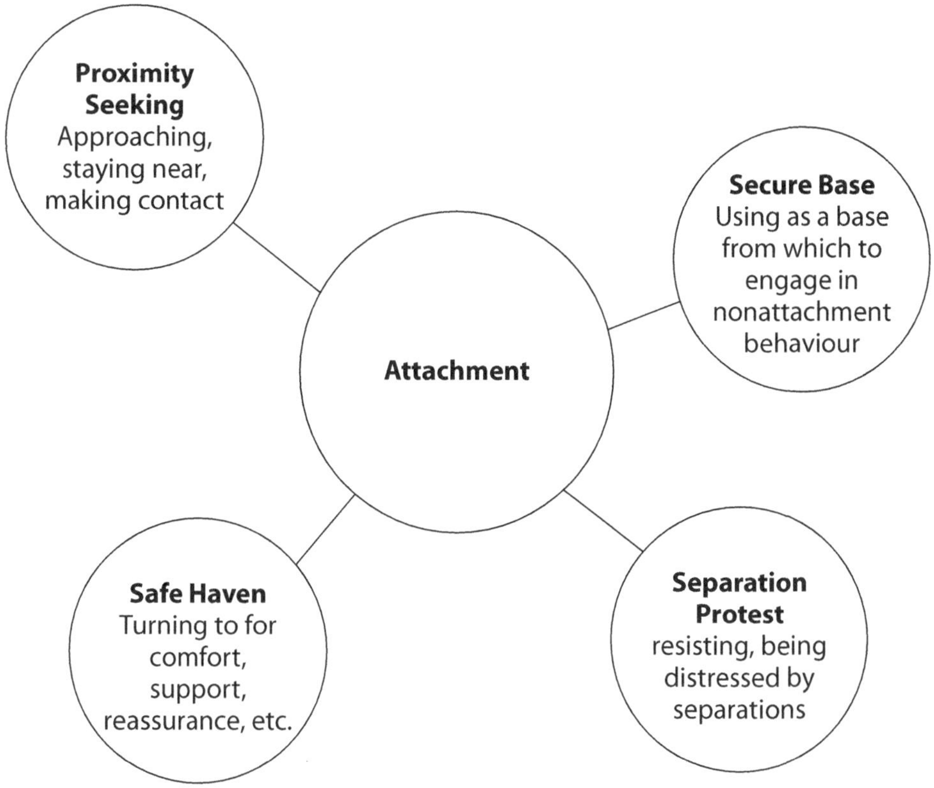

Figure 1. The components of attachment

Bartholomew, 1990; Collins & Read, 1990; Feeney & Noller, 1990; Hazan & Shaver, 1987; Kirk-patrick & Davis, in press; Kobak & Hazan, 1991; Main, Kaplan & Cassidy, 1985; Simpson, 1990). Results of these and other studies provide robust evidence in support of Bowlby's original claims concerning the nature of evidence in support of Bowlby's original claims concerning the nature of attachment relationships and their importance throughout life. Further, the findings are consistent with the claim that the *dynamics* of attachment (i.e., the activation and deactivation of the attachment system and its effects on other systems) as well as the *features and functions* of attachment relationships (e.g., safe haven, secure base) are essentially the same in infancy and adulthood.

Although infant and adult attachments are similar in many respects, they also differ in important ways (Weiss, 1982). One of the most significant developmental changes occurring between infancy and adulthood is in the *mutuality* of attachments. During infancy and childhood, attachment relationships are complementary (i.e., asymmetric). Infants seek security from their attachment figures but do not provide security in return; attachment figures provide care to, but do not typically seek care from, their infants. Two

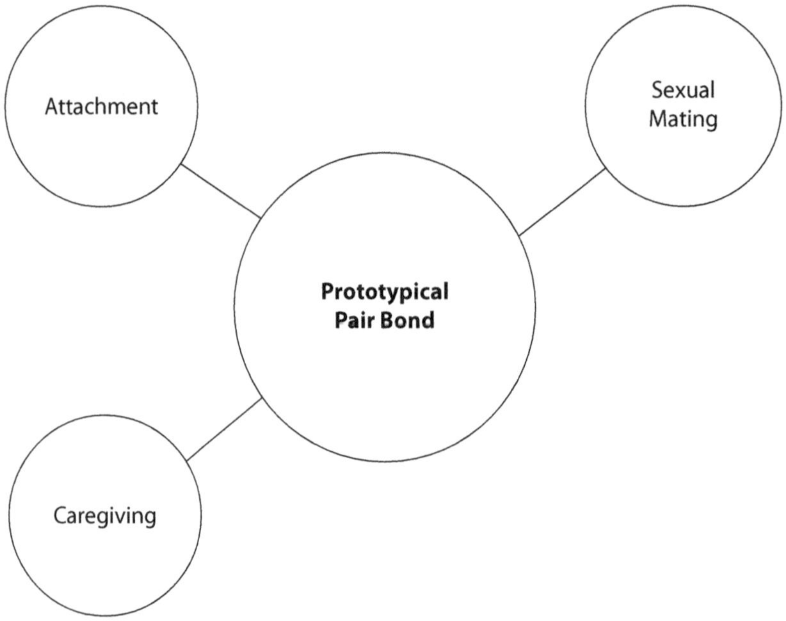

Figure 2. The components of a prototypical pair bond

different behavioral systems are presumed to be involved: the infant's attachment system and the attachment figure's caregiving system.

In contrast, adult attachment relationships are expected to be more reciprocal (i.e., symmetric), with each member of the dyad serving both as a provider and a recipient of care, a seeker of security as well as a target of security-seeking (Bowlby, 1969; Weiss, 1982). Another difference is that, in adulthood, reciprocal attachments are assumed to be formed primarily with sexual partners. Thus, in the course of normative development, sex becomes an integral part of attachment. The prototype of a reciprocal peer attachment (pair bond) is one that involves the integration of three behavioral systems - attachment, caregiving, and sexual mating (Bowlby, 1969; Shaver, Hazan & Bradshaw, 1988). (See Figure 2.)

There are, of course, other developmental changes in attachment. A typical 12-month old cries when his or her caregiver leaves the immediate vicinity, whereas a 36-month old can happily spend an entire day in nursery school. By adulthood, attached pairs can endure long separations without undue distress, although sudden, permanent, or greatly extended separations do evoke anxiety and protest behaviors (Weiss, 1988; Vormbrock, 1993). Most infants need actual physical contact when distressed but, by early childhood, can be soothed by telephone contact or even by verbal reassurances that contact is forthcoming. Adults can derive comfort from the mere belief that contact will be possible at some future point. Nevertheless, actual physical contact continues to serve as a necessary ingredient for maintaining the attachment bond and feelings of security for both children and adults.

Thus, attachment theory predicts developmental changes as well as continuities. Whereas the dynamics and functions of attachment are hypothesized to be similar across the lifespan, *structural* changes- specifically the shift from complementary to reciprocal attachments and the integration of sex - are predicted to occur as one moves from infancy, through childhood and adolescence, into adulthood.

Given the opportunity, all normal human infants become attached to their primary caregiver, typically within the first eight months of life. Whether secondary attachments to other people are formed simultaneously or only after a primary attachment has been established is open to debate, but there is no doubt that infants and children *do* form multiple attachments. Bonds that satisfy the criteria for being attachments - for instance that include proximity maintenance and safe haven and secure base behaviors - are commonly developed with several people.

Although multiple attachments are the norm, attachment figures are not treated equivalently Infants show clear discrimination and consistent preferences for the *primary* caregiver (Colin, 1985, 1987; Cummings, 1980; Farran & Ramey, 1977). Even if several caregivers are regularly available, infants reliably seek and maintain proximity to one, especially when tired or ill (Ainsworth, 1967,1982). Infants also exhibit more intense protest on being left by the primary attachment figure as compared to others (Schaffer & Emerson, 1964) and, in unfamiliar settings, are most reassured by the presence of the primary figure (Ricciuti, 1974; Shill, Solyom & Biven, 1984).

Bowlby (1969/1982) referred to this tendency of a child to form a special attachment to one person as 'monotropy'.

Multiple attachments are hypothesized to be hierarchically arranged. At the top of the hierarchy is the primary attachment figure. Over the course of development, many changes may occur in the content and structure of an individual's attachment hierarchy. People may be added to or dropped from the hierarchy. Parental figures tend to be permanent members of the hierarchy, although their positions naturally change as a child matures. Bowlby hypothesized that, with the formation of a pair bond in adulthood, the sexual partner assumes the position of primary attachment figure and ascends to the top of the hierarchy. When and by what process this change occurs is not specified within attachment theory.

Study 1: Age-Related Changes in the Target of Attachment Behaviors

Background and objectives

The shift from complementary to reciprocal attachments constitutes a major life transition but little is known about how and when primary attachment bonds are transferred from parents to peers, or how the bonds themselves are transformed in the process. What is known about this transition comes largely from the empirical literature on child and adolescent peer relations.

Peer relationships during this period of development are best characterized as affiliative relationships, which is functionally different from attachment relationships and believed to be regulated by a different behavioral system. The primary function of affiliative relationships is to provide stimulation and pleasure (as opposed to the comfort and security provisions of attachment relationships). However, a review of the existing research suggests that *some* components of attachment are evident in peer relationships during childhood and adolescence. For example, interest in and attraction to peers begins early in development. By about age 3, children are capable of engaging in complex social interactions with age-mates and show increasing interest in them (Gottman, 1983; Rubin, 1980). More and more time is spent in the company of peers relative to parents. Thus, one component of attachment - proximity seeking - is present in peer relationships by early childhood, although such relationships do not qualify as attachments in the full sense of the term.

By middle childhood, children become capable of developing intimate relationships with their peers (Furman & Buhrmester, 1985; Hartup, 1983; Lewis, 1982) and increasingly turn to each other for comfort. The confiding and emotional support evident in peer relationships at this age appears to be functionally similar to the safe haven behaviors observed in infancy. By late adolescence, peers come to be preferred over parents as sources of emotional support (Steinberg & Silverberg, 1986).

Thus, it appears that there may be developmental changes in the *target* of different attachment behaviors, such that between childhood and adolescence some components of attachment get shifted from parents to peers. The nature and timing of this transfer and the processes by which it is accomplished are not easily delineated on the basis of existing research or theory. Based on evidence that peer relationships do not typically satisfy all the definitional criteria of attachment but, depending on the age of the individuals, are characterized by some attachment features, we thought a key to understanding the transfer of attachment from parents to peers might lie in analysis of attachment at the level of components.

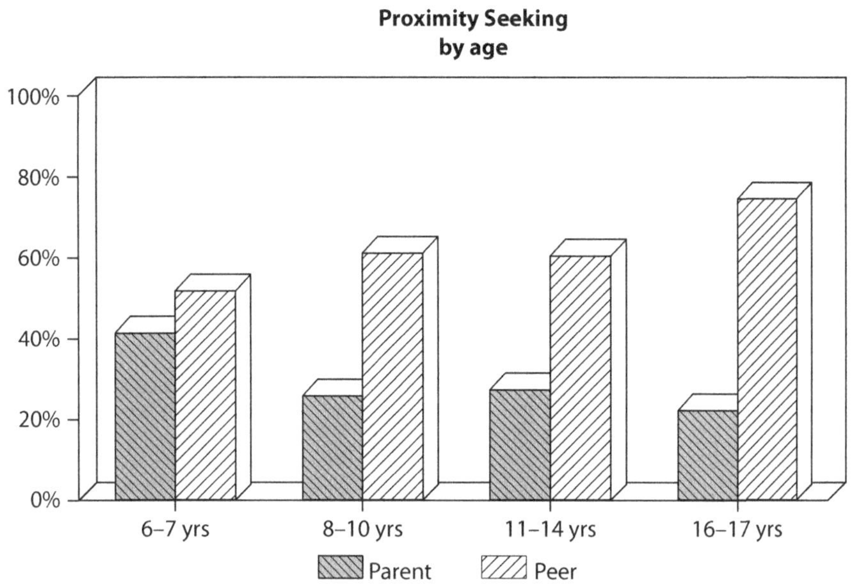

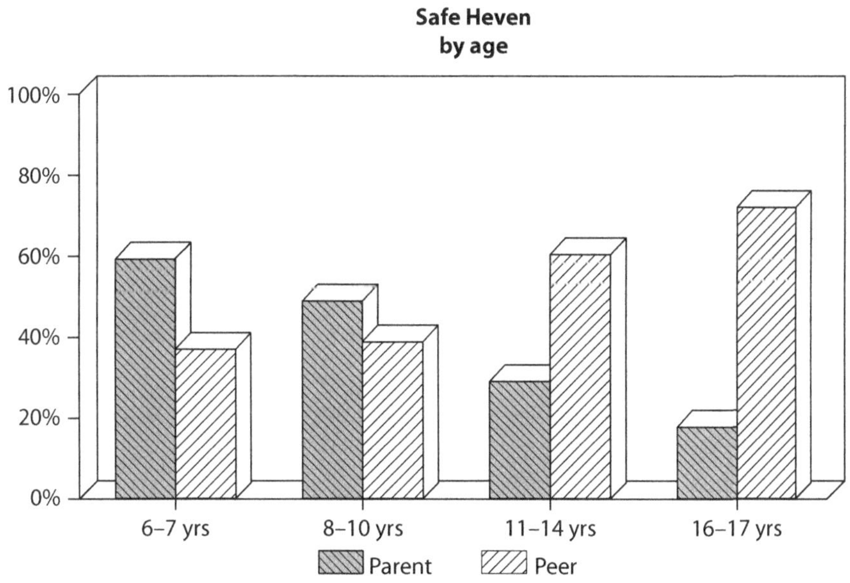

Figure 3. The target of four components of attachment by age

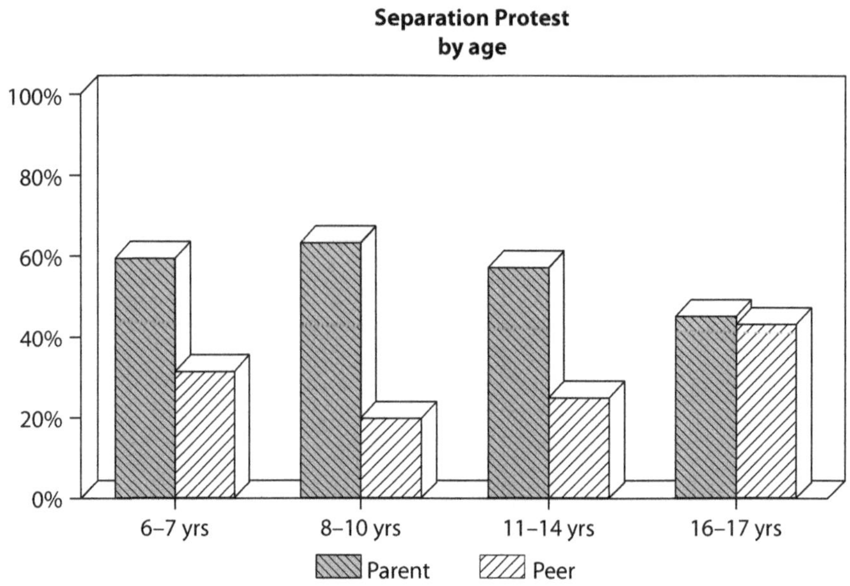

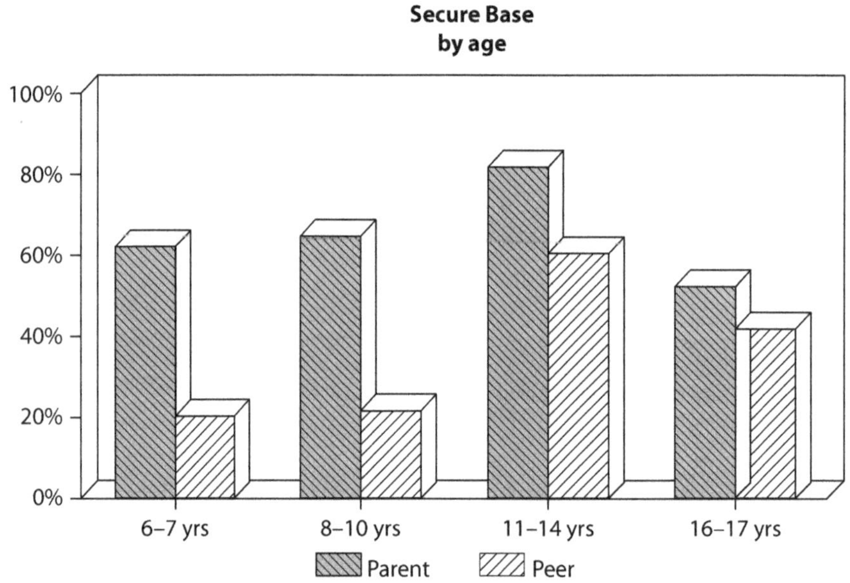

Figure 3. The target of four components of attachment by age (continued)

Method

We developed an interview measure of the four components of attachment and administered it to a cross-section of over 100 children and adolescents ranging in age from 6 to 17, Subjects were recruited through local public and private schools and community centers representing a wide variety of religious, ethnic, racial, and socioeconomic groups. Interviews were conducted individually by a trained interviewer and were videotaped.

In constructing the interview and the attachment-component items, we operated on the assumption that the components would be functionally and psychologically equivalent to their behavioral manifestations as observed in infants. For each component, we asked several questions: proximity seeking (Whom do you like to be close to, spend time with, etc.?); safe haven (Whom do you turn to for comfort when you're upset, feeling down, etc.?); separation protest (Whom do you not like to be away from, miss most during separations, etc.?); and secure base (Whom do you feel you can always count on, know will be available if needed, etc.?). Subjects were asked to respond to each of the questions by naming a single person (i.e., the *preferred* person in each situation).

Because we were primarily interested in the distinction between parental figures and peers, we categorized responses as either parent or peer and calculated proportions based on these two categories. The parent category included mothers, fathers, stepparents, and grandparents; the peer category included friends and romantic partners (i.e., boyfriends and girlfriends). Averaged across components, 91 per cent of all responses fell into one of these two categories. Uncommon responses (ranging from 2 to 9% across items) included siblings, teachers, aunts, uncles, and 'nobody'.

Whereas the consistency of responses to items within each component was generally high, consistency across components was not. The relatively low cross-component consistency was due to the fact that some subjects named a parent on all items; others named a parent on all questions for one component and a peer for all on another. This finding can be taken as evidence of the distinctiveness of the components. The results are presented in Figure 3.

Results and discussion

The most obvious trend in the data is evident in the differences between the first and second graphs, and between the top and bottom halves of the figure. All children and adolescents in the sample were peer-oriented in terms of proximity-seeking. That is, they preferred to spend their time in the company of peers rather than parents. If we look at the safe haven component (second graph), it is apparent that a marked shift occurs between the ages of 8 and 14, with peers coming to be preferred over parents as sources of comfort and emotional support. Comparing the top and bottom halves of the figure, it is evident that until late adolescence, parents continue to serve as bases of security and targets of separation protest. Only in late adolescence (the 15–17-year-old group) do we begin to see what can be considered full-blown attachments - that is, relationships that contain all the defining features of attachment. Further analysis of the late adolescence group revealed that of this minority (41 %) who considered a peer to be their primary attachment figure, the overwhelming majority (83%) named a romantic partner.

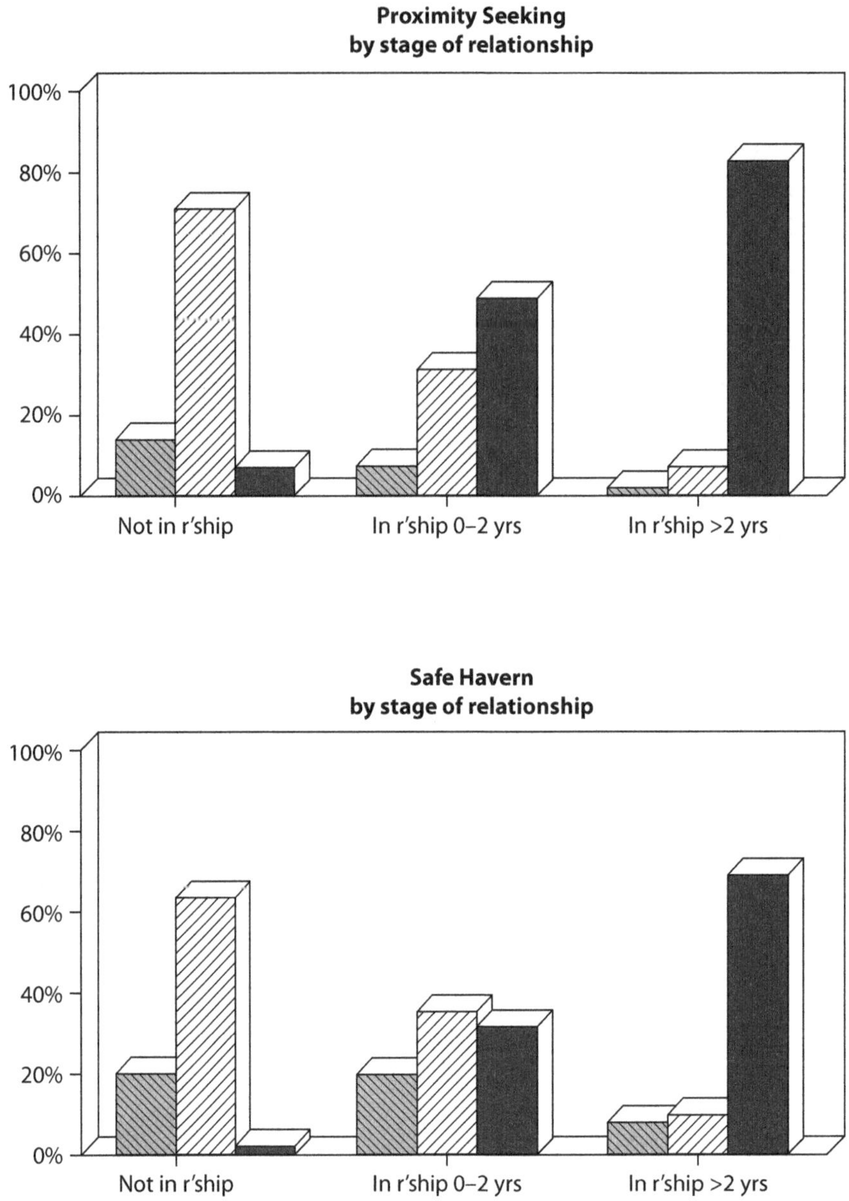

Figure 4. The target of four components of attachment by stage of relationship

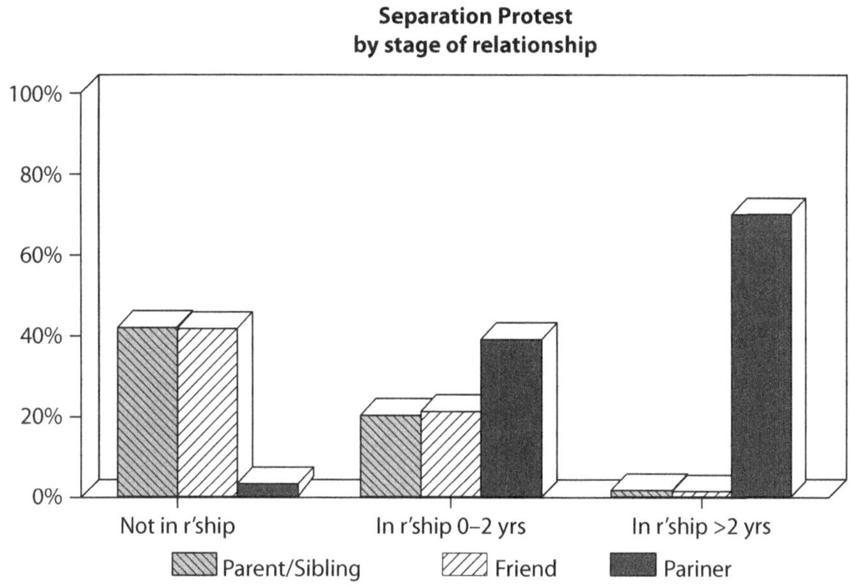

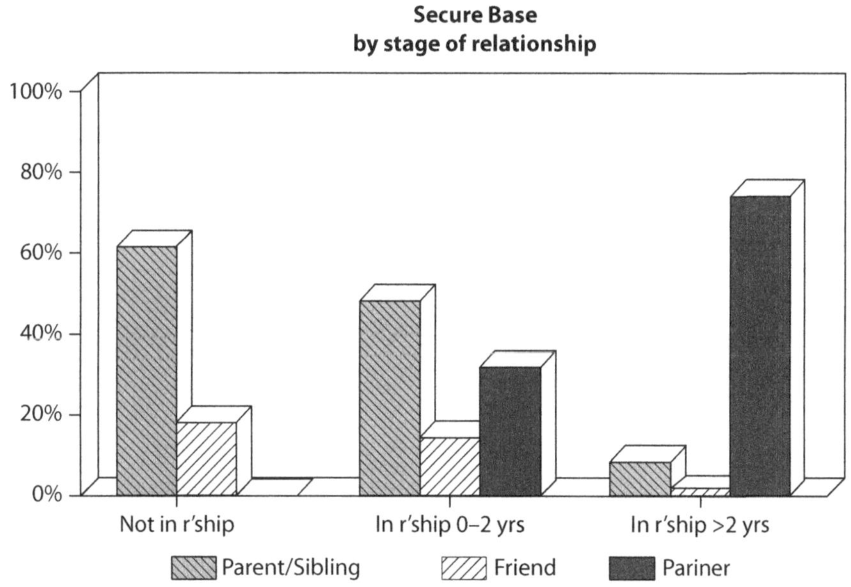

Figure 4. The target of four components of attachment by stage of relationship (continued)

We also assessed individual differences in attachment style with a modified version of Hazan and Shaver's (1987) attachment measure. The analyses of the individual differences data are not yet completed, but preliminary results show some reliable group differences. For example, of the small minority of the subjects who said they had 'nobody' to whom they could turn for comfort or on whom they could depend for support, over two-thirds were avoidantly attached. Although slightly less than half (48%) of the subjects were classified as insecurely attached (avoidant or ambivalent), they constituted the majority (71%) of adolescents who had formed romantic attachments. One interpretation of this finding is that insecure attachments to parents encourage early (perhaps premature) peer attachments.

According to the results of Study 1, attachments are transferred from parents to peers component by component in a sequence that begins with proximity seeking, followed by safe haven, and finally separation protest and secure base. In a sense, peer attachments are 'explored' from the parental base of security. It seems plausible that proximity seeking and safe haven behaviors are largely a matter of convenience. As children enter the school system and begin to spend the majority of their day in the company of peers, peers not only become the preferred targets of proximity seeking behaviors but also are convenient sources of emotional support and comfort. The true markers of attachment (i.e., separation protest and secure base) are reserved for parents or, in the case of the older adolescents, romantic partners. The first complete reciprocal peer attachments (i.e., those containing all four components) are romantic attachments, relationships in which sex or sexual attraction is an integral part.

Study 2: Relationship Status-Related Changes in the Target of Attachment Behaviors

Background and objectives

By what process are reciprocal attachments formed and what is the time course of this process? In infancy, attachment formation proceeds through a series of stages, beginning in the first weeks of life and ending sometime toward the end of the second year with the establishment of a 'goal-corrected partnership' (Bowlby, 1969/1982). The process begins with close proximity, maintained by the caregiver as well as by selective signaling on the part of the infant. By the eighth or tenth month, infants begin to engage in safe haven and secure base behaviors, and show strong resistance to being separated from their primary caregivers. Eventually, the relationship becomes more exclusive; by the end of the first year of life, infants vigorously reject the caregiving advances of strangers and, not uncommonly, even offers of comfort from secondary attachment figures. It is noteworthy that the components that together define the attachment bond do not emerge simultaneously, but rather in sequence. The emergence of separation protest and secure base behaviors indicate that an attachment bond is fully formed.

To date, there are no published studies of attachment formation in adulthood, but existing data on relationship formation and development suggest that whether and which attachment components are present may depend on how long a couple has been together.

For example, romantic couples typically experience a strong desire for physical proximity and contact, especially in the initial stages of a relationship (Berscheid, 1984). The provision of mutual support and caregiving appear to become more important in later stages (Reedy, Birren & Schaie, 1981; Sternberg, 1986). Similarly, the incidence and intensity of separation distress seems to vary according to relationship length and stage (Weiss, 1988). Thus, in adult relationships, as in infant-caregiver relationships, the presence or absence of attachment components may be partially determined by the stage of relationship development.

Method

To address the question of how reciprocal attachments are formed in adulthood, we administered the same interview used in Study One to an equally diverse sample of 120 adults, ranging in age from 18 to 82. Participants were recruited in a manner similar to the first study - that is, by posting notices in sociodemographically diverse settings (e.g., businesses and community centers). In this study, we grouped the adults by *stage* of romantic relationship development rather than by age. Three relationship status groups were identified: not in a romantic relationship, in a romantic relationship for less than two years, in a romantic relationship for two or more years. It is important to note that these cutoffs were empirically derived. Other cutoffs were examined, but the data indicated that relationships of fewer than two years duration were qualitatively different from those of longer duration, at least in the components we measured. The data also suggested response categories that differ in two ways from those used in Study One. First, siblings were named more often than they had been by younger subjects. (This was especially true for our oldest subjects, many of whose parents were no longer living.) Second, peers were subdivided into the two most common responses: friends and romantic partners. Averaging across components, 85 percent of all responses are covered by the following three categories: parent/sibling, friend, and romantic partner. Uncommon responses (e.g., therapist, God, a pet, a son or daughter) - interesting in their own right (Kirkpatrick & Shaver, 1990) but too few to analyze - were excluded from the analyses. Results are presented in Figure 4.

Results and discussion

The results of this study replicate those of Study One: Full-blown attachments are almost exclusively limited to parents or romantic partners. Like children and adolescents, adults seem to be peer-oriented in their proximity-seeking and safe haven behaviors (see first and second graphs), but either parent- or partner-oriented on separation protest and secure base, depending on whether and for how long they had a partner. Additionally, the results indicate that the process of reciprocal attachment formation takes approximately two years. Nearly all of the relationships of two or more years duration contained all four components of attachment, compared with only about one third of relationships in the under-two-years group.

We found gender differences on two of the components: Females who had partners were more likely than their male counterparts to name a sibling (most often, a sister) in response to the safe haven questions about whom they turn to for emotional support. On the separation protest items about who is missed during separations, 15 percent of the subjects named their children; of these, 90 per cent were women.

We also found some attachment style differences. Avoidantly attached subjects reported less interest in spending time with or being close to their partners, and were more likely than secure or ambivalent subjects to say they sought support from and counted on 'nobody'. Ambivalently attached subjects, more than secure or avoidant subjects, reported seeking support from someone other than their partners.

The overall pattern of results suggests that reciprocal attachments, like complementary attachments, begin with proximity seeking (a desire for closeness and contact). Eventually, the safe haven component (seeking emotional support and comfort) is added. If the relationship endures beyond two years, a fully developed attachment is likely to have formed. Complete attachments (i.e., containing all four components) are formed with either parents or romantic partners.

Although both parent and partner attachments begin with proximity-seeking, it is likely that the motivation for seeking closeness is different for infants and children than it is for adolescents or adults. In infancy, proximity-seeking is dominated by (though not limited to) the need to alleviate distress and maintain 'felt security' (Sroufe & Waters, 1977). In early childhood, contact with parents diminishes and peers are increasingly approached, albeit for their interest and stimulation value rather than for security. In late adolescence and in adulthood, proximity seeking is often directed toward romantic partners, suggesting sexual attraction as a primary motivating force.

The results of both studies are consistent with Bowlby's claims that, early in life, attachment relationships are formed with parental figures and, later in life, with sexual partners. Despite differences in the underlying motivation for seeking proximity (to parents or peers), such closeness provides a context that fosters intimacy and mutual caregiving and, in time, reliance on the relationship as a base of security from which separations are resisted. The establishment of a fully-developed attachment in infancy and childhood, the endpoint of complementary attachments to parents, may be the starting point of the process of reciprocal (peer) attachment formation. Sexual attraction and behavior appear to play a central role in the culmination of this process.

The very first relationship in the life of a typical human is one in which cuddling, suckling, kissing, prolonged skin-to-skin, face-to-face, and belly-to-belly contact, extended mutual gazing, and the touching of body parts otherwise considered 'private' are all permissible. Although some of these behaviors may occur in isolation within the context of other types of social relationships (e.g., kissing among friends), their joint occurrence in infancy is usually restricted to the infant-caregiver relationship. When this complex behavioral package later re-emerges, it is typically restricted to romantic relationships.

Physical Contact and Attachment

Until the 1950's, it was a widely-held belief among psychologists that the reason an infant becomes attached to his or her mother is because, through nursing, the mother becomes associated with the satisfaction of a basic hunger drive. The fact that mother love was inextricably tied to the provision of food was one of the few aspects of human psychology on which behaviorists and psychoanalysts agreed. Harlow (1958) simultaneously stunned the psychological community and revolutionized thinking about social attachments by demonstrating conclusively, through a series of studies with nonhuman primates, that the provision of contact comfort was a primary factor in attachment formation. By experimentally separating the provisions of food and contact comfort through the ingenious design of surrogate mothers, Harlow established that primates become attached to the supplier of opportunities to cuddle and cling.

Infant rhesus monkeys, like other nonhuman primates, spend their first weeks of life in continuous, mutually ventral contact with their mothers (Suomi, 1990). In this position, the infants not only experience the contact comfort that Harlow found to be so important for their development, but also have easy access to nourishment. Within weeks, the infant-mother relationship has many of the same features as those of human infant-caregiver dyads (Harlow & Harlow, 1965). Around the end of the first month of life, rhesus infants begin to use their mothers as a secure base for exploration, venturing away from her on forays of ever-increasing frequency, duration, and distance (Suomi, 1983). If, while exploring, the infant becomes frightened or fatigued, mother is immediately sought out for safe haven and comfort.

Often during periods of exploratory activity, infants initiate social interactions with peers and, through contact in the form of mutual grooming, establish affiliative ties. Naturally, as contact with peers increases, contact with the mother decreases. Eventually, peer contacts come to include sexual play (Suomi, 1990). Despite the dramatic change that occurs in time spent with mother relative to time spent with peers, mother continues to serve as the base of security for affiliative exploration. The infant's motivation for seeking proximity and contact with peers is different than the motivation for seeking contact with the mother; peers are approached for stimulation, whereas mothers are approached for comfort. The form of physical contact also differs between the two, with ventral contact being exclusive to the mother-infant relationship.

There is much more variability among human infants in the amount of physical contact they have with their caregivers. For example, Japanese infants are rarely separated from their mothers during the first months of life (Miyake, Chen & Campos, 1985), and do not typically sleep in a separate room or even a separate bed from the parents. Very young !Kung infants spend the whole of their day in physical contact with mother and, at night sleep next to her (Konner, 1982). In contrast, physical separations from caregivers are a common experience of infants in many Western cultures (e.g., Grossmann & Grossmann, 1981). Despite these cultural variations in amount of contact, the *nature and quality* of the contact between primary caregivers and their infants is quite similar. Compared to contact with others in the social group, contact with caregivers is more likely to be mutually ventral and of extended duration, and includes more kissing and nuzzling (Schaffer, 1971). Ventral contact tends to be more soothing than other forms of contact, especially when accompanied by opportunities for sucking. In this way the primary caregiver becomes associated with feelings of security and the alleviation of distress (Main, 1990). Thus, as in non-human primates, human attachments develop out of experiences of physical contact of a distinct nature.

In adulthood, close physical contact usually takes the form of sexual intimacy and is generally exclusive to marriage or romantic partnerships. Prohibitions against sexual behavior in other social relationships are rampant in Western society and religion, and seem to be present in some form or another in all cultures studied to date (Alcock, 1989). The fact that in most societies there are prohibitions against sex outside the pair bond relationship may be due in part to an implicit understanding that close physical contact with another could lead to an emotional bond that would jeopardize the primary one. Even in sub-cultures where extra-relationship sexual contact is permitted, efforts to avoid emotional involvement are common. For example, prostitutes commonly refuse to engage in kissing, nuzzling, and other forms of intimate face-to-face contact with their clients (Nass & Fisher, 1988). Gay males who regularly participate in extra-relationship sexual activities reserve kissing and cuddling for the primary partner (Blumstein & Schwartz, 1983). Ground rules among so-called 'swinging' heterosexual couples often forbid repeated sexual contact with the same person (O'Neill & O'Neill, 1972). A plausible interpretation of these findings is that repeated intimate physical contact naturally fosters attachment formation. If an emotional bond is not desired, special steps must be taken to protect against its formation.

In summary, there is abundant evidence that close physical contact is centrally important to attachment formation. Further, the contact that promotes and characterizes attachment relationships is qualitatively different from the various kinds of contact observed in other social relationships. Specifically, intimate (e.g., mutually ventral, face-to-face) contact and the feelings of security that it fosters appears to be the cornerstone of attachment formation.

The Biology of Attachment

The notion that attachment is a very real biological need rather than a luxury was established in studies of infants reared in orphanages and other institutional settings. Despite that fact that infants' nutritional and hygienic needs were being adequately met, because of high infant to nurse ratios and staff turnover rates, infants were not afforded an opportunity to develop attachment bonds. The results of attachment deprivation were shocking. Infants showed retarded growth and weight gain and displayed dulled affect characteristic of adult depression, and many died (Robertson, 1953; Spitz, 1946). Gardner (1972) studied the development of physically normal, nonabused infants who had received adequate physical care but were deprived of emotional care, especially physical affection. These home-reared infants showed many of the same abnormalities as institution-reared infants, including apathy, rigid body postures, and depression. Moreover, in the absence of organic abnormalities or nutritional deprivation, the infants were severely retarded in their physical growth - a condition Gardner called *deprivation dwarfism.* Thus, the fulfillment of attachment needs appears to be essential to the physical as well as the psychological well-being of human infants.

Bowl by stressed the importance of the protective functions of the attachment relationship and hypothesized that attachment behaviors developed because of their survival value in the environment of evolutionary adaptedness. Because human infants are incapable of caring for themselves at birth, it is adaptive for them to form an attachment to an adult who can provide food, care, and protection from predators. More recently, psychobiological researchers are discovering many additional ways in which attachment behaviors serve to enhance the health and well-being of infants. For example, Field and her colleagues demonstrated that premature infants who received tactile/ kinesthetic stimulation in the form of a body massage gained weight more rapidly, and were discharged from the hospital earlier, than infants in a standard care control group (Seafidi *et al.* 1990). Contact with a caregiver serves many biologically critical functions for human infants who have poorly developed mechanisms for temperature regulation and arousal modulation at birth. There is also evidence that caregiver contact helps to regulate other physiological systems, such as heartrate and REM cycles (Field, 1985; Hofer, 1987).

Although adults are clearly less dependent on an attachment bond for basic survival, there is ample evidence that adults incur health benefits from having close personal relationships, and suffer health decrements from the loss of an attachment relationship. Disruption, especially through divorce, makes one more susceptible to everything from automobile accidents to alcohol abuse to admission into a psychiatric facility (Bloom,

Asher & White, 1978). In addition, the grieving and lonely are more vulnerable to disease, according to studies of their hearts and immune systems (e.g., Keicolt-Glaser, Gamer, *et al* 1984; Kiecolt-Glaser, Ricker, *et al.* 1984; Lynch, 1977), and at greater risk of death from cancer (Goodwin, Hurt, Key & Sarret, 1987). Social deficiencies and losses jeopardize not only health and happiness but job performance and achievement as well (Baruch, Barnett & Rivers, 1983; Lee & Kanungo, 1984; Vaillant, 1977).

Like relationship dissolution, relationship formation can have real physiological effects, including changes in brain chemistry and activity. For example, the development of romantic relationships can be divided into two phases- the attraction phase and the attachment phase (Mellen, 1981; Walsh 1981). The two phases are hypothesized to correspond to distinct neurotransmitter and limbic system activity (Liebowitz, 1983). Evidence suggests that the experience of romantic love is mediated by naturally occurring amphetamine-like substances, especially phenylethylamine (PEA). Like other stimulants, PEA produces heightened arousal, awareness, and activity. It may be implicated in the 'high' that is experienced when an individual is in love, and the noticeable decrements in need for food and sleep. PEA also has mild hallucinogenic effects, which may be partially responsible for the well-known tendency of new lovers to idealize each other (Tennov, 1979; Walsh, 1981). Eventually, the brain habituates to the high PEA levels, at which time it is hypothesized that endogenous opiates - endorphins - take over and the so-called attachment phase begins. Endorphin release is accompanied by feelings of security and contentment, a sense that all is right with the world, and have long been associated with the formation of affectional bonds between infant and caregiver (Panksepp, Siviy & Normansell, 1985). For all romantic relationships, the point at which the attraction phase ends - approximately two years into the relationship according to our own data and findings reported by Tennov (1979) and Money (1980) - is the time when a relationship either begins to deteriorate or is transformed into a more enduring attachment bond.

Pair Bonds: The Integration of Attachment, Caregiving, and Sex

Attachment theory postulates that adult attachments involve the integration of three distinct behavioral systems: attachment, caregiving, and sexual mating. The term *integration* implies not only a dynamic coordination of the systems themselves but also that their regulation will be centered on one specific person. This person - the primary attachment figure - will serve simultaneously as the sexual partner and the primary provider and recipient of comfort and emotional support.

The hypothesized links between sex, caregiving, and attachment are strengthened by demonstrations that early attachment deprivation affects later sexual functioning and caregiving. For example, rhesus monkeys who were not given an opportunity to form attachments during infancy developed gross abnormalities in their sexual behavior as adults (Harlow & Harlow, 1965). Although they were reproductively normal in the physiological sense (e.g., sperm production, menstrual cycles), they showed severe deficits in the display and sequencing of the motor movements involved in copulation. When females deprived of early attachments were inseminated by artificial means (because they were sexually incompetent and incapable of being impregnated by natural means), they demonstrated highly abnormal and even violent caregiving responses toward their newborn young (Harlow & Harlow, 1962).

For obvious ethical reasons, there is no direct empirical evidence for the effects of early attachment experiences on sexual and caregiving functioning among humans, but there are some data that bear on the issue. According to retrospective accounts, for example, dysfunctional early attachment relationships are a common precursor of adulthood sexual deviance (Sroufe & Fleeson, 1986). A correlation has also been found between retrospective reports of maternal rejection during childhood and adult sexual promiscuity (Brennan, Shaver & Tobey, 1991). Securely attached adults appear to be more skilled at providing care to their offspring (Main *et al.* 1985), are more responsive to their infants' distress (Main, 1990), and are more caring and supportive toward their adult partners (Kunce & Shaver, see pages 205–237).

Although attachment bonds formed in adulthood typically include elements of attachment, caregiving, and sex, the relative importance of these different elements appears to change as a relationship develops (Berscheid & Walster, 1974; Levinger & Snoek, 1972; Lewis & Spanier, 1979; Taylor & Altman, 1987; Walster & Walster, 1978). In general, sex is more important in the initial phase of a relationship, when sexual attraction and interest are at their peak (Traupmann & Hatfield, 1981). As a relationship develops, the degree to which a partner provides comfort and emotional support becomes increasingly important (Reedy, Birren & Schaie, 1981). Kotler (1985) reported that sensitive and responsive care, not sexual attraction, was the most accurate predictor of relationship longevity. In attachment terms, what eventually comes to matter most is whether the partner serves as a haven of safety and a secure base.

Attachments at any age develop in the context of close physical proximity and intimate contact. Therefore, in order for an attachment to form, there must be a strong force promoting closeness. In infancy, proximity seeking is motivated by the need for security (Bowlby, 1969/1982); in adulthood, the primary motivating force is likely to be sexual attraction (Berscheid, 1988). In both types of relationships - between infants and caregivers and between adult romantic partners - the frequency and intensity of intimate contact diminishes somewhat once an attachment bond had been established. Nonetheless, sexual attraction is what brings two adults together, and sex is what holds them together long enough for an emotional bond - a psychological tether - to form. (See Table 1 for a summary of the attraction and attachment phases of a relationship.)

Table 1. A Summary of the Attraction and Attachment Phases of a Romantic Relationship

	Attraction Phase (attachment-in-the-making)	*Attachment Phase*	Sources
Time Course	0–2 years	beyond 2 years	Fisher, Hazan & Zeifman, Liebowitz, Money, Tennov
Attachment Components	proximity seeking, then safe haven	proximity seeking, safe haven, separation protest, secure base	Hazan & Zeifman
Importance of Sex	high	low to moderate	Berscheid & Walster, Reedy *et al.*
Importance of Caregiving	low to moderate	high	Kotler, Reedy *et al.*
Biology/ Neuro-chemistry	PEA, Amphetamine like substances	endorphins, opiate-like substances	Fisher, Leibowitz, Money, Panksepp *et al.*
Phenomenology	arousal, elation	calm, contentment	Berscheid, Liebowitz, Tennov
Evolutionary Function	bring couples together long enough to foster pregnancy	keep couples together to raise young	Eibl-Eibesfeldt, Fisher, Mellen, Walsh

The Evolution of Human Sexuality and Attachment

Evolutionary theory offers an explanation of the links between sex and attachment. In order for reproductive fitness to be maximized, individuals have to survive to reproductive age, successfully mate, and then provide care and protection to their offspring so that they, too, survive to reproduce (Mellen, 1981; Trivers, 1972). Successful human mating thus involves more than fertilizing an egg. Reproduction alone is not sufficient for the survival of a species whose young have a long period of dependency. Individuals not only need to be attracted to a sexual partner but also must remain with the partner long enough to see their progeny through the most vulnerable period of development—infancy.

It is likely that in the environment in which we evolved, caring for young was physically costly for the female and greatly reduced her mobility, thus increasing the importance of male caregiving for the survival of offspring. The natural cycle of conception, pregnancy, and weaning in non-Western human societies is approximately four years. Selection pressures, then, should have operated in such a way as to ensure that couples stay together for at least that long. Interestingly, worldwide census data show that more relationships end at the four-year mark than at any other time (Fisher, 1992). Of course, most couples remain together well beyond this point, some for reasons of love and attachment and others because the anticipated costs of breaking up are perceived to be too great (Levinger, 1976; Rusbult, 1983; Stanley & Markman, 1992). Nevertheless, the four-year point that marks the end of the natural child rearing cycle is a point at which relationships may be more vulnerable to dissolution.

Many unique features of human sexuality seem to have evolved so as to enhance the development and maintenance of emotional bonds between sexual partners. The most striking change in our reproductive physiology in comparison to other mammalian species is the loss of outward signs of estrus in the female. Mammals usually mate only during the short estrus periods of the female, whereas human sexual desire is not limited to certain seasons or reproductive cycles. Women may be sexually receptive during any phase of their reproductive cycle despite the fact that conception is possible only during a small fraction of the cycle. This physiological adaptation enables the couple to maintain a continuous tie on the basis of sexual reward (Eibl-Eibesfeldt, 1975).

The evolution of genital differences between us and our closest primate relatives also suggest the important role of sex in maintaining the integrity of the human pair bond. For example, the average length of the erect human penis is 13cm, compared with approximately 3 cm for the gorilla, a much larger animal in terms of overall body size. The large size of the erect human penis, in marked contrast to that of all the great apes, undoubtedly made possible a wide variety of copulatory positions (including more intimate face-to-face, mutually ventral positions) which may have served to enhance the sexual pleasure of both partners and increase the probability of female orgasm (Short, 1979). The ability of the human female to experience an orgasm comparable (at least!) to that of the male may then serve to increase the female's readiness to engage in sexual behavior and strengthen her emotional bond to her mate (Eibl-Eisbesfeldt, 1975).

Just as the continuous sexual receptivity of the human female strengthens the relationship bond by enhancing sexual rewards, hidden ovulation may strengthen the relationship bond by diminishing the apparent rewards of straying. Males of many diverse species guard their mates during periods of sexual receptivity so as to ensure fertilization by their own sperm and not that of another male's. When fertilization is accomplished or the fertile period has ended, the male is likely to move on to another receptive partner. However, if ovulation is hidden, making it impossible for the male to determine just when fertilization will be possible, the optimal male mating strategy may shift toward remaining with and guarding the same sexual partner for longer periods of time. This is a common strategy for humans, who employ exceptionally prolonged, culturally institutionalized mate-guarding in the form of marriage (Alcock, 1989).

To summarize, because of the demands of a greatly protracted period of infancy in humans, the maintenance of a strong bond between parents became critically important to the survival of their offspring (Mellen, 1981). Several unique features of human reproductive physiology and anatomy, especially hidden ovulation in females and large penis size in males, suggest that we may have exploited sex for this purpose (Eibl-Eisbesfeldt, 1975; Short, 1979). If this is so, sex serves more than a reproductive function in humans. Sex strengthens and maintains the emotional and psychological bond - the attachment - between two paired adults.

Conclusions

The links between sex and the emotional bond that is attachment are many and varied, and the links appear to be naturally-occurring ones with solid foundations in biology. When we compare the behaviors that typify lover and infant-caregiver dyads, the similarities are striking and also serve to set these relationships apart from other kinds of social ties. Relationships between lovers and between parents and their infants are, in a sense, the prototypes of close relationships, and both are grounded in repeated and intimate physical contacts. Additional evidence for links comes from research findings indicating that attachment experiences during infancy and childhood can have an organizing effect on adult sexual behavior and functioning.

Attachments promote healthy functioning in people of all ages, and serve to buffer individuals against the stressors of life. From an evolutionary perspective, the connections between sex and attachment are not surprising. It is highly adaptive for parents to be psychologically and emotionally bonded to each other because it helps ensure the survival of their vulnerable offspring. The attachment bond that forms between adults also makes an important contribution to their own well-being and adjustment.

We are currently investigating the role of sex in the formation and maintenance of adult attachment relationships, and the influence of individual differences on sexual behavior in relationships. Differences in attachment style have been related to individual sexual behavior (Simpson & Gangestad, 1992), but not to individual behavior within a relationship. An attachment model not only helps to predict how individual differences can influence the nature and course of relationships but also the critical periods when relationships of all types will be more vulnerable to breakup. These predictions can be examined empirically.

Attachment theory advanced the study of infant-mother interactions because it linked the psychological processes of attachment to their underlying motivational and biological states. The field of adult relationship research has yet to explore the links between sexual attraction and behavior and the psychological processes operating within attachment relationships. This omission is surprising because sex is the definitive behavior of adult romantic relationships, and sex provides the motivation for the kind of physical contact that fosters the formation and maintenance of affectional bonds between adult lovers. It is possible that this psychological tether between mates, which serves them and their progeny so well, would not develop were it not for the strong sexual forces that motivate them to seek each other out.

REFERENCES

Ainsworth, M.D.S. (1967) *Infancy in Uganda: Infant Care and the Growth of Attachment.* Baltimore: The Johns Hopkins press.

Ainsworth, M.D.S. (1982) Attachment Retrospect and prospect. In CM. Parkes & J. Stevenson-I Jinde (eds) *The Place of Attachment in Human Behavior* (pp.3–30). New York: Basic Books.

Ainsworth, M.D.S., Blehar, M.C, Waters, E. & Wall, S. (1978) *Patterns of Attachment: Assessed in the Strange Situation and at Home.* Hillsdale, NJ: Erlbaum.

Alcock, J. (1989) *Animal Behavior: An Evolutionary Approach.* Boston: Sinauer.

Bartholomew, K. (1990) Avoidance of intimacy: An attachment perspective. *Journal of Social and Personal Relationships, 7,*147–178.

Baruch, G., Barnett, R. & Rivers, C. (1983) *Lifeprints : New Patterns of Love and Work for Today's Women.* New York: McGraw-Hill.

Berscheid, E. (1984) Interpersonal attraction. In G. Lindzey & E. Aronson (eds) *Handbook of Social Psychology* (3rd ed., pp.413–484). Reading, MA: Addison-Wesley.

Berscheid, E. (1988) Some comments on love's anatomy or, whatever happened to old-fashioned lust? In R.J. Sternberg & M.L. Barnes (eds) *The Psychology of Love* (pp.359–374). New Haven, CT: Yale University Press.

Berscheid, E. & Walster, E (1974) A little bit about love. In T.L. Huston (ed) *Foundations of Interpersonal Attraction* (pp.355–381). New York: Academic Press.

Bloom, B.L., Asher, S.J. & White, S.W. (1978) Marital disruption as a stressor: A review and analysis. *Psychological Bulletin, 85,* 867–894.

Blumstein, P. & Schwartz, P. (1983) *American Couples: Money, Work and Sex.* New York: Morrow.

Bowlby, J. (1969/1982) *Attachment and Loss: Vol. I. Attachment* (2nd ed). New York: Basic Books.

Bowlby, J. (1973) *Attachment and Loss: Vol. II. Separation: Anxiety and anger.* New York: Basic Books.

Bowlby, J. (1979) *The Making and Breaking of Affectional Bonds.* London; Tavistock Publications.

Bowlby, J. (1980) *Attachment and loss: Vol. III Loss: Sadness and Depression.* New York: Basic Books.

Bowlby, J. (1988) *A Secure Base: Parent-child Attachment and Healthy Human Development.* New York: Basic Books.

Brennan, K.A., Shaver, PR. & Tobey, A.E. (1991) Attachment styles, gender, and parental problem drinking. *Journal of Social and Personal Relationships, 8,*451–466.

Colin, V. (1985) *Hierarchies and Patterns of Infants' Attachments to Parents and Day Caregivers: An Exploration.* Unpublished doctoral dissertation, University of Virginia, Charlottesville.

Colin, V. (1987) *Infant's Preferences Between Parents Before and After Moderate Stress Activates Behavior.* Presented at the biennial meetings of the Society for Research in Child Development, Baltimore, Maryland.

Collins, N.L. & Read, S.J. (1990) Adult attachment, working models, and relationship quality in dating couples. *Journal of Personality and Social Psychology, 58,* 644–663.

Cummings, EM. (1980) Caregiver stability and attachment in infant day care. *Developmental Psychology, 16,* 31–37.

Duck, S. (ed) (1988) *Handbook of Personal Relationships.* Chichester, UK: John Wiley & Sons.

Eibl-Eibesfeldt, I. (1975) *Ethology: The Biology of Behavior.* New York: Holt, Rinehart and Winston.

Farran, D.C. & Ramey, C.T. (1977) Infant day care and attachment behavior towards mothers and teachers. *Child Development, 48,*112–116.

Feeney, J A. & Noller, P. (1990) Attachment style as a predictor of adult romantic relationships. *Journal of Personality and Social Psychology, 58,* 281–291.

Field, T. (1985) Attachment as psychobiological attunement: Being on the same wavelength. In M. Reite & T. Field (eds) *The Psychobiology of Attachment* (pp.415–454). New York: Academic Press.

Fisher, H.E. (1992) *Anatomy of Love: The Natural History of Monogamy, Adultery, and Divorce.* New York: W.W. Norton.

Furman, W. & Buhrmester, D. (1985) Children's perceptions of the personal relationships in their social networks. *Developmental Psychology, 21,*1016–1024.

Gardner, L.J. (1972) Deprivation dwarfism. *Scientific American, 277,* 76–82.

Goodwin, J.S., Hurt, W.C., Key, C.R. & Sarret, J.M. (1987) The effect of marital status on stage, treatment and survival of cancer patients. *Journal of the American Medical Association, 258,* 3125–3130.

Gottman, J.M. (1983) How children become friends. *Monographs of the Society for Research in Quid Development, 48(3,* Serial No. 201).

Grossmann, K.E. & Grossmann, K. (1981) The mother-child relationship. *German Journal of Psychology, 5,* 237–252.

Harlow, H. (1958) The nature of love. *American Psychologist, 13,* 673–685.

Harlow, H. & Harlow, M.K. (1962) The effects of rearing conditions on behavior. *Bulletin of the Menniger Clinic, 26,* 213–224.

Harlow, H. & Harlow, M.K. (1965) The affectional systems. In A.M. Schrier, H.F. Harlow & F. Stollnitz (eds) *Behavior of Nonhuman Primates* (Vol. 2, pp.287–334). New York: Academic Press.

Hartup, W. (1983) Peer relations. In E.M. Hetherinton (ed) P.H. Mussen (Series Ed.), *Handbook of child psychology: Vol. 4. Socialization, Personality and Social Development* (pp.103–196). New York: John Wiley & Sons.

Hazan, C & Shaver, P.R. (1987) Romantic love conceptualized as an attachment process. *Journal of Personality and Social Psychology, 52,*511–524.

Hofer, MA. (1987) Early social relationships: A psychobiologist's view. *Child Development, 58, 663–647.*

Kiecolt-Glaser, J.K., Gamer, W., Speicher, C, Penn, G.M., Holliday, J. & Glaser, R. (1984) Psychological modifiers of immunocompetence in medical students. *Psychosomatic Medicine, 46,* 7–14.

Kiecolt-Glaser, J.K., Ricker, D., George, J., Messick, G., Speicher, G.E., Gamer, W. & Glaser, R. (1984) Urinary Cortisol levels, cellular immune competence, and loneliness in psychiatric inpatients. *Psychosomatic Medicine, 46,*15–23.

Kirkpatrick, LA. & Davis, K.E. (in press) Attachment style, gender, and relationship stability: A longitudinal analysis. *Journal of Personality and Social Psychology.*

Kirkpatrick, LA. & Shaver, P.R. (1990) Attachment theory and religion: Childhood attachments, religious beliefs, and conversion. *Journal for the Scientific Study of Religion, 29,* 315–334.

Kobak, R.R. & Hazan, C (1991) Attachment in marriage: The effects of security and accuracy of working models. *Journal of Personality and Social Psychology, 60,*861–869.

Konner, M. (1982) *The Tangled Wing: Biological Constraints on the Human Spirit.* New York: Holt, Rinehart & Winston.

Kotler, T. (1985) Security and autonomy within marriage. *Human Relations, 38,* 299–321.

Lee, M.D. & Kanungo, R.N. (eds) (1984) *Management of Work and Personal Life: Problems and Opportunities.* New York: Praeger.

Levinger, G. (1976) A social psychological perspective on marital dissolution. *Journal of Social Issues,* 32(1), 21–47.

Levinger, G. & Snoek, J.D. (1972) *Attraction in Relationship: A New Look at Interpersonal Attraction.* Morristown, NJ: General Learning Press.

Lewis, M. (1982) Social development in infancy and early childhood. In J.B. Osofsky (ed) *Handbook of Infant Development* (2nd ed., pp.419–493). New York: John Wiley & Sons.

Lewis, R.A. & Spanier, G.B. (1979) Theorizing about the quality and stability of marriage. In W.R. Burr, R. Hill, F.I. Nye & I.L. Reiss (eds) *Contemporary Theories About the Family* (Vol. 1, pp.268–294). New York: Free Press.

Liebowitz, M. (1983) *The Chemistry of Love.* New York: Berkley Books.

Lynch, J.J. (1977) *The Broken Heart: The Medical Consequences of Loneliness.* New York: Basic Books.

Main, M. (1990) Parental aversion to infant-initiated contact is correlated with the parent's own rejection during childhood: The effects of experience on signals of security with respect to attachment. In K.E. Barnard & T.B. Brazelton (eds) *Touch: The Foundation of Experience* (pp.461–495). Madison, CT: International Universities Press.

Main, M., Kaplan, N. & Cassidy, J. (1985) Security in infancy, childhood, and adulthood: A move to the level of representation. In I. Bretherton &. E. Waters (eds) *Growing points of attachment theory and research, Monographs of the Society for Research in Child Development,* 50(1–2, Serial No. 209), 66–104.

McKinney, K. & Sprecher, S. (eds) (1991) *Sexuality in Close Relationships.* Hillsdale, NJ: Erlbaum.

Mellen, S.L.W. (1981) *The Evolution of Love.* Oxford, England: Freeman.

Miyake, *K.,* Chen, S. & Campos, J.J. (1985) Infant temperament, mother's mode of interaction, and attachment in Japan: An interim report. In I. Bretherton & E. Waters (eds) *Crowing points of attachment theory and research. Monographs of the Society for Research in Child Development,* 50(1–2, Serial No. 209), 276–297.

Money, J. (1980) *Love and Love Sickness: The Science of Sex, Gender Differences, and Pair-bonding.* Baltimore: Johns Hopkins University Press.

Nass, G.D. & Fisher, M.P. (1988) *Sexuality Today.* Boston: Jones & Bartlett.

O'Neill, N. & O'Neill, C. (1972). *Open Marriage: A New Lifestyle for Couples.* New York: M. Evans.

Panksepp, J Siviy, S.M. & Normansell, LA. (1985) Brain opioids and social emotions. In M. Reite *& T.* Field (eds) *The Psychobiology of Attachment and Separation* (pp.3–50). London: Academic Press.

Perlman, D.& Jones, W.H. (eds) (1993) *Advances in Personal Relationships: A Research Annual* (Vol. 4), London: Jessica Kingsley Publishers.

Reedy, M.N., Birren, J.E. & Schaie, K.W. (1981) Age and sex differences in satisfying love relationships across the adult life span. *Human Development, 24,* 52–66.

Ricciuti, H.N. (1974) Fear and the development of social attachments in the first year of life. In M. Lewis & L. Rosenblum (eds) *Origins of Fear* (pp.73–106). New York: John Wiley & Sons.

Robertson, J. (1953) Some responses of young children to the loss of maternal care. *Nursing Times,* 49, 382–386.

Rubin, Z. (1980) *Children's Friendships.* Cambridge: Harvard University Press.

Rusbult, C.E. (1983) A longitudinal test of the investment model: The development (and deterioration) of satisfaction and commitment in heterosexual involvements. *Journal of Personality and Social Psychology, 45,*101 -117.

Scafidi, F.A., Field, T., Schanberg, S., Bauer, C, Tucci, K., Roberts, J., Morrow, C. *it* Kuhn, CM. (1990) Massage stimulates growth in preterm infants: A replication. *Infant Behavior and Development, 13,* 167–188.

Schaffer, H.R. (1971) *The Growth of Sociability.* Baltimore: Penguin Books.

Schaffer, H.R. & Emerson, P.E. (1964) The development of social attachments in infancy. *Monographs of the Society for Research in Child Development, 29(3).*

Shaver, P.R. & Hazan, C (1988) A biased overview of the study of love. *Journal of Social and Personal Relationships,* 5,473–501.

Shaver, P.R., Hazan, C & Bradsha w, D. (1988) Love as attachment: The integration of three behavioral systems. In R.J. Sternberg it M.L. Barnes (eds) *The Psychology of Love* (pp.68–99). New Haven, CT: Yale University Press.

Shill, M. A,, Solyom, P. & Biven, C (1984) Parent preference in the attachment exploration balance in infancy: An experimental psychoanalytic approach. *Child Psychiatry and Human Development, 15,*34–48.

Short, R.V. (1979) Sexual selection and its component parts, somatic and genital selection, as illustrated in man and the great apes. *Advances in the Study of Behavior, 9,*131–155.

Simpson, J.A. (1990) The influence of attachment styles on romantic relationships. *Journal of Personality and Social Psychology, 59,* 971–980.

Simpson J.A. &Gangestad, S.W. (l992) Sociosexuality and romantic partner choice. *Journal of Personality, 60,* 31–51.

Spitz, R. A. (1946) Anaclitic depression. *Psychoanalytic Study of the Child,* 2, 313–342.

Sroufe, L. A. & Fleeson, J. (1986) Attachment and the construction of relationships. In W.W. Hartup & Z. Rubin (eds) *Relationships and Development* (pp.51–72). Hillsdale, NJ: Erlbaum.

Sroufe, L.A. & Waters, E. (1977) Attachment as an organizational construct. *Child Development, 48,*1184–1199.

Stanley, S.M. & Markman, H.J. (1992) Assessing commitment in personal relationships. *Journal of Marriage and the Family, 54,* 595–608.

Steinberg, L. & Silverberg, S.B. (1986) The vicissitudes of autonomy in early adolescence. *Child Deployment, 57,* 841 -851.

Sternberg, R.J. (1986) A triangular theory of love. *Psychological Review, 93,*119–135.

Suomi, S.J. (1983) Social development in rhesus monkeys: Consideration of individual differences. In A. Oliverio & M. Zappella (eds) *The Behavior of Human Infants* (pp.71–83). New York: Plenum Press.

Suomi, S.J. (1990) The role of tactile contact in rhesus monkey social development. In K.E Barnard & T.B. Brazclton (eds) *Touch: The Foundation of Experience* (pp.129–164). Madison, CT: International Universities Press.

Taylor, D.A. & Altman, I. (1987) Communication in interpersonal relationships: Social penetration processes. In M. Roloff & G. Miller (eds) *Interpersonal Processes: Neio Directions in Communication Research* (pp.257–277). Newbury Park, CA: Sage.

Tennov, D. (1979) *Love and Limerence: The Experience of Being in hove.* New York: Stein and Day.

Traupmann, J. & Hatfield, E. (1981) Love: Its effects on mental and physical health. In R. Fogel, E. Hatfield, S. Kiesler & E. Shana (eds) *Aging: Stability and Change in the Family* (pp.253–274). New York: Academic Press.

Trivers, R. (1972) Parental investment and sexual selection. In B. Campbell (ed) *Sexual Selection and the Descent of Man,* 1871–1971 (pp.136–179). Chicago: Aldine.

Vaillant, G.E. (1977) *Adaptation to Life: How the Best and the Brightest Came of Age.* Boston: Little, Brown.

Vormbrock, J.K. (1993) Attachment theory as applied to war-time and job-related marital separation. *Psychological Bulletin, 114,*122–144.

Walsh, A. (1981) *Human Nature and Love.* Lanham, MD: University Press.

Walster, E. & Walster, G.W. (1978) *A New Look at Love.* Reading, MA: Addison-Wesley.

INITIATING RELATIONSHIPS: ATTRACTION AND FALLING IN LOVE

Thebusinessoflove.com

Relationship Initiation at Internet Matchmaking Services

By Susan Sprecher, Pepper Schwartz, John Harvey, and Elaine Hatfield

INTRODUCTION

Anytime a new form of communication is invented—the penny newspaper, Morse code and the telegraph, the ham radio, TV, or computers—men and women find ways to use that technology to find love (Joinson, 2003). The definitive history of commercial computer matching has yet to be written, but it is known that in the 1950s, almost as soon as computers appeared, commercial matchmaking services sprang up (CBC Archives, 1957). Recognized as the first widespread computer matching service was Operation Match, which was created in the mid-1960s by Harvard students after a discussion of the evils of blind dates and mixers. They distributed thousands of questionnaires to college students at several universities and asked them to rate themselves on looks, intelligence, and other dimensions and also to indicate what they would desire in a partner on these same dimensions. In return for the completed questionnaire and a fee of $3.00, they were promised a list of compatible matches. Data were entered on punch cards and analyzed with an Avco 1790 computer (which was probably the size of a small room). According to media reports, it took the computer 6 weeks to generate the lists. Not surprisingly, the business failed (for a description of this experiment, see Leonhardt, 2006).

Susan Sprecher, Pepper Schwartz, John Harvey, Elaine Hatfield; Susan Sprecher, Amy Wenzel, John Harvey, eds., "TheBusinessofLove.com: Relationship Initiation at Internet Matchmaking Services," from *Handbook of Relationship Initiation*, Pp. 249–265. Published by Psychology Press, 2008.

"Computer dates" were also conducted on university campuses in the 1960s and 1970s for academic research purposes. This was the heyday period for the study of interpersonal attraction in social psychology, and the focus was specifically on attraction that occurs between strangers. The bogus stranger experimental study (e.g., Byrne, 1971) was a common method used at the time to study attraction. In this method, people indicated how attracted they were to a stranger (a "bogus" person, unbeknownst to them) after receiving information about him or her. However, social psychologists also occasionally matched previously unacquainted students and sent them on "dates" in order to determine what factors predicted attraction after initial interaction (e.g., Byrne, Ervin, & Lamberth, 1970). One of the authors of this chapter (Hatfield, formerly Walster) conducted the best known of these studies (i.e., Walster, Aronson, Abrahams, & Rottman, 1966), a dance study with incoming freshmen at the University of Minnesota. Some such studies used a computer to assist with the matching, although the help was rudimentary and on the order of generating random numbers for the matching of questionnaires. Computers at the time were still not powerful enough to do sophisticated matching based on multiple variables.

Over time, as computers became faster and more powerful, people would eventually sit in front of computers, and the high-speed Internet was created. It was not long after these technological advances that the new generation of computer matchmaking businesses was created. Match.com was the first, launched in 1995. Match.com as well as Yahoo! Personals, two of the largest dating sites, began primarily as online personal advertisements, and "personal ads" continue today to be the primary service offered at these dating websites and many others. People post self-profiles, which include demographic information, personality descriptions, interests, and a photograph. They hope that potential eligibles will spot their posted information and want to communicate; they also browse the profiles of other members looking for possible dating prospects. Dating sites that offer this service have added many additional features over time, including keyword searches to narrow the pool, the ability to send preprogrammed icebreaker messages, voice and video greetings, anonymous instant messaging and e-mails, relationship advice, and personality testing. Whereas some sites, such as Match.com, are for the general population of singles, other sites target special niches of the population. There are those designed to appeal to various age groups (e.g., HookUp.com and SilverSingles.com), political groups (ConservativeMatch.com and LiberalHearts.com), religious groups (CatholicSingles.com, Jdate.com, ChristianCafe.com, and HappyBuddhist.com), and sexual orientation (GayWired.com and superEva. com). Dating sites also exist for people who possess mental and physical disabilities, unusual sexual preferences, and so forth. Even people who wish to find dates for themselves and their favorite pets can sign on to a site (DateMyPet.com). At the time this chapter was written, there may be almost 1,000 dating websites servicing the United States (e.g., Thompson, Zimbardo, & Hutchinson, 2005), and the technology available to create another one in an afternoon.

Whereas most dating websites are essentially an electronic version of personal advertisements, eHarmony.com (and founder, Dr. Neil Clark Warren) was the first to launch, in 2000, an alternative commercial matching website, followed by Perfectmatch.com in 2002. These sites distinguish themselves from the others by using a "scientific approach" to matching. Members complete a lengthy questionnaire, presumably based on scientific principles, and their questionnaire data are subjected to "matching algorithms" also developed based on scientific studies. For this effort and a monthly fee, members are promised a list of people who would make "perfect" or "compatible" matches. These sites have changed the online dating industry, with other major websites following suit. In 2005, Match.com launched Chemistry.com (which focuses on matching with "chemistry" in mind), and Yahoo! Personals now includes Yahoo! Premier, an in-depth matching service based on a relationship test. Independent research and development firms also market products and systems for multiple dating websites. Most notably, weAttract.com has developed personality-testing systems for both Match.com and Yahoo. com, and now has a scientific advisory board that includes American Psychological Association Past President Philip Zimbardo. Other social scientists who are involved as scientific advisors at some of the major dating sites include sociologist Pepper Schwartz (an author of this chapter) at Perfectmatch.com and anthropologist Helen Fisher (also an author in this volume) at Chemistry.com.

What scientific principles are being used to match people at the major relationship websites, such as eHarmony.com and Perfectmatch.com? How does relationship initiation through online dating websites differ from relationship initiation that occurs through more traditional ways of meeting, such as introductions from friends? Is it possible that commercial websites could help the scientific community of relationship scholars advance scientific knowledge about relationship initiation and development? These are some of the questions that our chapter will address. We will begin, however, by examining public attitudes toward online relationship initiation and a description of who is using the services and why.

Because online matching is relatively new, not much published, peer-reviewed research on the topic exists. Clearly, dating websites have developed faster than research agendas to investigate them. In order to write this chapter and review the process of relationship initiation at online matching services, it was necessary to draw upon other sources of information, including Internet reports, media accounts, and information provided on the matchmaking websites.

ATTITUDES ABOUT RELATIONSHIP INITIATION AT INTERNET MATCHING SERVICES

Only anecdotal evidence exists as to the public's attitudes toward Internet dating and Internet matching services when such online services first burst upon the scene in the mid- to late 1990s. The general public impression, reflected and perpetuated in newspaper accounts at the time, was negative. The people who used the services were assumed to be "lonely" and "desperate," and attention focused on those who lied about their marital status or gender and on cases of sexual predators who used the Internet to prey on innocent victims. Such negative media reports have continued to appear (e.g., Kleinfeld, 2003, as reported in Albright, 2007), although the media have also extolled the virtues of Internet dating.

More recently, research has been conducted on attitudes toward online dating, primarily with small convenience samples of young adults. Even though men and women in such samples are generally Internet experienced, their attitudes about online dating have been found to be more unfavorable than favorable. For example, Donn and Sherman (2002) conducted two studies examining college students' attitudes about online relationship formation. In Study 1, participants responded to several attitude statements about relationships formed over the Internet (e.g., "I would trust that the information people gave me about themselves over the Internet was true"). The sample overall was negative about online dating. For example, the participants indicated that they would worry that people on the Internet would not tell the truth, they were concerned about their safety when meeting someone online, and they generally thought it would take longer to get to know someone online than in person. In Study 2, the authors manipulated the level of information participants received about matching services (brief written description versus exposure by reviewing two matching websites) and found that greater exposure was associated with more positive (or less negative) attitudes. They also found that students with more frequent Internet usage had more favorable attitudes toward online dating.

Similar findings emerged in another survey study conducted with college students. Anderson (2005) asked the participants the degree to which it was right versus wrong, positive versus negative, and acceptable versus unacceptable for someone to enter into an online romantic relationship. Once again, the respondents had somewhat negative attitudes toward such "dating." However, greater Internet affinity, more time on the Internet, and being *less* romantic (as assessed on the Sprecher and Metts [1989] Romanticism scale) were associated with more positive attitudes.

In the research described above, the participants were relatively young and in college, and therefore likely to be surrounded by potential mates. Most had no prior exposure to matching services. A recent large-scale, national study assessed the attitudes of individuals across several ages, and included a subgroup of online daters. The Pew Internet and American Life project, a nonprofit research center that monitors the social effects of the Internet on Americans, conducted telephone interviews with a national representative sample of 3,215 adults, from age 18 to over 65 (reported in Madden & Lenhart, 2006). Of these, 2,252 (70%) were Internet users who were asked several questions about their attitudes about online dating.

Madden and Lenhart (2006) reported that their national sample of Internet users were divided in their views about whether online dating is a good way to meet people (44% agreed, and 44% disagreed). However, a greater percent (47%) agreed than disagreed (38%) with the statement "Online dating allows people to find a better match for themselves because they get to know a lot more people." Online dating was not viewed as easier and more efficient than other ways of meeting people (only 33% agreed that it was easier). Although people no longer believe that those who engage in online dating are desperate (61% disagreed), they do still worry that online dating can be dangerous (66% agreed with this statement). The subsample of respondents in the Pew Internet project who were classified as online daters (those who had gone to an online dating website or other sites where they could meet people) were more positive about online dating overall than were nonusers. For example, 79% of the online daters believed that using a dating website is a good way to meet people, and 64% agreed that online dating helps people find a better match. In addition, those who were classified as single and looking had a more positive attitude toward dating services than did the others.

The Pew data (Madden & Lenhart, 2006) suggest that Americans have a more positive attitude about online dating than is indicated by the earlier studies conducted with college students (Anderson, 2005; Donn & Sherman, 2002). Why the difference? It could be that post college singles are more positive than college students (perhaps because they have fewer opportunities than college students to meet others), but it could also be that attitudes about online dating have become more favorable in just a few years. The years from 2000 to 2005 experienced exponential growth in the number of visitors to dating websites (e.g., Madden & Lenhart, 2006; Thompson et al., 2005). Thus, relationship formation through dating websites has become increasingly main stream, and correspondingly, attitudes have likely become more positive.

Although the general public may be more accepting of online dating than they were several years ago, it has also been speculated that many consumers are becoming disillusioned, perhaps after experiencing several failed attempts at matching. In a 2005 report entitled "Consumers Are Having Second Thoughts About Online Dating," produced at weAttract.com and authored by Thompson and his colleagues (2005), one conclusion was that customer satisfaction with online dating has dropped. However, the evidence for that conclusion was indirect and based primarily on the leveling of revenue in the matching industry and on anecdotal evidence. Computer matching sites are probably here for the long haul. There will always be new groups of single adults who turn to the Internet after becoming disillusioned with other ways of meeting potential partners. A particular customer's attitudes toward online dating websites, however, are likely to depend on his or her personal success in finding a mate in cyberspace.

Obviously not all single adults are turning to the Internet to find a partner. It is difficult to know how many singles have subscribed to an Internet matching service in search of a partner and how they might be described demographically because the answer depends on *who* is doing the counting and *what* they are counting. The Pew Internet and American Life project survey referred to earlier (Madden & Lenhart, 2006) examined respondents' experiences with online dating. Most of the sample who were married or in a serious dating relationship had met their partners in more traditional ways (e.g., through friends, at work, or at school). Only 3% of the sample reported meeting through the Internet. However, about 15% of the total sample knew of someone who has been in a long-term relationship with or has married someone who he or she met online. Even more (31%) knew someone who had at least tried online dating sites. Of the total Internet users, 11% said they had gone to a dating website to meet people at least once (16 million people nationally). Within the smaller sample of online adults who were currently seeking romantic partners, 37% had tried a dating website (4 million nationally). Among these online daters, 43% (7 million nationally) reported going on a date with people whom they had met through dating websites.

The data from the Pew Internet project survey are not consistent with the numbers obtained from the web pages of the dating sites. In 2007, Match.com by itself indicates 15 million members, Yahoo.com has stated about 8 million, eHarmony.com over 5 million, and Perfectmatch.com about 3 million. However, as noted by Thompson et al. (2005), when dating sites refer to "millions," they are generally referring to their cumulated subscriptions. In addition, non-Americans can be included in these totals, as can people who have joined more than one website. On the other hand, the 3% of respondents from the Pew Internet project who said that they were in Internet-initiated relationships also include those relationships initiated in Internet venues other than matchmaking services, such as newsgroups and online support groups (Parks & Floyd, 1996; Parks & Robert, 1998).

Is there a demographic profile that distinguishes those who visit dating websites from their peers? According to the Pew national study (Madden & Lenhart, 2006), a greater percentage of men (12%) than of women (9%) visit dating websites. The proportion of Hispanics (14%) and Blacks (13%) who are Internet daters is higher than the proportion of Whites (10%). A higher proportion of urbanites (13%) as compared to suburbanites (10%) and those from rural areas (9%) visit dating websites. Most importantly, the age group of Internet daters in the sample seems to be heavily weighted to people ages 18 to 29 (18%), followed by those ages 30 to 49 (11%), then ages 50 to 64 (6%) and over 65 (3%). In addition, the Pew study found that the online daters were more liberal on most social attitudes than the general American public and, often, also other Internet users. More specifically, they found Internet daters to be less likely to define themselves as religious, less likely to believe in traditional gender roles, and more likely to try new things. Of course, the profile of users will be skewed in particular ways at the specialty sites. For example, religiosity will be higher at Christiansingles.com, and education will be more salient at TheRightStuff.com, a dating service for people at elite and Ivy League colleges and universities.

REASONS FOR USING MATCHING SERVICES

Although there is a large number of singles in the United States and worldwide, only a proportion of even the most computer savvy and love hungry of the singles turn to commercial dating sites in order to find a serious relationship, as noted in the previous section. Many factors may go into the decision to seek matchmaking assistance from an Internet commercial site, as well as into the decision about how long to remain a member of a site when a successful match does not occur. Most likely, individuals will weigh the attractions and advantages to online matching (or, conversely, the barriers to traditional ways of meeting others) against the financial costs and possible stigma of being an "online dater."

Attraction to Online Matching

Commercial matchmaking services are not a recent phenomenon and not limited to the Internet Before online matching services existed, there were matchmakers as well as printed personal advertisements, video-dating services, singles clubs, "lonely hearts clubs," singles travel clubs, and mail-order brides. Many of these alternative methods of meeting partners still exist, although they seem to have received less attention in recent years because of the increasing popularity of Internet matching services.

Several years ago, in a discussion of alternatives to traditional methods of relationship initiation, Woll and Cozby (1987) identified several barriers to traditional ways of meeting others that would motivate people to seek commercial alternatives, such as video-dating services, personal advertisements, and computer dating services. One factor that they mentioned was *lack of access* to available partners. They noted that as people become older (over 30), they have an increasingly difficult time meeting potential partners because they are usually removed from school settings and other locations with a large number of singles. A second barrier was *lack of time.* They wrote that "busy professionals who have many work and civic responsibilities simply do not have time to seek out others through 'normal channels'" (Woll & Cozby, 1987, p. 72). Woll and Cozby also referred to the limited time experienced by the single head of a household who is raising children. People with *special needs or interests* may also turn to alternative ways of meeting others because of the difficulty of finding a partner in the more traditional ways. For example, people whose work mandates brief stays in many different countries may need online help in locating potential dates because they will not have well-established friendship or work networks. *Shyness* may also lead some people to choose an alternative method over a traditional method of meeting others, although Woll and Cozby commented that, surprisingly, shyness appears to play a less motivating role than one might expect.

Although Woll and Cozby (1987) based their analysis of attraction to alternative methods for meeting others primarily on studies conducted with individuals who use personal advertisements and video-dating services, the same considerations likely apply also to users of online matching services. People are likely motivated to seek online matchmaking services because such services provide them with access to many eligible and available others and the process can be efficient and even begin in the convenience and privacy of one's home, day or night As Merkle and Richardson (2000) noted in a commentary about Internet dating, a person could sample scores of other potential partners via Internet matching services. The potential exists for connecting with large numbers of people, who may be spread across a large geographical region, in a relatively short period of time. Furthermore presumably, the people with whom one connects at matching services are "available," "eligible," and interested in making a connection—assumptions that often are less tenable for in-person meetings in diverse public settings. Given the millions of people using matching services in the early 21st century, the potential for contacts at this stage of relationship development is enormous. Another advantage is that people who have atypical interests or possess certain stigmata (such as being HIV positive) may be likely to find a partner or at least someone to chat with online by casting a wide net.

The degree to which people are attracted to the Internet is also related to the qualities (or lack thereof) of the "singles scene" in which they are currently searching. Some people live in geographical locations or work at jobs that make it difficult to find partners, particularly those who share their values and interests. Among the singles who were actively looking for a partner in the Pew sample, 55% said it was difficult to meet new people, and 47% said that there were very few single people nearby who they would be interested in dating (Madden & Lenhart, 2006). People in urban areas had an easier time finding potential dates and mates than did those in suburban or rural areas.

As another special attraction, Internet services provide considerable help in matching people according to age, occupation, wealth, physical looks, psychological qualities including values and attitudes, lifestyle preferences, and many other factors. The Internet increases one's chances of connecting with like-minded (or "like-bodied") people due to the computer s ability to rapidly sort along many dimensions. In fact, the biggest attraction to matching services may be the hope that one can obtain a soul mate, "the love of one's fife," a special partner who would unlikely be found through normal channels. Many matching services promote this hope. Finding a compatible mate through an Internet matching service may be possible, although it may take time and investment. In a 2003

New York Times article, "Online Dating Sheds Its Stigma as Losers.com," Amy Harmon describes a 33-year-old woman (name replaced by X below):

> Of the 120 men she traded messages with online in her first four months of Internet dating X talked to 20 on the telephone at least once and met 11 in person. Of those X dated four several times before realizing she had not found "the one." It is one of the first lessons learned by many in the swelling ranks of subscribers to Internet dating sites: soul mates are harder to come by than dinner and a movie. But like a growing number of single adults X remains convinced that the chances of finding her life partner are better online than off.

Barriers

With all the potential advantages to commercial services for matching, why would not all singles who are looking for a partner choose to use the Internet to find love? Some practical barriers to finding partners in this way for at least some people are the costs involved, illiteracy in the use of computers and online services, and time investment. Costs to belonging to an online dating service can be as high as $60 (in 2007) per month, plus the costs of owning a computer ($500 and beyond) and subscribing to an Internet service ($25 and up, depending on the speed of the Internet connection desired). These costs, however, may not be overwhelming for most, especially as compared to the costs of going to nightclubs and bars to meet others, taking cruises and trips with singles groups, and engaging in other elaborate ways of meeting people in person.

There is, however, a set of more imposing social psychological barriers to the use of the Internet for connecting. In particular, there still is a stigma associated with Internet matchmaking. Some people do not want the stigma and negative stereotypes that they believe might become associated with them if they use such services (e.g., Donn & Sherman, 2002). Although the stigma is dissipating with millions of Internet net users and the popularity of the Internet in television and movie portrayals (e.g., the movies *You've Got Mail* and Log *in for Love), It* still nonetheless affects some (29% of the Pew respondents agreed that people who engage in online dating are desperate, as reported by Madden & Lenhart, 2006).

Another barrier is that occasionally online searchers need to settle for matches who are at a geographical distance, which can introduce costs to the relationship. Although most online daters request that matches be within a nearby radius, those who do not live in geographical areas with high-density populations may need to expand the radius in order to have any matches. In contrast, traditionally people fell in love with the person next door (e.g., Bossard, 1932). Although it was unlikely that the person next door would have a similar score on the type of compatibility test completed at a popular Internet matching service today, neither person had to travel very far to see the other, and neither had to be uprooted in order to move in together. Now, people may be connected through Internet sites with people from other states or cities (or even countries), which creates all lands of logistic and financial challenges. The fact that these lands of relationships require commuting to see one another can exacerbate a related barrier: A pair formed over the Internet does not have the opportunity to possess support from family and friends. Often, family and friends do not know about the developing online relationship, and when they first learn about the Internet-initiated romance, they may not always be supportive (Wildermuth, 2004).

In addition, some singles may be reluctant to try online dating because they do not trust what online members post and say about themselves. Merkle and Richardson (2000) pointed to the anonymity of the Internet as a key issue for all parties in using this medium for communication. In particular, an abiding concern is that potential partners listing their wares on dating sites are not being honest about their marital status, their current romantic involvements, the age of photos posted, their financial status, their personal health, and the like. Singles have reason to be suspicious. Hortacsu, Hitsch, and Ariely (as reported in Levitt & Dubner, 2005) analyzed the profiles provided by 30,000 users at a dating website and compared their data with national averages. Men and women were an inch taller than the national average, and women reported weighing 20 pounds less than the national average. Most people reported themselves to be above average in looks; only 30% of users reported themselves as average in looks, and a mere 1% said they were "less than average." Of course, lying to get a date also occurs in face-to-face interactions (Boon & McCloud, 2001; Rowatt, Cunningham, & Druen, 1999), although in face-to-face situations it is difficult to be deceptive about such personal attributes as appearance and age.

There is also a more sinister side to the Internet that may serve as a formidable barrier to the most cautious of singles. Although they may be fewer in number now that the online dating industry has become mainstream and background checks exist at some sites, Internet predators still exist. Similar to what can occur in face-to-face interaction, some men may initiate a first date in order to isolate a woman and sexually assault her (Shotland, 1989). For further discussion of Internet stalking, see Spitzberg and Cupach (2007).

RELATIONSHIP INITIATION AT COMPUTER MATCHING SERVICES

This section discusses the process by which relationships begin through online matching services. We first discuss the formal role of computer matching services as a commercial market intermediary in relationship initiation. Second, we discuss more specifically how members search for compatible mates at the leading relationship-oriented Internet matching sites. Third, we discuss how relationship initiation that occurs through online matching sites is different from relationship initiation that occurs face-to-face, including through other commercial means.

Matching Services as a Formal Marriage Market Intermediary

Rarely have people formed intimate relationships completely unassisted by others. In some cultures, especially in past times, marriages were arranged by families. Even within societies that offer freedom in mate selection (e.g., those in North America), mating choices are influenced by family and friends. Friends, in particular, are helpful in providing social opportunities for people to meet others for romantic liaisons (e.g., Sprecher, Felmlee, Orbuch, & Willetts, 2002). To the degree that family and social networks help people initiate relationships, they serve as "informal marriage market intermediaries (MMIs)" (Ahuvia & Adelman, 1992).

The same social opportunities provided informally by social networks to facilitate potential pairings are also offered more formally and for a cost by commercial (formal) MMIs, such as Internet matching services. As we noted earlier, there has always been a commercial aspect to mate selection. However, a recent explosion has occurred in market functions that commercial niches offer to assist in relationship formation, especially for busy professionals (Ahuvia & Adelman, 1992; Bernard & Adelman, 1990).

Ahuvia and Adelman (1992) introduced a framework referred to as the "Searching-Matching-Interaction" (SMI) model to describe the marriage market functions served by these MMIs. The *searching* function refers to acquiring information on who is available. The *matching* stage refers to actual decision making for creating compatible matches. The third stage of the SMI framework refers to the "transaction," or *interaction,* which can lead to the development of a romantic relationship. MMIs can provide one, two, or all three marriage functions. Although informal MMIs (e.g., social networks) also serve these functions, they do so less efficiently (Ahuvia & Adelman, 1992).

Ahuvia and Adelman (1992) described computer dating services as potentially assisting in both searching and matching. We note that some online matching sites (e.g., Match.com) focus primarily on the searching function, others (e.g., eHarmony.com) focus primarily on the matching function, and still others (e.g., Perfectmatch.com) offer both. In the early 1990s, when Ahuvia and Adelman's review was written, computer dating services were limited to those developed by college researchers interested in studying interpersonal attraction processes (e.g., Coombs & Kenkel, 1966; Walster et al., 1966). The purpose of these computer dating studies was to match people based on certain criteria and then to see how much they were attracted to each other (as we noted earlier, the assistance of computers was minimal in these studies). Ahuvia and Adelman (1992, p. 459) summarized the findings of these studies in the following way: "physical attractiveness has shown to be highly correlated with attraction. ... Attempts to predict attraction based on personality variables and attitudes, however, have met with only limited success." At the time they wrote their review, Ahuvia and Adelman could find only two studies more specifically on commercial dating services. One was a conference paper by Woll (1987), who during the 1980s had conducted several studies on matching through video-dating services. As summarized in Ahuvia and Adelman, Woll (1987) presented "a compelling argument that a properly programmed computer would be better than a human matchmaker at predicting a couple's compatibility" (p. 459). In the other computer dating study available at the time, Sindberg, Roberts, and McClain (1972) compared a group of couples that had married after being matched by a computer matching agency with a control group of couples that met but did not marry. Generally, the couples in both groups were homogeneous on many traits, with homogamy on a few traits (e.g., degree of optimism versus pessimism) particularly associated with the likelihood of marrying.

Much has changed since Ahuvia and Adelman's (1992) theoretical review of market intermediaries was published. Computer services have advanced to the forefront of the market of formal intermediaries in matchmaking. The more general result of the popularity of matchmaking services is the increased social legitimacy of the marketing of the *searching* and *matching* functions of relationship formation. In addition, we predict that there soon will be a large number of scientific studies conducted with commercial dating services and the relationships that are formed from them, although currently there is a limited amount of published literature. In addition, future matching sites may also go beyond the searching and matching functions to offer more online interactions to facilitate singles finding an appropriate match (see work on "virtual dates" by Frost, as discussed in Evans, 2006).

From First Submission of Profile to the Development of the Relationship

How do people engage in relationship initiation through online relationship sites? In this section, we describe the process based on what we have gleaned from dating websites and popular articles (e.g., Gottlieb, 2006) and through the lens of a theoretical model from the relationship field, Levinger's (1974; see also Levinger & Snoek, 1972) model of pair relatedness. The model presents relationship development as progressing through the following stages: zero contact, unilateral awareness, surface contact, and a continuum of mutuality. We will refer to the two people who are meeting as P (person) and O (other).

Level 0 *(zero contact)* serves primarily as a benchmark, but the first stage (Level 1) in which relationship initiation occurs is *unilateral awareness.* At this stage, P becomes aware of O. O may become aware of P at nearly the same time, at a later time, or not at all. At Level 2, *surface contact,* P and O have initial contact. If positive impressions are formed between P and O at surface contact, the relationship may progress to Level 3, a stage representing increasing degrees *o£ mutuality,* during which more mutual disclosure, discovery, and investment occur (Levinger, 1974). Of course, the relationship could end at any time, and often does end after brief surface contact occurring through Internet interactions.

Below we discuss how P and O move through the stages of awareness, surface contact, and mutuality in the online world of matching services. We distinguish between relationship initiation on those sites that rely on members to make their own matches versus relationship initiation on sites uiat offer assistance in the matching process.

Relationship sites with member-initiated matches most websites facilitate searching by allowing people to post profile information as well as search the profiles of others. The profile information includes vital demographic information (e.g., age and gender), education, likes and dislikes, and usually a photograph. Online profile information is generally lengthier and more detailed man printed versions of personal advertisements (e.g., in the newspaper) because, in contrast to the printed version, there is no cost based on length. Some websites also allow video profiles.

If a P visiting one of the dating websites has the time and motivation, she could search many profiles, and therefore experience unilateral awareness with many Os. To narrow the field to those who are geographically accessible for offline relationships, she would likely search based on zip code, city, or state. To assist members in finding the most compatible matches, some sites (e.g., Match. com) offer keyword searches, in which members narrow their searches to those who mention in their profile a particular word or phrase (e.g., *dancer* or *like to travel).* Even so, a frustration that has been expressed by some members of large dating websites is that there are too many profiles to review. As noted by Thompson and his colleagues (2005), it can sometimes feel like "trying to find a needle in a bigger and bigger haystack" (p. 26).

From the pool of Os that P becomes aware of after searching through online profiles, she can decide with whom she would like to advance to surface contact. To our knowledge, research has not been conducted on the decision-making process that occurs during profile searches at online matching sites. However, an early study on decision strategies used in video dating is relevant. Woll (1986) instructed members of a video-dating service to read the profile sheets of other members of the video-dating service and describe into a tape recorder the exact factors they were considering in the decisions about whether to view their videotapes. He found that the members were most likely to refer to the age and physical attractiveness of the other members as affecting their choices.

Websites encourage their members to post a photo because the chances of being selected without a photo are small. Levitt and Dubner (2005) cited research by Hortacsu and his colleagues, who found men who included their photo in their profile receive three times the responses of men who did not; for women, the increase is sixfold. The photos allow "chemistry" to begin (or not), and the assumption among people who post their own photos is that the omission of a photo means that the person is unattractive. This may not be true (many of the profiles without photos insist that these members are quite good-looking), but in the absence of data to the contrary, searchers assume that photoless profiles hide less physically compelling candidates. Whitty's in-depth interviews with users of online dating also revealed the importance of posting a photograph (Whitty & Carr, 2006).

Surface contact on matching websites involves first engaging in a form of anonymous contact, which is usually controlled by the particular website. For example, at some sites, the first surface contact that members can have with others is to send a wink, "icebreaker," happy face, "spark," or another type of sign of interest. This represents a request from P to O to return the awareness, and serves as an invitation to move the relationship to surface contact. O may completely ignore the request or may read P's profile information and decide whether he or she wants to respond. O may not respond if he or she (a) is flooded with messages of interest from many others (has "alternatives") (b) does not think the other would make a good match after reviewing P's profile information, or (c) is not a paid member of the relationship site (some sites allow "visitors" to post profiles for free but not respond to messages from others until they pay).

If O responds to P, the surface contact stage of relationship initiation continues. Next, the two are likely to move to two-way online communication, which is usually in a structured anonymous format offered through the relationship site. For example, electronic messages can be exchanged between P and O without names or other identifying information. An interview study conducted with couples who met online (Baker, 1998) suggests that people s early attraction is influenced not only by what they learn about the other's attributes, but also by O's writing style and speed of responding to messages. Attraction and the likelihood of continuing the initiation process may also be influenced by how the social network is responding to the developing relationship—assuming they know about it (Wildermuth, 2004).

Similar to the surface contact stage that occurs in face-to-face interaction, two people who communicate for the first time online often begin with superficial information and then progress to sharing more personal information and disclosures. Research indicates that it is fairly easy to disclose online (Merkle & Richardson, 2000; Wysocki, 1996,1998; also see McKenna, this volume), and thus minor intersections of mutuality and interdependence can develop fairly easily even before there is a face-to-face meeting (e.g., Parks & Floyd, 1996; Parks & Robert, 1998). Experts on interaction in cyberspace have noted that individuals are often strategic in the presentation of the "self that they choose to emphasize in initial online interactions (Albright, 2007; Whitty, 2007; Whitty & Carr, 2006).

The P who has the time and motivation to have surface contact with many Os is likely to move to a stage of mutuality with at least one person but possibly several others. Initial stages of mutuality may begin online, but are likely to advance to phone calls; the exchange of cards, letters, and photographs through mail; and possibly a face-to-face meeting. When people decide to approach another person after an initial Internet screening, they are moving to another stage of cues and information. Each stage can involve different cues (e.g., voice cues in telephone contacts). Some sites now offer a way to make anonymous phone calls so that the recipient cannot have access to the callers phone number. If P and O meet in person, they are encouraged to do so in a public location. When P and O do meet offline, the relationship is likely to either move to deeper levels of mutuality or end if they discover the chemistry they had online does not transfer to face-to-face interaction. Merkle and Richardson (2000) noted that many online relationships fade away well before personal contact occurs, and many others are likely to end after a first meeting. Not only does lack of chemistry in face-to-face interaction cool what might have been a spark of romance occurring in online communication, but also so does any disappointment experienced if it is realized that the other misrepresented him or herself in the profile (e.g., Whitty, 2004).

Relationship Sites with Matching Assistance

As noted earlier, eHarmony.com, Perfect-match.com, Chemistry.com, and an increasing number of other sites offer "matching assistance." These sites require members to complete lengthy questionnaires, and based on the information provided in these questionnaires, the site sends members "compatibility matches" and a procedure to begin communicating if they wish. To match members based on their questionnaire data, matching sites are using what have been referred to in the business as "love or matching algorithms" (e.g., Orenstein, 2003), matching formulas based supposedly on scientific principles and translated into computer programs that can sift through the volumes of data collected from the members. Dating websites generally do not publish their matching formulas or subject them to peer review, but information on their websites and in the media (e.g., Gottlieb, 2006) suggests that the focus is on compatibility (mostly similarities, although occasionally differences too) in personality characteristics. The sites that offer scientific matching have been able to charge more, and as a result, other dating sites such as Match.com that have traditionally offered only the searching function are beginning to incorporate objective science into the matching process (e.g., Orenstein, 2003).

Some of the dating sites also offer a multiple-stage process for initiating contact, which is described to help two people learn more about each other in a nonthreatening way. For example, at eHarmony. com, this involves responding to multiple-choice items, sharing "must haves" and "can't stands," and writing and exchanging questions. The other sites recommend similar steps for initial interaction.

Regardless of the specific type of online dating world in which P and O maneuver through awareness, through surface contact, and on to minor intersections of mutuality, the pair may or may not migrate offline. Some friendships form online and remain online. Most people who become members of matching services, though, are interested in forming a romantic relationship, and therefore success is measured by a relationship that moves to face-to-face contact and on to a long-term commitment.

RELATIONSHIP FORMATION AT INTERNET SERVICES COMPARED TO OTHER WAYS OF FORMING RELATIONSHIPS

Above we discussed the specific steps of relationship initiation at online dating sites. In this section, we speculate how initiation steps and basic attraction processes may differ online versus offline.

Predictors of Attraction Online versus Offline

Some of the factors that have been found to affect attraction and the formation of relationships include similarity in attitudes and values, physical proximity, the physical attractiveness of potential partners, self-disclosure in the process of getting to know another person, and support from friends and family for the relationship (Berscheid & Reis, 1998; Hatfield & Rapson, 2005). Each of these factors may affect relationship formation, and each may work via the medium of the Internet (or e-mail) or via in-person interaction. However, these factors play out in different ways and points in time in the different means of meeting.

According to Merkle and Richardson (2000), the process of attraction in a face-to-face romantic relationship is likely to involve first the influence of spatial and physical attractiveness, and then the discovery of similarity and the role of self-disclosure. They stated that in contrast, Internet-initiated romantic relationships involve "an inverted developmental sequence," which first involves a high level of mutual and sometimes intense self-disclosure and an initial minimal role for physical attractiveness and proximity (see also Cooper & Sportolari, 1997). Physical attractiveness will still play a role once two people meet in person, as noted by Cooper and Sportolari (p. 9), but its impact may be less because it follows learning other information about each other. Cooper and Sportolari speculated that by the time two people meet, "the felt intensity and meaning of any unappealing physical traits are then more likely to be mitigated by the overall attraction that exists" (p. 9).

An interesting finding from early work on face-to-face versus online initiation is that Internet users may come to personally know one another better and share intimate knowledge more quickly than do persons who meet in person (Wysocki, 1998). In a survey of persons using the Internet for matchmaking, Wysocki found that people often spend a great amount of time writing about themselves and asking questions of others. Such activity may constitute a type of social penetration (Altman & Taylor, 1973). Presumably, the safety of anonymity and the alacrity of writing on the computer versus talking face-to-face may mediate such findings. Walther and Parks (2002) argued that not only does the intensity of self-disclosure lead to the development of closeness, but also closeness is enhanced by the ability to present oneself carefully by editing messages and by the tendency to make idealistic attributes of the (initially distant) other. Although closeness based on intense self-disclosure may develop more quickly in the Internet-developed relationships, the relationships may also more easily and quickly *dissolve* if there is not an adequate reward—cost ratio. That is, there may be fewer barriers to breaking up, which includes the influence of having many additional alternatives (Merkle & Richardson, 2000).

What do couples themselves say attracted them to the other when they first became acquainted online? In a small study of 18 couples who met online and then migrated offline, Baker (1998) reported that couples mentioned sense of humor, response time, interests, qualities described online, and writing style. Whitty and Gavin (2001) interviewed people who had developed online relationships and found that they valued many of the same relationship characteristics that people valued in face-to-face relationships, including trust, honesty, and commitment. In addition, people are attracted to those who were honest in how they presented themselves in their profile.

Getting Help from Friends versus an Internet Service

One common traditional way of meeting another is through friends. Friends assist in the mating process in a variety of ways, including by presenting social opportunities for others to meet and by actually making introductions (e.g., Sprecher et al., 2002). It is useful to compare relationship initiation that occurs through the assistance of computer matching services (and their scientific advisors) and relationship initiation that occurs through the assistance of friends.

Although in both cases there is assistance by a third party, there are differences between formal MMIs (e.g., computer matchmaking services) and informal MMIs (e.g., social networks) in addition to formality and cost. First, formal MMIs are typically more *efficient* (Ahuvia & Adelman, 1992). The online services often are always available and can be accessed as needed. Conversely, there is a limit to the degree that people can ask friends to host social events or introduce them to their friends. Furthermore, an almost unlimited number of people can be serviced by online matching services (millions are now members of some online dating services), whereas there is a limit in how many single friends are available through the network of one's friends.

A second difference between formal and informal MMIs is that the formal MMIs can be anonymous. One can remain anonymous to potential matches during the early stages of contact, revealing one's identity to the other only after trust has developed. In addition, in a way that might not be possible when one is searching for a partner in face-to-face interactions, people can search for a partner online without family and friends being aware.

The third difference is that the formal MMIs emphasize to a greater degree than the informal MMIs that mating is a transaction in which assets are exchanged and people possess market value (for a review of exchange and equity principles, see Hatfield, Rapson, & Aumer-Ryan, in press; Sprecher & Schwartz, 1994). As noted by Ahuvia and Adelman (1992), "[Sjocial scientists have long seen mate selection as occurring in a marriage market where both economic and interpersonal assets are exchanged. Commercial dating services, by making these assets explicit, further emphasize the relevance of market theory" (p. 454). The explicitness of the market value of individuals may be particularly evidenced in online personal advertisements, in which participants must emphasize their assets in a few sentences in order to appeal to potential seekers. To have others become interested enough to want to pursue them, members need to emphasize and even augment their professional status, appearance, and any other personal assets that they can offer. This is in contrast to relationships formed face-to-face, in which spatial and social proximity may naturally bring people together who have similar exchange assets and/or information about "exchange value" can be indirectly acquired through observations and information from the social network. On the other hand, some experts have argued that just the opposite occurs once there is online interaction. As noted by Cooper and Sportolari (1997, p. 9), "Electronic relating offers a different basis for interaction than that of the 'meat market' of the singles scene." People can get to know each other before there is an opportunity to exhaustively evaluate each others appearance.

Online Relationships versus Other Commercial Means for Meeting Others

We can also compare relationship initiation that occurs through online dating services with that which occurs in other commercial ways of meeting. Other commercial means include the now old-fashioned newspaper advertisements, as well as singles groups meetings, parties, dinners, dances, and so-called speed dating. Most of these other commercial means for meeting people focus on the 'interaction" aspect of the SMI framework presented above; less assistance is provided in matching decision making. Most of these other alternative ways also focus on finding matches within one particular geographic location. These activities may provide the advantages of information gained through in-person meetings. However, those attending these events also are dependent on who shows up and the ease of singling out any one individual for chatting. At singles functions, including dances, one may have to wade through a host of people to get to the one for whom there is attraction. Those who are shy or socially awkward, however, may have a difficult time in these settings (Sprecher & McKinney, 1987).

There is a plethora of variables associated with each type of in-person meeting, from random encounters to hookups at bars, meetings at singles' events, and setups by friends. These variables include the availability and density of singles, their interests in meeting others, and the amount of time and special interaction circumstances required for meeting (e.g., a man may want to ask one woman in a group of women to spend time with him, but be deterred by the size and nature of the group). These variables also speak to the delicate tactical and self-presentation considerations that frequently go into these in-person meetings (Goffman, 1959).

Speed dating is an interesting activity that has flourished in recent years. It is a commercially brokered service that involves advertising an event and then regulating the time each possible person has to talk to an "assigned date" (see chapter 11 in this book by Eastwick & Finkel). It usually is done in large meeting rooms in hotels or bars, and also involves a concluding questionnaire that asks persons to indicate which of the possible partners they might like to interact with further. Speed dating appears to be successful only to the degree that a host of well-qualified partners show up for the event. If advertising, practical matters such as the time and place of the event, geography in terms of density of the local singles population, or word-of-mouth commentaries are not favorable, then the event will not be successful, especially over the long run. Such events require capital and lots of organization. A sponsor may put on a few such events, not make enough money to continue, and thus leave at the doorstep users who began to rely on this means of meaning possible partners. On the other hand, speed dating has its admirers. It is ideal for people who feel that they know almost immediately whether they are interested in someone (see Eastwick & Finkel, this volume).

CONCLUSIONS AND FUTURE RESEARCH DIRECTIONS

Although relationships are still far more likely to be initiated offline than online, an increasing number of men and women are seeking the assistance of Internet matchmaking services (e.g., Madden & Lenhart, 2006). An interesting development that has occurred as a result of the popularity of matching services is the greater awareness by the media and lay public of the scientific study of relationships, particularly that of mate selection and attraction. Several dating websites (e.g., eHar-mony.com and Perfectmatch.com) claim to be utilizing the existing scientific literature on relationship initiation, mate choice, and factors leading to relationship success in crafting their compatibility questionnaires and in devising matching algorithms for pairing members. Some dating websites also seem genuinely interested in contributing to the scientific base of relationships. For example, eHar-niony.com has created a research laboratory and hired a team of scientists. Among other projects, they are conducting longitudinal research with couples who met through eHarmony.com matching (Gottlieb, 2006). Therefore, a mutually beneficial merger is being developed between the scientific field of relationships and the commercial matchmaking services. The sites have benefited from the scientific knowledge created in academe about personal relationships, but the scientific field also has the opportunity to benefit from the commercial websites' desire to make matchmaking a science. Nonetheless, whether the profit-making motive of the commercial enterprises will be compatible with the openness and objectivity required in scientific analysis is yet to be determined (e.g., Houran, Lange, Rentfrow, & Bruckner, 2004).

We would like to comment on three types of research that may be conducted in the future that will enhance our understanding of relationship initiation. First, the matchmaking sites are likely to (or likely to continue to, in some cases) conduct proprietary research that tests aspects of their matching algorithms or examines customer satisfaction and relationship success in response to matching innovations or online get-acquainted strategies. Although such findings may never be published in scientific journals, the findings may become available through the websites and in other reports and therefore have indirect implications for the scientific study of relationships.

Second, the scientific advisors and others who gain access to the matching services may be allowed to test theories about relationship initiation and development with a sample obtained from the website. The sample of online daters is not representative of singles who are at early stages of relationship development, but the generalizability of a sample of online daters may not be any more problematic, and may even be less problematic in some cases, than relying on college samples (Buchanan, 2000). In addition, the unique advantage of samples from matching websites is the ability to collect data from individuals in the midst of initial acquaintanceship, or even before they have noticed each other, something that is difficult to do even with convenient human subject pools in psychology. Furthermore, because members of websites often interact with many others before finding a successful relationship, within-subject comparisons can be conducted to examine the types of initial pairings and interactions that are most successful for the development of relationships, controlling for individual factors. Various innovative methods can be used, including interaction records (Wheeler & Reis, 1991), in which the members complete a brief record after each significant get-acquainted interaction. This approach has already been used in the Northwestern Speed-Dating Study (see Eastwick & Finkel, this volume).

A third type of research can compare later stages of successful relationships that had their origins in online matching with later stages of relationships that were initiated offline. If Dr. Warren, founder of eHarmony, is correct, relationships that are formed based on "the deep compatibility" that is claimed to be possible with compatibility matching at dating websites should have greater happiness and lower divorce rates than relationships that begin in more traditional ways, controlling for such critical variables as length of relationship, divorce status, and the presence of children. However, another viewpoint discussed in this chapter is that such cyberspace-initiated relationships will not benefit from the support that comes from being in a relationship that emerges through social networks and will have costs involved if at least one of the partners has to relocate in order for the pair to be in the same geographical region. Such comparison research has been conducted by eHarmony.com (Carter & Snow, 2004), but would be better conducted by independent research organizations or teams. One possible project could be to examine how the relationships that are formed online differ from relationships that are formed offline on a number of dimensions, including whether they are less homogeneous than relationships formed in more traditional dating practices, and also whether they differ on relationship satisfaction, longevity, and other indicators of quality. We speculate that once relationships that have begun through online dating services migrate offline, they may not be that different from relationships that form in other ways. The dissolution and divorce rates are likely to be the same, and probably the same factors will influence success versus dissolution. However, whether or not this is so is an empirical question that can be examined in future research.

In sum, commercial matching services are still in their infancy. In time—given the resources and money that are bound to be lavished on improving such commercial enterprises—it is reasonable to hope that matching sites will provide increased opportunities for men and women to find dating and marital relationships that are fulfilling. It is also hoped that in the future, the Busines-sofLove.com sites will use more complex versions of relationship science to inform their questionnaire construction, website construction, and matching algorithms; and that, in turn, Internet matching services will allow scholars to conduct the research needed to enrich understanding of attraction and love relationships.

REFERENCES

Ahuvia, A. C, & Adelman, M. B. (1992). Formal intermediaries in the marriage market: A typology and review. *Journal of Marriage and the Family,* 54,452—463.

Albright, J. M. (2007). How do I love thee and thee and thee: Self-presentation, deception, and multiple relationships online. In M. T. Whitty, A. J. Baker, & J. A. Inman (Eds.), *Online matching* (pp. 81–93). Hampshire, UK: Palgrave Macmillan.

Altman, I., & Taylor, D. (1973). *Social penetration: The development of interpersonal relationships.* New York: Holt, Rinehart & Winston.

Anderson, T. L. (2005). Relationships among Internet attitudes, Internet use, romantic beliefs, and perceptions of online romantic relationships. *Cyber Psychology & Behavior, 8,*521—531.

Baker, A. (1998, July). Cyberspace couples finding romance online then meeting for the first time in real life. *CMC Magazine.* Retrieved November 29,2007, from http://www.december.com/cmc/mag/1998/5ul/baker.html

Bernard, A. C, & Adelman, M. B. (1990). Market metaphors for meeting mates. In M. E. Goldberg, G. Gorn, & R. W. Pollay (Eds.), *Advances in consumer research* (Vol. 17, p. 78). Provo, UT: Association for Consumer Research.

Berscheid, E., & Reis, H. T. (1998). Attraction and close relationships. In D. Gilbert, S. Fiske, & G. Lindzey (Eds.), *The handbook of social psychology* (4th ed., Vol. 2, pp. 193–281). New York: McGraw-Hill.

Boon, S., & McCloud, B. (2001). Deception in romantic relationships: Subjective estimates at success at deceiving and attitudes toward deception. *Journal of Social and Personal Relationships, 18,*463–476.

Bossard, J. H. S. (1932). Residential propinquity in marriage selection. *American Journal of Sociology, 38,* 219–224.

Buchanan, T. (2000). Potential of the Internet for personality research. In M. H. Burnham (Ed.), *Psychological experiments on the Internet* (pp. 121–140). San Diego, CA: Academic Press.

Byrne, D. (1971). *The attraction paradigm.* New York: Academic Press.

Byrne, D., Ervin, C. R., & Lamberth, J. (1970). Continuity between the experimental study of attraction and real-life computer dating. *Journal of Personality and Social Psychology, 16,*157–165.

Carter, S., & Snow, C. (2004, May). *Helping singles enter better marriages using predictive models of marital success.* Paper presented at the 16th annual convention of the American Psychological Society, Chicago.

CBC Archives. (1957, July 17). *Clip: Computer matchmaker.* Retrieved November 29, 2007, from http://archives.cbc.ca/400i.asp?IDCat=75&IDDos=710&IDCli=4199&IDLan=l&NoCli=3&type=clip

Coombs, R. H., or Kenkel, W. F. (1966). Sex differences in dating aspirations and satisfaction with computer-arranged partners. *Journal of Marriage and the Family, 28,* 62–66.

Cooper, A., & Sportolari, L. (1997). Romance in cyberspace: Understanding online attraction. *Journal of Sex Education and Therapy, 22,* 7—14.

Donn, J. E., & Sherman, R. C. (2002). Attitudes and practices regarding the formation of romantic relationships on the Internet. *Cyber Psychology & Behavior, 5,*107–123.

Evans, D. (2006, September 6). Online matchmaking with virtual dates. *Online Dating.* Retrieved November 29,2007, from http://dating.corante.com/archives2006/09/06/online_matchmaking

Goffman, E. (1959). *The presentation of self in everyday life.* Garden City, NY: Doubleday.

Gottlieb, L. (2006, March). How do I love thee? *Atlantic Monthly,* 58–70.

Harmon, A. (2003, June 29). Online dating sheds its stigma as Losers.com. *New York Times.* Retrieved November 29, 2007, from http://www.nytimes.com/2003/06/29/national/29DATE.html?ex=1372219200&en=l 16d836a4d43845c&ei=5007&partner=USERLAND

Hatfield, E., & Rapson, R. L. (2005). *Love and sex: Cross-cultural perspectives.* Lanham, MD: University Press of America.

Hatfield, E., Rapson, R. L., & Aumer-Ryan, K. (in press). Social justice in love relationships: Recent developments. *Social Justice Research.*

Houran, J., Lange, R., Rentfrow, J. P., & Bruckner, K. H. (2004). Do online matchmaking tests work? An assessment of preliminary evidence for a publicized "predictive model of marital success." *North American Journal of Psychology,* 6, 507–526.

Joinson, A. N. (2003). *Understanding the psychology of internet behaviour: Virtual worlds, real lives.* New York: Palgrave Macmillan.

Kleinfeld, N. (2003, June 11). An officer and a gentleman? 50 women would disagree. *New York Times,* p. Al.

Leonhardt, D. (2006, March 28). The famous founder of Operation Match. *New York Times.* Retrieved December 22, 2007, from http://www.nytimes.com/2006/03/28/business/291eonside.html

Levinger, G. (1974). A three-level approach to attraction: Toward an understanding of pair relatedness. In T. L. Huston (Ed.), *Foundations of interpersonal attraction* (pp. 99–120). New York: Academic Press.

Levinger, G., & Snoek, J. D. (1972). *Attraction in relationships: A new look at interpersonal attraction.* Morristown, NJ: General Learning Press.

Levitt, S. D., & Dubner, S. J. (2005). *Freakonomics: A rogue economist explores the hidden side of everything* New York: William Morrow.

Madden, M., & Lenhart, A. (2006, March 5). *Online dating* (Report for the Pew Internet & American Life Project). Retrieved December 22, 2007, from http//www.pewintemet.org/pdTs/PIP_Online_Dating.pdf

Merkle, E. R., & Richardson, R. A. (2000). Digital dating and virtual relating: Conceptualizing computer mediated romantic relationships. *Family Relations, 490,*187—192.

Orenstein, S. (2003, August 1). The love algorithm Match.com thinks it has found a formula for ruling the online dating business: A scientific way to find Mr. or Ms. Right. *Business 2.0 Magazine.* Retrieved November 29, 2007, from http://money.cnn.com/magazines/business2/business2_archive/2003/08

Parks, M. R., & Floyd, K. (1996). Making friends in cyberspace. *Journal of Communication, 46,* 80–97.

Parks, M. R., & Roberts, L. D. (1998). "Making MOOsic": The development of personal relationships online and a comparison to their off-line counterparts. *Journal of Social and Personal Relationships, 15,*517–537.

Rowatt, W. C., Cunningham, M. R., & Druen, P. B. (1999). Lying to get a date: The effect of facial physical attractiveness on the willingness to deceive prospective dating partners. *Journal of Social and Personal Relationships, 16,*209–223.

Shotland, R. L. (1989). A model of the causes of date rape in developing and close relationships. In C. Hendrick (Ed.), *Close relationships* (pp. 247–270). Newbury Park, CA: Sage.

Sindberg, R. M., Roberts, A. E, & McClain, D. (1972). Mate selection factors in computer matched marriages. *Journal of Marriage and the Family, 34,*611–614.

Spitzberg, B. H., & Cupach, W. R. (2007). Cyber-stalking as (mis)matchmaking. In M. Whitty, A. Baker, & J. A. Inman (Eds.), *Online matchmaking* (pp. 127–146). Hampshire, UK: Palgrave Macmillan.

Sprecher, S., Felmlee, D., Orbuch, T. L., & Willetts, M. C. (2002). Social networks and change in personal relationships. In A. Vangelisti, H. Reis, & M. A. Fitzpatrick (Eds.), *Stability and change in relationships* (pp. 257–284). New York: Cambridge.

Sprecher, S., & Metts, S. (1989). Development of the "Romantic Beliefs Scale" and examination of the effects of gender and gender-role orientation. *Journal of Social and Personal Relationships, 6,*387–411.

Sprecher, S., & McKinney, K. (1987). Barriers in the initiation of intimate heterosexual relationships. *Journal of Social Work and Human Sexuality, 5,*97–110.

Sprecher, S., & Schwartz, P. (1994). Equity and balance in the exchange of contributions in close relationships. In M. J. Lerner & G. Mikula (Eds.), *Entitlement and the affectional bond* (pp. 11—42). New York: Plenum.

Thompson, M., Zimbardo, P., & Hutchinson, G. (2005, April 29). *Consumers are having second thoughts about online dating.* Unpublished report. Retrieved November 29, 2007, from http://weAttract.com

Walster, E., Aronson, V., Abrahams, D., & Rottman, L. (1966). Importance of physical attractiveness in dating behavior. *Journal of Personality and Social Psychology, 4,*508–516.

Walther, J. B., & Parks, M. R. (2002). Cues filtered out, cues filtered in: Computer-mediated communication and relationships. In M. L. Knapp & J. A. Daly (Eds.), *Handbook of interpersonal communication* (3rd ed., pp. 529–563). Thousand Oaks, CA: Sage.

Wheeler, L., & Reis, H. T. (1991). Self-recording of everyday life events: Origins, types, and uses. *Journal of Personality, 59,* 339–354.

Whitty, M. T. (2004, May). *Shopping for love on the Internet: Men and women's experiences of using an Australian Internet dating site.* Paper presented at the Communication Research in the Public Interest ICA meeting, New Orleans, LA.

Whitty, M. T. (2007). The art of selling one's "self on an online dating site: The BAR approach. In M. T. Whitty, A.]. Baker, & J. A. Inman (Eds.), *Online matching* (pp. 57–69). Hampshire, UK: Palgrave Macmillan.

Whitty, M. T., & Carr, A. N. (2006). *Cyberspace romance: The psychology of online relationships.* Basingstoke, UK: Palgrave Macmillan.

Whitty, M., & Gavin, J. (2001). Age/sex/location: Uncovering the social cues in the development of online relationships. *Cyber Psychology and Behavior, 4,* 623–630.

Wildermuth, S. M. (2004). The effects of stigmatizing discourse on the quality of on-line relationships. *Cyber Psychology & Behavior, 7,*73–84.

Woll, S. (1986, June). So many to choose from: Decision strategies in videodating. *Journal of Social and Personal Relationships, 3,*43–53.

Woll, S. B. (1987). *Improper linear models of matchmaking.* Paper presented at the Iowa Conference on Personal Relationships, Iowa City.

Woll S., & Cozby, P. (1987). Videodating and other alternatives to traditional methods of relationship initiation. In W. Jones & D. Perlman (Eds.), *Advances in personal relationships* (Vol. 1, pp. 69–109). Greenwich, CT: JAI.

Wysocki, D. K. (1996). *Somewhere over the modem: Relationships over computer bulletin boards.* Unpublished doctoral dissertation, University of California, Santa Barbara.

Wysocki, D. K. (1998). Let your fingers do the talking. Sex on an adult chat-line. *Sexualities, 1,*425–452.

The Drive to Love

The Neural Mechanism for Mate Selection

By Helen Fisher

Since the heaven and earth were created, you were made for me and I was made for you and I will not let you go," declared Chang Po to his beloved Meilan (Yutang, 1954, p. 73). The Chinese still cry over this twelfth-century Chinese fable, "The Jade Goddess," their version of Romeo and Juliet. "My beloved, the delight of my eyes," exclaimed Inanna of her beloved Dumuzi in a Sumerian poem recorded some four thousand years ago (Wolkstein, 1991, p. 51). An anonymous Kwakiutl Indian of southern Alaska recited these words in 1896: "Fires run through my body—the pain of loving you" (Hamill, 1996).

Paris and Helen, Orpheus and Eurydice, Abelard and Eloise, Troilus and Cressida, Tristan and Iseult, Shiva and Saci, Layla and Majnun: thousands of romantic poems, songs, and stories come across the centuries from Europe, the Middle East, Japan, China, India, and every other society that has left written or oral records. In a survey of 166 varied cultures, anthropologists found evidence of romantic love in 147 (Jankowiak and Fischer, 1992). There were no negative data; in the remaining nineteen societies, scholars had simply failed to examine this aspect of people's lives.

"What 'tis to Love?" Shakespeare asked in *As You Like It.* From the ancient Greeks to contemporary scholars, hundreds have offered theories about the components of love and styles of loving (Lee, 1988; Fehr, 198S; Aron and Westbay, 1996; Hatfield and Sprecher, 1986; Critelli, Myers, and Loos, 1986; Hendrick and Hendrick, 1986; Zick, 1970; Hazan and Shaver, 1987; Sternberg, 1986). And for good reason: love has myriad variations. Nevertheless, neuroscientists believe that the basic human emotions and motivations arise from distinct systems of neural activity, networks that derive from mammalian precursors

(Davidson, 1994; Panksepp, 1998). This article takes the neurological approach. It does not attempt to define one's idiosyncratic ways of loving that develop in childhood, nor why an individual chooses one person rather than another. Instead, it explores the underlying neural mechanisms associated with love, specifically romantic love.

Psychological studies indicate that romantic love is associated with a discrete constellation of emotions, motivations, and behaviors (Liebowitz, 1983; Hatfield and Sprecher, 1986; Tennov, 1979; Harris, 1995). Romantic love begins as an individual comes to regard another as special, even unique. The lover then intensely focuses his or her attention on this preferred individual, aggrandizing the beloved's better traits and overlooking or minimizing his or her flaws. Lovers experience extreme energy, hyperactivity, sleeplessness, impulsivity, euphoria, and mood swings. They are goal-oriented and strongly motivated to win the beloved. Adversity heightens their passion, in what is known as the Romeo and Juliet effect or "frustration attraction" (Fisher, 2004). Lovers become emotionally dependent on the relationship. They reorder their daily priorities to remain in contact with their sweetheart, and experience separation anxiety when apart. And most feel powerful empathy for their amour; many report they would die for their beloved.

A striking property of romantic love is "intrusive thinking." The lover thinks obsessively about the beloved. And, perhaps most central to this experience, the lover craves emotional union with his or her sweetheart. Plato wrote of this in *The Symposium* some twenty-five hundred years ago, saying the God of Love "lives in a state of need." Love-smitten individuals feel intense sexual desire, as well as extreme possessiveness of the beloved. Yet their craving for emotional union supersedes their longing for sexual contact. As a result, rejected lovers often go to extraordinary, inappropriate, even dangerous efforts to win back their sweetheart. Many spurned lovers suffer "abandonment rage" and depression as well, culminating in feelings of hopelessness, lethargy, resignation, and despair (Fisher, 2004). Last, romantic love is involuntary, difficult to control, and impermanent (Tennov, 1979; Hatfield and Sprecher, 1986; Harris, 1995). As Violetta sings in *La Traviata,* Verdi's tragic opera, "Let's live for pleasure alone, since love, like flowers, swiftly fades."

To further establish that the above assemblage of characteristics is accurate, I used these traits as domains in a questionnaire on romantic passion; 437 Americans and 402 Japanese filled out my questionnaire. The results indicate that romantic love does not vary considerably with age, gender, sexual orientiation, or ethnic group. For example, people over age forty-five and those under age twenty-five showed no significant statistical differences on 82 percent of the statements. On 87 percent of the queries, American men and women responded virtually alike. Heterosexuals and homosexuals gave statistically similar responses on 86 percent of the questions. American "whites" and "others" responded similarily on 82 percent of the questions. And where the above groups showed statistically significant differences in their responses, one group was usually just a little more passionate than the other. The greatest differences were between the Americans and the Japanese. On most of the forty-three questions where they showed statistically significant variations, these differences were small, however. And the twelve queries showing dramatic variance appeared to have cultural explanations (Fisher, 2004).

World poetry, myths and legends, many anthropological and psychological reports, and this questionnaire suggest that romantic love is a human universal (Jankowiak and Fischer, 1992; Fisher, 1998; Hatfield and Rapson, 1996). In fact, I have come to believe that romantic love is one of three discrete, interrelated emotion/motivation systems that all birds and mammals have evolved to direct courtship, mating, reproduction, and parenting. The other two are the sex drive and attachment. Each brain system is associated with different feelings and behaviors; each is associated with a different (and dynamic) constellation of neural correlates; each evolved to direct a different aspect of reproduction; and each interacts with the other two in myriad combinations to produce the range of emotions, motivations, and behaviors associated with all types of love (Fisher, 2004).

LUST, ATTRACTION, ATTACHMENT: THREE BRAIN SYSTEMS FOR LOVE

The sex drive (libido or lust) is characterized by the craving for sexual gratification; it is often directed toward many partners. In mammals, the sex drive is associated primarily with the estrogens and androgens; in humans, the androgens, particularly testosterone, are central to sexual desire in both men and women (Sherwin, 1994; Van Goozen, Wiegant, Endert, Helmond, and Van de Poll, 1997). Studies (fMRI) of human sexual arousal show that specific networks of brain activation are associated with the sex drive (Arnow, Desmond, Banner, Glover, Solomon, Polan, Lue, and Atlas, 2002; Beauregard, Levesque, and Bourgouin, 2001; Karama, Lecours, Leroux, Bourgouin, Joubert, and Beauregard, 2002; Tiihonen et al., 1994). These vary; but among them are the hypothalamus (Arnow et al., 2002; Beauregard et al., 2001; Karama et al., 1002) and the amygdala (Beauregard et at, 2001; Karama et al., 2002).

Attraction (the mammalian/avian counterpart to human romantic love) is characterized by increased energy, focused attention on a specific mate, obsessive following, affiliative gestures, possessive mate-guarding, and motivation to win a *preferred* mating partner (Fisher, Aron, Mashek, Strong, Li, and Brown, 2002, 2002a; Fisher, 2004). In humans, the developed form of animal attraction is known as romantic love, obsessive love, passionate love, or being in love. Recent data suggest this brain system is primarily associated with elevated activity of dopamine in the reward pathways of the brain. Most likely it is also associated with elevated activity of central norepinephrine and suppressed activity of central serotonin, as well as other brain systems acting together to produce the range of emotions, motivations, cognitions, and behaviors common to romantic love (Fisher, 1998, 2004; Fisher et al., 2002, 2002a).

Attachment is characterized in birds and mammals by mutual territory defense and/or nest-building, mutual feeding and grooming, maintenance of close proximity, separation anxiety, shared parental chores, and affiliative behaviors (Carter, DeVries, Taymans, Roberts, Williams, and Getz, 1997; Lim, Murphy, and Young, 2004; Lim and Young, 2004). In humans, partner attachment is known as companionate love (Hatfield, 1988, p. 191). Human attachment is associated with the above mammalian traits, as well as feelings of calm, security, social comfort, and emotional union with a long-term mate. Animal studies suggest this brain system is associated primarily with oxytocin and vasopressin in the nucleus accumbens and ventral pallidum, respectively (Lim et al., 2004; Lim and Young, 2004).

Each of these primary brain systems evolved to play a different role in courtship, mating, reproduction, and parenting (Fisher, 1998, 2004; Fisher et al., 2002, 2002a). The sex drive evolved to motivate our ancestors to seek coitus with a *range* of appropriate partners. Attraction (and its developed human form, romantic love) evolved to motivate individuals to select among potential mates, *prefer* a particular individual, and *focus* courtship attention on this favored mating partner, thereby conserving courtship time and energy. Attachment evolved primarily to motivate individuals to sustain an affiliative connection with this reproductive partner at least long enough to complete species-specific parental duties. Moreover, these three brain systems interact in myriad ways to direct many behaviors, emotions, and motivations associated with human reproduction.

FMRI STUDIES OF ROMANTIC LOVE

To investigate the biology of romantic love in humans, I and my colleagues Lucy L. Brown of the Albert Einstein College of Medicine, Arthur Aron of SUNY Stony Brook, and Stony Brook graduate students Greg Strong and Debra Mashek embarked on a neuroimaging study of men and women who had "just fallen madly in love" (Fisher et al., 1003; Aron, Fisher, Mashek, Strong, Li, and Brown, 2005). My hypothesis was that this phenomenon was associated with elevated activity of central dopamine and/ or norepinephrine and low activity of central serotonin (Fisher, 1998).

Using functional magnetic resonance imaging (fMRI), we collected data on ten women and seven men who reported being in love an average of 7.4 months (median 7; range 1–17 months); they ranged in age from eighteen to twenty-six. Each subject looked at a photograph of his or her beloved as well as a photograph of an emotionally neutral acquaintance, each viewing followed by a distraction task to cleanse the mind of strong emotion. This distraction task consisted of mentally counting backward from a large number, such as 9,471, in increments of seven. The protocol consisted of (1) positive stimulus (thirty seconds); (2) counting task (forty seconds); (3) neutral stimulus (thirty seconds); (4) counting task (twenty seconds). This process (or its reverse) was repeated six times; the experiment lasted about twelve minutes.

Group activation specific to the beloved occurred in several regions. Most significant was activity in the right ventral tegmental area (VTA) and right postero-dorsal body and dorsal tail of the caudate nucleus (Fisher, Aron, Mashek, Strong, Li, and Brown, 2003; Aron et al., 2005). The region activated in the VTA is rich in cells that produce and distribute dopamine to many brain regions, including the caudate nucleus. Moreover, the VTA is central to the brain's "reward system" (Schultz, 2000; Martin-Soelch, Leenders, Chevalley, Missimer, Kunig, Magyar, Mino, and Schultz, 2001; Breiter, Gollub, Weisskoff, Kennedy, Makris, Berke, Goodman, Kantor, Gastfriend, Riorden, Mathew, Rosen, and Hyman, 1997), the neural network associated with sensations of pleasure, general arousal, focused attention, and motivation to pursue and acquire rewards (Schultz, 2000; Delgado, Nystrom, Fissel, Noll, and Fiez, 2000; Elliott, Newman, Longe, and Deakin, 2003), The caudate nucleus is also associated with motivation and goal-oriented behaviors; it, too, is central to the dopaminergic reward system (Martin-Soelch et al., 2001; Schultz, 2000).

Using fMRI, Bartels and Zeki also investigated brain activity in seventeen men and women who reported being "truly, deeply, and madly in love" (2000, p. 3829). However, in this study, individuals reported being in love an average of 28.8 months, considerably longer. These subjects were less intensely in love. This was established (serendipitously) because both our participants and Bartels and Zeki's participants were administered the same questionnaire, the Passionate Love Scale (Hatfield and Sprecher, 1986), prior to scanning. Bartels and Zeki (2000, 2004) also found activation in a region of the dorsal caudate nucleus and the ventral tegmental area.

The above data suggest that the focused attention, motivation, and goal-oriented behaviors characteristic of romantic love are associated with elevated activity of central dopamine. Because specific activities of dopamine are also associated with ecstasy, intense energy, sleeplessness, mood swings, emotional dependence, and craving (see Fisher, 1998), dopamine most likely also contributes to these aspects of romantic love.

Elevated activity of norepinephrine and *low* activity of central serotonin may also be involved, although I have only corollary evidence at present. Norepinephrine is associated with a pounding heart, elevated blood pressure, and other physiological responses of the sympathetic nervous system, phenomena common to romantic love (Fisher, 1998, 2004). And scientists have recently studied concentrations of serotonin transporter in blood platelets of sixty individuals: twenty had fallen in love in the previous six months; twenty suffered from unmedicated obsessive-compulsive disorder (OCD); twenty normal (control) individuals were not in love (Marazziti, Akiskal, Rossi, and Cassano, 1999). Both the in-love participants and those suffering from OCD showed significantly lower concentations of the platelet serotonin transporter. Thus decreased activity of bodily (and perhaps also brain) serotonin most likely contributes to the lover's obsessive thinking and impulsivity.

Psychologists distinguish between emotions and motivations, which are brain systems oriented around planning and pursuit of a specific want or need. Arthur Aron had proposed that romantic love is not an emotion but a motivation system designed to enable suitors to build and maintain an intimate relationship with a preferred mating partner (Aron and Aron, 1991; Aron et al., 1995). Because the above-mentioned experiments indicate that this passion is associated with activity in the VTA and caudate nucleus, Aron's hypothesis is most likely correct: motivation and goal-oriented behaviors form the core of romantic love. These findings then suggested to me that romantic love is a *primary* motivation system—a fundamental mating drive (Fisher, 2004).

Donald Pfaff defines a drive as a neural state that energizes and directs behavior to acquire a particular biological *need* to survive or reproduce (Pfaff, 1999, pp. 7, 40). Romantic love shares many traits with basic drives: (1) Like all drives, romantic attraction is tenacious; emotions dissipate or change far more rapidly. (2,) Romantic love is focused on a specific reward (the beloved); emotions, such as joy and disgust, are focused on a range of phenomena instead. (3) This passion is not associated with any particular facial expression, while all of the primary emotions have characteristic facial poses. (4) Like all drives, romantic love is exceedingly difficult to control; it is harder to curb thirst, for example, than anger. (5) And, like all of the basic drives (Pfaff, 1999), romantic love is associated with elevated activity of central dopamine.

Drives lie along a continuum (Fisher, 1004). Some, such as thirst and the need for warmth, can rarely be extinguished until satisfied, while the sex drive and the maternal instinct can often be redirected. Falling in love appears to be near the base of this continuum. For example, romantic love is considerably stronger than the sex drive. Few people whose sexual advances are rejected proceed to kill themselves or someone else, whereas rejected lovers in cultures around the world commit suicide or homicide; many more become depressed. In a study of 114 Americans who had been romantically rejected in the past eight weeks, 40 percent were clinically depressed; 12 percent suffered moderate to severe depression (Mearns, 1991). Since romantic love is a universal and powerful human mating drive, it must have evolved.

EVOLUTION OF ROMANTIC LOVE: THE BRAIN NETWORK FOR "MATE CHOICE"

Ever since Darwin (1859,1871) proposed the concept of sexual selection to explain patterns of sexual dimorphism in birds and mammals, scientists have been describing physical and behavioral traits that birds and mammals have evolved to *attract* potential mates (Andersson, 1994; Miller, 2,000). The peacock's tail feathers are the standard example. But the corresponding brain mechanism by which the display chooser responds to these traits, comes to prefer a specific individual, and focuses his or her courtship time and energy on this *particular* conspecific has not been defined (Fisher et al., 2002, 2002a; Fisher, 2004),

Yet all birds and mammals express mate preferences; none copulate indiscriminately. The phenomenon of mate choice is so common in nature that the ethological literature regularly uses several terms to describe it, including "individual preference," "favoritism," "female choice," "sexual choice," "selective proceptivity," and "attraction." In most mammalian and avian species this mate preference is brief. In rats, for example, courtship attraction often lasts seconds; among elephants, it lasts three to five days; among foxes, it lasts about two weeks (Fisher, 2004). But all species display similar characteristics of attraction. Among these traits, attracted individuals focus their attention on a preferred mating partner and express heightened energy, obsessive following, sleeplessness, loss of appetite, possessive mateguarding, affiliative courtship gestures such as patting, stroking, and nuzzling, goal-oriented courtship behaviors, and intense motivation to win this *particular* individual (see Fisher, 2004). All these traits are also characteristic of human romantic love. Moreover, many creatures express this attraction instantly, what may be the forerunner of human "love at first sight."

Animal studies indicate that this mate preference (or attraction) is associated with elevated activities of central dopamine, another similarity with human romantic love. When a female lab-raised prairie vole is mated with a male, she forms a distinct preference for him associated with a 50 percent increase of dopamine in the nucleus accumbens, a region of the brain's reward system (Gingrich, Liu, Cascio, Wang, and Insel, 2000). When a dopamine antagonist is injected into the accumbens, the female no longer prefers this partner. And when a female is injected with a dopamine agonist, she begins to prefer the conspecific who is present at the time of infusion, even if she has not mated with this male (Gingrich et al., 2000; Wang, Yu, Cascio, Liu, Gingrich, and Insel, 1999). An increase in central dopamine is also associated with mate attraction in female sheep (Fabre-Nys, 1998).

This mammalian (and avian) attraction system most likely evolved for the same adaptive reason it evolved in humans: to enable individuals to *prefer* specific mating partners, thereby conserving valuable courtship time and energy (Fisher, 1998, 2004; Fisher et al., 2002, 2002a). Then, at some point in hominid evolution, this mammalian neural mechanism for mate preference developed into human romantic love. Perhaps this process initially began as early as 3.5 million years ago, along with the evolution of hominid pair-bonding (Fisher, 1992; Reno, Meindl, McCollum, and Lovejoy, 2003), then started to take its developed human form some two million years ago as the brain began to exhibit some characteristically human traits (Fisher, 2004).

To understand the range of emotions, motivations, and behaviors associated with human romantic love, my colleagues and I conducted a second fMRI study, this one of romantic rejection. We used functional magnetic resonance imaging (fMRI) to study ten women and five men who were still very much in love but had recently been rejected by their romantic partner (Fisher et al., 1005). We employed the same protocol as with our happily in love subjects. Rejected participants alternately viewed a photograph of their abandoning beloved and a photograph of a familiar, emotionally neutral individual, interspersed with a distraction attention task.

Preliminary analysis of the positive-neutral contrast showed significant group effects in the right nucleus accumbens/ventral putamen/paliidum, lateral orbitofrontal cortex, and anterior insular/operculum cortex (Fisher et al., 2005).

Other studies have shown that the nucleus accumbens/ventral pallidum/ putamen region where we found activity becomes more active as an individual chooses a high-risk investment associated with big gains or big losses (Kuhnen and Knutson, 2005) or anticipates a monetary reward (Zald, Boil-eau, El-Dearedy, Gunn, McGlone, Dichter, and Dagher, 2004). This region is also part of the dopaminergic reward system (Gingrich, Liu, Cascio, Wang, and Insel, 2000). The region of the anterior insula/operculum cortex where we found activity has been associated with skin and muscle pain and anxiety (Schreckenberger, Siessmeier, Viertmann, Landvogt, Buchholz, Rolke, Treede, and Bartenstein, 2005). The region of the orbitofrontal cortex where we found activity has been associated with "theory of mind" (Vollm, Taylor, Richardson, Corcoran, Stirling, McKie, Deakin, and Elliott, 2006), the human ability to muse on the thoughts and intentions of others; this brain region is also associated with evaluating punishers (Kringelbach and Rolls, 2004), implementing appropriate adjustments in behavior (Ridderinkhof, Van den Wildenberg, Segaiowitz, and Carter, 2004), obsessive/ compulsive behaviors (Evans, Lewis, and Iobst, 2004), and controlling anger (Goldstein, Alai-Klein, Leskovjan, Fowler, Wang, Gur, Hitzemann, and Volkow, 2005).

These results suggest that the dopaminergic reward system remains active in recently romantically rejected men and women, but the precise location of activity differs. These preliminary results also suggest that neural regions associated with taking risks for big gains or losses, physical pain, obsessive/ compulsive behaviors, ruminating on the intentions and actions of the rejecter, evaluating options, and emotion regulation increase their activity when someone is rejected by a beloved.

Ours is the second investigation of romantic rejection. Najib and colleagues (2004) studied nine women who were "actively grieving" a recent romantic breakup. Preliminary comparisons uncovered no commonalities; in fact, in several regions where we found activations, they found deactivations. Because our subjects regularly reported anger and hope for reconciliation, while the subjects in the Najib et al. study more regularly reported acceptance of the situation, I suspect that our participants were in the initial stage of romantic rejection, the protest phase, while their participants were in the subsequent resignation/despair phase.

PROTEST: THE INITIAL STAGE OF ROMANTIC REJECTION

Lewis, Amini, and Lannon divide romantic rejection into two general phases: protest and resignation/despair (2000). During the protest phase, abandoned lovers express intense energy, heightened alertness, and extreme motivation to win back their beloved. These psychiatrists theorize that this "protest response" evolved from a basic mammalian reaction to the rupture of *any* social tie. Moreover, they suggest that this protest response is associated with elevated activity of dopamine and norepinephrine, reasoning that these neurotransmitters most likely produce the heightened alertness, energy, and motivation that abandoned creatures exhibit as they call for help and search for their abandoner, generally their mother.

Our data on rejected lovers is preliminary evidence that the hypothesis of Lewis, Amini, and Lannon is correct: elevated activity in dopaminergic reward pathways are likely to be involved in the initial protest phase of romantic rejection. Our results may also help explain "frustration attraction"—why disappointed lovers begin to love their rejecting partner even more passionately (Fisher 2004). When a reward is delayed in coming, reward-expecting neurons *prolong* their activity (Schultz, 2000) and activity of the dopaminergic reward system is associated with feelings of intense romantic love. This phenomenon of frustration attraction appears to be maladaptive, but the intense energy, focused attention, extreme motivation, and goal-oriented behaviors that dopamine produce are useful biological tools for regaining a beloved (Fisher, 2004).

During the protest stage, rejected lovers often also experience "abandonment rage" (Meloy, 1998, 1999), another trait that may be linked to the dopaminergic reward system. The primary rage system has pathways to regions in the prefrontal cortex that anticipate rewards (Panksepp, 1998), and animal studies indicate that these reward and rage circuits are closely connected. For example, when you pet a cat, it expresses pleasure; when you withdraw the stimulation, it often bites (Panksepp, 1998), a response to unfulfilled expectations known as "frustration aggression." The data on our rejected lovers suggests one of the neural regions linked to this rage response, a region of the lateral orbitofrontal cortex associated with controlling anger.

These fMRI data on romantic rejection also suggest that the brain mechanisms for abandonment rage and romantic love can operate in tandem, biological data that corroborates current behavioral research. Ellis and Malamuth (2000) report that rejected men and women can be furious at a rejecting partner, while still being very much in love with him or her. Moreover, love and hate/rage have several behavioral similarities, including focused attention, obsessive thinking, heightened energy, and intense emotion, motivation, and craving (Fisher, 2004). So these data indicate that the opposite of love is not hate; more likely it is indifference. Like frustration attraction, abandonment rage appears to be maladaptive. It stresses the heart, raises blood pressure, and suppresses the immune system (Dozier, 2001). But it probably evolved to enable jilted lovers to depart a dead-end relationship faster; this way they could renew courtship sooner, a reproductive advantage (Fisher, 2004). Abandonment rage also motivates people to fight for the welfare of their offspring, as seen so often during divorce proceedings (Fisher, 2004).

RESIGNATION/DESPAIR; THE SECOND STAGE OF ROMANTIC REJECTION

The second general phase of romantic rejection, resignation/despair, may be associated with *reduced* activity in subcortical dopaminergic pathways. I hypothesize this for three reasons. First, a primate study indicates that when a monkey realizes an expected reward will *never* come, dopamine-making cells in the midbrain *decrease* their activity (Schultz, 2000). Second, the other recent fMRI investigation, of women suffering from a recent romantic breakup (Najib et al., 2004, p. 2253), reports decreased activity in parts of the dorsal caudate, a brain region rich in receptor sites for dopamine. Last, long-term stress suppresses the activity of dopamine and other monoamines, producing lethargy, despondency, and depression (Panksepp, 1998), which are traits of resigned and despondent lovers.

This despair response also seems counterproductive. But scientists argue that the high metabolic costs of depression are actually its benefits. They reason that depression is an honest, believable signal that something is desperately wrong, so it galvanizes friends and relatives to support the rejected person during his or her time of intense need (Hagen, Watson, and Thomson, in press). Depression also stimulates insight (Watson and Andrews, 2002), mental clarity that may spur the rejected lover to make difficult decisions that promote reproductive success (Nesse, 1991).

Love hurts. A recent neuroimaging study indicates that emotional pain induced by social exclusion affects some of the same brain regions that become active during physical pain (Eisenberger, Lieberman, and Williams, 2003). Some broken-hearted lovers even die from a heart attack or stroke caused by their depression (Rosenthal, 2002). Not everyone suffers from romantic rejection to the same degree, of course. Across the life course, individuals develop different feelings of competence or incompetence, different expectations of love, different sensitivities to rejection, and different coping strategies that predispose them to romantic rejection in different ways (Downey and Feldman 1996; Downey, Freitas, Michaelis, and Khouri, 1998; Leary, 2001). Moreover, some have more mating opportunities, options that mitigate feelings of protest, rage, and despair.

Men and women tend to express some differences in how they handle rejection, too (Baumeister, Wotman, and Stillwell, 1993; Buss, 1994; Hatfield and Rapson, 1996). Men are three to four times more likely to commit suicide after being rejected (Hatfield and Rapson, 1996) and are more likely to stalk a rejecting partner, as well as batter or kill her (Meloy, 2001; Meloy and Fisher, 2005), Rejected women report more severe feelings of depression (Mearns, 1991; Hatfield and Rapson, 1996), and more chronic strain and rumination after being rejected (Nolen-Hoeksema, Larson, and Grayson, 1999). Women are more likely to talk about their trauma as well, sometimes inadvertently re-traumatizing themselves in the process (Hatfield and Rapson, 1996).

But few people avoid the pain of romantic rejection. In one college community, 93 percent of both sexes queried reported that they had been spurned by someone they passionately loved; and 95 percent reported they had rejected someone who was deeply in love with them (Baumeister et al., 1993). These rejected lovers suffer for important evolutionary reasons. Discarded sweethearts have wasted precious courtship time and metabolic energy; and their reproductive future has been jeopardized, along with their social alliances, self-esteem, and happiness.

ROMANTIC LOVE: A COMBINATION OF BRAIN SYSTEMS

The above data suggest that central dopamine, norepinephrine, and serotonin, in various changing ratios and in conjunction with other neural systems, contribute to multiple aspects of romantic love. But these neurotransmitters also contribute to many other emotions and motivations; they are not specific to romantic love. This is to be expected. Pfaff (1999) proposes that all drives have two components: a *generalized* arousal system in the brain produces the energy and motivation to acquire any biological need; and a specific constellation of brain systems produces the feelings, thoughts, and behaviors associated with each *particular* biological need. The general arousal component of all drives, Pfaff reports, is associated with the actions of dopamine, norepinephrine, and serotonin, as well as several other brain chemicals. The specific constellation of brain systems associated with *each* particular drive varies. Our fMRI study may have uncovered only the "general arousal" component of romantic love.

We found activations and deactivations in many other brain regions and pathways, however, and some particular combination of these is probably specific to romantic love. Among them may be a region of the right antero-medial caudate body (Aron et al., 2005), because our happily in love subjects who scored higher on one of the questionnaires we administered prior to scanning, the Passionate Love Scale (Hatfield and Sprecher, 1986), also showed more activity in this brain region. Deactivation of the amygdala may also be central to the experience of being in love (Aron et al., 2005; Bartels and Zeki, 2,000), as well as activations and deactivations in other limbic and cortical regions. But the thoughts, emotions, and motivations associated with romantic love may be so varied across individuals, as well as across time within each individual, that the full set of dynamic, parallel neural systems involved may be impossible to record by group analysis.

CAN LOVE LAST?

Nevertheless, these fMRI experiments indicate some of the primary neurotransmitter systems involved in romantic love. They also suggest some things about the duration of intense, early stage romantic love, Nisa, a !Kung woman of the Kalahari Desert of Botswana, summed up love's trajectory succinctly: "When two people are first together, their hearts are on fire and their passion is very great. After a while, the fire cools and that's how it stays. They continue to love each other, but it's in a different way—warm and dependable" (Shostak, 1981, p. 168). Romantic love can be sustained in a long-term relationship, but it generally becomes less intense (Traupmann and Hatfield, 1981; Wallerstein and Blakeslee, 1995). And the characteristic impermanence of early-stage, intense romantic love is most likely an adaptive mechanism. Romantic love is metabolically expensive. So this brain system probably evolved primarily to enable our forebears to focus their courtship and mating energy on a preferred individual only long enough to conceive a child. Then this intense passion gradually subsided as most couples shifted into feelings of attachment so they could more calmly rear their child through infancy together (Fisher, 2004).

Two studies have explored the trajectory of intense, early stage romantic love. One investigation of blood platelet density of serotonin transporter indicates that intense romantic love lasts between twelve and eighteen months (Marazziti et al., 1999). And our between-subject analysis of happily in love individuals in longer relationships (eight to seventeen months) suggests how this passion changes across time. We initiated this secondary investigation because our group of happily in love subjects showed some different patterns of brain activation than did those of the Bartels and Zeki study. But, as mentioned earlier, our subjects were in love an average duration of 7.4 months, while those in the Bartels and Zeki study were in love an average duration of 28.8 months. So we separately analyzed only our happily in love participants who were in longer relationships. The results showed that these men and women exhibited brain activation patterns more closely resembling those of the subjects in the Bartels and Zeki study (Aron et al., 2005), specifically, activity in the anterior cingulate cortex and insular cortex. These data indicate that changes in cognition and emotion occur as love proceeds.

ROMANTIC LOVE: AN ADDICTION?

These fMRI studies of human romantic love have several implications for the medical and legal communities, as well as for individuals. Among them, romantic love is most likely highly addictive. Indeed, because romantic love is associated with focused attention, euphoria, craving, obsession, compulsion, distortion of reality, personality changes, emotional and physical dependence, inappropriate (even dangerous) behaviors, tolerance, withdrawal symptoms, relapse, and loss of self-control, psychologists have long regarded it as an addiction (Peele, 1975; Carnes, 1983; Halpern, 1982; Tennov, 1979; Hunter, Nitschke, and Hogan, 1981; Mellody, Miller, and Miller, 1992; Griffin-Shelley, 1991; Schaef, 1989; Findling, 1999). The above fMRI data on romantic love support this hypothesis. Those who are happily in love express neural activity in a region associated with the "rush" of cocaine, and those who are rejected in love appear to have neural activity in common with those who gamble for money, risking big gains and big losses.

Other studies also support the possible parallel between romantic love and addiction. When Barrels and Zeki compared the brain scans of their happily in love subjects with those of men and women who had injected cocaine or opioids, they found that some of the same brain regions became active (Barrels and Zeki, 2000). In addition, studies of cocaine addiction in animals (David, Segu, Buhot, Ichaye, and Cazala, 2004; Kalivas and Duffy, 1998; Wise and Hoffman, 1992.) and humans (fMRI) (Breiter et al., 1997) indicate that the VTA is involved in addiction, as it is in romantic love. Last, the decreasing desire for more chocolate (aversion) is associated with decreasing activity in the VTA (Small, Zatorre, Dagher, Evans, and Jones Gotman, 2001). Laymen generally consider that there are five major physiological addictions: food, alcohol, drugs, gambling, and nicotine. Romantic love may be another.

INDIVIDUAL VARIATIONS IN ROMANTIC LOVE

These fMRI data also suggest why some people fall in love more regularly and/or more passionately than others. Childhood, adolescent, and adult experiences unquestionably play a role. But baseline levels of dopamine and serotonin are directed by specific genes, and these genes are polymorphic; they produce individual variations in these neurotransmitter systems (Gibbons, 2004; Lesch, Bengel, Heils, Sabol, Greenberg, Petri, Benjamin, Mulier, Hamer, and Murphy, 1996). Hence some men and women can potentially inherit the biological proclivity to fall in love more often and/or more intensely than others.

One's habits and diseases can also affect one's biological susceptibility to romantic love. For example, daily drug use can alter the structure and function of the brain's reward system for weeks, months, or years (Nestler, 2001). Moreover, schizophrenia, Parkinson's disease, and other ailments alter dopaminergic pathways. Even environmental and social circumstances potentially contribute to one's romantic receptiveness. Novel situations, for example, can stimulate romantic feelings (Norman and Aron, 1995; Aron and Aron, 1996; Dutton and Aron, 1974), most likely because novelty (and danger) raise the activity of central dopamine (Fisher, 2004).

But the above fMRI studies can contribute nothing to the question of why we fall in love with one person rather than another. *Who* triggers this brain system is a different issue, directed largely by environmental and social forces. Timing plays a role; people tend to fall in love when they are ready (Hatfield, 1988). Proximity can spark this rapture (Pines, 1999). As the poet Ezra Pound wrote of this, "Ah, I have picked up magic in her nearness." Most men and women fall in love with individuals of the same ethnic, social, religious, educational, and economic background, those of similar physical attractiveness, a comparable intelligence, similar attitudes, expectations, values, interests, and those with similar social and communication skills (Rush-ton, 1989; Laumann, Gagnon, Michael, and Michaels, 1994; Pines, 1999; Buston and Emlen, 2003). People also gravitate toward those who fit within what I refer to as their love template or love map (Fisher, 2004) and Zentner (2005) refers to as an individual's ideal mate personality concept. This love template is an unconscious list of traits that an individual is looking for in an ideal partner; it develops as he or she grows up and then becomes refined as the person moves through life.

Biology also plays a role in whom we find attractive. People fall in love with individuals who are somewhat mysterious, perhaps in part because novelty elevates the activity of dopamine and norepinephrine. Women are more attracted to men with a different immune system (Wedekind et al, 1995), an evolutionary mechanism that may have evolved to rear more varied young. Like many creatures, humans also tend to be attracted to those who are symmetrical (Gangestad and Thornhill, 1997). When scientists recorded the brain activity of heterosexual men ages twenty-one to thirty-five as they looked at women with symmetrical faces, the ventral tegmental area became active (Aharon et al., 2001). I suspect that scientists will find many more biological mechanisms that contribute to attraction to a specific individual.

But whether all these environmental and biological stimuli trigger the brain circuitry associated with romance, or the brain circuitry of romance somehow sparks one's interest in a particular individual, is undetermined. The above fMRI data cannot solve the metaphysical issue of cause and effect between brain and mind.

LUST, ROMANCE, AND ATTACHMENT: INTERACTIONS

However, data collected from these fMRI studies can help to explain some of the psychobiological interactions among the three basic mating drives: lust, romantic love, and attachment. And they suggest at least one of the dangers of tampering with these three delicately balanced systems.

People who have fallen madly in love generally begin to find their beloved enormously sexually attractive, and biological interactions between romantic love and the sex drive may contribute. Increasing dopamine associated with romantic love can stimulate a cascade of reactions, including the release of testosterone, the hormone of sexual desire (Wenkstern,

Pfaus, and Fibiger, 1593; Wersinger and Rissman, 2000; Szezypka, Zhou, and Palmiter, 1998; Hull, Du, Lorrain, and Matuszewick, 1997). In fact, elevated activity of dopamine generally increases sex drive, sexual arousal, and sexual performance in humans (Clayton, McGarvey, Warnock, et al., 2000; Heaton, 2000; Walker, Cole, Gardner, Hughes, et al., 1993; Coleman, Cunningham, Foster, Batey, Donahue, Houser, and Ascher, 1999; Ascher, Cole, Colin, Feighner, Ferris, Fibiger, Golden, Martin, Potter, Richelson, and Sulser, 1995). This chemical connection between romantic love and lust makes evolutionary sense: if romantic love evolved to stimulate courtship with a preferred individual, it should also trigger the drive for sex, in order to start the mating process.

But can casual sex trigger feelings of romantic love? Most liberated adults have had sex with a friend or acquaintance and never fallen in love with him or her. But it can happen. The natives of rural Nepal say of this, "Naso pasyo, maya basyo," or "the penis entered and love arrived" (Ahearn, 2001), Perhaps this occurs because sexual activity increases the activities of dopamine in the brain (Damsma, Pfaus, Wenkstern, Phillips, and Fibiger, 1992; Plcim, Matochik, Barfield, and Auerbach, 1990; Yang, Pau, Hess, and Spies, 1996). In fact, women may be particularly vulnerable to falling in love with a casual sex partner because seminal fluid contains dopamine and tyrosine, a building block of dopamine (Burch and Gallup, in press). Sexual activity can also stimulate feelings of attachment via orgasm. Orgasm produces a flood of oxytocin and vasopressin, the neuropeptides associated with attachment in women and men (Carmichael, Humbert, Dixen, Palmisano, Greenleaf, and Davidson, 1987).

Because of the complex interactions among these three primary mating drives, the psychiatrist J. Anderson Thomson and I have proposed that serotonin-enhancing antidepressants (SSRIs) can jeopardize one's ability to feel romantic passion for a new partner or a deep attachment for a long-term mate (Fisher, 2004; Fisher and Thomson, in press). These medications *suppress* dopaminergic pathways; they also dull the emotions and curb obsessive thinking: All are associated with early-stage, intense romantic love. As many as 70 percent of patients taking these medications experience a decline in sexual desire, sexual arousal, and orgasm (anorgasmia). This anorgasmia may jeopardize the lover's feelings of attachment to a long-term partner too.

The negative biological effects of serotonin-enhancing antidepressants on feelings of romantic love and attachment were reported by a patient, who wrote: "After two bouts of depression in ten years, my therapist recommended I stay on serotonin-enhancing antidepressants indefinitely. As appreciative as I was to have regained my health, I found that my usual enthusiasm for life was replaced with blandness. My romantic feelings for my wife declined drastically. With the approval of my therapist, I gradually discontinued my medication. My enthusiasm returned and our romance is now as strong as ever. I am prepared to deal with another bout of depression if need be, but in my case the long-term side effects of antidepressants render them off limits" (Frankel, 2004).

The complex and dynamic interactions among these three brain systems suggest that *any medication* that changes their chemical checks and balances is likely to alter an individual's courting, mating, and parenting tactics, ultimately affecting fertility and one's genetic future.

BIOLOGICAL UNDERPINNINGS OF SERIAL MONOGAMY AND ADULTERY

The above fMRI data also bring understanding to the human tendency for serial monogamy and clandestine adultery. But to discuss the significance of these data, it is necessary to review the central elements of the human reproductive strategy.

Only 3 percent of mammals pair up to rear their young. *Homo sapiens* is among them. Today some 90 percent of women and men marry by age fifty in all but a few countries (Bruce et al., 1995), and cross-cultural data confirm that humans primarily practice social monogamy, forming a socially recognized pair-bond with a single mate at a time (Fisher, 1992). Although polygyny is permitted in 84 percent of human societies, in the vast majority of these cultures only about 10 percent of men actually maintain two or more wives simultaneously (Fisher, 1992). Moreover, because polygyny in humans is regularly associated with rank and wealth, Daly and Wilson propose that monogamy was even more prevalent in prehorticultural, unstratified societies (1983). In fact, anthropologists recently remeasured *Australopithecus afarensis* fossils for skeletal size, and reported that by 3.5 million years ago men and women exhibited roughly the same degree of sexual dimporphism as the sexes do today. Thus they propose that hominids lived in the same sorts of social units as modern *Homo sapiens;* these ancestral men and women were "principally monogamous" (Reno et al., 2003, p. 1073).

Humans are also adulterous. The National Opinion Research Center in Chicago reports that approximately 2.5 percent of men and 15 percent of women cheat at some point during marriage (Laumann et al., 1994). Other studies indicate that from 30 percent to 50 percent of married men and women philander (Gangestad and Thornhill, 1997). Scholars may never establish the true frequency of adultery in either sex, due to reporting bias. Nevertheless, studies of American adultery from the 1910s through the 1990s report its occurrence (Fisher, 1992). Extra-pair copulations occur frequently in every other society for which data are available (Frayser, 1985), as well as in many other socially monogamous species (Fisher, 1991, 1999). And human testes size, which varies according to a species' predominant reproductive strategy, suggests that adultery by both sexes was common in hominid prehistory (Miller, 2000).

Human divorce and remarriage, as well, and biological (as well as cultural) forces may be involved. Data on fifty-eight human societies, taken from the *Demographic Yearbook of the United Nations* between 1947 and 1989, indicate a worldwide divorce peak during and around the fourth year of marriage (Fisher, 1992). Because four years is the characteristic duration of birth spacing in hunting/gathering societies, and because many other socially monogamous avian and mammalian species form pair-bonds that Last only long enough to rear the young through infancy, I have hypothesized chat this human cross-cultural divorce peak represents the remains of a specific ancestral hominid reproductive strategy to remain together at least long enough to raise a single child through infancy (Fisher, 1991).

Children in hunting/gathering societies join a multiage play group soon after being weaned, becoming the responsibility of older siblings and other relatives in the band. So the ecological pressure on couples to remain pair-bonded was reduced after the weaning of a child, unless they had conceived another. Moreover, divorce most likely had an adaptive payoff in ancestral times: those who practiced serial monogamy in association with off-spring weaning would have created healthy genetic variety in their lineages (Fisher, 1992.).

Evolutionary hypotheses such as this are often regarded with skepticism by those unfamiliar with human ethology. I find this attitude shortsighted. Anthropologists, psychologists, sociologists, economists, primatologists, zoologists, and many other scholars have painstakingly accumulated a wealth of data on aspects of human behavior and its counterparts in many other species. Integra ting these disparate facts with logical, scientific reasoning can add understanding, stimulate discourse, and initiate new inquiry into this difficult puzzle: human nature.

But regardless of the reasons for the evolution of human serial monogamy, or the myriad biological and social forces that contribute to human divorce (Fisher, 1991), everywhere in the world that men and women have the economic resources to divorce, divorce and remarriage are common.

So clandestine adultery and serial monogamy are primary aspects of this "dual" human reproductive strategy. And the above MRI data on romantic love add insight to these human patterns.

Foremost, these fMRI data show that the brain circuitry for romantic love is distinct from that of the sex drive and that of attachment. Anecdotal data support this finding: one can feel deep attachment for one individual *while* feeling romantic passion for someone else *while* feeling the sex drive for a range of others. The relative biological independence of these three mating drives may have evolved to enable ancestral men and women to opportunistically engage in monogamy and adultery simultaneously and/or sequentially (Fisher, 2004). But the relative neurological *independence* of these three mating drives helps to explain contemporary cross-cultural patterns of philandering, sexual jealousy, stalking, spousal abuse, love homicide, love suicide, and the clinical depression associated with unstable and disbanded partnerships.

Wild is love. This passion can trigger the reward system in the brain at almost any time of life; even four-year-old children and senior citizens report this craving (Hatfield, Schmitz, Cornelius, and Rapson, 1988; Hatfield and Rapson, 1987; Purdy, 1995, Fisher 2004). Perhaps romantic love in children evolved to motivate them to practice at life's most essential task, choosing an appropriate mating partner. And romance in one's elder years keeps the body toned and the mind alert, and provides lovers with companionship, optimism, and energy.

As fMRI and other research techniques become more sophisticated, scientists will establish more about romantic love in children and the aging. Future research may also establish specifically how serotonin-enhancing antidepressants affect the brain activity of romantic passion; how diseases such as schizophrenia, Parkinson's disease, and various addictions affect this circuitry; why certain personality types fall in love more regularly than others; why some people suffer less from romantic rejection; how "talking therapies" or "twelve-step" programs affect brain circuitry in disappointed lovers; how the brain mechanisms for romantic love change across time; how this passion transforms into feelings of attachment for a long-term partner; how some couples sustain romantic love in long-term partnerships; and how novel situations, vacations, adultery, divorce, and childhood experiences and other life circumstances interact with brain mechanisms to affect whom we love, when we love, and how we express love. Future investigations may even help to explain the prevalence of some modern diseases that appear to be unrelated to romantic passion. For example, as the brain system for intense romantic love evolved, it may have contributed to the development of several obsessive-compulsive disorders and addictions as well.

The ancient Greeks called romantic love the "madness of the gods." It is important to investigate the biology of this passion in all its variations— because this madness is central to our lives. In a study of thirty-seven societies, men and women ranked love, or mutual attraction, as the first criterion for choosing a spouse (Buss, 1994). Everywhere people sing for love, pray for love, work for love, live for love, kill for love, and die for love. Even where marriages are arranged, spouses often fall in love. Nothing will extinguish the human drive to love.

References

Aharon, I., Etcoff, N., Ariely, D., Chabris, C. F., O'Connor, E., and Breiter, H. C. (2001). Beautiful faces have variable reward value: fMRI and behavioral evidence. *Neuron,* 32 (3): 537–551.

Ahearn, L, M. (2001). *Invitations to Love: Literacy, Love Letters and Social Change in Nepal.* Ann Arbor: University of Michigan Press.

Andersson, M. *(1994). Sexual Selection.* Princeton, N.J.: Princeton University Press.

Arnow, B. A., Desmond, J. E., Banner, L. L., Glover, G. H., Solomon, A., Polan, M. L., Lue, T, F., and Atlas, S. W. (2002). Brain activation and sexual arousal in healthy, heterosexual males, *Brain, 125* (5): 1014–1013,

Aron, A., and Aron, E. N. (1991). Love and sexuality. In K. McKinney and S. Sprecher (eds.), *Sexuality in Close Relationships,* pp. 15–48. Hillsdale, N.J.: Erlbaum.

Aron, A., Fisher, H. E., Mashek, D. J., Strong, G., Li, H. F., and Brown, L. L. (2005). Reward, motivation and emotion systems associated with early-stage intense romantic love: An fMRI study. *Journal of Neurospychology,* 94, 317–357.

Aron, A., Paris, M., and Aron, E. N. (1995). Falling in love: Prospective studies of self-concept change. *Journal of Personality and Social Psychology, 69, 1102–1112*

Aron, A., and Westbay, L. (1996). Dimensions of the prototype of love. *Journal of Personality and Social Psychology, 70,* 535–551.

Aron, E., and Aron, A. (1996). Love and expansion of the self: The state of the model. *Personal Relationships, 3,* 45–58.

Ascher, J. A., Cole, J. O., Colin, j. N., Feighner, J. P., Ferris, R. M., Fibiger, H. C, Golden, R. N., Martin, P., Potter, W. Z., Richelson, E., and Sulser, F. (1995). Bupropion: A review of its mechanism of antidepressant activity. *Journal of Clinical Psychiatry, 56* (9): 396–401.

Bartels, A., and Zeki, S. (2000). The neural basis of romantic love. *Neuro Report, 11,* 3829–3834.

------ (2004). The neural correlates of maternal and romantic love. *NeuroImage, 21,* 1155–1166.

Baumeister, R. F., Wotman, S. R., and Stillwell, A. M. (1993). Unrequited love: On heartbreak, anger, guilt, scriptlessness and humiliation. *Journal of Personality and Social Psychology, 64,* 377–394.

Beauregard, M., Levesque,J., and Bourgouin, P. (1001). Neural correlates of conscious self-regulation of emotion. *Journal of Neuroscience, 2.1* (18): RC165.

Breiter, H. C, Aharon, I., Kahneman, D., Dale, A., and Shizgal, P. (2001). Functional imaging of neural responses to expectancy and experience of monetary gains and losses. *Neuron, 30,* 619–639.

Breiter, H. C, Gollub, R. L., Weisskoff, R. M., Kennedy, D. N„ Makris, N., Berke, J. D., Goodman, J. M., Kantor, H. L., Gastfriend, D. R., Riorden, J. P., Mathew, R. T., Rosen, B. R., and Hyman, S. E. (1997). Acute effects of cocaine on human brain activity and emotion. *Neuron, 19,* 591–611.

Bruce, J., Lloyd, C. B., and Leonard, A. (1995). *Families in Focus: New Perspectives on Mothers, Fathers, and Children.* New York: The Population Council.

Burch, R. L., and Gallup, G. G., Jr. (in press). The psychobiology of human semen. In S. Platek and T. Shackelford (eds.), *Female Infidelity and Paternal Uncertainty.*

Buss, D. M. (1994). *The Evolution of Desire: Strategies of Human Mating.* New York: Basic Books.

Buston, P. M, and Emlen, S. T. (2003). Cognitive processes underlying human mate choice: The relationship between self-perception and mate preference in Western society. *Proceedings of the National Academy of Sciences of the United States of America, 100,* 8805–8810.

Carmichael, M. S., Humbert, R., Dixen, J., Palmisano, G., Greenleaf, W., and Davidson, J. M. (1987). Plasma oxytocin increases in the human sexual response, *journal of Clinical Endocrinology and Metabolism, 64* (1): 27–31.

Carnes, P. (1983). *Out of the Shadows: Understanding Sexual Addiction.* Minneapolis, Minn.: Comp Care.

Carter, C. S., DeVries, A., Taymans, S. E., Roberts, R. L., Williams, J. R., and Getz, L. L. (1997). Peptides, steroids, and pair bonding. In C. S. Carter, I. L Lederhendler, and B, Kirkpatrick (eds.), *The Integrative Neurobiology of Affiliation,* pp. 260–272. Annals of the New York Academy of Sciences, vol. 807. New York: New York Academy of Sciences.

Clayton, A. H., McGarvey, E. D., Warnock, J„ et al. (2000). Bupropion as an antidote to SSRI-induced sexual dysfunction. Poster presented at the New Clinical Drug Evaluation Unit Program, Boca Raton, Fla.

Coleman, C. C, Cunningham, L. A., Foster, V. J., Batey, S. R., Donahue, R. M. J., Houser, T. L., and Ascher, J. A. (1999). Sexual dysfunction associated with the treatment of depression: A placebo-controlled comparison of bupropion sustained release and sertraline treatment. *Annals of Clinical Psychiatry, 11,* 205–215.

Critelli, J. W., Myers, E. J., and Loos, V. E. (1986). The components of love: Romantic attraction and sex role orientation. *Journal of Personality, 54* (2): 354–370.

Daly, M., and Wilson, M. (1983). *Sex, Evolution and Behavior,* 2nd ed. Boston: Willard Grant.

Damsma, G., Pfaus, J. G., Wenkstem, D. G., Phillips, A. G., and Fibiger, H. C. (1992). Sexual behavior increased dopamine transmission in the nucleus accumbens and striatum of male rats: Comparison with novelty and locomotion. *Behavioral Neuroscience, 106,* 181–191,

Darwin, C. (1859/n.d). *The Origin of Species,* New York: The Modern Library/Random House.

------ (1871/n.d.). *The Descent of Man and Selection in Relation to Sex.* New York: Modern Library.

David, V., Segu, L., Buhot, M. C., Ichaye, M., and Cazala, P. (1004). Rewarding effects elicited by cocaine microinjections into the ventral tegmental area of C57BL/6 mice: Involvement of dopamine D(I) and serotonin (IB) receptors. *Psychopharmacology* (Berl), 174, 367–375.

Davidson, R. J. (1994). Complexities in the search for emotion-specific physiology. In P. Ekman and R. J. Davidson (eds.), *The Nature of Emotion: Fundamental Questions.* New York: Oxford University Press.

Delgado, M. R., Nystrom, L. E., Fissel, C., Noll, D. C, and Fiez, J. A. (1000). Tracking the hemodynamic responses to reward and punishment in the striatum, *journal of Neurophysiology, 84,* 3072–3077.

Downey, G., and Feldman, S. I. (1996). Implications of rejection sensitivity for intimate relationships. *Journal of Personality and Social Psychology, jo (6):* 1327–1343.

Downey, G., Freitas, A. L., Michaelis, B., and Khouri, H. (1998). The self-fulfilling prophecy in close relationships: Rejection sensitivity and rejection by romantic partners. *Journal of Personality and Social Psychology,* 75 (7): 545–560.

Dozier, R. W. (2002). *Why We Hate: Understanding, Curbing, and Eliminating Hate in Ourselves and Our World.* Chicago: Contemporary Books.

Dutton, D. G., and Aron, A. P. (1974)- Some evidence of heightened sexual attraction under conditions of high anxiety. *Journal of Personality and Social Psychology,* 30 (4): 510–517-

Eisenberger, N. I., Lieberman, M. D., and Williams, K. D. (1003). Does rejection hurt? An fMRI study of social exclusion. *Science,* 302, 190–292.

Elliott, R., Newman, J. L., Longe, O. A., and Deakin, J. F. W, (2003). Differential response patterns in the striatum and orbitofrontal cortex to financial reward in humans: A parametric functional magnetic resonance imaging study. *Journal of Neuroscience,* 23 (1): 303–307.

Eliis, B. J., and Malamuth, N. M. (2000). Love and anger in romantic relationships: A discrete systems mode!. *Journal of Personality, 68* (3): 525–556.

Evans, D. W., Lewis, M. D., and lobst, E. (2004). The role of the orbitofrontal cortex in normally developing compulsive-like behaviors and obsessive-compulsive disorder. *Brain and Cognition, 55* (1): 220–134.

Fabre-Nys, C, (1998). Steroid control of monoamines in relation to sexual behaviour. *Reviews of Reproduction,* 3 (1): 31–41.

Fehr, B. (1988). Prototype analysis of the concepts of love and commitment. *Journal of Personality and Social Psychology, 55* (4): 557–579.

"Findling, R. (1999). *Don't Call That Man!: A Survival Guide* to *Letting Go.* New York: Hyperion.

Fisher, H. (1992) *Anatomy of Love: The Natural History of Monogamy, Adultery and Divorce.* New York: Norton.

——(1998). Lust, attraction, and attachment in mammalian reproduction. *Human Nature,* 9 (I): 23–52.

——(1999). *The First Sex: The Natural Talents of Women and How They Are Changing the World.* New York: Random House.

——2004). *Why We Love: The Nature and Chemistry of Romantic Love.* New York: Henry Holt.

——(2006). Broken hearts: The nature and risks of romantic rejection. In A. Booth and C. Crouter (eds.), *Romance and Sex in Adolescence and Emerging Adulthood: Risks and Opportunities,* pp. 3–29. Mahwah, N.J.: Erlbaum.

Fisher, H., Aron, A., Mashek, D., Strong, G., Li, H., and Brown, L. L. (2002). The neural mechanisms of mate choice: A hypothesis. *Neuroendocrinology Letters, suppl. 4* (13): 91–97.

——(2002a). Defining the brain systems of lust, romantic attraction and attachment. *Archives of Sexual Behavior,* 31 (5): 413–419.

——(November 11, 2003). Early stage intense romantic love activates cortical-basal-ganglia reward/motivation, emotion and attention systems: An fMRI study of a dynamic network that varies with relationship length, passion intensity and gender. Poster presented at the annual meeting of the Society for Neuroscience, New Orleans.

——(2005). Motivation and emotion systems associated with romantic love following rejection: An fMRI study. Program no. 660.7. In *Abstract Viewer/Itinerary Planner.* Washington, D.C.: Society for Neuroscience.

Fisher, H., and Thomson, J. A. (in press). Lust, attraction, attachment: Do the sexual side effects of antidepressants jeopardize romantic love and marriage? In S. Platek (ed.), *Evolutionary Cognitive Neuroscience.* Cambridge, Mass.: MIT Press.

Frankel, J. (May 11, 2004). Reviving romance. *New York Times,* p. F4, Letters.

Frayser, S. (1985). *Varieties of Sexual Experience: An Anthropological Perspective on Human Sexuality.* New Haven, Conn.: HRAF.

Gangescad, S. W., and Thornhill, R. (1997). The evolutionary psychology of extrapair sex: The role of fluctuating asymmetry. *Evolution and Human Behavior, 18* (1): 69–88.

Gibbons, A. (2004). Tracking the evolutionaory history of a "warrior" gene. *Science,* 304, 818–819.

Gingrich, B-, Liu, Y., Cascio, C, Wang, Z., and Insel, T R. (2000). D2 receptors in the nucleus accumbens are important for social attachment in female prairie voles *(Microtus ochrogaster). Behavioral Neuroscience, 114* (I): 173–183.

Goldstein, R. Z, Alai-Klein, N., Leskovjan, A. C, Fowler, J. S., Wang, G. J., Gur, R. C, Hitzemann, R., and Volkow, N. D. (2005). Anger and depression in cocaine addiction: Association with the orbitofrontai cortex. *Psychiatry Research, 138* (1): 13–22.

Griffin-Shelley, E. (1991). *Sex and Love: Addiction, Treatment and Recovery.* New York: Praeger.

Hagen, E. H., Watson, P. J., and Thomson, j. A. (in press). Love's labours lost: Major depression as an evolutionary adaptation to obtain help from those with whom one is in conflict.

Halpern, H. M. (1982). *How to Break Your Addiction to a Person.* New York: McGraw-Hill.

Hamill, S. (ed.). *(1996). The Erotic Spirit: An Anthology of Poems of Sensuality, Love and Longing.* Boston: Shambhala.

Harris, H. *(1995)* Rethinking heterosexual relationships in Polynesia: A case study of Mangaia, Cook Island. In W. Jankowiak (ed.), *Romantic Passion: A Universal Experience?* New York: Columbia University Press.

Hatfield, E. (1988). Passionate and companionate love. In R. J. Sternberg and M. L. Barnes (eds.), *The Psychology of Love.* New Haven, Conn.: Yale University Press.

Hatfield, E., and Rapson, R. (1987). Passionate love/sexual desire: Can the same paradigm explain both? *Archives of Sexual Behavior, 16,* 259–278.

------ (1996). *Love and Sex: Cross-Cultural Perspectives.* Boston: Allyn and Bacon.

Hatfield, E., Schmitz, E., Cornelius, J., and Rapson, R. L. (1988). Passionate love: How early does it begin? *Journal of Psychology and Human Sexuality,* I (I): 35–51.

Hatfield, E., and Sprecher, S. (1986). Measuring passionate love in intimate relationships. *Journal of Adolescence, 9,* 383–410.

Hazan, C, and Shaver, P. (1987). Romantic love conceptualized as an attachment process. *Journal of Personality and Social Psychology, 52,* 511–514.

Heaton, J. P. (2000). Central neuropharmacological agents and mechanisms in erectile dysfunction: The role of dopamine. *Neuroscience and Biobehavioral Reviews,* 24 (5): 561–569.

Hendrick, C, and Hendrick, S. (1986). Research on love: Does it measure *up) Journal of Personality and Social Psychology, 56* (3): 784–794.

Hull, E. M., Du, J., Lorrain, D. S., and Matuszewick, L. (1997). Testosterone, preoptic dopamine, and copulation in male rats. *Brain Research Bulletin,* 44 (4): 317–333.

Hunter, M, S., Nitschke, *C,* and Hogan, L. (1981), A scale to measure love addiction. *Psychological Reports, 48,* 582.

Jankowiak, W. R., and Fischer, E. F. (1991). A cross-cultural perspective on romantic love. *Ethnology, 31* (2): 149.

Kalivas, P. W., and Duffy, P. (1998). Repeated cocaine administration alters extracellular glutamate in the ventral tegmenral area. *Journal of Neurochemistry,* 70, 1497- 1502.

Kapit, W., Macey, R. I., and Meisami, E. (2000). *The Physiology Coloring Book.* New York: Addison-Wesley Longman.

Karama, S., Lecours, A. R-, Leroux, J. M,, Bourgouin, P., Beaudoin, G., Jouben, S-, and Beauregard, M. (2002). Areas of brain activation in males and females during viewing of erotic film excerpts. *Human Brain Mapping, 16* (I): I-13.

Kringelbach, M. L., and Rolls, E. T. (2004). The functional neuroanatomy of the human orbitofrontal cortex: Evidence from neuroimaging and neuropsychology. *Progress in Neurobiology,* 72 (5): 341–372.

Kuhnen, C. M., and Knutson, B. (2005). The neural basis of financial risk taking. *Neuron, 46,* 763–770.

Langlois, J. H., and Roggman, L. A. (1990). Attractive faces are only average. *Psychological Science, I,* 115–121.

Laumann, E. O., Gagnon, J. H., Michael, R. T., and Michaels, S. (1994). *The Social Organization of Sexuality: Sexual Practices in the United States.* Chicago: University of Chicago Press.

Leary, M. R. (ed.). (2001), *Interpersonal Rejection.* New York: Oxford University Press.

Lee, J. A. (198S). Love-styles. In R. J. Sternberg, and M. L. Barnes (eds.), *The Psychology of Love,* pp. 38–67. New Haven, Conn.: Yale University Press.

Lesch, K. P., Bengel, D., Heils, A., Sabol, S. Z., Greenberg, B. D., Petri, S., Benjamin, J., Muller, C. R., Hamer, D. H., and Murphy, D. L. (1996). Association of anxiety-related traits with a polymorphism in the serotonin transporter gene regulatory region. *Science,* 274, 1527–1531.

Leshner, A. I. (1997). Addiction is a brain disease, and it matters. *Science, 278* (5335): 45–47.

Lewis, T., Amini, F., and Lannon, R. (2000). *A General Theory of Love.* New York: Random House.

Liebowitz, M. R. (1983). *The Chemistry of Love.* Boston: Little, Brown.

Lim, M. M., Murphy, A. Z., and Young, L. J. (2004). Ventral striatopallidal oxytocin and vasopressin Via receptors in the monogamous prairie vole *(Microtus ochrogaster). Journal of Comparative Neurology, 468,* 555–570.

Lim, M. M., and Young, L. J. (2004). Vasopressin-dependent neural circuits underlying pair bond formation in the monogamous prairie vole. *Neuroscience, 12.5,* 35- 45

Marazziti, D., Akiskal, H. S., Rossi, A., and Cassano, G. B. (1999). Alteration of the platelet serotonin transporter in romantic love. *Psychological Medicine,* 29, 741–745.

Martin-Soelch, C, Leenders, K. L., Chevalley, A. F., Missimer, J., Kunig, G., Magyar, S-, Mino, A., and Schultz, W. (2001.). Reward mechanisms in the brain and their role in dependence:

Evidence from neurophysiological and neuroimaging studies. *Brain Research Reviews, 36,* 139–149,

Mearns, J, (1991). Coping with a breakup: Negative mood regulation expectancies and depression following the end of a romantic relationship. *Journal of Personality and Social Psychology, 60,* 317–334.

Mellody, P., Miller, A. W., and Miller, J. K. (1992). *Facing Love Addiction.* New York: HarperSan Francisco.

Meloy, J. R. (2001). When stalkers become violent: The threat to public figures and private lives. *Psychiatric Annals,* 33 (10): 658–665.

Meloy, J. R., and Fisher, H. E. (2005). Some thoughts on the neurobiology of stalking. *Journal of Forensic Sciences, 50* (6): 1471–1480.

Miller, G. (2000). *The Mating Mind: How Sexual Choice Shaped the Evolution of Human Nature.* New York: Doubleday.

Najib, A., Lorberbaum, J. P., Kose, S., Bohning, D. E., and George, M. S. (2004). Regional brain activity in women grieving a romantic relationship breakup. *American Journal of Psychiatry, 161* (n).- 1145–1156.

Nemeroff, C. B. (1998). The neurobiology of depression. *Scientific American, 178* (6): 42–49.

Nesse, R. (1991). What good is feeling bad—The evolutionary benefits of psychic pain. *The Sciences: Journal of the New York Academy of Sciences, 31,* 30–37.

Nestler, E. J. (2001). Molecular basis of long-term plasticity underlying addiction. *Nature Reviews Neuroscience,* 2 (z): 119–128.

Netter, P., Hennig, J., Meier, B., and Rohrmann, S. (1998). Testosterone as an indicator of altered 5-HT responsivity in aggressive subjects. *European Psychiatry,* 73 (4):181–185.

Nolen-Hoeksema, S., Larson, J., and Grayson, C. (1999). Explaining the gender difference in depressive symptoms. *Journal of Personality and Social Psychology, 77,* 1061–1072.

Norman, C, and Aron, A. (1995). The effect of exciting activities on relationship satisfaction: A laboratory experiment. Paper presented at the International Network Conference on Personal Relationships, Williamsburg, Va.

Panksepp, J. (1998). *Affective Neuroscience: The Foundations of Human and Animal Emotions.* New York: Oxford University Press.

Peele, S. (1975). *Love and Addiction.* New York: Taplinger.

Pfaff, D. W. (1999). *Drive: Neurobiological and Molecular Mechanisms of Sexual Motivation.* Cambridge, Mass.: MIT Press.

Pines, A. M. (1999). *Falling in Love: Why We Choose the Lovers We Choose.* New York: Routledge.

Pleim, E. T, Matochik, J. A., Barfield, R. J., and Auerbach, S. B. (1950). Correlation of dopamine release in the nucleus accumbens with masculine sexual behavior in rats. *Brain Research, 524,* 160–163.

Purdy, M. (November 6, 1995). A sexual revolution for the elderly. *New York Times,* p. A16.

Reno, P. L., Meindl, R. S., McCollum, M. A., and Lovejoy, C. O. (2003). Sexual dimorphism in *Australopithecus afarensis* was similar to that of modern humans. *Proceedings of the National Academy of Sciences, 10,* 1073.

Ridderinkhof, K. R., Van den Wildenberg, W. P., Segalowitz, S. J., and Carter, C. S. (2004). Neurocognitive mechanism of cognitive control: The role of prefrontal cortex in action selection, response inhibition, performance monitoring, and reward-based learning. *Brain and Cognition, 56* (2): 129–140.

Robbins, T. W., and Everitt, B. J. (1996). Neurobehavioural mechanisms of reward and motivation. *Current Opinion in Neurobiology, 6,* 228–168.

Rosenthal, N. E. (2002). *The Emotional Revolution: How the New Science of Feelings Can Transform Your Life.* New York: Citadel Press. Rushton, J. P. (1989). Epigenesis and social preference. *Behavioral and Brain Sciences,*12, 31–32.

Schaef, A. W, (1989). *Escape from Intimacy; The Pseudo-Relationship Addictions.* New York: Harper & Row.

Schreckenberger, M., Siessmeier, T, Viertmann, A., Landvogt, C, Buchholz, H. G., Rolke, R., Treede, R. D., and Bartenstein, P. (1005). The unpleasantness of chronic pain is encoded by the insular cortex. *Neurology, 64* (7): 1175–1183.

Schultz, W. (2000). Multiple reward signals in the brain. *Nature Reviews. Neuroscience, 1,* 199–107.

Shakespeare, W. (1936). *As You Like It,* act V, scene *1.* In W. A. Wright (ed.), *The Complete Works of William Shakespeare.* New York: Doubleday.

Sherwin, B. B. (1994). Sex hormones and psychological functioning in postmenopausal women. *Experimental Gerontology,* 29 (3/4): 413–430.

Shostak, M. (1981). *Nisa: The Life and Words of a !Kung Woman.* Cambridge, Mass: Harvard University Press.

Small, D. M., Zatorre, R. J., Dagher, A., Evans, A. C, and Jones-Gotman, M, (2001). Changes in brain activity related to eating chocolate: From pleasure to aversion. *Brain, 124,* 1720–1733.

Sternberg, R. J. (1986). A triangular theory of love. *Psychological Review, 91* (2): 119–135.

Szezypka, M. S., Zhou, Q. Y., and Palmiter, R. D. (1998). Dopamine-stimulated sexual behavior is testosterone dependent in mice. *Behavioral Neuroscience, 112* (5): 1129–1135.

Tennov, D. (1979). *Love and Limerence: The Experience of Being in Love.* New York: Stein and Day.

Tiihonen, J., Kuikka, J., Kupila, J., Partanen, K-, Vainio, P., Airaksinen, J., Eronen, M., Hallikainen, T., Paanila, J., Kinnunen, I., and Huttunen, J. (1994). Increase in cerebral blood flow of right prefrontal cortex in men during orgasm. *Neuroscience Letters, 170,* 241–243.

Traupmann, J., and Hatfield, E. (1981), Love and its effect on mental and physical health. In R. Fogel, E. Hatfield, S. Kiesler, and E. Shanas (eds.), *Aging: Stability and Change in the Family,* pp, 253–174. New York: Academic Press.

Van Goozen, S., Wiegant, V. M., Endert, E,, Heimond, F. A., and Van de Poll, N. E. (1997). Psychoendocrinological assessment of the menstrual cycle: The relationship between hormones, sexuality, and mood. *Archives of Sexual Behavior,* 26 (4): 359–382.

Vollm, B. A., Taylor, A. N., Richardson, P., Corcoran., R., Stirling, J., McKie, S., Deakin, J. F., and Elliott, R. (2006). Neuronal correlates of theory of mind and empathy: A functional magnetic resonance imaging study in a nonverbal task. *NeuroImage,* 29 (1): 90–98.

Walker, P. W., Cole, J. O., Gardner, E. A., Hughes, A. R., et al. (1993). Improvement in fluoxetine-associated sexual dysfunction in patients switched to bupropion. *Journal of Clinical Psychiatry,* 54, 439–465.

Wallerstein, J. S, and Blakeslee, S. (1995). *The Good Marriage: How and Why Love Lasts.* Boston: Houghton Mifflin.

Wang, Z., Yu, G., Cascio, C, Liu, Y., Gingrich, B., and Insel, T. R, (1999). Dopamine Di receptor-mediated regulation of partner preferences in female prairie voles *(Microtus ochrogaster):* A mechanism for pair bonding? *Behavioral Neuroscience,* 113 (3): 601–611.

Watson, P. J., and Andrews, P. W. (2002). Toward a revised evolutionary adaptationist analysis of depression: The social navigation hypothesis, *journal of Affective Disorders,* 72, 1–14.

Wedekind, C, et al. (1995). MHC-dependent mate preferences in humans. *Proceedings of the Royal Society of London, 160,* 245–249.

Wenkstem, D., Pfaus, J. G., and Fibiger, H. C. (1993). Dopamine transmission increases in the nucleus accumbens of male rats during their first exposure to sexually receptive female rats. *Brain Research, 618,* 41–46.

Wersinger, S. R,, and Rissman, E. F. (2000). Dopamine activates masculine sexual behavior independent of the estrogen receptor alpha. *Journal of Neuroscience, 20* (II): 4248–4254.

Wise, R. A. (1996). Neurobiology of addiction. *Current Opinion in Neurobiology, 6,* 243.

"Wise, R. A., and Hoffman, D. C. (1992). Localization of drug reward mechanisms by intracranial injections. *Synapse, 10,* 147–163.

Wolkstein, D. (1951). *The First Love Stories.* New York: HarperCollins.

Yang, S. P., Pau, K. Y. F,, Hess, D. L., and Spies, H. G. (1996). Sexual dimorphism in secretion of hypothalamic gonadotropin-releasing hormone and norepinephrine after coitus in rabbits. *Endocrinology, 137* (7); 1683–2693.

Yutang, L. (1954). *Famous Chinese Stort Stories.* New York: Pocket Books.

Zald, D. H., Boileau, J., El-Dearedy, W., Gunn, R,, McGlone, P., Dichter, G. S., and Dagher, A. (2004). Dopamine transmission in the human striatum during monetary reward tasks. *Journal of Neuroscience, 14,* 4105–4111.

Zentner, M. R. (2005). Ideal mate personality concepts and compatibility in close relationships: A longitudinal analysis. *Journal of Personality and Social Psychology 89* (2): 142–256.

Zick, R. (1970). Measurement of romantic love. *Journal of Personality and Social Psychology, 16* (2): 265–273.

Safran, J. D. (1990). Toward a refinement of cognitive therapy in light of interpersonal theory: I. Theory. *Clinical Psychology Review, 10,* 87–105.

Safran, J. D., & Segal, Z. V. (1990). *Interpersonal process in cognitive therapy.* New York: Basic Books.

Schimek, J. (1983). The construction of the transference: The relativity of the "here and now" and the "there and then." *Psychoanalysis and Contemporary Thought,* 6, 435–456.

Schwarz, N., & Clore, G. L. (1983). Mood, misattribution, and judgments of well-being: Informative and directive functions of affective states. *Journal of Personality and Social Psychology, 45,* 513–523.
Seligman, M. E. P. (1975). *Helplessness: On depression, development, and death.* San Francisco: Freeman.
Shah, J. (2003a). Automatic for the people: How representations of significant others implicitly affect goal pursuit. *Journal of Personality and Social Psychology, 84,* 661–681.
Shah, J. (2003b). The motivational looking glass: How significant others implicitly affect goal appraisals. *Journal of Personality and Social Psychology, 85,* 424–439.
Showers, C. (1992). Compartmentalization of positive and negative self-knowledge: Keeping bad apples out of the bunch. *Journal of Personality and Social Psychology, 6'2,* 1036–1049.
Silver, R. C, &Wortman, C. B. (1980). Coping with undesirable life events. In J. Garber& M. E. P. Seligman (Eds.), *Human helplessness* (pp. 279–340). New York: Academic Press.
Singer, J. L. (1988). Reinterpreting the transference. In D. C. Turk & P. Salovey (Eds,), *Reasoning, interference, and judgment in clinical psychology* (pp. 182–205). New York: Free Press.
Smith, E. R. (1998). Mental representation and memory. In D. Gilbert, S. T. Fiske & G. Lindzey (Eds.), *Handbook of social psychology* (4th eel., Vol. 1, pp. 391–445). New York: McGraw-Hill.
Smith, E. R., Murphy, J., & Coats, S. (1999). Attachment to groups: Theory and management. *Journal of Personality and Social Psychology, 77,* 94–110.
Smith, E. R., & Zarate, M. A. (1992). Exemplar-based model of social judgment. *Psychological Review, 99,* 3–21.
Snyder, M„ Tanke, E. D., & Berscheid, E. (1977). Social perception and interpersonal behavior: On the self-fulfilling nature of social stereotypes. *Journal of Personality and Social Psychology, 35,* 656–666.
Steele, C. M. (1988). The psychology of self-affirmation: Sustaining the integrity of the self. In L. Berkowitz (Ed.), *Advances in experimental social psychology* (Vol. 21, pp. 261–302). New York: Academic Press.
Sullivan, H. S. (1953). *The interpersonal theory of psychiatry.* New York: Norton.
Taylor, S. E., & Brown, J. D. (1988), Illusion and well-being: A social psychological perspective on mental health. *Psychological Bulletin, 103,* 193–210.
Wachtel, P. L. (1981). Transference, schema, and assimilation: The relationship of Piaget to the psychoanalytic theory of transference. *Annual of Psychoanalysis, 8,* 59–76.
Watson, D., & Clark, L. A. (1984). Negative affectivity: The disposition to experience aversive emotional states. *Psychological Bulletin, 96,* 465–490.
Westen, D. (1988). Transference and information processing. *Clinical Psychology Review, 8,* 161–179.
White, R. W. (1959), Motivation reconsidered: The concept of competence. *Psychological Review, 66,* 297–333
Weiss, R.S. (1975) *Marital Separation.* New York: Basic Books

DEVELOPING AND MAINTAINING ROMANTIC TIES

Ties That Bind

Linking Personality to Interpersonal Behavior Through the Study of Adult Attachment Style and Relationship Satisfaction

By W. Steven Rholes, Ramona L. Paetzold, and Mike Friedman

Texas A&M University

Although relationship satisfaction may stem from many causes, one of its important correlates is having a secure attachment style—that is, having an attachment style that represents an appropriate balance between closeness to, and distance from, one's partner, an ability to have one's needs met for both security and autonomy. In this chapter we review the research that links attachment style to relationship satisfaction, primarily via a set of risk factors (some of which may be mediating variables) that have been shown to flow from an analysis of attachment styles and to be important for attaining or maintaining relationship satisfaction.

Since the mid-1980s, research on adult attachment has flourished, with a focus on its association with satisfaction in romantic relationships coming into full swing beginning in the 1990s. According to attachment theory, people develop beliefs about themselves and others (i.e., complex cognitive schema or working models) as a result of childhood and adolescent experiences with attachment figures (Bowlby, 1969, 1973; Ainsworth, Blehar, Waters, & Wall, 1978). Conceptualizations and operationalizations of attachment style may vary across researchers, but three primary attachment styles are relevant for the study of marital and romantic relationships: secure, anxious, and avoidant. We begin this chapter with a general discussion of the attachment system, explaining its evolutionary underpinnings and how it interacts with the other primary behavioral systems (caregiving, sexuality, and exploration). We describe the three basic attachment styles and briefly introduce evidence that they are associated with relationship satisfaction. We then turn to a discussion of the risk factors for relationship satisfaction. To complement this discussion, we also examine the implications for the partners of individuals having either secure or insecure attachment styles. Limitations of the existing literature and directions for future research are presented at the end of the chapter.

In this chapter we do not, and indeed could not, cover all of the literature suggesting connections between attachment style and relationship satisfaction. For example, we do not review the vast literature focusing on cognitive and affective processing as part of the working models of attachment (except for the literature clearly addressing anger, which to us is essential to understanding insecure attachment styles). Also largely absent from our chapter is the literature based on an assessment of attachment style according to the Adult Attachment Interview (AAI; Main & Goldwyn, 1998). This measurement technique originated in the developmental psychology literature and has to date been used much less extensively in the social psychology literature, particularly as it relates to relationship or marital satisfaction. Despite these and other lacunae in coverage, our presentation provides a substantial overview of the nature of adult attachment style and the major risk factors it appears to present for relationship dissatisfaction.

A BRIEF INTRODUCTION TO ATTACHMENT THEORY: EVOLUTION, ATTACHMENT STYLES, AND ITS RELATION TO OTHER BEHAVIORAL SYSTEMS

Among contemporary approaches to personality, attachment theory (Bowlby, 1969, 1973, 1980) may be the most thoroughly interpersonal. It includes the idea that involvement in close relationships is inherently motivated. It also asserts that personality (or attachment style) develops through social interaction with others in close relationships, and that attachment styles, in turn, play a life-long role in shaping behavior in close relationships. Although we briefly discuss inherent social motives and the development of attachment styles, our primary topic is the connection between attachment styles and interpersonal behavior, consistent with the theme of this volume. We argue that a history of insecure attachment relationships in infancy, childhood, and adolescence creates personal insecurities and habitual affective responses in adults that drive their maladaptive perceptions of partners (e.g., as unsupportive) and situations (e.g., as highly conflictual), as well as leading to their own maladaptive behaviors (e.g., resolving conflicts poorly). Insecure adults attribute their resulting dissatisfaction with relationships to aversive conditions (such as unresolved conflict), limited opportunities for intimacy and closeness, and alienation from their relationship partners, leading them to behave in ways that confirm their pessimistic perceptions and expectations and result in even further relationship dissatisfaction. Finally, we provide an overarching framework for understanding the perceptions, expectations, and behaviors of persons with insecure attachment styles, emphasizing how their habitual anger and egoistic concern with meeting their own needs for security and autonomy—to the exclusion of the needs of others—thwarts their ability to obtain higher levels of relationship satisfaction.

According to Bowlby (1969, 1973, 1980), humans have an innate attachment system that motivates infants to remain in close proximity to their caregivers, who serve as attachment figures. This system has evolved as a means of increasing the likelihood of survival and reproduction of a species whose members are relatively helpless at birth. Proximity to an attachment figure provides infants with comfort and security, allowing them to engage in other forms of essential behaviors such as exploration of their environments. While particularly critical during early stages of life, the attachment system remains active over a person's life span, from "the cradle to the grave" (Bowlby, 1973, p. 203), generating thoughts, feelings, and behaviors associated with the maintaining of proximity to attachment figures (Bowlby, 1988).

Although the proximity-seeking motive is posited to be universal as well as innate, not all attachment figures can or will provide the forms of caregiving that lead to feelings of security and safety in their offspring. As a result, different patterns of attachment emerge in infants (Ainsworth et al., 1978). Infants who receive consistent care and support from their primary attachment figure (typically, although not necessarily, their mother) tend to develop a *secure* attachment style. As demonstrated by Ainsworth et al., (1978), using what she called the Strange Situation Paradigm, these infants engage in high levels of exploration while using their mothers as a secure base when they become distressed or anxious. At the other extreme, when mothers are consistently unresponsive to their infants' needs to be comforted, the infants develop *avoidant* attachment styles. Ainsworth et al., (1978) noted that these infants did not seek care or support from their mothers when they were distressed; instead, they actively avoided their mothers and were prematurely self-reliant. Finally, when mothers were inconsistent in their care-giving, sometimes being highly responsive while at other times being inattentive, their infants developed an *anxious* (sometimes referred to as anxious/ambivalent or resistant) attachment style. Infants in this situation appeared to be conflicted, hypervigilant, and angry, engaging in less exploration while making inconsistent attempts to obtain support from their mothers when they became distressed.

Early attachment experiences generate mental working models of the self and others that give rise to attitudes, beliefs, and expectations about relationships, providing a framework for interpreting and influencing relationship experiences (Bowlby, 1973, 1980; Collins & Read, 1994; Simpson & Rholes, 1998). These working models represent complex cognitive and affective schemas that, by predicting the availability and responsiveness of others, allow individuals to generate their own behaviors. Because the attachment system, as an evolutionary device, is concerned with providing safety and security for individuals, each of the attachment styles has come to be characterized as a set of individual differences reflecting patterns of responses to significant threats to safety and security (Kobak & Sceery, 1988; Sroufe & Waters, 1977). Further, although the initial studies of adult attachment styles, including many reviewed in this chapter, assessed styles in terms of a typology or as prototypes (Bartholomew, 1990; Bartholomew & Horowitz, 1991; Hazan & Shaver, 1987), they are today typically assessed in terms of two continuous, orthogonal dimensions: avoidance and anxiety (Brennan, Clark, & Shaver, 1998; Simpson, 1990; Simpson, Rholes, & Nelligan, 1992). The anxiety dimension represents the extent to which the attachment system is activated in times of environmental or relationship threat or stress, whereas the avoidance dimension reflects the degree to which closeness with an attachment figure is desired. Nonetheless, for convenience throughout this chapter, persons who are high on the avoidance dimension are categorically referred to as avoidant, those high on the anxiety dimension are referred to as anxious, and those low on both avoidance and anxiety are referred to as secure.[1] No attempt is made to distinguish the method of assessing attachment style used in the research studies cited; the findings discussed in this chapter appear to be robust across measurement method except as otherwise noted.

In adults, attachment-related anxiety manifests itself in low levels of trust regarding the availability and responsiveness of attachment figures in times of need. Anxious adults hypervigilantly experience anxiety over the possibility of abandonment and having their needs for care and affection left unfulfilled in the future, while, at the same time, they are angry over having been rejected in the past (Bowlby, 1973). They tend to have low self-esteem (Brennan & Morris, 1997; Bylsma, Cozzarelli, & Suiner, 1997) and a negative self-image (Mikulincer, 1995), feeling that they are unworthy of better treatment; yet they may feel that they are entitled to receive higher levels of caregiving and love and engage in coercive attempts to get their needs met (Corcoran & Mallinckrodt, 2000).

Proximity and separation are particularly salient for anxious individuals, who find it difficult to obtain sufficient levels of "felt security" because of their concerns about abandonment (Sroufe & Waters, 1977). They feel insecure upon physical separation from their relationship partner, experiencing the joint needs for closeness and autonomy in a paradoxical manner that tends to favor excessive demands for physical and/or psychological closeness with their relationship partners (Brennan et al., 1998; Fraley & Shaver, 1998; Hazan & Shaver, 1987), yet at the same time report that their desired degree of closeness is not provided (Grabill & Kerns, 2000; Hazan & Shaver, 1987). Their obsessive search for security is associated with negative affect and rumination about the future of their close relationships (Mikulincer & Florian, 1998; Mikulincer & Orbach, 1995; Simpson, 1990). They have low levels of trust in their relationship partners (Levy & Davis, 1988) and are quick to see trust violations, attributing them to stable causes such as their partner's personality (Mikulincer, 1998b).

Attachment-related avoidance manifests itself in the almost certain expectation that attachment figures will not be available or responsive when needed and may be actively rejecting, causing them to be viewed as uncaring and untrustworthy. Particularly in times of stress, avoidant individuals tend to distance themselves from their relationship partners instead of seeking support from them (Collins & Feeney, 2000; Fraley & Shaver, 1998). At the same time, however, avoidant individuals can experience physiological arousal upon separation from their partners (B. C. Feeney & Kirkpatrick, 1996), indicating that distancing strategies for emotions and behaviors are the result of suppression of still intact attachment-related needs. Attachment theory predicts that the anger evident in anxious individuals should also exist in avoidant individuals, but that it is held in check through repressive defense mechanisms (Bowlby, 1988). Avoidant individuals tend to report having high self-esteem and may have a relatively positive view of self in spite of a history of rejection from attachment figures (Bartholomew, 1990; Bartholomew & Horowitz, 1991; Brennan & Morris, 1997; Mikulincer, 1995), but they tend to have low levels of trust and interdependence with their relationship partners (Levy & Davis, 1988).

Independence and autonomy are primary motives for avoidant individuals (Mikulincer, Florian, Cowan, & Cowan, 2002; Mikulincer & Naclison, 1991). They may be unresponsive and insensitive to relationship partners, preferring self-reliance and eschewing neediness, vulnerability, or dependence in their partners (Kazan & Shaver, 1987; Mikulincer & Shaver, 2003). This apparent desire for distancing, particularly during high levels of distress, can be viewed as the result of a need to avoid the re-experiencing of the pain of past rejection, as well as a strategy for avoiding future rejection (Bowlby, 1973, 1980, 1988). It can also he driven by anger, as will be described below. Their underlying need for close, emotional connection simply remains unfulfilled.

Individuals with a secure attachment style are able to manage their distress by accepting it and turning for support in a constructive fashion to close others, who are seen as available, trustworthy, and well-intended (Bowlby, 1988). They may also turn to "internalized" attachment figures as a means of coping with distress or threat (e.g., Mikulincer, Gillath, & Shaver, 2002; Mikulincer & Shaver, 2004). They balance their needs for closeness and autonomy, maintain high levels of self-esteem (Bartholomew & Horowitz;, 1991; Bylsma et al, 1997; Mikulincer, 1995), and are generally responsive to their partners (B. C. Feeney & Collins, 2003). Their positivity in cognition (Brennan & Morris, 1997; Mikulincer, 1995), affect (Tucker & Anders, 1998), and orientation toward their partners allows persons with a secure attachment style the cognitive and emotional resources to work on maintaining quality in their relationships (e.g., Collins & Feeney, 2000).

The attachment styles can be further delineated by a more nuanced consideration of anger and hostility. Bowlby (1973) distinguishes functional anger (the anger of hope) from dysfunctional anger (the anger of despair), noting that an individual can use functional anger to maintain attachment bonds by protesting that his or her needs are not being met and by serving to change the partner's negative behaviors. In contrast, dysfunctional anger can be destructive of attachment bonds and, in adults, can result from unresolved anger against earlier attachment figures. It can be manifested as hostility or resentment toward the partner and may incorporate revenge; dysfunctional anger can alienate the partner and may even result in aggression or violence (Bowlby, 1988).

Persons with all three attachment styles experience anger, particularly when their security is threatened or their needs are not met (Feeney, 1995,1999; Mikulincer, 1998a; Muris, Meesters, Morren, & Moorman, 2004), but their expression of anger differs. As expected, attachment security is associated with functional and adaptive manifestations of anger, coupled with the beliefs that the partner's negative behavior is well-intended and remediable (Feeney, 1999; Mikulincer, 1998a). Further, secure persons tend to acknowledge their angry emotion in a manner that is consistent with their physiological experience of anger (Mikulincer, 1998a).

Insecure attachment is associated with dysfunctional anger in ways that are consistent with the anxiety and avoidance working models. Anxious adults experience intense anger when they believe or fear that their relationship partners are unavailable to meet their needs (Creasey & Hesson-Mclnnis, 2001; Mikulincer, 1998a), ruminating on threat-related thoughts that may intensify and prolong their anger (Mikulincer, 1998a; Mikulincer & Shaver, 2003, 2005). Their anger may be associated with their tendency to make more negative attributions of their partners intent, even in ambiguous situations (Mikulincer, 1998a). These negative attributions may be the result of their tendency to project their own assumed negative characteristics onto their partner (Mikulincer & Horesh, 1999), which would include their own anger and hostility. Out of fear of losing their partner, however, they may fail to express their anger outwardly (Feeney, 1995, 1998; Mikulincer, 1998a), dysfunctionally controlling it and turning it inward (Mikulincer, 1998a). These findings have also been apparent in naturalistic interactions in a study by Simpson, Rholes, and Phillips (1996), who found that anxious persons felt greater anger and hostility toward their dating or marital partners during and after stressful, conflictual interactions.

Persons with an avoidant attachment style, consistent with their tendency to distance themselves from attachment-related distress and deactivate the attachment system, tend to experience what has been called "dissociated anger" (Mikulincer, 1998a). In other words, although avoidant persons self-report lower levels of anger than secure persons, physiological signs indicate the presence of intense anger and hostility. This approach to anger begins as an infant, according to Ainsworth et al., (1978), when, although avoidant babies were viewed as behaving angrily toward their rejecting mothers in a home environment, they later (in the Strange Situation, which was highly stressful) were noted as experiencing but suppressing their anger in order to avoid the expected rejection associated with seeking proximity to their attachment figure and thus reduce their angry arousal. Avoidant adults tend to attribute hostility to their partners, even in the presence of information suggesting non-hostile intent (Mikulincer, 1998a), a type of "defensive projection" that may serve the purpose of enhancing their own self-esteem (Mikulincer & Horesh, 1999).

Although in infants, direct expression of anger to the attachment figure can sometimes be a dangerous way of trying to get needs met (Ainsworth et al., 1978), as adults, avoidant persons need not fear distancing their partners by their angry behaviors, and so may he more likely to express strong anger in relationship interactions under circumstances that involve meeting their needs, such as trying to re-attain an optimal sense of distance that has been violated by a partner. They may also be likely to reciprocate anger. For example, Rholes, Simpson, and Oriña (1999) found that highly avoidant women displayed intense anger toward their partners during a stressful situation, particularly when they were highly distressed and their partners were themselves angry. Avoidant men displayed greater anger during the stressful period than did less avoidant men, particularly when their partners were distressed, sought more support from them, or displayed more anger.

To become angry at attachment figures necessarily involves understanding that one's legitimate needs have not been met. Even if socialized as children not to think about their attachment needs or the ways in which they have not been fulfilled (Bowlby, 1988), insecure individuals often still recognize at some level that they make legitimate claims on attachment figures. As a consequence, we suggest that they form a linkage between their anger and the knowledge that their needs can only be met through their own efforts (whether it be through the compulsive pursuit of their attachment figures for anxious persons or the compulsive distancing from their attachment figures for avoidant persons). This combination of anger and knowledge encourages or produces an egoistic stance; that is, insecure persons tend to focus on getting their needs met to the exclusion of the needs of those with whom they are angry, including their attachment figures. The conceptual models shown in Figure 5.1 depict schematically our understanding of attachment anxiety, avoidance, and anger as they pertain to processes linked to relationship satisfaction.

The attachment system is but one of four innate behavioral systems—attachment, caregiving, sexual, and exploration—described by Bowlby (1969). The first three systems are clearly interrelated in that they involve relationships between persons, while exploration is a system that provides for learning and individual growth through curiosity about the environment. Attachment researchers have focused primarily on the attachment system itself, although, as will be seen, some research has been conducted on the interaction between the attachment and care-giving and attachment and sexuality systems in adults. Though not discussed further in this chapter, romantic love has been conceptualized as an integration of the attachment, caregiving, and sexuality systems (Shaver, Hazan, & Bradshaw, 1988). Also not discussed in any detail in this chapter is the relationship between the attachment and exploration systems, except to note that persons having a secure attachment style, as opposed to an anxious or avoidant attachment style, are generally viewed as being best able to explore the social and physical environment (Ainsworth et al., 1978; Mikulincer et al., 2002). The "optimal balance" between dependence and

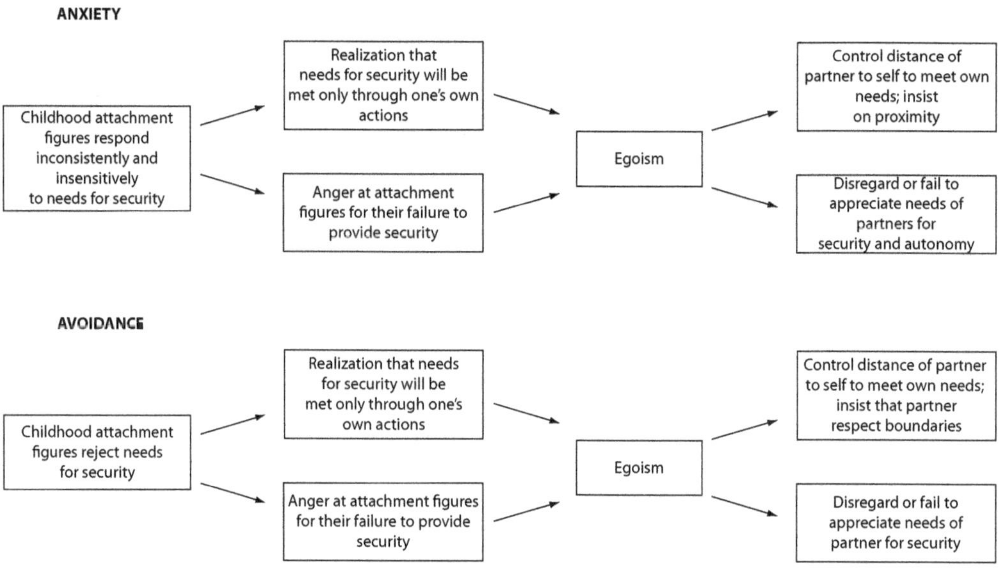

Figure 5.1 Models linking ttachment anxiety and avoidance of an individual to nature of interactions with partner.

autonomy allows such individuals to participate fully in close relationships while pursuing activities related to their own interests and personal development (Mikulincer et al., 2002).

ATTACHMENT STYLE AND RELATIONSHIP SATISFACTION

Satisfaction in relationships is related to a complex of interpersonal processes (e.g., Bradbury, Fincham, & Beach, 2000). For example, attributions about partner behaviors and intent, negative affect, behavioral interaction patterns, partner affection and support, and relationship violence are all processes that interest relationship and, particularly, marriage researchers (Bradbury et al., 2000). As suggested by the focus of tins chapter, there is a vast literature linking attachment style to dating and marital satisfaction. Because high-quality close relationships are essential to happiness and well-being, and because attachment theory provides a framework for understanding closeness and security in relationships in relation to caregiving and sexuality, which are important aspects of adult relationships, attachment researchers have studied a variety of individual characteristics and interpersonal processes that relate attachment style to relationship satisfaction.

The relationship literature investigates satisfaction as a function of individual behavior (e.g., conflict management) and as a function of situations and responses to them (e.g., periods of high stress, transition points in relationships). In this chapter, we discuss attachment research in each of these categories. Our analysis of behaviors focuses on support and caregiving, conflict management, violence, and the establishment of closeness through self-disclosure and sexual relations. Our examination of situations focuses on the transition made when couples first become parents. Finally, we also review the relatively few studies that have investigated individuals' satisfaction as a function of their partner's attachment styles. In each of these domains, our goal is to point out the linkage between attachment styles and risk factors for relationship dissatisfaction.

In general, studies have indicated that persons with secure attachment styles have greater commitment to and greater satisfaction with their (dating or marital) relationship partners than do those individuals who are either anxious or avoidant (e.g., Collins & Read, 1990, Feeney, Noller, & Roberts, 1998; Pistole, 1989; Simpson, 1990; but see Hollist & Miller, 2005, finding no relationship between attachment style and marital satisfaction in midlife marriage). Persons having an anxious attachment style tend to have the lowest levels of relationship satisfaction (e.g., Feeney, 1994; 1996; 1999; Feeney et al., 1998; Kobak & Hazan, 1991; Pistole, 1989; Rholes, Simpson, & Blakely, 1995; Simpson, 1990), although their levels of relationship satisfaction can be affected by factors such as perception of partner support (Campbell, Simpson, Boldry, & Kashy, 2005). Persons with avoidant styles typically fall between anxious and secure individuals (Mikulincer et al., 2002).

ATTACHMENT STYLE AND POTENTIAL RISK FACTORS FOR RELATIONSHIP (DIS)SATISFACTION: GIVING, SEEKING, AND PERCEIVING CARE AND SUPPORT

The fundamental purpose of the attachment system is to encourage infants, children, and adults to seek safety and comfort from attachment figures in times of distress. According to attachment theory, however, it should be relatively uncommon for people high in avoidance to seek support from attachment figures, because acknowledging a need for care from another undermines their desire to maintain psychological independence (Bowlby, 1973). Both self-report (Berant, Mikulincer, & Florian, 2001; Florian, Mikulincer, & Bucholtz, 1995; Mikulincer & Florian, 1995; Mikulincer, Florian, & Weller, 1993; Ognibene & Collins, 1998; Rholes, Simpson, Campbell, & Grich, 2001) and observational studies (Fraley & Shaver, 1998, Simpson, Rholes, & Nelligan, 1992) show that avoidant people are less likely to seek support from close others, thus limiting opportunities for interactions that could promote closeness. Individuals high in avoidance view others who seek their support in pejorative terms, as weak, immature, dependent, and unstable (Wilson, Simpson, & Rholes, 2000); thus, in addition to their desire to maintain independence, their reluctance to seek care may stem from its implications for self-perception. They also may hesitate to seek support because they believe that it will not be forthcoming (Florian et al„ 1995; Kobak & Sceery, 1988; Rholes et al., 2001),

Studies of support seeking among anxious individuals yield less consistent results. Retrospective self-report studies suggest that support seeking is positively correlated with anxiety (Florian et al., 1995; Mikulincer et al., 1993; Ognibene & Collins, 1998), but some observational studies and studies in which reports of support seeking are taken during a stressful period do not (Collins & Feeney, 2000; Mikulincer & Florian, 1995; Rholes et al, 2001; Simpson et al., 1992). Rholes et al., (2001) found that during the stressful months shortly before and after the birth of their first child, the more anxious women sought significantly less support than their less anxious counterparts. Anxious women perceive support to be less available, which may partially explain their behavior (cf. Florian et al., 1995). After stress subsides, self-perceptions and social desirability may encourage anxious people to perceive that they have sought support, but in the "heat" of a stressful episode their mistrust of relationships and relationships partners (Wallace & Vaux, 1993) appears to undermine actual support seeking.

Perceptions of the availability of support are strongly linked to attachment anxiety. Rholes et al., (2001) found that more anxious women going through the transition to parenthood were highly satisfied with their marriages if they perceived that their husbands were supportive. Unfortunately, however, most anxious women in this study reported that their husbands were not highly supportive. Several other studies also have found anxiety to be linked to the belief that relationship partners are unsupportive (Bartholomew, Cobb, & Poole, 1997; Florian et al., 1995; Priel & Shamai, 1995; Wallace & Vaux, 1993; Wilson, Rholes, Simpson, & Tran, 2007). Such perceptions can encourage denigration of partners, conflict, and anger and therefore constrain opportunities for relationship satisfaction.

Whether these perceptions accurately reflect at partner's behavior or whether they are constructions of supportiveness that are biased by the anxious working model is unclear. Rholes et al., (2001) found that husbands of more anxious women reported that they provided less support to them during the period surrounding the birth of their first child. Anxious women, however, reported that they received even less support than their husbands reported, but their non-anxious counterparts reported that they received more support than their husbands said they provided. This study thus indicates that support may actually be less available to anxious individuals, but also that the pessimistic working models of anxious individuals may further contribute to the perception that partners are unsupportive. Collins and Feeney's (2004) results strongly implicate perceptual bias. In their study, more anxious individuals who received a moderately unsupportive communication from their dating partners rated it as less supportive than their less anxious counterparts did and, after receiving the communication, remembered the behavior of their partner in a previous interaction as comparatively unsupportive, despite reports of objective raters to the contrary. Apparently, moderately unsupportive behavior by partners activates latent doubts among anxious individuals that impose a negative bias on their construction (or reconstruction) of their partners' behavior.

The primary purpose of the caregiving system is to encourage attachment figures to provide safety and care when sought by infants, children, or adult partners. Effective caregivers, according to attachment theory and research (e.g., Ainsworth et al., 1978), are able to "read" the internal states of others, provide care that is timed contingently on the other's signals and states of need, are warm and accepting of efforts to elicit help, and are consistently available to offer help when needed. Ineffective caregivers are intrusive, controlling, inconsistent, and unaccepting of the needs of others.

Insecure adults are generally ineffective caregivers. Attachment theory (Bowlby, 1988) argues that people with strong avoidant tendencies fear and distrust relationships in part because they do not want to be "trapped into" providing care to a relationship partner. Feeling at some level that no one ever has provided care to them, providing care to others may seem an unfair burden and may generate anger (Rholes et al., 1999). Consistent with the theory, more avoidant husbands indicated that they provided less support to their partners during labor and delivery (Wilson et al, 2007) and in general during the transition to parenthood (Rholes et al, 2001). Several observational studies also have linked avoidance to lower levels of supportive behavior (Rholes et al, 1995; Simpson et al,, 1992,1996; Westmaas & Silver, 2001), but at least one, Collins & Feeney (2000), did not. Avoidant people appear to be least supportive when they or their partners are comparatively distressed (Simpson et al., 1992, 1996). Thus, their behavior may reflect efforts to keep their attachment systems deactivated (Simpson et al., 1992). More proximal causes of their behavior appear to be less empathic and compassionate responses to the distress of others (Mikulincer et al, 2001; Mikulincer, Shaver, Gillath, & Nitzberg, 2005) and believing themselves to be less obligated to provide support and being more uncomfortable when asked to do so (Wilson et al, 2000).

There is little evidence that more anxious people provide less support to their partners overall. There is evidence, however, that they are less effective as caregivers and are motivated to help in part by egoistic concerns (e.g., B. C. Feeney & Collins, 2003; Kunce & Shaver, 1994). Consistent with the ineffective profile, anxious caregivers are described in the literature as providing less effective support overall, as being less emotionally and cognitively responsive to their partners, as being more dismissive and unhelpful to care-seekers, as being less able to perceive partners' needs for support, as being more controlling, and as becoming over-involved in their partners' problems (e.g., Collins & Feeney, 2000; B. C. Feeney & Collins, 2001; Kunce & Shaver, 1994). These differences in behavior may be partially explained by the greater endorsement of self-centered motives for helping partners by anxious caregivers (e.g., to keep their partner tied to them and to receive other benefits; B. C. Feeney & Collins, 2003). They also may result from the greater personal distress and less empathic responses that are characteristic of more anxious caregivers' response to the distress of others (Mikulincer et al, 2001, 2005; Westmaas & Silver, 2001).

Partners who receive more effective, responsive care and those who believe that support is available should they need it report that they feel loved and that they are more satisfied with their relationships (Collins & Feeney, 2000; Feeney, 1996; B. C. Feeney & Collins, 2003). Even highly anxious and avoidant individuals seem to benefit from partner support (Rholes et al., 2001; Simpson et al, 1992). Thus, the relationship dissatisfaction often experienced by insecure individuals and individuals involved in relationships with insecure partners may arise from their own inadequate care-seeking, inadequate caregiving by their partners, or perceptual biases that prevent them from perceiving support that is available to them.

Intimacy

Although the word "intimacy" is used widely in relationship research, often as a synonym for some forms of physical and psychological closeness (e.g., "a feeling of connectedness with another person"; Laurenceau, Troy, & Carver, 2005 , pp. 1123–1124), we prefer to think of intimacy as a strategy based on a capacity for negotiating closeness (cf. Cassidy, 2001). Hence, we do not view "seeking intimacy" as a relationship goal. Closeness (or its avoidance) is the goal, with different attachment styles being related to different processes or capacities for negotiating it. We focus here on two important strategies for negotiating closeness: self-disclosure (Keelan, Dion, & Dion, 1993; Laurenceau, Barrett, & Rovine, 2005; Mikulincer & Nachson, 1991) and sexual behavior (Cassidy, 2001; Feeney & Noller, 2004).

Self-Disclosure. Self-disclosure represents the process by which we reveal ourselves to others and is generally viewed as being critical to the establishment of closeness in relationships. Attachment researchers have studied a variety of aspects of self-disclosure, including its quantity, nature, flexibility, responsiveness, and target, as well as considering it both a trait and state construct. If self-disclosure is a means of attaining greater closeness, then persons with an avoidant attachment style should, because of their desire to maintain a controlled distance—i.e., independence and autonomy—from their partners, be expected to disclose less often, and less personally, than persons having a secure or anxious attachment style. This appears to be a robust finding in the attachment literature, regardless whether the self-disclosure is to relationship partners or strangers (Bartholomew & Horowitz, 1991; Bradford, Feeney, & Campbell, 2002; Mikulincer & Nachson, 1991). Their lack of self-disclosure presents fewer opportunities for their partners to feel close to them, thereby also limiting their partners' opportunities to engage in their own self-disclosure.

In Mikulincer and Nachson's (1991) experimental study using confederates as "partners," avoidant persons did not flexibly reciprocate self-disclosure and appeared insensitive to the nature of the confederate partner's self-disclosure. Further, although avoidant individuals had low levels of liking for self-disclosing partners regardless of the amount of personal information they revealed about themselves, self-disclosing partners who provided more personal details about themselves were liked less by avoidant individuals than by individuals who were secure or anxious. Avoidant individuals also tended to experience more negative emotion when interacting with partners who were high-disclosers than did secure or anxious individuals (Mikulincer & Nachson, 1991; Pistole, 1993). More recent research has found that avoidant persons have less desire to know personal information about their relationship partners than do secure or anxious persons (Rholes, Simpson, Tran, Martin, & Friedman, 2005). Thus, consistent with their working model, persons who are avoidant shun intimate strategies for self-disclosure on their own part and on the part of their partners, presumably as a means of controlling psychological and emotional distance.

Attachment theory would predict that anxious individuals engage in self-disclosure behaviors that are consistent with their desire to feel secure. In other words, they may enjoy self-disclosure from a partner if it signals that they are at low risk for rejection, but they may fail to reciprocate the nature of that self-disclosure if their focus is on their own neediness and fear of rejection instead of on their partner's needs. On the other hand, as a means of establishing security early in a relationship or during times of relationship threat, anxious persons may excessively self-disclose (even to persons who would find such intimate revelations inappropriate) and thus self-disclose more than either persons who are secure or avoidant. Thus, the self-disclosure of anxious persons should be based on contingency. In general, it has been found that in many ways the self-disclosure of anxious persons is like that of secure persons: high-disclosing partners tend to be more liked than low-disclosing partners, and the partner's level of self-disclosure tends to be reciprocated. However, an apparent lack of both flexibility and topical reciprocity on the part of anxious individuals suggests that they may be preoccupied with their own needs as part of their self-disclosure instead of fully attending to the needs of their partner; in other words, their self-disclosure does not represent an intimate strategy for obtaining mutual closeness (Mikulincer & Nachson, 1991).

By contrast, secure persons seek closeness in their close relationships and are more likely to self-disclose, and to disclose to relationship partners more than to others, as a means of obtaining closeness (Keelan et al., 1993; Mikulincer & Nachson, 1991; Pistole, 1993; Simpson, 1990). Additionally, secure individuals are more flexible and responsive in their self-disclosure and tend to engage in more topical reciprocity than persons who are anxious or avoidant, suggesting that they are more intimate in their relationships than the other two attachment styles (Mikulincer & Nachson, 1991).

Sexuality. Sexuality is another important aspect of intimacy in close relationships (Feeney & Noller, 2004). Research indicates that attachment style is associated with the way a person uses sexuality to meet his or her needs. For example, whereas procreation may provide a sexual motive for those who are secure or anxious, the effect is not as strong for avoidants (Davis, Shaver, & Vernon, 2004; Rholes, Simpson, Blakely, Lanigan, & Allen, 1997). For anxious persons, sexual motives are linked to feelings of closeness (for example, feeling loved by one's partner; Schachner & Shaver, 2004) and insecurity (Implett & Peplau, 2002; Schach-ner & Shaver, 2004). They tend to obsess and feel passionate about their sexual partners (Davis et al., 2004; Feeney & Noller, 1990), experience strong sexual jealousy (Buunk, 1997; Guerrero, 1998), prefer affectionate touching to genital contact (Hazan, Zeifman, & Middleton, 1994, as cited in Davis et al., 2004), and worry about the possibility of losing their partners to others (Schachner & Shaver, 2002). They may engage in sex as a means of pleasing their partner instead of as a way to meet their own needs (Davis et al., 2004; Tracy, Shaver, Albino, & Cooper, 2003).

Anxious women, in particular, may engage (or indicate willingness to engage) in unwanted but consensual sex (Gentzler & Kerns, 2004; Impett & Peplau, 2002). These behaviors may reflect manipulation instead of concern for one's partner; in other words, anxious persons may use sex as a form of self-protection from their partner's anger, to elicit caregiving from their partner, or to exert power over their partner (Davis et al, 2004),

Individuals with an avoidant attachment style have sexual motives that are linked to autonomy and self-enhancement among peers (Schachner & Shaver, 2002,2004; Tracy et al., 2003). They tend to eschew both the physical and psychological intimacy that accompany sex and thus may avoid sexual intercourse (Cooper, Shaver, & Collins, 1998; Hazan et al, 1994, as cited in Davis et al., 2004; Tracy et al., 2003); in addition, avoidance tends to be negatively related to passion (Davis et al, 2004) and love for one's partner (Tracy et al., 2003). They are more likely to engage in casual sex, including one-night stands (Brennan & Shaver, 1995; Feeney, Noller, & Patty, 1993; Fraley, Davis, & Shaver, 1998; Gentzler & Kerns, 2004; Schachner & Shaver, 2002). Avoidant persons tend to prefer physical genital contact via forms of sexual intercourse (e.g., oral or anal sex) to more emotional expressions of affection such as cuddling or kissing (Hazan et al., 1994, as cited in Davis et al,, 2004).

Both insecure attachment styles maintain consistent motivations for sexual intercourse when engaged in sexual activity outside of their primary relationships. In a study of extradyadic sexual involvement, anxious persons reported closeness motives while avoidant persons reported autonomy motives (Allen & Baucom, 2004). Although results are somewhat inconsistent across insecure attachment types, there is evidence that attachment insecurity is associated with having more affairs (Gangestad & Thornhill, 1997; Kirkpatrick, 1998), having sexual intercourse at an earlier age (Bogaert & Sadava, 2002; Gentzler & Kerns, 2004), and engaging in risky sexual behaviors (Bogaert & Sadava, 2002; Feeney, Peterson, Gallois, & Terry, 2000).

In contrast, attachment security is related to having a variety of sexual experiences within committed, long-term relationships (Hazan et al., 1994, as cited in Davis et al., 2004; Tracy et al., 2003) and having fewer partners in total (Brennan & Shaver, 1995; Cooper et al., 1998). Secure individuals also report more positive emotions regarding past sexual experiences than do anxious or avoidant persons (Tracy et al., 2003).

Conflict

Conflict has the potential to interfere with—i.e., reduce or enhance—marital or relationship satisfaction in various ways. For example, the mere presence of conflict could be viewed as either positive or negative, depending on the nature of the conflict, its frequency, how the partners attempt to resolve it, and how partners cope with the conflict; how partners communicate with each other during conflict is relevant as well (e.g., Gottman & Krokoff, 1989; Marchand & Hock, 2000; Noller, Feeney, Bonnell, & Callan, 1994). Attachment style has been demonstrated to be related to at least some of these features of conflict.

If conflict poses a potential threat to a relationship (e.g., Kobak & Duemmler, 1994; Pistole, 2003; Torquati & Vazsonyi, 1999), so that one partner may expect rejection or alienation, then attachment behaviors should be activated, leading to approaches to conflict consistent with attachment style. Persons with an avoidant attachment style would be expected to engage in strategies that would de-emphasize or avoid the conflict and facilitate emotional and psychological distancing from the partner (e.g., compromising to end the conflict, Pistole, 1989; withdrawing, Shi, 2003), while persons with an anxious attachment style would be hypervigilant to both the partner and associated distress during conflict and might be more likely to give in to the partner as a way of pleasing him or her instead of employing a strategy that would risk loss (e.g., Pistole, 1989; Shi, 2003). On the other hand, anxious persons are also concerned about getting their needs met and may therefore tend, at least to some degree, to be confrontational, demanding, and/or dominating and less able to engage in productive conflict resolution strategies (Corcoran & Mallinckroclt, 2000; Feeney, Noller, & Gallan, 1994; Shi, 2003; Simpson et al., 1996). Secure persons, because they have expectations that their partners will be available and responsive in times of need, may not even perceive conflict as a threat to the relationship and would be expected to be open and flexible with their partners during conflict (Kobak & Duemmler, 1994; Simpson et al., 1996).

For example, it has been demonstrated that, based on self-reports from college students in romantic relationships, positive conflict management skills such as displaying affection, validating the partner, staying focused on the positive nature of the specific conflict, and using effective arguing and/or a mutually integrating strategy were negatively related to anxiety and avoidance and positively related to being secure (e.g., Creasey & Hesson-Mclnnis, 2001; Pistole, 1989, 2003). At the same time, nonconstructive management skills involving negativity, escalation, and withdrawal were positively related to anxiety and avoidance (and negatively related to being secure), with persons who were anxious having the most difficulty in managing conflict (e.g., Creasey & Hesson-Mclnnis, 2001; Pistole, 2003).

Perceptions of and attitudes toward conflict have also been demonstrated to be related to attachment style. For example, although it might normally be expected that conflict would be viewed negatively by individuals having an anxious attachment style (i.e., as a threat to relationship security), Fishtein, Pietromonaco, & Feldman Barrett (1999) demonstrated that such persons may view high-conflict interactions more positively than others because of the overall potential for more responsiveness from their partners. In addition, while all persons in high-conflict relationships (regardless of attachment style) demonstrated more complex knowledge about negative attributes of their relationship, only anxious persons in high-conflict relationships showed greater complexity in knowledge of positive relationship aspects.

In a recent daily diary study of dating partners, persons high in attachment anxiety perceived more daily relationship conflict than others, even higher than would be expected given the level of relationship conflict reported by their partners (Campbell et al, 2005). Further, the perceived conflict was viewed by anxiously attached persons as escalating beyond the original topic of conflict and being more hurtful than persons who were not high in attachment anxiety considered it to be. No significant relationship was found between attachment avoidance and perceptions of conflict and hurtfulness. Further, in an accompanying observational study of conflict resolution for the dating partners, Campbell et al., (2005) found that anxious individuals were seen as escalating existing conflict and reacting too strongly to it, whereas avoidant individuals (and by implication, secure individuals) were not.

In addition to being associated with attachment style, conflict is clearly a risk factor for level of relationship satisfaction, as has been evidenced by several studies. For example, Feeney (1994) demonstrated that mutual understanding during conflict was related to both anxiety (negatively for both husbands and wives) and relationship satisfaction (positively for both husbands and wives), with mutuality fully mediating the relationship between anxiety and satisfaction for wives while only partially mediating the same relationship for husbands. Similarly, Carnelley, Pietromonaco, & Jaffe (1994), in a study of depression and relationship satisfaction, noted that women with insecure attachment styles were less likely than secure women to use constructive approaches to conflict resolution and were more likely to report less relationship satisfaction. Marchand's (2004) study of husbands and wives revealed that husbands who were anxious or avoidant engaged in significantly more attacking behaviors than those who were secure, whereas wives who were anxious or avoidant engaged in both more attacking and fewer compromising behaviors than their secure counterparts. Further, for wives, the negative relationship between their attachment anxiety and level of marital satisfaction was partially mediated by their attacking behaviors.

The study by Campbell et al., (2005) demonstrated that when anxious persons perceive more conflict, they themselves are less optimistic about the future of their relationship, believing that their partners are dissatisfied with the relationship and pessimistic about its future. Further, their work suggests that persons high in attachment anxiety attend carefully to daily events in their relationship when making assessments of relationship quality, thereby possibly perceiving it as less stable.

Violence

Studies of relationship violence can be divided into those that involve individuals whose abusiveness has brought them into the legal system and those that involve community samples of individuals or couples and (typically) less severe forms of violence. Studies in the later group, which include studies of adolescents and adults, routinely find that the anxious attachment style is related to the perpetration of verbal abuse and physical violence (e.g., Bookwala, 2002; Orcutt, Garcia, & Pickett, 2005; Roberts & Noller, 1998). Moreover, it is not the case that people with an anxious attachment style are more violent simply because they are less satisfied with their relationship generally or have more interpersonal problems with their spouse (Bookwala & Zdaniuk, 1998), which suggests that the dynamics of the anxious working model may affect violence regardless of general characteristics of marriage or other close relationships. In a study that focused only on violence perpetrated by women in dating relationships, Orcutt et al., (2005) found that women in relationships in which both partners were violent reported higher levels of attachment anxiety, and women who perpetrate violence in the absence of partner violence reported higher levels of attachment anxiety coupled with lower levels of avoidance. Other studies (e.g., Bookwala & Zdaniuk, 1998), however, report that violence is common among individuals who combine the anxious and avoidant attachment styles. Roberts and Noller (1998) report that men and women with an anxious attachment style are particularly likely to engage in violence if their partners' attachment styles are avoidant. Also highlighting the complexity of the relationship between attachment style and violence, Wekerle and Wolfe (1998) found that attachment styles moderate the relationship of childhood abuse to violence directed at adult partners. Men who were abused in childhood were more likely to act violently if their attachment styles were either anxious or avoidant, and women who were abused were more likely to he violent if their attachment style was anxious.

Studies involving male batterers referred to therapy report findings similar to those above. Pistole and Tarrant (1993) report that male batterers do not differ from controls on attachment style. Several other studies, however, challenge this finding (Dutton, Saunders, Starzomski, & Bartholomew, 1994; Dutton, Starzom-ski, & Ryan, 1996; Mauricio & Gormley, 2001; Tweed & Dutton, 1998). These studies report that attachment anxiety and a combination of anxiety and avoidance distinguish batterers from controls.

Bowlby (1973) argues that anger and violence toward partners is a response to real or threatened separation from attachment figures. He reports that parents who discipline their children by threatening separation or abandonment arouse both intense fear and intense anger. He further suggests that violence in adult couples is a reaction to separation, whether real, threatened, or imagined (Bowlby, 1988). From this perspective, it is easy to see why attachment anxiety is more broadly associated with violence than attachment avoidance: Anxious individuals' obsession with possible abandonment or with their partner's potential disregard of their needs makes violence and anger high in their hierarchy of responses (cf. Collins, 1996), and their tendency to see threats in many everyday behaviors can provide frequent triggers for such response. Concerns about separation and abandonment are much weaker among avoidant people, and the environmental conditions that may raise such concerns should be few. Avoidant people often are described by those who know them as hostile (Kobak & Sceery, 1988). That this hostility does not often manifest itself in relationship violence seems to attest to the control that avoidant individuals exercise over their behavior. This control may be broken down under very difficult, stressful circumstances (cf. Mayseless, 1991) or when their proclivity toward hostility is enhanced by childhood abuse (Wekerle & Wolfe, 1998).

The Transition to *Parenthood*

Whereas potentially vulnerable relationships (e.g., those in which one or both partners are insecure) may fare reasonably well during their early stages, the eventual encounter with difficult life circumstances may be an occasion in which destructive behaviors and perceptions are first unleashed. These events may thus mark the beginning of a long-term deterioration of relationship well-being. Simpson and Rholes (1994), however, argue that despite their destructive potential, difficulties that are met successfully through collaborative, mutually supportive and positive interactions may have a long-term "steeling" effect that encourages relationship well-being into the future. In support of their position, they cite research showing that recalling a time in which couple members helped one another through a difficult period encourages constructive problem-solving behavior and benevolent attributions (Holmes, 1991). They also note that friendships are strengthened when friends support each other through difficult times (Woolsey & McBain, 1987). Based on the material reviewed above, however, it seems likely that positive outcomes from encounters with stressors occur primarily among couples in which one or both partners are secure.

Becoming a parent for the first time occasions adaptation to new roles and identities, and for many couples these changes plus the responsibility for providing care to an infant make the transition to parenthood highly stressful (Heinicke, 1995). Because it is one of the most common experiences of marriage and other long-term relationships, the transition to parenthood may provide one of the best opportunities to study an event that may initiate processes that strengthen or weaken relationships over the long term. Given the challenges that the transition poses, it should not be surprising to find that conflict between new parents increases and companionate activities decline or that overall marital satisfaction declines during the transition to parenthood (Belsky & Pensky, 1988; Cowan & Cowan, 2000; see also Twenge, Campbell, & Foster, 2003). Not all couples show these trends, however. Tucker and Aron (1993) found that the variation in the quality of marital relationships increases during the transition, suggesting that although some couples find this period of time troubling, others maintain their equilibrium or even come through the transition with stronger relationships.

Anxious women are particularly vulnerable to declines in marital satisfaction across the transition, especially if they perceive that their partners do not adequately support their needs (Rholes et al., 2001). Support by partners may be particularly important to anxious women because they tend to appraise the threats attendant to pregnancy, motherhood, their health, and their infants as more severe than do other women and cope with these and other stressors less effectively (Alexander, Feeney, Hohaus, & Noller, 2001; Mikulincer & Florian, 1998). In addition to marital satisfaction, the combination of attachment anxiety and either inadequate caregiving by husbands (Feeney, Alexander, Noller, & Hohaus, 2003) or wives' perceptions that husbands were unsupportive (Simpson, Rholes, Campbell, Tran & Wilson, 2003) predicts increases in depressive symptoms across the transition period.

Rholes et al., (2001) found that more avoidant women also were less satisfied with their marriages just before and 6 months after the birth of their infants, but this did not worsen with the passage of time, and it did not interact with perceptions of support, as it did among anxious women. Avoidant women appraise the threats associated with the transition to parenthood as higher than secure women (Mikulincer & Florian, 1998), and both avoidant men and women find child care to be more stressful and less personally meaningful than do others (Rholes, Simpson, & Friedman, 2006). Avoidant men and women also cope with the stressors associated with the transition less effectively than their secure counterparts do (Alexander at al., 2001). Perhaps also contributing to their marital dissatisfaction during this period, avoidant parents engage in less relationship maintenance behavior (Curran, Hazen, Jacobvitz, & Feldman, 2005) and under some circumstances engage in higher levels of escalation of negative affect during problem-solving interactions (Paley et al., 2005). As is the case with anxiety, there are links between avoidance and depression during the transition (Simpson et al., 2003), but not all studies report this outcome (Feeney et al., 2003).

LIVING WITH SECURE AND INSECURE PARTNERS: THE EFFECTS OF PARTNER INSECURITY

Individuals involved in relationships with partners who have anxious attachment styles report themselves to be less satisfied with their relationships (Davila, Bradbury, & Fincham, 1998; Feeney, 1996; 1999; Lussier, Sabourin, &Turgeon, 1997; Rholes et al, 2001; Simpson, 1990). They experience more negative and fewer positive emotions (Davila et al., 1998; Simpson, 1990), including more sadness, depression, and anxiety and less happiness and love (Feeney, 1999). They also experience more distress in conflict-resolving discussions (Campbell et al., 2005) and evaluate everyday interactions with their partners more negatively (Bradford et al., 2002). In addition to dissatisfaction, Marcaurelle, Belanger, Marchand, Katerlos, & Mainguy (2005) report that, in a vulnerable clinical sample, individuals married to more anxious partners display more symptoms of clinical depression.

Involvement with an anxious partner, thus, appears to constitute a risk factor similar to those discussed above. These results may easily be seen as responses to the ways in which anxious people either perceive their partners (as unsupportive) or engage in interpersonal behaviors as discussed previously.

The adverse impact of anxiety appears to be most pronounced when anxious partners believe that their needs for support are not being met. In a study of the transition to parenthood, Rholes et al., (2001) found that husbands of anxious wives were dissatisfied with their marriages primarily when their wives believed that they were not receiving adequate emotional support, a common condition among anxious women in this study. In contrast, husbands whose anxious wives felt that their needs were being met reported high levels of satisfaction (as did the anxious wives themselves). This study did not address what anxious wives who felt unsupported might have done, if anything, to alienate their partners, but it does show how their partners behaved toward them. Anxious wives were disparaged as immature, unstable, dependent, and weak, with their husbands providing increasingly less support to them over time. Feeney and Hohaus (2001) also found that husbands provided less support to anxious wives, with Feeney and Collins (2003) indicating that one reason for this may be the belief that anxious partners are too needy. In other words, anxious people appear to generate reactions from partners that confirm the negative perceptions and expectations present in their working models of attachment anxiety.

There also are reports that partners of avoidant persons are less satisfied with their relationships, but they are fewer in number. In general, it appears that partner anxiety is more strongly and consistently linked to one's dissatisfaction than partner avoidance. Simpson (1990) found that female, but not male, college students who were paired with avoidant partners were less satisfied with their relationships; Rholes et al., (2001) found that partners of more avoidant individuals were more dissatisfied during the transition to parenthood; and Davila et al., (1998) found an indirect link between greater partner avoidance and lower marital satisfaction through the experience of negative affect in relationships. Collins, Cooper, Albino, & Allard (2002) measured attachment styles among a group of adolescents and examined their romantic relationships six years later. Partners of avoidant individuals were less satisfied with their relationships and reported their avoidant partners to be less disclosing, more critical and jealous, more likely to withdraw from discussions about problems, and (for male partners) more aggressive, consistent with the findings discussed above. Interestingly, this study also found that the partners of avoidant individuals were lower in agency, higher in negative emotionality, and had insecure attachment models of self. Thus, their dissatisfaction with their avoidant partners may have sources other than their partners' behavior.

CONCLUSIONS: GENERAL THEMES, LIMITATIONS OF EXISTING RESEARCH, AND DIRECTIONS FOR THE FUTURE

The year 2007 marked the fiftieth anniversary of Bowlby's initial presentation on attachment theory to his colleagues in the British psychoanalytic community. Hostility and incredulity best describe the reactions of his fellow psychiatrists to his ideas. Because he had abandoned key psychoanalytic concepts (secondary drives, psychic energy, libidinal phases, and the dependency theory of children's ties to their primary caregiver), his ideas were considered radical. Adding to his colleagues' confusion, he introduced concepts from unfamiliar disciplines (e.g., systems theory and ethology), and he conceptualized the bond between children and their caregivers as a species-general instinct that was not in principle different from those investigated among "lower" species. In short, Bowlby introduced a strikingly new conceptual framework into the conservative, insulated world of British psychoanalysis of the 1950s. Refining and advancing his framework was the central project of his professional life from the 1950s through the publication of his last major book in 1980. During these years, psychoanalytic theories of development changed markedly in response to the accumulation of empirical findings that link relationships with attachment figures to adaptive and maladaptive behavior in children and adults (Westin & Gabbarad, 1999). Attachment theory, however, has not completely turned away from its psychoanalytic roots. The substantial body of attachment research on implicit, uncontrolled cognitive processes, for example, shows its continuing influence (Shaver & Mikulincer, 2002).

One indication of just how far Bowlby's ideas were from those of his contemporaries is the number of connections they make to current trends in personality research. The most obvious link is to evolutionary approaches to personality (Buss, 1999). Like this approach, attachment theory begins by postulating inherent, species-wide behavioral dispositions among humans. An important difference between attachment and evolutionary approaches is the stronger emphasis that attachment research has placed on delineating the ways in which environmental factors alter the expression of innate motives on the formation of personality. The best known of this research is Ainsworth's pioneering study of the impact of maternal care on attachment to mothers (Ainsworth et al, 1978). Another point of difference is that attachment theory addresses only a limited number of inherent motivational systems, whereas contemporary evolutionary psychology has a much broader focus, investigating a wide range of cognitive and behavioral predispositions.

The other link is to "cognitive" approaches to personality (Cantor, 1990; Dweck & Leggett, 1988; Mischel & Shoda, 1995). The connecting concepts are attachment theory's internal working models and personality theory's schema. Sehemas and working models have almost identical functions. Like schemas, working models guide the interpretation of complex social events. They also are used to predict the behavior of others and select appropriate responses to these predictions or to observed behaviors, functioning as a set of If-Then rules (Mischel & Shoda, 1995). Working models shape interpersonal goals (e.g., to maintain psychological distance) and influence basic cognitive processes, including attention, perception, and memory (Cantor, 1990; Collins & Feeney, 2004). The centrality of the working model in attachment theory places it, along with most cognitive approaches, in the "doing" rather than the "having" tradition in personality theory and research.

Bowlby himself emphasized the dynamic nature of personality. To summarize his view of the impact of experiences with attachment figures on personality development, he wrote:

> [A]n individual who has been fortunate in having grown up in an ordinarily good home with ordinarily affectionate parents has always known people from whom lie [sic] can seek support, comfort, and protection. … So deeply established are his expectations and so repeatedly have they been confirmed that as an adult he finds it difficult to imagine any other kind of world. …
>
> For many more, the likelihood that a care-taking figure would respond in a supportive and protective way has been at best hazardous and at worst nil. When such people become adults it is hardly surprising that they have no confidence that a care-taking figure will ever be truly available and dependable. Through their eyes the world is seen as comfortless and unpredictable; and they respond either by shrinking from it or by doing battle with it. (Bowlby, 1973, p. 208)

In this chapter we have pointed out some of the consequences of not having grown up in an ordinarily good home as they pertain to relationship satisfaction—in particular, the realization that one's needs will be met only through one's own efforts and the anger that this realization and the experiences that led to it can engender. Avoidant adults have learned to withdraw from others to protect themselves and, as we suggest, to control their emotions, particularly anger. They find it difficult to leave their zone of comfort even though this means that the needs of others are ignored, and they appear to resent behavior that violates their boundaries or limits their control (e.g., emotions of partners that limit their control by forcing them to respond; appeals for help that have the same effect). Anxious adults, in contrast, have learned to do battle. They attempt to demand that others attend to their needs for security, often to the exclusion of any concern about the needs of others for autonomy and security.

We view egoism and the anger that is associated with it to be the linchpins for understanding attachment anxiety (see Figure 5.1). Although anxious persons can be characterized as having goals of obtaining closeness, these goals may be fueled in part by unresolved anger. Their compulsive focus on getting their needs for security met may make it more accurate to view anxious persons as seeking control over their partners in furtherance of their own egoistic concerns instead of seeking genuine closeness.

Anxious people are given to intense, often dysfunctional anger when partners are perceived to be unavailable, although their expression of anger may sometimes be blocked by a fear of alienating the partner. Presumably because they are more prone to anger, they also are more likely than their secure or avoidant counterparts to perpetrate violence against relationships partners. The way in which anxious people deal with conflicts also shows signs of both anger and egoism. They reveal less understanding of their partners' point of view during episodes of conflict, and they attack more and compromise with their partners less. They escalate conflict, and they perceive more conflict in their relationships than their partners. The literature on support and caregiving also reveals the egoism of anxious individuals. They appear to center their perceptions of their partners around what they receive from their partners, and they appear to be unable to perceive fully the support from their partners that is available to them. They are less empathic and as caregivers are less responsive, more controlling, and more often motivated to help by selfish concerns. As a consequence of their behavior, anxious individuals often find themselves in relationships with others who are dissatisfied. Their partners evaluate everyday interactions with them more negatively, report more negative and fewer positive emotions, and withdraw emotional support over time, which, ironically, anxious people appear to need in abundance to feel satisfied with their relationships.

Anger and egoism can also be seen to characterize avoidance (see Figure 5.1), even though the anger-prone nature of avoidant people appears largely to be kept below the level of consciousness as a result of defense mechanisms developed to accommodate their history of interaction with attachment figures. As noted by both Bowlby (1973) and Ainsworth et al., (1978), avoidant individuals experience anger early on in their lives as a result of rejection or abandonment by attachment figures. Consequently, they learn to experience proximity to an attachment figure as something to be avoided to reduce the risk of further rejection and to help to keep their anger over past rejections in check. Avoidant individuals develop attachment strategies to self-protectively avoid attachment figures in times of threat as a result of this anger; they also develop defense mechanisms to suppress the anger that is associated with closeness to their attachment figures. Thus, although the goal of maintaining distance appears to be the most salient aspect of their close relationships, this goal can be viewed in part as furthering a need to suppress anger.

Avoidant individuals do express anger at their partners under some circumstances, particularly when they are highly distressed or when their boundaries have been violated. Their desire to maintain distance from their partners appears to be the most salient aspect of their relationships. They do not often approach their partners and do not want their partners to approach them. They denigrate people who ask for their help and become angry when their partners seek their support. They engage in little self-disclosure and do not like others who disclose personal information to them. Their sex lives are characterized by less intimacy. They withdraw from problem-solving, presumably to minimize emotion-laden interaction with their partners. They seek less emotional support from partners and give less to them. Although their egoism may appear to be less obvious, avoidant individuals seem to be focused on their own needs and insensitive to the needs of their partners. Their desire to maintain a comfortable distance from others, even to the point of ignoring their needs, is a dominant theme in their relationships, and their ability to satisfy this desire may be the key to their relationship satisfaction.

As indicated earlier, anxious persons tend to report the greatest levels of relationship dissatisfaction, and secure persons report the lowest (Mikulincer et al, 2002). Thus, attachment anxiety appears to provide for a greater level of dysfunctionality than does attachment avoidance, particularly in conjunction with romantic relationships. However, caution must be used in interpreting these findings. First, it could be that avoidant individuals are just as unhappy with their relationships as anxious ones but report less unhappiness due to the defense mechanisms that suppress attachment-related affect. Thus, under sufficient levels of distress or cognitive load, avoidant persons may also reveal high levels of relationship dissatisfaction. Second, the findings may be affected by the nature of the relationships available for study. It could be, for example, that when secure persons become unhappy in their relationships, they are willing to end them sooner and move on to more fulfilling relationships. Avoidant persons, because they do not expect their partners to meet their needs for security and are accustomed to being self-reliant, may also be willing to end relationships that are unsatisfactory relatively quickly. Anxious persons, on the other hand, have needs for security and closeness as paramount and fear losing close relationships. They may tend to stay in relationships longer than either secure or avoidant persons, even though those relationships may not, or maybe perceived not, to meet their needs. Thus, at any point in time, there could be a greater probability that an anxious person's relationship is an unhappy one. Further research is needed to investigate these possibilities.

It is also possible that insecure persons, whether anxious or avoidant, lay the groundwork for their own dissatisfaction through partner selection. For example, it is clear that some psychological characteristics of partners (for example, a partner's depression) can adversely affect relationships (Joiner, Coyne, & Blalock, 1999). Most studies do not attempt to determine the mental health or other characteristics of the partners of insecure and secure adults and thus do not examine the extent to which individuals having different attachment styles may select the types of partners who themselves will pose difficulties for the relationship. One exception is Collins et al., (2002), who, as reported earlier, found that partners of avoidant adults were higher in negative emotionality, lower in agency, and had more negative self models. The extent to which insecure persons are engaged in relationships with troubled or otherwise problematic partners is therefore unclear, as are the processes through which such pairings might arise. For example, insecure individuals may select problematic partners because they are unable to perceive their potential partners accurately; they may be attracted to partners who exhibit behaviors that others recognize as signs of future problems; or, due to low self-esteem, they may believe that they do not deserve partners who might treat them better or make them happier. Self-verification theory (Swann & Read, 1981) suggests that insecure individuals, particularly those who are anxious, may select partners who confirm their negative self-views (cf. Brennan & Morris, 1997). They may also engage in behaviors motivated by a desire to create negative partner perceptions of them when the need for self-verification is high and other avenues for verification are unavailable.

Further, partners of anxious persons report more relationship dissatisfaction than do partners of avoidant persons. It is not a priori theoretically clear why this should be true. Both anxiety and avoidance are associated with risk factors that lead to dissatisfaction; from our point of view, both anxiety and avoidance are linked to an egoistic stance that allows the needs of the individual to supersede those of the partner. Part of the explanation may involve need for autonomy and the way in which egoism is manifested. Although neither anxious nor avoidant persons may excel at meeting the attachment needs of their partners, only anxious persons appear to be clingy and needy, sometimes "suffocating" their partners and denying them sufficient personal space. The explanation might also reside in the differential way in which anger is experienced and expressed. In other words, an avoidant individual's ability to suppress anger in most situations may lead to greater overall partner satisfaction. More research is needed to examine the joint role of anger and egoism in attachment style and the ways in which they act to produce relationship dissatisfaction.

Another area where research is needed is in the objective measure of behavioral risk factors. This is illustrated by findings from studies of partner support. Anxious individuals report that their partners do not provide adequate support, and partners of anxious adults report that they provide less support to them. Most studies of satisfaction, whether they focus on support, conflict, or other issues, are unable to determine whether the observed effects are driven by the intra-psychic dynamics of attachment models (i.e., dissatisfaction is linked to perceptions that the partner is behaving badly) or the objective behaviors of partners (dissatisfaction is linked to the fact that the partner is actually behaving badly). Assessing partners' self-reported behaviors can be helpful for providing a gauge against which to measure an individual's perceptions, but it has clear limitations. The partner's self-reported behaviors are subject to the same biases that the individual's reports of the partner's behavior are. Unfortunately, few studies to date have included objective assessments of behavior, so effects due to working models and partner behavior have been confounded.

There is also a need to examine further the kinds of behavior that anxious and avoidant individuals provoke that adversely affect their own satisfaction in relationships. This complex interdependent cycle of behaviors is only beginning to be studied. It could certainly be the case that insecure individuals, by making their partners dissatisfied, end up in a "dissatisfaction spiral." In order to break this cycle, studies of partner behaviors that could mitigate dissatisfaction for insecure persons are needed. For example, some individuals may provide naive "therapy" to their insecure partners to help reduce their relationship dissatisfaction. Studies of other factors that could encourage relationship satisfaction for insecure persons are also needed.

Finally, since the publication of the initial studies linking attachment style to relationship satisfaction (e.g., Simpson, 1990), a major goal of attachment researchers has been to identify factors that explain or mediate the association between these two variables; studies of conflict management and caregiving typify this effort. Less attention has been devoted to moderating variables. Level of stress is one moderating factor that has been addressed, with results often showing that the expected association between attachment styles and outcomes is stronger when stress levels are elevated. Because moderating factors have not been extensively studied, we do not know the range of conditions under which insecure adults may be satisfied with their relationships. We also do not know when or how processes, such as poor conflict management or the display of dysfunctional anger, that should mediate the effects of attachment style are triggered. Addressing these issues will provide a more nuanced understanding of the association between attachment style and relationship satisfaction.

NOTE

1. Persons who score high on both the anxiety and avoidance dimensions are sometimes referred to as "fearful." Although we do not refer to a "fearful" category, we do indicate when relationship effects are associated with a combination of both high anxiety and avoidance.

REFERENCES

Ainsworth, M. D. S., Blehar, M. C, Waters, E., & Wall, S. (1978). *Patterns of attachment.* Hillsdale, NJ: Erlbaum.

Alexander, R., Feeney, J., Hohaus, L., & Noller, P. (2001). Attachment style and coping resources as predictors of coping strategies in the transition to parenthood. *Personal Relationships, 8,* 137–152.

Allen, E. S., & Baucom, D. H. (2004). Adult attachment and patterns of extradyadic involvement. *Family Process, 43,* 467–488.

Bartholomew, K. (1990). Avoidance of intimacy: An attachment perspective. *Journal of Social and Personal Relationships, 7,* 147–178.

Bartholomew, K., Cobb, R. J., & Poole, J. A. (1997). Adult attachment patterns and social support processes. In G. R. Pierce, B. Lakey, I. G. Sarason, & B. R. Sarason (Eds.), *Sourcebook of social support and personality* (pp. 359–378). New York: Plenum Press.

Bartholomew, K„ & Horowitz, L. (1991). Attachment styles among young adults: A test of a four-category model. *Journal of Personality and Social Psychology, 61,* 226–244.

Belsky, J., & Pensky, E. (1988). Marital change across the transition to parenthood. *Marriage and Family Review, 13,* 133–156.

Berant, E., Mikulincer, M., & Florian, V. (2001). Attachment style and mental health: A one-year follow-up study of mothers of infants with congenital heart disease. *Personality and. Social Psychology Bulletin, 8,* 956–968.

Bogaert, A. F., & Sadava, S. (2002). Adult attachment and sexual behavior. *Personal Relationships, 9,*191–204.

Bookwala, J. (2002). The role of own and perceived partner attachment in relationship aggression. *Journal of Interpersonal Violence, 17,* 84–100.

Bookwala, J., & Zdaniuk, B. (1998). Adult attachment styles and aggressive behavior within dating relationships. *Journal of Social and Personal Relationships, 15,* 175–190.

Bowlby, J. (1969). *Attachment and loss: Vol. 1. Attachment.* New York: Basic Books.

Bowlby, J. (1973). *Attachment and loss: Vol. 2. Separation: Anxiety and anger.* New York: Basic Books.

Bowlby, J. (1980). *Attachment and loss: Vol. 3. Sadness and depression.* New York: Basic Books.

Bowlby, J. (1988). A *secure base: Clinical applications of attachment theory.* London: Routledge.

Bradbury, T. N., Fincham, F. D., & Beach, S. R. H. (2000). Research on the nature and determinants of marital satisfaction: A decade in review. *Journal of Marriage and the Family, 62,* 964–980.

Bradford, S. A., Feeney, J.A., & Campbell, L. (2002). Links between attachment orientations and dispositional and diary-based measures of disclosure in dating couples: A study of actor and partner effects. *Personal Relationships, 9,* 491–506.

Brennan, K., Clark, C, & Shaver, R (1998). Self-report measurement of adult attachment: An integrative overview. In J. A. Simpson & W. S. Rholes (Eds.), *Attachment theory and close relationships* (pp. 46–76). New York: Guilford.

Brennan, K. A., & Morris, K. A. (1997). Attachment styles, self-esteem, and patterns of seeking feedback from romantic partners. *Personality and Social Psychology Bulletin, 23,* 23–31.

Brennan, K. A., & Shaver, R R. (1995). Dimensions of adult attachment, affect regulation, and romantic relationship functioning. *Personality and Social Psychology Bulletin, 21,* 267–283.

Buunk, B. R (1997). Personality, birth order, and attachment styles as related to various types of jealousy. *Personality and Individual Differences, 23,* 997–1006.

Buss, D. M. (1999). Human nature and individual differences: The evolution of human personality. In L. Pervin & O. John (Eds.), *Handbook of personality: Theory and research* (pp. 31–57). New York: Guilford.

Bylsma, W. H., Cozzarelli, C, & Sumer, N. (1997). Relation between adult attachment styles and global self-esteem. *Basic and Applied Social Psychology, 19,* 1–16.

Campbell, L., Simpson, J. A., Boldry, J., & Kashy, D. A. (2005). Perceptions of conflict and support in romantic relationships: The role of attachment anxiety. *Journal of Personality and Social Psychology, 88,* 510–531.

Cantor, N. (1990). From thought to behavior: "Having" and "doing" in the study of personality and cognition. *American Psychologist, 45,* 735–750.

Carnelley, K. B., Pietromonaco, P. R., & Jaffe, K. (1994). Depression, working models of others, and relationship functioning. *Journal of Personality and Social Psychology, 66,* 127–140.

Cassidy, J. (2001). Truth, lies, and intimacy: An attachment perspective. *Attachment and Human Development, 3,* 121–155.

Collins, N. L. (1996). Working models of attachment: Implications for explanation, emotion, and behavior. *Journal of Personality and Social Psychology, 71,* 810–832.

Collins, N. L., Cooper, M. L., Albino, A., & Allard, L. (2002). Psychosocial vulnerability from adolescence to adulthood: A prospective study of attachment style differences in relationship functioning and partner choice. *Journal of Personality, 70,* 965–1008.

Collins, N. L„ & Feeney, B. C. (2000). A safe haven: An attachment theory perspective on support-seeking and caregiving in adult romantic relationships. *Journal of Personality and Social Psychology, 78,* 1053–1073.

Collins, N. L., & Feeney, B. C. (2004). Working models of attachment shape perceptions of social support: Evidence from experimental and observational studies. *Journal of Personality and Social Psychology, 87,* 363–383.

Collins, N. L., & Read, S. J. (1990), Adult attachment, working models, and relationship quality in dating couples. *Journal of Personality and Social Psychology, 58,* 644–663.

Collins, N. L., & Read, S .J. (1994). Cognitive representations of attachment: The structure and function of working models. In K. Bartholomew & D. Perlman (Eds.), *Advances in personal relationships* (Vol. 5, pp. 53–90). London: Jessica Kingsley.

Cooper, M. L., Shaver, P. R., & Collins, N. L. (1998). Attachment styles, emotion regulation, and adjustment in adolescence. *Journal of Personality and Social Psychology, 74,* 1380–1397.

Corcoran, K., & Mallinckrodt, B. (2000). Adult attachment, self-efficacy, perspective taking, and conflict resolution. *Journal of Counseling b- Development, 78,* 473–483.

Cowan, L. P., & Cowan, P. A. (2000). *When partners become parents: The big life change in couples.* Mahwah, NJ: Erlbaum.

Creasey, G., & Flesson-Mclnnis, M. (2001). Affective responses, cognitive appraisals, and conflict tactics in late adolescent romantic relationships: Associations with attachment orientations. *Journal of Counseling Psychology, 48,* 85–96,

Curran, M., Hazen, N., Jacobvitz, D., & Feldman, A. (2005). Representations of early family relationships predict marital maintenance during the transition to parenthood. *Journal of Family Psychology, 19,* 189–197.

Davila, J., Bradbury, T. N„ & Fincham, F. (1998). Negative affectivity as a mediator of the association between adult attachment and marital satisfaction. *Personal Relationships, 5,* 467–484.

Davis, D., Shaver, P. R., & Vernon, M. L. (2004), Attachment style and subjective motivations for sex. *Personality and Social Psychology Bulletin, 30,* 1076–1090.

Dutton, D. C, Saunders, K., Starzomski, A., & Bartholomew, K. (1994). Intimacy-anger and insecure attachment as precursors of abuse in intimate relationships. *Journal of Applied Social Psychology, 24,* 1367–1386.

Dutton, D. G., Starzomski, A., & Ryan, L. (1996), Antecedents of abusive personality and abusive behavior in wife assaulters. *Journal of Family Violence, 11,* 113–132.

Dweck, C. S., & Leggett, E. L. (1988). A social-cognitive approach to motivation and personality. *Psychological Review, 95,* 256–273.

Feeney, B. C, & Collins, N. L. (2001). Predictors of caregiving in adult intimate relationships: An attachment theoretical perspective. *Journal of Personality and Social Psychology, 80,* 972–994.

Feeney, B. C, & Collins, N. L. (2003). Motivations for caregiving in adult intimate relationships: Influences on caregiving behavior and relationship functioning. *Personality and Social Psychology Bulletin, 29,* 950–968.

Feeney, B. C, & Kirkpatrick, L, A. (1996). The effects of adult attachment and presence of romantic partners on physiological responses to stress. *Journal of Personality and Social Psychology, 70,* 255–270.

Feeney, J. A. (1994). Attachment style, communication patterns, and satisfaction across the life cycle of marriage. *Personal Relationships, 1,* 333–348.

Feeney, J. A. (1995). Adult attachment and emotional control. *Personal Relationships, 2,* 143–159.

Feeney, J. A. (1996). Attachment, caregiving, and marital satisfaction. *Personal Relationships, 3,* 401–416.

Feeney, J. A. (1998). Adult attachment and relationship-centered anxiety: Responses to physical and emotional distancing. In J. A. Simpson & W. S. Rholes (Eds.), *Attachment theory and close relationships* (pp. 189–218), New York: Guilford.

Feeney, J. A. (1999). Adult attachment, emotional control, and marital satisfaction. *Personal Relationships, 6,* 169–185.

Feeney, J. A., Alexander, R., Noller, P., & Hohaus, L. (2003). Attachment insecurity, depression, and the transition to parenthood. *Personal Relationships, 10,* 475–493.

Feeney, J. A., & Hohaus, L. (2001). Attachment and spousal caregiving. *Personal Relationships, 8,* 21–39.

Feeney, J. A., & Noller, P. (1990). Attachment style as a predictor of adult romantic relationships. *Journal of Personality and Social Psychology, 58,* 281–291.

Feeney, J. A., & Noller, P. (2004). Attachment and sexuality in close relationships. In J. H. Harvey, A. Weiizel, & S. Sprecher (Eds.), *Handbook of sexuality in close relationships* (pp. 183–201). Mahwah, NJ: Erlbaum.

Feeney, J. A., Noller, P., & Callan, V. J. (1994). Attachment style, communication and satisfaction in the early years of marriage. In K. Bartholomew & D. Perlman (Eds.), *Advances in personal relationships* (Vol. 5, pp. 269–308). London; Jessica Kingsley,

Feeney, J. A., Noller, P., & Patty, J. (1993). Adolescents' interaction with the opposite sex: Influences of attachment style and gender. *Journal of Adolescence, 16,* 169–186.

Feeney, J. A., Noller, P., & Roberts, N. (1998). Emotion, attachment, and satisfaction in close relationships. In P. A. Andersen & L. K. Guerrero (Eds.), *Handbook of communication and emotion: Research, theory, applications, and contexts* (pp. 473–505). San Diego, CA: Academic Press.

Feeney, J. A., Peterson, C, Gallois, C, & Terry, D. J. (2000). Attachment style as a predictor of sexual attitudes and behavior in late adolescence. *Psychology and. Health, 14,* 1105–1122.

Fishtein, J., Pietromonaco, P. R., & Feldman Barrett, L. (1999). The contribution of attachment style and relationship conflict to the complexity of relationship knowledge. *Social Cognition, 17,* 228–244.

Florian, V., Mikulhicer, ML, & Bucholtz, I, (1995). Effects of adult attachment style on the perception and search for social support. *The Journal of Psychology; Interdisciplinary and Applied, 129,* 665–676.

Fraley, R. C, Davis, K. E., & Shaver, P. R. (1998). Dismissing-avoidance and the defensive organization of emotion, cognition, and behavior. In J.A. Simpson &W.S. Rholes (Eds.), *Attachment theory and close relationships* (pp. 249–279). New York: Guilford.

Fraley, R. C., & Shaver, P. R. (1998). Airport separations: A naturalistic study of adult attachment dynamics in separating couples. *Journal of Personality and, Social Psychology, 75,* 1198–1212.

Gangestad, S. W., &Thornhill, R. (1997). The evolutionary psychology of extrapair sex: The role of fluctuating asymmetry. *Evolution and Human Behavior, 18,* 69–88.

Gentzler, A. L., & Kerns, K. A. (2004). Associations between insecure attachment and sexual experiences. *Personal Relationships, 11,* 249–265.

Gottman, J. M., & Krokoff, L. J. (1989). Marital interaction and satisfaction: A longitudinal *view. Journal of Consulting and Clinical Psychology, 57,* 47–52.

Grabill, C. M., & Kerns, K. A. (2000). Attachment style and intimacy in friendship. *Personal Relationships, 7,* 363–378.

Guerrero, L. K. (1998). Attachment-style differences in the experience and expression of romantic jealousy. *Personal Relationships, 5,* 273–291.

Hazan, C., & Shaver, P. R. (1987). Romantic love conceptualized as an attachment process. *Journal of Personality and Social Psychology, 52,* 511–524.

Heinicke, C. M. (1995), Determinants of the transition to parenthood. In M H. Bornstein (Ed.), *Handbook of parenting: Status and social conditions of parenting* (Vol. 3, pp. 277–303). Mahwah, NJ: Erlbaum.

Hollist, C. S„ & Miller, R. B. (2005). Perceptions of attachment style and marital quality in midlife marriage. *Family Relations, 54,* 46–57.

Holmes, J. G. (1991). Trust and the appraisal process in close relationships. In W. H. Jones & D. Perlman (Eds.), *Advances in personal relationships* (Vol. 2, pp. 57–104). London: Jessica Kingsley.

Impett, E. A., & Peplau, L. A. (2002). Why some women consent to unwanted sex with a dating partner: Insights from attachment theory. *Psychology of Women Quarterly, 26,* 360–370.

Joiner, T., Coyne, J. C, & Blalock, J. (1999). The interpersonal nature of depression: Overview and synthesis. In T. Joiner & J. C. Coyne (Eds.), *The interactional nature of depression* (pp. 3–20). Washington, D.C.: American Psychological Association.

Keelan, J. P. R., Dion, K. K., & Dion, K. L. (1993). Attachment style and relationship satisfaction: Test of a self-disclosure explanation. *Canadian Journal of Behavioural Sciences, 30,* 24–35.

Kirkpatrick, L. A. (1998). Evolution, pair-bonding, and reproductive strategies: A recon- ceptualization of adult attachment. In J. A. Simpson & W. S. Rholes (Eds.), *Attachment theory and close relationships* (pp. 353–393). New York: Guilford.

Kobak, R. R., & Duemmler, S. (1994). Attachment and conversation: Toward a discourse analysis of adolescent and adult security. In K. Bartholomew & D. Perlman (Eds.), *Advances in personal relationships* (Vol. 5, pp. 121–149). London: Jessica Kingsley.

Kobak, R. R., & Hazan, C. (1991). Attachment in marriage: The effects of security and accuracy of working *models. Journal of Personality and Social Psychology, 60,* 861–869.

Kobak, R. R., & Sceery, A. (1988). Attachment in late adolescence: Working models, affect regulation, and representation of self and others. *Child Development, 59,* 135–146.

Kunce, L. J., & Shaver, P. R. (1994). An attachment-theoretical approach to caregiving in romantic relationships. In K. Bartholomew & D. Perlman (Eds.), *Advances in personal relationships* (Vol. 5, pp. 205–237). London: Jessica Kingsley.

Laurenceau, J-R, Barrett, L. F., & Rovine, M. J. (2005). The interpersonal process model of intimacy in marriage: A daily-diary and multilevel modeling approach. *Journal of Family Psychology, 19,* 314–323.

Laurenceau, J. P., Troy, A. B., & Carver, C. S. (2005). Two distinct emotional experiences in romantic relationships: Effects of perceptions regarding approach of intimacy and avoidance of conflict. *Personality and Social Psychology Bulletin, 31,* 1123- 1133.

Levy, M. B., & Davis, K. E. (1988). Lovestyles and attachment styles compared: Their relations to each other and to various relationship characteristics. *Journal of Social and Personal Relationships, 5,* 439–471.

Lussier, Y., Sabourin, S., & Turgeon, C. (1997). Coping strategies as moderators of the relationship between attachment and marital adjustment. *Journal of Social and Personal Relationships, 14,* 777–791.

Main, M., & Goldwyn, R. (1998). Adult attachment scoring and classification system. Unpublished manuscript. University of California at Berkeley.

Marcaurelle, R., Belanger.C, Marchand, A., Katerlos, T. E,, & Mainguy, N. (2003). Marital predictors of symptom severity in panic disorder with agoraphobia. *Journal of Anxiety Disorders, 19,* 211–232.

Marchand, J. F. (2004). Husbands' and wives' marital quality: The role of adult attachment orientations, depressive symptoms, and conflict resolution behaviors. *Attachment and. Human Development, 6,* 99–112.

Marchand, J. R, & Hock, E. (2000). Avoidance and attacking conflict-resolution strategies among married couples: Relations to depressive symptoms and marital satisfaction. *Family Relations, 49,* 201–206.

Mauricio, A. M., & Gormley, B. (2001). Male perpetration of physical violence against female partners. *Journal of Interpersonal Violence, 16,* 1066–1081.

Mayseless, O. (1991). Adult attachment patterns and courtship violence. *Family Relations, 40,* 21–28.

Mikulincer, M. (1995). Attachment style and the mental representation of the self. *Journal of Personality and Social Psychology, 69,* 1203–1215.

Mikulincer, M. (1998a). Adult attachment style and individual differences in functional versus dysfunctional experiences of anger. *Journal of Personality and Social Psychology, 74,* 513–524.

Mikulincer, M. (1998b). Attachment working models and the sense of trust: An exploration of interaction goals and affect regulation. *Journal of Personality and Social Psychology, 74,* 1209–1224.

Mikulincer, M„ & Florian, V. (1995). Appraisal of and coping with a real-life stressful situation: The contribution of attachment styles. *Personality and Social Psychology Bulletin, 21,* 406–414.

Mikulincer, M., &: Florian, V. (1998). The relationship between adult attachment styles and emotional and cognitive reactions to stressful events. In J. A. Simpson & W. S. Rholes (Eds.), *Attachment theory and close relationships* (pp. 143–165). New York: Guilford.

Mikulincer, M., Florian, V„ Cowan, P. A., & Cowan, C. P. (2002). Attachment security in couple relationships: A systemic model and its implications for family dynamics. *Family Process, 341,* 405–434.

Mikulincer, M„ Florian, V„ & Weller, A. (1993). Attachment styles, coping strategies, and post-traumatic psychological distress: The impact of the Gulf War in Israel. *Journal of Personality and Social Psychology, 64,* 817–826.

Mikulincer, M„ Gillath, O., Halevy, V., Avihou, N„ Avidan, S., & Eshkoli, N. (2001). Attachment theory and reactions to others' needs: Evidence that activation of the sense of attachment security promotes empathic responses. *Journal of Personality and Social Psychology, 81,* 1205–1224.

Mikulincer, M., Gillath, O., & Shaver, P. R. (2002). Activation of the attachment system in adulthood: Threat-related primes increase the accessibility of mental representations of attachment figures. *Journal of Personality and, Social Psychology, 83,* 881–895.

Mikulincer, M., & Horesh, N. (1999). Adult attachment style and the perception of others: The role of projective mechanisms. *Journal of Personality and Social Psychology, 76,* 1022–1034.

Mikulincer, M., & Nachson, O. (1991). Attachment styles and patterns of self-disclosure. *Journal of Personality and Social Psychology, 61,* 321–331.

Mikulincer, M., & Orbach, I. (1995). Attachment styles and repressive defensiveness: The accessibility and architecture of affective memories. *Journal of Personality and Social Psychology, 68,* 917–925.

Mikulincer, M., & Shaver, P. R. (2003). The attachment behavioral system in adulthood: Activation, psychodynamics, and interpersonal processes. In M. P. Zanna (Ed.), *Advances in experimental social psychology* (Vol. 35, pp. 5.3–152). New York: Academic.

Mikulincer, M., & Shaver, P. R. (2004). Security-based self-representations in adulthood: Contents and processes. In W. S. Rholes & J. A. Simpson (Eds.), *Adult attachment: Theory, research, and clinical implications* (pp. 159–195). New York: Guilford.

Mikulincer, M., & Shaver, P. R. (2005). Attachment theory and emotions in close relationships: Exploring the attachment-related dynamics of emotional reactions to relational events. *Personal Relationships, 12,* 149–168.

Mikulincer, M., Shaver, P. R., Gillath, O., & Nitzberg, R. A. (2005). Attachment, caregiv-ing, and altruism: Boosting attachment security increases compassion and helping. *Journal of Personality and Social Psychology, 84,* 817–839.

Mischel, W., & Shoda, Y. (1995). A cognitive-affective system theory of personality: Recon- ceptu-alizing situations, dispositions, dynamics, and iuvariance in personality structure. *Psychological Review, 102,* 246–268.

Muris, P., Meesters, C, Morren, M., & Moorman, L. (2004). Anger and hostility in adolescents: Relationships with self-reported attachment style and perceived parental rearing styles. *Journal of Psychosomatic Research, 57,* 257–264.

Noller, P., Feeney, J. A., Bonnell, D., & Callan, V. J. (1994). A longitudinal study of conflict in early marriage. *Journal of Social and Personal Relationships, 11,* 233–252.

Ognibene, T. C, & Collins, N. L. (1998). Adult attachment styles, perceived social support and coping strategies. *Journal of Social and Personal Relationships, 15,* 323–345.

Orcutt , H. K., Garcia, M., & Pickett, S. M. (2005). Female-perpetrated intimate partner violence and romantic attachment style in a college student sample. *Violence and Victims, 20,* 287–302.

Paley, B., Cox, M. J., Kanoy, K. W., Harter, K. S. M., Burchinal, M„ & Margand, N. A. (2005). Adult attachment and marital interaction as predictors of whole family interactions during the transition to parenthood. *Journal of Family Psychology, 19,* 420–429.

Pistole, M. C. (1989). Attachment in adult romantic relationships: Style of conflict resolution and relationship satisfaction. *Journal of Social and Personal Relationships, 6,* 505–510.

Pistole, M. C. (1993). Attachment relationships: Self-disclosure and trust. *Journal of Mental Health Counseling, 15,* 94–106.

Pistole, M. C. (2003). Understanding attachment: Beliefs about conflict. *Journal of Counseling and Development, 81,* 318–328,

Pistole, M. C, & Tarrant, N. (1993). Attachment style and aggression in male batterers. *Family Therapy, 20,* 165–173.

Priel, B., & Shamai, D. (1995). Attachment style and perceived social support: Effects on affect regulation. *Personality and Individual Differences, 19,* 235–241.

Rholes, W. S., Simpson, J.A., & Blakely, B. S. (1995). Adult attachment styles and mothers' relationships with their young children. *Personal Relationships, 2,* 35–54.

Rholes, W. S., Simpson, J.A., Blakely, B. S„ Lanigan, L., & Allen, E. A. (1997). Adult attachment styles, the desire to have children, and working models of parenthood. *Journal of Personality, 65,* 357–385.

Rholes, W. S., Simpson, J.A., Campbell, L„ & Grich, J. (2001). Adult attachment and the transition to parenthood. *Journal of Personality and Social Psychology, 81,* 421–435.

Rholes, W. S., Simpson, J. A., & Friedman, M. (2006). Avoidant attachment and the experience of parenting. *Personality and Social Psychology Bulletin, 32,* 275–285.

Rholes, W. S., Simpson, J .A., Trans, S., Martin, A M., & Friedman, M. (2007). *Personality and Social Psychology Bulletin, 33,* 422–438.

Rholes, W. S., Simpson, J. A., & Orina, M. M. (1999). Attachment and anger in an anxiety-provoking situation. *Journal of Personality and Social Psychology, 76,* 40–957.

Roberts, N., & Noller, P. (1998). The association between adult attachment and couple violence: The role of communication patterns and relationship satisfaction, In J. A. Simpson & W.S. Rholes (Eds.), *Attachment theory and close relationships* (pp. 317–350). New York: Guilford.

Schachner, D. A., & Shaver, P. R. (2002). Attachment style and human mate poaching. *New Review of Social Psychology, 1,* 122–129.

Schachner, D. A., & Shaver, P. R. (2004). Attachment dimensions and sexual motives. *Personal Relationships, 11,* 179–195.

Shaver, P. R., Kazan, C., & Bradshaw, D. (1988). Love as attachment: The integration of three behavioral systems. In R.J. Sternberg & M. Barnes (Eds.), *The anatomy of love* (pp. 68–98). New Haven, CT: Yale University Press.

Shaver, P. R., & Mikulincer, M. (2002). Attachment-related psychodynamics. *Attachment and Human Development, 4,* 133–161.

Shi, L. (2003). The association between adult attachment styles and conflict resolution in romantic relationships. *The American Journal of Family Therapy, 31,* 143–157.

Simpson, J. A. (1990). Influence of attachment styles on romantic relationships. *Journal of Personality and Social Psychology, 59,* 971–980.

Simpson, J. A., & Rholes, W. S. (1994). Stress and secure base relationships in adulthood. In K. Bartholomew & D. Perlman (Eds.), *Advances in personal relationships* (Vol. 5, pp. 181–204). London: Jessica Kingsley.

Simpson, J. A., & Rholes, W. S. (1998). Attachment in adulthood. In J.A. Simpson & W. S. Rholes (Eds.), *Attachment theory and close relationships* (pp. 3–21). New York: Guilford.

Simpson, J. A., Rholes, W. S., Campbell, L., Iran, S., & Wilson, C. L. (2003). Adult attachment, the transition to parenthood, and depressive symptoms. *Journal of Personality and Social Psychology, 84,* 1172–1187.

Simpson, J. A., Rholes, W. S., & Nelligan, J. S. (1992), Support-seeking and support- giving within couples in an anxiety-provoking situation: The role of attachment styles. *Journal of Personality and Social Psychology, 62,* 434–446.

Simpson, J. A., Rholes, W. S., & Phillips, D. (1996). Conflict in close relationships: An attachment perspective. *Journal of Personality and, Social Psychology, 71,* 899- 914.

Sroufe, L. A., & Waters, E. (1977). Attachment as an organizational construct. *Child Development, 48,* 1184–1199.

Swann, W. B., Jr., & Read, S. J, (1981). Self-verification processes: How we sustain our self-conceptions. *Journal of Experimental Social Psychology, 17,* 351–372.

Torquati, J. C, & Vazsonyi, A. T. (1999). Attachment as an organizational construct for affect, appraisals, and coping of late adolescent females. *Journal of Youth and Adolescence, 28,* 545–562.

Tracy, J. L., Shaver, P. R., Albino, A. W., & Cooper, M. L. (2003). Attachment styles and adolescent sexuality. In P. Florsheim (Ed.), *Adolescent romance and sexual behavior: Theory, research, and practical implications* (pp. 137–159). Mahwah, NJ: Erlbaum.

Tucker, P., & Anders, S. L. (1998). Adult attachment style and nonverbal closeness in dating couples. *Journal of Nonverbal Behavior, 22,* 124–129.

Tucker, P., & Aron, A. (1993). Passionate love and marital satisfaction at key transition points in the family life *cycle. Journal of Social b- Clinical Psychology, 12,* 135–147.

Tweed, R. G., & Dutton, D, G. (1998). A comparison of impulsive and instrumental subgroups of batterers. *Violence and Victims, 13,* 217–230.

Twenge, J. M., Campbell, W. K., & Foster, C. A. (2003). Parenthood and marital satisfaction: A meta-analytic review. *Journal of Marriage and Family, 65,* 574–583.

Wallace, J. L., & Vaux, A. (1993). Social support network orientation: The role of adult attachment style. *Journal of Social and Clinical Psychology, 12,* 354–365.

Wekerle, C, & Wolfe, D. A. (1998). The role of child maltreatment and attachment style in adolescent relationship violence. *Development and Psychopathology, 10,* 571–586.

Westin, D., & Gabbard, G. O. (1999). Psychoanalytic approaches to personality. In L. Pervin & O. John (Eds.), *Handbook of personality: Theory and research* (pp. 57–101). New York: Guilford Press.

Westmaas, J. L., & Silver, R. C. (2001). The role of attachment in responses to victims of life crises. *Journal of Personality and Social Psychology, 80,* 425–438.

Wilson, C. L., Rholes, W. S., Simpson, J. A., & Tran, S. (2007). Labor, delivery, and early parenthood: An attachment theory perspective. *Personality and Social Psychology Bulletin, 33,* 505–518.

Wilson, C. L., Simpson, J. A., & Rholes, W. S. (2000). Attachment orientation and support giving. Poster presented at the Midwestern Psychological Association Annual Conference, Chicago, IL.

Woolsey, L. K., & McBain, L. (1987). Women's networks: Strengthening the bonds of friendship between women. In K. Storrie (Ed.), *Women, isolation, and. bonding* (pp. 59–76). Toronto; Methuen.

The Premarital Communication Roots of Marital Distress and Divorce

The First Five Years of Marriage

By Howard J. Markman, Galena K. Rhoades, Scott M. Stanley, and Erica P. Ragan
University of Denver
Sarah W. Whitton
University of Cincinnati

Using data from 210 couples who provided data across the first 5 years of marriage, we examined how premarital communication quality was related to divorce and later distress. The results showed that premarital observed negative and positive communication nearly reached significance as predictors of divorce, while self-reported negative communication was significantly associated with divorce. In terms of marital adjustment, we found that both premarital observed and self-reported negative premarital communication (but not observed positive communication) were associated with lower adjustment during the first 5 years of marriage. The most important questions addressed in this study pertain to how positive and negative dimensions of communication change over time and how these changes are related to being distressed or nondistressed after 5 years

Howard J. Markman, Galena K. Rhoades, Scott M. Stanley, Erica P. Ragan, Sarah W. Whitton, "The Premarital Communication Roots of Marital Distress and Divorce: The First Five Years of Marriage," from *Journal of Family Psychology*, Vol. 24, No. 3, Pp. 289–298. Published by Sage Publications, 2010.

of marriage. This is the first study, to our knowledge, to examine the changes in communication over time that are so central to theories of the development of marital distress and for research-based interventions. We found that all couples showed decreases in negative communication over time, but the nondistressed group declined significantly more than the distressed group in negative communication, suggesting they are handling negative emotions better. Implications for future research on the development of relationship distress and for enhancing research-based couples' intervention programs are provided.

Keywords: marriage, prediction, marital distress, communication, divorce

Millions of individuals experience marital distress, destructive conflict, and divorce every year. Evidence accumulates that marital distress and family fragmentation are associated with a broad spectrum of risks for adults and children, including problems with mental health and individual adjustment, child behavior, physical health, and economic success and stability (Booth & Amato, 2001; Halford & Bouma, 1997). The links between marital functioning and a wide range of outcomes has led to recognition that marriage has important public health consequences (Halford, Markman, & Stanley, 2008). As a result, the desire among policy makers to implement public sector programs that can help couples—especially high risk couples—achieve their own aspirations in marriage has grown dramatically in recent years (Seefeldt & Smock, 2004).

In part, such efforts have accelerated because evidence based programs have been built on findings from long-term studies on the risk factors for marital distress and divorce. These long-term (prediction) studies have spawned theories and tests of theories of marital success and dissolution as well as provided basic descriptive data on the course of marriages over time (e.g., Markman & Hahlweg, 1993). Although few individual studies have been cross-validated (Heyman & Slep, 2001), there is enough replication across studies to give us confidence in some of the major patterns of findings that link early risk and protective factors to later marital outcomes.

Most premarital couples, when they decide to marry, are happy with their relationship and expect to be happy together until "death do they part." However, these expectations are often not fulfilled (Glenn, 1998). Most couples say they decide to marry each other based on positive connections such as fun, friendship, and passion (Sternberg, 1998). When couples divorce, reasons include not enough commitment, too much conflict, infidelity, and growing apart (C. A. Johnson et al., 2002). Thus, we know most people decide to marry due to the presence of positives and divorce due to the presence of negatives or the absence of positives. However, we know very little about how negatives and positives before marriage influence the course of marriage and how changes in positive and negatives over time influence marital outcomes.

The overarching aim of the current paper is to assess how negative and positive communication before marriage predict future divorce and marital satisfaction. Starting before marriage enables us to detect patterns earlier in relationship development than in most previous studies and that may be apparent during the transitions associated with planning marriage but not afterwards. In addition, this study is the first, to our knowledge, to investigate how positive and negative communication, assessed by both behavioral and self-report measures, change over time, and how these changes predict marital outcomes.

Negative and Positive Communication as Risk and Protective Factors

Based on Heller and Monahan's (1977) pioneering work, Markman (1979) suggested that couples with communication-based risk factors (e.g., poor conflict management) and lower protective factors (e.g., low levels of positive communication) would be more vulnerable to the development of relationship problems. Since then, a series of cross-sectional and longitudinal studies of couples' interactions have identified a set of risk factors that have to do largely with the ability to handle negative emotions along with a smaller set of protective factors that have to do largely with positive connections (e.g., support, friendship; Karney & Bradbury, 1995). Early on, researchers questioned how well participants could report on their communication, leading to the addition of laboratory interaction tasks that allowed for both research participant and observer ratings of interactions (Markman & Notarius, 1987). The studies reviewed below focus on studies using objective observation of couples' communication.

Cross-Sectional Studies

Pioneered by Weiss and colleagues (e.g., Birchler, Weiss, & Vincent, 1975), early studies compared interaction patterns of distressed and nondistressed couples, and surprisingly found that negative patterns of interaction strongly differentiated happy from unhappy couples but that positive patterns did not (e.g., Birchler et al., 1975; Gottman, Markman, & Notarius, 1977). Here, we call this the "negativity effect," such that negatives are stronger risk factors than positives are protective factors. Building on cross-sectional studies, long-term studies of the development of marital distress emerged.

Prediction Research

There have been two general types of "prediction" studies using interaction tasks: Those predicting marital outcomes (usually dichotomous marital outcomes) from early marital (or in some cases premarital) variables and those predicting marital trajectories. We should note that none of these studies are actually true prediction studies in which outcomes are predicted before they are known (see Heyman & Slep, 2001). The first study predicting marital outcomes found that couples own ratings of their communication as they were talking during a conflict discussion predicted marital satisfaction up to 5 years later (Markman, 1981). Better communication ratings before marriage predicted higher satisfaction 5 years later (but were not associated with initial satisfaction). In a similar study, newlywed couples' ratings of communication quality predicted whether a couple was stable and satisfied versus divorced and/or unhappy 6 years later (Gottman, Coan, Carrere, & Swanson, 1998).

In studies using observer ratings of couples on conflict and/or support tasks, findings have supported the connections between early communication quality and future marital outcomes, with higher communication quality being associated with higher levels of marital quality up to 10 years into marriage for both premarital (e.g., Clements, Stanley, & Markman, 2004) and newlywed couples (e.g., Gottman & Krokoff, 1989; Pasch & Bradbury, 1998; Rogge and Bradbury, 1999). Pasch and Bradbury's (1998) study was among the first to add a social support task and found that observed social support by wives predicted marital outcomes 2 years later. Studies also have found inconsistent findings, such that early communication predicts later satisfaction but not divorce (e.g., Kiecolt-Glaser, Bane, Glaser & Malarkey, 2003), wives' communication predicts better than husbands' (e.g., Pasch & Bradbury, 1998), and negative communication tends to predict only when there are lower levels of positive communication (e.g., M. D. Johnson et al., 2005).

Many theories of the development of marital distress have a common focus on negatives and positives over time, and these share the general prediction that there will be declines in satisfaction. However, none of the studies reviewed above are able to test the developmental aspects of these theories because they only assess one time point at the beginning of the study and one at the end. More recently, researchers have added more follow-up points to examine how early marriage qualities predict trajectories of satisfaction over time.

Predictions of Marital Trajectories

Karney and Bradbury (1997) studied 60 newly wed couples over 4 years and assessed marital satisfaction and marital status at 6-month intervals. They found that more initial negative communication predicted steeper declines in satisfaction. Although newlywed interaction quality did not predict divorce, couples with steeper declines in satisfaction levels had a higher risk for divorce. For example, in stable marriages, satisfaction declined 3% per year whereas in unstable marriages satisfaction declined about 15% per year. M. D. Johnson et al. (2005) used the same sample and found that when there were high levels of positive affect, the predictive power of the negatives was mitigated. Thus, couples were most at risk for declines in satisfaction when there was high negative communication and low positive affect. Interactions were only collected at the initial assessment so they were not able to assess the impact of positives and negatives over time, as we do in the current study.

Huston, Caughlin, Houts, Smith, and George (2001) studied 168 newlywed couples over a 13-year period and tested two models (both of which offer a rich extension of exchange theory) of the development of marital distress relevant to the current study. The "enduring dynamics model" predicts that the negatives early in marriage (or before marriage) endure over time such that a couple's starting point predicts a couple's outcomes. In contrast, the emergent distress model" predicts that negatives increase over time to damage the positive connection for couples headed for problems. Support was found for the enduring dynamics model but not the emergent distress model (Huston et al., 2001). That is, couples who ended up unhappy were more negative initially than couples who ended up happy. Stronger tests of these models are possible when starting with couples before marriage (who then marry) because it is less likely that premarital couples have started down the pathway toward marital distress. For example, sociologists have found in long-term studies of the same cohort that the premarital stage is the when couples are the happiest (Van-Laningham, Johnson, & Amato, 2001), though a minority of couples start happy and stay happy over time (Kamp Dush, Taylor, & Kroeger, 2008). Studies starting after marriage, in contrast, are more likely to include already distressed couples because 21% of couples divorce within the first 5 years of marriage (Raley & Bumpass, 2003). Moreover, starting with premarital couples provides a research base for interventions during the transition to marriage, one of the best stages for divorce prevention and marriage enhancement programs (Halford et al., 2008).

In summary, the studies reviewed above show somewhat inconsistent findings, despite assessing similar constructs. The inconsistency of the findings are in part due to differences in data collection and data reduction, how interaction was measured (self-report vs. observation), time of follow-up, sample size and composition, level of initial satisfaction, difference in measures of outcome (stability, satisfaction, combinations of stability and satisfaction), and differences in coding systems and tasks used. Nevertheless, across time, labs, tasks, and outcomes, there are links between premarital and newlywed communication quality and later outcomes. Moreover, studies suggest that negative communication is a better predictor of marital outcomes than positive communication, and all the more so when combined with low levels of positive communication. Studies generally supported the enduring dynamics model, but because they typically start after marriage, research is needed regarding dynamics that endure from prior to marriage into marriage. In addition, none of the studies above have observed interactions over time, and thus the emergent distress theory has not yet been adequately tested.

Current Study

The overarching aim of the current study was to assess how negative and positive communication, assessed by both self-report and observational coding of interactions before marriage, predict future divorce and marital satisfaction. Starting before marriage provides a better test of the enduring dynamics model than starting after marriage. This study is also the first to investigate how positive and negative communication assessed by observational coding changes from before marriage to 5 years into marriage, and how these changes predict marital outcomes. The current study also provides a strong test of the emergent distress model because, for long-term analyses of communication, we are starting with couples when they are happy, before distress sets in. Observational coding of interactions are critical because they have consistently been found to be associated with both relationship outcomes and are indicators of changes following interventions (Markman & Hahlweg, 1993). Specifically, we present findings from an ongoing longitudinal study of premarital couples recruited from 1996 to 2001. Here we focus on findings from the premarital stage of development through the first 5 years of marriage. We chose 5 years because this is the point when we have the most data to test the hypotheses that are the focus of this paper.

Hypotheses

As noted above, starting before marriage enabled us to provide the best test to date of the enduring dynamics model, which predicts that marital distress and divorce are associated with premarital patterns. The first major hypothesis was that that both negative and positive dimensions of premarital communication would be associated with divorce and marital adjustment across the first 5 years of marriage and that negative communication would be more strongly related to divorce and marital adjustment than positive communication. Second, we focused on negative and positive communication trajectories as possible roots of the emergence of marital distress. Based on prior studies, we hypothesized that couples who were distressed after being married for 5 years would show and self-report more negative and less positive premarital communication initially, as well as steeper increases in negative communication over time and steeper decreases in positive communication over time.

Method

Participants

Participants were 208 couples (*N* = 416 partners) who had taken part in a larger study on the effectiveness of premarital education (see Markman et al., 2004; Stanley et al.,

2001). Couples who did not marry or who did not complete a premarital assessment were excluded, as were couples for whom we could not verify marital status at the time of their fifth wedding anniversary. When the study began, the participants were, on average, 26.55 years old *(SD* = 5.26) with a median education of 16 years and a median income of $30,000 to 39,999. The sample was 3.6% African American, 1.7% Asian American, 9.3% Hispanic or Latino, 0.7% Native American, and 84.7% White. At the couple level, 79% of the sample involved White partners paired with White partners, 11% involved White partners paired with non-White partners, and 10% involved non-White partners paired with non-White partners. Sixty-four percent of the couples lived together before marriage. Thirty-five couples (16.8%) divorced within the first 5 years of marriage; 173 (83.2%) remained married.

Procedures

Couples were recruited through the religious organizations (ROs) that would perform their wedding services. These ROs were randomly assigned to deliver naturally occurring premarital education, to deliver the Prevention and Relationship Enhancement Program (PREP; Markman et al., 2010), or send eligible couples to a university to receive PREP. Before receiving services, couples completed questionnaires and videotaped interaction tasks before marriage and before premarital education, 6 weeks following premarital education, and yearly thereafter. These visits lasted approximately 2 hours and couples were paid $40 to $100, depending on the time point. Data from all time points between the premarital assessment and the assessment that took place within 6 months of a couples' fifth wedding anniversary were used in the current study. On average, couples came in 5 months before their wedding day for the first assessment. For those who remained married, the average couple came in for five assessments starting before marriage and ending at their fifth wedding anniversary. Besides marital status, no longitudinal data from divorced couples are included in these analyses.

Measures

Observed negative and positive communication. As mentioned earlier, couples completed videotaped interaction tasks at every time point. For the current study, data from the problem-discussion task are used. For this task, couples identified their top problem area in their relationship on paper forms and then were instructed to discuss that issue for 10 to 15 minutes. These problem discussions were then coded using the global Interactional Dimensions Coding System (Kline et al., 2004). Using this system, coders rate each partner on nine dimensions that include affective, behavioral, and content cues and they assign a code to the couple for negative escalation. For the current study, negative and positive composite scores of these 10 dimensions were used. The negative composite score included negative affect, denial, dominance, conflict, withdrawal, and negative escalation ($\alpha = .87$). The positive composite included positive affect, problem-solving skills, support/validation, and communication ($\alpha = .88$). These composites were moderately correlated, $r = .56, p < .001$. Intercoder reliability for this sample was high, with intraclass correlations ranging from .66 to .95 (*Mdn* = .87; Kline et al., 2004).

Marital adjustment. The Marital Adjustment Test (Locke & Wallace, 1959) was used to assess marital adjustment. The internal consistency for the current sample was lower than in married couple samples ($\alpha = .61$), perhaps because the sample was relatively homogeneous and happy (*M* at T1 = 127.77, *SD* = 15.65, range = 84 to 156). This inventory was also used to create the distressed and nondistressed groups used in some analyses.

Self-reported negative communication. Participants rated the negativity of the communication they experience outside of the lab using the Communication Danger Signs Scale (Markman, Stanley, & Blumberg, 2010). This measure includes 7 items rated on a scale ranging from 1 *(almost never)* to 3 *(frequently)* scale. An example item is "My partner criticizes or belittles my opinions, feelings, or desires." This measure has demonstrated validity and reliability in a range of samples (e.g., Stanley, Markman, & Whit-ton, 2002). In this sample alpha was .73. This measure was significantly correlated with observed negative communication in this sample, $r = .26, p < .01$.

Results

Premarital Communication and Divorce

To test hypotheses about premarital communication and divorce, we used 2X2 analyses of variances (ANOVAs), with factors of divorced versus nondivorced and gender. We chose to use ANOVAs over logistic regressions because of the dependency between husbands' and wives' scores. By treating gender as a within-subjects variable in ANOVA, we were able to efficiently test whether gender moderated associations between premarital communication and divorce and were also able to collapse across men and women when there were no significant interactions. Results suggest that those who divorced were observed to have more negative communication before marriage ($M = 3.51, SD = 1.36$) than those who remained married ($M = 3.18, SD = 1.13$), but this difference only approached significance, $F(1, 205) = 2.40, p = .06$ (one-tailed), $d = .27$. Similarly, those who divorced were observed to have less observed positive communication before marriage ($M = 3.86, SD = 1.17$) than those who remained married ($M = 4.11, SD = 1.15$), but this difference only approached significance, $F(1, 205) = 1.68, p = .10$ (one-tailed), $d = .22$. For self-reported premarital negative communication, the difference between those who divorced ($M = 1.56, SD = 0.34$) and those who remained married ($M = 1.44, SD = 0.38$) was significant, $F(1, 178) = 4.40, p = .02$ (one-tailed), $d = .38$, and in the expected direction. Adding control variables as covariates in these ANOVAs (education, income, intervention status [received PREP or not], age, gender, and religiousness) did not change the results in meaningful ways.

Premarital Communication and Marital Adjustment Over Time

For the remaining hypotheses, we used multilevel modeling and HLM 6.02 software (Raudenbush, Bryk, & Congdon, 2004) because it allowed us to examine the trajectories of marital adjustment and communication over time. Following guidelines presented by Atkins (2005), we used three-level models in which time is nested within individuals who are in turn nested within couples.

Baseline model. We ran an initial unconditional model (below) before adding predictors to determine whether there was enough variation between partners within couples in marital adjustment intercepts and slopes (changes over time) to treat them as random effects.

Level 1: $Y_{tij} = \pi_{0ij} + \pi_{1ij}\,(\text{Time})_{tij} + \varepsilon_{tij}$ (1)

$\pi_{0ij} + \beta_{00j} + r_{0ij}$

Level 2: $\pi_{1ij} + \beta_{10j} + r_{1ij}$

Level 3: $\beta_{00j} + \gamma_{000} + u_{00j}$

$\beta_{10j} + \gamma_{100} + u_{10j}$

Here, t indexes time (in weeks) since the premarriage assessment; i indexes partners within a couple; and j indexes couples. There are four separate error terms, all of which are assumed to be normally distributed: ε_{tij} is the residual error term; r_{0ij} and r_{lij} are random intercept and slope terms at the individual level; and u_{00j} and u_{10j} are a random intercept and slope terms at the couple level. The Time variable was grand-mean centered, so the intercept term represents the average marital adjustment score across the first 5 years of marriage.

There was significant variation between partners in the level of marital adjustment, but not in slopes ($p > .50$). Therefore, we excluded random slope component in the Level 2 equations. In this baseline model we also tested whether there was significant variation between couples in marital adjustment intercept and slope. There was significant variability, so we treated the intercepts and slopes as random in Level 3 of the models testing our hypotheses. The fixed effects indicated that there were significant decreases in marital adjustment over time ($\gamma_{100} = 0.03$, $p < .001$) that were approximately equal to a 1.56 point drop in marital adjustment per year.

Hypotheses tests. We hypothesized that both negative and positive dimensions of premarital communication would be associated with marital adjustment across the first 5 years of marriage. To test these hypotheses, we added positive or negative premarital communication (grand-mean centered) to the baseline model (Equation 1). We ran three separate models including premarital observed negative communication (Model 1), premarital observed positive communication (Model 2), and premarital self-reported negative communication (Model 3) as predictors of marital adjustment (see Table 1). In Models 1 and 3, premarital observed and self-reported negative communications were significantly associated with lower average marital adjustment across the first 5 years of marriage. In the same models, premarital negative communication was also associated, unexpectedly, with less steep declines in marital adjustment over time. Premarital observed positive communication was not significantly associated with either average marital adjustment or changes in marital adjustment over time. Adding control variables to these models (education, income, intervention status [received PREP or not], age, gender, and religiousness) did not change the results in meaningful ways.

Differences in Trajectories of Communication Over Time by Marital Distress Status

In the next set of analyses we used a dichotomous outcome (distressed vs. nondistressed, as defined earlier) rather than a continuous outcome. We hypothesized that couples who were categorized as nondistressed (vs. distressed) after being married for 5 years would show less negative and more positive premarital communication, as well as less steep increases in negative communication over time and less steep decreases in positive communication over time. Married couples in which one or both partners had a score of 100 or less at the assessment nearest to their fifth wedding anniversary were considered distressed. We choose to use 100 as the cut-off because other research has found this to be a useful cut-off score for distinguishing between couples who are distressed and nondistressed (e.g., Clements et al., 2004; Rogge & Bradbury, 1999). Of the 173 couples who remained married through their fifth year of marriage, 32 (18.5%) were distressed; however, of these, 21 had been distressed at the premarital assessment and were therefore excluded from analyses so we could focus on couples before distress set in. This left 128 nondistressed and 24 (18.8%) distressed couples. Unconditional models (without predictors) in which Time was uncentered indicated that there was not significant variation between partners (at Level 2) in communication changes over time, so this random component (r_{1ij}) was excluded from the tests of hypotheses.

Table 1 Summary of Multilevel Models Predicting Marital Adjustment From Premarital Communication

	Observed negative communication			Observed positive communication			Self-reported negative communication		
Variable	Coefficient	SE	df	Coefficient	SE	df	Coefficient	SE	df
Intercept (7000)	124.79***	0.92	159	124.80***	0.94	159	141.83***	1.86	159
Observed negative communication (γ 010)	-2.45**	0.74	296	—			—		
Observed positive communication (γ010)	—			0.93	0.67	296	—		
Self-reported negative communication (γ010)	—			—			-7.77***	0.78	296
Time (“y100)	-0.03***	0.00	159	-0.03***	0.00	159	-0.07***	0.01	159
Observed Negative Communication X Time (γ010)	0.01*	0.00	1334	—			—		
Observed Positive Communication X Time (γ010)	—			0.01	0.00	1334	—		
Self-Reported Negative Communication X Time (γ010)	—			—			0.01**	0.00	1334

Note. Model 1 = observed negative communication; Model 2 = observed positive communication; Model 3 = Self-reported negative communication.

$^{*}p < .05$. $^{**}p < .01$. $^{***}p < .001$.

To test the ways in which communication changes over time related to whether couples ended up happy or unhappy at 5 years into their marriages, we used these equations.

$$\text{Level 1: } Y_{tij} = \pi_{0ij} + \pi_{1ij}\,(\text{Time})_{tij} + \varepsilon_{tij} \qquad (2)$$

$$\pi_{0ij} + \beta_{00j} + r_{0ij}$$

$$\text{Level 2: } \quad \pi_{1ij} + \beta_{10j}$$

$$\text{Level 3: } \quad \beta_{00j} + \gamma_{000} + \gamma_{001}\,(\text{Distress Status}) + u_{00j}$$
$$\beta_{10j} + \gamma_{100} + \gamma_{101}\,(\text{Distress Status}) + u_{10j}$$

We ran three separate models for these hypotheses: one with observed negative communication, another with observed positive communication, and a third with self-reported negative communication (Table 2; Figure 1). In these models, Time was uncentered so that the intercept term (γ_{000}) could be interpreted as the premarital communication score. Distress Status was also uncentered, so coefficients in the table represent values for those who were distressed in their marriages (i.e., those who were distressed were coded as 0). Results of the model with observed negative communication indicate that there were no differences in initial (premarital) negative observed communication between those who were distressed versus nondistressed 5 years into their marriages (γ_{001}), but that those who were nondistressed 5 years into their marriages experienced greater declines in negative communication than those who were distressed (γ_{101}). Similarly, there were not significant differences between groups on premarital positive communication (γ_{001}'), but distressed couples experienced decreases in positive communication over time (γ_{100}) whereas nondistressed couples experienced almost no change in positive communication over time (γ_{101}).

For self-reported negative communication, those who were nondistressed 5 years into their marriages reported lower premarital negative communication than those who were distressed (γ_{001}). Those who were distressed reported significant increases in negative communication over time (γ_{100}), while those who were nondistressed reported significantly smaller increases in negative communication over time (γ_{101}).

Discussion

The purpose of this study was to examine the ways in which observed and self-reported indicators of negative and positive premarital communication were related to marital adjustment and divorce 5 years into marriage. Specifically, we were interested in how changes in communication over time, starting before marriage, were associated with future marital quality.

In terms of divorce, consistent with the enduring dynamics model, we hypothesized that more negative and less positive communication before marriage (both observed and self-reported) would be associated with divorce. The results showed that observed negative and positive communication nearly reached significance in the predicted direction, while self-reported negative communication was significantly associated with later divorce. This study is one of the few that examines the hypothesis that divorce is associated with premarital communication quality. Most studies have focused only on marital quality as an outcome or have combined stability with marital quality; however, only a few have used divorce as an outcome (e.g., Clements et al., 2004; Huston et al., 2001).

Other studies also have reported relatively small effects of interaction on divorce (see Karney & Bradbury, 1995, for a review) for both positive and negative communication.

In our study we had a relatively small number of divorces and hence low power to detect effects. Also, we did not assess love. Given that Huston et al. (2001) showed reasonably strong prediction of divorce using measures of love, and that falling out of love is one of major reasons people give for divorce (Amato & Hohmann-Marriott, 2007), measures of love should be used in future research on divorce risk. More generally, events later in marriage, such as infidelity, can rapidly deteriorate a marriage that was otherwise doing well (e.g., Glass & Wright, 1997), and thereby have a far greater proximal effect on marital outcomes.

In terms of marital adjustment over time, higher levels of negative communication were significantly associated with lower levels of average marital adjustment across the first 5 years of marriage. Contrary to predictions, premarital positive observed communication was not significantly associated with marital quality. These findings are in line with other research that has highlighted the importance of negative communication in explaining future marital quality (e.g., Markman & Hahlweg, 1993) and add to the literature that somewhat different factors predict stability versus quality over time (Clements et al., 2004).

Table 2 Summary of Multilevel Models Analyzing Changes in Communication Over Time by Marital Distress Status at 5 Years Into Marriage

	Observed negative communication			Observed positive communication			Self-reported negative communication		
Variable	Coefficient	SE	df	Coefficient	SE	df	Coefficient	SE	df
Intercept (γ_{000})	3.09***	0.19	150	4.37***	0.20	150	1.51***	0.05	150
Distress status (γ_{001})	0.04	0.21	150	0.27	0.22	150	-0.16***	0.05	150
Time (γ_{100})	0.00	0.001	150	0.00	0.001	150	0.00***	0.00	150
Distress Status X Time (γ_{101})	0.00*	0.001	150	0.00*	0.002	150	0.00***	0.00	150

Note. Distress status was coded as 0 = distressed five years into marriage, 1 = nondistressed 5 years into marriage.

*p < .05. ***p < .001.

Taken together, the findings on the prediction of divorce and marital quality are consistent with Huston et al.'s (2001) enduring dynamics model, in that early risk is associated with later problems because the risk factors endure. The current study is one of the first that shows that some of the roots of distress lie in the couples' communication quality and such risk can be identified before marriage and as such, this study has important implications for interventions that focus on modifying communication patterns, such as PREP (Markman, Stanley, & Blumberg, 2010). However, the relatively small effect sizes of these findings also suggest a variety of dimensions are important to consider in the understanding and prevention of marital distress.

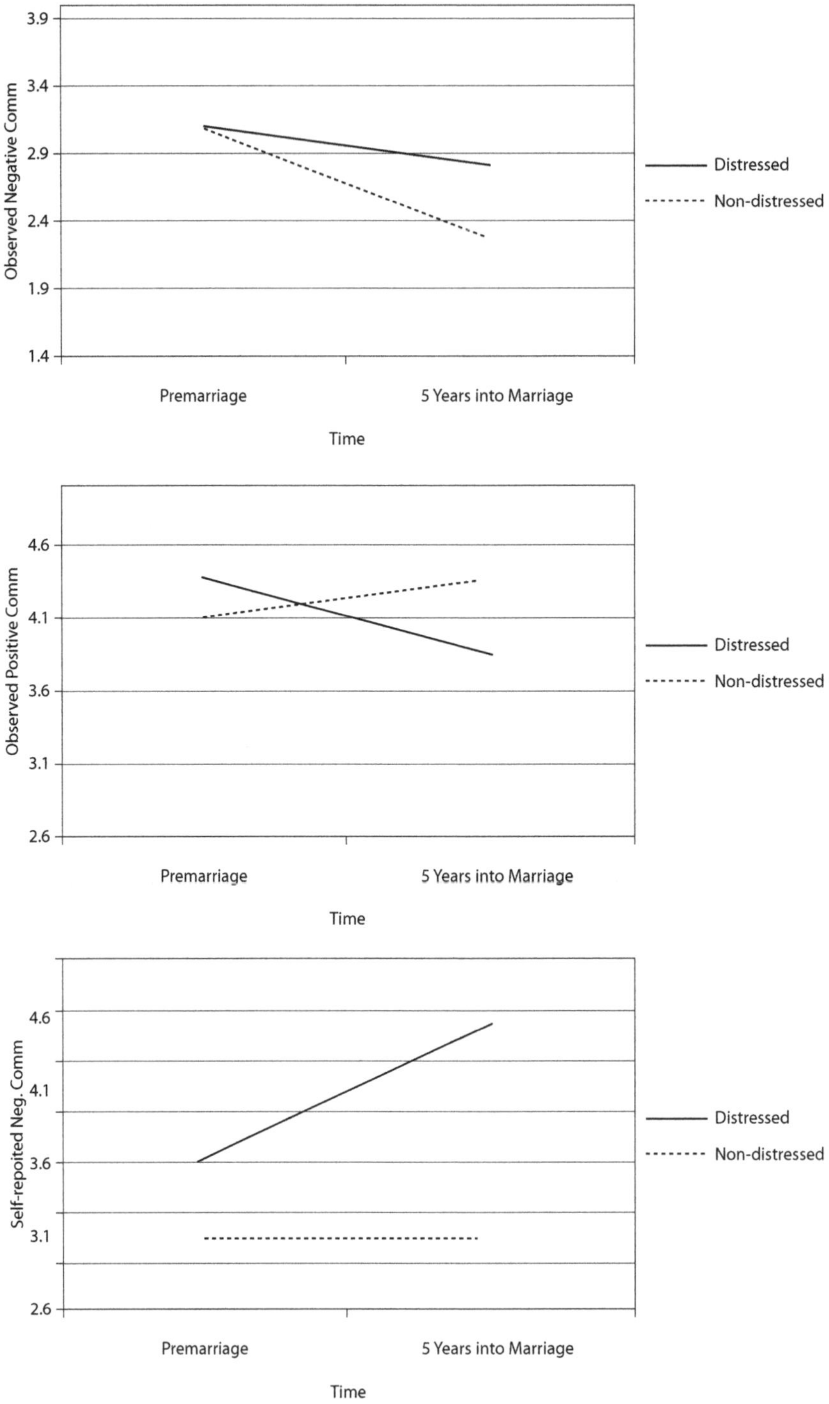

Figure 1. *Illustration of changes in communication over time by distress status. These figures are based on the intercept and slope values of the multilevel models presented in Table 2. Neg = negative.*

In terms of how premarital negative and positive observed communication were associated with changes in marital adjustment over the first 5 years of marriage, we found that, contrary to predictions, higher levels of observed and self-reported premarital negative communication were associated with less steep declines in marital adjustment. At first glance, these findings seem counterintuitive, but it is likely an artifact of the fact that those with high levels negative communication premaritally also have lower premarital adjustment scores. Thus, they have less room to decline than those who begin marriages with lower negative communication and higher marital adjustment scores. In addition, divorced couples were not included in the analyses because they have no end point data, and these couples likely would have had steep declines.

In regard to positive communication and decline in satisfaction, consistent with the general pattern of findings in the field, observed premarital positive communication was not associated with changes in marital adjustment over time.

Interaction Over Time

The most important set of questions addressed in this study pertain to how positive and negative dimensions of communication change over time and how these changes are related to being distressed or nondistressed after 5 years of marriage. This is the first study, to our knowledge, to examine the kinds of changes in communication over time that are consistent with the emergent distress model, which is central to most theories of the development of marital distress (Clements et al., 2004). The finding showing that the nondistressed couples declined more in negative communication over time than the distressed couples suggests that communication quality may be one of the important factors in determining the course of a couple's relationship over time. This is consistent with the emergent distress model, though it is not really possible to prove that the changes in communication precede the changes in adjustment. The finding is, however, consistent with one of the core assumptions underlying most research-based approaches to couples intervention: that negatives erode positives over time (Markman et al., 2010). These findings suggest that both overall level of negative communication (assessed by observational coding) as well as the perceived frequency of negative communication (assessed by the self-report measure) discriminate between couples who wind up distressed versus nondistressed. In addition, the finding that distressed compared to nondistressed couples show more negative communication over time is the first, to our knowledge, to support the emergent distress theory. This finding has important implications for interventions, because the basis of most couples prevention and therapy programs is, in part, that negatives will increase over time unless the couple learns skills to counteract them.

Perhaps the most interesting finding in the study is that couples who wound up distressed experienced more declines in positive communication compared to the couples who wound up nondistressed. This pattern is particularly important in that the nondistressed couples maintained high levels of positives while distressed couples declined. Many theories of marriage over time, suggest that the positives naturally decrease over time (e.g., Fisher, 2006), but our data do not support those contentions. Rather these finding support theories that suggest that marital distress is in part due to a decrease in positives. These findings are especially interesting to us because they emerge from a conflict task. It is probable that conflict tasks are not the best way to assess positives, and that the focus on conflict tasks in the history of this field may be one the reasons for the negativity effect (Fincham, Beach, & Stanley, 2007). The current findings not only suggest that positives do matter, but also that they can be assessed with some validity even when the context is a conflict task. In addition, we found support for positives, assessed by observational coding, predicting future marital outcomes using a traditional conflict task. Perhaps couples from more recent generations are putting more stock in the positive side of the relationship and when positives are low, couples are more reactive and this is seen in lower satisfaction (and to a degree, higher risk for divorce) later on.

Positives and Negatives in Marriage

Taken together, the results of this study do support previous findings that the negatives predict future marital distress and positives do not. Thus negatives may be stronger risk factors than the positives are protective factors. We coined the term the negativity effect to describe this pattern. Clinically, we describe the negativity effect by saying that it takes a number of positive "acts of kindness" to compensate for one negative "zinger" (Notarius & Markman, 1993). However, because we do not have a measure of self-reported positive communication, such as we do for negative communication, we need further research to solidify our suggestions. However, a similar finding emerges from health psychology where research reveals that negative emotions are stronger predictors of health problems than positive emotions (see Fredrickson & Losada, 2005, for a review). On the other hand, it has been noted that negative communication behavior has been much more robustly studied than positives, and that various forms of positives beyond mere positive communication behavior may have transformative properties (Fincham et al., 2007). To be clear, we are not saying that positives do not matter; they do, as we see from our current findings. Future research is needed on other forms of positive aspects of relationships, including fun, support, passion, commitment, and sacrifice. (Markman et al., 2010).

If negatives count more than positives when it comes to communication, why might this be so? Evolutionary perspectives would suggest that there is selection effect in favor of being more responsive to negatives. Negatives can really hurt us, so evolutionary psychologists suggest that we are selected for focusing more attention on the negatives in relationships and in life (e.g., Buss, 2000). The salience of negatives can also be explained in part by cognitive consistency theories (e.g., Aronson, 2008) where negatives are not expected (as in marriage) and cause stress that we are motivated to relieve. For example, in therapy, couples often report that the week was "really bad," and it turns out that one negative event colored the entire week that was otherwise filled with positives. Couples therapists can help partners work on decreasing the value of the negatives and increasing the value of the positives, as well as help couples decrease the number of negatives and increase the number of positives in day-to-day interactions (Markman et al, 2010).

There are several limitations with the study that must be taken into consideration when interpreting the current findings. First, all couples in the study completed a premarital intervention, and thus the patterning of the findings might be different for couples who did not participate in a premarital intervention. It is also possible that intervention effects may be affecting the pattern of findings in that the premarital data were assessed before the intervention and the postmarital data were assessed after the intervention. Thus, it is possible that the couples in this sample had higher levels of positives and marital quality over time and lower levels of negatives after the intervention, but this would not likely affect the pattern of findings. However, we controlled for intervention status and it did not affect the findings.

Second, because all the couples were marrying through religious organizations, it is possible that they were somewhat more religious than the average couple planning marriage. However, because the majority of first marriages take place through a religious organization (Stanley, Amato, Johnson, & Markman, 2006), the current sample is not all that different from most couples getting married for the first time. Nevertheless, the findings may not generalize to couples who do not marry through religious organizations. Third, we used a cutoff of 100 to define distress and non-distress. Although this is justified based on prior research, it is possible that included in the distressed group were some couples who were not all that distressed. Fourth, we did not include a self-report measure of positive communication. Future research should use such a scale to help better understand the roles of positive and negative communication in marriage. Fifth, we did not present data on communication over time for those couples who divorce. This is an important area for future research because there are no data to our knowledge on changes over time in communication of couples who go on to divorce. In the current study, we did not have enough couples and data to adequately examine this important question, but we plan to in the future as our sample of divorced couples increases in size and length of relationship. Sixth, many of the couples have had a child during the first 5 years of marriage and this transition likely affected their communication. Examining these effects was beyond the scope of the present paper, but a paper by Doss, Rhoades, Stanley, and Markman (2009) examined transition to parenthood in this sample. Finally, although there is some diversity in our sample, the couples are mostly White and middle class; thus the findings may not be generalizable to other groups.

In summary, the picture of nondistressed couples 5 years into marriage from an interaction perspective supports current theories of distress and intervention in that couples who start marriage with lower negatives and higher adjustment and who maintain high levels of positives are "at risk" for marital success. The findings support the use of prevention programs that focus on keeping happy couples happy by helping couples learn skills to handle the inevitable negatives in marriage and to protect and maintain positives (Markman et al., 2010) and suggest the use of these programs before marriage or early in marriage.

References

Amato, P. R., & Hohmann-Marriott, B. (2007). A comparison of high- and low-distress marriages that end in divorce. *Journal of Marriage and Family, 69,* 621–638.

Aronson, E. (2008). *The social animal* (10th ed.). New York, NY: Wirth/Freeman.

Atkins, D. C. (2005). Using multilevel models to analyze couple and family treatment data: Basic and advanced issues. *Journal of Family Psychology, 19,* 98–110.

Birchler, G. R., Weiss, R. L., & Vincent, J. P. (1975). Multimethod analysis of social reinforcement exchange between maritally distressed and nondistressed spouse and stranger dyads. *Journal of Personality and Social Psychology, 31,* 349–360.

Booth, A., & Amato, P. R. (2001). Parental predivorce relations and offspring postdivorce well-being. *Journal of Marriage & the Family, 63,* 197–212.

Buss, D. (2000). *The dangerous passion: Why jealousy is as necessary as love and sex.* New York, NY: Free Press.

Clements, M. L., Stanley, S. M., & Markman, H. J. (2004). Before they said "I do": Discriminating among marital outcomes over 13 years. *Journal of Marriage and Family, 66,* 613–626.

Doss, B. D., Rhoades, G. K., Stanley, S. M., & Markman, H. J. (2009). The effect of the transition to parenthood on relationship quality: An 8-year prospective study. *Journal of Personality and Social Psychology, 96,* 601–619.

Fincham, F. D., Stanley, S. M., & Beach, S. R. H. (2007). Transformative processes in marriage: An analysis of emerging trends. *Journal of Marriage and Family, 69,* 275–292.

Fisher, H. (2006). The drive to love: The neural mechanism for mate choice. In R. Sternberg & K. Weis (Eds.), *The new psychology of love.* New Haven, CT: Yale University Press.

Fredrickson, B., & Losada, M. (2005). Positive affect and the complex dynamics of human flourishing. *American Psychologist, 60,* 678–686.

Glass, S. P., & Wright, T. L. (1997). Reconstructing marriages after the trauma of infidelity. In K. W. Halford & H. J. Markman (Eds.), *Clinical handbook of marriage and couples intervention* (pp. 471–507). Hoboken, NJ: John Wiley and Sons.

Glenn, N. D. (1998). The course of marital success and failure in five American 10-year marriage cohorts. *Journal of Marriage & the Family, 60,* 569–576.

Gottman, J. M., Coan, J., Carrere, S., & Swanson, C. C. (1998). Predicting marital happiness and stability from newlywed interactions. *Journal of Marriage & the Family, 60,* 5–22.

Gottman, J. M., & Krokoff, L. J. (1989). Marital interaction and satisfaction: A longitudinal view. *Journal of Consulting and Clinical Psychology, 57,* 47–52.

Gottman, J. M., Markman, H. J., & Notarius, C. I. (1977). The topography of marital conflict: A sequential analysis of verbal and nonverbal behavior. *Journal of Marriage and the Family, 39,* 461–477.

Halford, W. K., & Bouma, R. (1997). Individual psychopathology and marital distress. In K. Halford & H. J. Markman (Eds.), *Clinical handbook of marriage and couples intervention* (pp. 291–321). Hoboken, NJ: Wiley.

Halford, W. K., Markman, H. J., & Stanley, S. (2008). Strengthening couples' relationships with education: Social policy and public health perspectives. *Journal of Family Psychology, 22,* 497–505.

Heller, K., & Monahan, J. (1977). *Psychology and community change.* Homewood, IL: Dorsey Press.

Heyman, R. E., & Slep, A. M. S. (2001). The hazards of predicting divorce without crossvalidation. *Journal of Marriage and Family, 63,* 473–479.

Huston, T. L., Caughlin, J. P., Houts, R. M., Smith, S. E., & George, L. J. (2001). The connubial crucible: Newlywed years as predictors of marital delight, distress, and divorce. *Journal of Personality and Social Psychology, 80,* 237–252.

Johnson, C. A., Stanley, S. M., Glenn, N. D., Amato, P. R., Nock, S. L., Markman, H. J., ... Dion, M. R. (2002). *Marriage in Oklahoma: 2001 baseline statewide survey on marriage and divorce (S02096 OKDHS).* Oklahoma City: Oklahoma Department of Human Services.

Johnson, M. D., Cohan, C. L., Davila, J., Lawrence, E., Rogge, R. D., Karney, B. R., ... Bradbury, T. M. (2005). Problem-solving skills and affective expressions as predictors of change in marital satisfaction. *Journal of Consulting and Clinical Psychology, 73,* 15–27.

Kamp Dush, C, Taylor, M., & Kroeger, R. (2008). Marital happiness and psychological well-being across the life course. *Family Relations, 57,* 211–226.

Karney, B. R., & Bradbury, T. N. (1995). The longitudinal course of marital quality and stability: A review of theory, method, and research. *Psychological Bulletin, 118,* 3–34.

Karney, B. R., & Bradbury, T. N. (1997). Neuroticism, marital interaction, and the trajectory of marital satisfaction. *Journal of Personality and Social Psychology, 72,* 1075–1092.

Kiecolt-Glaser, J. K., Bane, C, Glaser, R., & Malarkey, W. B. (2003). Love, marriage, and divorce: Newlyweds' stress hormones foreshadow relationship changes. *Journal of Consulting & Clinical Psychology, 71,* 176–188.

Kline, G. H., Julien, D., Baucom, B., Hartman, S. G, Gilbert, K., Gonzales, T., ... Markman, H. J. (2004). The Interactional Dimensions Coding System: A global system for couple interactions. In P. K. Kerig & D. H. Baucom (Eds.), *Couple observational coding systems* (pp. 113–127). Mahwah, NJ: Erlbaum.

Locke, H. J., & Wallace, K. M. (1959). Short marital-adjustment and prediction tests: Their reliability and validity. *Marriage and Family Living, 21,* 251–255.

Markman, H. J. (1979). Application of a behavioral model of marriage in predicting relationship satisfaction of couples planning marriage. *Journal of Consulting and Clinical Psychology, 47,* 743–749.

Markman, H. J. (1981). Prediction of marital distress: A 5-year follow-up. *Journal of Consulting and Clinical Psychology, 49,* 760–762.

Markman, H. J., & Floyd, F. (1980). Possibilities for the prevention of marital discord: A behavioral perspective. *American Journal of Family Therapy, 8(2),* 29–48.

Markman, H. J., & Hahlweg, K. (1993). The prediction and prevention of marital distress: An international perspective. *Clinical Psychology Review, 13,* 29–43.

Markman, H. J., & Notarius, C. I. (1987). Coding and marital family interaction: Current status. In T. Jacob (Ed.), *Family interaction and psychology* (pp. 329–390). New York, NY: Plenum.

Markman, H. J., Stanley, S. M., & Blumberg, S. L. (2010). *Fighting for your marriage* (3rd ed.). San Francisco, CA: Jossey-Bass.

Markman, H. J., Whitton, S. W., Kline, G. H., Thompson, H., St. Peters, M., Stanley, S. M., … Cordova, A. (2004). Use of an empirically-based marriage education program by religious organizations: Results of a dissemination trial. *Family Relations, 53,* 504–512.

Notarius, C. I., & Markman, H. J. (1993). *We can work it out: Making sense of marital conflict.* New York,

NY: Putnam.Pasch, L. A., & Bradbury, T. N. (1998). Social support, conflict, and the development of marital dysfunction. *Journal of Consulting and Clinical Psychology, 66,* 219–230.

Raley, E., & Bumpass, L. (2003). The topography of the divorce plateau: Levels and trends in union stability in the United States after 1980. *Demographic Research, 8,* 245–260.

Rogge, R. D., & Bradbury, T. N. (1999). Till violence do us part: The differing roles of communication and aggression in predicting adverse marital outcomes. *Journal of Consulting and Clinical Psychology, 67,* 340–351.

Seefeldt, K. S., & Smock, P. J. (2004). *Marriage on the public policy agenda: What do policy makers need to know from research?* (PSC Research Report No. 04–554). Ann Arbor, MI: Population Studies Center.

Stanley, S. M., Amato, P. R., Johnson, C. A., & Markman, H. J. (2006). Premarital education, marital quality, and marital stability: Findings from a large, random, household survey. *Journal of Family Psychology, 20,* 117–126.

Stanley, S. M., Markman, H. J., Prado, L. M., Olmos-Gallo, P. A., Tonelli, L., St. Peters, M., … Whitton, S. W. (2001). Community-based premarital prevention: Clergy and lay leaders on the front lines. *Family Relations, 50*(1), 67–76.

Stanley, S. M., Markman, H. J., & Whitton, S. W. (2002). Communication, conflict and commitment: Insights on the foundations of relationship success from a national survey. *Family Process, 41,* 659–675.

Sternberg, R. (1998). *Love is a story: A new theory of relationships.* New York, NY: Oxford University Press

VanLaningham, J., Johnson, D. R., & Amato, P. (2001). Marital happiness, marital duration, and the U-shaped curve: Evidence from a 5-wave panel study. Social Forces, 78, 1313–1341.

Howard J. Markman, Galena K. Rhoades, Scott M. Stanley, and Erica P. Ragan, Department of Psychology, University of Denver; Sarah W. Whitton, Department of Psychology, University of Cincinnati.

This research is funded by a grant from the National Institute of Child Health and Human Development, awarded to Howard J. Markman, Scott M. Stanley, and Elizabeth Allen (R01HD053314). The contents are solely the responsibility of the authors and do not necessarily represent the official views of NIH or NICHD. We thank all the couples who have shared their lives with us during our study as well as the anonymous reviewers for their excellent comments.

For Richer ... in Good Times ... and in Health

Positive Processes in Relationships

By Natalya C. Maisel and Shelly L. Gable

Abstract

Although psychologists have learned a great deal about negative and harmful processes in relationships, they have focused less on understanding the positive and beneficial processes in relationships. Of course, almost every close relationship offers the promise of both meaningful rewards and substantial risks, such as support, intimacy, companionship, conflict, rejection, and criticism. In this chapter, we attempt to highlight the complexities involved in relationships, with an emphasis on positive processes, with the goal of creating a picture that represents the dynamic reality of the social world. We first discuss the important role that intimate relationships play in human life and their strong links with health and well-being. We then highlight research on the positive processes in relationships, such as positive emotional expressions, shared novel experiences, intimacy, and the benefits of sharing positive events. This work complements previous literature which has tended to focus on the potential pitfalls in

Natalya C. Maisel, Shelly L. Gable; Shane J. Lopez, C.R. Snyder, eds., "For Richer ... in Good Times ... and in Health: Positive Processes in Relationships," from *Oxford Handbook of Positive Psychology*, Pp. 455–462.

relationships. For example, displaying low levels of negative emotions may not be enough to create a strong relationship—expressions of positive emotions are also beneficial. Finally, we point to future directions in the positive psychology of relationships, such as a greater focus on biology and health (e.g., examining hormones that promote bonding), and the need to examine other types of relationships, such as friendships.

Keywords: capitalization, emotions, interpersonal, intimacy, relationships

We know a great deal about processes that go awry in relationships, but we are still at the early stages of arriving at a nuanced understanding of what makes them work. In this chapter, we attempt to highlight the complexities involved in relationships (including the positive processes), with the goal of creating a picture that represents the dynamic reality of the social world.

We begin by making the obvious but still important point that intimate relationships constitute not just "an aspect of life" but one of the most important aspects of life. Next, we briefly review the literature on close relationships, which has tended to focus on negative and aversive processes, such as conflict and criticism. We then make a case for the importance of focusing on appetitive processes in relationships, such as positive emotional expressions, intimacy processes, and the benefits of sharing positive events. We review some of these exciting areas of research and suggest possible future directions for the positive psychology of interpersonal relationships.

Relationships, Health, and Psychological Well-Being

A large body of research has demonstrated that close relationships have a profound impact on health and well-being. For example, Berkman and Syme (1979) found that having a large social network was related to a decreased risk of mortality. In their review, House, Landis, and Umberson (1988) found that a lack of strong social ties was a mortality risk factor on the order of smoking and high blood pressure. More recently, Uchino, Cacioppo, and Kiecolt-Glaser (1996) reviewed 81 studies on social support and social integration and found a consistent association between social ties and increased positive physiological functioning of the cardiovascular, endocrine, and immune systems. Close relationships, the most important of our "social ties," are not only related to health and mortality, they also have been shown to have a strong association to subjective reports of happiness and life satisfaction (e.g., Diener & Seligman, 2002). Indeed, the need to connect with others has been proposed as a central motivation for human beings (Baumeister & Leary, 1995).

Although it is clear that having close social ties is important for health and well-being, research also has highlighted the negative consequences of interpersonal relationships (e.g., Rook, 1984). For example, losing a partner through death or divorce can be quite devastating, and such losses are often associated with large decreases in well-being (e.g., Stroebe, Stroebe, Abakoumkin, & Schut, 1996). Researchers have noted that negative social relationships can be a major source of stress and pain (e.g., Kiecolt-Glaser, 1999; Seeman, 2001). Although early epidemiological studies focused mainly on whether people were socially connected, researchers soon realized that the "quality" of these relationships must also be taken into account. For example, marriage seems to be related to positive health and psychological outcomes only if the marriage is happy and nondistressed (e.g., Kiecolt-Glaser & Newton, 2001). In short, the data suggest that having social bonds and close relationships are necessary for health and well-being. However, there is also risk involved; if these relationships are filled with negative emotions and conflict, they are detrimental to health and well-being.

Appetitive and Aversive Processes in Relationships

As noted above, although relationships are often a source of pleasure and joy, they can also be a major source of stress. A great deal of research in the field of close relationships has focused on these negative processes in relationships; however, more recently, researchers have begun to investigate the independent effects of negative and positive processes in relationships (e.g., Kiecolt-Glaser & Newton, 2001; Reis & Gable, 2003; Uchino, Holt-Lunstad, Uno, & Flinders, 2001). One particularly useful framework for making the distinction between these positive and negative aspects of relationships is a focus on appetitive and aversive dimensions of motivation, which differentiates between moving "toward" rewarding and desired outcomes (appetitive processes) and moving "away" from punishing and undesired outcomes (aversive processes; e.g., Carver, 1996). The appetitive dimension regulates approach-oriented behavior (e.g., focusing on potentially rewarding stimuli), whereas the aversive dimension regulates avoidance-oriented behavior (e.g., focusing on potentially punishing stimuli; see Gable, 2006).

This focus on appetitive and aversive processes has a long history of inquiry across various domains, and recent work suggests that separate biological systems underlie the two processes (see Elliot & Covington, 2001). Specifically, research on the brain has found that individual differences in behavioral activation system (BAS) and behavioral inhibition system (BIS) scores (e.g., Gray, 1987) differentially predicted prefrontal cortex activity, such that participants with higher BAS showed more resting activity in the left prefrontal cortex and participants with higher BIS showed more resting activity in the right prefrontal cortex (Sutton & Davidson, 1997). Moreover, the appetitive and aversive systems are seen as largely independent, as shown by Gable, Reis, and Elliot (2003) in the domains of motivation, affect, personality, attitude formation, and more. The distinction between the two systems can also be usefully applied to the research on interpersonal relationships.

Aversive Processes in Relationships

Research that has focused on the presence or absence of aversive social relationship behaviors, such as anger, violence, and conflict, has played an extremely important role in shedding light on interpersonal relationships (e.g., Bradbury, Fincham, & Beach, 2000). Studies of videotaped interactions between partners have highlighted negative patterns, such as demand-withdrawal patterns, where criticism and defensiveness create a detrimental cycle of handling conflict in relationships (e.g., Christensen & Heavey, 1990). Gottman's (1998) program of research has highlighted several predictors of divorce, such as contempt, negative affect reciprocity, stonewalling, belligerence, and criticism. In fact, conflict and negative affect management in relationships have been thought to be two of the most important factors influencing relationship satisfaction and stability (Christensen & Walczynski, 1997; Gottman, Coan, Carrere, & Swanson, 1998).

In addition to examining the presence of negative processes in relationships (e.g., conflict, criticism), researchers have examined the absence of negatives (e.g., trust, security). Research on trust in relationships has emphasized the importance of predictability and dependability in relationships, and trust in couples has been associated with a number of important relationship outcomes (Rempel, Ross, & Holmes, 2001). A related construct in this literature is "felt security" (e.g., Holmes, 2002). Research has demonstrated that feeling secure in one's relationships helps protect against the threat of rejection and leads to feeling more loved and accepted by one's partner (e.g., Murray, 2005). The research on criticism, conflict, trust, security, and other processes has been invaluable for our understanding of relationships. However, the importance of appetitive processes in relationships should not be overlooked, and we review some of these appetitive processes next.

Appetitive Processes in Relationships

Positive Emotions and Relationships

The bulk of research on emotions has focused on negative emotions, such as sadness, anger, and fear (see Fredrickson, 1998). However, in recent years, theorists have begun to examine the impact of positive emotions. Fredrickson (1998), in her broaden-and-build model of positive emotions, proposed that positive emotions serve adaptive functions, including promoting prosocial behavior and motivating people to build social resources. Although the focus of positive emotions was initially "intra"-personal, such as how these emotions could increase our attention capacity (e.g., Fredrickson, 2001), researchers have also begun to tackle the interpersonal or relational nature of these emotions (e.g., Shiota, Campos, Keltner, & Hertenstein, 2004).

Importantly, positive and negative emotions are largely independent dimensions that should not just be thought of as opposite ends of a single pole (e.g., Watson, Clark, & Tellegen, 1988). Along these lines, Updegraff, Gable, and Taylor (2004) found that people differed in terms of the frequency and impact of positive emotions in their daily lives. Specifically, they found that people who were higher in approach-oriented motivation tended to experience more positive emotions daily and tended to base more of their day-to-day subjective well-being on their positive emotional experiences. These effects were separate from the impact of any negative emotions, which is consistent with research demonstrating that trait-level positive and negative affect loaded onto separate appetitive and aversive dimensions (e.g., Gable et al., 2003).

What might be the interpersonal consequences of focusing more on positive emotional experiences? Research has demonstrated that people who generally reported greater positive affect were better at social interactions and had interactions of higher quality, whereas negative affect did not predict either of these outcomes (Berry & Hansen, 1996). In addition, Berry, Willingham, and Thayer (2000) conducted a daily diary study on friendship dyads and found that high positive affect was related to feelings of closeness, whereas high negative affect was related to feelings of irritation and occurrences of conflict in the relationship. As noted above, ignoring the appetitive processes (in this case, positive affect) would mean that a great deal of information about relationships is lost.

Many positive emotions are inherently social in nature. When one experiences emotions such as gratitude, compassion, and love, there is almost always an interpersonal target of these emotions. Emotions such as joy may trigger play behavior that solidifies relationships (Fredrickson, 2001). Even pride can have interpersonal consequences as it may motivate people to tell close others about their achievement, which can strengthen interpersonal connections (Lewis, 1993). Studies have demonstrated that when people experience positive emotions together, such as amusement and excitement, these shared experiences can result in potentially long-lasting social bonds (see Fredrickson, 2001). Additionally, the positive emotion of gratitude is associated with more prosocial activity and more empathy for others (e.g., McCullough, Emmons, & Tsang, 2002). Other important positive emotions in relationships are love and desire. In the current volume, there are excellent chapters on the topics of gratitude (see chap. 41) and love (see chap. 42) to which we refer the reader.

Social Support and Capitalization

Researchers often posit that the associations among social ties and positive outcomes in health and well-being have a great deal to do with social support, which refers to the aid, assistance, and emotional support we receive from friends, family members, and others (e.g., Barrera, Sandler, & Ramsay, 1981). Several observational coding guides for behavioral responses to social support disclosures have been developed which shed more light on the actual interaction processes of couples (e.g., Cutrona & Suhr, 1992). Additionally, researchers have attempted to uncover what support behaviors are helpful under different circumstances (e.g., Cutrona & Russell, 1990). Social support in close relationships tends to involve a complicated interaction between individual differences (e.g., attachment style), contextual factors (e.g., mood, severity of the stressor), relationship factors (e.g., satisfaction), and the actual support that is provided (e.g., Lakey, McCabe, Fisicaro, & Drew, 1996).

The classic focus of social support research has been on the disclosure of negative and stressful events to others. A much newer addition to the social support literature is the idea of capitalization, which is the process of sharing positive events with others and gaining additional benefits from this disclosure (Gable, Reis, Impett, & Asher, 2004). Extending Langston's (1994) research on the positive consequences of sharing positive experiences, Gable and colleagues (2004) have provided evidence for the importance of considering these positive event disclosures. These researchers conducted several studies demonstrating that people derive additional benefits, such as increased daily positive affect and daily well-being, when they share positive events with other people. These increases in positive affect and well-being are significant even when controlling for the benefits produced by the positive event itself. Additionally, this research suggests that capitalization interactions provide an important opportunity for people in relationships to foster intimacy and closeness through supportive exchanges without the drawback of risking one's self esteem or self-worth, as one might do when seeking support for a negative event (e.g., Bolger, Zuckerman, & Kessler, 2000).

Capitalization is a very common occurrence; Gable and colleagues (2004) found that people report sharing positive events with others on approximately 80% of days out of a 10-day period. Thus, the way that people "respond" to these positive event disclosures in everyday life is an important new area of research. For example, the benefits of capitalization were greatest when the person hearing the news reacted actively and constructively (e.g., enthusiastic, genuine responses; Gable et al., 2004). To further examine these reactions to capitalization attempts, Gable, Gonzaga, and Strachman (2006) examined responses to positive event disclosures in the lab. As predicted, active and constructive responses were significantly related to positive post-interaction reports and to other relationship well-being measures. Finally, another line of research on the importance of positive events includes the research on savoring, which describes one's ability to focus on and attend to positive emotions and experiences (Bryant, 1989). More recent studies have randomly assigned people to positive reminiscence conditions, and results indicated that positive reminiscences lead to greater savoring and increased reports of happiness (e.g., Bryant, Smart, & King, 2005).

Intimacy and Responsiveness

Another body of research that has focused on appetitive processes in relationships is the literature on intimacy and perceived partner responsiveness (e.g., Reis & Patrick, 1996). Humans not only have a need to belong, but they are also highly motivated to seek out intimacy with close others (Reis & Shaver, 1988). Reis and Shaver's model of intimacy begins with a person's self-disclosure to a romantic partner. His or her partner then interprets this disclosure (through the filter of individual differences and contextual factors) and responds to the disclosure. Finally, the disclosing person interprets his or her partner's response (again, through the filter of factors such as goals, personality traits, and context), and the outcome may be "perceived partner responsiveness," or the feeling that one is understood, validated, and cared for by one's partner (Reis & Patrick, 1996).

Self-disclosure and responsiveness are thus central aspects of intimacy. Although much attention in the past has been given to self-disclosure, disclosure alone is not enough to create intimacy (Reis & Patrick, 1996). A number of studies have now outlined the importance of perceived responsiveness to the self (e.g., Reis, Clark, & Holmes, 2004), including its association to relationship satisfaction (e.g., Reis & Patrick, 1996) and felt security (e.g., Holmes, 2002). Laurenceau, Barrett, and Pietromonaco (1998) used an event-contingent diary design to examine the effects of disclosure and responsiveness on evaluations of intimacy. They found perceived partner responsiveness to be a strong mediator of the link between self-disclosure and intimacy. Similarly, one study by Manne and colleagues (2004) examined couples where one partner had cancer and found that perceived partner responsiveness mediated the positive association between self-disclosure and increases in intimacy. An important next step in the literature on intimacy and responsiveness may be to see how widely applicable this process is across various types of interpersonal interactions (e.g., when partners share personal goals with each other; Feeney, 2004).

Shared Novel Experiences

Another important appetitive process in relationships is self-expansion (e.g., Aron, Aron, Tudor, & Nelson, 1991), which refers to the process of including a close other in one's conception of the self. This self-expansion process can include taking in a close other's "resources, perspectives and characteristics" (Aron et al., 1991, p. 243). Work by Aron and colleagues (e.g., Aron, Norman, Aron, McKenna, & Heyman, 2000) has demonstrated that partners' participation in novel, arousing experiences together can increase relationship satisfaction, presumably because these experiences offer opportunities for continued expansion. The importance of considering appetitive processes in relationships is especially clear in this body of research—partners who are motivated to engage in fun and exciting activities together, such as outdoor sports and travel, also tend to have high levels of marital satisfaction (e.g., Hill, 1988).

Experimental studies have also demonstrated that creating a novel and physiologically arousing task that couples participate in together leads to increases in relationship satisfaction (Aron et al., 2000). Further investigation into this effect has suggested that high positive affect (and not decreased negative affect) might be the mediating factor between these novel tasks and increased relationship satisfaction (see Strong & Aron, 2006). Other studies have since extended some of these findings in married couples to other relationships. Fraley and Aron (2004) found that closeness between strangers was increased through a shared humorous experience. Continued research on the ways that couples keep their relationships fun and exciting may prove to be a very beneficial strategy for guarding against decreased satisfaction.

Future Directions

Biology and Interpersonal Relationships

Researchers have begun to explore the biological systems underlying appetitive and aversive social processes. For example, Panksepp has proposed that an underlying reward system in the brain is thought to "mediate specific behavioral sequences related to appetitive engagements with the world" (Panksepp, Knutson, & Burgdorf, 2002, p. 462). This "seeking system" for social rewards is proposed to be distinct from a separation-distress system. Additionally, further research on the brain using electroencephalograms (EEGs) has supported the idea that different parts of the brain are activated when humans are approaching rewarding stimuli versus when they are avoiding punishing stimuli (e.g., Pizzagalli, Sherwood, Henriques, & Davidson, 2005). Research on the biological basis of affiliative behavior in humans is growing as well.

The hormone oxytocin appears to reduce anxiety and increase one's willingness to trust others and engage in prosocial behavior (Bartz & Hollander, 2006). As researchers explore the links between interpersonal relationships and biology in greater detail, neuroscience may be a productive new avenue of research (e.g., Fisher, Aron, Mashek, Li, & Brown, 2002).

Positive Emotions and Health

As noted previously, positive emotions have been shown to have a number of beneficial consequences for intrapersonal and interpersonal well-being. One burgeoning area of research in the field of positive emotions is examining the link between positive emotions and health. Relatively few studies to date have tackled this question directly, although there is evidence that positive emotions and dispositional positive affect are related to better health. For example, Harker and Keltner (2001) found that women who showed more positive affect in their college yearbook photos also reported better emotional and physical health 30 years later. In another interesting study, Danner, Snowdon, and Friesen (2001) coded autobiographies from Catholic nuns written when the women were in their early twenties. These researchers found a significant relationship between high positive emotional content in the autobiographies of the women and increased longevity. Research on positive emotions and health would likely benefit from an increasing focus on interpersonal relationships. Social relationships may prove to be one of the pathways through which positive emotions influence health. For example, people who are higher on trait levels of positive affect and agreeableness tend to have better social relationships (Watson, Clark, McIntyre, & Hamaker, 1992), which may then lead to improved health and well-being.

Other Relationships

Our review of the positive psychology of relationships has tended to focus on romantic relationships and the adult pair bond. Of course, there are many fascinating areas of research that focus on other types of relationships, which we have not had space to go into great detail here. The literature on the parent-child relationship is also beginning to focus on the positive psychology of relationships. In the past, much of the research on parents and children has focused on the outcomes of the children, and when researchers examined the outcomes of the parents, they often focused on the stress caused by the transition to parenthood. In particular, having children is thought to cause a significant decline in marital quality (e.g., Schulz, Cowan, & Cowan, 2006). But what are the benefits of having children? More research is needed to examine the factors that create positive parent-child relationships and the factors that help ease the adjustment to parenting (e.g., Demo & Cox, 2000).

Friendship relationships are another area of research where positive psychology can have a significant impact. The research cited on social support and social networks highlights the importance of friendship to health and well-being. Although there has not been a great deal of scholarship concerning friendships in adulthood, the research to date does suggest that relationships with friends have a number of important implications for health and well-being (see Bagwell et al., 2005). Interventions targeted at helping the elderly improve their friendship networks have been shown to decrease loneliness and increase well-being (e.g., Stevens & van Tilburg, 2000). Additionally, recent studies have begun to examine the effect of giving support in close relationships. For example, Brown, Nesse, Vinokur, and Smith (2003) examined mortality status in older individuals over a 5-year time period, and they found that providing emotional support to one's spouse was related to reduced mortality. Having a friendship network also might provide people with multiple opportunities to provide support, which may have a number of beneficial effects.

Concluding Comments

By focusing on appetitive relationship processes, such as positive emotions, capitalization, perceived partner responsiveness, and novel experiences, researchers are beginning to get a more complete picture about what makes relationships work. As this review of future directions indicates, there are still many unanswered questions regarding appetitive processes in interpersonal relationships. As both the fields of positive psychology and close relationships advance, we hope that researchers will continue to examine how the presence of positives in relationships can affect relationship well-being as well as individual functioning.

Questions about the Future of the Topic

1. How do couples maintain appetitive processes over time?
2. In addition to interventions aimed at reducing negative behaviors in relationships, are interventions to increase positive behaviors effective?
3. Under which circumstances are appetitive and aversive processes most important for interpersonal relationships?

References

Aron, A., Aron, E. N„ Tudor, M., & Nelson, G. (1991). Close relationships as including other in the self. *Journal of Personality and Social Psychology, 60(2)*, 241–253.

Aron, A., Norman, C. C, Aron, E. N., McKenna, C, & Heyman, R. E. (2000). Couples' shared participation in novel and arousing activities and experienced relationship quality. *Journal of Personality and Social Psychology, 78(2)* 273–284.

Bagwell, C. L., Bender, S. E., Andreassi, C. L., Kinoshita, T. L. Montarello, S. A., & Muller, J. G. (2005). Friendship quality and perceived relationship changes predict psychosocial adjustment in early adulthood. *Journal of Social and Personal Relationships, 22(2)*, 235–254.

Barrera, M., Sandler, I. N., & Ramsay, T. B. (1981). Preliminary development of a scale of social support: Studies on college students. *American Journal of Community Psychology,* 5>(4), 435–447.

Bartz, J. A., & Hollander, E. (2006). The neuroscience of affiliation: Forging links between basic and clinical research on neuropeprides and social behavior. *Hormones and Behavior, 50(4)*, 518–528.

Baumeister, R. F., & Leary, M. R. (1995). The need to belong: Desire for interpersonal attachments as a fundamental human motivation. *Psychological Bulletin, 117(5)*, 497–529.

Berkman, L. F., & Syme, S. L. (1979). Social networks, host resistance and mortality: A nine-yeat follow-up of Alameda County residents. *American Journal of Epidemiology, 109,* 186–204.

Berry, D. S., & Hansen, J. S. (1996). Positive affect, negative affect, and social interaction. *Journal of Personality and Social Psychology, 71(4),* 796–809.

Berry, D. S„ Willingham, J. K., & Thayer, C. A. (2000). Affect and personality as ptedictors of conflict and closeness in young adults' friendships. *Journal of Research in Personality, 34(\),* 84–107.

Bolger, N., Zuckerman, A., & Kessler, R. C. (2000). Invisible support and adjustment to stress. *Journal of Personality and Social Psychology, 79(6),* 953–961.

Bradbury, T. N., Fincham, F. D., & Beach, S. R. H. (2000). Research on the nature and determinants of marital satisfaction: A decade in review. *Journal of Marriage and the Family, 62(4),* 964–980.

Brown, S. L., Nesse, R. M, Vinokur, A. D., & Smith, D. M. (2003). Providing social support may be more beneficial than receiving it: Results from a prospective study of mottality. *Psychological Science, 14(4),* 320–327.

Bryant, F. B. (1989). A four-factor model of perceived control: Avoiding, coping, obtaining, and savoring. *Journal of Personality, 57(4), 773–797.*

Bryant, F. B., Smart, C. M., & King, S. P. (2005). Using the past to enhance the present: Boosting happiness through positive reminiscence. *Journal of Happiness Studies, 6(3),* 227–260.

Carver, C. S. (1996). Emergent integration in contemporary personality psychology. *Journal of Research in Personality, 30,* 319–334.

Christensen, A., & Heavey, C. L. (1990). Gender and social structure in the demand/withdraw pattern of marital conflict. *Journal of Personality and Social Psychology,* 5.9(1), 73–81.

Christensen, A., & Walczynski, P. T. (1997). Conflict and satisfaction in couples. In R. J. Sternberg & M. Hojjat (Eds.), *Satisfaction in close relationships* (pp. 249–274). New York: Guilford.

Cutrona, C. E., & Russell, D. W. (1990). Type of social support and specific stress: Toward a theory of optimal matching. In B. R- Sarason, I. G. Sarason, & G. R. Pierce (Eds.), *Social support: An interactional view* (pp. 319–366). Oxford: Wiley.

Cutrona, C. E., & Suhr, J. A. (1992). Controllability of stressful events and satisfaction with spouse support behaviors. *Communication Research, 19(2),* 154–174.

Danner, D. D., Snowdon, D. A., & Friesen, W. V. (2001). Positive emotions in early life and longevity: Findings from the nun study. *Journal of Personality and Social Psychology, 80(5),* 804–813.

Demo, D. H., & Cox, M. J. (2000). Families with young children: A review of research in the 1990s. *Journal of Marriage and the Family, 62(4),* 876–895.

Diener, E., & Seligman, M. E. P. (2002). Very happy people. *Psychological Science, 13(1),* 81–84.

Elliot, A. J., & Covington, M. V. (2001). Approach and avoidance motivation. *Educational Psychology Review, 13(2),* 73–92.

Feeney, B. C. (2004). A secure base: Responsive support of goal strivings and exploration in adult intimate relationships. *Journal of Personality and Social Psychology, 87(5),* 631—648.

Fisher, H. E., Aron, A., Mashek, D., Li, H., & Brown, L. L. (2002). Defining the brain systems of lust, romantic attraction, and attachment. *Archives of Sexual Behavior, 31(5),* 413–419.

Fraley, B., & Aron, A. (2004). The effect of a shared humorous experience on closeness in initial encounters. *Personal Relationships,* 7*I*(1), 61–78.

Fredrickson, B. L. (1998). What good are positive emotions? *Review of General Psychology, 2(3),* 300–319.

Fredrickson, B. L. (2001). The role of positive emotions in positive psychology: The broaden-and-build theory of positive emotions. *American Psychologist, 56(3),* 218–226.

Gable, S. L. (2006). Approach and avoidance social motives and *goals. Journal of Personality, 74(1),* 175–222.

Gable, S. L., Gonzaga, G. C, & Strachman, A. (2006). Will you be there for me when things go right? Supportive responses to positive event disclosures. *Journal of Personality and Social Psychology, 91(5),* 904–917.

Gable, S. L., Reis, H. T., & Elliot, A. J. (2003). Evidence for bivariate systems: An empirical test of appetition and aversion across domains. *Journal of Research in Personality, 37(5),* 349–372.

Gable, S. L., Reis, H. T., Impett, E. A., & Asher, E. R. (2004). What do you do when things go right? The intrapersonal and interpersonal benefits of sharing positive events. *Journal of Personality and Social Psychology, 87(2),* 228–245.

Gottman, J. M. (1998). Psychology and the study of marital processes. *Annual Review of Psychology, 49,* 169–197.

Gottman, J. M., Coan, J., Carrere, S., & Swanson, C. (1998). Predicting marital happiness and stability from newlywed interactions. *Journal of Marriage and the Family, 60(1),* 5–22.

Gray, J. A. (1987). *The psychology of fear and stress* (2nd ed.). New York: Cambridge University Press.

Harker, L., & Keltner, D. (2001). Express ions of positive emotion in women's college yearbook pictures and their relationship to personality and fife outcomes across adulthood. *Journal of Personality and Social Psychology, 80(1),* 112–124.

Hill, M. S. (1988). Marital stability and spouses' shared time: A multidisciplinary hypothesis. *Journal of Family Issues, 9(A), 427–451.*

Holmes, J. G. (2002). Interpersonal expectations as the building blocks of social cognition: An interdependence theory perspective. *Personal Relationships, 9(1),* 1–26.

House, J. S., Landis, K. R., & Umberson, D. (1988). Social relationships and health. *Science, 241,* 540–545.

Kiecolt-Glaser, J. K. (1999). Stress, personal relationships, and immune function: Health implications. *Brain, Behavior and Immunity, 13(1),* 61–72.

Kiecolt-Glaser, J. K., & Newton, T. L. (2001). Marriage and health: His and hers. *Psychological Bulletin, 127(A),* 472–503.

Lakey, B., McCabe, K. M., Fisicaro, S., & Drew, J. B. (1996). Environmental and personal determinants of support perceptions: Three generalizability studies. *Journal of Personality and Social Psychology, 70(6),* 1270–1280.

Langston, C. A. (1994). Capitalizing on and coping with daily-life events: Expressive responses to positive events. *Journal of Personality and Social Psychology, 67(6),* 1112–1125.

Laurenceau, J., Barrett, L. F., *&C* Pietromonaco, P. R. (1998). Intimacy as an interpersonal process: The importance of self-disclosure, partner disclosure, and perceived partner responsiveness in interpersonal exchanges. *Journal of Personality and Social Psychology, 74(5),* 1238–1251.

Lewis, M. (1993). Self-conscious emotions; Embarassment, pride, shame, and guilt. In M. Lewis & J. M. Haviland (Eds.), *Handbook of emotions* (pp. 563–573). New York: Guilford.

Manne, S., Ostroff, J., Rini, C, Fox, K., Goldstein, L., & Grana, G. (2004). The interpersonal process model of intimacy: The role of self-disclosure, partner disclosure, and partner responsiveness in interactions between breast cancer patients and their partners. *Journal of Family Psychology, 18(4),* 589–599.

McCullough, M. E., Emmons, R. A., & Tsang, J. (2002). The grateful disposition: A conceptual and empirical topography. *Journal of Personality and Social Psychology, 82(1),* 112–127.

Murray, S. L. (2005). Regulating the risks of closeness: A relationship-specific sense of felt security. *Current Directions in Psychological Science, 14(2),* 74—78.

Panksepp, J., Knutson, B., & Burgdorf, J. (2002). The role of brain emotional systems in addictions: A neuro evolutionary perspective and new "self-report" animal model. *Addiction. Special Issue: Evolutionary Psychobiological Approaches to Addiction, 97(4),* 459–69.

Pizzagalli, D. A., Sherwood, R. J., Henriques, J. B., & Davidson, R. J. (2005). Frontal brain asymmetry and reward responsiveness. A source-localization study. *Psychological Science, 16(\0),* 805–813.

Reis, H. T., Clark, M. S., & Holmes, J. G. (2004). Perceived partner responsiveness as an organizing construct in the study of intimacy and closeness. In D. J. Mashek & A. P. Aron (Eds.), *Handbook of closeness and intimacy* (pp. 201–225). Mahwah, NJ: Lawrence Erlbaum.

Reis, H. T., & Gable, S. L. (2003). Toward a positive psychology of relationships. In C. L. M. Keyes & J. Haidt (Eds.), *Flourishing: Positive psychology and the life well-lived* (pp. 129–159). Washington, DC: American Psychological Association.

Reis, H. T., & Patrick, B. C. (1996). Attachment and intimacy: Component processes. In E. T. Higgins & A. W. Kruglanski (Eds.), *Social psychology: Handbook of basic principles* (pp. 523–563). New York: Guilford.

Reis, H. T., & Shaver, P. (1988). Intimacy as an interpersonal process. In S. Duck & D. F. Hay (Eds.), *Handbook of personal relationships: Theory, research and interventions (pp.* 367–389). Oxford: Wiley.

Rempd J. K., Ross, M, & Holmes, J. G. (2001). Trust and communicated attributions in close relationships. *Journal of Personality and Social Psychology, 81(1),* 57–64.

Rook, K. S. (1984). The negative side of social interaction: Impact on psychological well-being. *Journal of Personality and Social Psychology, 46(5),* 1097–1108.

Schulz, M. S., Cowan, C. P., & Cowan, P. A. (2006). Promoting healthy beginnings: A randomized controlled trial of a preventive intervention to preserve marital quality during the transition to parenthood. *Journal of Consulting and Clinical Psychology,* 74(1), 20–31.

Seeman, T. (2001). How do others get under our skin? Social relationships and health. In C. D. Ryff & B. H. Singer (Eds.), *Emotion, social relationships, and health* (pp. 189—210). New York: Oxford University Press.

Shiota, M. N., Campos, B., Keltner, D„ & Hertenstein, M. J. (2004). Positive emotion and the regulation of interpersonal relationships. In P. Philippot & R. S. Feldman (Eds.), *The regulation of emotion* (pp. 127–155). Mahwah, NJ: Lawrence Erlbaum.

Stevens, N., & van Tilburg, T. (2000). Stimulating friendship in later life: A strategy for reducing loneliness among older women. *Educational Gerontology. Special Issue: International research and practice, 26(* 1), 15–35.

Stroebe, W., Stroebe, M., Abakoumkin, G., & Schut, H. (1996). The role of loneliness and social support in adjustment to loss: A test of attachment versus stress theory. *Journal of Personality and Social Psychology, 70(G),* 1241–1249.

Strong, G., & Aron, A. (2006). The effect of shared participation in novel and challenging activities on experienced relationship quality: Is it mediated by high positive affect? In K. D. Vohs & E. J. Finkel (Eds.), *Self and relationships: Connecting intrapersonal and interpersonal processes* (pp. 342–359). New York: Guilford.

Sutton, S. K., & Davidson, R. J. (1997). Prefrontal brain asymmetry: A biological substrate of the behavioral approach and inhibition systems. *Psychological Science, 8(3),* 204–210.

Uchino, B. N., Cacioppo, J. T., & Kiecolt-Glaser, J. K. (1996). The relationship between social support and physiological processes: A review with emphasis on underlying mechanisms. and implications for health. *Psychological Bulletin, 119(3),* 488–531.

Uchino, B. N., Holt-Lunstad, J., Uno, D., & Flinders, J. B. (2001). Heterogeneity in the social networks of young and older adults: Prediction of mental health and cardiovascular reactivity during acute stress. *Journal of Behavioral Medicine, 24(4),* 361–382.

Updegraff, J. A., Gable, S. L., & Taylor, S. E. (2004). NX/hat makes experiences satisfying? The interaction of approach-avoidance motivations and emotions in well-being. *Journal of Personality and Social Psychology, 86(3),* 496–504.

Watson, D„ Clark, L. A., Mclntyre, C. W., & Hamaker, S. (1992). Affect, personality, and social activity. *Journal of Personality and Social Psychology, 63(6),* 1011–1025.

Watson, D., Clark, L. A., & Tellegen, A. (1988). Development and validation of brief measures of positive and negative affect: The PANAS *scales. Journal of Personality and Social Psychology, 54(6),* 1063–1070.

WORKING IT OUT: COMMUNICATION, CONFLICT, AND AGGRESSION

Top 10 Greatest "Hits"

Important Findings and Future Directions for Intimate Partner Violence Research

By Jennifer Langhinrichsen-Rohling
University of South Alabama

In this article, the author highlights her choice of the 10 most important recent findings from the intimate partner violence research literature, which include (a) the creation of the Conflict Tactics Scale; (b) the finding that violent acts are most often perpetrated by intimates; (c) a series of findings that indicate that women also engage in intimate partner violence; (d) the finding that intimate partner violence typically evolves out of relationship dissatisfaction; (e) the finding that there are different subtypes of domestically violent men; (f) physiological measures that have added to our knowledge of intimate partner violence; (g) the evolving intergenerational transmission of violence theory; (h) the finding that verbal abuse, neglect, and psychological abuse need to be studied alongside physical violence; (i) research on leaving abusive relationships that may inform policy about sheltering battered women; and (j) the finding that alcohol plays an important role in the production of intimate partner violence. In the conclusion, the author describes a dyadic cycle of violence that may characterize some abusive couples. She also argues for a multi-modal theory that links findings obtained from individual, relationship, intergenerational, gender-specific, and cultural perspectives.

Jennifer Langhinrichsen-Rohling, "Top 10 Greatest 'Hits': Important Findings and Future Directions for Intimate Partner Violence Research," from *Journal of Interpersonal Violence*, Vol. 20, No. 1; January 2005, Pp. 108–118.

Whenever possible, I have used catchy or lyrical titles for my research publications (e.g., "Breaking up is hard to do," or "What's love got to do with it?"). Hence, in response to this invitation, I have highlighted my choice of the "top 10" most important research findings or the "greatest hits" in the intimate partner violence field. Throughout, I emphasize what I consider to be important methodological innovations, and I intersperse ideas about future directions that may expand our ability to understand, prevent, and intervene with both perpetrators and victims of intimate partner violence.

GREATEST HIT NUMBER 1: HE GAVE US A TOOL TO LOOK BEHIND CLOSED DOORS

In 1979, Straus created a measure, the Conflict Tactics Scale (CTS), which lit fire to the domestic violence field. The CTS was revolutionary because it allowed researchers to quantitatively study events that had often been ignored culturally and typically took place in private. Through the construction of the CTS, Straus also highlighted that violence often occurs within the context of family conflict. The CTS format was behavioral and act specific, which aided our ability to make comparisons across samples and studies. The CTS directions were normalizing (i.e., "Spouses also use many different ways of trying to settle their differences. . . . Tell me how often you did each of these things in the past year"), which facilitated reporting of socially undesirable events. Moreover, CTS-generated data were startling, indicating that one in six marriages had included an incident of physical violence (e.g., Straus & Gelles, 1990). CTS-generated data were also controversial. For example, rates of intimate violence by women, as measured by act perpetration, have been shown to be as high as or higher than rates of intimate violence by men (e.g., Archer, 2000). Perhaps as a consequence, researchers have been encouraged to contextualize the measurement of intimate partner violence to ensure gender sensitivity (i.e., adding impact, fear, injury, and motivations). Last, in its first major revision, (CTS2; Straus, Hamby, Boney-McCoy, & Sugarman, 1996), occurrences of sexual aggression were included, highlighting that operational definitions of what constitutes violence are still being articulated (e.g., Schumacher, Slep, & Heyman, 2001). For example, current questions include, "Does victim designation require fear, self-labeling, and/or experiencing certain frequency and/or type of violence?"

GREATEST HIT NUMBER 2: THE BOOGEY MAN IS MOST LIKELY TO BE SOMEONE YOU KNOW

Meanwhile, various researchers have demonstrated that perpetrators of other types of violence (e.g., stalking; see Douglas & Dutton, 2001) are also more likely to be family members or intimates than strangers, just as has been found with intimate partner violence. So we must continue delineating how and with whom close relationships are initiated, established, and maintained over time. Dating violence and rape research and relationship break-up research are also vital, as are longitudinal studies, because certain premarriage events may link family-of-origin violence to family-of-procreation violence (e.g., Jackson, 1999).

GREATEST HIT NUMBER 3: LAY MYTHS ABOUT VIOLENCE ARE NOT ALWAYS CONFIRMED

Empirical research functions both to confirm and disconfirm prevailing social beliefs. One prevailing belief is that men are the violent batterers and women are the victims (Jacobson & Gottman, 1998). Findings supporting this belief include that women are more likely than men to be injured and to express fear in response to intimate partner violence (Cascardi, Langhinrichsen, & Vivian, 1992; Jacobson et al., 1994). However, contrary to what could be expected from the "women are the victims" perspective, data indicate that women's perpetration of violence is surprisingly frequent, perhaps more so than men's, and it is not always in self-defense. Moreover, typical motivations for women's physical aggression include anger/tension release and retaliation for a partner's past behavior—including emotional abuse (Hamberger & Lohr, 1997). Recently, using meta-analysis, Archer (2000) also demonstrated that women even initiate dating violence more frequently than do men. Likewise, wives in violent marriages are as verbally hostile and negative during conflict situations as are their husbands (e.g., Jacobson et al., 1994). Finally, bidirectional violence is perhaps the most common pattern for violent couples (Vivian & Langhinrichsen-Rohling, 1994). As a whole, these controversial results have raised the question of whether male violence against women should always be the primary and/or exclusive focus of empirical investigation. Instead, I believe that women's violence also needs to be studied systematically, contextually, and scientifically. Gender-sensitive theories that account for both confirming and disconfirming findings need to be developed and rigorously tested to advance the field honestly.

GREATEST HIT NUMBER 4: DISSATISFIED RELATIONSHIPS ARE BREEDING GROUNDS FOR VIOLENCE

Perhaps because of fear of blaming the victim or increasing a victim's danger, both personal and institutional reluctance has been shown toward studying intimate partner violence dyadically. Reluctance has also been shown toward accepting theoretical models that imply that modifying dyadic exchanges (e.g., by teaching nonviolent conflict resolution processes) might reduce the occurrence of intimate violence. However, studies such as the one conducted by Aldarondo and Sugarman (1996) with 772 participants followed during a 3-year time period indicate that not only is marital conflict highly associated with the initial occurrence of violence, but it also predicts continued wife assaults.

Consistent with a relationship focus, O'Leary, Heyman, and Neidig (1999) empirically considered the differential effectiveness of conjoint couples therapy versus gender-specific therapy for intimate partner violence. In this research, 37 volunteering couples who had experienced at least two acts of husband-to-wife violence were randomly assigned to one of the two treatments. Contrary to expectation based on feminist theory, O'Leary et al.'s results indicated that both treatments were equally effective for reducing violence. Furthermore, improvements in marital communication were obtained only for spouses in the conjoint couples treatment, suggesting that dyadic processes and violence can and should be treated simultaneously in some couples. Worth noting, however, were the high dropout rate from both treatments and the noteworthy lack of eliminating domestic violence after either treatment (75% of the husbands had perpetrated some violence by the 1-year follow-up), suggesting much room for enhancing treatment efficacy in the future.

GREATEST HIT NUMBER 5: NOT ALL BATTERERS ARE BAD TO THE BONE

However, there may be important sample characteristics to consider before any firm conclusions about treatment efficacy can be drawn (Bograd & Mederos, 1999). Specifically, the battering that sends women to a domestic violence shelter might be qualitatively different from the type of violence perpetrated by men in volunteering community couples (e.g., men in the O'Leary et al. 1999 study). Thus, it seems likely that a one-size-fits-all model of violence intervention will be unsuccessful—and may be dangerous.

In fact, one of the most important recent advances in the domestic violence literature has been to empirically identify subtypes of batterers that may differentially respond to treatment. For example, Holtzworth-Munroe and Stuart (1994) delineated three subtypes of batterers: (a) generally violent/antisocial, (b) dysphoric/borderline, and (c) family only. Generally violent/antisocial batterers may be best served by legal rather than psychological interventions. Family-only batterers may be best served by conjoint or relationship-oriented interventions. Dysphoric/borderline batterers may need a treatment sequence that includes both individual and relationship components. Other researchers believe that batterers with psychopathic tendencies may also warrant specific intervention components (e.g., Huss & Langhinrichsen-Rohling, 2000).

Regrettably, recent work has called into question the degree to which paraprofessionals can accurately make subtype judgments, perhaps because practitioners typically assess one batterer at a time rather than in large groups that can be treated statistically

(Langhinrichsen-Rohling, Huss, & Ramsey, 2000). Thus, I believe the next decade must include research on how clinicians can reliably and validly determine batterer subtypes. Furthermore, we need to know if treatment efficacy can be enhanced if treatment modality is matched to batterer subtype. Researchers should also determine if sequential treatment (e.g., alcohol treatment, then individual batterer treatment, then couple treatment) can enhance our treatment success (Trute, 1998), which according to Babcock, Green, and Robie's (2004) recent meta-analysis have only a small effect size. Consequently, it is premature to mandate a particular type of treatment for all domestically violent perpetrators. Instead, researchers need to enhance treatment effectiveness with new strategies (e.g., motivational interviewing). New strategies will need community and institutional support for their development, implementation, and evaluation.

GREATEST HIT NUMBER 6: HEART RATE OFFERS CLUES TO INTERNAL PROCESSES DURING CONFLICT

Another recent methodological innovation within the intimate partner violence field has been to measure physiology, facial affect, and verbal exchanges concurrently as violent and nonviolent couples are arguing (e.g., Gottman et al., 1995), thus providing a rich multimodal context in which to understand intimate partner conflict. Use of physiological measures has led to perhaps the best-known sub typing scheme: the cobra (heart rate decelerators) and the pit-bull (heart rate accelerators) (Jacobson & Gottman, 1998).

In the past, microanalytic coding schemes were almost universally used as the sole assessment of couple interactions. In another advance, researchers have recently demonstrated the utility of coding interactions at multiple levels. For example, Vivian and colleagues have coded interactions between spouses both thematically and micro-analytically (e.g., Vivian, Langhinrichsen Rohling, & Heyman, in press). For some violent men, themes of engulfment, abandonment, and lack of power are central (e.g., Anglin & Holtzworth-Munroe, 1997). Thus, methodologically, I think continued advancements will involve collecting simultaneous and online indices of brain activity (e.g., evoked response potentials) and physiology in violent versus nonviolent partners while they are in conflict and then subjecting these data to a multilevel analysis.

GREATEST HIT NUMBER 7: THE INTERGENERATIONAL TRANSMISSION OF VIOLENCE THEORY MORPHS

Efforts to predict which individuals will be violent in their intimate relationships have included early childhood, personality, and relationship variables (e.g., O'Leary, Malone,

& Tyree, 1994). Consistently, clinicians and researchers have noted that many perpetrators had themselves been childhood victims of violence. This pattern became known as the intergenerational transmission of violence theory. Empirically, however, researchers have also gathered contrary data that showed that although there was a significant transmission effect, more individuals who were victims did not subsequently become perpetrators than did (Widom, 1989). This has led to ongoing efforts to better understand the nature and specificity of the transmission process (i.e., the effect of perpetrator and victim gender; age at victimization; frequency, severity, and type of abuse experienced). Continuing this line of inquiry, my colleagues and I have begun to delineate semantic mechanisms that might underlie the transmission process by using multidimensional scaling techniques (Langhinrichsen-Rohling, Hankla, & Dostal, 2004). This research indicates that the pathway from verbal abuse to physical violence is likely to be a focal point in understanding intergenerational violence transmission.

GREATEST HIT NUMBER 8: STICKS AND STONES MAY BREAK MY BONES, BUT WORDS REALLY HURT ME

Concurrently, other researchers have also demonstrated that psychological or verbal abuse needs to be elevated to a critical variable in the domestic violence field because it appears to have as great, if not greater, negative impact on victims than does physical violence (O'Leary, 1999). Moreover, psychological abuse occurring at 18 months of marriage has been shown to predict physical aggression in the marriage 1 year later (O'Leary et al., 1994). More recently, emotional neglect has also been shown to play an independent and important role in terms of its long-term impact on victims (Bevan & Higgins, 2002). Future work is likely to demonstrate that these types of abuse are particularly devastating to both child and adult victims, perhaps because they interfere with the development of self-esteem, self-acceptance, and/or emotional regulation.

GREATEST HIT NUMBER 9: LEAVING ABUSIVE RELATIONSHIPS IS ROUGH STUFF

In 1993, Barnett and LaViolette published a book titled *It Could Happen to Anyone: Why Battered Women Stay*. Answering this question is a central concern for many involved with intimate partner victims. Surprisingly, the evidence from community samples suggests that one of the main reasons that physically victimized married women give for staying is love—rather than fear or obstacles for leaving such as money or children (Kearney, 2001; Langhinrichsen-Rohling et al., 1998). However, safety concerns may also be paramount, in that leaving may be a particularly dangerous time because of escalating violence and stalking (Langhinrichsen-Rohling, Palarea, Cohen, & Rohling, 2000). In a review of this issue by Holtzworth-Munroe and colleagues (1997), two key points were made. First, most battered women do eventually leave violent relationships. Second, it is probably a mixture of safety and financial concerns, in conjunction with relationship commitment, that drives this decision. Efforts to predict which women will benefit most from being sheltered or encouraged to leave their partner immediately are needed. Furthermore, in terms of gender parity, no known research has focused on why unilaterally abused men stay in their violent relationships, which may shed additional light on the leaving process.

GREATEST HIT NUMBER 10: "HEY, BARTENDER"

Another reason that some battered women fail to leave their abusive relationship is that they may initially blame their partner's violence on transient reasons such as his drinking behavior (Holtzworth-Munroe, Smutzler, & Sandin, 1997). Consistent with this reasoning, many researchers have documented that a large proportion of domestically violent events do involve drinking and/or alcohol intoxication (e.g., Quigley & Leonard, 2000). Three models for the association between alcohol and violence have been proposed: (a) the spurious model, (b) the indirect effects model, and (c) the proximal effects model. In a groundbreaking study by Fals-Stewart (2003), the likelihood of physical aggression occurring on days of alcohol consumption was tracked for 15 months by men entering a domestic violence treatment program and by domestically violent men entering an alcohol treatment program. Data clearly supported the proximal effects model (i.e., alcohol consumption facilitates violence perhaps through its effects on cognitive processing); the odds of physical aggression were 8 times higher on drinking days for men from the domestic violence treatment program and 11 times higher on drinking days for domestically violent men in the alcohol treatment program. Thus, societal support of alcohol consumption may interfere with the efficacy of intimate partner violence prevention and/or intervention programs.

THE FINALE: ALL TOGETHER NOW?

So given this list of top 10 hits, where do we, as a field, go from here? Overall, I think we need to accept the finding that women can, at times, be violent and/or abusive. In current culture, many men (and women) learn to treat women's violence as laughable or inconsequential, even if it is quite serious. For most men, expressing fear toward or even concern or dismay about female violence is not an option. Men also receive conflicting messages about how to respond to women's violence. On one hand, they are told they can never hit women, and yet they simultaneously receive the message that if they are hit by someone, they must hit back (and beat them) or they are not "real men" (a proretaliation stance). Some of these cultural messages (Markowitz, 2001) may underlie what I am calling the "dyadic cycle of violence." In one version of this cycle, during the dating relationship, the woman initiates violence (usually of a minor nature) but does not view it as serious— although she is annoyed with the man prior to her perpetration. The man at first typically laughs it off. However, this response makes continued violence on her part more likely because it both trivializes her annoyance and legitimizes her impulsive aggression. Over time, however, the man's masculinity feels threatened if he does not respond in kind, particularly if her violence gets more frequent or severe—or her annoyance moves to anger and belittlement. His subsequent violent responses are more intense then hers, often involving more severe acts, and they are more likely to injure because of his size. He is going to "win," show her, and put an end to her attacking him. Under this scenario, however, this man may have some trouble taking full responsibility for his perpetration because, with some legitimacy, he can claim that she started it. Conversely, this woman might have more trouble leaving this relationship, perhaps out of some perhaps legitimate concern that she played a role in her victimization. I further assert that this dyadic cycle of violence is most likely to occur in retaliatory cultures and in cultures that view women's violence as funny or inconsequential. With this in mind, future research that links individual, relationship, intergenerational, and cultural theories about both men's and women's violence will be essential.

REFERENCES

Aldarondo, E., & Sugarman, D. B. (1996). Risk marker analysis of the cessation and persistence of wife assault. *Journal of Consulting and Clinical Psychology, 64*, 1010–1019.

Anglin, K., & Holtzworth-Munroe, A. (1997). Comparing the responses of martially violent and nonviolent spouses to problematic marital and nonmarital situations: Are the skill deficits of physically aggressive husbands and wives global? *Journal of Family Psychology, 11*, 301–313.

Archer, J. (2000). Sex differences in aggression between heterosexual partners: A meta-analytic review. *Psychological Bulletin, 126*, 651–680.

Babcock, J. C., Green, C. E., & Robie, C. (2004). Does batterers' treatment work? A meta analytic review ofdomestic violence treatment.*Clinical Psychology Review, 23*, 1023–1053.

Barnett,O. W.,& LaViolette, A. D. (1993).*It could happen to anyone: Why battered women stay.* Newbury Park: Sage.

Bevan, E., & Higgins, D. J. (2002). Is domestic violence learned? The contribution of five forms of child maltreatmentto men's violence and adjustment.*Journal of Family Violence, 17*, 223–245.

Bograd, M., & Mederos, F. (1999). Battering and couples therapy: Universal screening and selection of treatment modality. *Journal of Marriage and Family Therapy, 25*, 291–312.

Cascardi, M., Langhinrichsen, J., & Vivian, D. (1992). Marital aggression: Impact, injury, and health correlates for husbands and wives. *Archives of Internal Medicine, 152*, 1178–1184.

Douglas, K. S., & Dutton, D. G. (2001). Assessing the link between stalking and domestic violence. *Aggression and Violent Behavior, 6*, 519–546.

Fals-Stewart, W. (2003). The occurrence of partner physical aggression on days of alcohol consumption:A longitudinaldiary study. *Journal of Consulting and Clinical Psychology, 71*, 41–52.

Gottman, J. M., Jacobson, N. S., Rushe, R. H., Shortt, J. W., Babcock, J. C., LaTailade, J. J., et al. (1995). The relationship between heart rate reactivity, emotionally aggressive behavior, and general violence in batterers. *Journal of Family Psychology, 9*, 227–248.

Hamberger, L. K., & Lohr, J. M. (1997). An empirical classification of motivations for domestic violence. *Violence Against Women, 3*, 401–423.

Holtzworth-Munroe, A., Smutzler, N., & Sandin, E. (1997). A brief review of the literature on husband violence. *Aggression and Violent Behavior, 2*, 179–213.

Holtzworth-Munroe, A., & Stuart, G. L. (1994). Typologies of male batterers: Three subtypes and the differences among them. *Psychological Bulletin, 116*, 476–497.

Huss, M. T., & Langhinrichsen-Rohling, J. (2000). Identification of the psychopathic batterer: The clinical, legal, and policy implications. *Aggression and Violent Behavior, 5*, 403–422.

Jackson, S. M. (1999). Issues in the dating violence research: A review of the literature. *Aggression and Violent Behavior, 4*, 233–247.

Jacobson, N. S., & Gottman, J. M. (1998). *When men batter women: New insights into ending abusive relationships.* New York: Simon & Schuster.

Jacobson, N. S., Gottman, J. M., Waltz, J., Rushe, R., Babcock, J., & Holtzworth-Munroe, A. (1994). Affect, verbal content, and psychophysiology and the argument of couples with a violent husband. *Journal of Counseling and Clinical Psychology, 62*, 982–988.

Kearney, M. H. (2001). Enduring love: A grounded formal theory of women's experience of domestic violence. *Research in Nursing and Health, 24*, 270–282.

Langhinrichsen-Rohling, J., Hankla, M., & Dostal, C. (2004). Semantic networks of individuals from violent versus nonviolent families. *Journal of Family Violence, 19*, 139–151.

Langhinrichsen-Rohling, J., Huss, M. T., & Ramsey, S. (2000). The clinical utility of batterer typologies: A direct comparison of two typology strategies. *Journal of Family Violence, 15*, 37–53.

Langhinrichsen-Rohling, J., Palarea, R. E., Cohen, J., & Rohling, M. L. (2000). Breaking up is hard to do: Unwanted pursuit behaviors following the dissolution of a romantic relationship. *Violence and Victims, 15*, 1–17.

Langhinrichsen-Rohling, J., Schlee, K., Monson, C., Ehrensaft, M., & Heyman, R. (1998). What's love got to do with it? Perceptions of marital positivity in H-to-W aggressive, distressed, and happy marriages. *Journal of Family Violence, 13*, 197–212.

Markowitz, F. E. (2001). Attitudes and family violence: Linking intergenerational and cultural theories. *Journal of Family Violence, 16*, 205–218.

O'Leary, K. D. (1999). Psychological abuse: A variable deserving critical attention in domestic violence. *Violence and Victims, 14*, 1–21.

O'Leary, K. D., Heyman, R. E., & Neidig, P. H. (1999). Treatment of wife abuse: A comparison of gender-specific and conjoint approaches. *Behavior Therapy, 30*, 475–505.

O'Leary, K. D., Malone, J., & Tyree, A. (1994). Physical aggression in early marriage: Pre-relationship and relationship effects. *Journal of Consulting and Clinical Psychology, 62*, 594–602.

Quigley, B. M., & Leonard, K. E. (2000). Alcohol, drugs, and violence. In V. B. Van Hasselt & M. Hersen (Eds.), *Aggression and violence: An introductory text* (pp. 259–283). Boston: Allyn & Bacon.

Schumacher, J. A., Slep, A. M. S., & Heyman,R. E. (2001). Risk factors for male-to-female partner psychological abuse. *Aggression and Violent Behavior, 6*, 255–268.

Straus, M. A. (1979). Measuring intrafamily conflict and violence: The Conflict Tactics (CT) Scales. *Journal of Marriage and the Family, 41*, 75–88.

Straus, M. A., & Gelles, R. J. (1990). *Physical violence in American families: Risk factors and adaptations to violence in 8,145 families.* New Brunswick, NJ: Transaction.

Straus,M.A., Hamby,S.L., Boney-McCoy, S.,& Sugarman, D.B.(1996).The Revised Conflict Tactics Scales (CTS2). *Journal of Family Issues, 17*, 283–316.

Trute,B.(1998).Going beyond gender-specific treatments in wife battering: Pro-feminist couple and family therapy. *Aggression and Violent Behavior, 3*, 1–15.

Vivian, D., & Langhinrichsen-Rohling, J. (1994). Are bidirectionally violent couples mutually victimized? A gender sensitive comparison. *Violence and Victims, 9*, 107–124.

Vivian, D., Langhinrichsen-Rohling, J., & Heyman, R. E. (in press). The thematic coding of dyadic interactions (TCDI): Observing the context of couple conflict. In P. Kerig & D. Baucom (Eds.),*Couple observational coding systems.* Hillsdale, NJ: Lawrence Erlbaum.

Widom, C. S.(1989). Does violence beget violence? A critical examination of the literature. *Psychological Bulletin, 106*, 3–28.

Jennifer Langhinrichsen-Rohling obtained her Ph.D. from the University of Oregon in 1990. She also completed a 2-year, National Institute of Mental Health postdoctoral fellowship on marital violence at the State University of New York at Stony Brook. Her research areas include gender and marital violence, the prevention of violence in at-risk adolescents, the intergenerational transmission of violence, and stalking. She has authored more than 50 published articles and has been a principal investigator or co-investigator on a number of federally funded grants. She is currently a psychology professor at the University of South Alabama. She is also a licensed clinical psychologist.

Payback

The parameters of revenge in romantic relationships

By Susan D. Boon, Vicki L. Deveau, and Alishia M. Alibhai
University of Calgary, Canada

ABSTRACT

This investigation explored the provocations that spark intimates' desires for revenge, the kinds of vengeful responses they enact, and the motives that underlie decisions to retaliate. Eighty-five undergraduates were interviewed about incidents in which they "got even" with a current or former romantic partner. Both provocations and revenge responses predominately involved relationship rules violations, and most revenge responses were mild to moderate in severity and mundane in nature. In addition, most participants attributed their decisions to retaliate to the desire to bring about desired change in their partners (e.g., suffering, correction, or empathy), to redress their own unpleasant feelings, or to rectify injustice. Implications for research on revenge in romantic relationships are discussed.

KEY WORDS: dating relationships • provocations • responses to provocations • revenge acts • revenge motives • romantic partners • romantic revenge • wrongdoing

Susan D. Boon, Vicki L. Deveau, Alishia M. Alibhai, "Payback: The Parameters of Revenge in Romantic Relationships," from *Journal of Social and Personal Relationships*, Vol. 26, No. 6–7; September/November 2009 , Pp. 747–768.

On 13 September 2006 the London *Times* reported a story of a woman who sank her ex-husband's yacht in retaliation for divorcing her (Hoyle, 2006). That same year, a woman in New York City was charged with kidnapping and assault after arranging to have an ex-lover abducted and branded with the letter "R" because he failed to contact her after they had sex several years previously (Hamilton, White, & Bulliet, 2006). Such news stories demonstrate that people do not always initially respond to interpersonal offenses by forgiving the transgressor. Indeed, sometimes they respond by taking revenge, that is, by repaying harm with harm (Stuckless & Goranson, 1992). The purpose of the present study was to investigate the parameters (i.e., notable characteristics) of revenge as a response to wrongdoing in romantic relationships. In particular, we examined the kinds of negative events that precipitate acts of revenge among intimates, the kinds of actions intimates enact in response to such provocations, and the motives that impel them to retaliate when they believe they have been wronged. Our participants' stories about their acts of revenge may never make the front page of a newspaper but they have important implications for understanding relationship stability and satisfaction.

Revenge in romantic relationships

Relationship scholars have generally avoided the topic of revenge, despite the obvious importance of understanding the types of events that prompt retaliatory acts and how these responses might influence the quality or course of the affected relationships. Admittedly, a considerable body of research has examined behaviors and events that might serve as provocations (e.g., predicaments and relational transgressions; see Metts & Cupach, 2007). Research on relational accommodation has also explored, in a general sense, partners' willingness and inclination to respond to provocations in constructive versus destructive ways (Rusbult, Verette, Whitney, Slovik, & Lipkus, 1991). In addition, studies of jealousy have identified a number of revenge-type behaviors (e.g., the silent treatment, attempting to make a partner jealous) that jealous partners may enact to restore equity in their relationships (e.g., Guerrero & Andersen, 1998). Moreover, revenge is identified as a destructive communicative response to hurtful events (Bachman & Guerrero, 2006). However, despite these related areas of scholarship, very little research has aimed directly at understanding revenge in romantic relationships (for exceptions, see, Yoshimura, 2002, 2004) and the motives that generate such responses.

In contrast to the dearth of relational revenge research, the study of revenge in the workplace is fairly well established. Indeed, the workplace literature offers the richest descriptive base on when, and under what circumstances, people take revenge. For example, organizational researchers have examined the types of events that spark employees' desires for revenge (Bies & Tripp, 1996), the behaviors designed to exact revenge against co-workers (Bies & Tripp, 1996; Skarlicki & Folger, 1997; Tripp & Bies, 1997), the functional and dysfunctional consequences of revenge in a workplace setting (Skarlicki & Folger, 1997; Tripp & Bies, 1997), and the reasons employees cite for foregoing retaliation (Tripp & Bies, 1997).

There are ample grounds, however, for assuming that romantic revenge may differ (both in provocation and enactment) from workplace revenge. For example, in contrast to most workplace relationships, romantic relationships are *communal* in nature. To a much greater extent than among individuals in organizations, partners in romantic relationships are motivated to meet each other's needs and to protect each other's welfare. Moreover, norms that govern exchanges in romantic relationships tend to focus less on immediate reciprocity and "tit for tat" notions of fairness or equality than on ensuring the others' needs have been met (Clark & Mills, 1979). Romantic relationships also tend to be *voluntary* whereas workplace relationships tend to be ascribed. In Western societies, the freedom to choose co-workers is typically much more constrained when compared with the freedom to select romantic partners. Finally, romantic relationships are *attachment relationships* that fulfill important needs for emotional comfort and security (Shaver & Mikulincer, 2006). Although workplace relationships may also serve as attachment relationships, in most cases it is unlikely that they would rival romantic relationships in their importance in this regard. Given these important and varied differences between romantic and workplace relationships, romantic revenge deserves independent investigation.

Romantic relationships are one of the most important and enduring forms of adult relationships and the source of many of life's greatest joys. At the same time, problems arising from romantic relationships are among the most common reasons people seek psychological counseling (Pinsker, Nepps, Redford, & Winston, 1985) and can pose substantial threats to health and wellbeing (Kiecolt-Glaser & Newton, 2001). It is therefore important to investigate relational behaviors—such as revenge—which have significant potential to weaken or damage bonds between intimates. A strong descriptive base of knowledge concerning the parameters of those situations in which partners seek "an eye for an eye" would add considerably to our understanding of the means by which intimates deal with perceived wrongdoing in their relationships and lay the foundation for further research aimed at exploring questions of interest to researchers, counselors, and the general public. Answers to such questions would prove valuable to scholars seeking to study the processes by which partners decide how they will respond to perceived injury or offense, counselors treating couples in the aftermath of an act of revenge, and intimates trying to come to terms with their partners' perceived provocations.

The "when," "how," and "why" of getting even in romantic relationships

Despite the dearth of research on revenge per se in the relationships literature, the broader revenge literature provides direction for the generation of categories for purposes of coding data. For example, Bies, Tripp, and Kramer's (1997) analysis of workplace revenge suggests that revenge in organizations occurs in response to one of two main types of injury or offense: damage to the individual's sense of civic order (e.g., violations of an organization's formal rule structures, norms, or prevailing codes of ethics) and derogation of the individual's power, status, or identity (e.g., interpersonal attacks that undermine employees' status or power in the organization, that defame their reputations within their organizational networks, or which insult the individual or his or her collective). Goals oriented toward eliminating injustice and restoring the balance of power are also common among theoretical treatments of revenge motives (Miller & Vidmar, 1981; Solomon, 1994), suggesting that infringements of accepted rules or norms and acts that diminish an individual's relative power figure prominently among the main classes of events perceived as provocations. In addition, scholars (e.g., Baumeister, 1997; Frijda, 1994) echo Bies et al.'s claim that damage to an individual's prestige or self-esteem may play a central role in precipitating acts of revenge. We thus coded for both types of provocations in the present study (i.e., violation of norms and threat to the self).

Perhaps because they have not generally focused on revenge between intimates, however, scholars have not yet considered the possibility that, in a relationship context, affronts to the identity or social reputation of an individual's relationship may stimulate desires for vengeance. As research demonstrates that partners' social identities may derive in part from their membership in a couple (Agnew, Van Lange, Rusbult, & Langston, 1998), we examined this possibility in the present study, as well. Thus, in addition to coding for provocations involving violations of relationship rules and acts that threaten an individual's power, self-esteem, or social reputation, we also coded for provocations involving threats to the identities and social reputations of their relationships. In sum, the three superordinate categories that guided the coding process were: Violations of Relationship Rules, Affronts to the Relationship, and Threats to the Self.

Existing research (Bies & Tripp, 1996; Yoshimura, 2002, 2004) further suggests that there is at least as much variety in the ways people exact revenge as there is in the kinds of events that precipitate desires for revenge. For example, Yoshimura (2002, 2004) identified no fewer than 15 categories of revenge behaviors in his studies of revenge in romantic relationships. To simplify coding and to facilitate comparisons across provocations and responses in the present study (i.e., to determine if, generally speaking, the same classes of behavior that elicit desires for revenge also serve as the means for exacting reprisal), however, we applied the same three super-ordinate categories to the coding of revenge responses as to precipitating events rather than use Yoshimura's more extensive category system for revenge behaviors.

Finally, the literature contends that acts of revenge serve a diverse array of underlying goals and purposes. Specifically, retributive responses to perceived offense or injury have been attributed to desires to eliminate injustice (Bies et al., 1997; Miller & Vidmar,

1981; Solomon, 1994), restore a threatened or damaged self-image or sense of self-esteem (Baumeister, 1997; Bies et al., 1997; Frijda, 1994), make the harm-doer suffer (Baumeister, 1997; Frijda, 1994), equalize power (Bies et al., 1997; Crombag, Rassin, & Horselenberg, 2003; Frijda, 1994), deter future acts of harm (Crombag et al., 2003; Frijda, 1994), punish the harm-doer (Frijda, 1994; Miller & Vidmar, 1981; Yoshimura, 2007), escape pain (Frijda, 1994), teach the harm-doer a lesson (Baumeister, 1997), and balance gains and losses (Frijda, 1994). We also examined the possibility that participants might explain their vengeful responses by promoting the view that they had engaged in revenge for constructive, pro-relationship—possibly even prosocial—reasons (e.g., to restore, maintain, or enhance their relationships, or to benefit others). To the extent that societal attitudes condemn acts of revenge as petty, unethical, or morally repugnant (e.g.,Alibhai, Boon, & Deveau, 2008; Crombag et al., 2003; Uniacke, 2000), we thought participants might feel pressured to justify their retaliatory actions in ways that suggest these actions had achieved good for others beyond themselves.

In sum, we explore the following three research questions in this article:

- RQ1: What events or actions precipitate acts of revenge that occur between current or former romantic partners?
- RQ2: What kinds of behaviors do intimates enact to respond to such provocations?
- RQ3: How do individuals explain their decisions to take revenge following a provocation and do these explanations include motives intended to benefit their relationships or others more broadly?

Method

Participants

Ninety-six undergraduate psychology students (50 women, 46 men) responded to an ad on the Department of Psychology's research website seeking participants for a study on getting even in romantic relationships. Only individuals with past experience in a romantic relationship were eligible to participate. Participants received partial course credit for their time.

Six individuals attended the laboratory session but did not participate in the interview because they could not recall an instance in which they had gotten even with a romantic partner. We excluded the data for an additional five individuals from analysis because they failed to follow instructions (n = 4) or due to experimenter error (n = 1). The remaining 85 participants (43 women, 42 men) ranged in age from 18 to 42 (M = 22.60, SD = 4.24) and were primarily White (55.3%) or Asian (31.8%). Most (75.3%) were romantically involved at the time of the study, although only 37.6% were currently involved with the partners who provoked them in the episodes recalled in their interviews. The mean length of the relationships in which participants' revenge episodes occurred was 26.79 months (SD = 31.94).

Procedure

Using a methodology adapted from Tripp and Bies (1997), we randomly assigned participants to recall an instance in which they got even with a romantic partner and thought getting even was good (revenge-good), an instance in which they got even with a romantic partner and thought getting even was bad (revenge-bad), or an instance in which they wanted to get even with a romantic partner but elected not to do so (no revenge). As this experimental manipulation was designed for purposes beyond the present analysis, our discussion here focuses almost exclusively on the results for participants who took revenge (n = 58). However, because all participants described episodes in which they had been provoked, we included the data for no revenge participants (n = 27) in our analysis of the provocations.

Upon participants' arrival at the laboratory, the interviewer (the second author) reminded participants of the purpose of the study and encouraged them to be as open and honest as possible in their disclosures. She then provided them with additional instructions that specified the type of episode they were to recall for the interview:

> Please tell me of a specific time when you wanted to get even with a romantic partner and believed then or believe now that it was good (bad) to get even. If you can think of more than one incident, please choose the episode that was the most significant or memorable to you.

In the no revenge condition, the first sentence read, "Please tell me of a specific time when you wanted to get even with a romantic partner but chose not to."

Following assignment to instruction sets, the interviewer asked participants whether they needed time to identify a relevant revenge episode for discussion during the interview. If the participant answered in the affirmative, the interviewer left the laboratory for several minutes. As indicated previously, even with time for reflection, six participants could not recall an event. These participants were thanked for their time, awarded their course credit, and dismissed.

The interview proceeded in two phases. In the first, unstructured phase, the interviewer asked participants to tell their stories about getting even. The interviewer engaged in minimal prompting and questioning during this initial phase. In the second phase, the interviewer asked participants a series of specific questions designed to flesh out the details provided in the first, unstructured phase and, where necessary, to solicit those details that participants might have failed to divulge in their initial accounts. Interviews were audiotaped and later transcribed. Once the interview was finished, participants completed a brief questionnaire about the revenge episode they had discussed in the interview. The questionnaire data are not relevant to the purposes of this paper and are not discussed further.

We deliberately structured the recall instructions and interview questions to avoid the term "revenge," using instead the terms "repay harm with harm," "get even," and "get back." We were concerned that the term revenge might have negative connotations (perhaps especially given our focus on revenge in romantic relationships) which could heighten participants' concerns about the social desirability of their past actions and motives and lead them to edit their responses. In actuality, relatively few participants (n = 17 or 20%) spontaneously used the word revenge in their interviews (and one only used it to deny that her actions constituted revenge). Thus, whereas participants appeared reasonably comfortable admitting that they had "gotten even with" or "gotten back at" their partners, few described their behavior as revenge. Although other explanations are possible, this suggests that most participants did not perceive their actions as sufficiently severe to warrant that label or that they were uncomfortable acknowledging that it applied to their actions. In either case, it supports our decision to use other terms.

Coding

Three independent coders (an undergraduate student and the second and third authors) coded each interview. Preliminary examination of the transcripts indicated that the full richness and complexity of participants' accounts could not be captured unless coders were permitted to assign multiple codes to a given passage of text as, in some instances, failing to do so would result in loss of detail/depth. In the vast majority of cases, coders were able to classify content into one or more pre-determined categories generated from our literature review. However, a small number of novel categories were developed based on themes that emerged during coding.

We began with three super ordinate categories to code both precipitating events and revenge responses:"Violations of Relationship Rules", "Threats to Self" (which includes threats to an individual's self-esteem, social reputation, status, or public self-image, as well as acts that diminish the individual's power in relation to the partner), and "Affronts to the Relationship" (which includes acts that impugn the identity or the social reputation of the relationship with the partner).These categories roughly correspond to Bies et al.'s (1997) widely recognized typology (based on an inductive analysis of interviews with MBA students about acts of revenge they had committed in the workplace) with appropriate modifications reflecting the romantic relationship context.

First, studies of hurtful events, predicaments, and transgressions provided ample justification for construing violations of (often implicit) relationship rules, norms, and expected codes of relational conduct, or "Violations of Relationship Rules," as the romantic relationship analogs of acts that damage civic order. We thus developed a set of nine subcategories representing breaches of good relationship conduct identified in previous research or through examination of the interviews. These subcategories comprised violations of the norm of exclusivity (e.g., infidelity, flirting); failures to be responsive, to understand the participant's need to satisfy outside obligations and commitments, to treat the participants' families and friends in a considerate fashion, to be dependable, and to fight "fair;" improprieties involving disclosure of personal information (e.g., acts of deception, divulging the participants' secrets to others); acts causing damage to the participant's valued possessions; and acts of exploitation/manipulation.

The second super ordinate category of precipitating events/revenge responses, "Threats to Self," mirrored the second of Bies et al.'s (1997) classes of provocation and recognizes the revenge literature's emphasis on acts that challenge an individual's sense of self-worth or social reputation (e.g., Baumeister, 1997; Frijda, 1994). The distinction between self-esteem and social reputation is clearly non-trivial. Self-esteem concerns how an individual views him or herself, whereas social reputation concerns how an individual believes others view him or her. Nevertheless, it is commonplace for revenge scholars to treat them as closely related constructs when discussing the antecedents of vengeful behavior because both deal with threats to the individual's self and identity (e.g., Baumeister, 1997; Frijda, 1994). Moreover, both the workplace (e.g., Bies & Tripp, 2005; Bies et al., 1997; Tripp, Bies, & Aquino, 2002) and broader revenge literatures link decrements in power with threats to self-esteem and social reputation (e.g., Frijda, 1994; Miller & Vidmar, 1981). That is, these literatures often assume that acts that compromise an individual's sense of self—whether the private or public self—serve as inherent threats to his or her power in relation to the offender. Accordingly, we followed Bies et al.'s lead in combining threats to a partner's self-esteem or social reputation and acts that upset the balance of power between partners as provocations/revenge responses within the same super ordinate class. Importantly, coders' initial attempts to distinguish between threats to self-esteem and threats to social reputation (i.e., status or public self-image) failed. Therefore, we abandoned efforts to distinguish between different acts within this super ordinate category except to note partners' ploys to exert power or control over participants via coercion or acts of relational violence. Three additional subcategories emerged in our analysis of the interviews: hurtful messages, reputation defamation, and social exclusion.

We also coded for a third superordinate class of precipitating events/ revenge responses involving affronts to the identity or social reputation of an individual's relationship: "Affronts to the Relationship." Subcategories here represented provocations/retaliatory acts in which a partner terminated or suspended the relationship, flaunted a potential alternative relationship, feigned romantic interest in or involvement with the participant, or refused to tell others about the relationship.

Finally, we generated a set of categories to code participants' motives for getting even. These included superordinate categories reflecting desires to cause change, evoke feeling, or raise awareness in their partner (hereafter discussed under the label "Cause Desired Change") and motives associated with concerns about the injustice of the situation. Within the former category, "Cause Desired Change," we coded for the possibilities that getting even would educate, correct, or deter the partner (hereafter discussed under the label "correction") and/or cause the partner to experience hurt/suffering (hereafter discussed under the label "suffering"), empathy, regret/shame/ guilt (hereafter discussed under the label "regret"), humiliation, jealousy, and anger. Within the category, Justice, we identified three justice-related themes in participants' accounts: interests in reciprocating harm, punishing the partner, and restoring justice. Based on the literature, we also created categories representing desires to "redress the avenger's feelings," to "restore the participant's self-esteem/reputation," to "increase his/her power or control," to "help or protect others," and to "benefit the relationship" (the last two categories were generated to reflect motives that might serve to justify engaging in a morally questionable behavior). Finally, two novel motives emerged in analysis of the interviews, one predicated on the fact that the "opportunity to take revenge arose" and the other indicating that the "provocation had occurred previously."

Prior to coding, the second author trained coders in the use of the coding categories using 30 randomly selected interviews. Coders first met with the second author to identify those passages of text that contained content pertaining to the specific parameters under investigation. Inter-rater agreement was 75.3% with disagreements resolved via discussion. Next, coders classified the text passages into appropriate categories. Inter-rater agreement on the codes applied to the content was 75.2%; disagreements were again resolved via discussion.

Results

We performed χ^2 tests (where observed frequencies permitted) to determine whether our findings differed by experimental condition, sex, or whether the episode involved a current or former partner. Given the disparity in *n* across cells, we conducted separate tests for each of these independent variables. Of the 52 analyses performed, only two achieved conventional levels of significance. As the experiment-wise error rate for 52 tests at $\alpha = .05$ is 2.6, these associations (discussed briefly below where appropriate) should be interpreted with caution. More generally, it would appear that experimental condition had little effect on the content of participants' interviews, at least with respect to the parameters currently under examination.

TABLE 1 Precipitating events

Type of Event	Percentage (N = 85)
Violation of relationship rules	75.3 (64)
Norms of exclusivity	42.4 (36)
Failures to be responsive	21.2 (18)
Disclosure of personal information	16.5 (14)
Failure to be dependable	12.9 (11)
Failure to understand other obligations/commitments	5.9 (5)
Failure to be considerate to friends/family	3.5 (3)
Failure to fight in a fair fashion	0.0 (0)
Damage to valued possessions	0.0 (0)
Exploitation/manipulation	2.4 (2)
Affront to the relationship	23.5 (20)
Termination/suspension of relationship	18.8 (16)
Flaunted relationships with others	3.5 (3)
Feigned romantic interest in participant	4.7 (4)
Hid the relationship	2.4 (2)
Derogation of the self	17.6 (15)
Hurtful messages	9.4 (8)
Reputation defamation	3.5 (3)
Social exclusion	2.4 (2)
Violence/coercion	1.2 (1)
Other	9.4 (8)

Note. Frequencies reported in parentheses. As precipitating events could be classified into two or more categories, percentages do not add up to 100.

Precipitating events

Events that sparked participants' desires for revenge were coded into three broad categories: Violation of Relationship Rules, Affront to the Relationship, and Threat to Self. As is evident in Table 1, Violations of Relationship Rules were the most commonly identified provocations by a considerable margin, appearing in more than three times as many interviews as either of the other two classes of provocations examined.

Within the rule violation category, a diverse array of breaches of good relational conduct directed participants' thoughts toward vengeance. Violations of the norm of exclusivity—for example, extra-relationship sexual encounters and demonstrations of affection (e.g., kissing), dating, flirting, or spending time with others and so forth—were the most commonly reported rule infringements. Next most common were romantic partners' failures to be responsive. Participants reported retaliating—or wanting to retaliate—when, for example, their partners ignored them, gave them the cold shoulder, or engaged in behaviors they had previously told their partners upset them. Other less common categories of provocations within this class included breaches of rules concerning the disclosure of personal information (e.g., lying, revealing private information to others), failures to be dependable (e.g., breaking promises, failure to follow through on promises/commitments), and failures to understand the participant's need to fulfill external commitments and obligations. The remaining rule violations categories were observed in fewer than 5% of the interviews.

Affronts to the relationships were responsible for nearly one-quarter of the revenge episodes. Within this class, by far the most common events to elicit desires for vengeance involved the partner terminating or suspending the relationship (e.g., breaking up with the participant or insisting that they take a break). The remaining categories of provocations in this class—in which partners flaunted their relationships with others (often their ex-partners or people the participant disliked), feigned romantic interest in the participant, or hid the relationship from others—were each mentioned by fewer than 5% of our sample.

Finally, not quite 20% of participants identified acts that damaged the self as the trigger events that sparked their desires for revenge. The majority of provocations within this class involved the communication of hurtful messages (e.g., criticism, verbally abusive comments). Provocations involving reputation defamation, social exclusion, or violence/coercion were rare.

The two significant associations we obtained emerged in analyses of the frequencies for precipitating events. Participants reporting on events from past relationships (32.7%) were more than five times more likely than participants reporting on events from ongoing relationships (6.3%) to recall provocations involving affronts to their relationships, χ^2 (1, N = 84) = 7.91, $p < .01$, Cramer's V = .31. This is not surprising given that, as indicated earlier, the bulk of provocations in this category involved dissolving or suspending a relationship. In addition, females (27.9%) were significantly more likely than males (9.5%) to report that their desires for revenge had been sparked by acts that derogated the self, χ^2 (1, N = 85) = 4.70, $p < .05$, Cramer's V = .24.

TABLE 2 Revenge responses

Type of Response	Percentage (N = 58)
Violation of relationship rules	63.8 (37)
Norms of exclusivity	25.9 (15)
Failure to be responsive	17.2 (10)
Disclosure of personal information	25.9 (15)
Failure to be dependable	8.6 (5)
Failure to understand other commitments/obligations	1.7 (1)
Failure to be considerate to friends/family	0.0 (0)
Failure to fight in a fair fashion	0.0 (0)
Damage to valued possessions	5.2 (3)
Exploitation/manipulation	3.4 (2)
Affront to the relationship	20.7 (12)
Termination/suspension of relationship	1.7 (1)
Flaunting relationships with others	19.0 (11)
Feigned romantic interest in participant	1.7 (1)
Hid the relationship from others	0.0 (0)
Derogation of the self	32.8 (19)
Hurtful messages	13.8 (8)
Reputation defamation	17.2 (10)
Social exclusion	6.9 (4)
Violence/coercion	3.4 (2)
Other	13.8 (8)

Note. Excludes participants in the no revenge condition. As revenge responses could be classified into two or more categories, percentages do not add up to 100.

Revenge responses

Coders employed the same three broad classes to the categorization of participants' revenge responses as they used in analysis of the provocations. Table 2 reveals some important similarities in findings across the two parameters. First, in the same way that violations of relationship rules dominated participants' reports of the kinds of acts that precipitated their desires to get even with their partners, participants were more than twice as likely to indicate that they had retaliated by violating relationship norms themselves as they were to indicate having retaliated in ways categorized in either of the remaining classes of revenge response. Second, participants who avenged themselves by breaking relationship rules tended to abuse the same four rules that were identified as the most commonly violated rules in the coding of the provocations: rules concerning the exclusive nature of the relationship, the disclosure of personal information, responsiveness, and being dependable. Of the remaining relationship rule-based subcategories of revenge responses, only one (damaging valued possessions) was observed in more than 5% of the interviews.

The similarities disappear, however, when we consider the findings for the next most common class of revenge response, Affronts to the Relation-ship. Whereas the dissolution or suspension of the relationship was the most commonly reported provocation classified in this category (18.8% of our sample), only one participant avenged herself by terminating her relationship or taking a break from her partner. Instead, participants were apt to report getting even by flaunting new relationships (or potential relationships) and ensuring that the offending partner either witnessed their behavior or learned of it from others. None of the remaining subcategories in this class of revenge responses were identified in more than one interview.

Finally, acts of revenge in which participants caused harm to the partner's sense of self were only about half as common as acts of revenge in which participants bent or broke the rules of good relationship conduct as their means of repaying harm with harm. Nevertheless, despite their considerably lower frequency, the revenge responses classified in this category comprise some of the nastiest retaliatory behaviors observed in this study, at least in terms of their probable scope of impact. For example, participants reported publicly defaming their partner's character or attributes (often, but not always, his or her sexual attributes or sexual prowess) and forming coalitions with others in their mutual social networks to exclude the partner from important events (e.g., parties, graduation celebrations) or from the network itself. One woman even wrote letters to professional degree programs to which her ex-partner applied to inform them of the malicious actions he had perpetrated against her (withdrawing her from all her fall term courses after their relationship dissolved). More generally, most revenge behaviors classified in this category fall into one of two broad subcategories: hurtful messages and reputation defamation. Acts involving social exclusion or the use of coercion or abusive forms of control were slightly more common as revenge responses than as provocations, but still rare.

Revenge motives

In addition to discussing what their partners had done to provoke them and how they had responded to these provocations, participants in the two revenge conditions were also asked to describe what they hoped to achieve by getting even. Coders classified statements pertaining to motives into eight broad categories derived from our review of the revenge literature.All but one of the themes captured in these categories were observed in 5% or more of the interviews (see Table 3).

TABLE 3 Motives underlying participants' desires to get even

Motive	Percentage (N = 58)
Cause desired change in partner	81.0 (47)
Correction	46.6 (27)
Suffering	32.8 (19)
Empathy	31 (18)
Regret	6.9 (4)
Humiliation	6.9 (4)
Jealousy	5.2 (3)
Angry	0.0 (0)
Redress the avenger's feelings	69.0 (40)
Justice	46.6 (27)
Reciprocate harm	36.2 (21)
Punish the partner	3.4 (2)
Restore justice	6.9 (4)
Increase power and control	12.1 (7)
Opportunity arose	10.3 (6)
Restore self-esteem/face	8.6 (5)
Repeated provocation(s)	8.6 (5)
Help or protect others	5.2 (3)
Benefit the relationship	0.0 (0)
Other	27.6 (16)

Note. Excludes participants in the no revenge condition. Frequencies reported in parentheses. As motives could be classified into two or more categories, percentages do not add up to 100.

According to their interview responses, the majority of participants hoped to use revenge to cause desired change in the partner who had provoked them. Correction, suffering, and empathy were the changes in attitudes, feelings or behavior that participants most often reported hoping to elicit in their partners. Less common were reports that participants wanted to get even, to cause their partners to experience regret, to humiliate their partners, or to make their partners jealous. We also coded for the possibility that participants' revenge responses may have been motivated by the desire to make their partners angry, but found no evidence of this in our interviews.

Second most common were motives related to the desire to redress the negative feelings the avengers experienced in the aftermath of the provocation, followed by motives oriented around justice concerns (e.g., restoring justice, punishing the partner, and reciprocating harm). Interestingly, when participants appealed to notions of justice to explain their acts of vengeance, they were much more likely to frame their motives in terms of reciprocating harm than either punishing their partners or restoring justice.

Motives predicated on the participants' desire to use revenge to increase his or her power or control in the relationship were identified as the fourth most frequent class of motives but, contrary to expectations based on the literature, were observed in just over 10% of revenge accounts. Even less common were instances of revenge that participants attributed to motives directed toward restoring self-esteem or social reputation, helping others, or benefiting their relationships. Indeed, none of our participants explained their vengeful responses as enacted to repair or enhance their relationships with the partners who had harmed them.

Finally, a small minority of participants indicated that they got even with their partners simply because the opportunity to do so arose. A similar minority reported that their act of vengeance was a response to multiple or repeated provocations.

Discussion

A lover scorned: acts that precipitate romantic revenge

We sought answers to three related research questions in this study. RQ1 explored the actions and events that trigger acts of vengeance between current or former romantic partners. Our analysis indicated that participants' desires for revenge tended to occur primarily in response to perceived violations of relationship rules, especially rules surrounding relationship exclusivity and partner responsiveness. In contrast, provocations involving actions that threatened or damaged participants' selves (which included acts that damaged their self-esteem, social reputation, or the balance of power between partners) or affronts to their relationships were much less common in participants' accounts.

This pattern of results corroborates, extends, and stands in contrast to previous findings and theorizing. First, the finding that violations of expected codes of relational conduct served to generate desires for revenge for many of our participants mirrors earlier findings in the organizational literature which point to acts that violate organizational rules, norms, or ethical standards as a primary source of the thoughts and feelings that stimulate desires for vengeance. Although the rules that guide partners' behavior in romantic relationships may often be unspoken (Metts, 1994), our results clearly suggest that partners flout such rules at their peril.

Second, our results suggest that a complete understanding of the kinds of events that inspire revenge in romantic contexts must move beyond a simple consideration of threats to an individual's *personal* identity, threats well represented in the revenge literature, to consider threats to his or her *social identity* as part of a couple, as well. A substantial minority of respondents identified affronts to the identities or social reputations *of their relationships* as the provocations that fuelled their desires for revenge. Much of the "sting" associated with such events may result from their implications for the individual's sense of self-worth or public self-image. Nevertheless, people's self-concepts extend well beyond their personal identities (Brewer, 1991; Tajfel & Turner, 1986). It may thus prove important in understanding partners' responses to relational offenses and injuries to recognize that they frequently see themselves not only as a "me" or an "I" but also as part of a "we" (Agnew et al., 1998).

Finally, precipitating events involving threats to participants' self-esteem or social reputations and the balance of power between partners were identified in our interviews much less frequently than our review of the revenge literature might have led us to expect. However, before we conclude that this pattern of results calls into question assumptions in the literature that threats involving the self and power serve to motivate retaliatory responses, two facts bear consideration.

First, a careful consideration of the provocations participants recalled suggests that many of these events would almost certainly have undermined their self-esteem/social reputations (e.g., a partner's infidelity might serve as a potent threat to an individual's sense of self-worth) and/or left them in a one-down position relative to their partners (e.g., being excluded from important social occasions might diminish individuals' sense that they have the power to control their associations with members of their social networks). We coded the interviews in a fairly literal manner, however, and cautioned coders against drawing inferences that could not be firmly based in participants' actual speech. The fact that we observed comparatively few provocations classifiable in this superordinate category may thus be more an artifact of the fact that participants tended not to refer directly and explicitly to power, self-esteem, or social reputation in their responses than an indication that such threats played little role in precipitating their acts of vengeance. Second, most theoretical discussions of the role of the self and power in revenge treat such potential provocations in abstract terms, arguing, for example, that interpersonal offenses involve inherent threats to an individual's power by virtue of the fact that the offender has demonstrated that he or she has the power to harm the victim, whereas the victim does not possess the power to prevent such harm (e.g., Frijda, 1994). Considerations such as these suggest that researchers might be wise to ask questions directed specifically at examining the role of the self and power even in instances where participants report provocations which, at least on the surface, appear to reflect other sorts of concerns (e.g., rule violations).

Getting even in romantic relationships: an eye for an eye?

RQ2 examined the specific means participants employed to retaliate in the revenge episodes they recalled. Two interesting findings emerged in our analysis of the relevant data.

First, more participants described getting even with their partners by flouting the rules of good relationship conduct than by engaging in any of the other classes of vengeful response we explored. Indeed, participants were nearly twice as likely to report taking revenge by bending, breaking, or ignoring the tacit rules that regulate partners' behavior in romantic relationships than by engaging in the next most commonly reported class of revenge response. Moreover, the same four subcategories of rule violations observed most frequently as the events that precipitated their desires for revenge (rules concerning exclusivity, disclosure, responsiveness, and dependability) were also the four most frequently observed subcategories of rule violations in their descriptions of their retaliatory responses to these events.

This pattern of results suggests that people may be relatively more inclined to respond to a romantic partner's provocation by breaching relationship rules (and certain kinds of relationship rules, in particular) than by engaging in other kinds of retaliatory behaviors. Given that participants overwhelmingly reported violations of relationship rules as the events that precipitated their desires for revenge, it is tempting to interpret this as evidence that individuals seek symmetry between provocation and response in deciding how to react to a current or former partner's injury or offense. Unfortunately, our sample is too small and the observed frequencies across categories too uneven to permit investigation of this possibility. Future studies with larger samples will be required to test such hypotheses. More generally, researchers should explore the process by which individuals determine how they will get even with a current or former partner. What considerations direct their selections? What barriers constrain their choices?

Our data may also have important implications for the way we conceptualize romantic revenge. For example, Yoshimura's (2002, 2004) participants reported acts of revenge that varied widely in terms of the probable severity and breadth of their consequences for the partner (e.g., from dressing more sexily and acting happy in a former partner's presence to kidnapping the partner's children or pets, getting the partner fired, and poisoning the partner). We also observed considerable variation in the severity of the actions our participants undertook to repay a partner's harm with harm (everything from the silent treatment to sexual infidelity). Importantly, however, few of their responses could properly be considered severe. Instead, they tended to be mild to moderate in severity and mundane in nature.

We conducted face-to-face interviews, asked participants to describe a time when they themselves got even with a romantic partner, and avoided the term "revenge" in our instructions. In contrast, Yoshimura's participants completed an anonymous questionnaire, reported on their own or another's vengeful response, and responded to instructions that explicitly equated getting even with revenge. Our results may thus differ from Yoshimura's for several reasons. First, our participants may have experienced greater apprehension about admitting that they had engaged in serious forms of retaliation. Second, some of Yoshimura's participants may have reported events of an apocryphal nature (e.g., "I once heard about this guy who …"). Third, to the extent that people view "getting even" as less severe than "taking revenge," his instructions may have primed participants to recall events of a more severe nature than did our instructions.

Differences in methodology notwithstanding, the important point here is that participants in our study described what might best be termed instances of "everyday" revenge rather than the more sensationalistic varieties of romantic revenge that make headlines in newspapers and which inspire popular films such as *Fatal Attraction* (Lyne, 1987) and *The War of the Roses* (DeVito, 1989). If the kinds of revenge responses we observed in this study reflect the kinds of vengeful behaviors in which individuals engage when seeking to retaliate against their (current or former) romantic partners, researchers and theorists may need to broaden their understandings of romantic revenge to incorporate these milder, more "ordinary" ways of getting even.

Motives behind repaying harm with harm in an intimate context

How do individuals explain their decisions to take revenge? Do these explanations justify getting even with a romantic partner by suggesting that taking revenge may benefit their relationships or people outside their relationships? RQ3 sought answers to these questions.

Consistent with past research and theorizing, participants reported a diverse array of goals they hoped to achieve by acting vengefully. Only three of these, however, appeared with noteworthy frequency in our interviews: participants tended to cast their motives in language that emphasized desires to bring about change in their partners, redress their own feelings, and/or manage concerns with justice.

In hindsight, we recognize that a fair degree of conceptual overlap may exist between certain of the categories we established to code for justice motives and at least two of the sub-categories in the "cause desired change" category. In particular, the latter category included motives predicated on desires to cause the offending partner to suffer and to correct his or her behavior. The former of these motives may share important points of similarity with the "reciprocate harm" justice category and the latter may appropriately be construed as a desire for rehabilitative justice.

In support of this possibility, χ^2 analyses revealed a significant tendency for coders to cross-categorize motives reflecting the desire to make the partner suffer as also reflecting the goal of reciprocating harm (χ^2 (1, N = 58) = 22.35, p < .001) and a near-significant tendency to cross-categorize motives emphasizing correction as also reflecting concerns with justice, collapsing across subcategories (χ^2 (1, N = 58) = 3.55, p = .06). As the correction and suffering motives were the two most frequently identified motives within the broader desired change category, these results suggest—not surprisingly, given emphases on justice in both the revenge (Bies et al., 1997; Miller & Vidmar, 1981; Solomon, 1994) and relationships (Hatfield, 1983; Sprecher & Schwartz, 1994) literatures—that concerns with justice may play a particularly formative role in directing responses to provocations perpetrated by romantic partners. Future research might target partners' concerns about justice and the relation of these to their experiences in revenge episodes more directly.

After hoping to educate, correct, or deter their partners or make their partners suffer as much as they themselves had, the most common motive within the "cause desired change" category reflected participants' desire to induce empathy in the partner. A substantial proportion of our participants spoke of wanting their partners to know—that is, to appreciate—what it felt like to be treated as they had been treated. Participants' emphasis in such cases appeared to be less on ensuring that the partner *suffer*, however, than it was on ensuring that the partner *knew what it felt like to suffer as a result of being treated the way they had been treated*. Further research is needed to determine whether such comments should be interpreted literally or whether they reflect individuals' attempts to couch their desires to make their partners suffer in terms that make their motives appear more palatable.

Consistent with the finding that relatively few participants identified acts that threatened their self-esteem, social reputations, or the balance of power in their relationships as provocations (or, indeed as revenge responses), we also found that few participants spoke explicitly of desires to restore self-esteem or their social reputations or to reassert their power or control as motives that guided their decisions to retaliate. Unfortunately, the present data cannot speak to whether this pattern of results indicates that these sorts of motives rarely serve as the goals behind acts of revenge between (current or former) romantic partners or whether it is an artifact of the particular discourses our participants used and our literal approach to coding. Future research might explore this issue with alternative methods that do not require inference.

Finally, in answer to the second part of RQ3, we found little evidence to support our expectation that participants might justify their vengeful responses by ascribing their retaliatory actions to motives aimed at relationship maintenance or improvement or the benefiting of others. This is an interesting finding, particularly in light of evidence elsewhere in the interviews which strongly suggests that participants' attitudes toward revenge were, indeed, quite mixed (i.e., both condemning and condoning; Alibhai et al., 2008) and which shows, moreover, that at least a small proportion of participants reported that the revenge episode brought about positive change in their relationships (Boon, Alibhai,

& Deveau, 2008). To the extent that they recognized that societal attitudes toward revenge are ambivalent (e.g., Crombag et al., 2003; Uniacke, 2000), we thought participants might experience pressures to justify their vengeful responses in ways that promoted the view that they had engaged in their actions to restore, maintain, or build their relationships or to help or protect others. The fact that so few of our participants advanced such claims (even though a few reported relational benefits of revenge) suggests that the connections between people's attitudes toward revenge in romantic contexts, the motives that direct their responses to provocations, and the outcomes they associate with a decision to repay a partner's harm with harm may be more complex than we had initially anticipated. Future research should examine the interplay between these phenomena in more detail.

The importance of investigating everyday revenge

Previously we concluded that the majority of the vengeful acts in which our participants engaged were rather milder and more mundane than they were severe and extraordinary. This raises an important question: Are such acts of "everyday" revenge worthy of investigation?

We can think of at least three reasons to answer in the affirmative. First, theorists generally believe that the processes involved in calibrating vengeful response to provocation are fraught with difficulties (e.g., Baumeister, 1997; McLean Parks, 1997) and that systematic perceptual biases often lead victims to see provocations as more severe and unjustified than do offenders (Baumeister, Stillwell, & Wotman, 1990). Victims may thus tend to over-compensate for harms incurred, a tendency that might promote a cycle of revenge in which a provocation results in a retaliatory response that is itself perceived as a provocation. The potential for escalation of conflict and therefore for harm to self, partner, and relationship may thus be considerable even when the initial provocation or revenge response is mild.

Second, although the revenge responses most commonly reported in this study represent the low to moderate end of the severity continuum, research on related behaviors in other domains (i.e., rudeness at work, workplace incivilities, etc.) suggests that it is often the smaller, milder, everyday kinds of aversive interpersonal behaviors that cause the greatest harm (e.g., Andersson & Pearson, 1999; Johnson & Indvik, 2001). To the extent that the effects of such recurrent acts of revenge may build over time or in the aggregate, even mild revenge responses could come to cause substantial relationship conflict and result in significant and enduring decreases in commitment and loyalty, satisfaction with the relationship, and partners' willingness to draw charitable attributions for each others' behavior.

Finally, some scholars have argued that the sorts of dramatic, often violent acts people stereotypically associate with the terms revenge and retaliation may represent just the tip of the iceberg where responses to perceived injustice are concerned (Skarlicki & Folger,

1997). Milder, more mundane acts may be far more common, the rule rather than the exception. If this reasoning is correct and less extreme, more commonplace acts—though less "newsworthy" than their more severe counterparts—are capable of adversely affecting relations between the parties involved, they clearly merit empirical investigation on the basis of their sheer prevalence alone.

Limitations

The present study builds on previous revenge research but offers a base of descriptive knowledge concerning the key parameters of revenge as it occurs between current and former romantic partners. To be fair, however, our contribution to this initial knowledge base is founded on the responses of people involved in dating relationships of reasonably short duration. Future research should examine revenge as it occurs among partners from longer, more established relationships and relationships with greater barriers to dissolution (e.g., marital relationships). In addition, although we observed little or no difference in responses as a function of whether participants discussed acts of revenge against current or former partners, researchers would be wise to consider this distinction in future research and, where possible, restrict participants to recall revenge episodes that have occurred in their current, ongoing relationships.

Our conclusions are also based entirely on people's recollections of episodes that may have occurred weeks, months, or perhaps years in the past (unfortunately, we inadvertently neglected to ask participants how much time had elapsed since the episodes they recounted in their interviews). Our findings must thus be considered in light of the fact that participants' interview responses may reflect distortions of memory borne of the passage of time and the occurrence of intervening events. Moreover, given that our data were obtained in face-to-face interviews, other forms of distortion—of a motivated nature—may also be reflected in participants' responses. Researchers might want to explore the feasibility of alternative methods that would enable romantic revenge to be studied in a prospective fashion and which would decrease concerns with social desirability.

Conclusion

Revenge is a phenomenon of universal human significance, with the potential to cause great harm and—as some (Bies et al., 1997) have argued—the potential to benefit social relations, as well. The present investigation explores this phenomenon in the context of important interpersonal relationships and provides a useful descriptive base for understanding some of the key parameters of romantic revenge. Our findings also highlight how much we have yet to learn about this important, but neglected topic of inquiry. We hope our research will inspire others to undertake investigations of revenge, especially as it unfolds between members of close relationships where the stakes—for good or for ill—may often be higher than in other interaction contexts.

REFERENCES

Agnew, C. R., Van Lange, P. A. M., Rusbult, C. E., & Langston, C. A. (1998). Cognitive interdependence: Commitment and the mental representation of close relationships. *Journal of Personality and Social Psychology, 74*, 939–954.

Alibhai, A. M., Boon, S. D., & Deveau, V. L. (2008). An investigation into ambivalent attitudes toward revenge. Unpublished Manuscript, University of Calgary.

Andersson, L., & Pearson, C. M. (1999).Tit for tat? The spiraling effect of incivility in the workplace. *Academy of Management Review, 24*, 452–471.

Bachman, G. F., & Guerrero, L. K. (2006). Relational quality and communicative responses following hurtful events in dating relationships: An expectancy violations analysis. *Journal of Social and Personal Relationships, 23*, 943–963.

Baumeister, R. F. (1997). *Evil: Inside human cruelty and violence*. New York: W. H. Freeman.

Baumeister, R. F., Stillwell, A., & Wotman, S. R. (1990). Victim and perpetrator accounts of interpersonal conflict: Autobiographical narratives about anger. *Journal of Personality and Social Psychology, 59, 994–1005.*

Bies, R. J., & Tripp, T. M. (1996). Beyond distrust: "Getting even" and the need for revenge. In R. Kramer & T. Tyler et al. (Eds.), *Trust in organizations: Frontiers of theory and research* (pp. 246–260). Thousand Oaks, CA: Sage.

Bies, R. J. & Tripp, T. M. (2005). The study of revenge in the workplace: Conceptual, ideological, and empirical issues. In S. Fox & P. E. Spector (Eds.), *Counterproductive work behavior: Investigations of actors and targets* (pp. 65–81). Washington, DC: American Psychological Association.

Bies, R. J., Tripp, T. M., & Kramer, R. M. (1997). At the breaking point: Cognitive and social dynamics of revenge in organizations. In J. Greenberg & R. Giacalone (Eds.), *Antisocial behavior in organizations* (pp. 18–36). Thousand Oaks, CA: Sage.

Boon, S. D., Alibhai, A. M., & Deveau, V. L. (2008). A taste of their own medicine: Consequences following acts of revenge in romantic relationships. Unpublished Manuscript, University of Calgary.

Brewer, M. B. (1991).The social self: On being the same and different at the same time. *Personality and Social Psychology Bulletin, 17*, 475–482.

Clark, M. S., & Mills, J. (1979). Interpersonal attraction in exchange and communal relationships. *Journal of Personality and Social Psychology, 37*, 12–24.

Crombag, H., Rassin, E., Horselenberg, R. (2003). On vengeance. *Psychology, Crime, and Law, 9*, 333–344.

DeVito, D. (Director).(1989). *The war of the roses* [Film].

Frijda, N. H. (1994). The lex talionis: On vengeance. In S. H. M. van Goozen, N. E. Van de Poll, & J. A. Sergeant (Eds.), *Emotions: Essays on emotion theory* (pp. 263–289). Hillsdale, NJ: Lawrence Erlbaum.

Guerrero, L. K., & Andersen, P. A. (1998). Jealousy experience and expression in romantic relationships. In P. A. Andersen & L. K. Guerrero (Eds.), *Handbook of communication and emotion: Research, theory, applications and contexts* (pp. 155–188). San Diego, CA: Academic Press.

Hamilton, B., White, P., & Bulliet, M. (2006, October 29). Brand ex: Gal busted for leaving a mark on old flame. *New York Post* (Online), http://www.nypost.com/p/news/brand_ex_gal_busted_for_leaving_g09wkLzHRL0Ma7hbkdHkiM (accessed 7 November 2009).

Hatfield, E. (1983). Equity theory and research: An overview. In H. H. Blumberg, A. P. Hare, V. Kent, & M. Davies (Eds.), *Small groups and social interaction*, Vol. 2 (pp. 401–412). Chichester, England: Wiley.

Hoyle, B. (2006, September 13). Wife "sank" £90,000 yacht as marriage hit the rocks. *The Times Online*, http://www.timesonline.co.uk/tol/news/uk/article637540.ece (accessed 7 November 2009).

Johnson, P. R., & Indvik, J. (2001). Rudeness at work: Impulse over restraint. *Public Personnel Management, 30*, 457–465.

Kiecolt-Glaser, J. K., & Newton, T. L. (2001). Marriage and health: His and hers. *Psychological Bulletin, 127*, 472–503.

Lyne, A. (Director).(1987). *Fatal Attraction* [Film].

McLean Parks, J. (1997). The fourth arm of justice: The art and science of revenge. *Research on negotiation in organizations*, Vol. 6 (pp. 113–144). Greenwich, CT: JAI Press.

Metts, S. (1994). Relational transgressions. In W. R. Cupach & B. H. Spitzberg (Eds.), *The dark side of interpersonal communication*, 1st edn. (pp. 217–239). Hillsdale, NJ: Erlbaum.

Metts, S., & Cupach, W. R. (2007). Responses to relational transgressions: Hurt, anger, and sometimes forgiveness. In B. H. Spitzberg & W. R. Cupach (Eds.), *The dark side of interpersonal communication*, 2nd edn.(pp. 243–273). Mahwah, NJ: Erlbaum.

Miller, D. T., & Vidmar, N. (1981). The social psychology of punishment reactions. In M. J. Lerner & S. C. Lerner (Eds.), *The justice motive in social behavior: Adapting to times of scarcity and change* (pp. 145–172). New York: Plenum.

Pinsker, H., Nepps, P., Redfield, J., & Winston, A. (1985). Applicants for short-term dynamic psychotherapy. In A. Winston (Ed.), *Clinical and research issues in short-term dynamic psychotherapy* (pp. 104–116). Washington, DC: American Psychiatric Association.

Rusbult, C. E., Verette, J., Whitney, G. A., Slovik, L. F, & Lipkus, I. (1991). Accommodation processes in close relationships: Theory and preliminary empirical evidence, *Journal of Personality & Social Psychology. 60*, 53–78.

Shaver, P. R., & Mikulincer, M. (2006). Attachment theory, individual psychodynamics, and relationship functioning. In A. L. Vangelist & D. Perlman (Eds.), *The Cambridge handbook of personal relationships* (pp. 251–271). New York: Cambridge University Press.

Skarlicki, D. P., & Folger, R. (1997). Retaliation in the workplace: The roles of distributive, procedural, and interactional justice. *Journal of Applied Psychology, 82*, 434–443.

Solomon, R. C. (1994). Sympathy and vengeance:The role of the emotions in justice. In S. H. M. van Goozen, N. E. Van de Poll, & J. A. Sergeant (Eds.), *Emotions: Essays on emotion theory* (pp. 291–311). Hillsdale, NJ: Lawrence Erlbaum.

Sprecher, S., & Schwartz, P. (1994). Equity and balance in the exchange of contributions in close relationships. In M. J. Lerner & G. Mikula (Eds.), *Entitlement and the affectional bond: Justice in close relationships* (pp. 11–41). New York: Plenum.

Stuckless, N., & Goranson, R. (1992). The vengeance scale: Development of a measure of attitudes toward revenge. *Journal of Social Behavior and Personality, 7*, 25–42.

Tajfel, H., & Turner, J. C. (1986). The social identity theory of intergroup behavior. In S. Worchel & W. Austin (Eds.), *Psychology of intergroup relations* (2nd ed.) (pp. 7–24). Chicago: Nelson-Hall.

Tripp, T. M., & Bies, R. J. (1997). What's good about revenge? In R. J. Lewicki, R. J. Bies, & B. H. Sheppard (Eds.), *Research on negotiation in organizations*, Vol. 6 (pp. 145–160). Greenwich, CT: JAI Press.

Tripp, T. M., Bies, R. J., & Aquino, K. (2002). Poetic justice or petty jealousy? The aesthetics of revenge. *Organizational Behaviour and Human Decision Processes, 89*, 966–984.

Uniacke, S. (2000). Why is revenge wrong? *The Journal of Value Inquiry, 34*, 61–69.

Yoshimura, S. M. (2002).An evolutionary approach to communicating vengeance in romantic relationships. Unpublished doctoral dissertation, Arizona State University, Tempe.

Yoshimura, S. M. (2004). Fifteen types of revenge activities enacted against current and past romantic partners. Paper presented at the meeting of the International Association for Relationship Research. Madison, Wisconsin, July.

Yoshimura, S. (2007). Goals and emotional outcomes of revenge activities in interpersonal relationships. *Journal of Social and Personal Relationships, 24*, 87–98.

Vicki Deveau is now with Provoke, Calgary. This article is based on the second author's doctoral thesis conducted under the first author's supervision. Portions of the data reported in this paper were presented at the June 2006 Canadian Psychological Association Social Personality Section preconference in Calgary, Alberta, and the July 2006 conference of the International Association for Relationship Research in Crete, Greece. The authors would like to thank Paola San Juan and Verlyne Nzojibwami for assistance with transcription, Melissa van Hal for assistance with coding, and Eddie Sheppard for his comments on an earlier draft of this paper. *All correspondence concerning this article should be addressed to Susan D. Boon, Department of Psychology, University of Calgary, 2500 University Dr. NW, Calgary, AB, T2N 1N4, Canada [e-mail: sdboon@ucalgary.ca].*

GENDER, SEXUALITY, AND SEXUAL ORIENTATION

Men, Women, and Sexual Stereotypes

By R.W. Firestone, L.A. Firestone, and J. Catlett

At this contentious moment in the history of male-female relationships, it is important for us to note that there is not one set of elements for men and another for women. Society has wounded and rewarded men and women differently. But when it comes to practicing the art and discipline of love, we are equally challenged.

—Keen (1997, p. 32)

During the past 50 years, a significant transformation has taken place in the way men arid women relate sexually (Hyde & Oliver, 2000; Schoenewolf, 1989; Solomon & Levy, 1982; Walsh, 1997; Young, 1999). Numerous cultural developments have contributed to these changes, among them the feminist movement, the men's movement, and women's ongoing and increasing involvement in the workplace (Bly, 1990; Sheehy, 1998). Since the 1960s, surveys indicate that many men have become more sensitive and less detached while many women have become more self-assertive and less dependent than their predecessors (Rubin, 1990). Commenting on the many real gains for both men and women that may be attributed to the "sexual revolution" Rubin stated,

> For the first time in our history, women were not just permitted but exhorted to experience the full force of their sexuality, to take pleasure in its expression, to celebrate it publicly rather than to conceal it as some private shame. … [For men] there was the possibility for sex among equals, sex with a "good" woman who made a free choice, a woman who was neither guilt-ridden nor shamed by the expression of her sexuality, a sexual connection that was also a freely given emotional exchange. (p. 93)

However, as social critic Young (1999) observed, these gains are far from complete: "Too many countries around the world still deny women the basic rights of adult members of society (though it's worth remembering that men's lot in these countries usually is not too enviable either)" (pp. 265–266).

Despite the movement toward gender equality, many people still lack a fully developed sense of self and the autonomy necessary to sustain a loving and sexually fulfilling relationship. Men and women are currently living within a society that is in transition between a traditional patriarchal social structure and a system that reflects more equality between the sexes (Silverstein, Auerbach, & Levant, 2002). As a result, many are confused about their gender roles, relationships, and sexuality.

It is beyond the scope of this book to examine the multitude of recent societal changes with respect to gender roles and expectations or to comment on their implications for sexual relationships. However, in this chapter, we describe an overall view of sexual stereotyping in our society and show bow these distorted views create animosity between men and women. We provide a brief review of findings from gender studies and a critique of gender studies that we believe may perpetuate stereotypic attitudes. We offer our views regarding similarities and differences between the sexes. Our focus is on exploring these similarities and differences in terms of men's and women's psychosexual development, adult sexual functioning, and ways of expressing their sexuality in relationships. In addition, we explore how boys and girls learn their parents' defensive styles of relating with each other through the process of imitation. Also we examine conflicting hypotheses about how children are socialized into their respective gender roles and the differential developmental tasks they encounter during their formative years. Lastly, we briefly review several conjectures proposed by evolutionary psychologists regarding differences in male and female sexual strategies and preferences in mate selection.

SEXUAL STEREOTYPES: AN OVERVIEW

Psychological defenses established early in life later combine with the defenses of other individuals to produce cultural attitudes and social mores that shape a society. Once established, cultural prerogatives and social institutions reflect back on each member of society (Billig, 1987; Billig et al., 1988; G. Mead, 1934/1967). Sexist attitudes and sexual stereotypes are a significant part of this defensive apparatus and are transmitted through succeeding generations within the family context. If parents have sexist attitudes, their children assimilate these views, both explicitly through verbal communications and implicitly through the processes of identification and imitation. These defensive views are then projected into the social mores and institutions of the larger society. Sexism essentially represents the extension of each individual's biased, hostile attitudes toward the opposite sex into a social framework. Negative attitudes toward lesbian, gay, bisexual, or transsexual orientations are also still commonplace in our culture {Friedman & Downey, 2002).

Although changes have occurred in the roles of men and women in our society, there are still remnants of sexist views that portray men as masterful and powerful yet paternalistic and uncommunicative, and women as emotionally responsive and communicative yet childlike, helpless, and incompetent (Aries, 1997; Beyer & Finnegan, 1997; Kupers, 1997).[1] Sexual stereotypes are confusing because they assign men and women to artificial categories. Clearly, some stereotypes do correspond to research findings regarding specific differences between men and women. However, when these findings are exaggerated or overgeneralized in the popular media (Tiefer, 2000); and when perceptions of men and women take on a connotation of cynicism and denigration, they generate hostility between people and undermine their relationships.

According to Lott (1997), some gender research has perpetuated biased attitudes toward women and men. She commented that, in general "Cataloging sameness and differences does not serve the interests of a science of psychology, first, because we well know that behavior always occurs in a context and that the situation or circumstance makes a significant difference" (p. 19). Lott went on to note that societies that encourage beliefs "in gender-related traits (regardless of whether they are said to be learned or innate)" tend to justify the continuation of "separate spheres for women and men" (p. 22).

The majority of adults have been raised in families in which they learned inaccurate information about themselves and about the opposite sex. Social psychologist Geis (1993) noted that people hold numerous implicit hypotheses and beliefs about men and women that they use to "interpret perceptions of males and females from the time they are born" (p. 14). Moreover, these beliefs about gender differences influence people's behavior in ways that are limiting or restrictive (Deaux, 1999). For example, Fiske, Bersoff, Borgida, Deaux, and Heilman (1997) have pointed out that *"prescriptive* or normative sex stereotypes (e.g., women should be nice and passive; men should be strong and aggressive)" (p. 322) are harmful for both women and men.

Despite changes in family life because of increased equality between the sexes, the ways that many boys and girls are socialized into their respective gender roles may still adversely affect the quality of their relating in adult associations. For example, Ickes (1993) has reported "a growing *body of research evidence indicating* that the relationships of men and women with traditional gender roles are far from optimal" (p. 71).

In general, sexist attitudes tend to foster a "us/them" polarization and reflect an underlying negativity and hostility that can be as damaging to human relations as racial prejudice. In a recent interview (American Association of Marriage and Family Therapy Staff, 2002), Keen strongly criticized sexist attitudes and traditional gender role expectations of men and women that remain in popular thought today: "I would no longer use words like masculinity and femininity. They are very deceptive" (p. 33).

> People go into therapy asking the questions they've been taught to ask, so you get these simplistic things, like "men are from Mars and women are from Venus." Come on! I have 2 daughters and 2 ex-wives—don't tell me that women are always from Venus. In some of the groups I've worked with, I've met good, assertive women, making their place in the world and after a while they say, "I don't feel feminine." And there are the men who are very sensitive and tell me that they don't feel masculine. … They have all these stereotypes. I try to lead them to their own stories—to own their own autobiography, rather than think in terms of these archetypes. (p. 35)

DISTORTED VIEWS OF MEN AND WOMEN

In exploring the sources of stereotypic views of men and women, it is worthwhile to briefly summarize recent social and economic trends.

A Historical Perspective on Men

During the late 1960s, a number of social forces converged to set into motion a cultural movement that has come to be known as the "men's movement." The movement evolved in part as a response to the women's liberation movement and was also inspired by the youth movement's opposition to the status quo and the Vietnam War. Currently, the men's movement is divided among several major organizations that promote differing ideologies and have diverse psychological underpinnings and political agendas.

Distorted Views of Men

Despite the efforts of many factions in the men's movement to promote gender equality and challenge sexual stereotypes, there are still strong tendencies to malign and depreciate men in contemporary society. Glide and Fiske (2001) have cited findings showing that men and women alike have more positive views of women than of men. Some early proponents of the feminist movement also expressed hostile attitudes toward men. As feminist bell hooks *[sic]* (1984/2001) observed, many women liberationists originally insisted on a '"woman only' feminist movement and a virulent anti-male stance" (p. 527). "Men, they argued, were all-powerful, misogynist oppressors—the enemy. Women were the oppressed—the victims" (p. 527). According to Young (1999), "The new feminism [beginning in the 1980s] ... focuses on the evil that men do to women" (p. 5).

Many people still view men as powerful, aggressive, insensitive, non-communicative, and misogynous and as being interested only in sex, not in intimacy or close relationships (Allen, 1997; Aries, 1997; Felson, 2002; Kupers, 1997; Rubin, 1983). It is not uncommon to see gender issues discussed, in both the professional and popular literature, from a biased point of view that perceives men as being less sensitive, feelingful, communicative, and empathic than women. For example, in attempting to make people more aware of the ways that commonly accepted stereotypes about men affect the raising of boys, Levant (1992) delineated the "seven traditional male role norms" (p. 380). Among the characteristics he described that fit these male role norms are "restrictive emotionality" and "nonrelational attitudes toward sexuality" (p. 380).

Linguist Tannen (1990), who bases her work on findings from selected gender studies, has argued that women feel that men do not communicate. Tannen (1997) attributes the problem to differences in conversational style. Her use of the terms *"report-talk* and *rapport-talk"* to depict these differences may have the effect of supporting stereotypic views. She contended that "For most men, talk is primarily a means to preserve independence and negotiate and maintain status in a hierarchical social order. ... For most women ... conversation is primarily a, ... way of establishing connections and negotiating relationships" (p. 88).

Such discussions also tend to portray men as generally being less willing than women to commit to a relationship. This same bias depicts men as being primarily interested in their careers, sporting activities, and practical matters and as being less interested than women in marriage and parenthood. We believe that these sexist attitudes prevent people from developing a genuine understanding or a realistic picture of men's personal qualities. Moreover, many men accept these generalizations as foregone conclusions and have internalized the associated negative emotional loading or bias. As a result, they subscribe to society's stereotypical and negative views of themselves, which causes them to turn against themselves and other men.

For example, in comparing men and women in terms of self-esteem, it is interesting to note that a study by Rudman and Goodwin (2004) showed that "women strongly implicitly prefer their own gender, whereas men do not" (p. 508). In an interview, Rudman further explained, '"A clear pattern shown in all four studies is that men do not like themselves automatically as much as women like themselves'. ... 'This contradicts a lot of theoretical thinking … [and suggests] that negative male stereotypes can promote greater liking for women'" (quoted in Dittmann, 2004, p. 11).

During the developmental years and throughout their lives, boys and men attempt to adjust their behavior according to these negative stereotypes about men (Pleck, 1995).[2] For example, Silverstein et al. (2002) have emphasized that men develop gender role identity as a result of strong social pressure to conform to cultural norms and stereotypes.[3] According to Pollack (1998), the myth that boys are "toxic" includes a perception of men as "psychologically unaware, emotionally unsocialized creatures" (p. 62). In his work, Pollack stresses the fact that men and women alike are damaged by accepting these stereotypes as real representations of boys and men.

There are also numerous stereotypes about men pertaining to their sexuality. In our society, men are generally perceived as being more sexually oriented than women, having more sexual experiences and fantasies than women, being more sexually aggressive, more random, more impersonal in their sexual encounters than women, and relating to women as sex objects (Levant, 1992; Pleck, 1995). Although research does tend to support the premise that men indicate more interest in sex than women,[4] the information is often misinterpreted or exaggerated. The same is true when people over' generalize or exaggerate research findings suggesting that men have more sexual experience and more sexual fantasies than their female counterparts, are more random in selecting partners, and desire more variety (Buss & Schmitt, 1993).

In relation to child-rearing, many men who believe that they are less nurturing or loving toward children than women may retreat from the paternal role and leave most of child-rearing functions to women. Some women reinforce this stereotype by subtly conveying that women understand better than men how best to raise a child (Pollack, 1998).[5] In describing how traditional gender roles based on cultural stereotypes have been manifested in fathering, Silverstein et al. (2002) commented, "Because a 'real' man must avoid 'sissy stuff,' a traditional father limits his involvement in child care. He might 'baby-sit' if his wife has to be away, but he does not actively manage the children" (p. 362).

Although family life has changed in recent years, partly as a result of women's increasing involvement in the workplace, internalized stereotypes and behaviors based on these biased views are difficult to overcome because they are deeply entrenched in people's thinking. In a series of interviews and discussion groups, several men and women revealed the ways in which distorted views of men were transmitted to them in the context of early interactions within their family-of-origin.

Colin: I've been thinking lately about how my mother's attitude toward men. affected me while I was growing up and how I'm still struggling with that in my adult life. I had a view of my father through my mother's eyes, and it was not a very good view. She really saw him as a critical, angry man. So I grew up seeing him, and almost all men, through her eyes, I didn't even know what a strong man was. To me, viewed through her eyes, strong men were mean. Strength was meanness.

Evan: I can identify totally with what Colin said. Anything that I do that feels male, I identify as being mean. I grew up in a household in which my father was at work all the time. When I was 8 years old, my father died and from then on I was surrounded by women who saw men as lechers. I picked up their point of view, and I've got that point of view toward other men. I've taken on that point of view toward myself, and it really restricts me. If I have a sexual urge that I feel like acting on, not even necessarily the physical act of sex per se, but just talking with a woman that I'm attracted to sexually, I feel totally constrained. I feel like if I make a move that I'm infringing on someone else's territory. I feel that it's wrong for me to do, it's mean for me to do and that I just don't belong there.

Kimberly: Whenever I feel interested in meeting a man or pursuing a relationship, I have a lot of cynicism about my prospects. I remember my mother lecturing me about men. I never thought much about her lectures at that point and I thought they had no effect on me whatsoever. But now I find myself thinking things like: "You're never going to find any man who is nice because there are no men who are like that. They're all horrible. They all want to make a fool out of you. They all do. They're all just going to drop you and toss you aside for somebody else. They all are."

Jennifer: My father didn't have any sexual experience before he married my mother when he was 23. He really believed the stereotype that men were out of control sexually. He was always telling me "You have to be really careful with men, because the least little thing you do to them is going to trigger them and they're going to be out of control and they won't be able to stop themselves."

Eric: Up until I was about six or seven, my sisters and I slept in the same room, and then we were separated. At that time, my younger sister was my best friend. I remember I could not understand what was going on. Also I remember 1 had a feeling I was being separated because I was changing into a person that could not control himself and I was going to do something bad. There was this unspoken feeling in my family that "Men get to a stage where once they become a sexual person it's something they can't control. They become like an animal, and you have to separate them from girls really early so that nothing happens in the family." And I know that as I grew older, I kept on waiting for this mysterious thing to happen to me that I was going to turn into an animal in terms of being sexual and not be able to hold myself back.

A Historical Perspective on Women

The feminist movement (a revival of the original 19th century women's movement) has lobbied for better child care, abortion rights, and ratification of the Equal Rights Amendment and has taken an aggressive stand against patriarchism (Yanak, 2004).[6] On the socioeconomic level, feminists have contributed significantly to women's goals of achieving personal freedom and equal status with men (Showalter, 2001).

Living within a patriarchal society has indeed had a significant impact on women's lives (Bigler, 1999; Gilligan, 1982, 1996). For many centuries, women were denied access to power and influence in many important spheres of life and therefore many adopted indirect or passive means in attempting to fulfill their human potentialities (Chesler, 2001). As Rubin (1983) noted more than twenty years ago, "Not only are women economically and socially disadvantaged when compared to men, but social definitions insist that passivity and dependency are the core of femininity while aggressiveness and independence are the central features of masculinity" (p. 141). Today, many women still find it difficult to break out of this stereotypic mold, often for reasons that are more psychological than social (Gilligan, 1991).[7]

Distorted Views of Women

Women are continually being shaped and directed by stereotypes in destructive ways that cause alienation between the sexes. For example, in Western society, attitudes that portray females as helpless and unstable are still commonplace and have both a direct and indirect influence on economic as well as sexual equality between the sexes. Many feminists predict that it will take considerably more time to alter basic attitudes about being a woman in a patriarchal society (Chodorow, 1978; J. Miller, 1976; Spence, 1999; Young, 1999).

Admittedly, it is difficult to alter, within one or two generations, deeply held sexist beliefs based on a centuries-old patriarchal social order. One reason for this difficulty lies in the fact that many sexist attitudes are implicit and exist on an unconscious level. As noted previously, unconscious, implicit beliefs held by parents are internalized by their children and, in turn, are

reinforced by stereotypic views still prevalent in most modern societies. In fact, some theorists argue that sexist views against women based on patriarchism have changed little during the past 100 years. For example, according to Rosenberger (1998), "Freud's … [1905/1953] evaluation of women as possessing weaker superego development reflected the prevailing social context of womanhood. … This paradigm is little changed today and little varied across cultures" (p. 66).

In terms of physical strength and overall body size, women are clearly the weaker sex. Originally, these biological factors undoubtedly contributed to the formation of an unequal power structure based on the division of labor by sex difference. However, women who exhibit overly passive or compliant traits and behaviors have probably been influenced more by suppression, social prejudice, and stereotypic views than by these biological determinants. Fiske et al. (1997) described the effects on women of trying to follow "prescriptive" stereotypes or "female role norms": "[Women's] competence is undervalued if they behave in traditionally feminine ways, while their interpersonal skills are derogated and their mental health is questioned if they behave in traditionally masculine ways" (p. 322).

In the area of sexuality, women are invariably thought of as having less sexual desire and fewer sexual fantasies, and as being more passive sexually than men. They are viewed as having little interest in casual sexual encounters and as only wanting sex if they are in love or involved on a deep level (Buss & Schmitt, 1993; Daly & Wilson, 1983; Ridley, 1993). In their relationships, they are believed to be more loving and faithful than men. Society views with criticism and suspicion those women whose sexual preferences and behaviors fail to conform to these stereotypes. According to Reid and Bing (2000), most people still rely on these stereotypes when defining women's roles:

> Women have been represented on one polarity as asexual madonnas, and at the other end as highly sexual, alluring sirens. ... They are either good or evil. The good woman will be represented biologically as virginal (i.e., pure, innocent, and naive) and psychologically as a self-effacing, self-denying earth mother. The evil woman is seen as a whore; she is a scheming, ambitious, and a clever seductress. (pp. 141–144)

Clearly, not all of the social prejudice that women face is hostile; some paternalistic attitudes toward women as the weaker sex are seemingly positive. For example, although women are typically perceived as more childish, melodramatic, scatterbrained, or irrational than men, on the positive side, they are seen as sensitive, empathic, and intuitive, as easily forming deep emotional attachments, and as primarily interested in a long-term relationship and parenthood. As Glick and Fiske (2001) pointed out, "Benevolent sexism (a subjectively favorable, chivalrous ideology that offers protection and affection to women who embrace conventional roles) coexists with hostile sexism (antipathy toward women who are viewed as usurping men's power)" (p. 109). (Views of men as strong, masterful, and rational are also "benevolent.")

According to Glick and Fiske, many women willingly accept this stereotypic view of themselves. "Benevolent sexism, after all, has its rewards; chivalrous men are willing to sacrifice their own well-being to provide for and to protect women" (p. 115). Indeed, both men and women tend to endorse "benevolent" sexist beliefs that perceive women as basically weaker than men in areas that go beyond size and strength and as needing special protection and care.[8]

We have found that although most women believe on a conscious level that they are as competent and as intelligent as their male counterparts, on an unconscious level, many still hold internalized stereotypic beliefs that are diametrically opposed to their conscious attitudes. Despite the fact that women are increasingly assuming leadership positions in the business and professional world, in their personal lives and in their intimate relationships, some women continue to relate to men as "ultimate rescuers" and feel they need to be taken care of on some level. In a meta-analysis that investigated gender differences in helping behaviors, Eagly and Crowley (1986) found indications of this tendency. "In general men. helped more than women and women received more help than men" (p. 283).

In calling attention to traditional stereotypes and conventional views of gender roles that alienate men and women, Keen (1997) argued that "Women, we are told, want to talk about their feelings and problems, and men just want to solve them. Women want relationship, and men need to maintain autonomy. We suffer from different communication strategies, tongues, languages" (p. 12). Keen went on to say that

> There is widespread resentment about the ways we [are] wounded by the gender roles we inherited. Men were taught that they could earn love only by providing, taking charge, being in control, and protecting women and children. Women were taught that they could earn love only by being nurturing, sexy, submissive, and passive. (p. 26)

In a similar vein, Marmor (2004) has criticized the negative sexist views of women still promulgated in society, many of which were based on findings in previous research: "The degree of cultural and/or intellectual accomplishment on the part of women as compared to men is not dependent on any presumptive inherent biological or psychosexual inferiority, nor has it ever been" (p. 19).

In recent years, a number of researchers have critiqued many of the widely publicized findings obtained from gender studies. We suggest that the ways in which some studies were designed probably contributed to the contradictory and inaccurate findings previously reported in the literature. For example, Grossman and Wood (1993) manipulated instructions to subjects in two experiments. They discovered that any gender differences in emotional expressivity were largely related to subjects' endorsement of gender-role expectations. In other words, subjects in the two experiments responded as they believed they were "supposed" to respond, according to the popular gender stereotypes.

In addition, Burn (1996) reported that measures of empathy used in some studies found larger sex differences on self-report questionnaires than on physiological measures.

Her finding suggested that males may "be unwilling to portray themselves as empathic on a self-report measure, because doing so is inconsistent with the male gender role" (p. 57). We contend that this finding could also be explained by the fact that men may be reluctant to reveal feelings of empathy or be emotionally expressive because they have come to accept without question the stereotypical view of themselves as being less empathic and emotionally expressive than women.

Other recent gender studies have shown that many stereotypes negatively comparing men with women in terms of their ability to express emotion are blatantly inaccurate, while others have interpreted inconclusive findings as being definitive (Barrett, Robin, Pietromonaco, & Eyssell, 1998; Carpenter & Addis, 2000; Conway, 2000).

In studies that examined men's and women's communication styles, Burleson, Kunkel, Samter, and Werking (1996) found few differences in key aspects of communication. In particular, Dindia and Allen (1992), in their meta-analysis of 205 studies involving 23,702 subjects, found that "sex differences in self-disclosure are small" (pp. 117–118). These findings contradicted Tannen's (1990) hypotheses regarding differences between men and women in their communications styles as described in the previous section. Hook, Gerstein, Detterich, and Gridley (2003) concluded that "Men and women were similar in their level of comfort with both giving and receiving emotional support in relationships" (p. 471). In relation to men's and women's views of love, Fehr and Broughton (2001) found that "Unexpectedly, both women and men embraced companionate kinds of love as representing their view of love" (p. 134).

In terms of sexuality, it does not appear that women are innately less interested in sex or more sexually inhibited than men. In fact, when men and women are surveyed, there is tremendous overlap in their sexual propensities and preferences. For example, contrary to the popular stereotype that men have far more sexual experiences than women, a recent survey (Smith, 1998) showed that since the early 1900s, women have gradually become more experienced sexually. In 1998, 51.5% of women between the ages of 15 and 19 had engaged in premarital sex, as compared with 60% of the men in the same age group.

In a meta-analysis of research in this area, Hyde and Oliver (2000) concluded that "The bottom line is that the theories reviewed … do not make strong differential predictions regarding patterns of gender differences in sexuality. Rather, they yield similar if not identical predictions" (p. 73).[9] In other words, there appear to be more similarities than differences between men and women in areas pertaining to sexual interest and sexual behavior.

Attachment research has provided conflicting findings regarding differences between men and women in their attachment patterns in adult romantic relationships. For example, Shaver, Papalia, et al. (1996) found some gender differences in attachment styles, particularly in individuals categorized as being insecurely attached, while others (Gentzler & Kerns, 2004; Schmitt, Alcalay, et al., 2003) found no gender differences in individuals categorized as avoidantly attached.

Lastly, in terms of child-rearing, Silverman (2003) reported findings from numerous studies, including research conducted by Lamb, showing no differences between fathers' and mothers' desire and ability to parent their children. For example, in summarizing their research, Lamb and Lewis (2004) reported, "Most men in a variety of cultural settings clearly adapt positively to parenting" (p. 278).

We believe that it is important to explore the differences that do exist between the genders, separate from the stereotypic biases, overgeneralizations, and frequently politicized interpretations of research findings regarding such differences.

OUR VIEWS

Our observations of men and women have led to the conclusion that many gender stereotypes are exaggerated and destructive. Our interviews and discussions with individuals, couples, and family members resulted in information that often contradicted widely accepted generalizations about how women and men view emotions, sex, relationships, and childrearing, and how they relate in an intimate association. For example, we found that although most males traditionally have been taught to mask their emotions, including feelings of empathy, compassion, and sadness, they are as emotionally expressive as females in settings where such feelings are acceptable. In spite of this, some of the men we interviewed still tended to underestimate their sensitivity and their capacity for experiencing emotion and, to some extent, they idealized women with respect to these qualities.

In terms of committing to a relationship, the large majority of men reported that they desired a long-term association with another person, were as interested in marriage and raising children as their female counterparts, and wanted to share the responsibilities of child-rearing with their partner. We also found that, contrary to stereotypic thinking, men were not indifferent to women's feelings and moods. In fact, most of the men we interviewed showed a consistent concern for their partner's well-being and reported feeling the most happy and contented when their partners were feeling strong and self-confident.

In relation to child-rearing, both men and women indicated a strong interest in and feeling for children. Moreover, many women reported having the same anxieties about handling newborns as men did. They did not feel that they possessed an inherent maternal quality that made them more sensitive or attuned to their infants and children than their mates. In fact, there tended to be wide variation among mothers as well as fathers in their capability to care for their offspring. We also noted that many men gave child-rearing functions a high priority and tried to spend as much time as possible with their children. Our findings with respect to men's involvement in child-rearing functions are supported in part by Pleck's (1997) findings that there have been "Clear increases in paternal engagement and responsibility, especially over the past three decades" (p. 75).

We also found that in general, both men and women reported feeling guilty and were self-critical when they felt they were not living up to popular societal stereotypes. Moreover, many said that they felt resentful and angry when a partner failed to conform to certain gender role expectations.

We suggest that there may be differences between men and women with respect to the ways that they express themselves in a sexual situation. For example, a sexually healthy, emotionally mature man would be comfortably assertive and responsive during sex. This term refers to the capacity to respond spontaneously and sensitively to indications of the woman's increasing excitement and to an ability to remain emotionally close throughout the experience and afterward. This emotional contact can be preserved through verbal and/or nonverbal communication.

Being comfortably active indicates an absence of self-doubts, feelings of inadequacy, and anxieties related to feeling completely responsible for satisfying one's partner. It also implies a freedom from the fear that some men experience in the presence of a passionate, wanting woman.

In fact, many men report experiencing the highest levels of sexual arousal when their partner becomes excited or aroused. At the same time they enjoy receiving physical affection, touching, and sexual caressing from their partner.

A sexually healthy, emotionally mature woman would tend to be actively receptive during lovemaking. This implies a willingness to remain fully open to her partner during sex and the ability to stay in touch with one's bodily sensations and feelings rather than to retreat into one's mind. Women who are self-possessed and able to remain emotionally close to their partner during sex can be described as being actively receptive. During lovemaking, they are neither overly aggressive nor passive. Active receptivity as described here is representative of an internal state of wanting and the desire to enter into an equal physical and emotional transaction with another person. It is important to emphasize here that receptivity does not mean passivity. As Marmot (2004) noted, "Receptivity and passivity are not synonymous. It is a striking commentary on the power of a cultural prejudice that both male and female classical Freudians have always assumed that the vagina, as a hollow organ, *had* to be a passive receptacle" (p. 16).

If a woman is in this receptive state, that is, allowing herself to completely experience feelings of sexual desire, she tends to elicit a strong sexual response from her partner. Ideally, this receptivity and openness are part of her overall style of relating to her partner. In other words, these behaviors and traits of openness and vulnerability would extend beyond the bedroom into the couple's daily life and significantly contribute to harmony in their relationship. When making love, ideally both partners, if emotionally mature and sexually healthy, would be fully engaged in an equal transaction in terms of both giving and receiving affection and sexual pleasure, and each would be responsible for asking for what he or she wanted sexually.

In a discussion group, Ken talked about feeling that his girlfriend, Lauren, was not open to receiving pleasure from him.

> *Ken;* The one thing I've had a hard time saying is that I don't see our sex life as being as exciting as I would like it to be. I don't feel excited when 1 think about making love. I feel that some of the things you do make me not want to be with you. When I thought more about it, I realized that it seems difficult for you to receive pleasure from me during the sexual act. I haven't been able to explain it very well or talk about it with you until now.
>
> I don't feel critical of you, or critical about the reasons why I don't feel attracted to you. I have an idea of what it is. I think it's difficult for you to let me make you feel good, to have an orgasm. It's hard for me to feel like I can give you an orgasm. 1 feel like you take it from me [sad]. Then I feel gypped out of being able to make you feel good. I feel upset, different than how I like to feel with you. Instead, what I end up doing is avoiding being sexual with you.

We also learned that a man's emotional and sexual responses appeared to be strongly related to the woman's genuine sexual desire. A woman may act interested or aggressively pursue sex, but without feeling and genuine desire for the man, her partner will have difficulty responding sexually. Most men blame themselves for sexual failures and tend to deny their partner's influence, even when intellectually aware of her potential effect. We also found that the way women feel about themselves and their physical appearance has considerable impact on their partner's sexual desire. Women also revealed that they experienced less sexual desire and often found it difficult to feel excited or aroused when their partner was cold or withdrawn, became overly dependent, seemed to value work over personal and family life, or felt victimized.

Therefore, there are several definitive differences between men and women and these differential behaviors and propensities are influenced by a multitude of biological, environmental, and cultural factors. As Chiland (2004) argued,

> Mead [Mead, 1948] shows that every society has a concept of how males and females should feel and behave and how, through the educative and other child-rearing procedures it sets up, it shapes children in such a way that they become the men and women that society expects. (p. 86)

The socialization process within the family, differential developmental tasks, and social learning through identification with and imitation of parental role-models are all formative influences that interact to generate different sexual attitudes and behaviors in men and women.

PARENTAL IMPACT ON ADULT SEXUALITY

In this section, we focus on the dynamics operating in the earliest relationships of both male and female children that impact their later development as sexual beings. It is important to note that social learning in relation to sexuality and differential sexual behavior takes place in the context of role modeling and imitation, especially of the traits, attitudes, and behaviors manifested by the same-sex parent. Hogben and Byrne (1998) stressed the fact that "As children are more likely to be reinforced for same-sex imitation, they tend to pick up same-sex behaviors, which leads to the cognitive association of particular behaviors with male versus female sexuality" (Hogben & Byrne, 1998, Theoretical Models and Research Outcomes section, ¶ 9). According to learning theory, "children imitate same-gender adults more than other-gender adults, so that the gender-role behavior of the previous generation perpetuates itself in the next generation" (Hyde & Oliver, 2000, p. 61). Thus, an exploration of parent-child relations can facilitate a better understanding of same-sex identification and imitation processes that contribute to adult sexual functioning of individuals of both genders.

Fathers and Sons

In attempting to establish a relationship with their father, many boys experience serious inner conflicts: they long for tenderness, love, and nurturance from their fathers, yet in some families, there may be a taboo against fathers being physically affectionate to their sons. According to Pollack (1998), "Because of the way we as a society view boys and men … many fathers, especially in public settings, may feel inhibited about showing the empathy they *naturally* feel for their sons" (p. 116).[10]

Competitive feelings between family members can have a negative effect on boys' sexual development. Boys may experience envy, hostility, and feelings of rivalry directed toward them from their fathers and may have competitive feelings toward their fathers as well (Firestone, 1994a). We have found that both sets of feelings can contribute to the sense of alienation that many boys feel in relation to their fathers. As adults, their friendships and associations with other men are often influenced by emotional residuals of this conflict. For example, a son's awareness that as an adult he is now enjoying a more satisfying intimate relationship than his father had can lead to guilt and anxiety about surpassing his father. Men's achievements in their professional and personal lives and in their relationships can activate powerful feelings of fear and guilt, as well as a sense of loss.

In addition, fathers serve as role models for their sons in terms of both positive and negative behaviors they exhibit. For example, in a study of more than 80 adolescent boys, D'Angelo, Weinberger, and Feldman (1995) found that sons of fathers who were aggressive and who lacked self-control exhibited numerous problems as adolescents and adults. Included in these problematic behaviors were "poor peer relations ... at-risk behaviors ... multiple sexual partners ... [and] poor conflict resolution skills" (p. 883).

Boys observe and identify with a father's hostile and defensive attitudes toward their mother and other women, as noted in chapter 3. A father's weakness as a role model poses a serious limitation on the son's ability to develop a strong sense of male identity. Moreover, many fathers unknowingly support the mother's stereotypic views of men as uncommunicative, harsh, and unfeeling. Many women reinforce this sexist attitude when they use their husbands as agents of punishment. As a result, many children, boys and girls alike, learn to view male strength in a negative light. With respect to these conflicting views of masculinity that boys are presented with, Park (1995) emphasized that

> What the boy needs is a father's help in dealing with the emotional pressures that come from his mother. He needs to learn that there are other views of masculinity than those which she propounds, and that what she says to him has more to do with her own past experiences than with him. (p. 23)

Some fathers manifest intrusive child-rearing practices when relating to their sons. Barber and Harmon (2002) have described a form of "psychological control" that they observed in many family constellations. According to Barber and Harmon, psychological control includes such parental behaviors as possessiveness, protectiveness, love withdrawal, control of the child's personal life, and erratic emotional behavior. Barber and Harmon reported preliminary findings from a number of studies that investigated the negative effects of paternal psychological control on male adolescent behaviors, particularly tendencies to be aggressive in peer relationships. Although their results are still inconclusive because of the limited number of samples studied thus far, there are indications that this type of control on the part of fathers is detrimental to the psychosocial development of their male offspring.

Other fathers exert harsher forms of behavioral control in interactions with their sons. For example, in his work, G. Parker (1983) observed a number of fathers who exerted "affectionateless control" over their sons.[11] Parker defined affectionless control as a harsh parenting style that appears to represent a diminished caring on the part of fathers. For example, Jain, Belsky, and Crnic (1996) reported a group of fathers who they described as traditional in their child-rearing practices. "The traditional men were those classified as disciplinarians and as uninvolved. ... [They were] over-reactive to typical toddler behavior, resulting in almost exclusively disciplinary interactions or avoidance of their sons altogether" (p. 440).

As a result of these influences, many men feel isolated and alone in their suffering and may try to mask their pain with a tough, defensive exterior (Jolliff & Home, 1999; Pollack, 1998; Silverstein et al., 2002). They are convinced that other men do not experience the same feelings of inadequacy, desperation, and fear that torment them. Because they feel alienated, they often find it difficult to relate to other men on more than a superficial level.

Pollack (1998) delineated several negative consequences in male development stemming from absent or uninvolved fathers. He noted that "Father absence has been correctly linked to a host of ills for boys ... [including] difficulties with emotional commitments" (pp. 124–125). As noted, interactions between parents can have both positive and negative effects on their male offspring. Alienation between parents, argumentative interactions, and marital distress in general can interfere significantly with a boy's relationship with his father. For example, one study reported by Cummings, Goeke-Morey, and Raymond (2004) showed that "Marital conflict predicted more disruptions in father-son than in mother-son interactions" (p. 200).

In general, the anxiety and insecurity from these early childhood experiences with their fathers are perpetuated in men's adult relationships. The defenses that they formed to cope with this pain and hurt interfere with their achieving real intimacy and adult sexual relating.

Mothers and Daughters

In the traditional family constellation, the mother still has the role of primary caregiver and therefore exerts the greater influence on children (Mendell, 1998). Mothers' strengths as well as their weaknesses are transmitted intergenerationally to their daughters through the processes of identification and imitation. In general, girls tend to form a stronger identification with their mothers than do boys (Chodorow, 1978; Fenchel, 1998; Hudson & Jacot, 1995). According to Genevie and Margolies (1987), mothers "form this primary relationship more readily with their daughters whom they view as extensions of themselves" (p. 291). This phenomenon has the potential for perpetuating mature, positive personality characteristics through succeeding generations of women. However, the negative effects of this identification process often outweigh the positive (Fenchel, 1998; Firestone, 1990b; Welldon, 1988).

Mothers who are intrusive and violate the boundaries of their children damage their daughters' ability to develop independence and autonomy as adult women. For example, an emotionally immature mother may attempt to merge her identity with her daughter and overstep the boundaries between them (Fenchel, 1998; Rubin, 1983; Westkott, 1997).[12] If a mother seeks to fulfill herself through her children, her daughter often feels drained of her emotional resources and angry at the mother's intrusiveness and control. Many girls react to their mother's exaggerated focus by repressing their anger and becoming more passive and compliant. As adults, they tend to unconsciously hold back their affection and sexual responses in intimate relationships, with little or no understanding of the underlying reasons.

> *Emily:* Recently I started thinking about my relationship with my mother and how I was always her baby and I was her best friend and I was her everything. I remember going to the store in high school and crossing the street and her holding my hand and feeling totally humiliated and being so afraid my friends were going to see me holding my mother's hand crossing the street. And she'd always make a big deal about it. Anything I did, she was right there.
>
> One time my boyfriend and I—we were totally in love— we were at my Mom's house and we laid down on the floor to watch TV, and my mother came and laid right between us. Then she laughed and said, "Oh silly me. What have I done?" Today I feel still guilty about falling in love. Getting to know a man is okay, but once the relationship deepens, then I feel guilty and I want to step back. Each time this happens, it's hard for me to maintain the closeness. Something comes between us. It sounds strange, but it's almost like she gets in the way. It's like somehow she possesses me or something like that. I feel like she's still here, she's still getting in my way, and she still wants me. She doesn't want me to have anything, except for her.

Paradoxically, the more the daughter resents the mother and suffers in interactions with her, the more she tends to imitate her behavior. Her attempts to remain close to the mother lead to the formation of a fantasy bond or imagined connection with her (Firestone, 1990b). As a result of this negative identification, the daughter tends to incorporate and compulsively act out her mother's most negative characteristics, traits that were not necessarily representative of her- mother's personality as a whole. This alliance or imagined fusion with the mother can play a significant part in limiting the daughter's ability to assume the role of an adult sexual woman. For example, some women experience profound separation anxiety when they symbolically or literally move away from the mother as they reach higher levels of self-differentiation and become more individuated.

In other cases, a daughter may fear her mother's feelings of hostility, jealousy, and envy as she moves toward sexual maturity. She may actually be afraid of retaliation from the mother for seeking adult sexual fulfillment. In our experience, we have found that both separation anxiety and fear of the mother's envy or vindictiveness are often experienced by women at crucial points in their sexual development. Caplan (1981) has described how a daughter may adjust to her mother's envy: "Often, she does one of two things (or tries both at different times): she reduces her efforts to achieve (or at least begins to conceal them from her mother), and she puts emotional or physical distance between herself and her mother" (p. 120).

Guilt reactions may also become more evident as young women take tentative steps toward independence or move away from emotional ties with the family. In the case of adolescent girls, the guilt involved in breaking away or "leaving her mother behind" is often intense and debilitating, especially when the mother is depressed, self-denying, self-destructive, or immature in her orientation (Richman, 1986).

Thus, each step in the daughter's movement toward self-differentiation and separation from the mother, entering into a sexual relationship with a man, getting married, starting a family of her own, can create varying degrees of guilt, fear, and separation anxiety. During such critical periods, these powerful emotions often cause women to retreat to a sameness with the mother. Similarly, each step that women take toward sexual maturity is filled with conflict. Most women are necessarily ambivalent; they are torn between expressing their love and sexual desire in relation to a man, which represents a symbolic separation from the mother, and holding back their loving responses, which affirms the imaginary connection with her (Firestone, 1990b; Rubin, 1983). In reporting data from interviews with pregnant women, Rheingold (1964) described the consequences of preserving the imagined connection with one's mother:

> A woman may bring any number of assets to marriage—compassion, wisdom, intelligence, skills, an imaginative spirit, delight-giving femininity, good humor, friendliness, pride in a job well done—but if she does not bring emancipation from her mother, the assets may wither or may be overbalanced by the liability of the fear of being a woman, (p. 451)

Over many generations, women have tended to internalize compliant, yet inwardly defiant, behavior patterns that have been as detrimental to their personal development as the social forces that made their use necessary. These passive-aggressive tendencies often give rise to withholding patterns that may only be partially conscious; yet these behaviors act as barriers to harmonious relations between men and women. Although many women still feel restricted or oppressed by the inequities that continue to exist within society, we believe that much of the damage to their initiative and sexuality can be traced to limitations imposed by identification with negative traits in the mother and fears of separating from the imagined connection or fantasy bond with her (Firestone, 1990b).

Mothers and Sons

A significant aspect of maternal influence on male offspring is the propensity of some mothers to be overprotective, overly involved, intrusive, or nervously focused on their children, and on their sons in particular. This overprotective stance may originate from benevolent maternal attitudes, however, it can also arise because of a mother's lack of involvement in other parts of her life. As French psychoanalyst and social critic Kristeva (Oliver, 2002) commented,

> Nobody knows what the good-enough mother is ... but I would try to suggest that maybe the good-enough mother is the mother who has something else to love besides her child; it could be her work, her husband, her lovers, etc. If for a mother the child is the meaning of her life, it's too heavy. (p. 336)

Investigations into the long-term effects on boys of maternal overprotection and control have shown that "psychological control was positively related to both depression and antisocial behavior" in older boys (Barber & Harmon, 2002, p. 19). As adults, men who were affected by their mothers' anxious concern, intrusiveness, and exaggerated focus may exhibit a wide range of defensive reactions. To varying degrees, they may experience painful feelings of inadequacy or have a fear of being smothered or dominated by a woman. They may even become critical of sexually responsive women and unconsciously averse to forming relationships with them.

We have found that men tend to experience feelings of sexual inferiority when the mother has been inappropriate or seductive in her behavior during the formative years. It has been shown that a seductive relationship with the mother often stimulates intense oedipal rivalry and leads to increased fear of competing and powerful feelings of inadequacy in the growing boy (Love, 1990; A. Miller, 1979/1981; Park, 1995). This type of provocative relationship on the part of some mothers can predispose sexual problems in adult males, including either an avoidance of sex, or a tendency to be overly compliant or submissive in relationships with women. In general, these family dynamics lead to considerable hostility between men arid women and can seriously undermine their sexual relationships. On the basis of 150 in-depth interviews with men during a period of two years, Park (1995) found that for many men, "The experience of being truly close to someone else, whether man or woman, puts him at risk of experiencing again the same bewildering emotions that he knew in infancy" (p. 3). Specifically, with respect to overly solicitous and emotionally seductive mothers, Park noted that

> Men [from these enmeshed families], who generally have so much of mother, tend to experience her presence as sometimes smothering, stifling and demanding. In their later relationships, the pull towards intimacy and sexual union is powerfully countered by the fear of being submerged or swallowed up. They cannot get close because they do not think they will survive the experience. (p. 125)

In some families where the mother tends to form an exclusive relationship with her son, the father is often pushed into the periphery of the boy's life. We have found that although the father may feel distressed and angry at the way his son is being overprotected or indulged, he also feels excluded from the relationship and finds it difficult to intervene, and he may develop resentment toward both his wife and son (Firestone, 1990b).

A mother who is intrusive in this way exerts a strong pull on the son that leaves him feeling empty. The same person that a son would naturally turn to for love and care is instead seeking nurturance, care, and love from him (Love, 1990). Therefore, as an adult, he may self-protectively pull back from women and turn away from potential sources of gratification in close relationships (Firestone & Catlett, 1999). Men who have been damaged in this way may develop habitual patterns of holding back their affection and sexual responses because they perceive their partner's sexual interest as a demand.

Emotional unavailability, rejection, or withholding on the part of mothers also have detrimental consequences for male children (Fenchel, 1986; Park, 1995; Pollack, 1998; Pollack & Levant, 1998). For example, if a mother withholds her affection and love from her son, his hurt and angry response may cause him to suppress his affectionate feelings for her. In other cases, he may become clingy, desperate, and overly dependent on her. Subsequently, as an adult, he may be uncomfortable with dependent feelings in himself.

Many men continue to search for gratification of their unfulfilled longings for affection, tenderness, and love. The desperation and dependency they felt toward their mother is now directed toward the primary woman in their lives. In their adult associations, these men seek symbolic safety and reassurance in an imagined connection or fantasy bond with women (maternal substitutes) to their own detriment and that of their sexual relationship (Firestone, 1985). According to Rubin (1983), the man's sexual involvement with a woman

> Calls up the memory of the infantile attachment to mother along with the old ambivalence about separation and unity, about emotional connection and separateness. It's likely therefore that it will elicit an intense emotional response—a response that's threatening even while it's gratifying. ... It's also what they fear. For it threatens their defenses against the return of those long-repressed feelings for that other woman—the first connection in their lives. So they hold on to the separation between the sexual and emotional and thereby keep the repression safe. (pp. 105–106)

Fathers and Daughters

Fathers also play a significant role in their daughters' development. It has been found that paternal warmth and involvement in the family are important factors influencing the development of femininity in young girls (Cramer, 1997). In explaining the importance of fathers in the lives of their female offspring, Rubin (1983) stresses that fathers are crucial in helping their daughters successfully differentiate from the mother. She noted that

> In childhood, a girl handles the threat [of separation from the mother] by turning to father to help her make and maintain the necessary separation. ... It's this difference, and the importance it holds in her separation struggle, that helps to define a girl's sexual orientation. ... A father affirms the femaleness of his daughter. (pp. 147–148)

There is also some evidence showing that paternal neglect, emotional unavailability, or indifference are hurtful to female children. One study (Manlove &. Vernon-Feagans, 2002) of fathers and infant sons and daughters found that fathers were available to their sons significantly more than to their daughters. The fathers in this sample were also much more involved in caregiving or child-tearing tasks in relation to their sons than their daughters.

In a seminal article, Ellis et al. (2003) posed the question: "Does father absence place daughters at special risk for early sexual activity and teenage pregnancy?" These researchers conducted longitudinal studies in the United States and New Zealand in which community samples of girls were followed prospectively from early in life (5 years) to approximately age 18. It was found that the answer to this question is yes. "First, in both the U.S. and New Zealand samples, there was a dose-response relationship between timing of onset of father absence and early sexual outcomes," (p. 815), including teenage pregnancy. Cramer (1997) also emphasized that "fathers contribute heavily to their daughter's representations of gender identity and of relations between the sexes," but she qualified her statement as follows: "The degree of cohesion [agreement] or of conflict between female images carried by mother and father will in great part determine the future woman's fate" (p. 388).

In many areas of female psychosexual development, it appears that on the one hand, fathers can provide confirmation of their daughter's feminine characteristics, while on the other, they can denigrate these same potentialities. For example, several women participants in our seminars reported feeling humiliated by fathers who depreciated or ridiculed them. Often these humiliating events occurred early in the girl's life:

> Jacqueline: When I was about five years old, my sister and 1 were arguing in our bedroom while we were getting dressed and my father was yelling for me to come into the living room. I didn't have any clothes on yet, but I was so afraid to not respond right away when he called that 1 went out into the living room. I was naked when 1 walked in there, and when he saw me, he started laughing. I remember feeling humiliated and there was nothing I could do to cover myself up either.
>
> Paula: My father teased me all the time about my body, especially when I got to be a teenager. If I got dressed up to go to a party and was wearing a padded bra, he would notice and invariably say "Hey, it looks like you're getting help today." I was always very embarrassed about my breasts being small anyway, so I would feel totally humiliated when

he said that. His teasing made me feel terrible about myself and I thought 1 was so inadequate, that something was really wrong with me, that my body wasn't right somehow.

Obviously, in families where the father has an overly sexualized involvement or actually acts out incestuous feelings, he has a profoundly harmful effect on his daughter's developing sexuality. In relation to father-daughter incest, Herman (1981) suggested that: "The actual sexual encounter may be brutal or tender, painful or pleasurable; but it is always, inevitably, destructive to the child. The father, in effect, forces the daughter to pay with her body for affection and care which should be freely given" (p. 4).

In summarizing this section, we suggest that the psychodynamics operating in the father-daughter and father-son dyads described above are complicated and often difficult to untangle. As Lamb and Lewis (2004) commented, "Because the two parents' behaviors, attributions, and attitudes are complexly interrelated, it is hard to identify paternal effects" (p. 290). However, these researchers also stressed the fact that "The evidence to date suggests that ..., earlier paternal involvement predicts their adult children's feelings of satisfaction in spousal relationships" (p. 290).

GENDER-ROLE SOCIALIZATION AND DEVELOPMENTAL TASKS

The ways that children learn to conform to their gender roles are largely determined by familial and cultural influences; however, there is considerable controversy regarding how male and female children are socialized into their respective gender roles. Some theorists suggest that society's patriarchal influences still direct the socialization of boys and girls (Nealer, 2002; Pollack, 1998), whereas others claim there is little difference in how male and female offspring are being raised in today's families (Geary, 1998). In addition, social learning theorists have hypothesized that differences in mothers' and fathers' styles of relating to each other must "somehow help boys and girls acquire gender-appropriate behavioral repertoires" (Lamb & Lewis, 2004, p. 287).

A number of research studies have been conducted addressing the question of whether or not remnants of patriarchism have differential effects on boys and girls. In particular, many researchers have focused their attention on how society and families influence young children's development of emotional expressiveness and empathy. These personal qualities and/or behaviors are important because they affect one's ability to establish and maintain intimacy in an adult romantic relationship as well as influencing one's style of sexual relating.

Male Psychosexual Development and Gender-Role Socialization

Research findings related to the ways that boys are raised in our culture are contradictory. There are at least three competing theories that attempt to explicate the socialization of a male child into the masculine gender role. For example, in a review of research into child-rearing practices in the traditional family, Pollack (1998) asserted, "Studies show that boys at a very early age are pushed to suppress their vulnerable and sad feelings, they also demonstrate that boys are pressured to express the one strong feeling allowed them—*anger*" (p. 44). In other words, Pollack's findings showed that in more traditional families, boys are taught to act brave, strong, and tough and to not show weakness, and therefore to stay away from tender feelings. In Pollack's opinion, our patriarchal society also places a strong emphasis on male children separating emotionally from the mother at an early age. Other research (Levant, 1998) has indicated that male infants may be more emotionally expressive than female infants before this separation.[13] According to Levant, this research also showed that "Despite this initial advantage in emotional expressivity, males learn to tune out, suppress, and channel their emotions" (p. 39).

In contrast, Kiselica (2001) has criticized Pollack's and Levant's findings and their interpretations of such findings. According to Kiselica, boys and girls differ only in *how* they express feelings of empathy. In his work, Kiselica observed that "boys are just as likely as girls to help a crying peer" and concluded that male children and adolescents are "quite capable of responding prosocially when their fellow human beings are in some kind of trouble" (p. 15).

Geary's (1998) findings also contradict Pollack's and Levant's position. Geary discovered no differences between male and female infants and toddlers in their expressions of empathy in situations where they had caused the distress in another baby. In addition, he reported studies showing that the ways boys and girls are socialized to their gender roles are becoming increasingly similar, and that in general, parents "treat boys and girls in very similar ways" (p. 252).

Thus, it appears that many of the findings regarding socialization practices briefly reviewed here are ambiguous and largely inconclusive. We suggest that there is a need for further, carefully designed, observational studies of emotional expressiveness and empathy in adult males and their proposed antecedents in infants, toddlers, and young boys.

Psychoanalytic and object relations theorists have suggested that the different developmental pathways by which boys and girls attain sexual maturity may contribute to gender differences with respect to emotional responsiveness, attitudes toward sex, and sexual behavior (Benjamin, 1995; Chodorow, 1978, 1989; Kernberg, 1995).[14] For example, Kernberg (1995) contended that the developmental tasks faced by hoys (resolving the oedipal conflict) are substantially different from those that girls encounter. However, Kernberg also noted that all children, regardless of gender, face a similar developmental task—that of emancipating themselves from the effects of their parents' attitudes toward the opposite sex and their prohibitions regarding sexuality: "In short, overcoming fear and envy of the other gender represents, for both men and women, the exhilarating experience of overcoming the prohibitions against sexuality" (p. 54).

Mendell (1998) also stressed similarities between male and female development: "Both girls and boys must grapple with the issue of separating from the mother, first in order to attain object constancy and its associated autonomy and then in the service of becoming separate, differentiated, genital sexual beings" (pp. 231–232). The son, in differentiating himself from the mother, gradually shifts his identification to the father.

Female Psychosexual Development and Gender-Role Socialization

In contrast to theoretical approaches to male development, there is considerable agreement about the important social and cultural factors that continue to affect girls and women through the life span. Hyde and Oliver (2000) observed that "Central to the message conveyed to girls and women is that sex for them is legitimate only in the context of a committed relationship, whereas men are allowed more sexual freedom" (p. 71).

The results of this differential socialization would indicate that "women are punished for sexual activities such as having numerous partners or engaging in casual sex, whereas men are less likely to be punished, or perhaps are positively reinforced (through admiration or increased social status), for such behaviors" (p. 61). Hyde and Oliver (2000) noted, however, that this "double standard" has eased in recent years, being replaced by a more relaxed standard in which premarital or extramarital sex is tolerated for both men and women, yet these sexual involvements are acceptable for women only if they are in love or engaged.[15] Social role theory proposes that throughout childhood and beyond, girls learn implicitly and explicitly what will be expected of them as sexual women., including expectations based on the double standard described above (Bussey & Bandura, 1984; Fagot & Hagan, 1991). In addition, according to Reid and Bing (2000), girls are taught that they need to be cared for and protected because they are the "weaker" sex.

Attachment researchers have also explored gender differences in studies comparing the personality traits and behaviors in infants who are securely attached to their mothers with those of infants categorized as insecurely attached. One study found that at age 4, insecurely attached girls showed greater compliance and less assertive behavior than insecurely attached boys (Turner, 1991). However, Gilligan (1982) found that compliant behavior is manifested at a later stage in girls' development than was suggested by Turner.[16]

Psychoanalytic and psychodynamic theorists have approached the issue of female psychosexual development from a number of different perspectives. Early psychoanalysts proposed that girls needed to maintain their original identification with the mother in order to attain a decisive female identity and appropriate feminine gender role. At the same time, they also needed to make "libidinal connections to the father and'—unlike boys—[girls need] ... to overcome the rivalry with the mother" (Fenchel, 1998, p. xvi).

In contrast to classical psychoanalytic perspectives, early revisionists and critics of Freud's male-oriented theories (Chodorow, 1978; Homey, 1967) asserted that the most significant factor is not how girls resolve the triangular situation of the oedipal complex but rather how they respond to events and experiences that occur much earlier, during the pre-oedipal phase. Recently, Benjamin (1999) who endorses Horney's revisionist views, argued that "The girl reaches the [oedipal] complex by way of her libidinal strivings toward the father rather than through the narcissistic injury of not having a penis" (p. 88). Benjamin also noted that the anxiety of separating from the mother is more important than castration anxiety as a formative influence in female sexual development.[17]

French psychoanalyst Chodorow (1978, 1989) concluded that boys and girls have different gender-related experiences because women care for children. She contended that,

> As a result of being parented by a woman, both sexes are looking for a return to this emotional and physical union, A man achieves this directly through the heterosexual bond which replicates for him emotionally the early mother-infant exclusivity which he seeks to recreate. ... Women have different and a more complex set of relational needs, in which exclusive relationship to a man is not enough. This is because women experience themselves as parr of a relational triangle in which their father and men are emotionally secondary, or at most equal, in importance to their mother and women. Women, therefore, need primary relationships to women as well as to men. (1989, p. 77)

Chodorow further asserted that, in contrast to boys, it is not necessary for girls to sever the attachment to the mother in order to develop a feminine identity; instead they need to preserve the attachment to the mother.[18]

We agree, albeit only in part, with Chodorow's analysis of the differential outcomes of early developmental tasks for boys and girls. We contend that because male and female children face differential developmental tasks during their formative years, as adults they tend to have a conflict of interest when they enter into a sexual relationship with one another. As Chodorow asserted, for a man, a close sexual relationship can symbolize the fulfillment of his desire for close, affectionate contact with the mother that he has longed for since early childhood. However, this illusion that he is achieving a reunion with the mother is often based more on a childlike fixation than on a healthy, adult desire for companionship. We emphasize that for a woman, a mature sexual relationship with a man can symbolize separation and a loss of fantasized connection with the mother, which arouses consider-able fear, guilt, and anxiety. In such instances, men and women are at odds with each other in forming a committed sexual relationship, especially one that includes emotional closeness and satisfying sexuality. To avoid the blending of love and sexuality, one or both partners may withdraw either sexually or emotionally from the other person.

EVOLUTIONARY PSYCHOLOGISTS' CONJECTURES ABOUT DIFFERENTIAL MATING STRATEGIES

One difference between men and women suggested by evolutionary psychologists is that men and women employ different strategies in selecting mates (Buss & Barnes, 1996; Buss & Schmitt, 1993; Kriegman, 1999). These psychologists propose that prehistoric men and women needed to solve different types of adaptive problems (Buss, 1994; G. Miller, 2000). Describing the reasoning behind their conjectures, Buss and Schmitt (1993) explain that for more than two million years, our ancestors' choices evolved through a process of natural selection. During evolutionary history, both women and men have pursued short' and long-term mating strategies necessary for solving problems of adaptation. Their preferences for desirable qualities in a potential mate evolved from those strategies that best solved problems related to each gender's reproductive constraints, that is, strategies that essentially favor gene survival.

For example, Buss and Schmitt (1993) reported that men's tendencies to be more random and women's tendencies to be more selective have been observed to be universal across human societies. They conjectured that men tend to seek sexual variety and pursue a larger number of sexual relationships to ensure the replication of their genes in future generations. In attempting to identify which women were fertile, primitive man had to rely on cues indicating youth and physical health; "full lips, clear skin, smooth skin, clear eyes, lustrous hair, symmetry [breasts, waist and hips in proper proportions], good muscle tone, an absence of lesions ... sprightly, youthful gait and high activity level" (p. 208).

In order to allocate their limited resources to the offspring that carried their genes, our male ancestors also needed assurance that they were the rightful parent. According to Buunk, Angleitner, Oubaid, and Buss (1996), "Over human evolutionary history, men have faced a profound adaptive problem that has not been faced by women: uncertainty in their parenthood of children" (p. 359). In modern times, men still tend to prefer "women who are young and physically attractive as indicators of reproductive value (see Buss, 1989b) and who are sexually loyal and likely to be faithful as indicators of paternity certainty" (Buss & Schmitt, 1993, p. 226).

These theorists (Buss &. Schmitt, 1993) found that for the most part women are highly selective in choosing a mate. Their selectivity is partly a function of a biological imperative to find both the best genes for their children (Wilson, 1981) as well as the resources and parental interest necessary for assisting in the rearing of offspring to reproductive age. According to Buss and Schmitt, "*women in long-term mating* contexts, *more than men, will desire cues to a potential mate's ability to acquire resources, including ambition, good earning capacity, professional degrees, and wealth.* This prediction has been confirmed extensively across cultures" (p. 223). Although different groups value different characteristics, this general pattern appears to hold up across cultures.[19] According to evolutionary psychologists, men and women also have different strategies in relation to short-term partner selection and casual sex (Schmitt et al., 2003). For example, in "choosing partners for a sexual liaison, men reliably indicated lower criteria than did women" (Kenrick & Trost, 1993, p. 154).

The hypotheses set forth by evolutionary theorists are not without their critics, especially when the theory is applied to assumed differences in male and female mating strategies. Moore and Travis (2000) argued that,

> As applied to human culture, this view [that males benefit by mating with as many females as possible] supports the notion of promiscuous behavior in men as being adaptive, when in reality there is no evidence that promiscuous men have more offspring than men who invest heavily in the nurturing of their children. (p. 48)[20]

In our opinion, although certain evolved sexual or reproductive strategies and tendencies may still persist in individuals of both genders, other factors including cultural and psychological factors and the availability of potential partners probably have more influence in shaping people's sexual behavior and preferences (Hazan 6k Diamond, 2000). Gender researchers Eagly and Wood (1999) tend to agree with our point of view. They found that "a re-analysis of Buss's [1989] ... study of sex differences in the attributes valued in potential mates in 37 cultures yielded cross-cultural variation that supports the social structural account of sex differences in male preferences" (p. 408). In a more general sense, rather than attributing sex differences in human behavior primarily to evolved dispositions that differ by sex, it may well be that these differences lie "mainly in the differing placement of women and men in the social structure" (p. 408).

More importantly, human beings are far from being passive recipients of certain inclinations that may have helped their ancestors survive. In other words, we have some choice in the matter, our destiny is not predetermined, and our behavior and propensities are continually being influenced by a myriad of other factors.

CONCLUSION

In most aspects of their psychological makeup, men and women cannot be easily categorized according to their gender identity. Their behavior should not be evaluated or judged by conventional criteria that stress gender differences. Clinically, it is important to work with clients to facilitate an understanding that they do not have to comply with these gender expectations and stereotypes. It is helpful to explore with them the similarities between women and men, describe their mutual strengths, and to demonstrate through attitude and action that it is possible to change destructive, traditional sexist attitudes.

Although considerable effort has gone into attempts to delineate early environmental influences on gender-role behaviors and different sexual attitudes and behaviors observed in men and women, it appears that many findings from gender research are ambiguous or inconclusive. In any case, these findings and popular interpretations of such findings should not be used to support destructive stereotypes that still exist in our culture.

On a social level, proponents in the men's and women's movements have contributed to the struggle to achieve personal freedom while developing a sense of kinship with members of the opposite sex. Yet, because sexist attitudes are internalized so early in the developmental sequence, people still face a difficult task in challenging and transcending sexual stereotyping, traditional gender roles, and the defensive behaviors embedded in these roles. This struggle requires boldness and determination when confronting internal conflicts and external social pressures that support conformity to rigidly defined sex roles.

We believe that women and men can develop themselves personally and become equal partners in all aspects of their relationships, including sexually. Women can take responsibility for their sexual desire and fulfillment and ask more directly for what they want sexually. Men can view their partners as equal and not take a paternalistic attitude toward them. Men can challenge their idealization of women especially in their role as mothers. Women can challenge their idealization of men as "rescuers" who should protect and take care of them. Women can break the negative aspects of their identification with their mothers and face the anxiety of living as separate individuals. Men can break the negative aspects of their identification with their fathers and overcome fears of achieving intimacy in their relationships, even if their fathers did not.

By becoming more aware of the sexism and the distortions of men and women still prevalent in Western culture, people can gradually move beyond these views and develop closer, more congenial relationships. As they relinquish defensive attitudes about themselves and their sexuality, they can achieve higher levels of self-differentiation and experience more fulfillment in their sexual lives.

NOTES

1. Aries (1997) noted that "Decades of research has shown widespread agreement among people about the characteristics of men and women" (p. 96). Men are characterized by a cluster of instrumental traits: they are seen to be leaders, to be dominant, aggressive, independent, objective, and competitive. Women, in contrast, are characterized by a cluster of affective traits: they are seen to be emotional, subjective, tactful, and aware of the feelings of others. Gender stereotypes have changed relatively little over the past twenty years despite considerable changes in women's status in society. (p. 96)
2. Pleck (1995) and Levant (1992) have discussed the effects of "gender-role strain" on males, that is, the inconsistent and contradictory roles they are supposed to fill.

According to Walsh's (1997) description of this concept, "For example, men are expected to be independent and competitive at work and caring and cooperative at home. Failure to fulfill male role expectations can lead to 'low self-esteem and other negative consequences'" (pp. 399–400).

3. Silverstein et al. (2002) commented that Gender roles were seen as culturally defined on the basis of cultural stereotypes rather than as emanating from an intrinsic biological feminine or masculine essence. ... Attempts to conform to these role norms, therefore, inevitably lead to psychological stress rather than to psychological well-being. (p. 362)
4. Although differences between men's and women's levels of sexual desire have been reported by a number of researchers and clinicians (H. Kaplan, 1995; Love & Robinson, 1994), it has also been shown that these differences appear to be a matter of degree and are influenced by a wide range of factors, including social, psychological, and biological influences.
5. Observing this pattern in the families he studied, Pollack (1998) attributed some of the father's difficulties to what he termed "gatekeeper mothers": Gatekeeping is what happens when mothers, despite their very best intentions, unwittingly maintain so close a bond with their sons that there is simply little room left for the father to play a meaningful role— the emotional "gate" has been kept closed. (p. 125)
6. Currently, many feminists continue to focus on inequities between the sexes, both politically and economically. Others, particularly feminists in academia, have concentrated their efforts on altering stereotypic attitudes and beliefs about women, as well as developing a "relational" therapy approach. Notable among these are a group of clinicians and researchers at the Stone Center for Developmental Studies at Wellesley College {Jordan, Kaplan, Miller, Stiver, 6k Surrey, 1991; J. Miller & Stiver, 1994; Rogers, 1994).
7. According to Gilligan (1991), women's struggle to resist complying with restrictive, traditional patriarchal prescriptions is a psychological battle that begins in preadolescence. "Girls are pressed at adolescence to take on images of perfection as the model of the pure or perfectly good woman: the woman whom everyone will promote and value and want to be with" (p. 24).
8. In recent years there have been concerted efforts on the part of many women to move past "benevolent" stereotypic views. For example, Dowling (2000) documented a significant countertrend where women are refusing to accept these paternalistic, condescending views of themselves. In her book *The Frailty Myth,* she emphasized the strides made by many women to correct these sexist views of women as inherently weak, frail, or helpless in relation to men. Drawing on various studies in the sports world, including statistics from Women's Olympics, Dowling noted that "Women of all ages have begun trading in the crimped 'femininity' of the past for a bold new female bravado" (p. xxxi).
9. However, there are a few gender differences in other areas of sexual functioning. Smith (1998) found that 54% of men think about or fantasize about sex every day or several

times a day, whereas only 19% of women think about sex with this same frequency. Results from the Laumann et al. (1994) large-scale survey indicated that 26.7% of men, compared with 7.6% of women, reported that they had masturbated at least once a week during the past year. According to Hyde and Oliver (2000), "Many other gender differences were moderate in magnitude ... Males were more sexually permissive ... and females reported more anxiety, fear, and guilt about sex. ... Still other behaviors showed no gender difference" (p. 68).

10. Kindlon and Thompson (1999) have emphasized how important it is for fathers to be able to make an "emotional connection" with their sons. They noted that Even though fathers in two-parent families today tend to be slightly more involved in child care than they were twenty years ago (a gain of about 15 percent), their involvement doesn't always translate into the kind of emotional connection that boys want. ... We find that boys feel shortchanged, not only in terms of time but also in terms of affection, and this loss remains with them into adulthood. (p. 100)
11. According to G. Parker (1983), There are two broad types of overprotection: a caring form labeled "affectionate constraint," which is not clearly associated with psychiatric disorder; and a form in which there is an associated decrement in care, labeled "affectionateless control" which appears to be strongly associated with several psychiatric disorders and with several anomalies in psychosocial development, (pp. ix-x) See also the study by Jain, Belsky, and Crnic (1996), in which four groups of fathers were identified by cluster analysis: caretakers, playmates-teachers, disciplinarians, and disengaged fathers.
12. See Westkott's (1997) critique of Stone Center's New Psychology of Women: The Stone Center writers do not question what they describe as "the mother's interest in being understood and cared for" by her daughter. ... Instead, they accept it as a given ... implying that it is "natural" or unproblematic. However, by doing so, they close off the possibility for interpreting it as a parent's *use* of her child, a practice which others ... have argued has harmful developmental consequences. (p. 367)
13. Findings from a number of infant studies tend to support Levant's (1998) observations and hypotheses regarding emotional expressiveness in male infants. For example, Tronick (1980) reported that "When mothers held a frozen posture and a still face while looking toward their [2-month-old] infants, the babies looked away and eventually slumped away with a hopeless facial expression" (p. 7). According to Tronick and Weinberg (1997), Infant boys are more emotionally reactive than girls. They display more positive as well as negative affect, focus more on the mother, and display more signals expressing escape and distress and demand for contact than do girls. Girls show more interest in objects, (p. 61). See also Lyons-Ruth and Zeanah (1993). However, in other observational studies, female infants and toddlers tended to surpass male infants and toddlers in maintaining eye contact with caregivers and peers, recognizing faces,

and reacting with empathy to another infant's crying (Zahn-Waxier, Radke-Yarrow, Wagner, &. Chapman, 1992; Zahn-Waxler, Robinson, & Emde, 1992).

14. Critics have argued that "outdated" psychoanalytic theories generally "ignore individual circumstances and assume an essentialist position (i.e., the belief that there exists a basic female nature that remains relatively impervious to contextual factors)" (Reid & Bing, 2000, p. 145). In particular, these critiques strongly disagree with approaches suggesting that daughters have "difficulty identifying with their mothers because they held sexual desires for their fathers" (p. 145). For example, Reid and Bing claimed that "In light of current incidents of family sexual abuse and reexaminations of Freud's notes, researchers now give less credence to the notion of female gender emanating from penis envy or childhood feelings of female inferiority" (p. 145). Similarly, in relation to male development, Silverstein and Auerbach (1999), in criticizing the essentialist assumption "that boys need a heterosexual male parent to establish a masculine gender identity" (p. 403), noted that "a significant amount of research on the children of lesbian and gay parents has shown that children raised by lesbian mothers (and gay fathers) are as likely as children raised in heterosexual, two-parent families to achieve a heterosexual gender orientation" (p. 403).
15. From a cross-cultural perspective, Morokoff (2000) has asserted that "women's sexual behavior is subject to social control in most if not all societies" (p. 308). Morokoff noted, however, that recent social changes have reduced the power exerted by some of these techniques, for example, "The advent of effective contraception has [led to] ... a steadily increasing percentage of adolescent women [who] become sexually active with each new survey conducted" (p. 309).
16. According to Gilligan, only when girls reach preadolescence (sometime between the ages of 9 through 13) do they become compliant, give up their opinions, and lose a sense of who they are and what they know. In comparing the different developmental crises that boys and girls must navigate, Gilligan (1991) emphasized that "The relational crisis of boys' early childhood and of girl's adolescence is marked by a struggle to stay in relationship—a healthy resistance to disconnections which are psychologically wounding (from the body, from feelings, from relationships, from reality)" (p. 24).
17. Benjamin (1995) further explained that Once core gender identity is established in the first twelve to eighteen months of life, the child proceeds to elaborate gender role identity in conjunction with separation-individuation issues, hence in a conflictual and variable context. ... Children continue throughout the second and third years to identify with both parents, even though their roles are somewhat differentiated and the father may assume special importance. (p. 127)
18. Classical psychoanalytic theories of male psychosexual development and the oedipal conflict have been articulated for more than 100 years; whereas theories of female psychosexual development were not explicated until the latter half of the 20th century.

19. Buss (1994) also asserted that "In evolutionary terms, men and women are identical in many or most domains, differing only in the limited areas in which they have faced recurrently different adaptive problems over human evolutionary history" (p. 18). Thus, men and women also evolved a number of similar personality characteristics and behaviors that they prefer in potential partners, such as intelligence, affection, generosity, and altruism. These traits can also be hypothesized to have evolved through the process of sexual selection, because in modern times these traits are among those that appear to be equally distributed statistically between the two genders. As Ridley (1993) put it, "Not everything is different; most things, in fact, are identical between the sexes. Much of the folklore about differences is merely convenient sexism" (p. 248).
20. Moore and Travis (2000) cite numerous examples of media "hype" surrounding supposedly scientific findings based on sociobiological or evolutionary principles. For example, in describing an ABC television news program on the reality of sex differences, they commented: "The message of the program was that men and women are 'just biologically hard-wired to be different,' and, accordingly, expectations of gender specific behaviors and attitudes should be different as well" (p. 49).

Sex Differences in Mate Preferences Revisited

Do People Know What They Initially Desire in a Romantic Partner?

By Paul W. Eastwick and Eli J. Finkel

Northwestern University

In paradigms in which participants state their ideal romantic-partner preferences or examine vignettes and photographs, men value physical attractiveness more than women do, and women value earning prospects more than men do. Yet it remains unclear if these preferences remain sex differentiated in predicting desire for real-life potential partners (i.e., individuals whom one has actually met). In the present study, the authors explored this possibility using speed dating and longitudinal follow-up procedures. Replicating previous research, participants exhibited traditional sex differences when stating the importance of physical attractiveness and earning prospects in an ideal partner and ideal speed date. However, data revealed no sex differences in the associations between participants' romantic interest in real-life potential partners (met during and outside of speed dating) and the attractiveness and earning prospects of those partners. Furthermore, participants' ideal preferences, assessed before the speed-dating event, failed to predict what inspired their actual desire at the event. Results are discussed within the context of R. E. Nisbett and T. D. Wilson's (1977) seminal article: Even regarding such a consequential aspect of mental

Paul W. Eastwick, Eli J. Finkel, "Sex Differences in Mate Preferences Revisited: Do People Know What They Initially Desire in a Romantic Partner?," from *Journal of Personality and Social Psychology*; Vol. 94, No. 2, Pp. 245-264.

life as romantic-partner preferences, people may lack introspective awareness of what influences their judgments and behavior.

Keywords: sex differences, mate preferences, speed dating, empathy gap, a priori theories

After decades of research, it is now well established that men and women differ in their reports of the importance of certain characteristics in a romantic partner. Such assessments of *ideal partner preferences* or *mate preferences* have consistently revealed two key sex differences: A greater male (compared with female) desire for romantic partners who are physically attractive and a greater female (compared with male) desire for romantic partners who have good earning potential. These findings are frequently (but not always, see Eagly & Wood, 1999) discussed as part of an evolutionary psychological perspective on mate selection, which suggests that men and women possess different evolved, domain-specific psychological adaptations that guide their mate preferences and their romantic-partner choices accordingly (Buss, 1989, 1994; Buss & Kenrick, 1998; Buss & Schmitt, 1993).* In the present study, we replicated these ubiquitous sex differences in romantic-partner preferences and attempted to follow them to their anticipated conclusion: sex-differentiated romantic interest in real-life potential romantic partners depending on the partner's physical attractiveness and earning prospects. In fact, the data never pointed toward such a conclusion; instead, they led us on a detour that raised fascinating new questions about the meaning of romantic-partner preferences and shed new light on the processes underlying romantic-relationship initiation.

Sex Differences in Stated Mate Preferences

The foundation of the modern empirical study of mate preferences dates back to the first half of the 20th century. Sociologist Reuben Hill asked participants to rate the importance of certain qualities in a mate and found that men placed more importance on good looks than did women, whereas women placed more importance on good financial prospects than did men (Hill, 1945). The best-known study of mate preferences in this "stated preference" tradition was published by David Buss (1989), who surveyed 10,047 participants spread across 37 different cultures and documented consistent sex

* Some evolutionary perspectives also predict that other sex differences will emerge within the domain of human mating, such as the desired age of a mate or interest in short-term sexual relationships (Buss, 1989; Buss & Schmitt, 1993; Kenrick & Keefe, 1992; Symons, 1979). The present report focuses exclusively on the sex differences in the stated importance of physical attractiveness and earning prospects in a romantic partner.

differences in the importance of physical attractiveness and good earning prospects. Buss interpreted these data in an evolutionary framework, appealing largely to Trivers's (1972) parental-investment theory. Buss suggested that (a) men (more than women) value physical attractiveness in a mate because a woman's physical attractiveness confers information about her reproductive value, and (b) women (more than men) value earning prospects in a mate because a woman's offspring are more likely to survive given a man's economic contributions. Many evolutionary psychologists argue that these preferences persist today because they increased the reproductive success of ancestral humans who possessed them, presumably because such preferences facilitated mate choice by directing ancestral men and women to select attractive and successful mates, respectively (see Buss & Schmitt, 1993).

These two sex differences in stated mate preferences have withstood a number of additional empirical tests. For example, the differences have proven robust in meta-analyses of the stated-preference paradigm (Feingold, 1990, 1992), in a nationally representative sample (Sprecher, Sullivan, & Hatfield, 1994), and among men and women who anticipated having high incomes (Townsend, 1989; Wiederman & Allgeier, 1992). Other researchers have asked participants to evaluate photographs or descriptions of opposite-sex individuals; the attractiveness of these stimuli affected men's liking more than women's, and the earning prospects of these stimuli affected women's liking more than men's (e.g., Stroebe, Insko, Thompson, & Layton, 1971; Townsend & Wasserman, 1998). In addition, a naturalistic program of research explored the content of personal advertisements (e.g., Harrison & Saeed, 1977), revealing these same sex differences in the mate characteristics sought by ad placers (see meta-analyses by Fein-gold, 1990, 1992). Finally, recent research investigating online dating has found that (a) men's (but not women's) incomes predicted the number of opposite-sex emails received (Hitsch, Hortaçsu, & Ariely, 2006), and (b) the physical attractiveness of users' online photographs predicted email receipt better for women than for men (Olivola et al., 2007).

Several evolutionary psychologists have also posited that distinct psychological adaptations guide people's behavior in short-term versus long-term romantic relationships; therefore, men and women are likely to value different characteristics in a romantic partner depending on whether they are currently in a short-term or a long-term mating mindset (Buss & Schmitt, 1993). For example, women should be more likely to prefer men who exhibit cues to their genetic fitness (e.g., physical attractiveness) for short-term compared with long-term relationships (Gangestad & Simpson, 2000). Some research has in fact demonstrated that men and women converge in the strength of their preference for physically attractive individuals in short-term contexts (Kenrick, Groth, Trost, & Sadalla, 1993; Li & Kenrick, 2006; but see Buunk, Dijkstra, Fetchenhauer, & Kenrick, 2002; Regan, Levin, Sprecher, Christopher, & Cate, 2000). Similarly, women tend to prioritize earning prospects when seeking a long-term compared with a short-term partner (Li & Kenrick, 2006). In general, the extant data support those evolutionary perspectives that predict that sex differences in mate preferences will be especially robust when individuals consider a long-term compared with short-term relationship.

All of the above studies have helped build a strong case for the existence of sex differences in mate preferences with respect to physical attractiveness and earning prospects. Although much of the support derives from the stated preferences of men and women as reported on questionnaires or in response to experimental stimuli (e.g., photographs), the personal-ad and online-dating findings suggest that these sex differences continue to emerge in some actual dating contexts. In addition, participants' stated preferences are meaningfully moderated by the short-term versus long-term distinction, as predicted by several prominent evolutionary perspectives (Buss & Schmitt, 1993; Gangestad & Simpson, 2000). Nevertheless, the functional importance of these preferences would be bolstered by demonstrations that they predict what happens when men and women actually meet one another, either in a live dating context or even when considering real-life potential marriage partners. Surprisingly, in prior studies in which the targets of participants' romantic interest were not hypothetical ideals or photographs but rather live, flesh-and-blood human beings, the sex differences in physical attractiveness and earning prospects have proven empirically evasive. We now turn our attention to these curious findings.

Equivocal Evidence for Sex Differences

If men (more than women) prefer physical attractiveness and women (more than men) prefer earning prospects, this could conceivably result in a marriage "tradeoff such that attractive women will tend to marry rich men. Two studies are often cited as providing evidence for this hypothesis. In the first, Elder (1969) presented data showing that women's physical attractiveness positively predicted marrying a high-status mate. In the second, Udry and Eckland (1984) found that attractiveness was positively related to household income (but not own income) for women; the reasonable inference is that the additional income is a result of marrying successful husbands. However, it is difficult to draw any firm conclusions from these studies for two reasons. First, neither study examined sex *differences* in the correlation between attractiveness and spousal earning prospects. Second, attractive people tend to accrue many extra benefits in life, including better occupational success (see meta-analysis by Langlois et al., 2000); therefore, an association between women's attractiveness and men's earning prospects could emerge if attractive people simply marry other attractive people (see Buller, 2005). In other words, it could be the attractiveness of certain men (not their accompanying income and success) that successfully attracts good-looking women. In fact, Stevens, Owens, and Schaefer (1990) assessed the attractiveness and education levels (an indicator of earning prospects) of recently married women *and* men and indeed found that, after controlling for the fact that attractive women marry attractive men, the apparent association between men's education and women's attractiveness disappeared. In short, there is no strong evidence demonstrating that men and women engage in a marriage tradeoff between physical attractiveness and earning prospects.

Several other creative research paradigms have failed to show that men and women differ in their romantic interest toward opposite-sex others who are physically attractive or have good earning prospects. Speed and Gangestad (1997) asked college students to nominate friends and acquaintances who were romantically popular, who were physically attractive, and who were likely to have future financial success. Results revealed no sex difference in either the (large) correlation between popularity and physical attractiveness or the (negligible) correlation between popularity and future financial success. Recently, researchers have started to investigate romantic preferences using *speed-dating* (Eastwick & Finkel, in press-b; Finkel & Eastwick, in press; Finkel, Eastwick, & Matthews, 2007), a paradigm in which opposite-sex individuals meet for short dates and then decide whether they would ("yes") or would not ("no") be interested in meeting one another again. Data on individuals (M_{age} = 32 years, SD = 5.3) who attended professional speed-dating events revealed that (a) income did not make either sex significantly more desirable, and (b) athough men indeed had a strong preference for women with attractive faces, bodies, and a lower body mass index (BMI), women had a similarly strong preference for men with attractive faces, bodies, and an average BMI (Kurzban & Weeden, 2005). Finally, a speed-dating study with graduate-student participants did find that men were more likely than women to "yes" the dates they found physically attractive (Fisman, Iyengar, Kamenica, & Simonson, 2006). Regarding earning prospects, however, women and men did not differ in their likelihood of "yessing" the dates they judged to be ambitious or the dates who came from wealthy hometowns. Especially fascinating are data presented by Iyengar, Simonson, Fisman, and Mogilner (2005) revealing that speed-daters' stated preferences correlated poorly (r s ranging from .00 to .17) with their actual yes/no decisions—we return to this point shortly.

With regard to the importance of physical attractiveness, Feingold's (1990) meta-analysis summarized findings from several different research paradigms, two of which (stated preferences and personal ads) are mentioned above. Although men clearly exhibit a stronger preference for physical attractiveness in these two paradigms, the evidence for the physical-attractiveness sex difference is less robust when participants are actually interacting with a potential partner. Feingold (1990) reported that being physically attractive was (a) positively associated with dating activity more strongly for women than for men but (b) positively associated with the number of opposite-sex interactions per day more strongly for men than for women. Feingold speculated that these findings might actually reflect a sex difference in the *strategies* that men and women use to initiate a romantic relationship (i.e., attractive men have more interactions because many of their female friends are attempting to initiate a relationship through friendship). Thus, these data do not unambiguously demonstrate a sex difference in the importance of physical attractiveness. Feingold also examined data from seven studies in which men and women actually went on dates with one another (e.g., the well-known "computer dance" study conducted by Walster, Aronson, Abrahams, & Rottmann, 1966). The correlation between romantic liking for and physical attractiveness of one's date was positive for both men and women, but the meta-analyzed sex difference between these correlations was small and not significant. Although Feingold's (1990) review is often cited as providing clear evidence for the sex difference in the importance of physical attractiveness, a closer look reveals substantial ambiguity in paradigms in which participants actually interact.

Have Participants Told More Than They Know?

It initially seems strange that the sex differences that emerge so consistently in the literature on stated preferences become so erratic when examining live dating contexts. Fortunately, the extant social psychological literature could shed light on this quandary. One possibility is suggested by the classic Nisbett and Wilson (1977) demonstrations that people are often unable to correctly report how features of a stimulus affect their evaluations of it (known as a "causal judgment"). Their studies revealed that participants do not use true introspection to answer such "why" questions (e.g., "Why do you like this particular pair of stockings?")—they instead defer to their a priori theories about whether a certain feature might plausibly lead to such an evaluation. Although these a priori theories may be correct at times, Nisbett and Wilson made their case by exposing the inaccuracy of participants' theories across a variety of contexts.

Nevertheless, the Nisbett and Wilson (1977) experiments tested preferences and judgments that did not hold tremendous meaning in participants' lives (e.g., stocking preferences). Might something as important as mate selection be subject to their critique? Could mate preferences reflect participants' potentially inaccurate a priori theories about the characteristics they would find appealing in a romantic partner or why they would choose a certain potential mate over another? This suggestion is plausible for three reasons. First, although it may seem odd to equate mate preferences with Nisbett and Wilson's problematic causal judgments, one of the original introspective inaccuracy studies (Nisbett & Bellows, 1977) conceived of physical attractiveness in precisely this way. Physical attractiveness was a *reason* participants might like or dislike a job candidate in that study, just as it is a reason that participants might like or dislike a potential romantic partner. Second, although several subsequent articles demonstrated that participants were aware of what influenced their judgments when the data were analyzed using alternative statistical procedures (e.g., Smith & Miller, 1978), this awareness typically emerged only when those judgments were made in rapid succession in a controlled laboratory setting (e.g., Wright & Rip, 1981; cf. Wilson, Laser, & Stone, 1982). People still tend to have difficulty reporting what influences their judgments in everyday life; for example, participants demonstrated virtually no insight about how their mood judgments were affected by the amount of sleep they got (Wilson et al., 1982). These difficulties are likely to be compounded in the romantic domain, given how rarely individuals select a romantic partner or must choose among several interested and available partners (compared with how often they sleep!). Third, because mate preferences are typically assessed when a participant is in a state of cool rationality, such preferences may not reflect what inspires actual desire during the emotional throes of romantic attraction. For example, it is easy to imagine an individual acknowledging (while calmly chatting with friends) the benefits of dating an individual who is loyal and reliable but soon thereafter experiencing strong romantic desire in the presence of someone who is unpredictable and exciting. This is an example of a cold-to-hot prospective empathy gap (Ariely & Loewenstein, 2005; Loewenstein, 1996, 2005) and similarly hints that stated mate preferences might not map onto priorities in live dating contexts.

For these three reasons, it is plausible that men and women show consistent sex differences in their stated mate preferences because they are reporting consensual a priori theories about what characteristics in a romantic partner will inspire their interest. If individuals were to report not on hypothetical ideal partners but instead on the actual people they were currently romantically pursuing, it is an open question (based on the previous literature) whether sex differences would emerge—and the a priori theories account presents a strong case for why they may not.

The Current Research

To explore how the traditionally sex-differentiated characteristics of physical attractiveness and earning prospects predict initial romantic attraction, we took a broad, panoramic snapshot of participants' romantic lives. Our procedures covered two distinct contexts: (a) a speed-dating event designed specifically for undergraduate students and (b) an intensive one-month follow-up. During this follow up, we examined in detail how participants' potential relationships developed, both with respect to their speed-dating "matches" and with respect to other romantic interests whom participants met outside of speed-dating ("write-ins"). If stated mate preferences serve the function of directing romantic interest, we should confirm the following three hypotheses:

H1. *Sex differences in stated preferences.* Men will state that they prefer physical attractiveness in a romantic partner more than women do, and women will state that they prefer earning prospects in a romantic partner more than men do. These established sex differences will be evident in reports of both an ideal partner and an ideal speed-date.

H2. *Sex differences in initiation.* Given H1, men (compared with women) will demonstrate greater interest in and pursuit of potential partners they find attractive, and women (compared with men) will demonstrate greater interest in and pursuit of potential partners they judge to have good earning prospects. In addition, as partner preferences differ depending on the degree to which men and women approach potential partners with a short-term versus a long-term mindset, these sex differences might prove especially robust among individuals who are more (rather than less) interested in pursuing a long-term, serious relationship (this short-term/long-term mindset hypothesis is called H2A).

H3. *Individual differences in initiation.* A participant who states a preference for physical attractiveness (or earning prospects) in a romantic partner will also demonstrate greater interest in and pursuit of potential partners he/she judges to be physically attractive (or to have good earning prospects). In other words, stated preferences will correlate with in vivo preferences (those revealed within the actual dating context).

However, if stated preferences do not reflect participants' genuine introspective insight but rather their inaccurate a priori theories about what characteristics in a potential partner might inspire their romantic interest, H2, H2A, and H3 might not be confirmed.

One shortcoming of previous live dating research is that those studies have often employed only a single dependent variable (sometimes consisting of only a single item). Of course, there are many intervening steps between meeting someone and forming/ maintaining a romantic relationship with that person; these steps include the initial spark of interest, sharing contact information, initiating and enjoying time spent together, feelings of romantic passion, and so forth. Therefore, in the present report, we employ 17 different dependent variables (collectively referred to as *relationship-initiation dependent variables)* and draw conclusions by meta-analyzing results across these diverse measures.

Method

Participants

Using flyers posted around campus and informational e-mails sent to the freshmen, sophomore, and junior class Listservs, we recruited 163 undergraduate students (81 women, 82 men) to participate in a study of romantic-attraction processes, including a speed-dating component (for greater procedural detail, see Finkel et al., 2007). Participants were 19.6 years old on average *(SD* = 1.0 years); 36.2% were freshmen, 38.7% were sophomores, 21.5% were juniors, and 3.7% were seniors. (We recruited seniors less aggressively because they were scheduled to graduate approximately 6 weeks after the events.) The sample was

73.6% White/ Caucasian, 10.4% Asian, 5.5% South Asian, 4.3% Hispanic, 2.5% African American, 1.2% Middle Eastern, and 2.5% unreported.

Participants were paid $5 at the end of the speed-dating event and $3 for every follow-up questionnaire (out of 10) completed. In addition, those who completed at least 9 of the 10 follow-up questionnaires were paid a bonus of $10.

Procedure

Part 1: Pre-event questionnaire. The first part of the study consisted of a 30-min online pre-event questionnaire assessing background variables about the participants. Participants completed this questionnaire 6–13 days before attending a speed-dating event.

Part 2: Speed-dating. The second part of this study consisted of a full-fledged 2-hr speed-dating event at which participants pursued "matches" with opposite-sex participants. Events were modeled loosely on procedures used by professional speed-dating companies and took place in a secluded art gallery located in Northwestern University's student union. Tables and chairs were positioned throughout the room such that each pair of speed-daters could communicate easily with one another while seated a comfortable distance away from other pairs. Nonalcoholic beverages, lighting, and music were selected to make the event elegant and were held constant across all speed-dating events.

Upon each participant's arrival at the event, one research assistant gave him or her a name tag, clipboard, pen, a set of interaction-record questionnaires, and a unique ID (letters for women, numbers for men). The research assistant instructed participants to write their ID and first name on their name tag. Next, a second research assistant took a digital photo of the participant and was willing to take additional photos until the participant was happy with one. Once all participants had arrived, the experimenter explained how the speed-dating event would proceed.

For three randomly determined speed-dating events, men remained seated while women rotated from man to man; for the remaining four speed-dating events, women remained seated while men rotated. Each speed-date lasted for 4 min; participants conversed freely during this time. After each speed-date, the experimenter blew a whistle to signal that participants should rotate to the location for their next speed-date. Before beginning this next speed-date, however, participants completed an interaction record about the previous date and jotted notes to themselves to take home. After 2 min passed, the experimenter signaled for participants to complete their interaction records and begin their next 4-min date. Participants dated all opposite-sex individuals present and had between 9 and 13 dates, depending on event attendance. Once all dates had been completed, the experimenter explained to the participants how to complete the matching process and remaining questionnaires.

After the event, participants returned to the speed-dating Web site, where they indicated whether they would be interested in meeting again each person they had speed-dated.

Participants clicked "yes" or "no" next to the photograph and ID of each speed-dater. When two speed-daters replied "yes" to one another, this was called a "match"; only matches were later provided with the ability to contact one another (see below). Participants also indicated whether they would allow "missed matches" (speed-daters who had said "no" to the participant but to whom the participant had said "yes") to learn that the participant had said "yes" to them. If the participant allowed this option, the missed match was given the option of changing his/her previous "no" response to a "yes," thus securing an extra match for both the participant and the missed match. In total, 100% of participants completed the matching process, and 54% chose the missed-matches option. Participants generated a total of 206 matching pairs (average number of matches per participant = 2.53, *SD* = 2.0).

At 5 p.m. the day following the speed-dating event, participants received an e-mail directing them to a Web site where they could view their matches. The Web site displayed the photograph, ID, and first name of each speed-dater with whom the participant had a match. Participants were also given the ability to change their "no" to a "yes" for any speed-daters who agreed to the missed-matches option described above. After completing a brief post-match questionnaire, participants could then click on a button next to each match's photograph to get to the speed-dating messaging page. Participants could use this page to send a message to a match and to view messages received from that match.

Part 3: Follow-up. Twenty-four hr after they had access to their match information (and 48 hr after the speed-dating event), participants received an e-mail directing them to a Web site where they could complete the first of 10 follow-up questionnaires. They received similar e-mails every 72 hr until the follow-up portion of the study was completed (30 days after the speed-dating event). They were instructed to complete each questionnaire before going to bed that night, although we accepted late questionnaires. Of the 92% of speed-dating participants who elected to take part in the follow-up portion of the study, 69% completed at least 9 of the 10 questionnaires.

On each of the 10 follow-up questionnaires, participants responded to items about each speed-dating match. In addition, participants were asked to provide the name of anyone else (aside from their matches) whom they considered to be a romantic interest. After providing the name of this "write-in" target, they completed follow-up questions about this individual, in addition to their matches, at each wave. Participants could provide multiple write-in targets; altogether, participants reported on 143 write-ins over the course of the month. Most of the write-ins (78%) attended Northwestern University or lived in the Chicago/Evanston, Illinois area, whereas 20% were currently living or going to school elsewhere in the United States (no information was available for the remaining 2%). According to the participants' reports, the write-ins were 20.1 years old on average (*SD* = 2.0 years), participants had known the write-ins for an average of 380 days (*Mdn* = 180 days), and they had been romantically interested in them for an average of 245 days (*Mdn* = 68 days). We refer to follow-up questionnaire targets as either a "speed-date/match" or "write-in" to reflect the two different ways a target could be included in the data set. Write-ins are useful because they can address whether any of the follow-up results can be explained away as strange anomalies that are only characteristic of relationships that grow out of a speed-date (see Eastwick & Finkel, in press-b; Finkel et al., 2007). Therefore, data pertaining to write-ins are presented separately from those pertaining to speed-dating matches.

Materials

All measures included in the present report (except for "yes-sing") were assessed on four different questionnaires: pre-event, interaction-record, postmatch, and follow-up. The present report focuses on the following three traits that might describe a romantic partner: *physically attractive* (assessed by the items "physically attractive" and "sexy/hot"), *earning prospects* ("good career prospects," "ambitious/driven"), and *personable* ("fun/exciting," "responsive," "dependable/trustworthy," "friendly/nice"). The first two constructs were examined because of their relevance to the literature on sex differences in mate preferences; the third serves as a useful comparison and includes characteristics that both men and women desire in a romantic partner (e.g., Fletcher, Simpson, Thomas, & Giles, 1999; see factor analysis that follows).

Stated mate preferences. Stated mate preferences were assessed in two different ways (ideal partner and speed-date) at two different times (pre-event and Wave 10 follow up). First, as part of the pre-event questionnaire, participants rated the importance of physically attractive ($\alpha = .83$), earning prospects (Times New Roman = .75), and personable (Times New Roman = .71) characteristics in an ideal romantic partner on a scale from 1 *(not at all)* to 9 *(extremely).* We refer to these reports as *pre-event ideal partner* stated preferences.

Given that the present study was inspired by the literature on ideal partner preferences, these pre-event ideal partner reports seemed the most logical measures to use for construct validation. We conducted a factor analysis (principal axis factoring with promax rotation) on the eight items (see above) that were intended to assess the three ideal partner constructs of interest. Inspection of the scree plot revealed a three-factor solution: The two items assessing Physically Attractive loaded primarily on the first factor, the four items assessing Personable loaded primarily on the second, and the two items assessing Earning Prospects loaded primarily on the third (all factor loadings > .5 with no double loadings).

Of course, an ideal partner preference is context-free, and the principle of attitude-behavior compatibility (Ajzen & Fishbein, 2005) suggests that such a preference would best predict behavior when it refers to the same, specific context in which the behavior will take place. Therefore, also on the pre-event questionnaire, participants received the following instructions: "How much do you think the following characteristics will matter in your decision to 'yes' or 'no' someone after your 4-minute date?" Participants then responded to the identical items reported above that assessed Physically Attractive (α =

.84), Earning Prospects (α = .72), and Personable (α = .44) characteristics.* We refer to these reports as *pre-event speed-date* stated preferences.

On the tenth and final follow-up questionnaire, participants again reported their ideal romantic partner preferences for Physically Attractive (α = .76), Earning Prospects (α = .79), and Personable (α = .77), just as they had on the pre-event questionnaire. In addition, participants reported the likelihood that Physically Attractive (α = .76), Earning Prospects (α = .73), and Personable (α = .58) characteristics would matter in their decision to "yes" or "no" someone after a 4-min date should they go speed-dating again. These reports are referred to as *Wave 10 ideal partner* and *Wave 10 speed-date* stated preferences, respectively.

Partner characteristics. As part of the interaction record, participants rated on a scale from 1 *(not at all)* to 9 *(extremely)* the extent to which they thought each speed-dating partner was characterized by the identical items reported above that assessed Physically Attractive (α = .95), Earning Prospects (α = .86), and Personable (α = .84) characteristics. In addition, on each follow-up questionnaire, participants used a 1–9 scale to rate the extent to which they thought each speed-dating match and write-in was characterized by the items assessing Physically Attractive (α = .92), Earning Prospects (α = .79), and Personable (α = .81) characteristics.

Relationship initiation dependent variables. On a scale from 1 *(strongly disagree)* to 9 *(strongly agree),* the interaction record assessed participants' reports of *romantic desire* for the speed-dating partner ("I really liked my interaction partner," "I was sexually attracted to my interaction partner," and "I am likely to say 'yes' to my interaction partner"; α = .88) and *chemistry* with him or her ("My interaction partner and I seemed to have a lot in common," "... seemed to have similar personalities," and "... had a real connection"; α = .91).

All postmatch questionnaire and follow-up questionnaire relationship-initiation dependent variables were assessed on scales from 1 *(strongly disagree)* to 7 *(strongly agree).* As part of the postmatch questionnaire, participants indicated for each match their level of match *excitement* ("I am extremely excited that I matched with [name]"), their *initiation plans* ("I am very likely to initiate contact with [name]"), and their *initiation hopes* ("I hope that [name] initiates contact with me").

On each of the 10 follow-up questionnaires, participants responded to items pertaining to each speed-dating match and to each write-in. Furthermore, the items about each match/write-in were customized depending on the participants' answer to the following pivot question: "What is the current status of your relationship with [name]?" Participants

* Although we were dismayed by the low alpha of the Personable index for the speed-date preferences, we included it because the alphas for the Personable ideal-partner preferences and partner characteristics were acceptable. Although dropping the item fun/exciting might have produced a factor more similar to the Warmth/Trustworthiness factor identified by Fletcher et al. (1999), doing so actually reduced all relevant alphas in the present data set. Regardless, changing the Personable factor by dropping this item did not substantially alter the results reported in this article.

were given the following response options to this question: (a) dating seriously, (b) dating casually, (c) friend *with* romantic potential, (d) acquaintance *with* romantic potential, (e) friend *without* romantic potential, (f) acquaintance *without* romantic potential, (g) no relationship at all. Participants completed the pivot question about each match/ write-in every time they completed a follow-up questionnaire. If a participant selected option a, b, c, or d, this match/write-in was considered *romantic,* and if a participant selected option e, f, or g, this match/write-in was considered *nonromantic.* If a participant selected option g on two (or more) consecutive waves, no items were assessed for that match/write-in at that wave. A smaller subset of items was required for nonromantic compared to romantic matches/write-ins (for greater detail, see Finkel et al., 2007).

If participants selected either a romantic or a nonromantic response to the pivot question, participants completed an item assessing to what degree this particular match/write-in was someone they wanted to *get to know better* ("I am eager to get to know [name] better"). In addition, if participants responded "yes" that they had "hung out with [name] in person or corresponded with [name] not in person (e-mail, instant messaging, phone, etc.)" since the last time they completed a follow-up questionnaire, they completed a one-item measure of *date initiation* ("For the most part, I was the one to initiate correspondence/ hanging out with [name]") and a one-item measure of *date enjoyment* ("Corresponding/ hanging out with [name] has been enjoyable").

If participants selected a romantic response to the pivot question, they completed the following additional measures: a five-item measure of romantic *passion* ("I feel a great deal of sexual desire for [name]," "I think [name] and I have 'soulmate' potential," "I am romantically interested in [name]," "[name] is the only person I want to be romantically involved with," and "[name] always seems to be on my mind"; α = .84), three items assessing to what extent the participant desired a *one-night stand,* a *casual relationship,* and a *serious relationship* with the match/write-in ("I would like to have a one-night stand with [name]," "… a casual relationship with [name]," "… a serious relationship with [name]"), and an item assessing *commitment* to the match/write-in ("I am committed to pursuing/ maintaining a relationship with [name]").

Finally, if participants responded "yes" that they had "engaged in any romantic physical contact (kissing or other sexual activities) with [name]" since the last time they had completed a follow-up questionnaire, they completed a one-item measure of *sexual initiation* ("I basically initiated the physical contact with [name]"), a one-item measure of *sexual enjoyment* ("I enjoyed the romantic physical contact with [name]"), and an item assessing to what extent the physical contact was a *good idea* ("having romantic physical contact with [name] was a bad idea [reverse scored]").*

* Responses to these three items are only reported for write-ins, because participants rarely reported engaging in romantic physical contact with a fellow speed-dater.

Potential moderator constructs. In the present report, we explore five moderators of H2 and H3. First, we describe the three constructs that were measured at the level of the individual participant (i.e., person-level moderators). Two of these three were intended to address H2A: Perhaps sex differences in the association between the relationship-initiation dependent variables and physical attractiveness or earning prospects will be larger for individuals who are more (compared with less) interested in acquiring a serious romantic relationship (Buss & Schmitt, 1993; Gangestad & Simpson, 2000). The first moderator was *desire for a serious relationship (target-general),* assessed on the pre-event questionnaire by the item: "These days, how much would you like to have a serious relationship" (1 = *not at all,* 7 = *very much).* The second moderator is a three-item measure of *sociosexuality,* a construct that assesses an individual's willingness to engage in short-term sexual relationships (Simpson & Gangestad, 1991). The three items were assessed on the pre-event questionnaire (1 = *strongly disagree,* 7 = *strongly agree)* and were selected from the original Simpson and Gangestad (1991) inventory: "Sex without love is okay," "I would have to be closely attached to someone (both emotionally and psychologically) before I could feel comfortable and fully enjoy having sex with him or her" (reverse scored), and "I can imagine myself being comfortable and enjoying 'casual' sex with different partners" (α = .86). The third was *self-perceived mate value* and was assessed on the pre-event questionnaire (1 = *strongly disagree,* 7 = *strongly agree)* by the items "I am a desirable dating partner," "In general, I tend to have many options for romantic partners," and "Members of the opposite sex that I like tend to like me back" (α = .68). We used this construct to probe H3: Perhaps individuals are more likely to demonstrate interest in and pursue potential partners who approximate their ideals to the extent that they are high (or perhaps low) in self-perceived mate value.

In the present report, we explored two additional moderators that were assessed on the follow-up questionnaire about each match/write-in classified as romantic (i.e., target-specific moderators). The first is *desire for a serious relationship (target-specific),* which also serves as one of the relationship-initiation dependent variables (see above). The second is *partner-specific attachment anxiety,* assessed by the items "I need a lot of reassurance that [name] cares about me," "I worry that [name] doesn't care about me as much I care about him/her," and "I feel uncertain about [name]'s true feelings for me" (α = .80). This construct represents the uncertainty and need for reassurance that individuals often experience in romantic relationships. Elsewhere (Eastwick & Finkel, in press-a), we have explored this construct in detail and argued that it is a common experience during the early stages of a romantic relationship. For the purposes of the present report, we hypothesized that partner-specific attachment anxiety could foster an empathy gap (Loewenstein, 2005) between participants' stated preferences (which they likely reported in a "cool" cognitive state) and the characteristics that actually inspire their passion for potential romantic partners. For simplicity, the analyses for the two target-specific moderators were conducted on the dependent variable *romantic attraction* (α = .87); this DV is an average of the seven romantic-initiation dependent variable items (the five items encompassing *passion,* the *get to know better* item, and the *commitment* item), which (a) were necessarily assessed for that match or write-in at that wave and (b) were not obviously redundant with either moderator (e.g., the *one-night stand* and *casual relationship* items).

Analysis strategy. We used multilevel data-analytic strategies to examine the present data (Kenny, Kashy, & Bolger, 1998; Raudenbush & Bryk, 2002). Data collected prior to the follow-up questionnaires have a two-level structure: Measures assessed about each speed-date/match (Level 1) are nested within participant (Level 2). Data collected on the follow-up questionnaires have a three-level structure: Measures assessed on each of the 10 follow-up questionnaires (Level 1) are nested within each match/ write-in (Level 2), which are nested within participant (Level 3). For example, a participant who was a "friend with romantic potential" with two different matches for all 10 follow-up questionnaires would provide 20 different associations between partner characteristics and passion (10 for each match). All analyses were carried out in SAS with either the NLMIXED procedure (to predict "yessing" using logistic regression) or the MIXED procedure (for all remaining dependent variables). The intercept was permitted to vary randomly at Level 2 and Level 3 (where applicable). All variables were left unstandardized (unless indicated otherwise); participant sex was coded male = —.5, female = .5.

Results

Stated Mate Preferences

Table 1 presents means for stated mate preferences separately by sex. In line with H1, the expected sex differences emerged. On the pre-event questionnaire, men (more than women) reported that the characteristic *physically attractive* was important in an ideal romantic partner and would matter in their decision to say yes to a speed-date. In addition, the same sex difference emerged 1 month later when participants again reported these ideal partner and speed-date stated preferences. The sex differences for *physically attractive* were medium to large in size (mean d = —.55), according to Cohen's (1992) conventions. In addition, women (more than men) estimated on the pre-event questionnaire that the characteristic *earning prospects* was important in an ideal romantic partner and would matter in their decision to say yes to a speed-date. One month later, this sex difference was marginally significant for participants' reports of an ideal partner but did not reach significance for the speed-date stated preferences. The sex differences for *earning prospects* were small to medium in size (mean d = .35). As expected, men and women did not differ in the importance they ascribed to *personable* characteristics, either in an ideal romantic partner or on a speed-date (mean d = .07).

Table 1 Sex Differences in Stated Mate Preferences Among Speed-Daters

	Participant sex						
	Male		*Female*		*Sex difference*		
Stated preference	*M*	*SD*	*M*	*SD*	*t*	*df*	*d*
Physically attractive							
Pre-event ideal partner	8.04	1.10	7.18	1.31	—4.52***	156	—0.71
Pre-event speed-date	7.78	1.08	7.00	1.60	—3.64***	140	—0.57
Wave 10 ideal partner	8.01	0.81	7.62	1.22	—2.02*	109	—0.36
Wave 10 speed-date	7.64	1.20	6.90	1.46	—2.85**	110	—0.54
Earning prospects							
Pre-event ideal partner	6.91	1.53	7.73	1.36	3.61***	161	0.57
Pre-event speed-date	4.42	1.96	5.05	2.19	2.47*	161	0.30
Wave 10 ideal partner	7.34	0.96	7.72	1.03	1.93†	109	0.38
Wave 10 speed-date	5.12	1.94	5.42	1.93	0.79	110	0.16
Personable							
Pre-event ideal partner	8.10	0.73	8.10	0.71	0.01	161	0.00

Pre-event speed-date	7.03	1.06	7.21	1.09	1.05	161	0.17
Wave 10 ideal partner	8.12	0.68	8.20	0.74	0.60	109	0.11
Wave 10 speed-date	7.21	0.94	7.20	1.27	0.06	110	0.01

Note. *ns* ranged from 45 to 82 men and from 66 to 81 women. On a 1–9 scale, higher numbers indicate greater stated importance of *physically attractive, earning prospects,* or *personable* characteristics in an ideal romantic partner or in the hypothetical decision to "yes" someone after a 4-min date. Variables were assessed both before the speed-dating event and at the 10th follow-up wave (1 month later). d = difference between the male and female means divided by the pooled standard deviation. $^{\dagger}p < .10$. $^{*}p < .05$. $^{**}p < .01$. $^{***}p < .001$.

Sex Differences in Relationship Initiation

H2 states that sex differences should emerge in the partner characteristics that predict relationship initiation. First, we would expect that finding a potential romantic partner physically attractive should better predict relationship initiation for men than for women. To test this hypothesis, we regressed the relationship-initiation dependent variables (one at a time) onto *physically attractive* judgments separately for reports of speed-dating partners/matches and write-ins and separately for men and women. The *B*s representing the associations between *physically attractive* and each dependent variable are presented separately by sex in the first four columns of Table 2. For dependent variables assessed prior to the follow-up questionnaire (above the dashed line), *physically attractive* judgments were assessed on the interaction record, whereas for dependent variables assessed on the follow-up questionnaire (below the dashed line), *physically attractive* judgments were assessed at the same follow-up wave.

Overall, participants' judgments of a potential romantic partner's physical attractiveness positively and significantly predicted the relationship-initiation dependent variables. In addition, for each dependent variable, the significance of the difference between the male and female *B*s was tested by the interaction term in a supplementary regression analysis that entered *physically attractive,* participant sex, and their interaction as predictors (Cohen, Cohen, West, & Aiken, 2003). Sporadic sex differences emerged for *physically attractive* (see bolded *B*s in Table 2); for example, men were more likely than women to initiate correspondence/hanging out with matches they found physically attractive (.35 vs. 10), whereas women were more likely than men to enjoy corresponding/hanging out with matches they found physically attractive (.22 vs. 11). A count of these sex differences reveals two cases in which the *B* was significantly more positive for men and three cases in which the *B* was significantly more positive for women out of 25 pairs of male/female regression *B*s.

Table 2 Associations (Regression Bs) Between Partner Characteristics and Relationship-Initiation Dependent Variables

	Physically attractive				Earning prospects				Personable			
	Speed-date/match 5 *B*		Write-in 2 *B*		Speed-date/match *SB*	*IB*	Write-in		Speed-date/match		Write-in	
Dependent variable	♂ *B*	♀ *B*	♂ *B*	♀ *B*	♂ *B*	♀ *B*	♂ *B*	♀ *B*	♂ *B*	♀ *B*	♂ *B*	♀ *B*
Interaction record												
Romantic desire	.76 ***	74 ***			.49***	.29***			.90***	.95***		
Chemistry	.44 ***	.51 ***			.50***	.32***			.89***	1.02***		
"Yessing"	1.01***	.80***			.44***	.17***			.94***	1.11***		
Postmatch												
Excitement	.49***	.44***			.14†	.17*			.28**	.37***		
Initiation plans	.44***	.41***			.07	.16*			.10	.38***		
Initiation hopes	.40***	.48***			.00	.20**			.00	.38***		
Follow-up (all)												
Get to know better	.46***	.39***	.48***	.37***	.27***	.28***	.34***	23***	.64***	60***	.56***	.44***
Date initiation	.35***	.10	.09	.18*	.20*	.06	.16†	.24*	.10	— .07	.07	.16
Date enjoyment	.11†	.22***	.35***	37***	.22**	.3.1***	.30***	.26***	.63***	.65***	.77***	.64***
Follow-up (romantic)												
Passion	.31***	.39***	.30***	43 ***	.13*	.16*	.08	.10†	.27**	.26**	.31**	.39***
One-night stand	— .07	.28***	—.14	.07	.01	— .25*	.16†	— .19*	— .26†	— .23*	— .09	.09
Casual relationship	.26***	.42***	.12	.05	.20**	.25*	.09	— .12	.32**	.32**	.32**	.06

	Physically attractive				Earning prospects				Personable			
	Speed-date/match 5 B		Write-in 2 B		Speed-date/match		Write-in		Speed-date/match		Write-in	
					SB	IB						
Serious relationship	.58***	.37***	.41 ***	43 ***	.26**	.17	.27**	.07	.40**	.23*	.65***	.39***
Commitment	.28**	.45**	.32**	.41***	.12	.14	—.01	.20*	.31*	.40***	.39**	.48***
Follow-up (sexual)												
Sexual initiation			.22	.31*			.19	.03			.08	.37*
Sexual enjoyment			.36***	33 ***			.11	.10			.17	.14
Contact good idea			.27	.42**			.44*	53***			.14	.66***
Overall r	.43***	.46 ***	.26***	.31***	.19***	16 ***	.16**	.18**	.29***	32***	.25***	.27***
Sex difference r	.03		.05		—.04		.02		.	03	.02	

Note. Regression *B*s indicate the relationship between *physically attractive, earning prospects,* or *personable* partner characteristics and 17 relationship-initiation dependent variables (each characteristic was regressed separately). Partner characteristics were measured on a 1–9 scale with higher numbers indicating greater presence of the characteristic in the partner. Relationship-initiation dependent variables were measured on a 1–7 scale, except for *romantic desire* and *chemistry,* which were measured on a 1–9 scale, and "yessing," which is coded 1 for *yes* and 0 for *no. Bs* in the speed-date/match column were calculated on potential partners whom the participants met while speed-dating; *B*s in the write-in column were calculated on potential partners whom the participants met independently of speed-dating. Bolded *B*s indicate a significant or marginally significant sex difference; the bolded *B* is always the more positive of the two. Partner characteristics *(physically attractive, earning prospects, personable)* were assessed either at the speed-dating event (above the dashed line) or at each follow-up wave (below the dashed line). The overall *r* row indicates the meta-analyzed effect size *r* across all *B*s reported in the column. The sex difference *r* row indicates the size of the difference between men's reports *(S)* and women's reports (2); a negative *r* indicates that the characteristic was a stronger determinant of men's romantic interest. $^{\dagger}p < .10$. $^{*}p < .05$. $^{**}p < .01$. $^{***}p < .001$.

To gain a formal, less impressionistic sense of the big picture, we calculated the overall effect size r for the association between *physically attractive* and the relationship-initiation variables (see bottom of Table 2). We calculated these correlations using meta-analytic models that included each relationship-initiation variable as a random effect and participant sex as a fixed effect (Cooper & Hedges, 1994; Konstantopoulos & Hedges, 2004). For example, each of the 28 speed-date/match *B*s (see first two columns in Table 2) was first standardized and then weighted by the reciprocal of its variance (calculated from the Huber-White sandwich standard error);* the intercept given by the model is the average r, and the fixed effect for sex indicates the average size of the sex difference across the DVs. This same procedure was implemented separately for speed-dating partners/matches and write-ins. In general, physical attractiveness predicted relationship initiation quite well: Correlations were .43 (men) and .46 (women) for reports of speed-dating partners/matches and .26 (men) and .31 (women) for reports of write-ins.† Finally, the size of the sex difference (i.e., the fixed effect of sex in the meta-analytic model, similar to the effect size q, which can be interpreted like a correlation, see Cohen, 1992) is presented in the final row of Table 2. For both speed-dating partners/matches and write-ins, the sex difference was nonsignificant. Descriptively speaking, both sex differences were extremely small (r = .03, p = .673, and r = .05, p = .499, for speed-dating partners/matches and write-ins, respectively) and, if anything, trending such that physical attractiveness was a more important determinant of *women's* relationship initiation. Although physical attractiveness appears to predict romantic interest in the early stages of potential relationships, we found no evidence for sex differences in its importance.

H2 also suggests that finding a potential romantic partner to have good earning potential should better predict relationship initiation for women than for men. The four middle columns of Table 2 present the associations between participants' judgments of *earning prospects* and each dependent variable separately by sex and separately for speed-dating partners/matches and write-ins. Overall, participants' judgments of a potential romantic partner's earning prospects positively and significantly predicted the relationship-initiation dependent variables. Again, sporadic sex differences emerged for *earning prospects* (see bolded *B*s in Table 2); surprisingly, at the event itself, men seemed especially interested (compared with women) in the speed-dating partners they felt had good earning prospects.

---

* For "yessing," the B estimate given by NLMIXED was first converted to a d(B X /3/π) and then to an r(d 2/d2 + 4), and finally the variance of this correlation was calculated with the formula (1 — r2)2/(N — 2) (Had dock, Rindskopf, & Shadish, 1998; Rosenthal, 1994).

† Note that the smaller effect size for write-ins compared with matches is probably because of differences in variables assessed for these two kinds of targets; many of the largest effects were found for dependent variables assessed either on the interaction record or the postmatch questionnaire (which did not apply to write-ins), and effects for the eight dependent variables assessed for both matches and write-ins are roughly comparable in size.

A count of these sex differences across the 25 pairs of male/female regression *B*s reveals five cases in which the *B* was significantly more positive for men and one case in which the *B* was significantly more positive for women. Again, more formally, we calculated the overall *r* for the association between *earning prospects* and relationship initiation using the same meta-analytic procedures described above. As displayed at the bottom of Table 2, *earning prospects* predicted relationship initiation, although the correlations were smaller than those found for *physically attractive:* Correlations were .19 (men) and .16 (women) for reports of speed-dating partners/matches and .16 (men) and .18 (women) for reports of write-ins. Again, there were no significant sex differences in these overall associations; the difference between the male and female *rs* were again descriptively very small (r = — .04, p = .480, and r = .02, p = .825, for speed-dating partners/matches and write-ins, respectively), with one trending in the male direction and one trending in the female direction. Although *earning prospects* did positively predict romantic interest, again we found no evidence for sex differences in the importance of this variable.

Finally, for comparative purposes, we examined the relationship between *personable* characteristics and the relationship-initiation variables, although we would not expect to find systematic sex differences in these associations. The final four columns of Table 2 present the associations between participants' judgments of *personable* and each dependent variable separately by sex and separately for speed-dating partners/matches and write-ins. Overall, participants' judgments of a potential romantic partner's *personable* characteristics positively and significantly predicted the relationship-initiation dependent variables. Three sex differences (out of 25) emerged for *personable* in the female direction (see bolded *Bs* in Table 2). Again, we calculated the overall *r* for the association between *personable* and relationship initiation using the same meta-analytic procedures described previously. As displayed at the bottom of Table 2, *personable* predicted relationship initiation moderately well: Correlations were .29 (men) and .32 (women) for reports of speed-dating partners/ matches and .25 (men) and .27 (women) for reports of write-ins. As expected, there were no significant sex differences in these overall associations (r = .03, p = .714, and r = .02, p = .812, for speed-dating partners/matches and write-ins, respectively).

The preceding analyses revealed that participants' *own* judgments of the physical attractiveness and earning prospects of potential romantic partners predicted their romantic interest in those partners equally well for men and women. However, it could still be true that men (compared with women) are more romantically interested in *objectively* attractive potential partners and that women (compared with men) are more romantically interested in *objectively* ambitious potential partners. To explore this possibility, we obtained several alternative measures of partner characteristics. Because each speed-dater was rated by 9–13 other speed-daters on the characteristics *physically attractive, earning prospects,* and *personable,* we could create consensus ratings of these three characteristics for each target by averaging these 9–13 judgments. Interrater reliabilities for these judgments were strong:

The *physically attractive* reliability was α = .92, the *earning prospects* reliability was α = .77, and the *personable* reliability was α = .79.

For each analysis presented in the "speed-date/match" columns of Table 2, these consensus ratings were substituted in place of the subjective *physically attractive, earning prospects,* and *personable* judgments (no consensus ratings were available for write-ins). Using the same meta-analytic procedure reported above, we calculated overall *rs* that describe the association between each target's consensus characteristics and participants' reports on the relationship-initiation dependent variables with respect to that target. Overall *rs* and sex-difference *rs* are presented in the first three rows of Table 3. *Physically attractive, earning prospects,* and *personable* consensus ratings were positively and significantly associated with the relationship-initiation dependent variables for both men and women. As with the subjective judgments, however, the sex differences in these associations were small and nonsignificant.

All speed-daters had their photographs taken at the speed-dating event, affording an additional measure of physical attractiveness. Six independent coders (three women and three men) rated each photo on physical attractiveness (α = .76); for each analysis presented in the first two columns of Table 2, these coder ratings were substituted in place of the subjective attractiveness judgments (photos were not taken of write-ins, so no coder-ratings were available). As shown in the fourth row of Table 3, the overall meta-analyzed *rs* for men and women were again positive and significant, but as with the subjective physical-attractiveness judgments, the sex difference was again small and nonsignificant.

Table 3 Overall Associations Between Alternative Measures of Partner Characteristics and Relationship-Initiation Dependent Variables

Independent variable	Male *r*	Female *r*	Sex difference *r*
Consensus physically attractive	.27***	.29***	.02 (p = .714)
Consensus earning prospects	.13***	.14***	.01 (p = .817)
Consensus personable	.14***	.13***	—.01 (p = .817)
Coder-rated physical attractiveness	.14**	.17***	.03 (p = .612)
Hometown average income	—.08**	—.02	.06 (p = .134)

Note. Male and female *r* columns present the meta-analyzed effect size *r* between the independent variable (calculated with respect to speed-dates/ matches only) and all relationship-initiation dependent variables (see Table 2) for male and female participants, respectively. The sex difference *r* column indicates the size of the difference between men's reports and women's reports; a negative *r* indicates that the characteristic was a stronger determinant of men's romantic interest.

** $p < .01$. *** $p < .001$.

Finally, similar to an analysis conducted by Fisman et al. (2006), we used the 2000 census data (United States Census Bureau, 2000) to calculate the natural log of the median income of each participant's hometown (hometown was reported by zip code on the pre-event questionnaire). For each analysis presented in the fifth and sixth columns of Table 2, these ratings were substituted for the subjective earning-prospects judgments (no hometown zip codes were assessed for write-ins, so no income measure was available for these targets). As shown in the fifth row of Table 3, women demonstrated neither greater nor lesser romantic initiation toward men who were from wealthy hometowns, and men appeared to dislike women from wealthy hometowns, although this correlation was small (r = —.08). As with the subjective earning-prospects judgments, the sex difference was nonsignificant (r = .06, p = .134). Taken together, these five auxiliary analyses suggest that men and women did not differ in how these alternative measures of partner characteristics inspired their romantic interest, which is the same pattern of results revealed by participants' own subjective judgments (see Table 2). (We explore H2A regarding participants' short-term versus long-term orientations in the *Moderator Construct Analyses* section below.)

Individual Differences in Relationship Initiation

Considering that male and female participants differed in how important they rated physical attractiveness and earning prospects in an ideal partner and an ideal speed-date (H1), how is it that no sex differences emerged when predicting relationship-initiation variables from these same characteristics (H2)? This intriguing null finding suggests the possibility that stated ideal partner preferences may have been unrelated to what actually inspired romantic interest in the live dating context of this study (see also Iyengar et al., 2005). Therefore, we examined H3: If some participants reported an especially strong preference for a certain partner characteristic (e.g., physically attractive), did those same participants also demonstrate especially strong romantic interest in and pursuit of those romantic partners they judged to possess that characteristic? The context of the speed-dating event provides a rare opportunity to examine this individual-differences hypothesis; because participants met between 9 and 13 potential romantic partners at an event, we can assign each participant a unique B for how well his/her judgments of *physically attractive* (or *earning prospects,* or *personable)* predicted his/her reports of romantic desire, chemistry, or likelihood of "yessing" across all dates.* If the stated preferences have predictive validity, a participant who stated that physical attractiveness was important in an ideal romantic partner or a speed-date should have shown a strong association (i.e., a large *B*) between judgments of his/her dates' physical attractiveness and his/her romantic desire for, chemistry with, and likelihood of "yessing" those dates. In other words, a participant's stated preferences and the in vivo preferences revealed by his/her own individual *B*s should be positively correlated.

Table 4 Correlations Between Participants' Romantic Desire, Chemistry, and "Yessing" Bs and Stated Preferences for Physically Attractive

Variable	Romantic desire *B*	Chemistry *B*	"Yessing" *B*	Pre-event ideal partner	Pre-event speed-date	Wave 10 ideal partner	Wave 10 speed-date
Romantic desire *B*	—	.62***	.24**	.02	.07	—.04	— .01
Chemistry *B*	.62 ***	—	.16*	— .02	— .03	—.10	— .08
"Yessing" *B*	.24**	.16*	—	.10	.12	.02	.00
Pre-event ideal partner	.03	.07	.09	—	.62***	68***	55***
Pre-event speed-date	.02	.06	.14	.61***	—	60***	62 ***
Wave 10 ideal partner	— .08	— .06	.06	.68***	.61***		55***
Wave 10 speed-date	.00	.00	.01	.55***	67***	70***	

Note. Romantic desire, chemistry, and "yessing" *B*s were calculated for each participant across

* Bs for "yessing" could not be computed for participants who said "yes" (n = 6) or "no" (n = 3) to all dates. Also, because a B for "yessing" is the natural log of an odds ratio, a number of large outliers emerged; participants who had "yessing" Bs beyond Tukey's inner fences (Myers & Well, 1995; Tukey, 1977) were considered missing (ns = 12 for physically attractive, 15 for earning prospects, 25 for personable). Even with the inclusion of these outliers, however, none of the 24 nonsignificant correlations between a stated preference and the "yessing" Bs in Tables 4, 5, and 6 (the correlations of interest) became significant.

all 9–13 of his/her speed-dates. Stated-preference items were assessed on a 1–9 scale with higher numbers indicating greater self-reported importance of *physically attractive* in an ideal romantic partner or in the hypothetical decision to "yes" someone after a 4-min date. Stated preferences were assessed both before the speed-dating event and at the 10th follow-up wave (1 month later). Stated preferences above the diagonal were within-person centered; stated preferences below the diagonal were left as their raw values.

$^{*}p \leq .05$. $^{**}p \leq .01$. $^{***}p \leq .001$.

Tables 4, 5, and 6 present all correlations among participants' individual *B*s (romantic desire, chemistry, and "yessing") and his/her stated preferences (ideal partner and speed-date, both pre-event and Wave 10) for *physically attractive, earning prospects,* and *personable,* respectively. There are two ways of scoring stated preferences in these analyses: Stated preferences can be within-person centered (i.e., the raw, 1–9 values minus the participant's mean rating across all traits, also called an ipsative measure), or they can be left as their raw values. A high value for a within-person centered stated preference indicates that the participant claimed to value that trait more than he/she values other traits, whereas a high value for a raw stated preference indicates that the participant claimed to value that trait more than other participants did. Because both approaches are meaningful, we present the within-person centered correlations above the diagonal and the raw-values correlations below the diagonal in Tables 4, 5, and 6. (Of course, the correlations among the three *B*s do not change whether they are below or above the diagonal.)

Across Tables 4, 5, and 6, the three *B*s correlated significantly with one another. For example, if a participant tended to romantically desire those dates he found physically attractive, he also tended to experience chemistry with those same dates he found attractive ($r = .62$, $p < .001$; see Table 4). Also, the four stated-preference assessments (both within-person centered and raw values) correlated highly with one another. If a participant reported a strong ideal partner preference before the event for someone with good earning prospects, she was more likely than other participants to also report a preference for such a partner while speed-dating ($r = .52$, $p < .001$), and at the Wave 10 follow-up as an ideal partner ($r = .53$, $p < .001$), and while speed-dating ($r = .39$, $p < .001$; see Table 5). However, the correlations between the *B*s (in vivo preferences) and the stated-preference measures (both within-person centered and raw values) were small: Out of 72 correlations, only 2 were significant and positive and 1 was actually significant and negative. For example, participants who reported at pretest that they would be more likely to say yes to a date who they felt was personable were in fact *not* significantly more likely to say yes to those dates ($r = .05$, $p = .578$; see Table 6). In summary, although participants' stated preferences were consistent across four different assessments, and although participants' in vivo preferences were consistent within a live dating context (i.e., the *B* correlations), participants' stated preferences were unrelated to their in vivo preferences.

Tables 4, 5, and 6 present results aggregated across sex; however, it is possible that this presentation could obscure sex differences in these correlations. To test for sex differences, we conducted regressions that predicted each variable in Tables 4, 5, and 6 from one of the remaining six variables in that table, participant sex, and their interaction. (We report this analysis on the within-person centered stated preferences to keep the presentation manageable, but our conclusions were identical when we used the raw-values preferences.) Because the interaction with sex may differ depending on which variable is considered the independent variable and which is considered the dependent variable, we examined all possible regression combinations, giving a total 42 regressions for each of the three tables. For *physically attractive,* only 3 of these 42 regressions revealed a sex interaction (at $p < .05$), for *earning prospects,* only 4 of these 42 regressions revealed a sex interaction, and for *personable,* only 6 out of these 42 regressions revealed a sex interaction. Furthermore, only 1 of these 13 sex-differentiated correlations was between a *B* and a stated preference (the correlations of interest), and this correlation remained nonsignificant for both men and women. Therefore, we find little evidence to suggest that the sexes differ in how well their stated preferences correlate with their in vivo preferences.

Table 5 Correlations Between Participants' Romantic Desire, Chemistry, and "Yessing" Bs and Stated Preferences for Earning Prospects

Variable	Romantic desire *B*	Chemistry *B*	"Yessing" *B*	Pre-event ideal partner	Pre-event speed-date	Wave 10 ideal partner	Wave 10 speed-date
Romantic desire *B*	—	.71***	59***	.07	.09	.03	— .03
Chemistry *B*	.71***	—	.48***	.11	.13	.13	— .02
"Yessing" *B*	59***	.48***		.04	.08	.07	.12
Pre-event ideal partner	.14	.16*	.07	—	53***	.60***	.41***
Pre-event speed-date	.10	.16*	.08	52***	—	.44***	.53***
Wave 10 ideal partner	.13	.15	.09	53***	.38***		.47****
Wave 10 speed-date	.03	.03	.18	39***	53***	.44***	

Note. Romantic desire, chemistry, and "yessing" *B*s were calculated for each participant across all 9–13 of his/her speed-dates. Stated-preference items were assessed on a 1–9 scale with higher numbers indicating greater self-reported importance of *earning prospects* in an ideal romantic partner or in the hypothetical decision to "yes" someone after a 4-min date. Stated preferences were assessed both before the speed-dating event and at the 10th follow-up wave (1 month later). Stated preferences above the diagonal were within-person centered; stated preferences below the diagonal were left as their raw values.

* $p < .05$. *** $p < .001$.

Finally, we subjected the three in vivo preferences and the four within-person centered stated preferences (separately for Physically Attractive, Earning Prospects, and Personable) to a factor analysis to more formally test whether in vivo and stated preferences reflect two independent factors. (Again, results do not change appreciably when using the raw-values preferences.) The results of these three factor analyses (principal axis factoring with promax rotation) are presented in Table 7. In all three cases, two-factor solutions were suggested by parallel analyses (Humphreys & Montanelli, 1975; see also Fabrigar, Wegener, MacCallum, & Strahan, 1999) in which the eigenvalues of the actual data are compared with eigenvalues of an equivalently sized set of random data. As expected, for all three sets of preferences, the three in vivo preferences loaded on one factor and the four stated preferences loaded on the other. Furthermore, the promax rotation is oblique and therefore permits the factors to be correlated; however, as shown in Table 7, the correlation between the two factors was generally quite weak across the three sets of preferences.

Table 6 Correlations Between Participants' Romantic Desire, Chemistry, and "Yessing" Bs and Stated Preferences for Personable

Variable	Romantic desire *B*	Chemistry *B*	"Yessing" *B*	Pre-event ideal partner	Pre-event speed-date	Wave 10 ideal partner	Wave 10 speed-date
Romantic desire *B*	—	59***	39***	.14	.04	.09	.02
Chemistry *B*	.59***		.25**	—.02	.08	—.20*	—.07
"Yessing" *B*	39***	.25**	—	—.03	—.06	—.01	—.10
Pre-event ideal partner	—.04	.05	.14	—	.35***	.52***	.25**
Pre-event speed-date	—.13	.05	.05	32***	—	.44***	.51***
Wave 10 ideal partner	—.05	—.12	.06	.49***	.35***	—	.47***
Wave 10 speed-date	—.07	.05	.08	.18*	.48***	47***	—

Note. Romantic desire, chemistry, and "yessing" *B*s were calculated for each participant across all 9–13 of his/her speed-dates. Stated-preference items were assessed on a 1–9 scale with higher numbers indicating greater self-reported importance of *personable* in an ideal romantic partner or in the hypothetical decision to "yes" someone after a 4-min date. Stated preferences were assessed both before the speed-dating event and at the 10th follow-up wave (1 month later). Stated preferences above the diagonal were within-person centered; stated preferences below the diagonal were left as their raw values.

$^{*}p \leq .05$. $^{**}p \leq .01$. $^{***}p \leq .001$.

Similarity Effects?

It is plausible that participants' awareness of their own standing on these partner characteristics *(physically attractive, earning prospects,* and *personable)* inhibited the pursuit of their ideals. In other words, stated preferences may have failed to correlate with in vivo preferences not because participants' stated preferences were inaccurate, but instead because they anticipated rejection to the degree a partner outshined them on a particular characteristic. To explore this possibility, we conducted a series of regression equations with the following form: where SelfChari is person i's self-rating on a characteristic (physically attractive, earning prospects, or personable, assessed on the pre-event questionnaire on a scale from 1–9), PartnerChar_{ij} is person i's interaction-record rating of speed-dating partner j on that characteristic, StatedPref_i is the average of person i's four within-person centered stated preferences (ideal partner and speed-date from both the pre-event questionnaire and the Wave 10 follow-up questionnaire) for that characteristic, and DV_{ij} is person i's romantic desire, chemistry, or yes/no decision regarding speed-dating partner j. We regressed each of these three dependent variables on each of the three characteristics (nine total regressions).

Table 7 Factor Loadings of Participants' Romantic Desire, Chemistry, and "Yessing" Bs and Stated Preferences

	Physically attractive		Earning prospects		Personable	
Variable	Factor 1	Factor 2	Factor 1	Factor 2	Factor 1	Factor 2
In vivo preferences						
Romantic desire *B*	.04	.89	—.11	.86	.11	.80
Chemistry *B*	—.06	.69	.04	.81	—.10	.63
"Yessing" *B*	.04	.21	.08	.71	—.04	.52
Stated preferences						
Pre-event ideal partner	.78	.06	.79	.06	.53	.04

Pre-event speed-date	.74		.02	.75		—.03	.66		.08
Wave 10 ideal partner	.82		—.06	.67		.01	.73		—.07
Wave 10 speed-date	.71		.00	.62		—.03	.56		—.09
Factor correlation		*r* = .01			*r* = .09			*r* = .02	

Note. Loadings of .2 and above are bolded. Stated preferences are within-person centered.

$$DV_{ij} = \gamma_0 + \gamma_1 \text{SelfChari} + \gamma_2 \text{ PartnerChar}_{ij}$$

$$+ \gamma_3 \text{StatedPref}_i + \gamma_4 (\text{PartnerChar}_{ij} \text{ X StatedPrefi}) + e_{ij}, \ (1)$$

To examine similarity effects, we conducted each of the nine regressions twice, as suggested by Griffin, Murray, and Gonzalez (1999): once for all reports in which participants scored higher than their speed-dating partner ($\text{SelfChar}_i > \text{PartnerChar}_{ij}$) and once for all reports in which participants scored lower ($\text{Self-Char}_i < \text{PartnerChar}_{ij}$). If y_2 is positive when $\text{SelfChar}_i > \text{PartnerChar}_{ij}$ but negative when $\text{SelfChar}_i < \text{PartnerChar}_{ij}$, this would indicate that participants desired similarity on that characteristic. Furthermore, stated-preference effects could emerge after accounting for these similarity effects: A positive PartnerChar_{ij} X Stated-Pref_i interaction would indicate that having a strong stated preference leads participants to either (a) strongly deselect partners who fall below them on that characteristic or (b) strongly select partners despite the fact that they lie above them on that characteristic.

None of the nine regressions revealed any evidence that participants desired similarity. Whether speed-dating partners scored below or above the participant on a characteristic, participants significantly liked the partner more to the extent that he/she possessed greater levels of that characteristic (all γ_2s were positive; ts > 2.68). Furthermore, none of the PartnerChar_{ij} X Stated-Pref_i interactions were both positive and significant ($p < .05$), although two were $p < .10$ and negative and three were $p < .10$ and positive. These analyses suggest that participants did not experience inhibited romantic interest in speed-dating partners who exceeded them on a characteristic; on the contrary, higher physical attractiveness, earning prospects, or personable ratings were consistently romantically inspiring regardless of self ratings, and stated preferences did not play a consistent role in moderating these effects.

Moderator Construct Analyses

At this point, the data suggest a disconnect between the characteristics that participants claim to prefer in a romantic partner and the characteristics that participants actually value in a live dating context. To get a better sense of what might or might not be accounting for the effects reported above, we conducted several theoretically sensible moderational analyses.

Desire for a serious relationship (target-general). Some prominent evolutionary theories (Buss & Schmitt, 1993; Ganges-tad & Simpson, 2000) would suggest that the null results for H2 (missing sex differences) are not meaningful without considering participants' short-term versus long-term mating orientations. After all, several previous reports have suggested that men's and women's ideal partner preferences change depending on whether they are considering a short-term or long-term relationship (e.g., Li & Kenrick, 2006). Therefore, we explored H2A: Might sex differences in the associations between the relationship-initiation dependent variables and physical attractiveness or earning prospects have emerged for participants who were more (compared with less) interested in having a long-term relationship? If so, we would expect to consistently find significant Partner Characteristic X Sex X Desire for a Serious Relationship (Target-General) interactions predicting the relationship-initiation dependent variables.* We tested whether this three-way interaction was significant for every male/female pair of *B*s displayed in Table 2 (with the exception of those pertaining to the dependent variables *desire for a serious relationship/casual relationship/one-night stand,* which are theoretically ambiguous in this case). In other words, we explored 11 possible three-way interactions in which speed-dating matches served as targets and 8 possible three-way interactions for the write-ins for each partner characteristic.

For the characteristic *physically attractive,* H2A predicts that these three-way interactions will be negative. That is, the two-way Physically Attractive X Desire for a Serious Relationship (Target-General) interaction (which tests whether *physically attractive* better predicts the dependent variable among individuals more compared with less interested in a serious relationship) should be more positive for men than for women. However, out of 11 possible three-way interactions for the speed-dating matches, 0 were significant and negative and 1 was actually significant and positive (i.e., the two-way interaction was more

* This three-way interaction tests whether any sex difference in the association between a partner characteristic and romantic interest is smaller for participants who experienced low compared with high desire for a serious relationship. Given ambiguities in the previous literature (e.g., Kenrick et al., 1993, vs. Li & Kenrick, 2006), we did not specifically hypothesize whether the sex differences would be reduced, nonexistent, or reversed for participants experiencing low desire for a serious relationship. Indeed, the three-way interaction could detect any of these patterns, and all of them would support prominent evolutionary models of mating (Buss & Schmitt, 1993; Gangestad & Simpson, 2000); we therefore tested for three-way interactions across all relevant moderator analyses.

positive for *women).* Out of eight possible three-way interactions for the write-ins, two were significant and negative and two were significant and positive. For the characteristic *earning prospects,* H2A predicts that these three-way interactions will be positive. That is, the two-way Earning Prospects X Desire for a Serious Relationship (Target-General) interaction (which tests whether *earning prospects* better predicts the dependent variable among individuals more compared with less interested in a serious relationship) should be more positive for women than for men. Only 1 out of 11 possible three-way interactions for the speed-dating matches was significant and positive, and one out of eight possible three-way interactions for the write-ins was actually significant and negative (i.e., the two-way interaction was more positive for *men).* Finally, H2A would not necessarily predict the emergence of significant three-way interactions for the characteristic *personable.* In this case, 1 out of 11 possible three-way interactions was significant (and positive) for the speed-daters, and three out of eight possible three-way interactions were significant (and positive) for the write-ins. In short, these analyses did not reveal compelling evidence that the sex differences predicted by H2 emerged more strongly for participants who were especially interested in acquiring a serious romantic relationship.

Sociosexuality. Sociosexuality refers to the degree to which individuals are willing (unrestricted) or unwilling (restricted) to engage in short-term, sexual relationships (Simpson & Gangestad, 1991). Again, we examined H2A: It is possible that sex differences in Table 2 might emerge for individuals at the restricted (low) compared with the unrestricted (high) end of the sociosexuality scale. To explore this possibility, we conducted analyses identical to those reported above for desire for a serious relationship (target-general). (Note that the predicted direction of effects reverses for sociosexuality because of how the items are scored.)

None of the 11 Physically Attractive X Sex X Sociosexuality interactions was significant for the speed-dating matches, and two of the eight possible three-way interactions for the write-ins were significant and negative (i.e., the opposite of the predicted direction). For the characteristic *earning prospects,* 0 of the 11 possible three-way interactions was significant for the speed-dating matches, and for the write-ins, 1 was significant and negative (the predicted direction) and 1 was significant and positive (the opposite of the predicted direction). For the characteristic *personable,* 1 out of 11 possible three-way interactions was significant (and negative) for the speed-dating matches, and one out of eight possible three-way interactions was significant (and negative) for the write-ins. Again, the data did not suggest that the sex differences predicted by H2 emerged more strongly for participants who were less (compared with more) willing to engage in short-term, sexual relationships.

Desire for a serious relationship (target-specific). We also explored whether one of the relationship-initiation dependent variables, desire for a serious relationship, could serve as a moderator of the effects reported in Table 2. Because participants completed this item with regard to a specific target, it provides a more focused test of H2A than does the general, person-level desire-for-a-serious-relationship item. However, because this target-specific desire-for-a-serious-relationship measure was assessed on each follow-up questionnaire for matches/write-ins classified as romantic (see Method section), it cannot be used to predict many of the relationship-initiation dependent variables (e.g., those assessed at the level of the target, such as "yessing"). For simplicity, we examined whether the three-way Partner Characteristic X Sex X Desire for a Serious Relationship (Target-Specific) interaction significantly predicted the amalgamated dependent variable *romantic attraction,* which was made up of all the romantic-initiation items that had to be available at each follow-up wave for each match or write-in classified as romantic (see Method section).

For the characteristic *physically attractive,* this three-way interaction was marginally significant and positive (the opposite of the predicted direction) for matches and was marginally significant and negative (the predicted direction) for write-ins. For the characteristics *earning prospects* and *personable,* the three-way interactions did not reach marginal significance for either speed-dating matches or write-ins. In total, we did not find compelling evidence for H2A using this target-specific desire-for-a-serious-relationship item. (Null or inconsistent results also emerged when we examined the moderational role of the two target-specific variables that assessed desire for a casual relationship and desire for a one-night stand.)

An astute reader might notice that in the first two columns of Table 2, *physically attractive* predicts desire for a one-night stand more strongly for women than for men but predicts desire for a serious relationship more strongly for men than for women. This pattern is consistent with H2A, and indeed, the Physically Attractive X Sex interaction is significant if used to predict the difference between these two items (serious minus one-night stand). However, the Physically Attractive X Sex interaction is not significant for the write-ins, and neither of the Earning Prospects X Sex interactions is significant. Oddly, the Personable X Sex interaction is significant for the write-ins; the sex-differentiated pattern is especially pronounced in this case but is not consistent with H2A. In short, one of the four predicted interactions was significant, and one of the two nonpredicted interactions was significant.

Finally, it is worth noting that the three moderators used above to test H2A all demonstrated healthy variability in this sample. Desire for a serious relationship (target-general) had a mean of 5.0 (SD = 1.6), sociosexuality had a mean of 3.2 (SD = 1.8), and desire for a serious relationship (target-specific) had a mean of 4.8 (SD = 1.8; across matches and write-ins). The range of all three variables included the entire 1–7 scale, and none had any outliers outside of Tukey's inner fences (Myers & Well, 1995; Tukey, 1977). It is also unlikely that all participants had solely short-term romantic goals in mind: For speed-dating matches, participants were most interested in a casual relationship (M = 5.08), followed by a serious relationship (M = 3.89), and were least interested in a one-night stand (M = 3.20; all three means differ significantly at $p < .001$). For write-ins, participants were most interested in a serious relationship (M = 5.39), followed by a casual relationship (M = 5.14), and were again least interested in a one-night stand (M = 3.10; all three means differ significantly *at* $p < .03$). In sum, the data suggest that participants' short-term versus long-term orientations had no bearing on our failure to confirm H2 in this study.

Partner-specific attachment anxiety. We also conducted an exploratory analysis examining whether partner-specific attachment anxiety (e.g., Eastwick & Finkel, in press-a) might serve as a moderator of the effects presented in Table 2. We hypothesized that participants might show traditional sex differences on the characteristics that predict the relationship-initiation variables when they are *not* feeling particularly anxious or uncertain about what a potential romantic partner thinks of them. In other words, anxiety could be one emotion that fosters an empathy gap (e.g., Loewenstein, 2005) between the cool, rational mindset in which stated preferences are typically reported and the desire participants feel toward a real-life potential romantic partner. Perhaps it is easier to compare a target's qualities with some ideal romantic-partner template (a template which typically differs by sex) when one is not preoccupied with thoughts about whether that target is romantically interested in the self.

To illustrate, imagine a male participant who is not caught up in the throes of anxiety with respect to a certain physically attractive female target, yet he still remains romantically interested in her and recognizes that she is an "objectively" good catch. It is easy to imagine that, in such a nonanxious state, men (compared with women) might be more inspired by a target's physical attractiveness and women (compared with men) might be more inspired by a target's earning prospects. However, as participants report increasing levels of partner-specific attachment anxiety, the traditional sex differences should become attenuated. This hypothesis suggests that a three-way Partner Characteristic X Sex X Partner-Specific Attachment Anxiety interaction should emerge for the traditionally sex-differentiated characteristics *physically attractive* and *earning prospects* but not for *personable* in predicting romantic attraction. (We use this amalgamated dependent variable again because partner-specific attachment anxiety, like desire for a serious relationship [target-specific], was assessed only for matches/ write-ins classified as romantic.)

For the characteristic *physically attractive,* this three-way interaction was marginally significant and positive for matches; this suggests that, as predicted, *physically attractive* was a better predictor of romantic interest for men (compared with women) at low rather than high levels of partner-specific attachment anxiety. However, the three-way interaction did not achieve significance for the write-ins. For the characteristic *earning prospects,* the three-way interaction was marginally significant and negative for matches and significant and negative for write-ins; this suggests that, as predicted, *earning prospects* was a better predictor of romantic interest for women (compared with men) at low rather than high levels of partner-specific attachment anxiety. Finally, for the characteristic *personable,* the three-way interaction was not significant for either matches or write-ins, as expected.* Although we view these results as preliminary and we await future research before drawing definitive conclusions, it is possible that the uncertainty or anxiety often associated with developing relationships may attenuate traditional sex differences in the characteristics that men and women consider important in a romantic partner.

H3 moderation. Finally, we attempted to identify significant moderators of the 72 stated/in vivo correlations presented in Tables 4, 5, and 6. For example, it is plausible that participants showed greater correspondence between their stated and in vivo preferences to the extent that they were interested in having a long-term, serious relationship or to the extent that they had a restricted sociosexual orientation (these H3 moderational analyses can only be conducted with moderators measured at the level of the individual participant). If this were true, we would expect to find that desire for a serious relationship (target-general) positively interacted (and sociosexuality negatively interacted) with stated preferences to predict in vivo preferences. Separately for these two possible moderators, we conducted two regressions for each of the 72 correlations (total regressions per moderator = 144), once with the stated preference serving as the dependent variable and once with the in vivo preference serving as the dependent variable (just as above when we explored sex differences in these correlations). The interaction of desire for a serious relationship (target-general) and these preferences was never significant and positive (the predicted direction) and was actually significant and negative in two cases. In addition, sociosexuality was only a significant and negative (the predicted direction) moderator in 1 of these 144 regressions; it was never significant and positive. Therefore, it appears unlikely that participants' desire for a serious relationship or their sociosexuality orientation were factors that could explain why their stated and in vivo preferences were uncorrelated.

We also explored the possibility that self-perceived mate value could moderate these 72 stated/in vivo correlations. Two patterns are plausible. For one, perhaps stated and in vivo preferences correlated poorly in this study because participants with low mate value felt they had little to offer in the dating arena and were therefore more likely to express interest in real-life potential partners who fell short of their stated ideal. On the other hand, perhaps individuals with high mate value possessed unrealistic ideals regarding romantic partners,

---

* Of the three marginal or significant three-way interactions involving partner-specific attachment anxiety, only the following two-way simple slope of interest was reliable: The Physically Attractive X Sex interaction was significant and positive for individuals scoring one standard deviation above the mean on partner-specific attachment anxiety (e.g., physically attractive predicted romantic attraction better for women than for men at high levels of anxiety). Thus, the present results do not allow for definitive conclusions about the precise pattern of these interactions.

and it would therefore be the low-mate-value participants who would be in a position to select partners who approximated their attainable ideals. The first hypothesis predicts that self-perceived mate value will positively interact with stated preferences to predict in vivo preferences (and vice versa), and the second hypothesis predicts that these interactions will be negative. Again, we conducted 144 regressions. The interaction of self-perceived mate value and these preferences was never significant and positive, and in nine cases (6% of the analyses), the interaction was significant and negative. We therefore find little consistent evidence that participants' self-perceived mate value (i.e., their own general self-assessment of success with the opposite sex) significantly inhibited or augmented the pursuit of their ideals at the speed-dating event.

Table 8 briefly summarizes the outcomes of each of the analyses reported in this article that tested a possible explanation for our failure to confirm H2 and H3.

Discussion

In the present study, we examined how participants' judgments of potential romantic partners' physical attractiveness, earning prospects, and personable characteristics predicted the romantic interest they felt toward those individuals. We advanced three hypotheses: Given that (a) participants demonstrated traditional stated-preference sex differences on the characteristics *physically attractive* and *earning prospects,* data should have revealed (b) sex differences in the associations between those characteristics and romantic interest in potential partners and (c) meaningful correlations between stated preferences and in vivo preferences revealed at the speed-dating event. The latter two hypotheses were unsupported. First, although physical attractiveness, good earning prospects, and personable characteristics were all positively and significantly associated with romantic interest, the data revealed no evidence of sex differences in these associations. We were also unable to find any evidence that these missing sex differences were related to participants' long-term versus short-term orientations, as might be predicted by some prominent evolutionary theories (e.g., Buss & Schmitt, 1993). Second, stated preferences were largely independent of in vivo preferences: For example, a participant who claimed to value physical attractiveness highly in a romantic partner was not significantly more likely than other participants to like, feel chemistry with, or say "yes" to the dates he found physically attractive.

These data offer support for the idea that mate preferences as reported in the typical stated-preference paradigm might reflect participants' a priori theories about the characteristics of a person that might inspire their romantic interest (Nisbett & Wilson, 1977; see Sprecher, 1989, for a similar perspective). Recall one Nisbett and Wilson (1977) example: Some participants watched a film while distracted by a noisy power saw and claimed that the noise negatively affected their impression of the film. In fact, participants who watched the movie without the distraction did not rate the film any more favorably. Although the power saw seemed like a plausible explanation for participants' dislike of the film, it actually had no discernable impact. Similarly, participants' stated mate preferences might overweight (or underweight) factors that seem like plausible (or implausible) reasons for liking one particular romantic partner more than another. If indeed participants' stated preferences derive from such plausibility judgments in lieu of genuine introspection, this could explain why they failed to predict judgments and behavior in this study.

It may initially seem absurd that something as important as one's mate preferences (as opposed to beliefs about distracting power saws) might merely reflect a priori theories constructed from naive plausibility judgments. One possible resolution to this puzzle is that stated mate preferences may be subject to the empathy gap (Loewenstein, 2005) if one's preferences are reported coolly and rationally without fully accounting for the affect that often characterizes romantic processes. According to this theoretical perspective, we might expect that a priori theories will play a role in partner selection in the instances when participants somehow elude the powerful affect often associated with romantic attraction. In the present study, we found suggestive evidence that traditional sex differences in relationship initiation emerged for participants reporting low (compared with high) levels of one indicator of such affect: partner-specific attachment anxiety.

However, the a priori theories and (closely related) empathy-gap accounts are not the only plausible interpretations of the present data. For example, the closed field of eligible partners at the speed-dating event itself might have inspired individuals not to act on their preferences but rather to simply pursue the best of the available options. Individual preferences might exert more of an influence in an open-field situation in which participants are not guaranteed a face-to-face interaction with all the desirable individuals present.* Nor does the a priori theories account suggest that stated mate preferences are not worthy of empirical study. Quite the contrary, the present results highlight new research possibilities that will facilitate a better understanding of (a) when and how romantic-partner ideals impact partner selection and (b) how those ideals come to be sex differentiated in the first place. Below, we explicate some of these possibilities and highlight what the present work does and does not say about the processes underlying romantic-partner selection.

Table 8 Plausible Explanations for the Failure to Confirm Hypotheses 2 and 3

Alternative explanation	Supported?
For missing sex differences (Hypothesis 2)	
• Sex differences might emerge using consensus or objective measures of partner characteristics	Unsupported

* Of course, the write-in targets came from an open field of eligible partners, and we did not find evidence for sex differences among those data (i.e., H2 was unsupported). Nevertheless, we could only directly test H3 using the in vivo preferences calculated at the speed-dating event.

• Sex differences might emerge for participants who are more (compared to less) interested in a serious relationship in general	Unsupported
• Sex differences might emerge for participants who have a restricted (compared to an unrestricted) sociosexual orientation	Unsupported
• Sex differences might emerge for participants reporting high (compared to low) interest in a serious relationship with a specific partner	Unsupported
• Sex differences might emerge for participants reporting low (compared to high) levels of partner-specific attachment anxiety	Modestly supported
For poor correlation of stated and in-vivo preferences (Hypothesis 3)	
• Participants might exhibit diminished interest in partners who exceeded their self-ratings on a particular characteristic (i.e., they anticipated rejection)	Unsupported
• Correlations might be stronger for participants who are more (compared to less) interested in a serious relationship in general	Unsupported
• Correlations might be stronger for participants who have a restricted (compared to an unrestricted) sociosexual orientation	Unsupported
• Correlations might be stronger for participants who are especially high (or especially low) in self-perceived mate value	Unsupported

Alternative Explanations, Limitations, and Future Directions

Comparison with previous literature. Although on the surface it appears anomalous that these data revealed no evidence of sex differences in the importance of physical attractiveness and earning prospects, the results are actually quite consistent with previous findings. As reported in the introduction section, other studies have found that physical attractiveness is a similarly strong determinant of men's and women's desirability in speed-dating (Kur-zban & Weeden, 2005) and regular dating (Feingold, 1990) contexts. Kurzban and Weeden (2005) and Fisman et al. (2006) did not find a significant sex difference in the (weak) effect of income (or hometown income) on speed-daters' desirability; we, too, found weak effects for this variable and no significant sex difference. Iyengar et al. (2005) also reported small correlations between speed-daters' stated preferences and their "yessing" *B*s, very similar to those reported here. In an article that specifically explored sex differences in a speed-dating context, Fisman et al. (2006) reported that men were more likely than women to say "yes" to a speed-dating partner they found to be physically attractive. In fact, our data showed this same sex difference (see Table 2, third row, first vs. second columns), but we would hesitate to conclude that this sex difference alone demonstrates that physical attractiveness is more important to men. It does suggest that men may be more eager than women to obtain the contact information of a physically attractive other, but as illustrated by our range of dependent variables, exchanging contact information is merely one step on the road to relationship initiation. The fact that this particular sex difference reverses at other points in the process (e.g., feeling chemistry, date enjoyment) recommends employing a range of dependent variables as investigators to further unravel how partner characteristics impact the process of selecting a romantic partner. Last, although we found no evidence that participants preferred similarity on these particular characteristics, other researchers have in fact had similar difficulty uncovering similarity effects (especially on physical attractiveness) in live dating contexts (Walster et al., 1966, cf. Berscheid, Dion, Walster, & Walster, 1971).

Moreover, we are not the first to recommend examining whether participants' stated mate preferences predict their interest in real-life romantic partners. The sex difference in the preferred age of one's mate has enjoyed such validation: For example, Buss (1989) reported substantial correlations between national averages of men's and women's preferences for a younger/older mate and national statistics on age difference at marriage (see also Kenrick & Keefe, 1992). At this time, it is unclear why preferences for characteristics such as physical attractiveness or earning prospects in a mate operate differently in live romantic contexts compared with age preferences. Future reports that directly compare the functional role of preferences for romantic partners' characteristics and for romantic partners' age (perhaps at different points in women's ovulatory cycles; e.g., Haselton & Miller, 2006) are sure to reveal fascinating insights.

Sample considerations. The participants in this sample were all undergraduate students at a medium-sized private university in the midwestern United States. In addition, all participants were willing to go speed-dating, an activity that probably does not appeal to everyone (cf. Eastwick & Finkel, in press-b; Finkel et al., 2007). It would be a tremendous stretch from the current data to suggest that physical attractiveness or earning prospects are never associated with sex-differentiated romantic interest in actual dating partners. Our sample may have been especially egalitarian; sex differences might have emerged had our sample been composed of participants with more traditional values or perhaps socialites actively striving to date individuals who closely approximate the cosmopolitan ideal. However, the most important threat to the generalizability of the present sample was successfully dodged: Traditional sex differences did emerge on the ideal partner and speed-date stated preferences. This sample may have been unusual in various ways, but it was not unusual in this key respect. In fact, because these are bright, motivated college students who probably enjoy introspecting about their romantic lives, it is reasonable to suggest that the individual-differences hypothesis (H3) was probably especially *likely* to receive support in this sample. The fact that these students seemed to have little introspective access to their own romantic-partner preferences does not bode well for less psychologically curious individuals. And although it may be true that college students are less likely than adults to have figured out what they want in a romantic partner, this work was intended to address previous studies on sex differences, the better part of which employed college student samples. Nevertheless, firm conclusions await replication across diverse samples.

One aspect of this sample leaves open a strong form of a hypothesis originally advanced by Li, Bailey, Kenrick, and Lin-senmeier (2002): It may be that the characteristics that are considered necessities (as opposed to luxuries) in a mate are especially sex differentiated. For example, if women consider earning prospects to be a necessity in a mate, they may be especially unwilling (compared with men) to consider a potential partner who falls below some acceptable threshold on this trait. Because all of the men in this sample were attending a respectable university, it is possible that all the men exceeded this threshold. Thus, the present data show that men and women do not differ in their earning-prospects preference once this threshold is met but cannot establish whether there are sex differences in the threshold itself. This necessities-versus-luxuries interpretation, however, is unlikely to apply to physical attractiveness, as it would be difficult to argue that all of our participants were above some minimal standard on this dimension.

Mate selection versus mate retention. An emerging body of research has recently demonstrated that romantic-partner ideals are important within established romantic relationships (Fletcher & Simpson, 2000). For example, romantic partners who idealize one another are less likely to break up (Murray, Holmes, & Griffin, 1996), and participants report greater satisfaction with their present relationship to the extent that their partner matches their ideals (Fletcher et al., 1999). Although the present report casts some doubt on the notion that mate preferences serve the function of mate *selection,* this extant research on ideals suggests that mate preferences may instead serve the function of mate *retention.* Although this selection/retention distinction is surely not a strict dichotomy, it allows for the possibility that at moments of deliberative choice during the course of one's relationship (e.g., whether to marry one's partner), an individual might compare his or her partner to a set of ideal preferences and decide whether or not the relationship is worth continuing (Fletcher & Simpson, 2000; Gagne & Lydon, 2004). It is certainly plausible that traditional measures of stated mate preferences (e.g., Hill, 1945) might predict mate retention—this may indeed be how such preferences play a functional role.

Two pieces of evidence will be critical to confirm this mate-retention hypothesis. First, the mate-retention account suggests that sex differences should emerge in how the characteristics *physically attractive* and *earning prospects* are associated with relationship dissolution. We know of no data indicating that (a) men are more likely than women to end a relationship with a partner who is judged unattractive or (b) women are more likely than men to end a relationship with a partner who is judged to have poor earning prospects, but these hypotheses are certainly reasonable and testable. Second, for understandable reasons, studies that have examined the role of partner ideals in established romantic relationships typically assess participants' ideals after they are already in a relationship. Although it would certainly be difficult to assess ideals before participants meet a long-term romantic partner, such a procedure would avoid the problem of participants' ideals becoming "contaminated" by the characteristics of a current partner. In fact, one recent study indeed found that participants changed their ideals such that they placed more importance on the positive characteristics of their current romantic partner, even after dating for only a few months (Fletcher, Simpson, & Thomas, 2000). Research that explores whether partner ideals (a) predict sex differences in relationship dissolution and (b) persist before, during, and after the initiation of a relationship will be critical for the argument that mate preferences serve the function of mate retention.

Accuracy and awareness. We cannot establish definitively that participants are wholly unaware of the qualities that initially appeal to them in a romantic partner. The strongest evidence for such a claim in the present data set comes from the speed-date preferences, which required participants to report what qualities would appeal to them on a 4-min date. Even this focused set of items failed to predict participants' judgments and behavior reliably (see Tables 4, 5, and 6). (These results also suggest that the problem of attitude compatibility, Ajzen, 2005, does not explain why stated mate preferences failed to translate into sex differentiated romantic interest.) On the other hand, our participants were likely aware that characteristics such as physical attractiveness have a positive (as opposed to negative) impact on their liking for someone. A distinction raised by Wilson and Gilbert (2003) in their review of the affective-forecasting literature is perhaps relevant: People are generally good at predicting the *valence* of their emotions but make interesting and systematic errors when predicting the *intensity* of their emotions. Had we assessed unappealing characteristics in this study, our participants' predictions might have been accurate regarding valence (I like reliability and dislike laziness) but inaccurate regarding intensity

(I like reliability more than I like physical attractiveness). To be sure, this conjecture will require additional research.

Conclusions and Future Directions

What role do mate preferences play in the process of early romantic-relationship development? The implicit and consensual answer has until now been simple: Preferences guide behavior by directing men and women to select and pursue whatever potential romantic partner most closely approximates their typically sex-differentiated ideals. Support for this account had been demonstrated in paradigms in which participants were provided with written or visual stimuli (e.g., personal ads, photos), but support was less robust once participants interacted with flesh-and-blood potential romantic partners. In the present study, we took a comprehensive snapshot of participants' romantic lives in an effort to improve understanding of how exactly people go about the process of romantic-partner selection. Our efforts revealed no discernable functional role for mate preferences in determining whom participants desired and pursued for a romantic relationship.

We have suggested that participants' stated mate preferences may reflect their a priori theories about the characteristics of a potential romantic partner that will inspire their interest—in other words, people do not truly know what they desire in a romantic partner. However, there are two related interpretations of the current data that are decidedly less extreme: Participants' stated mate preferences may have validity (e.g., they predict mate retention), but participants either (a) do not compare a potential romantic partner with an ideal until after a relationship has begun or (b) do attempt such a comparison but it is flawed in some respect. We hope that these possibilities will inspire future research and shed new light on the processes underlying romantic-partner selection.

References

Ajzen, I. (2005). *Attitudes, personality, and behavior* (2nd ed.). Milton-Keynes, England: Open University Press.

Ajzen, I., & Fishbein, M. (2005). The influence of attitudes on behavior. In D. Albarrac´ın, B. T. Johnson, and M. P. Zanna (Eds.), *The handbook of attitudes* (pp. 173–221). Mahwah, NJ: Erlbaum.

Ariely, D., & Loewenstein, G. (2005). The heat of the moment: The effect of sexual arousal on sexual decision making. *Journal of Behavioral Decision Making, 18,* 1–12.

Berscheid, E., Dion, K., Walster, E., & Walster, G. W. (1971). Physicalattractiveness and dating choice: A test of the matching hypothesis. *Journal of Experimental Social Psychology, 7,* 173–189.

Buller, D. J. (2005). *Adapting minds: Evolutionary psychology and the persistent quest for human nature.* Cambridge, MA: MIT Press. Buss, D. M. (1989). Sex differences in human mate preferences: Evolutionary hypotheses tested in 37 cultures. *Behavioral and Brain Sciences, 12,*1–49.

Buss, D. M. (1994). *The evolution of desire: Strategies of human mating.* New York: Basic Books.

Buss, D. M., & Kenrick, D. T. (1998). Evolutionary social psychology. In D. T. Gilbert, S. T. Fiske, and G. Lindzey (Eds.), *The handbook of social psychology* (4th ed., Vol. 2). New York: McGraw-Hill.

Buss, D. M., & Schmitt, D. P. (1993). Sexual strategies theory: An evolutionary perspective on human mating. *Psychological Review, 100,* 204–232.

Buunk, B. P., Dijkstra, P., Fetchenhauer, D., & Kenrick, D. T. (2002). Age and gender differences in mate selection criteria for various involvement levels. *Personal Relationships, 9,* 271–278.

Cohen, J. (1992). A power primer. *Psychological Bulletin, 112,* 155–159.

Cohen, J., Cohen, P., West, S., & Aiken, L. (2003). *Applied multiple regression/correlation analysis for the behavioral sciences* (3rd ed.). Hillsdale, NJ: Erlbaum.

Cooper, H., & Hedges, L. V. (Eds.). (1994). *The handbook of research synthesis.* New York: Russell Sage Foundation.

Eagly, A. H., & Wood, W. (1999). The origins of sex differences in human behavior: Evolved dispositions versus social roles. *American Psychologist, 54,* 408–423.

Eastwick, P. W., & Finkel, E. J. (in press-a). The attachment system in fledgling relationships: An activating role for attachment anxiety. *Journal of Personality and Social Psychology.*

Eastwick, P. W., & Finkel, E. J. (in press-b). Speed-dating: A powerful and flexible paradigm for studying romantic relationship initiation. In S. Sprecher, A. Wenzel, and J. Harvey (Eds.), *The handbook of relationship initiation.* New York: Erlbaum.

Elder, G. H. (1969). Appearance and education in marriage mobility. *American Sociological Review, 34,* 519–533.

Fabrigar, L. R., Wegener, D. T., MacCallum, R. C, & Strahan, E. J. (1999). Evaluating the use of exploratory factor analysis in psychological research. *Psychological Methods, 4,* 272–299.

Feingold, A. (1990). Gender differences in effects of physical attractiveness on romantic attraction: A comparison across five research paradigms. *Journal of Personality and Social Psychology, 59,* 981–993.

Feingold, A. (1992). Gender differences in mate selection preferences: A test of the parental investment model. *Psychological Bulletin, 112,* 125–139.

Finkel, E. J., & Eastwick, P. W. (in press). *Current Directions in Psychological Science.*

Finkel, E. J., Eastwick, P. W., & Matthews, J. (2007). Speed-dating as an invaluable tool for studying initial romantic attraction: A methodological primer. *Personal Relationships, 14,* 149–166.

Fisman, R., Iyengar, S. S., Kamenica, E., & Simonson, I. (2006). Gender differences in mate selection: Evidence from a speed-dating experiment. *Quarterly Journal of Economics, 121,* 673–697.

Fletcher, G. J. O., & Simpson, J. A. (2000). Ideal standards in close relationships: Their structure and functions. *Current Directions in Psychological Science, 9,* 102–105.

Fletcher, G. J. O., Simpson, J. A., & Thomas, G. (2000). Ideals, perceptions, and evaluations in early relationship development. *Journal of Personality and Social Psychology, 79,* 933–940.

Fletcher, G. J. O., Simpson, J. A., Thomas, G., & Giles, L. (1999). Ideals in intimate relationships. *Journal of Personality and Social Psychology, 76,* 72–89.

Gagné, F. M., & Lydon, J. E. (2004). Bias and accuracy in close relationships: An integrative review. *Personality and Social Psychology Review, 8,* 322–338.

Gangestad, S. W., & Simpson, J. A. (2000). The evolution of human mating: Trade-offs and strategic pluralism. *Behavioral and Brain Sciences, 23,* 573–644.

Griffin, D. W., Murray, S. L., & Gonzalez, R. (1999). Difference score correlations in relationship research: A conceptual primer. *Personal Relationships, 6,* 505–518.

Haddock, C. K., Rindskopf, D., & Shadish, W. R. (1998). Using odds ratios as effect sizes for meta-analysis of dichotomous data: A primer on methods and issues. *Psychological Methods, 3,* 339–353.

Harrison, A. A., & Saeed, L. (1977). Let's make a deal: An analysis of revelations and stipulations in lonely hearts advertisements. *Journal of Personality and Social Psychology, 35,* 257–264.

Haselton, M. G., & Miller, G. F. (2006). Women's fertility across the cycle increases the short-term attractiveness of creative intelligence compared to wealth. *Human Nature, 17,* 50–73.

Hill, R. (1945). Campus values in mate-selection. *Journal of Home Economics, 37,* 554–558.

Hitsch, G. J., Hortacsu, A., & Ariely, D. (2006). *What makes you click? Mate preferences and matching outcomes in online dating.* Unpublished manuscript, University of Chicago Graduate School of Business.

Humphreys, L. G., & Montanelli, R. G. (1975). An investigation of the parallel analysis criterion for determining the number of common factors. *Multivariate Behavioral Research, 10,* 193–205.

Iyengar, S. S., Simonson, I., Fisman, R., & Mogilner, C. (2005, January). *I know what I want but can I find it? Examining the dynamic relationship between stated and revealed preferences.* Paper presented at the Society for Personality and Social Psychology Annual Meeting, New Orleans, LA.

Kenny, D. A., Kashy, D. A., & Bolger, N. (1998). Data analysis in social psychology. In D. T. Gilbert, S. T. Fiske, and G. Lindzey (Eds.), *The handbook of social psychology* (4th ed., Vol. 1). New York: McGraw-Hill.

Kenrick, D. T., Groth, G. E., Trost, M. R., & Sadalla, E. K. (1993). Integrating evolutionary and social exchange perspectives on relationships: Effects of gender, self-appraisal, and involvement level on mate selection criteria. *Journal of Personality and Social Psychology, 64,* 951–969.

Kenrick, D. T., & Keefe, R. C. (1992). Age preferences in mates reflect sex differences in human reproductive strategies. *Behavioral and Brain Sciences, 15,* 75–133.

Konstantopoulos, S., & Hedges, L. V. (2004). Meta-analysis. In D. Kaplan (Ed.), *Handbook of quantitative methodology for the social sciences* (pp. 281–297). New York: Sage.

Kurzban, R., & Weeden, J. (2005). Hurrydate: Mate preferences in action. *Evolution and Human Behavior, 26,* 227–244.

Langlois, J. H., Kalakanis, L., Rubenstein, A. J., Larson, A., Hallam, M., & Smoot, M. (2000). Maxims or myths of beauty? A meta-analytic and theoretical review. *Psychological Bulletin, 126,* 390–423.

Li, N. P., Bailey, J. M., Kenrick, D. T., & Linsenmeier, J. A. W. (2002). The necessities and luxuries of mate preferences: Testing the tradeoffs. *Journal of Personality and Social Psychology, 82,* 947–955.

Li, N. P., & Kenrick, D. T. (2006). Sex similarities and differences in preferences for short-term mates: What, whether, and why. *Journal of Personality and Social Psychology, 90,* 468–489.

Loewenstein, G. (1996). Out of control: Visceral influences on behavior. *Organizational Behavior and Human Decision Processes, 65,* 272–292.

Loewenstein, G. (2005). Hot-cold empathy gaps and medical decision making. *Health Psychology, 24,* S49-S56.

Murray, S. L., Holmes, J. G., & Griffin, D. W. (1996). The self-fulfilling nature of positive illusions in romantic relationships: Love is not blind, but prescient. *Journal of Personality and Social Psychology, 71,* 1155– 1180.

Myers, J. L., & Well, A. (1995). *Research design and statistical analysis.* Hillsdale, NJ: Erlbaum.

Nisbett, R. E., & Bellows, N. (1977). Verbal reports about causal influences on social judgments: Private access versus public theories. *Journal of Personality and Social Psychology, 35,* 613–624.

Nisbett, R. E., & Wilson, T. D. (1977). Telling more than we can know: Verbal reports on mental processes. *Psychological Review, 84,* 231–259.

Olivola, C. Y., Todorov, A., Eastwick, P. W., Finkel, E. J., Hortacsu, A., & Ariely, D. (2007). *A picture is worth a thousand inferences: First impression and mate selection in Internet matchmaking and speed-dating.* Unpublished manuscript, Princeton University.

Raudenbush, S. W., & Bryk, A. S. (2002). *Hierarchical linear models: Applications and data analysis methods* (2nd ed.). Thousand Oaks, CA: Sage.

Regan, P. C, Levin, L., Sprecher, S., Christopher, F. S., & Cate, R. (2000). Partner preferences: What characteristics do men and women desire in their short-term sexual and long-term romantic partners? *Journal of Psychology & Human Sexuality, 12,* 1–21.

Rosenthal, R. (1994). Parametric measures of effect size. In H. Cooper and L. V. Hedges (Eds.), *The handbook of research synthesis* (pp. 231–244). New York: Sage.

Simpson, J. A., & Gangestad, S. W. (1991). Individual differences in sociosexuality: Evidence for convergent and discriminant validity. *Journal of Personality and Social Psychology, 60,* 870–883.

Smith, E. R., & Miller, F. D. (1978). Limits on perception of cognitive processes: A reply to Nisbett and Wilson. *Psychological Review, 85,* 355–362.

Speed, A., & Gangestad, S. W. (1997). Romantic popularity and mate preferences: A peer-nomination study. *Personality and Social Psychology Bulletin, 23,* 928–936.

Sprecher, S. (1989). The importance to males and females of physical attractiveness, earning potential, and expressiveness in initial attraction. *Sex Roles, 21,* 591–607.

Sprecher, S., Sullivan, Q., & Hatfield, E. (1994). Mate selection preferences: Gender differences examined in a national sample. *Journal of Personality and Social Psychology, 66,* 1074–1080.

Stevens, G., Owens, D., & Schaefer, E. C. (1990). Education and attractiveness in marriage choices. *Social Psychology Quarterly, 53,* 62–70.

Stroebe, W., Insko, C. A., Thompson, V. D., & Layton, B. D. (1971). Effects of physical attractiveness, attitude similarity, and sex on various aspects of interpersonal attraction. *Journal of Personality and Social Psychology, 18,* 79–91.

Symons, D. (1979). *The evolution of human sexuality.* New York: Oxford University Press.

Townsend, J. M. (1989). Mate selection criteria: A pilot study. *Ethology and Sociobiology, 10,* 241–253.

Townsend, J. M., & Wasserman, T. (1998). Sexual attractiveness: Sex differences in assessment and criteria. *Evolution and Human Behavior, 19,* 171–191.

Trivers, R. L. (1972). Parental investment and sexual selection. In B. G Campbell (Ed.), *Sexual selection and the descent of man, 1871–1971* (pp. 136–179). Chicago: Aldine.

Tukey, J. W. (1977). *Exploratory data analysis.* Reading, MA: Addison Wesley.

Udry, J. R., & Eckland, B. K. (1984). Benefits of being attractive: Differential payoffs for men and women. *Psychological Reports, 54,* 47–56.

United States Census Bureau. (2000). Census 2000 summary file 3. Retrieved Febrauary 13, 2006, from http://factfinder.census.gov

Walster, E., Aronson, V., Abrahams, D., & Rottmann, L. (1966). Importance of physical attractiveness in dating behavior. *Journal of Personality and Social Psychology, 4,* 508–516.

Wiederman, M. W., & Allgeier, E. R. (1992). Gender differences in mate selection criteria: Sociobiological or socioeconomic explanation? *Ethology and Sociobiology, 13,* 115–124.

Wilson, T. D., & Gilbert, D. T. (2003). Affective forecasting. In M. P. Zanna (Ed.), *Advances in experimental social psychology* (Vol. 35, pp. 345–411). San Diego, CA: Academic Press.

Wilson, T. D., Laser, P. S., & Stone, J. I. (1982). Judging the predictors of one's own mood: Accuracy and the use of shared theories. *Journal of Experimental Social Psychology, 18,* 537–556.

Wright, P., & Rip, P. D. (1981). Retrospective reports on the causes of decisions. *Journal of Personality and Social Psychology, 40,* 601–614.

Paul W. Eastwick and Eli J. Finkel, Department of Psychology, Northwestern University.

This research was facilitated by National Science Foundation Grant 0719780 to Eli J. Finkel and by grants from the University Research Grants Committee at Northwestern University and the Dispute Resolution Research Center at the Kellogg School of Management to Paul W. Eastwick and Eli J. Finkel, as well as a grant from the National Science Foundation Graduate Research Fellowship Program to Paul W. Eastwick.

We thank Jacob Matthews and Mike Machenry for their programming genius, and we gratefully acknowledge Alice Eagly, Mike Bailey, Spyros Konstantopoulos, Joan Linsenmeier, and William Revelle for their insightful comments on this article. We also thank the following individuals for their assistance with the speed-dating study: Layla Bermeo, Debra Blade, Christine Brooks, Bonnie Buik, Madelaine Eulich, Megan Graney, Jeff Jablons, Kristin Jones, Julie Keller, Jennifer Leyton, Kaidi Liu, Mallory Martino,

Ashley Mason, Jesse Matthews, Abby Mtchell, Jennifer Rosner, Seema Saigal, Sarah Scarbeck, David Sternberg, Laura Thompson, Ashley Treadway, Stephanie Yang, and the Northwestern Class Alliance.

The Close Relationships of Lesbians and Gay Men

By Letitia Anne Peplau and Adam W. Fingerhut
University of California, Los Angeles

Key Words: division of household labor, gay-related stressor, power, second-parent adoption, sexual orientation, homosexuality, social stigma, social support, stress-related psychological disorders

Abstract

This article reviews empirical studies of same-sex couples in the United States, highlighting consistent findings, drawing comparisons to heterosexual couples, and noting gaps in available research. U.S. Census data indicate that there were more than 600,000 same-sex couples living together in 2000. Research about relationship formation, the division of household labor, power, satisfaction, sexuality, conflict, commitment, and relationship stability is presented. Next, we highlight three recent research topics: the legalization of same-sex relationships through civil unions and same-sex marriage, the experiences of same-sex couples raising children, and the impact of societal prejudice and discrimination on same-sex partners. We conclude with comments about the contributions of empirical research to debunking negative stereotypes of same-sex couples, testing the generalizability of theories about close relationships, informing our understanding of gender and close relationships, and providing a scientific basis for public policy.

INTRODUCTION

In the past half century, the close relationships of lesbians and gay men have moved from the shadows of society as a "love that dares not speak its name" to center stage in a national and international debate about same-sex marriage. The increasing visibility of same-sex couples has challenged researchers to provide scientific information that can illuminate the relationship experiences of lesbians and gay men. Research findings can also inform legal and policy questions that have been raised by ongoing efforts to achieve equal rights for same-sex couples.

This review focuses on the experiences of same-sex couples in the United States. We begin with up-to-date estimates about the number of same-sex couples. Next, we review the research literature on same-sex couples and identify major empirical findings. When possible, we compare the experiences of same-sex couples to those of heterosexual couples in order to indicate areas of commonality and of difference. It is noteworthy that research on same-sex couples began slowly in the 1970s, grew in the 1980s, and then diminished as researchers shifted their attention to the impact of the AIDS epidemic on the gay community. Much of the research we review was conducted 10 or 20 years ago.

In the past few years, however, research on same-sex couples has been revitalized and has shifted to a new set of topics. We highlight three recent research directions: the legalization of same-sex relationships through civil unions and same-sex marriage, the experiences of same-sex couples raising children, and the impact of societal prejudice and discrimination on same-sex partners. We conclude with general comments about the role of empirical research in four areas: debunking negative stereotypes about same-sex couples, testing the generalizability of theories about close relationships, informing our understanding of gender and close relationships, and providing a scientific basis for public policy.

COUNTING SAME-SEX COUPLES

Although same-sex couples have a clear and growing presence in American society, several factors make it difficult to provide an accurate estimate of the number of lesbians and gay men who are currently in a same-sex relationship. First, some lesbians and gay men are reluctant to reveal their sexual identity or the nature of their romantic attachments. Second, lacking the equivalent of legal heterosexual marriage and divorce, we have no public records of how many lesbians and gay men are currently in a serious relationship or have experienced the loss of a serious relationship through breakup or the death of a partner. Third, researchers have used differing and noncomparable questions to assess the relationship status of lesbians and gay men, asking, for instance, if an individual is in a romantic/sexual relationship, has a steady partner, has been together with a partner for six months or more, or currently lives with a romantic partner.

Nonetheless, available evidence suggests that many gay men and lesbians are in couple relationships. Recently, the U.S. Census and other national surveys added the category "unmarried partner" to their household roster, making it possible to estimate the number of gay and lesbian adults who live together with a same-sex partner. According to the 2000 Census, there were approximately 600,000 same-sex couples living together in the United States, with roughly equal numbers of men and women (Gates & Ost 2004). Approximately 16% of same-sex couples included at least one Hispanic partner, and 14% included at least one black partner. One estimate is that about 28% of gay men and 44% of lesbians are currently living with a same-sex partner (Black et al. 2000). Although same-sex couples are more common in urban areas, they are located in all parts of the United States.

BASIC FINDINGS ABOUT SAME-SEX COUPLES

In the sections that follow, we review major findings from research on same-sex couples and offer suggestions about areas in need of further investigation. Prior to turning to these findings, it is useful to comment briefly on the sources of data that have been used in research on same-sex couples. Most studies have been conducted in the United States with individuals who self-identify as gay or lesbian, for instance by volunteering to participate in a study about gay and lesbian couples. Like many studies of heterosexual couples, studies of same-sex couples have typically recruited younger, well-educated, middle-class, white volunteers. Many studies have relied on questionnaires and have obtained reports from only one partner in a couple.

In addition to many small-scale studies, there have been a few major research programs focusing on same-sex couples. For example, in a project known as the American Couples Study, Blumstein & Schwartz (1983) obtained responses to lengthy questionnaires from both partners in 957 gay male, 772 lesbian, 653 heterosexual cohabiting, and 3656 heterosexual married couples. A subset of participants also completed an 18-month follow-up questionnaire. More recently, Kurdek conducted two longitudinal studies involving repeated assessments of both partners in same-sex couples and married heterosexual couples (see reviews in Kurdek 1994a, 2004a). Our review encompasses both small-scale studies and larger programs of research.

Relationship Formation

Several studies have compared the qualities that lesbians, gay men, and heterosexuals seek in romantic partners (see review by Peplau & Spalding 2000). Regardless of sexual orientation, most individuals value affection, dependability, shared interests, and similarity of religious beliefs. Men, regardless of sexual orientation, are more likely to emphasize a partner's physical attractiveness; women, regardless of sexual orientation, give greater emphasis to personality characteristics. Like their heterosexual counterparts, lesbians and gay men report that they often meet potential dates through friends, at work, at a bar, or at a social event (e.g., Bryant & Demian 1994). Urban areas with visible gay and lesbian communities provide expanded opportunities to meet potential partners. In addition, the Internet has rapidly become a way for gay men and lesbians to meet each other. There is some evidence that lesbians and gay men, like their heterosexual counterparts, rely on fairly conventional scripts when they go on dates with a new partner (Klinkenberg & Rose 1994).

For lesbians and gay men, the boundaries between friendship and romantic or sexual relationships may be particularly complex (e.g., Diamond & Dube 2002, Nardi 1999). Rose et al. (1993), for example, found that many lesbian romantic relationships began as a friendship, then developed into a love relationship, and later became sexual. Some women reported difficulties with this pattern of relationship development, such as problems in knowing if a relationship was shifting from friendship to romance and in gauging the friend's possible sexual interest. In addition, lesbians and gay men may be especially likely to remain friends with former sexual partners (Solomon et al. 2004, Weinstock 2004). In a recent study (Harkless & Fowers 2005), lesbians and gay men were more likely than were heterosexuals to agree, "When a relationship is ending, one of my biggest fears is that I will lose the friendship" or that it is important "to remain friends with someone with whom I've had a serious relationship." Lesbians and gay men were also more likely than were heterosexuals to report continued phone calls and social contacts with ex-partners. The factors that encourage same-sex ex-partners to remain friends are not well understood but may include the small size of some gay and lesbian social networks, the norms of particular gay and lesbian communities, and the benefits that can accrue from transforming ties with ex-lovers into friendship (Nardi 1999, Weinstock 2004).

The Division of Household Labor and Power

Traditional heterosexual marriage is organized around two basic principles: a division of labor based on gender and a norm of greater male power and decision-making authority. Researchers have investigated how same-sex couples, who lack biological sex as a basis for assigning tasks and status, organize their lives together (see review by Peplau & Spalding 2000).

Turning first to the division of labor, it is important to emphasize that most gay men and lesbians are in dual-earner relationships, so neither partner is the exclusive breadwinner and each partner has some measure of economic independence. When it comes to housework, same-sex couples are likely to divide chores fairly equitably. For example, Kurdek (1993) compared the division of housework (e.g., cleaning, cooking, and shopping) in cohabiting same-sex couples and married heterosexual couples, none of whom had children. In heterosexual couples, wives typically did most of the housework. In contrast, lesbian and gay couples divided the household tasks more equally (see also Kurdek 2006). Lesbian partners tended to share tasks; gay male partners were more likely to have each partner specialize in certain tasks. In a review of research on this topic, Kurdek (2005, p. 252) concluded that "although members of gay and lesbian couples do not divide household labor in a perfectly equal manner, they are more likely than members of heterosexual couples to negotiate a balance between achieving a fair distribution of household labor and accommodating the different interests, skills, and work schedules of particular partners."

Questionnaire studies may not capture the nuanced complexities of domestic work for cohabiting couples. An in-depth study of dual-earner heterosexual families (Hochschild & Machung 1989) showed that although most wives did the bulk of housework, many couples found ways to characterize their allocation of housework as balanced. Similarly, based on in-depth interviews and home observations, Carrington (1999) suggested that same-sex couples' reports of equal sharing of household activities may reflect their ideals but often mask substantial observable differences between partners' actual contributions. He found that equal sharing of domestic activities was far from universal: It was most common among affluent couples who relied on paid help, and when both partners had less demanding jobs with more flexible schedules.

When researchers assess power in close relationships, they typically try to characterize the overall pattern of dominance to determine whether one partner is more influential than the other is. The lesbians and gay men who participate in psychological research tend to be advocates of power equality in their relationships. In an early study, 92% of gay men and 97% of lesbians defined the ideal balance of power as one in which both partners were "exactly equal" (Peplau & Cochran 1980). In a more recent study, partners in gay and lesbian couples rated power equality as important in an ideal relationship, although lesbians scored significantly higher on the value of equality than did gay men (Kurdek 1995a). This strong endorsement of power sharing may reflect, in some measure, the tendency for researchers to recruit participants who are well educated and generally liberal in their attitudes.

Not all couples who strive for power equality achieve this ideal. Reports of the actual balance of power vary from study to study. For example, when Peplau & Cochran (1980) asked lesbians and gay men "who has more say" in your relationship, only 38% of gay men and 59% of lesbians characterized their current relationship as "exactly equal." Equal power was reported by 59% of the lesbians studied by Reilly & Lynch (1990) and by 60% of the gay men studied by Harry & DeVall (1978).

Social exchange theory predicts that greater power accrues to the partner who has relatively greater personal resources, such as education, money, or social standing. Studies of gay men have supported this hypothesis. For example, Harry found that gay men who were older and wealthier than their partner was tended to have more power (Harry 1984, Harry & DeVall 1978). Blumstein & Schwartz (1983, p. 59) concluded that "in gay male couples, income is an extremely important force in determining which partner will be dominant." For lesbians, research results are less clear-cut, with some studies finding that income is significantly related to power (Caldwell & Peplau 1984, Reilly & Lynch 1990) and others not (Blumstein & Schwartz 1983). Dunne (1997, p. 180) concluded that "lesbian women are comfortable neither with dominating nor with being dominated in their partnerships." Further research on the balance of power is needed to clarify these inconsistent results and to broaden our knowledge about correlates of power imbalances.

Love and Satisfaction

Stereotypes depict gay and lesbian relationships as unhappy and dysfunctional, especially in comparison with heterosexual relationships (e.g., Crawford & Solliday 1996, Testa et al. 1987). In fact, empirical research finds striking similarities in the reports of love and satisfaction among contemporary lesbian, gay, and heterosexual couples. Peplau & Cochran (1980) found no significant differences in scores on standardized Love and Liking scales among matched samples of lesbians, gay men, and heterosexuals who were all currently in a romantic/sexual relationship. In a longitudinal study of married heterosexual and cohabiting homosexual couples, Kurdek (1998) found similar results. Controlling for age, education, income, and years cohabiting, the couples did not differ in relationship satisfaction at initial testing. Over the five years of this study, all types of couples tended to decrease in relationship satisfaction, but no differences were found among gay, lesbian, or heterosexual couples in the rate of change in satisfaction. A survey of African American lesbians and gay men in committed relationships (Peplau et al. 1997) also found high levels of relationship satisfaction and closeness. Further, the partner's race was unrelated to relationship satisfaction: Interracial couples were no more or less satisfied, on average, than same-race couples.

Researchers have begun to identify factors that enhance or detract from satisfaction in same-sex relationships. Like their heterosexual counterparts, gay and lesbian couples generally benefit when partners are similar in background, attitudes, and values (Kurdek & Schmitt 1987). Additionally, consistent with social exchange theory, happiness tends to be high when partners perceive many rewards and few costs from their relationship (e.g., Beals et al. 2002, Duffy & Rusbult 1986). A study of lesbian relationships found support for another exchange theory prediction, that satisfaction is higher when partners are equally involved in or committed to a relationship (Peplau et al. 1982). For lesbian couples, greater satisfaction has also been linked to perceptions of greater equity or fairness in the relationship (Schreurs & Buunk 1996). Finally, several studies of lesbians and gay men have found that satisfaction is higher when partners believe they are relatively equal in power and decision-making (reviewed by Peplau & Spalding 2000).

Sexuality

Sexuality has been a popular topic of investigation in studies of gay and lesbian couples. A comprehensive review of this literature is provided by Peplau et al. (2004). Research on the frequency of sex in relationships has identified several consistent patterns. Among same-sex and heterosexual couples, there is wide variability in sexual frequency and a general decline in frequency as relationships continue over time. In the early stages of a relationship, gay male couples have sex more often than do other couples. Further, research consistently finds that lesbian couples report having sex less often than either heterosexual or gay male couples.

Considerable attention has been given to the low frequency of sex reported by lesbians, in part because this pattern may reflect broader issues about female sexuality (Fassinger& Morrow1995,Peplau&Garnets 2000). One suggestion is that gender socialization leads women to repress and ignore sexual feelings, and this effect is magnified in a relationship with two female partners. Another view is that women have difficulty taking the lead to initiate sexual activities with a partner, resulting in low levels of sexual activity. A third possibility is that men are generally more interested in sex than are women, leading to higher levels of sexual activity in couples that include a male partner. A fourth possibility is that traditional conceptions of sexuality, which equate "sex" with penile penetration, may not adequately capture lesbian women's sexual experiences. Finally, there may be methodological problems with the ways researchers have asked questions about women's sexuality (Rothblum 2000).

In addition to studying sexual frequency, researchers have also investigated sexual satisfaction in gay and lesbian couples. High levels of sexual satisfaction have been reported in studies of students and young adults (e.g., Peplau & Cochran 1981, Peplau et al. 1978), predominantly white adult samples (e.g., Blumstein & Schwartz 1983, Kurdek 1991, McWhirter & Mattison 1984), and samples of African American lesbians and gay men (e.g., Peplau et al. 1997). Not surprisingly, sexual satisfaction and sexual frequency are linked. In the American Couples sample, for example, the correlation between sexual frequency and sexual satisfaction was $r = 0.50$ for gay men and $r = 0.48$ for lesbians (controlling for age and duration of relationship). Sexual satisfaction is also associated with global measures of relationship satisfaction in gay and lesbian as well as heterosexual couples (e.g., Bryant & Demian 1994, Eldridge & Gilbert 1990, Peplau et al. 1997).

Research has documented differences between gay, lesbian, and heterosexual couples concerning the issue of sexual exclusiveness versus openness. First, there are differences in attitudes about monogamy(Baileyetal. 1994). In the American Couples Study, only 36% of gay men indicated that it was important to be sexually monogamous, compared with71% of lesbians, 84% of heterosexual wives, and 75% of husbands. Second, there are major differences in reports of actual behavior (Bryant & Demian 1994, McWhirter & Mattison 1984). In the American Couples Study, only a minority of lesbians (28%), wives (21%), and husbands (26%) reported having engaged in extradyadic sex, compared with 82% of gay men. Third, among those individuals who had engaged in extradyadic sex, gay men reported having a greater number of sex partners. Finally, Kurdek (1991) found that sexual fidelity was positively related to relationship satisfaction for lesbian and heterosexual couples, but not for gay male couples. This may reflect the norms of the gay male community and the fact that some male couples have agreements that extradyadic sex is acceptable (Hickson et al. 1992).

We know little about possible changes in sexual attitudes and behavior that may have occurred among lesbians and gay men in recent years, both in response to the AIDS epidemic and the greater attention being given to same-sex marriage. Rutter & Schwartz (1996) suggested that from the 1970s to the 1990s gay men's attitudes shifted toward greater endorsement of monogamy but their actual sexual behavior did not undergo a corresponding change.

Conflict and Partner Violence

Few couples avoid occasional disagreements and conflicts. Lesbian, gay male, and heterosexual couples report a similar frequency of arguments and tend to disagree about similar topics, with finances, affection, sex, criticism, and household tasks heading the list (Kurdek 1994a, 2005, 2006; Metz et al. 1994). How well do lesbians and gay men solve problems that arise in their relationships? Available research indicates that their problem-solving skills are at least as good as are those of heterosexual couples. In a study of homosexual and heterosexual couples, Kurdek (1998) found no differences in the frequency of using positive problem-solving styles such as negotiating or compromising. Nor were differences found in the use of poor strategies, such as launching personal attacks or refusing to talk to the partner. A study that observed couples discussing relationship conflicts in a laboratory setting found that gay and lesbian partners used somewhat more positive communication styles than did heterosexual couples (Gottman et al. 2003). Finally, as with heterosexual couples, happy lesbian and gay male couples are more likely than are unhappy couples to use constructive problem-solving approaches (Kurdek 2004, Metz et al. 1994).

Recently, researchers have begun to document the existence and nature of violence in same-sex relationships (see review by Potoczniak et al. 2003). It is impossible to estimate accurately the frequency of same-sex domestic violence, not only because of underreporting to the police but also because research studies have been based on small, unrepresentative samples. Interviews with abused gay and lesbian individuals (e.g., Potoczniak et al. 2003, Renzetti & Miley 1996) have documented a cycle of escalating abuse in some same-sex couples. This pattern, in which one partner uses violence and threats of violence to intimidate and control the other, bears many similarities to violence in heterosexual couples that Johnson (2006) has characterized as "intimate terrorism." We know less about other types of violence in same-sex relationships, including violent resistance to abuse by a partner and situational violence that occurs when a verbal conflict turns physical. We also lack information about the correlates of domestic violence among same-sex couples. In male-female couples, traditional attitudes about gender roles, differences in physical size and strength, and differences in financial resources can all contribute to patterns of abuse. How do these factors affect same-sex couples? In addition, are there other factors unique to lesbians and gay men that contribute to violence, including experiences of discrimination or the stress of belonging to a sexual minority group (Balsam & Szymanski 2005)?

Commitment and Relationship Stability

Three general factors contribute to partners' psychological commitment to each other and to the longevity of their relationship; all three appear to be relevant to same-sex couples (see reviews by Kurdek 2000, Peplau & Spalding 2000). Of obvious importance are positive attraction forces, such as love and satisfaction, that make partners want to stay together. A second factor is the availability of alternatives to the current relationship, most often a more desirable partner. Partners who perceive few alternatives are less likely to leave a relationship. Finally, barriers that make it difficult for a person to leave a relationship also matter (Kurdek 1998, 2000). Barriers include investments that increase the psychological, emotional, or financial costs of ending a relationship, as well as moral or religious feelings of obligation or duty to one's partner. A model including all three predictors of commitment was tested by Beals et al. (2002) using data on lesbian couples from the American Couples Study. Their analyses found that relationship satisfaction, the quality of alternatives, and investments each predicted psychological commitment, which in turn predicted relationship stability.

There is evidence that married heterosexual couples perceive more barriers than do gay, lesbian, or cohabiting heterosexual couples (e.g., Kurdek 1998, Kurdek & Schmitt 1986). A relative lack of barriers may make it less likely that lesbians and gay men will be trapped in miserable and deteriorating relationships. On the other hand, weaker barriers may also allow partners to end relationships that might have improved if given more time and effort. In a longitudinal study, Kurdek (1998) found that barriers to leaving the relationship were a significant predictor of relationship stability over a five-year period. Today, as lesbians and gay men gain greater legal recognition for their relationships, the barriers to ending same-sex relationships may become more similar to those of heterosexuals. The impact of such trends on the stability of same-sex relationships is an important topic for future investigations.

Given the weaker barriers to ending same-sex relationships, we might anticipate that there would be fewer long-term relationships among lesbians and gay men compared with heterosexuals. Unfortunately, we currently know little about the longevity of same-sex relationships. No information comparable to divorce statistics for heterosexual marriages is available. Several studies have documented the existence of very-long-lasting gay and lesbian relationships (e.g., Johnson 1990, McWhirter & Mattison 1984). Longitudinal studies provide further clues about relationship stability. In a five-year prospective study, Kurdek (1998) reported a breakup rate of 7% for married heterosexual couples, 14% for cohabiting gay male couples, and 16% for cohabiting lesbian couples. Controlling for demographic variables, cohabiting gay and lesbian couples were significantly more likely than were married heterosexuals to break up (see also Kurdek 2004).

In this section, we reviewed empirical research describing basic features of same-sex relationships and comparing them with heterosexual relationships. In the next section, we consider three new directions in research on same-sex couples.

RECENT RESEARCH DIRECTIONS

The twenty-first century has seen renewed interest in research on same-sex couples, spurred by the increasing visibility of lesbians and gay men and by public policy debates about same-sex marriage and gay adoption. A shift has also occurred from viewing same-sex couples through the lens of abnormality and dysfunction toward viewing lesbians and gay men as members of a sexual minority group dealing with social stigma and discrimination.

Legalizing Same-Sex Relationships: Marriage, Civil Unions, and Domestic Partnerships

For heterosexual couples, marriage represents both a public sign of commitment and a legal status affecting many aspects of life. The General Accounting Office (2004) has estimated that marriage affects 1138 federal rights, including taxes, Social Security, and veterans' benefits. Not surprisingly, lesbians and gay men have actively sought to make legal recognition of their relationships a reality. In a national survey (Kaiser Family Foundation 2001), 74% of lesbians and gay men said that if they could legally marry someone of the same sex, they would like to do so someday. In recent decades, advances have been made in achieving formal recognition for same-sex relationships. Within gay and lesbian communities, same-sex couples are holding commitment ceremonies to celebrate their relationships, and some religious groups now perform same-sex wedding ceremonies. Additionally, increasing numbers of employers provide domestic partner benefits to same-sex partners. Despite this progress, the substantial social and legal benefits and protections accorded to legally married couples by state and federal laws are still beyond the reach of most same-sex partners in the United States.

Efforts to legalize same-sex relationships have met with considerable opposition. Reflecting public sentiment, President Clinton signed the Defense of Marriage Act in 1996, clarifying that for the federal government, marriage is defined as "a legal union of one man and one woman as husband and wife" and that spouse should be defined only as "a person of the opposite sex who is a husband or a wife." A majority of state governments have also taken steps to restrict marriage to heterosexual couples (Human Rights Campaign 2006). Recent national poll data indicate that a 53% majority of Americans oppose allowing gay men and lesbians to marry legally, with only 36% in favor of same-sex marriage and 11% uncertain (The Pew Forum on Religion and Public Life 2005). For many Americans, opposition to same-sex marriage is strongly correlated with the belief that homo-sexuality is immoral (Lewis 2006). Despite opposition to same-sex marriage, an increasing percentage of Americans endorses extending legal rights and protections to lesbians and gay men. In national surveys (e.g., Kaiser Family Foundation 2001), more than two-thirds of Americans support providing inheritance rights, health insurance, and social security benefits to same-sex domestic partners. For the first time in 2005, a 53% majority of those polled favored permitting lesbians and gay men to enter into civil unions that would give them many of the same rights as married couples (The Pew Forum on Religion and Public Life 2005). Public attitudes and governmental policies differ from state to state. Currently, only Massachusetts offers legal marriage to same-sex couples, and six other states recognize some form of same-sex civil union.

In addition to information about heterosexuals' attitudes toward same-sex marriage, researchers have also gathered information about the attitudes of gay men and lesbians. Lannutti (2005) used an open-ended Web-based survey to examine the attitudes of 288 lesbians and gay men toward same-sex marriage. Her findings revealed complex and nuanced views. Virtually all participants emphasized fairness and equal rights: Legal marriage would be a sign that lesbians and gay men had achieved first-class citizenship. Many positive aspects of same-sex marriage were noted. Marriage would help couples feel closer and strengthen their relationships, in part by creating structural barriers to relationship dissolution. Respondents also suggested that marriage would reduce the stress that same-sex couples experience, by increasing legal rights and benefits, reducing societal prejudice, and diminishing internalized homophobia among lesbians and gay men. At the same time, respondents expressed concerns that the availability of legal unions might put pressure on individuals to get married "for the wrong reasons" or might create status hierarchies within the gay/lesbian community that could stigmatize those who choose not to marry. Another concern was that legalizing same-sex marriage might lead to assimilation into mainstream heterosexual norms and values that would change and harm unique features of the gay/lesbian community.

Currently, we have very little information about American couples who seek civil unions or same-sex marriage. Solomon, Rothblum and colleagues (e.g., Solomon et al. 2004, 2005; Todosijevic et al. 2005) studied the first cohort of couples to obtain civil unions in Vermont. For comparison purposes, the researchers asked gay and lesbian respondents to nominate a married heterosexual sibling and the sibling's spouse as well as a gay or lesbian couple from their friendship circle who were not in a civil union. Results from this research replicated many findings from previous studies concerning sexuality, conflict, and the division of housework and childcare among same-sex couples. Few differences were found among same-sex couples based on their civil union status.

As time goes by, researchers will be able to investigate the impact of civil unions and same-sex marriage on gay and lesbian couples more thoroughly. An important goal will be to identify factors that distinguish same-sex couples who seek legal recognition from those who do not, including their motives and the extent to which couples emphasize the symbolic and psychological meaning of legal recognition or the financial and legal benefits that recognition may confer. A further question concerns the impact of legal recognition itself on the nature and longevity of same-sex relationships. Will legalization increase the stability of same-sex relationships? Data from Norway and Sweden, where registered same-sex partnerships have been available since the 1990s, indicate that the rate of dissolution within five years of entering a legal union is higher among same-sex partnerships than among heterosexual marriages, with lesbian couples having the highest rates of dissolution (Andersson et al. 2006). Unfortunately, the Scandinavian data do not permit comparisons with the longevity of same-sex couples who did not seek legal recognition. Many other questions remain unanswered (Patterson 2004a). For example, do the social and economic benefits of legal recognition affect relationship functioning and satisfaction? Does legal recognition change the way in which couples or their family and friends think about their relationship? Does legalization lead to better physical and mental health for gay and lesbian people (Herdt & Kertzner 2006, Herek 2006, King & Bartlett 2006)? Finally, does the form of legal recognition marriage, civil union, domestic partnership— make a difference?

Same-Sex Couples with Children

Based on data from the 2000 U.S. Census (Gates & Ost 2004), it has been estimated that among adults aged 22–55, 34% of lesbian couples who live together and 22% of gay male couples who live together are raising children. Consequently, approximately 250,000 children under the age of 18 are being raised by same-sex couples. Although the experiences of these children are beyond the scope of our review, it is important to note that research has documented that they are comparable to children of heterosexual parents on measures of psychological well-being, self-esteem, cognitive abilities, and peer relations (see reviews by Fulcher et al. 2006, Patterson 2003, Tasker 2005).

Gay- and lesbian-headed families are created in a variety of ways (Patterson 1995a). Some lesbians and gay men, perhaps the majority at present, had children in a previous heterosexual relationship. Growing numbers of lesbians and gay men are choosing to have children within the context of a same-sex relationship. In a national poll, 49% of gay men and lesbians who were not parents said they would like to have or adopt children of their own (Kaiser Family Foundation 2001). Given the obstacles to parenthood faced by self-identified gay men and lesbians, there is a high likelihood that their children are strongly desired and planned.

Several paths to parenthood are available to same-sex couples, each affecting the biological relatedness of the child to the parents. Some couples adopt, in which case neither parent is biologically related to the child. Some gay male couples turn to surrogacy, so that the partner who provides the sperm is biologically related to the child. Some lesbian couples use donor insemination, so that the lesbian who carries the child is biologically related to the child. Other lesbian couples use in vitro fertilization so that one woman contributes the egg and the other woman is the birth mother. There are also differences in the legal relations between parents and children. Some states permit two same-sex partners to be the legal parents of a child, whereas many others do not. In states that do not allow second-parent adoption by a same-sex partner, only one partner in the couple is a legal parent. It is likely that the family experiences of lesbians and gay men differ, depending on how they become parents and the nature of their biological and legal relationship to their children.

Although census data provide basic information about same-sex couples with children, small-scale studies provide richer details about the experiences of these couples. Several studies have investigated relationship satisfaction among lesbian couples with children (see review by Patterson 1995a). There is some evidence that relationship satisfaction may decline shortly after the birth of a child, as is generally true for heterosexual couples. A recent longitudinal study followed lesbian couples from one month before the birth of a child to three months after the birth (Goldberg & Sayer 2006). All couples used donor insemination. For both the biological and nonbiological mother, love for the partner typically declined and conflict increased with the transition to parenthood. Patterns of change were affected by the women's neuroticism, expectations about social support from family, and features of the partners' interaction. Other studies have compared lesbian parenting couples with other couples. In an illustrative study, Flaks et al. (1995) compared 15 lesbian couples to 15 heterosexual couples, all with children between the ages of three and nine who were conceived through donor insemination. No significant differences were found between the lesbian and heterosexual couples on the Dyadic Adjustment Scale, a standard measure of relationship quality.

Does the egalitarian division of household labor typically found among gay and lesbian couples without children hold for those with children? Although limited, available research indicates that parenthood does not change the general pattern of shared household responsibilities for same-sex couples (see review on lesbian parenthood by Parks 1998). This is particularly true for the allocation of household chores and decision-making (e.g., Patterson 1995b, Patterson et al. 2004). The division of childcare responsibilities, on the other hand, is less clear-cut.

Research consistently demonstrates that lesbian couples with children endorse an egalitarian division of childcare as their ideal (Chan et al. 1998, Patterson 1995b, Patterson et al. 2004). This is in contrast to heterosexual couples, who tend to endorse a nonegalitarian division, with the wife ideally doing more childcare than the husband does. Research on the actual division of childcare among lesbian mothers is less consistent. Some studies have reported that lesbian partners share equally in childcare (Hand 1991, Patterson et al. 2004), but others have reported that lesbian couples adopt a less-than-egalitarian division of childcare (Ciano-Boyce & Shelley-Sireci 2002, Patterson 1995b). The reasons for these differences are not understood. They may result from the use of relatively small samples. It seems likely, however, that other factors are also at play. In particular, the biological and legal relationship of each parent to the children may make a difference. It may be, for example, that biological mothers tend to be more involved in childcare than are nonbiological mothers. Research systematically examining these issues is needed.

Currently, research on same-sex couples with children is quite limited. Research on gay fathers is rare (Patterson 2004b). Studies of ethnic minority families and low-income families are also needed. Further, it would be useful for researchers to go beyond studying relationship satisfaction and the division of labor to address a broader set of issues in the lives of same-sex couples raising children and to go beyond description toward specifying underlying mechanisms affecting couples' functioning. Longitudinal approaches to studying same-sex couples as they transition into parenthood may prove especially useful.

Societal Stigma: Stress and Social Support

The stigma of homosexuality affects lesbians, gay men, and their relationships in many ways. Personal experiences of rejection and discrimination are common. In a national survey (Kaiser Family Foundation 2001), 74% of lesbians and gay men reported experiencing discrimination based on sexual orientation, with 23% reporting that discrimination occurred "a lot." Additionally, 34% reported that their family or a family member had refused to accept them because of their sexual orientation. Discrimination often comes in the form of minor daily hassles, such as derogatory remarks or poor service. Swim (2004) utilized daily experience accounts to assess gay and lesbian people's experience with these everyday hassles. Over a one-week period, participants reported experiencing an average of two hassles related to their sexual orientation. Two-thirds of these hassles were verbal, including jokes, comments based on stereotypes, hostile or threatening comments, and comments expressing general dislike of gay men and lesbians. In an experimental study, Jones (1996) demonstrated that same-sex couples requesting a hotel room with a shared bed were denied a room significantly more often than were other-sex couples making an identical request. Lewis et al. (2001) identified several types of gay-related stressors that are specific to lesbians and gay men. One type concerned family reactions and included rejection, lack of support, or ignoring the person's sexual orientation. Other gay-related stressors involved the need to hide one's sexual orientation, fear of being exposed as homosexual, violence and harassment, lack of societal acceptance, and discrimination.

Gay and lesbian couples are also vulnerable to hate crimes based on their sexual orientation. In 2002, a lesbian couple and their infant son barely escaped with their lives when arsonists set their home on fire, only days after the women had sued the University of Montana for failing to provide domestic partner benefits.In1999, two brothers claiming to be carrying out God's will brutally murdered long-term gay partners Gary Matson, 50, and Winfield Mowder, 40, while they slept in their home. In a national survey, 32% of lesbian and gay respondents reported having been the target of physical violence against them or their property because of their sexual orientation (Kaiser Family Foundation 2001).

Researchers have consistently shown that lesbians and gay men who experience greater levels of discrimination are at greater risk for poor psychological adjustment and stress-related psychological disorders (e.g., Mays & Cochran 2001; Meyer 1995, 2003). Indeed, researchers are now testing the applicability of models of minority stress, first developed with regard to ethnic minorities, to the experiences of lesbian and gay individuals (Meyer 1995, 2003). Unfortunately, we currently have little information about how social stigma and discrimination affect same-sex couples. Research with heterosexual married couples has clearly demonstrated that high levels of stress from sources outside a relationship (e.g., financial difficulties, lack of social support) are associated with lower marital satisfaction and declines in satisfaction over time (Karney & Bradbury 2005). Further, during times of high stress, married couples report experiencing more marital problems.

It is reasonable to assume that discrimination based on sexual orientation places strains on gay and lesbian couples (Mays et al. 1993, Otis et al. 2006). A study of same-sex couples in civil unions (To do sijevic et al. 2005) found a significant association between reports of more gay-specific stressors and lower relationship satisfaction for lesbian couples but not for gay male couples. The effects of gay-related stress on couple functioning may be direct, for example, through limited access to important resources such as jobs and housing, or rejection of the couple or their children by family, neighbors, or peers at work or school. Discrimination may also affect couples indirectly, by diminishing the self-esteem or mental health of the partners or their ability to function effectively in a relationship. Research to determine the ways in which discrimination affects same-sex couples is needed.

Equally important will be studies of the resilience of same-sex couples in the face of prejudice and discrimination. Central to understanding how couples cope with discrimination will be analyses of social support. Research consistently shows that, compared with heterosexuals, lesbians and gay men perceive less social support from their family of origin (Elizur & Mintzer 2003; Kurdek 2004, 2006). Of course, these average differences can be misleading. Some gay men and lesbians have strong and supportive family ties that are undoubtedly a valuable source of aid and comfort in times of need. At the other extreme, some lesbians and gay men have negative relations with their families, ranging from grudging acceptance to outright rejection of them and/or their partner. There is evidence that greater social support from relatives is associated not only with greater personal well-being but also with greater relationship satisfaction in same-sex couples (Kurdek 1988, 1995b). In addition, there may be distinctive types of social support that are of special relevance to lesbians and gay men. Preliminary evidence that support for a woman's lesbian identity may be particularly important to psychological well-being comes from a two-week-long daily experience study of lesbians (Beals & Peplau 2005).

A further consistent finding is that lesbians and gay men may compensate for lower levels of family support by establishing closer ties with friends. Some lesbians and gay men create "families of choice," that is, a network of friends who provide love and support, celebrate holidays and rituals, share leisure activities, and offer assistance in time of need (Carrington 1999). Oswald (2002) referred to the creation of these families as "choosing kin" and noted commonalities between these flexible family networks and the fictive kinship patterns seen in African American and Latino communities. Studies of the impact of supportive friends on the well-being of same-sex couples would be valuable (Elizur & Mintzer 2003).

Social relations can be a mixed blessing (Rook 1998). On the one hand, supportive relationships are a source of aid and comfort in times of stress. On the other hand, social relations can be powerful sources of conflict, hostility, and disappointment that create stress. Further research on sources of stress and support for same-sex couples is needed, along with explicit analyses of how models of minority stress may apply to same-sex couples.

In this section, we have reviewed three relatively new topics of research about same-sex couples: legal recognition of same-sex relationships, same-sex partners as parents, and the impact of gay-related stress on gay and lesbian couples. An important direction for future research will be to use better and more varied research methodologies. The recent availability of information about same-sex couples gathered from large, representative samples including the U.S. Census and other major surveys has been a major advance. Survey research can fruitfully be augmented with daily experience methods, longitudinal assessments, behavioral observations in controlled settings, and experimental designs. In-depth interviews, participant observations, and ethnographies can provide rich descriptions of the daily lives of same-sex couples within a specific cultural, historical, and social context. Studies specifically focusing on couples from diverse ethnic and social class backgrounds would fill an important gap in existing knowledge.

CONCLUDING COMMENTS

The growing body of research on same-sex couples has contributed to our understanding of close relationships in several important ways. One contribution has been to challenge the accuracy of negative social stereotypes about gay and lesbian relationships and to provide more reliable information (see review by Peplau 1991). For decades, the media have depicted homosexuals as unhappy individuals who are unsuccessful in developing stable romantic ties and so end up frustrated and lonely. Both the women lovers in Radclyffe Hall's popular 1928 novel, *The Well of Loneliness* (Hall 1928), and the male lovers in the recent award-winning film, *Brokeback Mountain,* reflected this theme. Contrary to these media images, research has documented that many contemporary lesbians and gay men establish enduring intimate relationships. Research has also debunked a second stereotype, that gay and lesbian relationships are dysfunctional or inferior in quality to those of heterosexuals. Instead, studies have shown that on standardized measures of love, satisfaction, and relationship adjustment, same-sex and heterosexual couples are remarkably similar. This is not to say that all same-sex relationships are happy and problem-free, but rather that gay and lesbian couples are not necessarily more prone to relationship difficulties than are heterosexuals. A third stereotype, that same-sex relationships universally mimic heterosexual marriages by creating "husband" and "wife" roles, has also been discredited. Historical and anthropological accounts have documented that masculine-feminine distinctions have sometimes been important in structuring same-sex relations, and this may continue to be true among some Americans today (Murray 2000, Peplau 2001, Peplau et al. 1999). However, most contemporary gay and lesbian couples in the United States share homemaking tasks and financial provider responsibilities, rather than dividing them such that one partner is the "husband" and the other partner is the "wife" (Kurdek 2005).

A second contribution of research on gay and lesbian relationships has been to test the generalizability of relationship concepts and theories that were based, implicitly or explicitly, on heterosexual couples. We reviewed research showing the applicability of social exchange models of commitment and stability to same-sex couples. Although same-sex couples may differ from heterosexual couples in their mean level of exchange variables, such as barriers to dissolution, the hypothesized associations among key constructs have been strongly supported. This research provides evidence for the general usefulness of exchange models. It also suggests that researchers studying gay and lesbian relationships can build on the existing theoretical literature about close relationships, rather than having to start anew. We agree with Kurdek (2005, p. 253), who observed that "despite external differences in how gay, lesbian and heterosexual couples are constituted, the relationships of gay and lesbian partners appear to work in much the same way as the relationships of heterosexual partners." A promising new direction is provided by studies applying ideas from adult attachment theory to same-sex couples (e.g., Elizur & Mintzer 2003, Kurdek 2002, Ridge & Feeney 1998).

A third contribution of research on same-sex relationships has been to provide a new way to investigate how gender affects close relationships. For example, by comparing how women behave with male versus female partners, we can begin to disentangle the effects on social interaction of an individual's own sex and the sex of their partner. This comparative research strategy is obviously not identical to an experiment, but can nonetheless be informative. Research on social influence in close relationships is illustrative. Studies of heterosexuals have shown that men and women tend to use somewhat different tactics when trying to influence an intimate partner, but could not clarify if these differences were due to the sex of the influence agent, the sex of the target, or some other factor such as relative power in the relationship. Studies including gay, lesbian, and heterosexual couples (Falbo & Peplau 1980, Howard et al. 1986) have demonstrated that regardless of gender or sexual orientation, partners with relatively less power in a relationship tend to use "weak strategies" such as withdrawal or supplication. In contrast, partners with relatively more power tend to use "strong strategies" including bargaining or bullying.

A fourth contribution of empirical research on same-sex relationships has been to provide a scientific basis for policy and legal decisions. Activities of the American Psychological Association (APA) are illustrative. In July 2004, the APA Council of Representatives issued a resolution on sexual orientation and marriage. It stated, "APA believes that it is unfair and discriminatory to deny same-sex couples legal access to civil marriage and to all its attendant benefits, rights and privileges." The resolution explicitly referred to research on same-sex couples and concluded that research provides no evidence to justify discrimination against same-sex couples. The APA has also submitted research-based legal briefs *amicus curiae* for court cases challenging state marriage laws in Nebraska, New Jersey, New York, Oregon, and Washington (Herek 2006).

As this review suggests, research on same-sex couples has been reinvigorated by the continuing public debate about same-sex marriage, by the availability of improved research methods, and by general theoretical advances in the field of close relationships.

ACKNOWLEDGMENT

We are grateful for advice and assistance provided by David Frederick, Negin Ghavami, Andrew Galperin, Gary Gates, Gregory Herek, Natalya Maisel, Cristina Nguyen, Danny Osborn, Kelly Turner, and Curtis Yee.

LITERATURE CITED

Am. Psychol. Assoc. 2004. Resolution on sexual orientation and marriage. http://www. apa.org/pi/lgbc/policy/marriage.pdf

Andersson GT, Noack T, Seierstad A, Weedon-Fekjaer H. 2006. The demographics of same-sex marriages in Norway and Sweden. *Demography* 43:79–98

Bailey JM, Gaulin S, Agyei Y, Gladue BA. 1994. Effects of gender and sexual orientation on evolutionarily relevant aspects of human mating psychology. *J. Personal. Soc. Psychol.* 66:1081–93

Balsam KF, Szymanski DM. 2005. Relationship quality and domestic violence in women's same-sex relationships: the role of minority stress. *Psychol. Women Q.* 29:258–69

Beals KP, Impett EA, Peplau LA. 2002. Lesbians in love: why some relationships endure and others end. *J. Lesbian Stud.* 6:53–63

Beals KP, Peplau LA. 2005. Identity support, identity devaluation, and well-being among lesbians. *Psychol. Women Q.* 29:140–48

Black D, Gates G, Sanders S, Taylor L. 2000. Demographics of the gay and lesbian population in the United States. *Demography* 37:139–54

Blumstein P, Schwartz P. 1983. *American Couples.* New York: Morrow. 656 pp.

Bryant AS, Demian. 1994. Relationship characteristics of American gay and lesbian couples: findings from a national survey. In *Social Services for Gay and Lesbian Couples*, ed. LA Kurdek, pp. 101–17. New York: Haworth

Caldwell MA, Peplau LA. 1984. The balanceof power inlesbian relationships. *Sex Roles*10:587– 600

Carrington C. 1999. *No Place Like Home: Relationships and Family Life Among Lesbians and Gay Men.* Chicago: Univ. Chicago Press. 273 pp.

Chan RW, Brooks RC, Raboy B, Patterson CJ. 1998. Division of labor among lesbian and heterosexual parents: associations with children's adjustment. *J. Fam. Psychol.* 12:402–19

Ciano-Boyce C, Shelley-Sireci L. 2002. Who is mommy tonight? Lesbian parenting issues. *J. Homosex.* 43:1–13

Crawford I, Solliday E. 1996. The attitudes of undergraduate college students toward gay parenting. *J. Homosex.* 30:63–77

Diamond LM, Dube EM. 2002. Friendship and attachment among heterosexual and sexual-minority youths. *J. Youth Adolesc.* 31:155–66

Duffy SM, Rusbult CE. 1986. Satisfaction and commitment in homosexual and heterosexual relationships. *J. Homosex.* 12:1–24

Dunne GA. 1997. *Lesbian Lifestyles: Women's Work and the Politics of Sexuality.* Toronto: Univ. Toronto Press. 258 pp.

Eldridge NS, Gilbert LA. 1990. Correlates of relationship satisfaction in lesbian couples. *Psychol. Women Q.* 14:43–62

Elizur Y, Mintzer A. 2003. Gay males intimate relationship quality: the roles of attachment security, gay identity, social support, and income. *Pers. Relat.* 10:411–36

Falbo T, Peplau LA. 1980. Power strategies in intimate relationships. *J. Personal. Soc. Psychol.* 38:618–28

Fassinger RE, Morrow SL. 1995. Overcome: repositioning lesbian sexualities. In *The Psychology of Sexual Orientation, Behavior, and Identity: A Handbook*, ed. L Diamant, RD McAnulty, pp. 197–219. London: Greenwood

FlaksDK, FicherI,MasterpasquaF,JosephG.1995. Lesbians choosingmotherhood:acompar-ative study of lesbian and heterosexual parents and their children. *Dev. Psychol.* 31:105–14

Fulcher M, Sutfin EL, Chan RW, Scheib JE, Patterson CJ. 2006. Lesbian mothers and their children. In *Sexual Orientation and Mental Health: Examining Identity and Development in Lesbian, Gay, and Bisexual People*, ed. AM Omoto, HS Kurtzman, pp. 281–99. Washington, DC: Am. Psychol. Assoc.

Gates G, Ost J. 2004. *The Gay and Lesbian Atlas.* Washington, DC: Urban Inst. Press. 232 pp.

Gen. Account. Off. 2004. Defense of Marriage Act: update to prior report. Document GAO-04–353R. Washington, DC: GAO

Goldberg AE, Sayer A. 2006. Lesbian couples' relationship quality across the transition to parenthood. *J. Marriage Fam.* 68:87–100

Gottman JM, Levenson RW, SwansonC,SwansonK,TysonR, YoshimotoD. 2003. Observing gay, lesbian and heterosexual couples' relationships: mathematical modeling of conflict interaction. *J. Homosex.* 45:65–91

Hall R. 1928. *The Well of Loneliness.* New York: Bard Avon. 506 pp.

Hand SI. 1991. *The lesbian parenting couple.* PhD thesis. San Francisco: Prof. School Psychol.

Harkless LE, Fowers BJ. 2005. Similarities and differences in relational boundaries among heterosexuals, gay men, and lesbians. *Psychol. Women Q.* 29:167–76

Harry J. 1984. *Gay Couples.* New York: Praeger. 151 pp.

Harry J, DeVall WB. 1978. *The Social Organization of Gay Males.* New York: Praeger. 223 pp.

Herdt G, Kertzner R. 2006. I do, but I can't: the impact of marriage denial on the mental health and sexual citizenship of lesbians and gay men in the United States. *J. Sex. Res. Soc. Policy* 3(1):33–49, online ISSN 1553–6610

Herek GM. 2006. Legal recognition of same-sex relationships in the United States: a social science perspective. *Am. Psychol.* 61:In press

Hickson FC, Davies PM, Hunt AJ, Weatherburn P, McManus TJ, Coxon AP. 1992. Maintenance of open gay relationships: some strategies for protection against HIV. *AIDS Care* 4:409–19

Hochschild A, Machung A. 1989. *The Second Shift: Working Parents and the Revolution at Home.* New York: Viking

Howard JA, Blumstein P, Schwartz P. 1986. Sex, power, and influence tactics in intimate relationships. *J. Personal. Soc. Psychol.* 51:102–9

Human Rights Campaign. 2006. *Statewide marriage laws.* http://www.hrc.org/Template. cfm?Section=Center&CONTENTID=2822.5&TEMPLATE=/ContentManagement/ContentDisplay.cfm

Johnson MP. 2006. Violence and abuse in personal relationships: conflict, terror, and resistance in intimate partnerships. In *The Cambridge Handbook of Personal Relationships*, ed. A Vangelisti, D Perlman, pp. 557–78. New York: Cambridge Univ. Press

Johnson S. 1990. *Staying Power: Long-Term Lesbian Couples.* Tallahassee, FL: Naiad Press. 333 pp.

Jones DA. 1996. Discrimination against same-sex couples in hotel reservation policies. *J. Homosex.* 31:153–59

Kaiser Family Found. 2001. *Inside-Out: A Report on the Experiences of Lesbians, Gays and Bisexuals in America and the Public's View on Issues and Policies Related to Sexual Orientation*, Menlo Park, CA

Karney BR, Bradbury TN. 2005. Contextual influences on marriage: implications for policy and intervention. *Curr. Dir. Psychol. Sci.* 14:171–74

King M, Bartlett A. 2006. What same-sex civil partnerships may mean for health. *J. Epidemiol. Community Health* 60:188–91

Klinkenberg D, Rose S. 1994. Dating scripts of gay men and lesbians. *J. Homosex.* 26:23–35

Kurdek LA. 1988. Perceived social support in gays and lesbians in cohabitating relationships. *J. Personal. Soc. Psychol.* 54:504–9

Kurdek LA. 1991. Correlates of relationship satisfaction in cohabiting gay and lesbian couples. *J. Personal. Soc. Psychol.* 61:910–22

Kurdek LA. 1993. The allocation of household labor in gay, lesbian, and heterosexual married couples. *J. Soc. Issues* 49(3):127–39

Kurdek LA. 1994a. The nature and correlates of relationship quality in gay, lesbian, and heterosexual cohabiting couples. In *Lesbian and Gay Psychology: Volume 1*, ed. B Greene, GM Herek, pp. 113–55. Thousand Oaks, CA: Sage

Kurdek LA. 1994b. Areas of conflict for gay, lesbian, and heterosexual couples: What couples argue about influences relationship satisfaction. *J. Marr. Fam.* 56:923–34

Kurdek LA. 1995a. Developmental changes inrelationship qualityin gay and lesbian cohabiting couples. *Dev. Psychol.* 31:86–94

Kurdek LA. 1995b. Lesbian and gay couples. In *Lesbian, Gay, and Bisexual Identities over the Lifespan*, ed. AR D'Augelli, CJ Patterson, pp. 243–61. New York: Oxford

Kurdek LA. 1998. Relationship outcomes and their predictors: longitudinal evidence from heterosexual married, gay cohabiting, and lesbian cohabiting couples.*J. Marr. Fam.*60:553–68

Kurdek LA. 2000. Attractions and constraints as determinants of relationship commitment: longitudinal evidence from gay, lesbian, and heterosexual couples. *Pers. Relat.* 7:245–62

Kurdek LA. 2002. On being insecure about the assessment of attachment styles. *J. Soc. Personal. Relat.* 19:811–34

Kurdek LA. 2004. Are gay and lesbian cohabiting couples *really* different from heterosexual married couples? *J. Marr. Fam.* 66:880–900

Kurdek LA. 2005. What do we know about gay and lesbian couples? *Curr. Dir. Psychol. Sci.* 14:251–54

Kurdek LA. 2006. Differences between partners from heterosexual, gay, and lesbian cohabiting couples. *J. Marr. Fam.* 68:509–28

Kurdek LA, Schmitt JP. 1986. Relationship quality of partners in heterosexual married, heterosexual cohabiting, and gay and lesbian relationships. *J. Personal. Soc. Psychol.* 51:711–20

Kurdek LA, Schmitt JP. 1987. Partner homogamy in married, heterosexual cohabitating, gay, and lesbian couples. *J. Sex Res.* 23(2):212–32

Lannutti PJ. 2005. For better or worse: exploring the meanings of same-sex marriage within the lesbian, gay, bisexual and transgendered community. *J. Soc. Personal. Relat.* 22:5–18

Lewis GB. 2006. *Thinking about gay marriage: putting the moral condemnation back into morality policy*. Presented at Williams Inst. 5th Annu. Update Sex. Orientation Law Public Policy, Univ. Calif., Los Angeles

Lewis RJ, Derlega VJ, Berndt A, Morris LM, Rose S. 2001. An empirical analysis of stressors for gay men and lesbians. *J. Homosex.* 42(1):63–88

Mays VM, Cochran SD. 2001. Mental health correlates of perceived discrimination among lesbian, gay, and bisexual adults in the United States. *Am. J. Public Health* 91:1869–76

Mays VM, Cochran SD, Rhue S. 1993. The impact of perceived discrimination on the intimate relationships of black lesbians. *J. Homosex.* 25:1–14

McWhirter DP, Mattison AM. 1984. *The Male Couple: How Relationships Develop*. Englewood Cliffs, NJ: Prentice-Hall. 341 pp.

Metz ME, Rosser BRS, Strapko N. 1994. Differences in conflict-resolution styles among heterosexual, gay, and lesbian couples. *J. Sex Res.* 31:1–16

Meyer IH. 1995. Minority stress and mental health in gay men. *J. Health Soc. Behav.* 36:38–56

Meyer IH. 2003. Prejudice, social stress, and mental health in lesbian, gay, and bisexual populations: conceptual issues and research evidence. *Psychol. Bull.* 129:674–97

Murray SO. 2000. *Homosexualities*. Chicago: Univ. Chicago Press. 507 pp.

Nardi PM. 1999. *Gay Men's Friendships*. Chicago: Univ. Chicago Press. 253 pp.

Oswald RF. 2002. Resilience within the family networks of lesbians and gay men: intentionality and redefinition. *J. Marr. Fam.* 64:374–83

Otis MD, Rostosky SS, Riggle EDB, Hamrin R. 2006. Stress and relationship quality in same-sex couples. *J. Soc. Personal. Relat.* 23:81–99

Parks CA. 1998. Lesbian parenthood: a review of the literature. *Am. J. Orthopsychiatry* 68:376– 89

Patterson CJ. 1995a. Lesbian mothers, gay fathers, and their children. In *Lesbian, Gay, and Bisexual Identities over the Lifespan: Psychological Perspectives*, ed. AR D'Augelli, CJ Patterson, pp. 262–90. New York: Oxford Univ. Press

Patterson CJ. 1995b. Families of the baby boom: parents' division of labor and children's adjustment. *Dev. Psychol.* 31:115–23

Patterson CJ. 2003. Children of lesbian and gay parents. In *Psychological Perspectives on Lesbian, Gay, and Bisexual Experiences*, ed. LD Garnets, DC Kimmel, pp. 497–548. New York: Columbia Univ. Press. 815 pp. 2nd ed.

Patterson CJ. 2004a. What difference does a civil union make? Changing public policies and the experiences of same-sex couples: comment on Solomon, Rothblum, and Balsam 2004. *J. Fam. Psychol.* 18:287–89

Patterson CJ. 2004b. Gay fathers. In *The Role of the Father in Child Development*, ed. ME Lamb, pp. 397–416. New York: Wiley. 4th ed.

Patterson CJ, Sutfin EL, Fulcher M. 2004. Division of labor among lesbian and heterosexual parenting couples: correlates of specialized versus shared patterns. *J. Adult Dev.* 11:179–89

Peplau LA. 1991. Lesbian and gay relationships. In *Homosexuality: Research Findings for Public Policy*, ed. JC Gonsiorek, JD Weinrich, pp. 177–96. Newbury Park, CA: Sage

Peplau LA, Spalding LR, Conley TD, Veniegas RC. 1999. The development of sexual orientation in women. *Annu. Rev. Sex Res.* 10:70–99

Peplau LA. 2001. Rethinking women's sexual orientation: an interdisciplinary, relationship-focused approach. *Pers. Relat.* 8:1–19

Peplau LA, Cochran SD. 1980. *Sex differences in values concerning love relationships.* Presented at Annu. Meet. Am. Psychol. Assoc., Montreal

Peplau LA, Cochran SD. 1981. Value orientations in the intimate relationships of gay men. *J. Homosex.* 6:1–19

Peplau LA, Cochran SD, Mays VM. 1997. A national survey of the intimate relationships of African American lesbians and gay men: a look at commitment, satisfaction, sexual behavior, and HIV disease. In *Ethnic and Cultural Diversity among Lesbians and Gay Men*, ed. B Greene, pp. 11–38. Thousand Oaks, CA: Sage

Peplau LA, Cochran SD, Rook K, PadeskyC.1978. Women in love: attachment and autonomy in lesbian relationships. *J. Soc. Issues* 34(3):7–27

Peplau LA, Fingerhut AW, Beals KP. 2004. Sexuality in the relationships of lesbians and gay men. In *Handbook of Sexuality in Close Relationships*, ed. J Harvey, A Wenzel, S Sprecher, pp. 350–69. Mahwah, NJ: Erlbaum

Peplau LA, Garnets LD, eds. 2000. Women's sexualities: new perspectives on sexual orientation and gender. *J. Soc. Issues* 56(2):181–364

Peplau LA, Padesky C, Hamilton M. 1982. Satisfaction in lesbian relationships. *J. Homosex.* 8:23–35

Peplau LA, Spalding LR. 2000. The close relationships of lesbians, gay men and bisexuals. In *Close Relationships: A Sourcebook*, ed. C Hendrick, SS Hendrick, pp. 111–24. Thousand Oaks, CA: Sage

Potoczniak MJ, Mourot JE, Crosbie-Burnett M, Potoczniak DJ. 2003. Legal and psychological perspectives on same-sex domestic violence: a multi systemic approach. *J. Fam. Psychol.* 17:252–59

Reilly ME, Lynch JM. 1990. Power-sharing in lesbian partnerships. *J. Homosex.* 19:1–30

Renzetti CM, Miley CH. 1996. *Violence in Gay and Lesbian Domestic Partnerships.* New York: Haworth. 121 pp.

Ridge SR, Feeney JA. 1998. Relationship history and relationship attitudes in gay males and lesbians: attachment style and gender differences. *Aust. NZ J. Psychiatry* 32(6):848–59

Rook KS. 1998. Investigating the positive and negative sides of personal relationships: through a lens darkly? In *The Dark Side of Close Relationships*, ed. BH Spitzberg, WR Cupach pp. 369–93. Mahwah, NJ: Erlbaum

Rose S, Zand D, Cini M. 1993. Lesbian courtship scripts. In *Boston Marriages: Romantic but Asexual Relationships Among Contemporary Lesbians*, ed. ED Rothblum, KA Brehony, pp. 70–85. Amherst: Univ. Mass. Press

Rothblum ED. 2000. Sexual orientation and sex in women's lives: conceptual and methodological issues. *J. Soc. Issues* 56(2):193–204

Rutter V, Schwartz P. 1996. Same-sex couples: courtship, commitment, context. In *The Diversity of Human Relationships*, ed. AE Auhagen, M von Salisch. pp. 197–223. New York: Cambridge Univ. Press

Schreurs KMG, Buunk BP. 1996. Closeness, autonomy, equity and relationship satisfaction in lesbian couples. *Psychol. Women Q.* 20:577–92

Solomon SE, Rothblum ED, Balsam KF. 2004. Pioneers in partnership: lesbian and gay male ouples in civil unions compared with those not in civil unions and heterosexual married siblings. *J. Fam. Psychol.* 18:275–86

Solomon SE, Rothblum ED, Balsam KF. 2005. Money, housework, sex, and conflict: same-sex couples in civil unions, those not in civil unions, and heterosexual married siblings. *Sex Roles* 52:561–75

Swim JK. 2004. *Day to day experiences with heterosexism: heterosexist hassles as daily stressors.* Work. Pap., Dept. Psychol., Penn. State Univ.

Tasker F.2005. Lesbian mothers, gay fathers, and their children: a review.*J. Dev. Behav. Pediatr.* 26(3):224–40

Testa RJ, Kinder BN, Ironson G. 1987. Heterosexual bias in the perception of loving relationships of gay males and lesbians. *J. Sex Res.* 23:163–72

The Pew Forum on Religion and Public Life. 2005. *Abortion and rights of terror suspects top court issues; strong support for stem cell research.* http://pewforum.org/docs/index.php?Doc ID=91

Todosijevic J, Rothblum ED, Solomon SE. 2005. Relationship satisfaction, affectivity, and gay-specific stressors in same-sex couples joined in civil unions. *Psychol. Women Q.* 29:158–66

Weinstock JS. 2004. Lesbian FLEX-ibility: friend and/or family connections among lesbian ex-lovers. *J. Lesbian Stud.* 8(3/4):193–238

JEALOUSY AND INFIDELITY

Affairs and Infidelity

By Graham Allan and Kaeren Harrison

INTRODUCTION

This chapter is concerned with people's emotional responses to extradyadic relationships and in particular the hurt that is experienced when they occur. Given the enormous interest in popular culture about such relationships and the potential impact they have on family dynamics, including of course separation and divorce, surprisingly little research has been concerned directly with understanding the patterning and consequences of different forms of extrapartnership involvement. Some related topics have been researched more than others. For example, the incidence of extramarital sex has been examined in a number of studies (Haavio-Mannila & Kontula, 2003; Laumann, Gagnon, Michael, & Michaels, 1994; Treas & Giesen, 2000; Wellings, Fields, Johnson, & Wadsworth, 1994; Wiederman, 1997), as have feelings of jealousy in response to the discovery of a partner's infidelity (e.g., Buss, Larsen, Westen, & Semmelroth, 1992; Buunk & Dijkstra, 2006; Harris, 2003). But there has been limited research explicitly examining the social or psychological impact of extrapartnership involvement, particularly outside clinical settings (Olson, Russell, Higgins-Kessler, & Miller, 2002). Perhaps this is not surprising given the secret as well as sensitive nature of the topic, but as a consequence extensive or detailed information about people's actual experiences of extrapartnership involvement, including the hurt they experience, is not readily available.

The overall aim of this chapter is to raise questions about the nature of the hurt experienced during and after an affair. After briefly reflecting on the different elements that the concept of "hurt" entails, the chapter discusses some of the forms of hurt that being in an extradyadic relationship can generate. Most importantly it examines the different responses to the discovery of an affair. Although recognizing the complexity of these responses, it focuses particularly on three frequently interrelated themes: jealousy, betrayal, and loss. Before concluding with suggestions about key areas for future research, the chapter addresses the question of how recent changes in patterns of partnership formation and dissolution are likely to influence people's understandings of extradyadic sexual involvement.

Before proceeding to consider the notion of "hurt" more systematically, two other matters need to be raised. The first concerns the issue of terminology and language (Allen et al, 2005). The different terms used to describe extra-partnership sexual involvement are indicative of the changing understandings of these matters within Western culture. For many, terms like *adultery* and *infidelity* now seem both old-fashioned and overly moralistic. They were suitable for an era in which a traditional form of marriage was the key institution of partnership. They seem far less apposite now in an era when there is greater diversity and flexibility in the "rules" governing different partnerships. For some, even the term *affair* carries connotations linked too heavily to a form of marital commitment that is no longer appropriate to many partnerships. Within some of the research literature, the terms *extradyadic relationship* and *extradyadic sex* have come to be used as more value-free concepts, though clearly these terms do not have much cultural resonance.

Second, there is the question of what now constitutes "cheating," "infidelity," or an "affair." Under traditional "marital blueprints" (Cancian, 1987), infidelity was clearly premised on marriage and signified a breaking of the marital contract. Now with changes in the patterning of partnership, these issues are somewhat less straightforward. Being unfaithful (or whatever term is favored) implies a relational commitment, but that commitment is no longer synonymous with marriage. For example, couples cohabiting together can also be unfaithful, though whether they regard each other's extradyadic involvements as infidelity in part depends on the understandings they have mutually negotiated with each other. In addition to the circumstances of the couple, responses to extradyadic involvement are also likely to depend on the characteristics of the "infidelity." In general, the deinstitutionalization of marriage (Cherlin, 2004) and the concomitant individualization of partnerships mean that reactions to intimate/sexual involvement with others are likely to be more varied than they were in an era when marriage was more firmly embedded, both morally and structurally.

HURT AND "INFIDELITY"

The idea of "hurt" has been discussed fully in different chapters in this book (see particularly the chapters in Part II). Although in comparison to other emotions, the idea of hurt has received relatively little scholarly attention, previous research has identified several processes that can generate feelings of hurt (e.g., Leary, Springer, Negel, Ansell, & Evans, 1998; Vangelisti, 1994). In Chapter 15 in the present volume, Feeney posits five forms of behavior that are liable to generate such feelings within romantic/sexual partnerships:

1. Active disassociation—behaviors that indicate disinterest in the partner, including denial of love and commitment
2. Passive disassociation—being ignored or excluded from activities, conversations, and disclosures
3. Criticism—negative comments about behavior, appearance, or personality
4. Infidelity—extrarelationship sexual involvement
5. Deception—misleading acts, lying, and breaking promises

The fourth of these, infidelity, is the central issue of this chapter, though it is also evident that extradyadic involvement can encompass the other categories, especially active disassociation, deception, and criticism. This complex of hurtful behaviors makes infidelity an intriguing topic for examining the character of hurt feelings.

Leary (2001) argued that the defining feature of hurtful events is perceived relational devaluation. In a similar vein, Vangelisti (2001) saw relational transgression as the central component of hurt feelings. Certainly the idea of relational transgression is core to any understanding of the hurt generated by involvement in extradyadic relationships. Feeney (2005 and Chapter 15, this volume) adds to this conception by noting that relational transgressions that evoke a sense of personal injury, as infidelity so frequently does, are particularly liable to generate feelings of hurt. As she writes (this volume, p. 316), "Hurt is associated with events that damage the victim's view of the self as worthy of love, or core beliefs about the availability and trustworthiness of others or both." Despite the evident connection between infidelity arid these emotional reactions, little research has specifically examined the patterning of hurt consequent on extradyadic involvement.

Accordingly, in this chapter we are taking a broad perspective on "hurt." Its focus is on the range of painful emotional responses that direct or indirect involvement in extrapartnership intimate and sexual interactions generates. Rather than conceptualizing "hurt" as a specific emotional response (Leary & Springer, 2001), we are concerned with overlapping constructions of painful feelings (Feeney, 2005), some being well defined but others less clear-cut. Thus, although aspects of jealousy, betrayal, trust, emptiness, anger, abandonment, and the like could all in theory be distinguished, for our purposes a generic idea of "hurt" portrays well these different negative outcomes that may result from extrapartnership involvement. Of course, not all the negative emotional responses that can be subsumed under the term *hurt* necessarily arise in any particular instance, but nonetheless this broad conceptualization provides a useful framework for the discussion that follows.

There is one rider to add here. Intimate relationships by their nature are generally not "emotion-free." That is, although sexual interactions may at times be quite casual, relationships sustained for any period of time usually do entail a degree of emotional commitment. Consequently, they also have the potential to involve elements of hurt, particularly when they are in the process of ending. People can, for example, feel resentful or angry at the way they are or have been treated, upset, and mournful that the relationship is over and jealous of any new relationship that the ex-partner later forms. Consequently, in looking at hurt caused through extrapartnership involvement, it is important to separate out elements that are rooted in the circumstances of intimate and sexual relationships per se from those that stem from the fact of an extrapartnership liaison. Similarly, the hurt of extrapartnership involvement needs to be kept distinct from the pain consequent on any separation or divorce that may follow. Often in particular instances these elements are difficult to separate, but in what follows the focus is on the extrapartnership dimension.

INVOLVEMENT IN AN "AFFAIR"

In this section we turn briefly to consider the experiences of those who have been directly involved in an extradyadic relationship, particularly in a sustained relationship, which is more likely to entail strong emotional feelings than an episodic sexual encounter. In addition to issues involved in any intimate relationship, a portion of the additional emotional strain experienced in significant, longer term affairs stems from their being clandestine. Only a proportion of infidelities and affairs ever become known to the established partner. Clearly the more short term the extrapartnership involvement and the less emotional attachment it entails, the more likely it is to remain hidden and the less likely it is to cause evident hurt for any of those involved.

At the early stages of the relationship, the "forbidden" character of the involvement may add an exciting *frisson* to the experience (Reibstein & Richards, 1992). However over time, feelings of anxiety and resentment are likely to come more to the fore as a consequence of having to be on guard against discovery. The need for secrecy, difficulties of arranging meetings, uncertainties about the timing of them, and limitations to spontaneity are liable to produce tensions in the relationship that would otherwise not be there. Although these tensions might be accepted as the cost of being involved in an extrapartnership liaison, at the same time they run somewhat counter to conventional conceptions of how romantic relationships are normally celebrated.

Many of those involved in sustained extrapartnership relationships experience feelings of guilt about their actions although these feelings are not always associated directly with ideas of "hurt" (Allan & Harrison, 2004; Allen et al, 2005; Lawson, 1988). Sometimes this guilt leads to a confession that brings the extrapartnership relationship into the open and changes its character. Other times, individuals devise ways of coping with these feelings, sometimes by framing their actions in ways that minimize any sense of betrayal they generate. This framing may involve emphasizing the lack of passion, love, or satisfaction in their regular partnership or taking the view that their partner is not being hurt so long as the affair remains secret. Further feelings of guilt may be experienced when the extrapartner relationship involves people who are known to each other as part of the same social group. In particular, the dynamics of affairs become particularly complex when the affair is between an individual and a friend of the spouse/partner. Here there is in effect a double betrayal as well as a greater need for monitoring and vigilance if the affair is to be kept clandestine.

As noted earlier, the ending of a significant extrapartnership relationship carries with it many of the problems associated with the ending of any emotionally close sexual attachment. However, it can also entail additional difficulties especially if the ending is undesired. In particular, if the relationship is discovered and becomes public, the person having the relationship is likely to have to deal with a wide range of emotional distresses—their own as well as those of the other people involved—and potentially conflicting pressures for action. In many cases he or she may be required to come to a decision as to which of the relationships to continue. For some, this decision may be a relief from the pressures of having a secret affair; for others, though, either decision will represent a significant loss, the costs of which may be borne over a lengthy period. As Amato and Previti (2003) among others indicate, a partner's knowledge of an affair is a prime ground for divorce. Moreover, the hurt felt by the uninvolved partner will often cause the person having the affair to experience a heightened sense of guilt and recrimination, as indeed may the hurt feelings of the other party to the affair.

Some of those involved in an affair will accept the "loyalty" of the other person in the relationship to their original partner—and may have a similar "loyalty" to their own long-term partner (Allan, 2004; Richardson, 1988). Others will feel more resentful and hurt at the ending of the relationship yet have few ways of challenging or channeling their distress. One important issue is the extent to which any grief or upset at the end of the relationship can be expressed socially. For some, the illicit and clandestine character of the relationship will mean that few others will be able to offer support. Being unable to express the hurt experienced to others or even talk through and reevaluate the events leading to the ending of the affair may make "closure" more difficult. This issue of social nonrecognition can be experienced particularly strongly in instances where the relationship ends through death. As Richardson (1985) notes, the bereaved lover in an affair is often unable to participate in the funeral or grieve publicly.

RESPONSES TO DISCOVERY

The most obvious and extensive hurt arising from extrapartnership liaisons occurs when the liaison becomes known to the other partner. However, people's responses to a partner's unfaithfulness are not uniform; a wide range of factors will influence them. Although at an individual level any act of infidelity can cause hurt, it is likely that the nature of the involvement of the extradyadic pair will be of consequence. Thus, it is generally easier to accept a one-time encounter presented as an unfortunate and regrettable aberration than a continuing relationship based on emotional attraction. Similarly, a relationship that is now ended will be easier to reconcile than one that is known to be continuing. Moreover, as Vangelisti and Gerstenberger (2004) emphasize, the response of the partner who has been unfaithful is also likely to influence the reaction to the affair. Expressions of culpability and regret by the "guilty" partner for what has happened, especially if it is not part of a familiar cycle of infidelity within the relationship, are likely to generate different responses from those where no sense of remorse or guilt is expressed or where it seems evident an emotional attachment continues even if the relationship is "over" and sexual involvement has ceased.

Responses to infidelity will also be influenced by cultural understandings of partnership, marriage, and sexuality. In some cultural settings, exclusivity in marriage may play a less significant part than it does in others (Haavio-Mannila & Kontula, 2003). In particular, as part of normatively accepted sexual double standards in those societies, men's extramarital involvements may be seen as less damaging to marital commitment, especially where patriarchal control of economic and material resources is deeply embedded. Similarly among certain social groups, marriage may be more a mechanism for alliance and continuity of the lineage than for personal or romantic fulfillment. This would, for instance, appear to have been the case in aristocratic circles in Britain in the 19th and early 20th centuries. Some sexually libertarian groups may espouse an explicit ideology of open sexual relationships, as for example with the Bloomsbury set in Britain in the 1920s and Californian (and other) "swingers" in the 1960s and 1970s. In these and other such cases, emotional and social responses to a partner's sexual involvement with others are clearly going to be different than when sexual exclusivity is taken as the cornerstone of a successful partnership.

The form of emotional hurt that has received most attention in the research literature as a result of infidelity becoming "known" is jealousy. As White (1981, p. 24) indicates, jealousy itself comprises "a complex of thoughts, feelings and actions" that can be expressed in a wide variety of ways (cited in Vangelisti & Gerstenberger, 2004, p. *69;* see also Guerrero, Spitzberg, & Yoshimura, 2004). But numerous other forms of hurt have also been reported in the literature, including betrayal, rejection, worthlessness, shame, and a sense of loss about self, relationship, and identity. Of course, such feelings are not experienced uniformly. Much depends on the history of the partnership, as well as on the dynamics of the infidelity and its aftermath.

Jealousy

Buunk and Dijkstra (2006) provide a good summary of research into jealousy as a response to extrapartnership sexual involvement. As they point out, although there are indications that young women in Western societies are now beginning to behave more like men (Laumann et al., 1994; Wiederman, 1997), a double standard has applied around extra-partnership sexual activity in most societies, with men being far more open to engaging in such activity than women. Whatever its roots, the existence of such a double standard as part of normative understandings of masculinity and femininity are likely to have an impact on emotional responses to the discovery of a partner's infidelity. Given this, it is not surprising that gender differences in jealousy on the discovery of an affair have regularly been reported in the literature, though often this research has relied on the measurement of hypothetical, experimental responses among young populations rather than on people's actual responses to known extrapartnership involvement (e.g., Becker, Sagarin, Guadagno, Millevoi, & Nicastle, 2004; Buss et al, 1992; Cramer, Abraham, Johnson, & Manning-Ryan, 2001; Harris, 2003). Women are often thought to be more jealous than men, though this may be because they are more liable to discuss their feelings openly. But equally they are given more cause to be jealous by their partners. In this, the operation of the double standard—its institutional incorporation into routine social relations and personal identities, based at least in part on men's greater control of economic and material resources—could be argued to result in jealousy being constructed differently for men and women. As Buunk and Dijkstra (2004) write,

> Men, more than women, seem to have a tendency to reduce the chances of their partner's infidelity by being possessive, by spending as much time with their partner as possible, by exhibiting controlling forms of jealousy, and by threatening their partner with undesirable consequences, such as desertion and violence if she were to be unfaithful, even when this would constitute only a single sexual act. (p. 108)

Thus, even if women appear to be more jealous than men, the consequence of men's jealousy with regard to partner unfaithfulness can be the more severe. Of relevance here are not only the punishments metered out by some religious groupings for wives' adultery, such as executions by stoning in some parts of the rural Muslim world, but also the acts of "patriarchal terrorism" (Johnson, i995)> including murder, that sometimes follow suspicion of unfaithfulness by jealous male partners (Harris, 2003). Clearly in these instances, the hurt involved in actual or suspected infidelity is more than just emotional.

Various researchers have also pointed out that there are differences in the degree to which different aspects of infidelity make men and women jealous (Becker et al., 2004; Buss et al., 1992). The prime argument has been that men's jealousy is aroused most by their partner's *sexual* involvement with another person, whereas women are more likely to experience strong feelings of jealousy when their partner is being *emotionally* unfaithful. That is, for men it is the act of sex itself that generates jealousy. Although sexual involvement may lead to jealousy in women too, they feel most threatened when their partners are involved with someone else at an emotionally intimate and not just a sexual level. Different explanations can be offered to account for this finding. Evolutionary psychologists have suggested that males' dominant concerns with potentially uncertain paternity lead them to focus most on sexual exclusivity, whereas females, for whom maternity is rarely an issue, focus instead on emotional commitment as a way of ensuring continued access to the material resources their partners control (Buss et al. 1992; Buunk 8c Dijkstra, 2006; Cann, Mangum, & Wells, 2001).

Others would agree that women often need to be concerned with relational commitment as a means of protecting their economic welfare, but would see this focus more as a consequence of socioeconomic structure than innate genetic drives. That is, in many societies, women's inferior economic position means that they (and their children) are materially dependent on their male partners, with separation and divorce generally resulting in significant economic deprivation. Consequently, within the normative blueprint of marriage/ partnership in question, men's involvement in sexual activity with others may be tolerated, provided that they remain committed socially and economically to the original union. The threat, in other words, is not the sex—indeed culturally such infidelity may come to be expected of men as part of the routine construction of masculinity. The threat comes from the possibility that sexual involvement may lead to emotional commitment and from there to a more permanent alternative relationship. In contrast, men's status and honor as men, within the same normative blueprint, are likely to be more dependent on maintaining the sexual exclusivity- "purity"—of their committed partner. In line with other aspects of the sexual double standard, to be cuckolded is of itself threatening to their masculine identity.

Given this, we might expect gender differences in the facets of infidelity that generate jealousy to be less marked in societies like the United States in which women have greater economic opportunity. In this regard, the methodological criticisms of the evolutionary perspective made by researchers like DeSteno and Salovey (1996); DeSteno, Bartlett, Salovey, and Braverman (2002); and Harris (2003) seem particularly relevant. They argue that findings about gender differences on the impact of emotional or sexual infidelity are largely a consequence of respondents being required to select one or other of these possibilities through the use of forced-choice questions. In their own research, DeSteno and his colleagues (DeSteno, Bartlett, Salovey, 8c Braverman, 2002; DeSteno & Salovey, 1996) found that questions using continuous rating scales eliminated these differences. They suggest the reasons for this finding are that women are less likely to view sexual and emotional infidelity as independent events, instead usually assuming that emotional infidelity also implies sexual infidelity. In consequence, they argue that women select emotional infidelity as more jealousy provoking in forced-choice questions, as emotional infidelity signifies a "double-shot" infidelity, incorporating both emotional and sexual betrayal. In other words, at least for women in the United States, the apparent differences in jealousy response revealed in forced-choice studies arise as a result of such double-shot understandings of the different modes of infidelity specified rather than being valid reflections of gender differences in jealousy patterns.

Betrayal

Jealousy is only one of the responses that people experience when they find out that their partners have been unfaithful (Allen et al., 2005; Becker et al., 2004; Boekhout, Hendrick, & Hendrick, 1999). Often people also experience a strong sense of betrayal and a feeling that trust has been broken, perhaps in a way that seems irreparable. As with other responses to a partner's infidelity, the extent to which these feelings arise obviously depends on the principles -implicit as well as explicit—around which the relationship has been negotiated. Where, as is usually the case with contemporary Western couples, there is an assumption of sexual exclusivity, knowledge that a partner has "cheated" can undermine the belief that the relationship is "special." However idealistic such a belief might be, part of the romantic construction of committed intimate relationships lies in the symbolism of the unity and bounded exclusivity of the couple. Thus, infidelity can represent a betrayal not just of a commitment to sexual exclusivity but more importantly of the essential "coupleness" that is the partners' relationship.

Such a betrayal can significantly undermine the degree of trust that is felt in the relationship. Frequently this undermining of trust is a consequence not just of betrayal but also a result of the lying and deceit that generally accompany an affair if it is prolonged over any period of time. Indeed sometimes the deliberate lies and planned deceits are felt most heavily. Whether suspicions have previously been raised matters little; deception is as damaging to trust as straightforward lies. Either way, the partner who finds out about the extradyadic relationship is left feeling deceived, often wondering how he or she could have been so foolish as not to recognize the tell-tale signs now so apparent with hindsight. Moreover, the erosion of trust is difficult to overcome. Many people whose partners have had an affair find themselves, willingly or otherwise, unable to trust again as fully as they did in the past. Determined not to repeat previous naivete, their default position is now suspicion rather than trust, a situation that over time can generate its own tensions and relationship deterioration (Knapp, 2006).

Loss and Identity

Discovering a partner is involved in an extradyadic relationship also frequently leads to an undermining of the individual's sense of self (Olson et al, 2002). In essence, the betrayal also comes to represent a personal rejection. In seeking to understand why the affair developed, what it was that led to it, and what made the attraction so great, questions about what is missing in the partnership inevitably get raised. And these questions about the relationship are themselves liable to be turned into questions about the self. In other words, individuals with partners who are involved in an extradyadic relationship end up doubting their own adequacy and pondering what it is they are lacking that makes the other person so compelling in comparison. This doubting can entail a range of different elements. It can certainly raise doubts i about sexual performance and adequacy. But it can also cast doubts about other characteristics of the self, including physical attractiveness, personality, and overall worth. Thus within contemporary constructions of "coupledom," the evident desire of the partner for someone else, even if only temporarily, can represent personal rejection and significantly undermine confidence in the self.

Moreover, public knowledge of a partner's sustained involvement with another can lead to feelings of failure and even humiliation (Allen et al., 2005; Olson et al., 2002). Pride can suffer as a result of the rejection being known by others in the couple's social network. People may also experience a sense of shame in these circumstances. In part this stems from knowing others are gossiping about them. But this shame, in turn, can be compounded by a sense that people judge them as partially responsible for what has happened in their relationship. In other words, knowledge of an affair leaves partners open to public scrutiny and gossip issues that are normally bounded by privacy. In addition, similar feelings of shame can arise through awareness that others have known—or suspected—about the affair before they knew about it themselves. In these circumstances, they may feel anger at friends for not revealing what they suspected sooner. As above, individuals' pride may be further hurt through awareness of others perceiving them as gullible and foolish for not recognizing sooner what was happening.

Overall, people can experience a wide range of emotions when a partner's extradyadic involvement comes to light. However, many of them can be recognized as at least partially rooted in a significant sense of loss (Boekhout et al., 1999). As we have seen, there can be feelings of worthlessness and loss of self. There can also be a loss of "relationship," not so much through its ending but more through reinterpreting its meaning, though of course this loss is compounded if separation or divorce follows (Orbuch, 1992). That is, even if the relationship continues, it may no longer be seen as it was. In a sense its innocence may be lost in a way that is impossible to recapture. As a number of the respondents in the study reported by Allan and Harrison (2002) recognized, they felt they could possibly forgive but not forget. Their trust had been broken, their belief in their partner damaged. Even though they did not seek to dwell on whatever pain they had experienced at the time, it remained a vivid memory. For these people, this represented a consciousness of loss in their relationship, notwithstanding its continuation.

EXCLUSIVITY IN LATE MODERNITY

People's expectations of partnerships have been changing in recent years throughout much of the Western world. One powerful indication of this change is the way in which patterns of partnership formation and dissolution have shifted, initially with increases in divorce and then with rises in cohabitation (Cherlin, 2004; Smock, 2004). These changes reflect, first, the demise of ideas of intimate partnerships necessarily being lifelong, "one-and-only" type relationships and, second, the increasing acceptance that individuals have the right to expect happiness and personal fulfillment through these partnerships (Giddens, 1992). Although symbolically marriage continues to be seen as a lifelong, "for better or worse" commitment, in reality cultural assumptions are increasingly informed by a belief that continuing personal happiness is the key rationale for any intimate partnership. Although there are religious and ethnic variations in this belief, staying unhappy in a long-term union for its own sake receives considerably less moral endorsement now than it did under previous marital blueprints.

A remaining question for this chapter concerns the impact of these changes in patterns of commitment on understandings of and responses to extrapartner sexual involvement. The increased emphasis on personal satisfaction in contemporary partnerships, along with the premise of increasing individualization generally, would suggest that partnerships are more fragile and less socially embedded than they once were. On this basis, emotional hurt stemming from partnership indiscretion or violation is liable to result more readily in the ending of the relationship. In other words, the expectation of achieving personal fulfilment and self-realization through one's intimate partnership may render sexual congress outside the partnership increasingly unacceptable. In line with this expectation, there is some evidence that younger cohorts are less accepting of infidelity than older ones, though obviously their views may change over time (Kontula & Haavio-Mannila, 2004; Laumann etal., 1994).

In contrast, it is conceivable that the emphasis on partnerships as individually negotiated relationships rather than socially prescribed sets of responsibilities and obligations will lead to partnership infidelity being understood within a different framework. In particular, although it seems likely that knowledge of a partner's involvement in another intimate relationship will be experienced as painful, it may be that particular episodes of infidelity come to be accepted as something that is liable to happen in long-term relationships. In other words, where there is an increasing emphasis on the *quality* of relationships, different understandings of sexual infidelity may emerge. This is not an argument about the liberalization of sexual mores. It is more a question of whether in certain circumstances contemporary forms of commitment lead to a readier acceptance that individuals may have competing "needs" or "desires" that cannot always be met within the confines of their established partnerships. Is it, for example, possible for people to become sexually involved with others in ways that, although painful, do not inevitably undermine their commitment to the existing partnership? What sort of tolerances are acceptable under what sorts of circumstances?

Given the high levels of ideological commitment to monogamy currently claimed, especially in the United States (Allen et al., 2005; Treas & Giesen, 2000), this changed conception may seem far-fetched, though clearly there have always been some couples who do not feel sexual exclusivity is important within their partnership. But many other shifts in sexual expression and behavior—including acceptance of "uncommitted" sexual relations, cohabitation, and gay marriage—would also have seemed far-fetched not that long ago. Moreover, there is a great deal more variation in the organization of coupledom now than was found in much of the 20th century. The growth of cohabitation is an example of this variation. So too, more couples are now choosing to have commitment without coresidence ("living apart together"), not solely for work reasons but also because this arrangement ensures a greater degree of personal autonomy than more standard couple arrangements. Similarly a significant number of gay couples have relationships that permit extrapartnership sexual involvement, with the proviso that such sexual involvements are just that—sexual rather than emotionally intimate. In these relationships, commitment requires emotional fidelity but not sexual exclusivity (Weeks, Heaphy, & Donovan, 2001).

A major demographic shift that may have some bearing here is the increased numbers of people experiencing more than one committed partnership over their life course. That is, the prevalence of remarriages and other forms of repartnering as a result of increased levels of separation and divorce may lead to some further reevaluation of monogamy and extrapartnership involvement. Clearly people's understandings of marriage as necessarily a lifelong commitment are shifting. In this context, it may be that acts of betrayal within partnerships are increasingly "resolved" through separation. It is possible though that there will be an increasing propensity for some people, perhaps especially those with greater relationship experience, to interpret some forms of extrapartnership sexual involvement as not necessarily indicative of an act of betrayal. Although such openness may not be regarded as routine or acceptable in the way some gay couples perceive it, the distinction between sexual and intimate involvement may come to have increased salience for heterosexual couples in the changed sexual climate of late modernity. Of course, this is highly speculative but understandings of partnership and commitment, and consequently feelings of emotional hurt in cases of known extrapartnership involvement, can be interpreted as culturally framed rather than psychologically or biologically given. At the very least, the ways in which such involvements are symbolically constructed and interpreted will be of consequence for the reactions generated.

FUTURE RESEARCH

It is clear that we need a great deal more research on the emotional impact of different forms of extrapartnership involvement. As things stand, research knowledge is not only extremely limited but also frequently based on questionable methodologies. This applies to most aspects of extrapartnership involvement, including the emotional responses of those directly or indirectly party to it. Although we know that extrapartnership involvement is relatively common (despite high levels of expressed disapproval), knowledge of its patterning and consequences is largely missing. Clearly there are major methodological difficulties in generating high-quality information about people's experiences of the topic, largely as a result of its furtive and morally suspect character. Nonetheless if we are to understand the varied course of these events and the different responses they evoke, we need to find better ways of collecting appropriate data on them.

There are a number of different issues here. To begin with, there is the question of sampling. Much of the research concerned with people's responses to infidelity, including that on different aspects of jealousy, relies on samples drawn from undergraduate populations. Typically those involved are asked questions about how they would respond to a partner being unfaithful. From these types of data, extrapolations are made to a wider population. Although such an approach may be useful for many topics, it seems questionable with regard to extrapartnership sexual liaisons. Among the key issues here are the respondents' age and experience. Certainly it seems dubious to take the views and perspectives of people who have relatively little—and sometimes no—experience of long-term committed relationships as being indicative of the views of a wider population with its quite diverse histories of relationship commitment, especially about a subject matter that resonates with moral injunctive.

As important, research concerned with partnership infidelity that relies on hypothetical responses to presented scenarios, as much experimental research on undergraduate populations does, can also be questioned. Although this is an established and useful procedure for many topics, its utility for discerning people's actual responses to direct or indirect involvement in partnership infidelity is limited. What we undoubtedly need are more studies that focus on real rather than hypothetical extradyadic involvement. Obtaining an adequate sample of those with such experience is certainly difficult. In particular, why should those whose extrapartnership involvement remains covert choose to reveal their emotions, activities, and histories for the sake of scientific knowledge? Even if the extrapartnership involvement is more openly known, not everyone would choose to share his or her experiences about such a personal and private issue. Paradoxically though, it is precisely because of the sensitive and morally charged nature of these experiences that reliance on data derived from hypothetical constructions of them is so questionable.

Data drawn from clinical populations are also problematic for a range of reasons, including the selectivity of those who end up undertaking some form of counseling after direct or indirect experience of extrapartnership involvement. However, studies based on clinical populations frequently have the advantage of being able to focus on process rather than relying on onetime accounts. It would seem imperative that we have fuller accounts of the processes involved in extrapartnership liaisons if we are to understand them adequately, not least when the focus is on hurt and other emotional impacts. To begin with, we need to know more than we currently do about the natural histories of different forms of extradyadic involvements, whether these be short lived or long term, emotionally empty or emotionally charged, known about or secret, a single episode/relationship or serial infidelity. We need to understand better the structural and contextual factors that influence their different pathways and how decisions are made by those involved about their relationships' continuation or ending.

In this regard, there would be many benefits from having a longitudinal research design, though the practical difficulties of ever conducting such studies, given the secrecy surrounding many extrapartnership liaisons, are huge. Such a longitudinal design could focus not only on the natural histories of the extradyadic relationships but also on the longer term consequences for the committed partnerships, including how successful couples are in their various attempts to repair any damage done to their relationship by the extradyadic liaison. The key issue here is that people's emotional responses to significant episodes in their lives are not static; their understandings change over time, for better or worse, as they reflect on the issues involved and gain further insight into them. Thus, whether directly or indirectly involved in the extradyadic relationship, their interpretation and emotional responses to the liaison are emergent over time and not necessarily consistent.

In particular, the emotions aroused when a partner comes to learn about an extradyadic involvement, the hurt and distress experienced, the arguments, rows, and discussions, as well as the resulting calm or resolution that follows, are dynamic and consequential. Frequently, especially when the infidelity has been prolonged and emotionally meaningful, the significance of past events and the accounts given of them are reconsidered, mulled over, and in the process reinterpreted (Olson et al., 2002). In turn, these emotionally charged musings and reinterpretations serve to generate new understandings of the infidelity, its history, and consequences for the existing relationship. Such account construction is central to the generally fluid process that informs future attitudes, decisions, and actions (Weber, 1992). Consequently we need to research individuals' emergent accounts of their experiences—whether direct or indirect—as they are key to the construction of whatever resolution is realized. A longitudinal design allows them to be studied as process rather than as single "fixed" accounts.

CONCLUSION

If relational transgression is accepted as being a prime component of hurt feelings, then as noted earlier extradyadic involvement is a particularly apt phenomenon for examining processes of hurt. What makes it especially relevant is the fact that it involves actions as much as words. The hurt experienced is not just a consequence of people saying hurtful things; it arises from their behavioral acts transgressing their agreed relationship expectations. Although current research has focused on hurt experienced as a result of extradyadic involvement, much of it has been specifically concerned with jealousy, an important though partial aspect of the hurt feelings that can be provoked. And as discussed in the previous section, some of the studies investigating jealousy are open to question for drawing conclusions from what are effectively hypothetical data.

It would be valuable to have more analyses of the hurt experienced by all those involved in extradyadic relationships, despite the many methodological difficulties entailed in such research. Currently the focus tends to be on the betrayed party. In some cases those who are betrayed are the only ones who experience hurt as a result of the extradyadic liaison. But in other cases, those directly involved may also feel degrees of emotional pain. Whether this pain is defined as "hurt" depends on the breadth of definition used. But if the emotionally disruptive consequences of extradyadic relationships are to be understood properly, then the responses of the different actors as the events unfold all need to be studied. Although not discussed explicitly in this chapter, this would also include any hurt experienced by children as a consequence of parental discord arising from the extradyadic involvement.

From a social science perspective, it is important to research the bases of the hurt that extradyadic involvement creates, including its personal, cultural, and historical variations. But it is equally important that the resolutions to such hurt are better understood. Often, of course, the outcome is separation or divorce. In other cases though, the relationship is sustained, perhaps with renegotiated understandings of its framing. How long the hurt is experienced, how it is overcome, whether levels of trust are reestablished, what strategies are used to achieve a form of reconciliation, and the like are all key questions that warrant further research. Moreover in an era of rapid change in normative expectations of sexuality and intimacy, shifts in the patterning of hurt generated through extradyadic relationships also comprises an important topic for future research.

REFERENCES

Allan, G. (2004). Being unfaithful: His and her affairs. In J. Duncombe, K. Harrison, G. Allan, & D. Marsden (Eds.), *The state of affairs: Explorations in infidelity and commitment* (pp. 121–140). Mahwah, NJ: Erlbaum.

Allan, G., & Harrison, K. (2002). Marital affairs. In R. Goodwin & D. Cramer (Eds.), *Inappropriate relationships* (pp. 45–63). Mahwah, NJ: Erlbaum.

Allen, E. S., Atkins, D. G, Baucom, D. H., Snyder, D. K., Gordon, K. C., & Glass, S. P. (2005). Intrapersonal, interpersonal, and contextual factors in engaging in and responding to extramarital involvement. *Clinical Psychology-Science and Practice, 12,* 101–130.

Amato, P. R., & Previti, D. (2003). People's reasons for divorcing: Gender, social class, the life course, and adjustment. *Journal of Family Issues,* 24, 602–626.

Becker, D. V., Sagarin, B. J., Guadagno, R. E., Millevoi, A., & Nicastle, L. D. (2004). When the sexes need not differ: Emotional responses to the sexual and emotional aspects of infidelity. *Personal Relationships, 11,* 529–538.

Boekhout, B. A., Hendrick, S. S., &Hendrick, C. (1999). Relationship infidelity: A loss perspective. *Journal of Personal and Interpersonal Loss, 4,* 97–123.

Buss, D. M., Larsen, R. J., Westen, D., & Semmelrofh, J. (1992). Sex differences in jealousy: Evolution, physiology, and psychology. *Psychological Science,* 3, 251- 255.

Buunk, B. P., & Dijkstra, P. (2004). Men, women and infidelity: Sex differences in extradyadic sex and jealousy. In J. Duncombe, K. Harrison, G. Allan, & D. Marsden (Eds.), *The state of affairs: Explorations in infidelity and commitment* (pp. 103–120). Mahwah, NJ: Erlbaum.

Buunk, B. P., & Dijkstra, P. (2006). Temptations and threat: Extradyadic relations and jealousy. In A. L.Vangelisti & D. Perlman (Eds.), *The Cambridge handbook of personal relationships* (pp. 533–555). New York: Cambridge University Press.

Cancian, F. (1987). *Love in America: Gender and self-development.* New York: Cambridge University Press.

Cann, A., Mangum, J. L., & Wells, M. (2001). Distress in response to relationship infidelity: The roles of gender and attitudes about relationships. *Journal of Sex Research, 38,*185–190.

Cherlin, A. J. (2004). The deinstitutionalization of American marriage. *Journal of Marriage and Family, 66,* 848–861.

Cramer, R. E., Abraham, W. T., Johnson, L. M., & Manning-Ryan, B. (2001). Gender differences in subjective distress to emotional and sexual infidelity: Evolutionary or logical inference explanation? *Current Psychology, 20,*327–336.

DeSteno, D. A., Bartlett, M. Y., Salovey, P., & Braverman, J. (2002). Sex differences in jealousy: Evolutionary mechanism or artifact of measurement? *Journal of Personality and Social Psychology, 83,*1103–1116.

DeSteno, D. A., & Salovey, P. (1996). Evolutionary origins of sex differences in jealousy? Questioning the "fitness" of the model. *Psychological Science,* 7, 367–372.

Feeney, J. A. (2005). Hurt feelings in couple relationships: Exploring the role of attachment and perceptions of personal injury. *Personal Relationships, 12,* 253- 271.

Giddens, A. (1992). *The transformation of intimacy.* Cambridge: Polity Press.

Guerrero, L., Spitzberg, B. H., & Yoshimura, S. (2004). Sexual and emotional jealousy. In J. Harvey, A. Wenzel, & S. Sprecher (Eds.), *The handbook of sexuality in close relationships* (pp. 311–345). Mahwah, NJ: Erlbaum.

Haavio-Mannila, E., & Kontula, O. (2003). Single and double sexual standards in Finland Estonia, and St. Petersburg. *Journal of Sex Research, 40,*36–49.

Harris, C. R. (2003). A review of sex differences in sexual jealousy, including self-report data, psychophysiological responses, interpersonal violence, and morbid jealousy. *Personality and Social Psychology Review,* 7,102–128.

Johnson, M. P. (1995). Patriarchal terrorism and common couple violence: Two forms of violence against women. *Journal of Marriage and the Family) 57,* 283–294.

Knapp, M. (2006). Lying and deception in close relationships. In A. L. Vangelisti & D. Permian (Eds.), *The Cambridge handbook of personal relationships* (pp. 517—532). New York: Cambridge University Press.

Kontula, O., & Haavio-Mannila, E. (2004). Renaissance of romanticism in the era of increasing individualism. In J. Duncombe, K. Harrison, G. Allan, & D. Marsden (Eds.), *The state of affairs: Explorations in infidelity and commitment* (pp.; 79–102). Mahwah, NJ: Erlbaum.

Laumann, E., Gagnon, J., Michael, R.> & Michaels, S. (1994). *The social organization of sexuality: Sexual practices in the United States.* Chicago: University of Chicago Press.

Lawson, A. (1988). *Adultery: An analysis of love and betrayal.* New York: Basic Books.

Leary, M. R. (2001). Toward a conceptualization of interpersonal rejection. In M. R. Leary (Ed.), *Interpersonal rejection* (pp. 3–20). New York: Oxford University.

Leary, M. R., & Springer, C. A. (2001). Hurt feelings: The neglected emotion. In R.M. Kowalski (Ed.), *Behaving badly: Aversive behaviors in interpersonal relationships* (pp. 151–175). Washington, DC: American Psychological Association.

Leary, M. R., Springer, C, Negel, L., Ansell, E., & Evans, K, (1998). The causes, phenomenology, and consequences of hurt feelings. *Journal of Personality and Social Psychology, 74,*1225–1237.

Olson, M. M., Russell, C. S., Higgins-Kessler, M., & Miller, R. B. (2002). Emotional processes following disclosure of an extramarital affair. *Journal of Marital and Family Therapy, 28,* 423–434.

Orbuch, T. (1992). A symbolic interactionist approach to the study of relationship loss. In T. Orbuch (Ed.), *Close relationship loss: Theoretical approaches* (pp. 192–204). New York: Springer-Verlag.

Reibstein, J., & Richards, M. (1992). *Sexual arrangements: Marriage and affairs.* London: Heinemann.

Richardson, L. (1985). *The new other woman: Contemporary single women in affairs with married men.* New York: Free Press.

Richardson, L. (1988). Sexual freedom and sexual constraint: The paradox for single women in liaisons with married men. *Gender and Society, 2,* 368–384.

Smock, P. (2004). The wax and wane of marriage: Prospects for marriage in the 21st century. *Journal of Marriage and Family, 66,* 966–973.

Treas, J., & Giesen, D. (2000). Sexual infidelity among married and cohabiting Americans. *Journal of Marriage and the Family, 62,* 48–60.

Vangelisti, A. L. (1994). Messages that hurt. In W. R. Cupach 8c B. H. Spitzberg (Eds.), *The dark side of interpersonal communication* (pp. 53–82). Hillsdale, NJ: Erlbaum.

Vangelisti, A. L. (2001). Making sense of hurtful interactions in close relationships. In V. Manusov & J. H. Harvey (Eds.), *Attribution, communication behavior and close relationships* (pp. 38–58). New York: Cambridge University Press.

Vangelisti, A. L., & Gerstenberger, M. (2004). Communication and marital infidelity. In J. Duncombe, K. Harrison, G. Allan, 8c D. Marsden (Eds.), *The state of affairs: Explorations in infidelity and commitment* (pp. 59–78). Mahwah, NJ: Erlbaum.

Weber, A. (1992). An account-making process: A phenomenological approach. In T, Orbuch (Ed.), *Close relationship loss: Theoretical approaches* (pp. 174–191). New York: Springer-Verlag.

Weeks, J., Heaphy, B., & Donovan, C. (2001). *Same sex intimacies: Families of choice and other life experiments.* London: Routledge.

Wellings, K., Fields, J., Johnson, A., &Wadsworth, J. (1994). *Sexual behaviour in Britain.* London: Penguin.
White, G. L. (1981). Jealousy and partner's perceived motives for attraction to a rival. *Social Psychology Quarterly, 44,* 24–30.
Wiederman, M. W. (1997). Extramarital sex: Prevalence and correlates in a national survey. *Journal of Sex Research, 34,*167–174.

Sex Differences in Jealousy

A Matter of Evolution or Attachment History?

By Kenneth N. Levy, Kristen M. Kelly, and Ejay L. Jack

Jealousy is a powerful and painful emotion with pernicious effects on romantic relationships (White & Mullen, 1989). It has been implicated as the leading cause of spouse battering and homicide across many cultures (Daly & Wilson, 1988; Gibbens, 1958; Wolfgang, 1958). Historically, jealousy has been conceptualized as a consequence of low self-esteem or even neurosis (Mathes, Phillips, Skowron, & Dick, 1982; Pines & Aronson, 1983). Nearly two-thirds of romantic couples reported that jealousy posed a significant problem in their relationship, sometimes leading to assaults or battery (Gayford, 1975, 1979). Research has linked spousal abuse, rapes, and stalking behavior to feelings of jealousy (Davis, Ace, & Andra, 2000; Dutton, van Ginkel, & Landolt, 1996; Tjaden & Thoennes, 1998). If jealousy can be understood through developmental analysis rather than attributed to biological evolution, it might be easier to manage through education and clinical treatment. Although evolutionary psychologists (e.g., Thornhill & Palmer, 2000) have argued that evolutionary analyses of sex differences in socially undesirable behaviors do not imply that the behaviors cannot be socially controlled, viewing these behaviors as strongly attributable to evolved genetic mechanisms clearly makes them seem virtually inevitable and hence difficult to change.

Evolutionary psychologists have distinguished between two kinds of jealousy: sexual and emotional (e.g., Buss, Larsen, Westen, & Semmelroth, 1992). Sexual jealousy is evoked by a perceived threat concerning a partner's sexual infidelity, whereas emotional jealousy arises from a perceived threat of a partner's emotional infidelity. Sexual jealousy is reportedly more common in men than in women. Across a wide variety of cultures, men are more likely than women to divorce partners who are sexually unfaithful (Betzig, 1989) and even to batter and kill such partners (Daly & Wilson, 1988). Given the seriousness and pervasiveness of these effects of male sexual jealousy, it is important to understand its causes and dynamics. In this chapter we argue that attachment theory provides a framework for understanding jealousy and for changing attitudes and beliefs in ways that may reduce the tragic consequences of jealousy that occurs in the context of romantic relationships.

THE EVOLUTIONARY EXPLANATION OF SEX DIFFERENCES IN JEALOUSY

David Buss and his colleagues have offered an evolutionary explanation of sex differences in jealousy. They and other proponents of the evolutionary perspective assert that men and women evolved different sexual strategies (Buss, 1995; Daly & Wilson, 1988; Daly, Wilson, & Weghorst, 1982; Symons, 1979). For male mammals, gamete production is relatively inexpensive, because sperm are continuously and copiously produced. For female mammals, however, gamete production is more limited, there being only a few hundred gametes that become mature over a female's relatively short reproductive life cycle. Thus, even at the time of fertilization, women have contributed a greater proportion of net resources to future offspring than men have; women typically go on to invest more bodily resources in nursing and caring for offspring than men do. From these facts, evolutionary psychologists conclude that there is likely to be conflict between men and women due to differences in their mating strategies (Buss, 1995). Men can maximize their evolutionary fitness by impregnating as many women as possible while investing as little as possible in rearing any individual offspring. In contrast, women can maximize their fitness by carefully choosing a mating partner who will maximize their offspring's survival by providing support, protection, and "good genes" that get passed on to offspring. For women, it matters a great deal that some men more than others may be willing to provide the extended support and biparental care that increase the likelihood of offspring survival and health.

These differences in reproductive strategies are thought by evolutionary psychologists to produce inherent sex differences in types of jealousy. Whereas women bear the greater reproductive costs, the fact that fertilization occurs inside a woman's body means that men have always faced a profound adaptive problem not faced by women: uncertainty of paternity. Women are virtually certain which offspring are their own, but DNA studies indicate that between 9 and 13% of children have a putative father who is not the man who impregnated their mother (Baker & Bellis, 1995). Being uncertain of paternity presents substantial reproductive costs to men in the form of time, energy, nuptial gifts, and opportunity costs. The adaptive problem of uncertain paternity is exacerbated in species such as ours in which males often engage in post fertilization parental investment (Trivers, 1972). A man risks investing resources in a putative child who is not (genetically speaking) his own, thereby investing in another male's offspring while reducing his own evolutionary fitness. Evolutionary psychologists believe that male sexual jealousy evolved as a solution to this problem (Wilson & Daly, 1992).

In contrast, although women do not experience much uncertainty with regard to maternity, they do risk losing time, resources, and commitment from a man if he deserts her or channels investments to alternative mates (Trivers, 1972). Therefore, the evolutionary story says, women exercise more vigilance to prevent other women from absconding with their mates, rather than responding to specific acts of sexual infidelity, because a man's continued presence aids in successfully rearing offspring. Consistent with this notion that men are more bothered by sexual infidelity and women by emotional infidelity or loss of interest and commitment, research has found that men across a wide variety of cultures are more likely than women to divorce partners who are sexually unfaithful (Betzig, 1989) and possibly to batter or even kill partners who are unfaithful (Daly & Wilson, 1988). Conversely, women manifest greater distress while imagining their male partner's emotional infidelity (Buss et al., 1992), viewed as an important warning sign that their mate may withdraw his resources from the relationship and child.

In two large-sample tests of this line of reasoning, Buss et al. (1992) found that men tend to view sexual infidelity as more distressful than women do, and women tend to view emotional infidelity as more distressful. They also found that men displayed greater physiological distress than did women while imagining a mate's sexual infidelity, as reflected by increased electromyographic activity (i.e., muscle tension), increased electrodermal response (indicating autonomic arousal), and elevated heart rate.

These findings have been replicated by other researchers in the United States, Germany, the Netherlands, and China (Buunk, Angleiter, Oubaid, & Buss, 1996; Geary, Rumsey, Bow-Thomas, & Hoard, 1995; Wiederman & Allgeier, 1993). Buss and his colleagues (Buss, Kirkpatrick, Shackelford, & Bennett, 1996) interpret the cross-cultural replicability of the sex differences as good evidence for their basis in genes and evolution.

ALTERNATIVES TO THE EVOLUTIONARY PERSPECTIVE

A number of researchers have challenged the evolutionary interpretation of sex differences in jealousy (DeSteno & Salovey, 1996a; Harris, 2003; Harris & Christenfeld, 1996; Rabinowitz & Valian, 2000). First, although cross-cultural data are crucial for testing the evolutionary hypothesis, they alone are not sufficient to support it. Second, it is especially important to rule out plausible alternative explanations in quasi-experimental studies such as these, in which biological sex serves as the independent variable, because men and women obviously cannot be randomly assigned to male and female conditions. In such studies, unmeasured variables are major threats to the validity of results and can lead to accepting spurious findings (Abelson, 1995). Third-variable correlations often cannot be accounted for, so it is quite possible that the replicable sex differences in types of jealousy are a result of other, nongenetic variables. Third, although a higher percentage of men than women report being more distressed by sexual infidelity, in many studies the majority of both genders are more distressed by emotional infidelity (Buss et al., 1992; Buunk et al., 1996; Geary et al., 1995; Wiederman & Allgeier, 1993). For instance, American men are equally divided on which form of infidelity is more distressing; the majority of Chinese, Dutch, and German men find emotional infidelity more distressing (see Buller, 2005, for a review). Thus Buss's theory does not fully or conclusively explain the data, and there are a number of reasonable alternative hypotheses. An evolutionary perspective on sex differences in jealousy cannot, without invoking additional constructs, explain these international differences within the sexes. Finally, evolutionary psychologists make "predictions" about events that have already occurred, based on assumptions and inferences about environments that generally cannot be tested. For instance, Eagly and Wood (1999) found a great deal of cross-cultural variability in the relative contributions of men and women to subsistence, with women sometimes contributing more. This variability makes it difficult to infer from evidence at hand what conditions prevailed for our ancestors.

TESTS OF ALTERNATIVE THEORIES

DeSteno and Salovey (1996a, 1996b) and Harris and Christenfeld (1996) considered most of the alternative explanations of sex differences in jealousy. Harris and Christenfeld's (1996) "rational belief hypothesis" suggests that sex differences may be based on a difference between the sexes in how they interpret evidence of infidelity, that is, a difference in reasoning or in operative rationality. They argue that, for cultural reasons, men are more likely to believe that women engage in sexual behavior when in love; and conversely, women are more likely to believe that men engage in sexual behavior independently of love. Thus men are more bothered by sexual infidelity because it signals that their mate has fallen in love with another man. Women, in contrast, may be bothered by sexual infidelity less than by emotional infidelity because sexual infidelity alone does not necessarily mean that her mate has fallen in love with someone else. These authors found support for their hypothesis in a survey of 137 people (Harris & Christenfeld, 1996). DeSteno and Salovey (1996a) proposed a "double-shot hypothesis." They contended that beliefs about types of infidelity are not as separable as might be expected. Instead, they argued, sex differences are due to different beliefs about the conditional probabilities that either sexual or emotional infidelity implies the occurrence of the other kind of infidelity. They found that both men and women selected the infidelity event that they believed was more likely to signal the concurrence of the other type of infidelity as well. Additionally, women more than men believed that emotional infidelity implied sexual infidelity. Thus the forced-choice dichotomy used by Buss and colleagues to study jealousy may not actually separate two interrelated kinds of jealousy.

It is important to realize, however, that the rational-belief and double-shot hypotheses do not explain cultural variation in sex differences in types of jealousy (Buss, Larsen, & Westen, 1996). Buss and colleagues noted that both hypotheses wrongly imply that socialization rather than genetics is the causal agent responsible for observed sex differences. They pointed out that biologically evolved sex differences might, in fact, explain the processes responsible for the rational-belief and double-shot phenomena. In support of their arguments, a recent series of empirical studies controlling for the correlated nature of infidelity types failed to replicate the findings reported by Harris and Christenfeld (1996) and DeSteno and Salovey (1996; Buss et al., 1999). The continued failure to resolve the debate between groups of theorists who favor an evolutionary explanation of sex differences in jealousy and groups who favor a nonbiological explanation suggests a need for a theory that explains both between- and within-sex differences, that distinguishes between socially and genetically mediated conditional probabilities of various implications of acts of infidelity, and that reveals why men often find sexual infidelity more distressing than emotional infidelity, whereas women often find emotional infidelity more distressing.

Rabinowitz and Valian (2000) and Eagly and Wood (1999) offered additional alternative explanations for sex differences in jealousy. They suggested that the differences are rooted in social and economic structures and the associated internalization of and adherence to gender roles. Although Eagly and Wood (1999) provided evidence for certain parts of their critique of evolutionary psychological theories (showing, for example, that there is a great deal of cross-cultural variability in the relative contributions of men and women to subsistence, with women sometimes contributing more), there have been no direct tests of their account of sex differences in jealousy.

ATTACHMENT PROCESSES AS THE ALTERNATIVE EXPLANATION

Bowlby's (1969, 1973, 1980) attachment theory offers a parsimonious alternative explanation for the existence of sex differences in jealousy. According to the theory, the affective bond that develops between the child and caretaker affects the child's emerging self-concept and view of the social world. Bowlby (1969) conceptualized human motivation in terms of "behavioral systems," a concept borrowed from ethology, and proposed that attachment-related behavior in infancy (e.g., clinging, crying, smiling, monitoring caregivers, and developing a preference for a few reliable caregivers or "attachment figures") is part of a functional biological system that increases the likelihood of protection from predation, provides comfort during times of stress, and offers a foundation for social learning. Central to attachment theory is the concept of internal working models—mental representations formed through repeated transactions with attachment figures. These working models subsequently act as heuristic guides through the world of relationships and organize personality development.

Based on Bowlby's theory, Ainsworth and her coworkers (Ainsworth, Blehar, Waters, & Wall, 1978) identified three major styles of attachment in infancy—secure, avoidant, and anxious-ambivalent—and traced these styles to caregivers' behavior. Subsequently, Hazan and Shaver (1987) extended Ainsworth's framework to the study of romantic love, which they conceptualized as an attachment process. They created a pencil-and-paper measure of adult attachment styles, which asked respondents to say which of three descriptions of relationship styles fit them best: secure, avoidant, or anxious-ambivalent. In a host of studies conducted since 1987, this brief measure and various extensions of it have significantly predicted relationship outcomes (e.g., satisfaction, breakups, commitment), patterns of coping with stress, couple communication, and even phenomena such as religious experiences and patterns of career development (see reviews by Shaver & Hazan, 1993, and Mikulincer & Shaver, 2003).

Bartholomew (Bartholomew & Horowitz, 1991) revised Hazan and Shaver's (1987) three-category classification scheme, proposing a four-category model that differentiated between two types of avoidant adults: fearful and dismissive. Consistent with Bowlby's (1969) analysis of working models of self and relationship partners, the four categories could be arrayed in a two-dimensional space, with one dimension being "model of self" (positive vs. negative) and the other being "model of others" (positive vs. negative). For secure individuals, the models of self and other are both positive. For anxious-ambivalent (or preoccupied, to use Bartholomew and Horowitz's term) individuals, the model of others is positive (i.e., relationships are attractive), but the model of self is not. For dismissing individuals, the reverse is true: The somewhat defensively maintained model of self is positive, whereas the model of others is not (i.e., intimacy in relationships is regarded with caution or avoided). Fearful individuals have relatively negative models of both self and others.

Attachment research indicates that attachment styles are mainly attributable to experiences in close relationships, not to genes. Numerous studies have linked children's developing attachment patterns to patterns of parenting behavior (see Main, 1995, for a review), but researchers have failed to find genetic influences on children's attachment styles (e.g., Bokhorst et al., 2003). The stability or instability of attachment patterns across the childhood and adolescent years is largely attributable to stability or instability of relationships with attachment figures during that same period (see Fraley, 2002, for a review). Moreover, adult romantic attachment styles are related to people's descriptions of childhood relationships with parents (e.g., Levy, Blatt, & Shaver, 1998) and can change systematically over time as a function of relationship experiences (e.g., Kirkpatrick & Hazan, 1994). In addition, behavior genetic studies of relationship styles in adult twins show that these styles are attributable more to environmental factors than to genetic factors (e.g., Waller & Shaver, 1992).

Although there are no replicable sex differences in attachment security measured in infancy or in adulthood, there are sex differences among the insecure styles that may help explain sex differences in jealousy. More men than women have an insecure dismissive-avoidant attachment style (e.g., Bartholomew & Horowitz, 1991; Levy et al., 1998; Shaver et al., 1996). Dismissive-avoidant individuals tend to be unemotional, to deny their needs for intimacy, to be strongly invested in autonomy, and to exhibit greater sexual promiscuity (e.g., Bartholomew & Horowitz, 1991; Brennan & Shaver, 1995; Schachner & Shaver, 2002, 2004; Simpson, 1990). However, this counter dependent and compulsively self-reliant style is not as strong as its possessors let on. Instead, it appears to be a defense against unconscious feelings of vulnerability (e.g., Bowlby, 1988; Mikulincer, Dolev, & Shaver, 2004).

ATTACHMENT STYLE AND SEX DIFFERENCES IN JEALOUSY

Recognizing the limitations discussed earlier concerning simple evolutionary models of sex differences in jealousy, we (Levy & Kelly, 2006) proposed an attachment theory perspective on sex differences in jealousy. We hypothesized that observed sex differences in types of jealousy were actually due to sex differences in adult romantic attachment style. First of all, we hypothesized, in line with most of the previous research, that there would be a significant sex difference in the type of jealousy that was experienced as most distressing. Second, we predicted a significant difference between men and women in the degree of dismissive attachment, with men being more dismissive than women. Although sex differences in attachment security in infancy and early childhood are not theoretically predicted in attachment theory, by late adolescence and early adulthood, sex differences in attachment are typically found when using the self-report romantic attachment measures typically employed by personality and social psychologists. More men are found to be dismissing, and more women are found to be preoccupied. Gender-specific parental socialization practices may contribute to these gender differences in attachment style. For example, research has shown that parents use more positive emotion words in conversation and joint play with their girl children than with their boy children (Dunn, Bretherton, & Munn, 1987; Fivush, Brotman, Buckner, & Goodman, 2000; Goodnow, 1988). Over time, the cumulative absences of such experiences may result in a greater likelihood of dismissive attachment for men. Additionally, with progressive development, gender roles may be increasingly internalized. However, the data are mixed with regard to the influence of gender roles. For example, Shaver et al. (1996) found that feminine gender roles were negatively correlated with avoidance; however, Servello and Bartholomew (1996) were unable to confirm a relationship between gender roles and dismissive attachment in men (although gender role was related to preoccupied attachment in women). These findings suggest a link between gender roles and attachment patterns but indicate that other factors are also likely to be influential in explaining sex differences in adult attachment.

Third, we expected a significant difference in reactions to different jealousy-provoking situations between people with different attachment styles. Specifically, we expected dismissive individuals to find sexual infidelity more distressing and securely attached individuals to find emotional infidelity more distressing. There are two main reasons for hypothesizing that dismissive individuals would find sexual infidelity more distressing. First, previous research has found that dismissive individuals, compared with people with the other attachment styles, tend to be more concerned with the sexual aspects of relationships than with emotional intimacy (Schachner & Shaver, 2004)[1] For example, dismissive men report more sexual interests in extradyadic relationships, more promiscuous behavior, and poaching the mates of others, and they are more likely to describe relationship partners in terms of physical and sexual attributes rather than internal and emotional ones (Allen & Baucom, 2004; Schachner & Shaver, 2002; Simpson & Gangestad, 1991). Additionally, dismissive men report a short-term, low investment exploitive sexual strategy that includes engaging in sexual behavior to regulate negative affect and to control and coerce others (Davis, Shaver, & Vernon, 2004; Levy, 1990, 1999). Second, consistent with psychodynamic theories of projection, research has shown that dismissive individuals are more likely to engage in defensive projection of negative information about the self, which seems also to serve the secondary purpose of maintaining interpersonal distance (Mikulincer & Horesh, 1999). Taking these points together, we hypothesized that dismissive individuals would be more concerned about their partner's sexual investments than their partner's emotional investments. In addition, they were expected to be more likely to project their own motives and interests in extradyadic relationships onto their partners. Thus differences in jealousy that appear to be rooted in sex differences might actually reflect differences in attachment style. That is, dismissing individuals, who are more likely to be men, might be more likely to report jealousy regarding sexual infidelity. In contrast, secure individuals, regardless of sex, were hypothesized to be more likely to experience jealousy in response to a partner's emotional infidelity.

Using the Buss Infidelity Questionnaire (Buss et al., 1992) and Bartholomew's Relationship Questionnaire (Bartholomew & Horowitz, 1991), we assessed 416 undergraduate students enrolled in introductory psychology classes at two large northeastern urban universities. As predicted, we replicated Buss et al.'s (1992) finding of sex differences in jealousy reactions to sexual and emotional infidelity. Men were more likely to find sexual rather than emotional infidelity distressing, and women were more likely to find emotional infidelity rather than sexual infidelity distressing. In our study, this difference, shown in Table 6.1, was highly significant, $\chi^2(1) = 29.93, p < .001$.

Also, as predicted, we found a significant sex difference in the distribution of attachment types, $\chi^2(3) = 10.67, p < .01$. Men were more likely than women to exhibit dismissive attachment, and women were slightly more likely than men to exhibit fearful attachment (Figure 6.1).

TABLE 6.1. Relation between Sex and Type of Jealousy Experienced as Most Distressing

	Sex			
Jealousy type	Male	Female	Row total	
Emotional	44 (18.1) (46.5%)	240 (81.9) (75.7%)	284	100%
Sexual	55 (44.4) (53.5%)	77 (53.3) (24.3%)	132	100%
Column total	99 (27.0%) 100.0%	317 (73.0%) 100.0%	416 100.0%	100%

Note: Cell entries are n's, row percentages, and column percentages. $\chi^2(1) = 29.93, p < .001$. Data from Levy and Kelly (2006).

These results are consistent with previous research, in which men were more likely than women to be dismissingly avoidant in attachment style (Brennan, Shaver, & Tobey, 1991; Brennan & Morris, 1997; Levy et al., 1998; Shaver et al., 1996). Consistent with our (Levy & Kelly, 2006) main hypothesis that sex differences in jealousy would be explicable in terms of differences in attachment style, we found that dismissive individuals, who were more likely to be men, were also more likely to report distress regarding sexual infidelity (Figure 6.2).

In contrast, secure individuals, including secure men, reported more jealousy than did dismissive individuals in response to emotional infidelity (Figure 6.3). In line with our reasoning, we (Levy & Kelly, 2006) also found that the association between dismissive attachment and sexual jealousy was significant for both men and women, $\chi^2(3)$ - 27.84, $p < .001$, and $\chi^2(3) = 16.29, p < .001$, respectively.

We computed odds ratios separately for each variable to evaluate the specific effects of sex and attachment style on jealousy. Overall, men were between three and four times more likely than women to endorse sexual jealousy. However, when odds ratios were computed separately by attachment style, the sex differences in jealousy for secure and preoccupied individuals were weak and not significant according to simple chi-square tests. The sex differences in jealousy were dramatically heightened, however, in the fearful and dismissive groups, with men being roughly 5 and 26 times, respectively, more likely to endorse sexual jealousy. A Mantel-Haenszel test showed that the odds ratios, taken together, were significantly greater than 1, consistent with a main effect of sex on jealousy type, $\chi^2(1) = 24.07, p < .001$. However, the Breslow-Day test suggested significant heterogeneity between the stratified odds ratios, $\chi^2(3) = 8.03, p < .05$, consistent with a moderating effect of attachment style on the relationship between sex and jealousy type. Odds ratio analyses also revealed the importance of attachment style overall, and within each sex,

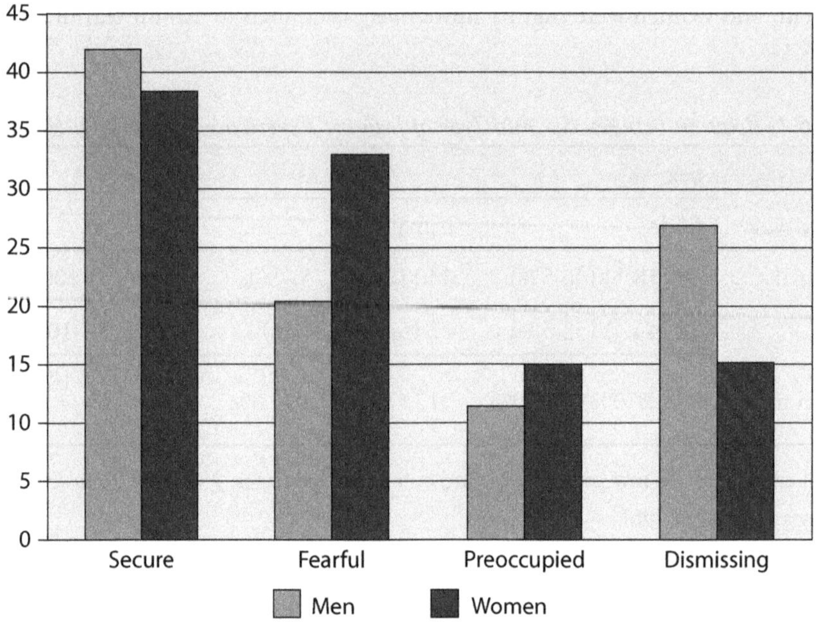

FIGURE 6.1. *Percentage of each of four attachment styles in samples of men and women. Data from Levy and Kelly (2006)*

especially with regard to secure versus dismissing styles. Dismissive women, for example, were roughly 4 times more likely to endorse sexual jealousy than were their secure counterparts, whereas dismissive men were nearly 50 times more likely than secure men to endorse sexual jealousy. Simple chi-square analyses were significant for the relationship between overall attachment style and jealousy for both sexes.

To determine the relative strength of effect of each variable, as well as the significance of the moderating effect, we (Levy & Kelly, 2006) performed a series of sequential logistic regression analyses, which revealed that sex and attachment style were both significant predictors of jealousy individually and, after accounting for the effects of the other variable, consistent with independent main effects for each. The interaction term led to significant improvement in the model over and above sex and attachment style variables, suggesting significant moderation of the sex-jealousy relationship by attachment style. The full model, containing both variables and the interaction term, was statistically reliable when compared with a constant-only model, $\chi^2(7, n = 411) = 75.70, p < .001$, and performed well, correctly classifying 75% of cases according to jealousy type.

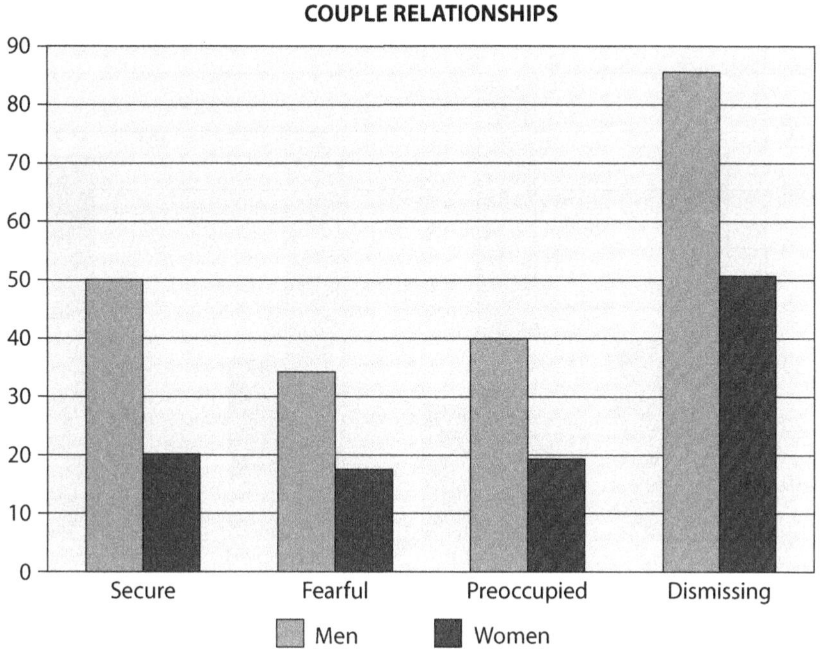

FIGURE 6.2. *Percentage of respondents in each attachment-style category who were more distressed by sexual than by emotional infidelity. Data from Levy and Kelly (2006).*

IMPLICATIONS AND CONCLUSIONS

Levy and Kelly's (2006) findings suggest that observed sex differences in jealousy are more complex than simple evolutionary models imply. Although Buss and colleagues (Buss et al., 1992; Buss, Larsen, & Westen, 1996) found that men are more likely than women to find sexual infidelity more distressing than emotional infidelity, there is no evidence that this replicable sex difference is due solely to biological sex. Levy and Kelly's findings indicate that adult romantic attachment style plays an important part in determining which kind of infidelity elicits more jealousy. Secure individuals, including secure men, are more likely to find emotional infidelity than sexual infidelity distressful, whereas dismissing individuals, especially dismissing men, are more likely to find sexual infidelity to be the bigger problem. The psychological and cultural/environmental mechanisms underlying sex differences in jealousy may be more important than evolutionary psychologists have supposed. Nevertheless, our findings do not completely rule out Buss's hypothesis, because a significant sex difference in jealousy type remained even after controlling for the contribution of attachment style. Both sex and attachment style differences made significant unique and interactive contributions to the distress caused by sexual and emotional infidelity. However, it is also important to keep in mind that sex differences may not

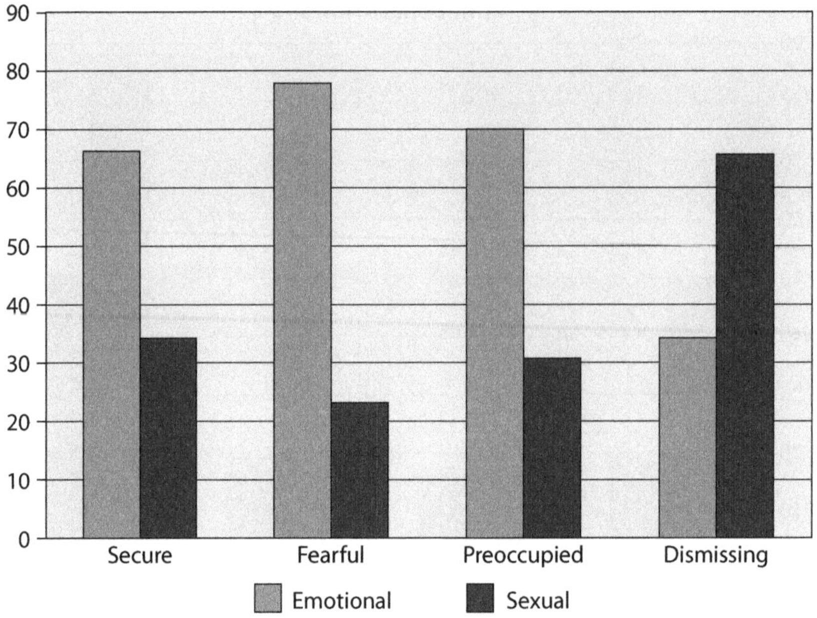

FIGURE 6.3. *Percentage of respondents in each attachment-style category who were more distressed by sexual or by emotional infidelity. Data from Levy and Kelly (2006).*

operate as Buss and colleagues suggest but could be the function of a variable that covaries with sex, such as gender role identification (Rabinowitz & Valian, 2000).

We are not opposed to evolutionary perspectives in general: Attachment theory is, in fact, an evolutionary, ethological theory. However, we are concerned with the way evolutionary theory has been applied to explain a broad array of complex human behaviors in close relationships, such as romantic attraction, parenting, gender differences, and emotions such as jealousy. We believe that current discussions of evolved sex differences in jealousy could easily lead to a misunderstanding of evolutionary theory.

First, evolutionary theory holds that an organism's survival potential is enhanced by being supple and responsive to the environment rather than being as rigid as evolutionary psychologists typically portray it. Organisms need to be sensitive to cues from the environment, as well as flexible and adaptable in response to a wide range of environmental phenomena (Buller, 2005). For example, if maternal rejection is induced by a competitive social situation, offspring who develop aggressive, nonaltruistic, or "dismissing" personality styles may do better than those who are altruistic and cooperative (Belsky, 1999; Chisholm, 1999). On the other hand, infants brought up in a supportive social environment may benefit from developing a more altruistic, cooperative, and "secure" personality style. Therefore, it would not make evolutionary sense for either men or women to be locked into a particular mode of behavior (i.e., sexual jealousy vs. emotional jealousy).

Second, every human activity invariably involves inherited biological components, but evolution is possible only where there is variation among individuals. Any explanation that implies that an intraspecies or intragender behavior is invariant runs counter to basic principles of evolutionary theory.

Third, the existence of a behavior does not necessarily indicate that it evolved through natural selection. Cultural evolution does not depend on genetic change; it depends primarily on the development of new ideas and occurs much more quickly than biological evolution. Thus dramatic changes in how men and women behave have occurred during the past 25,000 years, although virtually no genetic changes have occurred during that time. Anthropological evidence, for example, suggests that patriarchy is a relatively recent phenomenon (Lerner, 1986) and thus cannot be accounted for by genetic explanations.

Fourth, evolutionary theory does not minimize the importance of environments to the extent implied in the explanations common in evolutionary psychology. Evolutionary psychological models tend to inflate the explanatory weight of biological processes. Instead of accepting such reductionistic notions, we need to look more closely at the environments in which genes and the processes they influence function. Both intrasex and interattachment style variations for both kinds of jealousy we studied suggest that men have the same biological potential for emotional jealousy as do women and, conversely, that women have the same biological potential for sexual jealousy as do men. If evolutionary models are going to be of maximal value, they must specify the conditions and processes of organism-environment interactions through which genotypes are transformed into phenotypes. Genotypes are never expressed independently of environment.

In contrast, an attachment theory perspective provides a broad yet parsimonious explanation of sex differences in type of jealousy perceived as most distressing. Unlike simple evolutionary explanations, attachment theory can explain both between and within-sex differences, as well as differentiate between environmentally and genetically based interpretations.

Another advantage of an attachment theoretical perspective on sex differences in jealousy is that it offers suggestions for prevention and intervention. An important goal of theoretical understanding is to enable change. That male sexual jealousy has been implicated as the leading cause of spouse battering and homicide across many cultures (Daly & Wilson, 1988) highlights the importance of understanding the dynamics of sexual jealousy. Unfortunately, the evolutionary perspective put forth by Buss and his colleagues offers little advice for reducing sexual jealousy in men. At its worst, it supplies a quietist justification for male violence by viewing it as rooted in nature. An attachment perspective, however, offers an understanding of jealousy that is rooted in internal working models of self and relationships based on past experiences. This perspective suggests a number of ways to reduce and prevent sexual jealousy in both men and women through establishing and enhancing secure attachment relationships throughout the lifespan. Good ideas about how to accomplish these goals can be found in writings by clinicians (e.g.,

Bowlby, 1988; Slade, 1999) and researchers (e.g., Gillath, Shaver, 8c Mikulincer, 2005; Mikulincer & Shaver, 2001).

In conclusion, jealousy is a complex and multidetermined emotional reaction (White & Mullen, 1989). Although evolutionary psychology can contribute to explaining between-sex differences in the elicitation of emotional versus sexual jealousy, it is limited in a number of respects. First, the evolutionary psychology perspective cannot systematically explain within-sex differences. Second, it cannot explain the full complexity of the emotional experience of jealousy. We believe that attachment theory offers a coherent and parsimonious explanation of kinds of jealous reactions with greater scope and better predictive power than explanations based in evolutionary psychology. Approaching the study and amelioration of jealousy from an attachment perspective helps us understand its sources, points to new research possibilities, offers suggestions for educational and clinical interventions, and promises to alleviate important social problems. Our own work leaves open a number of questions, such as why dismissing attachment is more common among men than women, which suggests that avoidant parenting interacts with either genetic factors or with societal sex-role stereotypes. If these remaining questions are tackled by researchers, we will be able to provide an even better set of guidelines for parents, educators, and clinicians.

NOTE

1. We do nor want to suggest that secure individuals are not interested in the sexual aspects of relationships. In fact, research has shown that secure men and dismissive men report having comparable amounts of sex; however, secure men report having this sex in long-term committed relationships as a way of expressing intimacy and increasing closeness, whereas dismissive men report having sex in multiple, short-term uncommitted relationships as a way of conquering and coercing others (Brennan & Shaver, 1995; Davis, Shaver, 8t Vernon, 2004; Schachner & Shaver, 2004).

REFERENCES

Abelson, R. P. (1995). *Statistics as principled argument.* Hillsdale, NJ: Erlbaum.

Ainsworth, M. S., Blehar, M. C, Waters, E., & Wall, S. (1978). *Patterns of attachment: A psychological study of the Strange Situation.* Hillsdale, NJ: Erlbaum.

Allen, E. S., & Baucom, D. H. (2004). Adult attachment and patterns of extradyadic involvement. *Family Process, 43,* 467–488.

Baker, R. R., & Bellis, M. A. (1995). *Sperm competition: Copulation, masturbation, and infidelity.* London: Chapman & Hall.

Bartholomew, K., & Horowitz, L. (1991). Attachment styles among young adults: A four-category model of attachment. *Journal of Personality and Social Psychology, 61,226–241.*

Belsky, J. (1999). Modern evolutionary theory and patterns of attachment. In J. Cassidy & P. R. Shaver (Eds.), *Handbook of attachment: Theory, research, and clinical applications* (pp. 141–161). New York: Guilford Press.

Betzig, L. (1989). Causes of conjugal dissolution: A cross-cultural study. *Current Anthropology, 30,* 654–676.

Bokhorst, C. L., Bakermans-Kranenburg, M. J., Fearon, R. M. P., van IJzendoorn, M. H, Fonagy, P., *&* Schuengel, C. (2003). The importance of shared environment in mother-infant attachment security: A behavioral genetic study. *Child Development, 74,* 1769–1782.

Bowlby, J. (1969). *Attachment and loss: Vol. 1. Attachment.* New York: Basic Books.

Bowlby, J. (1973). *Attachment and loss: Vol. 2. Separation.* New York: Basic Books.

Bowlby, J. (1980). *Attachment and loss: Vol. 3. Loss: Sadness and depression.* New York: Basic Books.

Bowlby, J. (1988). *A secure base.* New York: Basic Books.

Brennan, K. A., & Morris, K. A. (1997). Attachment styles, self-esteem, and patterns of seeking feedback from romantic partners. *Personality and Social Psychology Bulletin, 23,* 23–31.

Brennan, K. A., & Shaver, P. R. (1995). Dimensions of adult attachment, affect regulation, and romantic relationship functioning. *Personality and Social Psychology Bulletin,* 22,267–283.

Brennan, K. A., Shaver, P. R., & Tobey, A. E. (1991). Attachment styles, gender, and parental problem drinking. *Journal of Social and Personal Relationships, 8,*451–466.

Buller, D. J. (2005). *Adapting minds: Evolutionary psychology and the persistent quest for human nature.* Cambridge, MA: MIT Press.

Buss, D. M. (1995). Evolutionary psychology: A new paradigm for psychological science. *Psychological Inquiry, 6,* 1–30.

Buss, D. M., Kirkpatrick, L., Shackelford, X, & Bennett, K. (1999). *On the nature of sex differences in jealousy: Testing alternative hypotheses about origins.* Unpublished manuscript, University of Texas, Austin.

Buss, D. M., Larsen, R. J., & Westen, D. (1996). Sex differences in jealousy: Not gone, not forgotten, and not explained by alternative hypotheses. *Psychological Science,* 7, 373–375.

Buss, D. M., Larsen, R. J., Westen, D., & Semmelroth, J. (1992). Sex differences in jealousy: Evolution, physiology, and psychology. *Psychological Science, 3,*251–255.

Buunk, B. P., Angleiter, A., Oubaid, V., & Buss, D. M. (1996). Sex differences in jealously in evolutionary and cultural perspective: Tests from the Netherlands, Germany, and the United States. *Psychological Science,* 7, 359–363.

Chisholm, J. S. (1999). *Death, hope, and sex: Steps to an evolutionary ecology of mind and morality.* New York: Cambridge University Press.

Daly, M., Sc Wilson, M. (1988). *Homicide.* New York: Aldine de Gruyter.

Daly, M., Wilson, M., & Weghorst, S. J. (1982). Male sexual jealousy. *Ethology and Sociobiology, 3,* 11–27.

Davis, D., Shaver, P. R., & Vernon, M. L. (2004). Attachment style and subjective motivations for sex. *Personality and Social Psychology Bulletin, 30,* 1076–1090.

Davis, K. E., Ace, A., & Andra, M. (2000). Stalking perpetrators and psychological maltreatment of partners: Anger-jealousy, attachment insecurity, need for control, and break-up context. *Violence and Victims, IS,* 407–425.

DeSteno, D. A., & Salovey, P. (1996a). Evolutionary origins of sex differences in jealousy: Questioning the "fitness" of the model. *Psychological Science, 7,* 367–372.

DeSteno, D. A., & Salovey, P. (1996b). Genes, jealousy, and the replication of misspecified models. *Psychological Science, 7,* 376–377.

Dunn, J., Bretherton, I., & Munn, P. (1987). Conversations about feeling states between mothers and their young children. *Developmental Psychology, 23,* 132–139.

Dutton, D. G., van Ginkel, C, & Landolt, M. A. (1996). Jealousy, intimate abusive-ness, and intrusiveness. *Journal of Family Violence, 11,* 411—423.

Eagly, A. H., & Wood, W. (1999). The origins of sex differences in human behavior: Evolved dispositions versus social roles. *American Psychologist, 54,* 408—423.

Fivush, R., Brotman, M. A., Buckner, P. J., & Goodman, S. H. (2000). Gender differences in parent-child emotion narratives. *Sex Roles, 42,* 233- 253.

Fraley, C. R. (2002). Attachment stability from infancy to adulthood: Meta-analysis and dynamic modeling of developmental mechanisms. *Personality and Social Psychological Review, 6,* 123–151.

Gayford, J. J. (1975). Wife battering: A preliminary survey of 100 cases. *British Medical Journal, 1,* 194–197.

Gayford, J. J. (1979). Battered wives. *British Journal of Hospital Medicine, 22,* 496–503.

Geary, D. C, Rumsey, M., Bow-Thomas, C. C, & Hoard, M. K. (1995). Sexual jealousy as a facultative trait: Evidence from the pattern of sex differences in adults from China and the United States. *Ethology and Sociobiology, 16,* 355–383.

Gibbens, T. C. N. (1958). Sane and insane homicide. *Journal of Criminal Law, Criminology, and Police Science, 49,* 110–115.

Gillath, O., Shaver, P. R., & Mikulincer, M. (2005). An attachment-theoretical approach to compassion and altruism. In P. Gilbert (Ed.), *Compassion: Conceptualizations, research, and use in psychotherapy* (pp. 121–147). London: Brunner-Routledge.

Goodnow, J. J. (1988). Children's household work: Its nature and functions. *Psychological Bulletin, 103, 5–26.*

Harris, C. R. (2003). A review of sex differences in sexual jealousy, including self-report data, psychophysiological responses, interpersonal violence, and morbid jealousy. *Personality and Social Psychology Review,* 7, 102–128.

Harris, C. R., & Christenfeld, N. (1996). Gender, jealousy, and reason. *Psychological Science,* 7, 364–366.

Hazan, C, & Shaver, P. R. (1987). Romantic love conceptualized as an attachment process, *journal of Personality and Social Psychology, 52,* 511–524.

Kirkpatrick, L. A., & Hazan, C. (1994). Attachment styles and close relationships: A four-year prospective study. *Personal Relationships, 1,* 123–142.

Lerner, G. (1986). *The creation of patriarchy.* New York: Oxford University Press.

Levy, K. N. (1990). [Narrative descriptions of significant others]. Unpublished raw data.

Levy, K. N. (1999). Attachment style, representations of self and others, and affect regulation: Implications for the experience of depression (Doctoral dissertation, City University of New York, 1999). *Dissertation Abstracts International, 60,* 4895.

Levy, K. N, Blatt, S. J., & Shaver, P. R. (1998). Attachment style and parental representations. *Journal of Personality and Social Psychology, 74,* 407—419.

Levy, K. N., & Kelly, K. M. (2006). *Sex differences in jealousy: Evolutionary style or attachment style?* Manuscript submitted for review.

Main, M. (1995). Recent studies in attachment. In S. Goldberg, R. Muir, & J. Kerr (Eds.), *Attachment theory: Social, developmental, and clinical perspectives* (pp. 404–474). Hillsdale, NJ: Analytic Press.

Mathes, E. W., Phillips, J. T., Skowron, J., & Dick, W. E. (1982). Behavioral correlates of the interpersonal jealousy scale. *Educational and Psychological Measurement, 42,* 1227–1231.

Mikulincer, M., Dolev, X, & Shaver, P. R. (2004). Attachment-related strategies during thought-suppression: Ironic rebounds and vulnerable self-representations. *Journal of Personality and Social Psychology, 87,* 940–956.

Mikulincer, M., & Horesh, N. (1999). Adult attachment and the perception of others: The role of projective mechanisms. *Journal of Personality and Social Psychology, 76,* 1022–1034.

Mikulincer, M., & Shaver, P. R. (2003). The attachment behavioral system in adulthood: Activation, psychodynamics, and interpersonal processes. In M. P. Zanna (Ed.), *Advances in experimental social psychology* (Vol. 35, pp. 53–152). New York: Academic Press.

Pines, A., & Aronson, E. (1983). Antecedents, correlates, and consequences of sexual jealousy. *Journal of Personality, 51,* 108–136.

Rabinowitz, V. C, & Valian, V. (2000). Sex, sex differences, and social behavior. In P. Moller & D. LeCroy (Eds.), *Evolutionary perspectives on human reproductive behavior* (pp. 196–207). New York: New York Academy of Sciences.

Schachner, D. A., & Shaver, P. R. (2002). Attachment style and human mate poaching. *New Review of Social Psychology, 1,* 122–129.

Schachner, D. A., & Shaver, P. R. (2004). Attachment dimensions and sexual motives. *Personal Relationship, 11,* 179–195.

Servello, S., & Bartholomew, K. (1996, August). *Sex, gender roles, and attachment patterns in young adults.* Paper presented at the International Conference on Personal Relationships, Banff, Alberta, Canada.

Shaver, P. R., & Hazan, C. (1993). Adult romantic attachment: Theory and evidence. In D. Perlman & W. Jones (Eds.), *Advances in personal relationships* (Vol. 4, pp. 29–70). London: Kingsley.

Shaver, P. R., Papalia, D., Clark, C. L., Koski, L. R., Tidwell, M. C, & Nalbone, D. (1996). Androgyny and attachment security: Two related models of optimal personality. *Personality and Social Psychology Bulletin, 22,* 582–597.

Simpson, J. A. (1990). Influence of attachment styles on romantic relationships, *journal of Personality and Social Psychology, 59,* 971–980.

Simpson, J. A., & Gangestad, S. W. (1991). Influences of attachment styles on romantic relationships. *Journal of Personality and Social Psychology, 59,* 971–980.

Slade, A. (1999). Attachment theory and research: Implications for the theory and practice of individual psychotherapy with adults. In J. Cassidy & J. R. Shaver (Eds.), *Handbook of attachment: Theory, research, and clinical applications* (pp. 575–594). New York: Guilford Press.

Symons, D. (1979). *The evolution of human sexuality.* New York: Oxford University Press.

Thornhill, R., & Palmer, C. T. (2000). *A natural history of rape: Biological bases of sexual coercion.* Cambridge, MA: MIT Press.

Tjaden, P., & Thoennes, N. (1998). *Stalking in America: Findings from the National Violence Against Women survey.* Denver, CO: Center for Policy Research.

Trivers, R. (1972). Parental investment and sexual selection. In B. Campbell (Ed.), *Sexual selection and the descent of man: 1871–1971* (pp. 136–179). Chicago: Aldine.

Waller, N. G., & Shaver, P. R. (1992). Importance of nongenetic influences on romantic love styles: A twin-family study. *Psychological Science, 5,* 268–274.

White, G. L., & Mullen, P. E. *(1989). Jealousy: Theory, research, and clinical strategies.* New York: Guilford Press.

Wiederman, M. W., & Allgeier, E. R. (1993). Gender differences in sexual jealousy: Adaptationist or social learning explanation? *Ethology and Sociobiology, 14,* 115–140.

Wilson, M. I., & Daly, M. (1992). The man who mistook his wife for a chattel. In J. Barkow, L. Cosmides, & J. Tooby (Eds.), *The adopted mind* (pp. 289–322). New York: Oxford University Press.

Wolfgang, M. E. (1958). *Patterns in criminal homicide.* Philadelphia: University of Pennsylvania Press

More Information than You Ever Wanted

Does Facebook Bring Out the Green-Eyed Monster of Jealousy?

By Amy Muise, M.Sc., Emily Christofides, M.Sc., and Serge Desmarais, Ph.D.

Abstract

The social network site Facebook is a rapidly expanding phenomenon that is changing the nature of social relationships. Anecdotal evidence, including information described in the popular media, suggests that Face-book may be responsible for creating jealousy and suspicion in romantic relationships. The objectives of the present study were to explore the role of Facebook in the experience of jealousy and to determine if increased Facebook exposure predicts jealousy above and beyond personal and relationship factors. Three hundred eight undergraduate students completed an online survey that assessed demographic and personality factors and explored respondents' Facebook use. A hierarchical multiple regression analysis, controlling for individual, personality, and relationship factors, revealed that increased Facebook use significantly predicts Facebook-related jealousy. We argue that this effect may be the result of a feedback loop whereby using Facebook exposes people to often ambiguous information about their partner that they may not otherwise have access to and that this

Amy Muise, Emily Christofides, Serge Desmarais, "More Information than You Ever Wanted: Does Facebook Bring Out the Green-Eyed Monster of Jealousy?," from *CyberPsychology & Behavior*, Vol. 12, No. 4, Pp. 441–444.

new information incites further Facebook use. Our study provides evidence of Facebook's unique contributions to the experience of jealousy in romantic relationships.

Introduction

In young relationships, a glance at a rival or a small token of affection is sometimes enough to send those involved into a giddy high or momentary despair. In the past, flirty gestures of interest or signs of subtle disregard remained entirely within a person's own control, and partners in close relationships were most often not subjected to the daily scrutiny of their exchanges with members of their social circle. The development of online social network sites such as Facebook has created a fundamental shift in this practice. Has this new reality resulted in all aspects of our lives becoming open for all to see? If so, what potential negative outcomes can result from this degree of social openness?

Facebook, by its very nature, provides easy access to friends' and partners' information, including changes to their profile, additions of new contacts (termed "friends"), and messages posted on their page (on their virtual "wall"). Lee and Boyer[1] report that Facebook can play a role in maintaining long-distance friendships but that college students do not need Facebook to maintain most of their close friendships. In fact, some of their friends on Facebook may be quite superficial, with students reporting having friends that they have encountered only briefly outside of Facebook. [1,2]

While social network sites provide the opportunity to reunite with long-lost friends, they also allow people to make information public within their circle of friends and to make their list of friends itself open to public scrutiny.[3] Anecdotal evidence from discussions with undergraduates points to a common perception that Facebook causes jealousy and negatively impacts romantic and sexual relationships. Similarly, in a recent popular media article, Persch suggests that Facebook is responsible for creating jealousy and suspicion in romantic relationships.[4] These informal sources suggest that exposing one's social network activities in a public domain appears to have some negative implications for romantic and sexual relationships. For these reasons, we became interested in Facebook as a unique environment for the experience of jealousy.

Past research has indicated several personality and relationship factors that contribute to the experience of jealousy. Feelings of jealousy in a specific situation, such as the imagined situation of a partner's infidelity, are predicted by general levels of emotional jealousy,[5] or trait jealousy, suggesting that some individuals are more prone than others to jealousy. Individual levels of trust and self-esteem have also been associated with the experience of jealousy, where lower levels of trust are related to more intense and frequent experiences of jealousy,[6,7] and self-esteem mediates the intensity of jealousy experienced following a relationship threat.[8] In addition, White includes self-esteem in his definition of jealousy, describing jealousy as a "complex of thoughts, feelings and actions which follow threats to self-esteem and=or threats to the existence or quality of the relationship." [9(p24)] Relational uncertainty, and more specifically, doubt about a partner's involvement in the relationship, also produces jealous responses from individuals in romantic relationships.[10,11] Type of relationship and level of commitment have also been shown to contribute to the experience of jealousy; in general, people in committed relationships experience less jealousy than those in newer, more casual ones.[12]

Exposure to information about a romantic partner's friends and social interactions may result in an environment that enhances jealousy. Sheets et al.[13] identified four categories of jealousy-evoking situations: when one's partner shows interest in another person, when another person shows interest in one's partner, when one's partner talks about or interacts with prior relational partners, and ambiguous scenes involving the partner. The ease of making connections on Face-book may increase contact with past romantic and sexual partners, creating the potential for jealousy in current relationships. Facebook also assists in maintaining relationships that may otherwise be only ephemeral,[2] and it may in fact connect people who would not otherwise communicate. In the context of a romantic relationship, exposing one's partner to all of these individuals, many of whom may be unknown to the partner, may increase the potential for jealousy and suspicion.

Social network sites such as Facebook have changed the nature of public and private in the sense that much more information is available to individuals about their partner's relationships and interactions than they would have with other online or offline methods of communication. This lack of privacy in the traditional sense may expose individuals to more information about their partner than they would access otherwise.

In light of past research, we believed it important to control for personal factors such as trait jealousy, trust, and self-esteem and for relational factors such as relational uncertainty and commitment in our exploration of the links between Facebook use and jealousy. We predicted that time spent on Facebook would uniquely contribute to Facebook-specific jealousy beyond the effects of the personal and relational factors described in the jealousy literature.

Methods

Data were collected as part of a larger study on undergraduate student use of Facebook. The study was an anonymous online survey, and data were collected according to the criteria described in Christofides et al.[14] After removing 35 participants (n = 31 female; n = 4 male) due to missing data regarding their Facebook usage, 308 respondents (n = 231 female; n=77 male), ranging in age from 17 to 24 years (M = 18.70, SD = 0.97), were retained for analysis. At the time of the survey, the majority of the participants were in a relationship in which they were seriously dating one person (50.5%); other participants were casually dating one or more partners (8.3%), in an open relationship (3.7%), living with a partner but not married (3.0%), married (0.7%), or divorced=separated (0.3%). The remaining 33.6 percent of participants were not currently dating anyone.

The Facebook Jealousy scale (Cronbach's α = 0.96) was created for the current study in order to assess the experience of jealousy in the specific context of Facebook. We compiled a list of items to reflect aspects of Facebook that have the potential to contribute to sexual and romantic jealousy. A group of Facebook users in the target demographic then reviewed these items for readability and inclusiveness. The scale was administered to the current sample, and exploratory factor analysis (EFA) revealed a one-factor solution with the first factor yielding an eigenvalue of 12.68 and accounting for 47.0% of the variance. All items were retained because the factor loadings ranged from 0.432 to 0.821. The final scale consisted of 27 items, measured on a 7-point Likert scale (1, *very unlikely* to 7, *very unlikely),* that assess Facebook-related jealousy. Sample items include "How likely are you to become jealous after your partner has added an unknown member of the opposite sex?" and "How likely are you to monitor your partner's activities on Facebook?"

Other factors include general propensity toward jealousy,[15] levels of trust,[6],[16] self-esteem (Rosenberg Self-Esteem scale, as used by Ellison et al.[2]), relational uncertainty,[17] and commitment.[18] One item measured the amount of time participants spent on Facebook. Participants were also asked to provide demographic information and descriptive information about their use and their partners' use of Facebook, and they were asked one open-ended question to allow them to provide qualitative data about their experience of jealousy on Facebook.

Results

Descriptive data

Participants in the current sample reported spending an average of 38.93 minutes on Facebook each day *(SD* = 32.13) and had between 25 and 1000 Facebook friends (M = 296.19, *SD* = 173.04). The majority of participants (74.6%) were at least somewhat likely to add previous romantic or sexual partners as friends on Facebook, and 78.9% reported that their partner has added previous romantic or sexual partners as friends. Almost all of the participants in the current sample (92.1%) reported that their partner was at least somewhat likely to have Facebook friends who they do not know. Past research has indicated that jealousy may be differentially experienced based on gender, [(eg,19)] and such differences were found in the current sample. Women, M = 40.57, SD = 26.76, in our sample spent significantly more time on Facebook than men, M = 29.83, SD= 23.73; t(305) = -3.32, p<0.01, and women, M = 3.29, SD=1.24, scored significantly higher on Facebook jealousy than men, M = *2.81*, SD =*1.09;* t(305) = -3.32, p < 01. Therefore, gender was controlled for in the regression analysis.

Multiple regression

We hypothesized that Facebook use uniquely contributes to the experience of jealousy, and we therefore tested a model of Facebook jealousy that took into account a variety of personal and relationship factors known to be associated with the general experience of jealousy. We tested our model using a hierarchical multiple regression analysis consistent with the theoretical model that we outlined based on past research into relational jealousy. Gender and trait jealousy were entered into block 1, personality and relational factors were entered in blocks 2 and 3 respectively, and Facebook use was entered in block 4. As expected, we found that trait jealousy was a significant predictor of Facebook jealousy, which, along with gender, accounted for 46% of the variance. When personality and relational factors were added to our model, only trust significantly added to our prediction of Facebook jealousy scores (for trust, β = —2.03, p = 0.04; for all other factors, $\beta < 0.07$, $p > 0.16$). The inclusion of the blocks 2 and 3, the personality and relational factors, accounted for only 2% of additional variance and therefore did not contribute significantly to the model. Time spent on Facebook was a significant predictor of Facebook jealousy (β = 2.59, p = 0.01). While this variable added only 2% of variance to the prediction model, it did uniquely predict scores on the Facebook jealousy scale beyond gender, trait-based jealousy, and other personality and relationship factors. This finding is notable considering the predictive power of trait jealousy. The final model explains 48% of the variance in Facebook jealousy.

Qualitative data

While only a portion of the participants responded to our open-ended question (68 participants), their answers provided some additional information about potential cues regarding the process associated with Facebook jealousy. The statements of these individuals were analyzed for themes relating to the experience of jealousy on Facebook by the first and second authors, and four themes emerged. An independent rater who was blind to the purpose of the study coded the data using these four themes and demonstrated high interrater reliability (Cohen's k = 0.93). The first theme, which we called *accessibility of information* (described by 19.1% of participants) included statements about the increased amount of information available through Facebook about the relationship one's partner has with other individuals. The second theme, *relationship jealousy* (16.2%), explicitly linked Facebook use to participants' own or their partner's experiences of jealousy. The third theme, *Facebook as an addiction* (10.3%), indicated participants' difficulty in limiting the time they spent on their partner's Facebook page or on Facebook in general. The final theme, *lack of context* (7.4%) consisted of references to the ambiguous nature of Facebook and the role of this ambiguity in potential negative consequences such as jealousy.

For all of the positive aspects of the increased social connection that Facebook enables, there may also be some costs for those individuals involved in romantic and sexual relationships. Our data showed a significant association between time spent on Facebook and jealousy-related feelings and behaviors experienced on Facebook. Is time spent on Facebook increasing jealousy, or is the heightened level of jealousy that may emerge as a result of the information found on partners' Facebook postings resulting in increased time on Facebook? We argue that both options are inevitably intertwined and that the findings are most likely due to dual causation. The qualitative feedback we collected provides some preliminary support for this argument.

The open nature of Facebook gives people access to information about their partner that would not otherwise be accessible. As one participant reported, "It turns people into nosey parkers ... all of that personal information is totally unnecessary, but no one can help themselves." Moreover, the information listed on one's Facebook page may be interpreted in a variety of ways given its frequent lack of context. As some participants explained, "I have enough confidence in her [his partner] to know my partner is faithful, yet I can't help but second-guess myself when someone posts on her wall....It can contribute to feelings of you not really 'knowing' your partner." Ambiguous scenes involving a partner and contact with past romantic and sexual partners are among the common triggers of jealousy in romantic relation-ships,[13] and these ambiguous scenes are a regular occurrence on Facebook. Real or imagined negative situations invoke feelings of jealousy, and participants felt the Facebook environment created these feelings and enhanced concerns about the quality of their relationship. As one participant noted, "It definitely invokes a false sense of jealousy." Another participant explained that "I was already a bit jealous and insecure, but I think that Facebook has definitely made me much much much worse."

Our results suggest that Facebook may expose an individual to potentially jealousy-provoking information about their partner, which creates a feedback loop whereby heightened jealousy leads to increased surveillance of a partner's Facebook page. Persistent surveillance results in further exposure to jealousy-provoking information. For many, the need for knowledge about their partner's intent becomes indispensable, and several participants specifically mentioned the word "addiction" in relation to their own Facebook usage. One participant who had recently broken up with her boyfriend stated, "It's addictive. ...I always find myself going on there checking new pictures and screening them. I can't help it!" Our finding of a link between jealousy triggers on Facebook and increased surveillance of a partner's profile has also been discussed in some popular media,[4] suggesting that this phenomenon is not limited to the current sample. However, our study is the first to test this hypothesis and to control for personality and social factors that may have confounded the results.

With the vast majority of our sample reporting that their partners have unknown individuals and past romantic and sexual partners as friends on Facebook, the potential for jealousy in this environment is evident. The qualitative data we collected indicates that participants recognize that increased exposure to information on Facebook without proper context can increase their experience of jealousy. What is perhaps more puzzling is that despite this knowledge, many of these same participants also engage in a high degree of personal disclosure on Facebook.[14] These findings are consistent with past research that college-aged students practice high self-disclosure on Facebook,[1] suggesting that individuals may not adequately recognize that their own information disclosure may be a cause for concern for their partner. As a result, personal disclosures may foster a vicious cycle whereby a person's acontextual disclosure on Facebook may only increase the likelihood that one's partner may also do the same, thus increasing the likelihood of causing one's own experience of jealousy.

This study provides evidence of a relationship between Facebook use and the experience of jealousy in that context, though further research is needed to better understand this feedback loop because the nature of our data could not fully explain this process. Future research must directly examine the effects of various triggers on the experience of jealousy and on the time individuals spend on Facebook. Ideally, this research would directly assess the process by which time spent on Facebook and the experience of jealousy on Face-book are related. In addition, it would be interesting to learn whether these same relationships hold true in samples of adults who are outside of the university context. Unlike most young undergraduate student relationships, adult relationships are more likely to have developed before Facebook became popular, and one could argue that partners in that age group may be less well equipped to deal with the challenges that Facebook poses to relationships. In addition, adults may have a longer past to uncover, with more old friends and partners with whom to connect, thus potentially exposing members of couples to a greater potential for jealousy. One thing is sure: Facebook provides a superb forum for the study of relational jealousy, and our study only serves as a starting point.

Disclosure Statement

The authors have no conflict of interest.

References

1. Lee S-Y, Boyer L. A place of their own: an exploratory study of college students' uses of Facebook. Paper presented at the 57th International Communication Association Annual Meeting, San Francisco, CA, 2007.

2. Ellison NB, Steinfeld C, Lampe C. The benefits of Facebook "friends": social capital and college students' use of online social network sites. Journal of Computer-Mediated Communication 2007; 12. http://jcmc.indiana.edu/vol12/issue4/ ellison.html (accessed Jan. 25, 2009).
3. boyd dm, Ellison NB. Social network sites: definition, history, and scholarship. Journal of Computer-Mediated Communication 2007; 13:article 11. http://jcmc.indiana. Edu/vol13/issue1/boyd.ellison.html (accessed Jan. 25, 2009).
4. Persch JA. Jealous much? MySpace, Facebook can spark it. MSNBC Online. www.msnbc.msn.com/id/20431006/ (accessed Jan. 25, 2009).
5. Russel EB, Harton HC. The "other factors": using individual and relationship characteristics to predict sexual and emotional infidelity. Current Psychology: Developmental, Learning, Personality, Social 2005; 24:242–57.
6. Couch LL, Jones WH. Measuring levels of trust. Journal of Research in Personality 1997; 31:319–36.
7. Xiaojun W. Relationship between jealousy and personality. Act Psycholologica Sinica 2002; 34:175–82.
8. DeSteno DA, Salovey P. Evolutionary origins of sex differences in jealousy? Questioning the "fitness" of the model. Psychological Science 1996; 7:367–72.
9. White GL. Jealousy and partner's perceived motives for attraction to a rival. Social Psychology Quarterly 1981; 44:24–30.
10. Afifi WA, Reichert T. Understanding the role of uncertainty in jealousy experience and expression. Communication Reports 1996; 9:93–103.
11. Theiss JA, Solomon DH. Coupling longitudinal data and multilevel modeling to examine the antecedents and consequences of jealousy experiences in romantic relationships: a test of the relational turbulence model. Human Communication Research 2006; 32:469–503.
12. Aylor B, Dainton M. Antecedents in romantic jealousy experience, expression, and goals. Western Journal of Communication 2001; 65:370–91.
13. Sheets VL, Fredendall LL, Claypool HM. Jealousy evocation, partner reassurance, and relationship stability: an exploration of the potential benefits of jealousy. Evolution & Human Behavior 1997; 18:387–402.
14. Christofides E, Muise A, Desmarais S. Information disclosure and control on Facebook: are they two sides of the same coin or two different processes? CyberPsychology & Behavior 2009; 12. http:// www.liebertonline.com/doi/pdfplus/10.1089/cpb.2008.0226 (accessed March 27, 2009).
15. Pfeiffer SM, Wong PTP. Multidimensional jealousy. Journal of Social & Personal Relationships 1989; 6:181–96.
16. Couch LL. The development of the Trust Inventory. Unpublished master's thesis, University of Tennessee, 1994.
17. Knobloch LK, Solomon DH. The sources and content of relational uncertainty. Communication Studies 1999; 50:261–79.

18. Rusbult CE, Martz JM, Agnew CR. The investment model scale: measuring commitment level, satisfaction level, quality of alternatives and investment size. Personal Relationships 1998; 5:357–91.
19. Buss D, Larsen R, Westen D, Semmelroth J. (1992). Sex differences in jealousy: evolution, physiology, and psychology. Psychological Science 1992; 3:251–55.

STRESS, SOCIAL SUPPORT, AND HEALTH

The Unrecognized Stereotyping and Discrimination Against Singles

By Bella M. DePaulo and Wendy L. Morris
University of California, Santa Barbara, and *McDaniel College*

ABSTRACT: A widespread form of bias has slipped under our cultural and academic radar. People who are single are targets of singlism: negative stereotypes and discrimination. Compared to married or coupled people, who are often described in very positive terms, singles are assumed to be immature, maladjusted, and self-centered. Although the perceived differences between people who have and have not married are large, the actual differences are not. Moreover, there is currently scant recognition that singlism exists, and when singlism is acknowledged, it is often accepted as legitimate.

KEYWORDS—singles; stigma; discrimination; stereotypes; relationships

For years, we have been studying what we call singlism, the stigmatizing of adults who are single. We have found evidence of singlism in the negative stereotypes and discrimination faced by singles (DePaulo, 2006; DePaulo & Morris, 2005a; DePaulo & Morris, 2005b). Although singlism is a nonviolent, softer form of bigotry than what is often faced by other stigmatized groups such as African Americans or gay men and lesbians, the impact of singlism is far ranging. Unlike more familiar isms such as

Bella M. DePaulo, Wendy L. Morris, "The Unrecognized Stereotyping and Discrimination Against Singles," from *Current Directions in Psychological Science*, Vol. 15, No. 5, Pp. 251–254. Published by Blackwell Publishing, 2006.

racism, sexism, or heterosexism, singlism is not often recognized, and when it is pointed out, it is often regarded as legitimate.

WHO IS "SINGLE?"

We can define singles as legally single or socially single, though the two often overlap. According to the U.S. Census Bureau, over 40% of adults are legally single, including people who are divorced or widowed and those who have always been single. In everyday interactions, what matters most often is whether a person is socially single or socially coupled. People who are in sexual partnerships regarded as serious by themselves and others are socially coupled. Impressions of seriousness are shaped by factors such as the length of time the twosome has been together, the regularity and exclusivity with which they see each other, whether they seem to intend to stay together, and whether they live together.

EVIDENCE OF SINGLISM

Negative Stereotypes of the Socially Single

We asked nearly 1,000 undergraduates to list the characteristics that came to mind when they thought about people who were married (in one condition) or single (in the other). Married people were more likely than singles to be described as mature, stable, honest, happy, kind, and loving. Singles were more often called immature, insecure, self-centered, unhappy, lonely, and ugly (but also, on the positive side, independent). The perceived differences between single and married people were often quite large. For example, married people were described as caring, kind, and giving almost 50% of the time, compared to only 2% of the time for singles (Morris, DePaulo, Hertel, & Ritter, 2006).

Next, we wanted to know whether singles are perceived even more negatively after they have passed the age at which most people marry. Groups of undergraduates and community members rated descriptions of single and married people. The targets were described as men or women and as 25 or 40 years old. All groups rated the singles as less socially mature, less well-adjusted, and more self-centered and envious than the married people (though also more independent and career-oriented). As we expected, the differences favoring married people were even greater when the targets were described as 40 years old than when they were described as 25. Still, though, there were significant differences even at the younger age.

Why should 25-year-olds be derogated simply because they are not yet married? As of the year 2004, at least half of all American women, and even more men, had not married by age 25. Maybe, we thought, young adults needed to show that they were at least working at coupling, to avoid getting stigmatized. In another experiment, undergraduates read profiles describing students who were currently coupled, currently single, previously coupled, or always single. Working at coupling did matter. Students who were described as having current or past relationship experience were regarded as more socially mature, better-adjusted, and less self-centered than the others.

Discrimination Against Singles

Discrimination against single people is often legal. As of 2004, 23 states offered no protections from marital-status discrimination, and others offered only partial protections. Employers can legally subsidize health benefits for spouses of married employees (and sometimes domestic partners), while offering no comparable benefits to a parent, sibling, or friend of their single employees. That amounts to unequal compensation for the same work. Similarly, a married person in need of care can receive it from a spouse who is covered by the Family and Medical Leave Act (FMLA), but singles who need care do not have anyone in their own generation who is eligible for FMLA benefits.

Single men are paid less than their married male colleagues even when they are of similar age and have comparable work experience. Marriage also brings increased tax benefits and social security benefits and discounts on automobile insurance, travel packages, and club memberships (reviewed in DePaulo, 2006).

We have also found experimental evidence of housing discrimination against singles (Morris, Sinclair, & DePaulo, 2006). In three studies, participants read descriptions of three applicants for a rental property and indicated their preferred lessee. Rental agents were much more likely to choose a married couple (60%) over a cohabiting romantic couple (23%) or a pair of friends (17%). Undergraduates' preference for the married couple was even stronger: 80% chose the married couple, as compared to just 12% choosing the cohabiting couple and 8% who chose the friends. Undergraduates also overwhelmingly favored a married couple (70%) over a single woman (18%) or a single man (12%). The preferences of the rental agents are particularly significant, as they raise the possibility that singles may be at a disadvantage when trying to find housing. Future research should explore this.

Byrne and Carr's (2005) analysis of a nationally representative sample found that people who have always been single and are not cohabiting with a romantic partner are more likely than married people to report experiencing (for example) poorer service in restaurants or condescending attitudes in everyday life. The authors controlled for many factors such as age, race, sexual orientation, and health, making a convincing case that singles really are slighted in their interpersonal experiences. But we still wondered whether singles themselves think they are discriminated against based upon their relationship status.

SINGLISM IS UNACKNOWLEDGED

What is especially interesting about singlism is that most people are unaware that singles are stigmatized at all. When we asked adults to list any groups to which they belonged that might be targets of negative stereotypes or discrimination, only 4% of singles spontaneously mentioned singles as such a category. When explicitly asked whether they thought singles might be a stigmatized group, only 30% of singles and 23% of coupled people said that they were. This level of awareness is low compared to the 100% of gay people, 90% of obese people, 86% of African Americans, and 72% of women who acknowledged their groups' stigma (Morris, 2005).

The practice of singlism is often considered acceptable. While many are outraged by discrimination based on race, gender, or sexual orientation, few people feel any injustice has occurred when a single person is targeted. When participants in an experiment read about housing discrimination against singles, they thought the practice was more legitimate and fair than when they read that the housing discrimination targeted a member of a recognized stigmatized group such as an African American person, a gay person, or an obese person (Morris, Sinclair, & DePaulo, 2006).

WHYARE SINGLES STIGMATIZED?

Unfounded Stereotypes or Accurate Perceptions? What if marriage really does transform people, such that they become strikingly happier than they were when they were single and much happier than their peers who have always been single? Then negative perceptions of single people as unhappy would seem more like accurate assessments than like unfair characterizations.

Meta-analytic reviews (summarized by DePaulo & Morris, 2005a) are sometimes said to support the claim that getting married makes people happier, because currently married people score higher on happiness than other groups. But the biggest differences are between the currently married and those who were previously married but are currently divorced or widowed. Getting married cannot account for those differences, because currently married, divorced, and widowed people all got married. The smallest difference ($r = .09$) is between the currently married and those who have always been single.

Nor can it be said that getting married and staying married makes people happy. The meta-analytic reviews summarize studies in which the single, married, and previously married people are all different people. So, the people who stayed married may have been happier than the other people even before they got married. A recent review suggests that happiness may indeed come first in the causal chain leading to other life outcomes (Lyubomirsky, King, & Diener, 2005).

Definitive causal statements about marriage and happiness can never be made, because people cannot be randomly assigned to get married or stay single. Still, longitudinal research can provide an answer to an important question: When people marry, do they become happier than they were when they were single?

An 18-year longitudinal study of thousands of German adults analyzed by Richard Lucas and his colleagues suggests that the long-term answer is no (Lucas, 2005; Lucas, Clark, Georgellis, & Diener, 2003). People who got married and stayed married experienced a small increase in happiness around the year of the wedding, but then their happiness returned to the level it was before. People who married and later divorced were already becoming less happy as the wedding day approached, a trend that did not reverse until the year before the divorce became final. (Their happiness then continued to increase; on the average, though, divorced people did not become as happy as they had been when they were single.)

People who stayed single throughout the study started out slightly less happy (0.2 points on an 11-point scale) than the people who would eventually get married and stay married. However, their mean happiness level was always squarely on the happy end of the scale (never more than 0.6 points lower than the continuously married). It was never as low as that of the divorced people the year before their divorce became official (and it was slightly higher than that of the divorced people for most other years, too). Also, the mean happiness level of the single people was never as low as that of the widowed people right after they were widowed.

The pattern of results is similar for health. People who have always been single are typically just as healthy, or only slightly less healthy, than people who have always been married. When there is a difference related to marital status, it is likely to be the previously married, not the continuously single, who are disadvantaged (DePaulo, 2006; Rook & Zettel, 2005).

Crandall and Warner (2005) argue that negative evaluations are indicative of prejudice, regardless of whether they are accurate. Claims about the transformative power of marriage, though, seem to be grossly exaggerated or just plain wrong. Getting married does not make people lastingly happier or definitively healthier.

Can Singlism Be Explained From an Evolutionary Perspective?

Evolutionary psychologists Pillsworth and Haselton (2005) have noted that we need "adaptations that promote successful mating, such as the basic desire to find a mate and have sex" (p. 98). Thus, people pay attention to whether others are single or coupled because this information is relevant to reproduction. However, the cultural assumption that coupling is the key to happiness is more difficult to explain. As Pillsworth and Haselton note, "the evolutionary perspective does not suggest that coupling will result in a healthier or more satisfying life for any particular individual. ... In the modern world, coupling does not guarantee an on-average fitness benefit to couple members or their children" (p. 101).

A Cultural Lag in Perceptions?

As recently as the mid-20th century, there were big differences between single and married adults. Then, having sex or children outside of marriage was considered shameful. Women were more dependent on marriage for financial security. Adults married younger, and divorced less often, than they do now. In contrast, Americans today spend more years of their adult lives single than married. Many women earn enough to support themselves and sometimes children, too. Because of advances in birth control and reproductive technology, women can have sex without having children, and they can have children without having sex. Perhaps, then, the negative appraisals of single people are signs of cultural lag: Perceptions of single people have not yet caught up with their rapidly changing place in society (Byrne & Carr, 2005).

Singles as a Threat to Cultural Beliefs

DePaulo (2006) suggests that there is more than just cultural lag at work. In contemporary American society, there is a glorification of marriage and coupling that many single and married people accept uncritically. According to the marital mythology, finding a soul-mate is a transformative experience: Marrying that all-purpose, all-important partner can make a person happy and healthy and fulfill all emotional and social needs. The marital mythology is powerfully attractive, offering as it does a seemingly simple path to a rewarding and meaningful life. Singles—especially those who clearly lead fulfilling lives—challenge that belief system. Singlism serves to maintain cultural beliefs about marriage by derogating those whose lives challenge those beliefs.

THE PARADOX OF SINGLEHOOD

Singles are targeted with stereotyping and discrimination, and married people are glorified. Yet, paradoxically, getting married does not result in lasting improvements in well-being, and people who have always been single are not very different in health or happiness from people who have been continuously married. How is this possible?

Singles often maintain a diversified relationship portfolio, rather than investing so much in just one person. Even in their later years, when others expect them to be lonely and alone, they often enjoy networks of supportive relationships (Zettel, 2005). Social scientists who study adult relationships have focused overwhelmingly on romantic relationships. Perhaps it is time to give relationships with friends, siblings, and everyone else their due.

Single people who have the resources and opportunities to do so can pursue their passions and excel at work that they love. They can embrace solitude as well as interpersonal engagement. If singles are increasingly living their lives fully, rather than marking time waiting for "the one," then the paradox begins to resolve itself. Maybe singles more often respond to stereotyping and discrimination with resilience than with victimization. Much more research will be needed to know for sure.

FUTURE RESEARCH

In our own work, we found evidence of singlism in the United States and Germany (Hertel, Schütz, DePaulo, Morris, & Stucke, in press). But as Pillsworth and Haselton have noted, "In most cultures around the globe, your spouse is not your best friend, or even your primary social partner" (p. 102). How are singles perceivedin those cultures? Even within the United States, there is much left to learn about how singlism is shaped by factors such as gender, ethnicity, sexual orientation, and social class.

Reams of research reports have examined marital status as a predictor of well-being. Marital status, though, may be a poor proxy for more important predictors. Do people have the degree of social connectedness that they need and want, whether that is attained by cohabitation, embeddedness in a network of friends, or some other means? Are they living a life that they find engaging and meaningful?

The development of a new field of study offers great promise. Many of the most fundamental questions about singles and singlism have yet to be addressed, or even framed. The answers are likely to have implications for public policy and even for the way people conduct their everyday lives.

Recommended reading

Byrne A., & Carr, D. (2005). (See References)

DePaulo, B. (2006). (See References)

DePaulo, B.M., & Morris, W.L. (2005a). (See References)

DePaulo, B.M., & Morris, W.L. (2005b). (See References)

Gillis, J.R. (1997). The perfect couple. In J.R. Gillis, A world of their own making (pp. 133–151). Cambridge, MA: Harvard University Press.

Byrne, A., & Carr, D. (2005). Caught in the cultural lag: The stigma of singlehood. Psychological Inquiry, 16, 84–91.

Crandall, C.S., & Warner, R.H. (2005). How a prejudice is recognized. Psychological Inquiry, 16, 137–141.

DePaulo, B. (2006). Singled out: How singles are stereotyped, stigmatized, and ignored, and still live happily ever after. New York: St. Martin's Press.

DePaulo, B.M., & Morris, W.L. (2005a). Singles in society and in science. Psychological Inquiry, 16, 57–83.

DePaulo, B.M., & Morris, W.L. (2005b). Should singles and the scholars who study them make their mark or stay in their place? Psychological Inquiry, 16, 142–149.

Hertel, J., Schütz, A., DePaulo, B.M., Morris, W.L., & Stucke, T.S. (in press). She's single, so what? How are singles perceived compared to people who are married? Journal of Family Research.

Lucas, R.E. (2005). Time does not heal all wounds: A longitudinal study of reaction and adaptation to divorce. Psychological Science, 16, 945–950.

Lucas, R.E., Clark, A.E., Georgellis, Y., & Diener, E. (2003). Re-examining adaptation and the set point model of happiness: Reactions to changes in marital status. Journal of Personality and Social Psychology, 84, 527–539.

Lyubomirsky, S., King, L., & Diener, E. (2005). The benefits of frequent positive affect: Does happiness lead to success? Psychological Bulletin, 131, 803–855.

Morris, W.L. (2005). The effects of stigma awareness on the self-esteem of singles (Doctoral dissertation, University of Virginia, 2005). Dissertation Abstracts International, 66(03), 1785B.

Morris, W.L., DePaulo, B.M., Hertel, J., & Ritter, L. (2006). Perception of people who are single: A developmental life tasks model. Manuscript submitted for publication.

Morris, W.L., Sinclair, S., & DePaulo, B.M. (2006). The perceived legitimacy of civil status discrimination. Manuscript submitted for publication.

Pillsworth, E.G., & Haselton, M.G. (2005). The evolution of coupling. Psychological Inquiry, 16, 98–104.

Rook, K.S., & Zettel, L.A. (2005). The purported benefits of marriage viewed through the lens of physical health. Psychological Inquiry, 16, 116–121.

Zettel, L.A. (2005). Aging alone: Do the social support resources of never-married individuals place them at risk? Dissertation Abstracts International, 65(10), 5441B.

Invisible Support and Adjustment to Stress

By Niall Bolger, *New York University*
Adam Zuckerman, *International Survey Research Corporation*,
Ronald C. Kessler, *Harvard Medical School*

Although there is abundant evidence that perceived availability of support buffers the effects of stressors on mental health, the relatively meager research on support transactions has failed to show an association between actual receipt of support and adjustment to stressors. The authors examined a possible explanation for this inconsistency, that awareness of receiving support entails an emotional cost and that the most effective support is unnoticed by the recipient. Using data from a daily diary study of support provision and receipt in couples, the authors show that many transactions reported by supporters are not reported by recipients. They also show that these invisible support transactions promote adjustment to a major stressor.

It is now well established that perceptions of social support availability predict better adjustment to stressful events (Cohen, 1992; Hobfoll & Vaux, 1993; House, Landis, & Umberson, 1988; Sarason, Sarason, & Gurung, 1997; Stroebe & Stroebe, 1996; Wills, 1990). It is less clear, however, how these protective effects come about and thus how one might intervene to enhance support during times of stress. Given this uncertainty, social support researchers have increasingly turned their attention to identifying the specific interpersonal processes thought to underlie social support availability effects (Cutrona, 1986; Cutrona & Suhr, 1994; Eck-enrode, 1983; Eckenrode & Wethington, 1990; Gottlieb, 1988; Heller, Swindle & Dusenbury, 1986; Reis, 1984).

Although this line of investigation is still relatively new, studies up to now have found that actual support transactions do not improve adjustment to stressful life experiences (Barrera, 1986; Bolger, Foster, Vinokur, & Ng, 1996; B. B. Brown, 1978; Dunkel-Schetter & Bennett, 1990; Eckenrode & Wethington, 1990; Lieberman, 1986; Wethington & Kessler, 1986). Indeed, most studies have documented that support receipt is either associated with poor adjustment or, at best, leaves the recipient no better off than if support had not been received.

We do not yet understand why receiving support appears to be ineffective in reducing distress, although three possibilities have been suggested as explanations. One is that people who receive support are under more stress than those who do not receive support. Consistent with this view, Barrera (1986) has shown that the seemingly bad effect of receiving support on mental health is substantially reduced when individual differences in stress severity are controlled. A second possibility is that people's attempts to give support may be miscarried; that is, their well-intentioned efforts may fail to be helpful or may even make matters worse for the person under stress. Coyne, Wortman, and Lehman (1988) documented that this kind of miscarried helping is not uncommon. A third possible reason why received support may be ineffective is that receiving help entails a cost to self-esteem because it makes salient to recipients that they are having difficulties coping with a stressor (Fisher, Nadler, & Whitcher-Alagna, 1982; Shapiro, 1978).

Whatever the explanation, it is hard to reconcile the ineffectiveness of received support with the well-established buffering effects of more traditional measures of perceived support availability. If received support is ineffective, why is it that perceived support availability buffers the effects of stress on health?

To reconcile this inconsistency, it has been proposed that the stress-protective effects of perceived support availability do not involve actual support transactions. B. B. Brown (1978), for example, found that people with the best social and personal resources—those who are known to adjust better to stress—are the least likely to report seeking support when they are under stress. Thus, the perception that one could get support if one wanted it might be sufficient to help one deal with many stressful situations. Advancing this view, Wethington and Kessler (1986) argued that this perception of support availability may either be comforting in itself or provide the kind of psychological safety net that helps motivate self-reliant coping efforts. In either case, the best psychological outcomes appear to be associated with perceiving that support is available rather than seeking it out.

Although Wethington and Kessler's (1986) account explains how perceived support availability can have a beneficial effect independent of enacted support, it does not explain why enacted support appears to have a neutral or negative effect on adjustment to stress. To make sense of this finding, our approach in this article is to posit that support transactions are most likely to be beneficial when they are accomplished without being visible to the recipient. This proposition is in line with Lieberman's (1986) suggestion that the high-resource group in the B. B. Brown (1978) study may have been getting support so smoothly that it was invisible to them. What do we mean by *invisible* in this context? There are at least two types of situations in which support may be invisible to recipients. First, the supportive act may occur outside of the recipient's awareness, for example, when one spouse takes care of unexpected housework without telling the other. Second, the recipient may be aware of the act but may not code it as support, for example, when a friend purposefully gives advice in an indirect way so as not to draw attention to the recipient's distress or his or her inability to deal with the stressful situation.

Such invisible supportive acts would not only buffer the effects of stressors on the recipient, but they would also circumvent any self-esteem or self-efficacy cost of receiving help. Perhaps the reason, then, why traditional received support measures do not appear to be beneficial is that they confound two opposing effects, the benefits people experience when support is provided to them and the costs they experience when they perceive—accurately or inaccurately—that support has been provided.

If recipient accounts of support confound these two opposing effects, then such measures alone will never uncover the benefits of receiving support. However, combining recipient accounts with provider accounts may provide a way of doing so. It is known that provider and recipient accounts are, at best, only moderately correlated (Abbey, Andrews, & Halman, 1995; Antonucci & Israel, 1986; Coriell & Cohen, 1995). Using both measures may allow one to disentangle the benefits of support, which we hypothesized are captured by the unique effects of the provider's account of support, from the costs of support, which we hypothesized are captured by the unique effect of the recipient perceiving that support has occurred.

Figure 1 illustrates these ideas. It shows that support provision and receipt are positively related, reflecting the idea that providers and recipients are likely to agree that instances of support have occurred. However, it also shows that provider and recipient accounts have unique and opposite effects on distress in stressful situations. This causal pattern implies that the most effective type of support transaction is one in which the provider reports providing support but the recipient does not believe that support has occurred, namely, when the benefits of provision are accrued and the costs of receipt are avoided. This is the type of support that we refer to as *invisible.* By the same token, this causal pattern implies that the least effective type of support is one in which the provider does not report providing support but the recipient reports receiving it.

To test these ideas, we conducted a daily diary study that questioned couples about support given and received across a series of weeks. Specifically, we studied 68 couples in which one member was preparing to undergo a major stressful event, the New York State Bar Examination. This is a 2-day examination that all prospective lawyers must pass before practicing law in New York State. Over a 35-day period leading up to and beyond

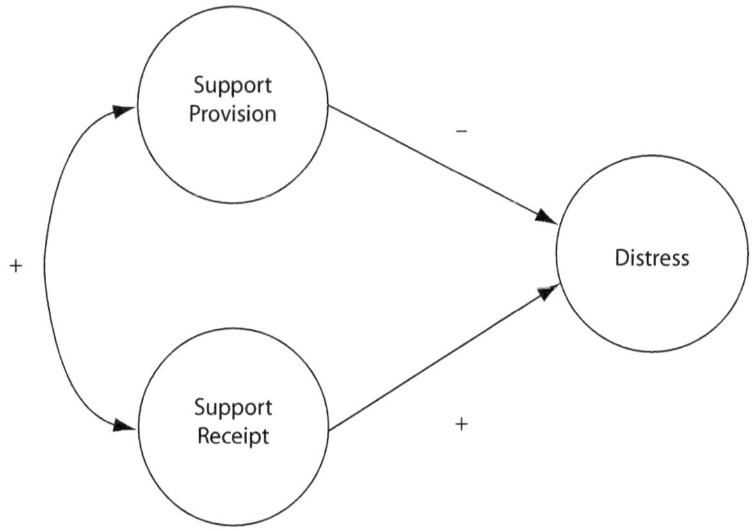

Figure 1. Model of support effects in stressful situations.

the examination, examinees and partners in these couples each completed a brief daily questionnaire. Partners reported their daily provision of emotional support, and examinees reported their daily receipt of emotional support as well as their daily levels of anxiety and depression. We focused on emotional support in the current study because emotional support has been consistently found to be the most effective in reducing distress (Cohen & Wills, 1985; Stroebe & Stroebe, 1996).

We chose to study couples facing this major stressor not only because it allowed us to obtain provider and recipient accounts of enacted support, but also because it allowed us to rule out two other possible explanations for the absence of enacted support effects in prior studies. First, because the objective features of the stressor are the same for each examinee, our design allowed us to circumvent a pervasive problem in identifying enacted support effects, namely that enacted support is confounded by unmeasured differences in stressor severity (Barrera, 1986).

Second, we could examine the validity of the miscarried-helping explanation, that is, that many well-intentioned support attempts fail to meet the needs of those under stress and may even make matters worse (Coyne et al., 1988). If support attempts are frequently miscarried, then our prediction that adjustment will be best when support is given and invisible to the recipient should not be borne out. Rather, adjustment should be best in situations in which the recipient rather than the provider feels that support has occurred.

In summary, then, our study enabled us to investigate a particular explanation for the failure of prior studies to find beneficial effects of enacted support. Our goal was to determine whether these beneficial effects are confined to acts that are invisible to recipients and therefore cannot be captured by traditional measures of enacted support. We did so while at the same time considering two other possible explanations, one based on unmeasured differences in stressor severity and the other based on the view that support attempts are often miscarried.

Method

Design and Sample

To recruit couples, we asked officials at all 15 New York State law schools to distribute recruitment letters to their graduating students. Nine of the schools agreed to do so. The recruitment letters described the study and specified our inclusion criteria. To be eligible, examinees had to be in a romantic relationship with a partner of the opposite sex for at least the last 6 months and had to expect to be living with their partner at the time of the study. Couples in which both members were taking the test were excluded from participation. Our recruitment letters also indicated that couples completing all materials would receive $50.

Because information about the relationship status of graduating law students was not available from law schools, we distributed recruitment letters to all final-year students. Each letter was accompanied by a postcard to be returned to the investigators if the student met the study's eligibility requirements and was interested in finding out more about the study. One hundred forty postcards were returned.* Interested students were then contacted by phone and given more complete details of the study. Of these, 99 couples agreed to participate.

Two months before the examination, couples were sent a background questionnaire that obtained a variety of demographic, social, and personality information not relevant to the current investigation. One month before the examination, couples were sent two booklets of seven daily diaries, one each for the examinee and partner. The daily diary forms for the examinee and partner were identical and consisted of a single sheet of paper. The entire form was designed to be completed in less than 5 min, and participants were instructed to complete a diary form each day at bedtime. The diary period ran from 32 days before to 3 days after the examination. A daily diary procedure such as this is well suited to documenting the effect of support on adjustment because it allows investigators to obtain reports of stressors, support, and distress near the time they occur, thereby minimizing retrospective recall problems (Eckenrode & Bolger, 1997). After completing the 1st week of diaries, participants returned the diary booklet to the investigators using

* Note that because the proportion of graduating law students who met our inclusion criteria was unknown, the number of returned postcards cannot be used to calculate response rates.

an included prestamped envelope. This procedure was repeated for the entire 5 weeks of the diary period.

Of the 99 couples who initially agreed to participate, a final sample of 68 couples (69%) completed all of the materials. Of this final sample, 45 couples (66%) had male examinees. Examinee mean age was 29.4 years *(SD* = 5.1), and partner mean age was 29.5 *(SD* = 5.9). Two thirds of the couples were married, and couples had been living together for an average of 3.3 years *(SD* = 3.8). Eighty-one percent of partners had at least a BA-level education.

Our focus in this article is on the 32 diary days leading up to and including the examination; we did not analyze data from the 3 days following the event. Complete data were obtained on 2,138, or 98%, of the 2,176 (68 X 32) couple-days potentially available for analysis. Thus, the proportion of completed daily diary reports was very high.

Measures

*Examinee distress.*Examinee anxiety and depression were measured daily with items from the Profile of Mood States (Lorr & McNair, 1971). For each affect, the four highest loading items from a factor analysis conducted by Lorr and McNair (1971) were used. The items tapping anxiety were "on edge," "uneasy," "anxious," and "nervous." The items tapping depression were "sad," "discouraged," "hopeless," and "worthless." Examinees were asked to rate the extent to which they had felt or experienced these feelings in the past 24 hr. They responded by circling the appropriate number on a 5-point scale ranging from *not at all* (0) to *extremely* (4). Daily scores for each affect were obtained by averaging the ratings of the relevant items.

Support provision and receipt. Partners' provision of emotional support to the examinees was assessed on each diary day. This measure consisted of a single item, in which each partner reported whether he or she had "listened to and comforted" the examinee within the previous 24 hr. This dichotomous variable was coded .5 if partners reported providing support and —.5 if they did not. Similarly, each day examinees completed a parallel item, in which they reported whether they had received emotional support (as defined above) from their partners. Again this variable was coded .5 if examinees reported receiving support and —.5 if they did not.

The bar examination as a stressor. Our prospective design was intended to capture increases in the perceived threat of the bar examination as the event approached. In particular, we expected that the final week before the examination would be a time of high threat, when the examination was imminent and the possibilities for further preparatory study were almost over. Preliminary inspection of our data revealed that, as was found in a previous study of students preparing to take the Medical College Admission Test (Bolger & Eckenrode, 1991), appreciable increases in distress were evident only in the final week before the examination. Therefore, to distinguish a period of high threat from a period of more moderate threat, we divided the preexamination period into two phases, one involving the first 25 days of the diary period and the other involving Days 26 to 32. For analysis purposes (see *Multilevel Statistical Model),* Phase 1 was coded —.5 and Phase 2 was coded .5. The mean levels of anxiety in the first and second phases were 1.83 and 2.62, respectively, paired $t(67) = 18.87$, $p < .001$. Comparable means for depression were 0.58 and 0.70, paired $t(67) = 5.06$, $p < .001$.

Multilevel Statistical Model

The goal of the analysis was to examine the stress-protective effect of *enacted support,* defined as the reduction in the relationship between stressor onset and distressed mood as a function of supportive interactions with one's partner. As discussed earlier, we hypothesized that the unique effect of support from the provider's perspective would be to reduce the negative effects of a stressor, whereas the unique effect of support from the recipient's perspective would be to increase its effects.

The analysis was accomplished using a multilevel or hierarchical linear model (Bryk & Raudenbush, 1992; Goldstein, 1995; Kenny, Kashy, & Bolger, 1998; Kreft & De Leeuw, 1998; Snijders & Bosker, 1999). A multilevel model allowed us to obtain separate estimates of the effects of support provision and receipt on adjustment to the bar examination for each couple and to efficiently aggregate these estimates such that results for the average couple were obtained. In addition, it allowed us to test the possibility that couples differ significantly in these effects and to take account of this variability in constructing tests of significance.

Our statistical model specifies that each couple in the population has its own characteristic relationship between support provision and receipt and adjustment to a stressor, in this case, the approach of the bar examination. Note that a within-couple analysis approach ensures that any between-couples factors, such as average examinee distress or personality, cannot account for any associations found (see Kenny et al., 1998, for a discussion of this point).

Because cross-sectional associations between support and adjustment are likely to reflect in part the effects of adjustment on support (as found, e.g., by Bolger et al., 1996), we focused on longitudinal associations, specifically, those with a 1-day lag.* Thus, support provision and receipt and their interactions with stressor phase on day t are all hypothesized to affect change in distress from day t to day $t + 1$. To rule out the possibility that any lagged effect of support on adjustment might be an artifact of initial adjustment (see Bolger et al,, 1996), initial distress was included in the model as a control variable. In such

* In preliminary analyses we examined 2- and 3-day time lags, but we found no evidence of effects beyond a 1-day lag.

a model the dependent variable can be interpreted as residualized change in distress from day t to day $t + 1$ (Kessler & Greenberg, 1981).

The analysis model for each couple can be written as follows:

$$\Delta D_{t+1} = b_0 + b_1 D_t + b_2 S_t + b_3 P_t + b_4 R_t + b_5 (P_t \times S_t) + b_6 (R_t \times S_t) + e_{t+1}, \quad (1)$$

where ΔD_{t+1} is the change in examinee's distress between day t and day $t + 1$; D_t is the examinee's distress on day t (with the grand mean across all couple-days subtracted); S_t is the stressor phase (coded —.5 for the first 25 days of the diary period and .5 for the final week up to and including the examination*); P_t is the partner's report of providing emotional support on day t (coded .5 if the partner reported providing support and —.5 if he or she did not); R_t is the examinee's report of receiving emotional support on day t (coded .5 if the examinee reported receiving support and -.5 if he or she did not); $(P_t \times S_t)$ and $(R_t \times S_t)$ are the interactions between phase and the provision and receipt of support on day f, respectively; and e_{t+1} is a residual component of change in the examinee's distress. The coefficient b_0 is the regression intercept, and the coefficients b_1, through b_6 are the effects of the six independent variables.

We hypothesized that the coefficient for $(P_t \times S_t)$ would be negative, reflecting that support provision reduces the effect of the stressor on distress. In contrast, we hypothesized that the coefficient for $(R_t \times S_t)$ would be positive, reflecting that support receipt exacerbates the effect of the stressor on distress.

Although our model allowed for each couple to have unique estimates of support effects, the focus of the current study was on support effects for the average couple. To obtain estimates of these effects, we used a maximum likelihood (ML) approach, as implemented in SAS Institute's PROC MIXED software (Littell, Milliken, Stroup, & Wolfinger, 1996; SAS Institute, 1997; see Kenny et al., 1998, for a discussion of alternative approaches to estimation of these models). Thus, the results presented for Equation 1 are ML estimates for the average couple.

Results

Table 1 shows the frequency of emotional support provision and receipt and the degree of concordance between the two. On 65% of the days on which partners reported providing

* The more usual type of effect coding in linear models is — 1, 1, but -.5, .5 has the advantage of making the coefficient for the effect-coded variable more interpretable. With —1, 1, the coefficient is interpreted as half the mean difference in the dependent variable associated with the two categories of the predictor variable. With -.5, .5, the coefficient is simply the mean difference itself.

support, examinees agreed that the support had been provided. On 56% of the days on which partners did not report providing support, examinees agreed that it had not been provided. In all, concordant days accounted for 61% of diary days. Although these results show that there was appreciable agreement between partners on the occurrence of emotional support, they also demonstrate that providers and recipients often had discordant perceptions of such support interactions.

Table 1 Partner's Report of Emotional Support Provision by Examinee's Report of Emotional Support Receipt (N = 2,138 Couple-Days)

	Support provision					
	No		Yes		Total	
Support receipt	*N*	%	*N*	%	*N*	%
No	503	56	434	35	937	44Yes
Yes	395	44	806	65	1,201	56
Total	898	100	1,240	100	2,138	100

We next examined the effects of support provision and receipt on adjustment in the two diary phases, as specified in Equation 1. We estimated this equation twice, once for each of the distress variables, anxiety and depression.* Recall that phase, emotional support provision, and emotional support receipt were effect coded (- .5, .5), distress on day *t* had the sample mean subtracted, and the dependent variable was change in distress from day *t* to day *t* + 1 (see Aiken & West, 1991, for a discussion of the desirability of this type of coding in regression analyses involving interaction effects). Given that change in distress for Day 32 would involve using data obtained on the day after the examination had ended,

* In preliminary analyses, we examined whether the estimates for Equation 1 differed depending on whether the examinee was male or female. No evidence of gender differences emerged. Also, we initially estimated models that included (a) a two-way interaction between support provision and receipt and (b) a three-way interaction between support provision, support receipt, and stressor phase. Neither of these effects was statistically significant.

we omitted Day 32 from the analysis.* The number of couple-days available for analysis was reduced from 2,138 to 2,072.

Table 2 Effects of Emotional Support Provision and Receipt on Adjustment to the Bar Examination: Multilevel Model Results for Examinee Daily Anxiety and Depression (N = 68 Couples [2,072 Couple-Days])

	Change in anxiety from day	*t* to day *t +1*		Change from day	in depression *t* to day *t* + 1	
Predictor on day *t*	*b*	t(67)	*P*	b	t(67)	*P*
Intercept	0.14	3.22	.002	0.01	0.38	.702
Initial anxiety/ depression	-0.50	-18.30	.000	-0.62	-18.36	.000
Stressor phase	0.40	9.57	.000	0.07	2.38	.020
Support provision	-0.04	-0.94	.350	-0.07	-2.67	.008
Support receipt	0.12	2.29	.025	0.04	1.57	.117
Provision X Phase	-0.03	-0.32	.748	-0.18	-3.45	.001
Receipt X Phase	0.17	2.02	.047	0.13	2.59	.010

Note. The analysis is based on the 31 days up to and including the examination. Stressor phase contrasts the final week (Days 26–31) with the previous 25 days (Days 1–25). Emotional support provision and receipt and stressor phase are effect-coded variables (-.5, .5). The initial level of anxiety/depression has the sample mean (across couples and days) subtracted.

Anxiety

In the left-hand side of Table 2 are the estimates for Equation 1 for anxiety.† The intercept indicates that for average days (average in terms of initial anxiety, phase, and support

---

* Distress on Days 33 to 35 was very low compared with distress at any point during the previous 32 days (see Thompson & Bolger, 1999); thus, we did not wish to confound support effects on Day 32 with the sharp decline in distress associated with the end of the examination.

† We noted earlier that our analysis approach allowed for each couple to have unique estimates of the coefficients in Equation 1. However, results showed that only three of the coefficients differed across couples: the intercept (b0), the coefficient for today's dependent variable (b1,), and the coefficient for support receipt (b4). The standard deviations of these differences were 0.306, 0.147, and 0.229, respectively. In a multilevel model such as this, in which some coefficients vary randomly across couples and some are fixed, tests of significance for the fixed coefficients can be based on the degrees of freedom for

provision and receipt), anxiety increased by 0.14 units from one day to the next, *t(67)* = 3.22, $p = .002$. The phase effect indicates that, on average, this increase in anxiety was 0.40 units higher in the high-stress than in the moderate-stress phase, t(67) = 9.57, $p = .000$. There was no evidence that, averaging over stressor phase, support provision on a given day predicted subsequent declines in anxiety, $b = -0.04$, t(67) = -0.94, $p = .350$, nor was there evidence that this effect varied by stressor phase, $b = -0.03$, t(67) = -0.32, $p = .748$.

There was evidence, however, that support receipt on a given day predicted subsequent increases in anxiety, $b = 0.12$, t(67) = 2.29, $p = .025$, and that this effect varied by stressor phase, $b = 0.17$, t(67) = 2.02, $p = .047$. Specifically, when recipients reported receiving support on a given day, the likelihood of their anxiety increasing the following day was 0.17 units greater in the high-stress phase than in the moderate-stress phase.

These estimates can be used to calculate the separate effect of support provision and receipt in each stressor phase.* In the moderate-stress phase, support effects of either kind are negligible: provision $b = -0.03$, *t(61)* = -0.73, $p = .467$; receipt $b = 0.04$, t(67) = 0.81, $p = .418$. In the high-stress phase, the provision effect is once again negligible, b = —0.06, t(67) = —0.73, $p = .468$, but the receipt effect is substantial and statistically significant, b = 0.21, r(67) = 2.53, $p = .014$.†

Figure 2 shows predicted mean anxiety change for various combinations of provision and receipt in the high-stress phase. Consistent with the effects reported above, examinee reports of emotional support receipt are associated with larger anxiety increases, whereas partner reports of support provision are associated with smaller (and nonsignificant)

---

days, 1,864, rather than for couples, 67. Clearly, using the former degrees of freedom would result in smaller p values in significance tests. This approach presumes that the coefficients truly do not vary in the population, but it is known that power to detect such random effects is small in many empirical studies (Kenny et al., 1998). Therefore, we chose to take a conservative approach to significance testing and used a df of 67 for tests on all coefficients.

* Given the coding used in the analysis, the support provision effect in Phase 1, for example, is the main-effect coefficient for provision (fc3) minus 0.5 times the Provision X Phase interaction coefficient (fc5), that is, -0.04 - 0.5(-0.03) = -0.03.

† Our analysis approach emphasized the unique effects of provision and receipt, but it could be argued that what is common in these reports is a more valid measure of support actually exchanged. To take account of this concern, we conducted a parallel set of analyses in which, instead of provision and receipt as predictors, we used (a) the mean of the provision and receipt (a measure of what is common to the two reports) and (b) the difference between provision and receipt (a measure of discrepancy). Although it may not be obvious, this parallel analysis explains exactly the same variance in the dependent variables. For anxiety, what this analysis revealed is that the mean of provision and receipt is relatively unimportant; rather, what is important is the extent to which provision is greater than receipt. In the high-stress phase, the effect of the mean of provision and receipt was 0.08, t(67) = 1.54, p = .128, whereas the effect of the difference (provision minus receipt) was —0.27, t(61) = —2.20, p = .032.

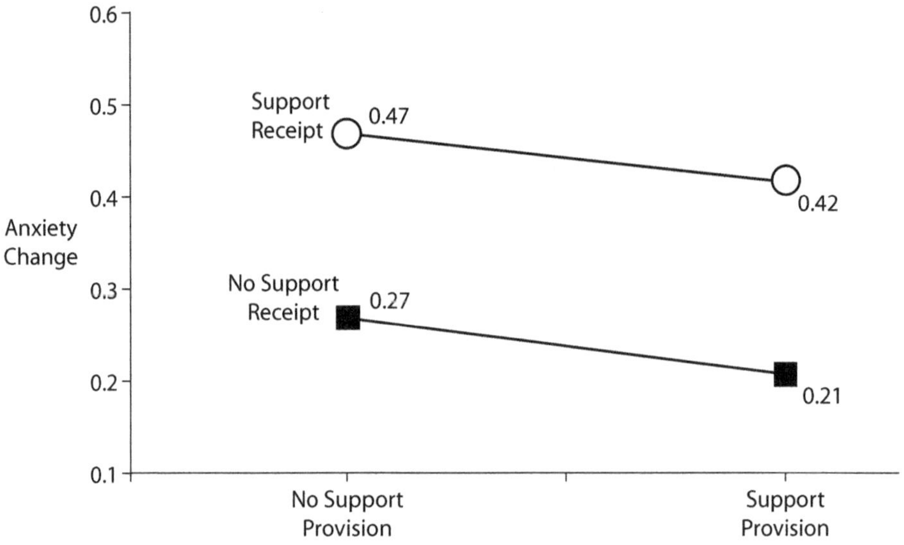

Figure 2. Emotional support effect in the high-stress phase: anxiety.

anxiety increases. Interestingly, although the effects of provision were not significant, note that the lowest levels of anxiety increase were found in the invisible support condition, that is, the condition involving provision but no receipt.

Depression

The results for depression are presented in the right-hand side of Table 2.* The intercept shows that for days that were average in terms of initial depression, phase, and support provision and receipt, depression did not increase from one day to the next, b = -0.01, t(67) = 0.38, p = .702. The phase effect shows that, on average, the day-to-day increase in depression was 0.07 units higher in the high-stress phase than the moderate-stress phase. Averaging across phase, support provision predicted relative declines in depression over time, b = —0.07, t(67) = —2.67, p = .008, and this effect was greater in the high-stress as compared with the moderate-stress phase, b = —0.18, f(67) = -3.45, p = 001. Averaging across phase, there was some evidence that support receipt predicted a relative increase in

* As in the case of anxiety, only three of the seven coefficients in Equation 1 varied across couples: the intercept (b0), the coefficient for today's depression (h,), and the coefficient for phase (b3). The standard deviations of these couple differences were 0.251, 0.191, and 0.123, respectively. Once again we took a conservative approach to significance testing and used the degrees of freedom for couples, 67, for tests on all coefficients.

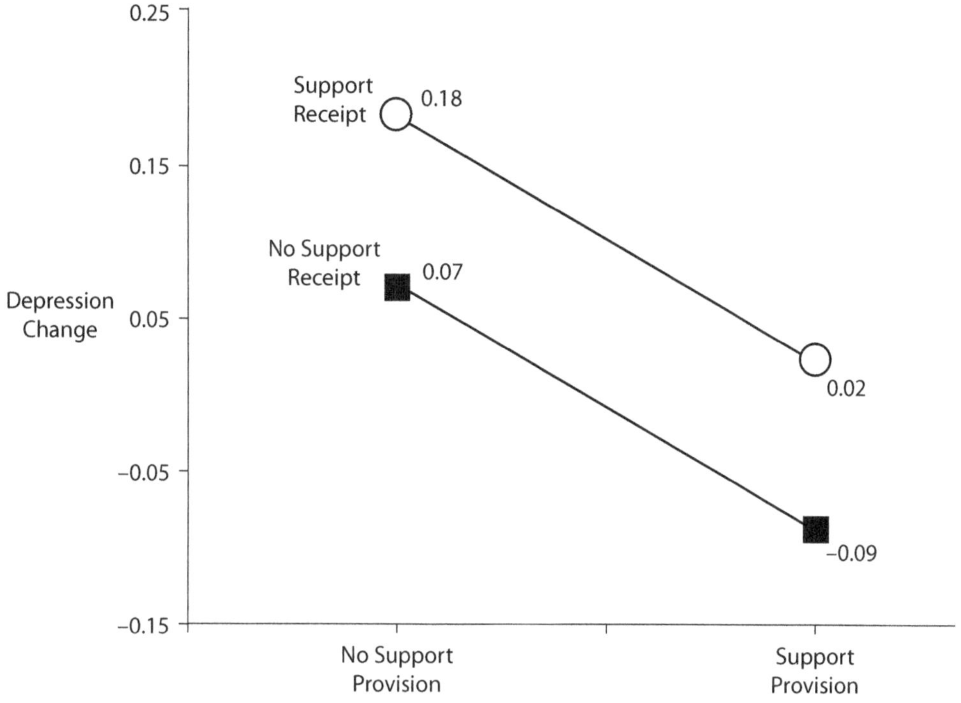

Figure 3. Emotional support effect in the high-stress phase: depression.

depression over time, b = 0.04, t(67) = 1.57, p = .117, and this effect was greater in the high-stress compared with the moderate-stress phase, b = 0.13, f(67) = 2.59, p = .010.

Once again, it is useful to examine the provision and receipt effects in each stressor phase. In the moderate-stress phase, support effects of either kind are again negligible: provision b = 0.01, t(67) = 0.61, p = .544; receipt b = -0.02, t(67) = -0.92, p = .362. In the high-stress phase, however, both effects are substantial, opposite in sign, and statistically significant: provision b = -0.16, t(67) = -3.41, p = .001; receipt b = 0.11, t(67) = 2.31, p = .024. Thus, in the high-stress phase, when partners reported providing support on a given day, the change in recipients' depression from that day to the next was 0.16 units lower than it was when partners did not report providing support. By contrast, when recipients reported receiving support on a given day, the change in their depression was 0.11 units higher than it was when they did not report receiving support.*

* Again we conducted a parallel analysis that estimated the effects of the mean support and the discrepancy in support (provision minus receipt). This analysis revealed results similar to those found for anxiety: The average level of support was unimportant in predicting depression; rather, depression declined most when providers' accounts of support exceeded those of recipients. For depression in the

Figure 3 shows predicted mean depression change for various combinations of provision and receipt in the high-stress phase. The extremes in the figure are most notable. The best situation is the one we would label as *invisible support,* in which partners said they provided emotional support but examinees said they did not receive it. In this situation, depression tended to decrease over time by 0.09 units, $t(67) = -1.73$, $p = .088$. The worst situation was one in which providers said they did not provide support but recipients said they received it. Here, examinees experienced the costs of receipt, failed to experience the benefits of provision, and their depression increased by 0.18 units, $t(67) = 3.30$, $p = .002$.

Discussion

This research helps resolve a puzzle in the social support literature: Although the perception that support is available is associated with better adjustment, the perception that one has been the recipient of specific supportive acts is not. Given that individual supportive acts are the presumed building blocks of generalized beliefs about support availability, why do such acts not appear to benefit the recipient? Our findings suggest that such acts do, infact, benefit the recipient. However, relying solely on recipients' reports of support receipt masks this beneficial effect, because there is a cost to adjustment of feeling that one has received support.

Specifically, using a daily diary design to study couples in which one member was preparing for the New York State Bar Examination, we obtained the examinee's reports of receiving emotional support from the partner and the partner's reports of providing emotional support to the examinee. By capitalizing on the fact that couples' reports of provision and receipt did not always agree, it was possible in the case of depression to show that reports of support provision were associated with increased examinee adjustment, whereas reports of support receipt were associated with decreased examinee adjustment. Thus, these results suggest that the most beneficial support is that which is invisible to the recipient. In this situation, the recipient reaps the benefits of support provision without incurring the cost of support receipt.

Whereas the hypothesized pattern was found for depression, only part of the pattern was found for anxiety. Emotional support receipt increased anxiety, but emotional support provision did not decrease anxiety. How can one make sense of this pattern? The ineffectiveness of support in alleviating anxiety is interpretable if one considers the high degree of threat posed by the bar examination. Because so much career success is at stake, this event is considered highly stressful by almost all who take it. Thus, for an event as threatening as this, there may be little partners can do to lower the anticipatory anxiety it

---

high-stress phase, the effect of the mean of provision and receipt was -0.03, $t(67) = —0.87$, $p = .386$, whereas the effect of the difference (provision minus receipt) was —0.27, $t(67) = -3.63$, $p = .001$.

provokes. However, it does appear that partners can help alleviate symptoms of anticipatory depression and discouragement.

It is important to note that the pattern of results found here cannot be explained by processes involving unmeasured stressor severity or miscarried helping. Although the null or negative effects of support receipt found in previous studies could have been due to unmeasured differences in stressor severity, this seems unlikely in the current study because the stressor was objectively the same for each participant. Similarly, our results are inconsistent with the idea of miscarried helping, whereby the provider's efforts to be helpful are perceived as unhelpful and thus unlikely to be coded as support (Coyne et al., 1988). Recall that this is precisely the situation we labeled *invisible support* and one that we found to be associated with the lowest distress. If miscarried helping was a common form of invisible support then it seems unlikely we would have found the results we did.

Issues for Future Research

These findings raise several important issues for future research. First, whereas the findings help explain why traditional measures of enacted support (those based on recipient accounts) fail to buffer the effects of stressors on adjustment, they do not explain the beneficial effects of perceived support availability. Some have suggested that perceptions of support availability are an aspect of personality and may have little bearing on how much support has been received in the recent past (Lakey & Cassady, 1990; Sarason, Pierce, & Sarason, 1990). Our findings, however, leave open the possibility that perceived support availability measures capture, to some extent, support that has been provided. Thus, it will be important in future research to examine the relation between perceived support availability and partner reports of support provision, especially of invisible support provision.

Second, we have not directly examined why the perception that one has been supported is associated with heightened distress. It has been suggested that the receipt of aid can entail a self-esteem cost to the extent that it challenges the recipient's sense of personal competence in a valued domain. A number of classic laboratory studies bolster this view (Fisher et al., 1982; Shapiro, 1978). Support receipt can also amplify distress by making recipients aware that their distress and incompetence are publicly visible, thereby prompting concern that others will evaluate them negatively. Finally, it is possible that support receipt may have a negative effect by unintentionally drawing recipients' attention toward rather than away from their negative mood. In so doing, it may increase the impact of the negative mood on subsequent cognitions and behavior, thereby leading to an increasing spiral of negativity. Future studies will need to assess the extent to which these possible explanations can account for the effects reported here.

Third, it is important to reiterate that we do not believe that invisible support, as identified in this study, is a single type of support. Rather, we believe that it involves at least two types. The first is composed of acts that are beneficial to the recipient but which occur outside of the recipient's awareness. That is, the provider does something in the background that the recipient never finds out about, such as dealing with problems that would have distressed the recipient had he or she known about them or had to deal with them. This type of support has been referred to by Coyne as *protective buffering* (see, e.g., Coyne & Smith, 1991). The data were not available in our study to determine what proportion of invisible support is of this type, but such data could be obtained in future daily diary studies.

The second type of invisible support is one that is accomplished in such a skillful way that, although information about the transaction is available to the recipient, the transaction is not coded as enacted support. Because the supportive act is not made salient, recipients avoid me accompanying increase in the salience of then-distress, their doubts about their competence in the problem domain, and their perception that their distress and incompetence are publicly visible. This type of invisible support, whereby information that support has been given is available but is not coded as received, is likely to characterize the expert face-to-face social support that is the essence of good parenting, good mentoring, and good friendships, and being a good clinician or social worker.

What is involved in such expert support? Politeness theory (P. Brown & Levinson, 1987) provides one potential answer, suggesting that such support is indirect, which involves providing support without drawing attention to the recipient's need. For example, indirect instrumental support might involve providing the solution to an instrumental problem in such a way that recipients think they have discovered it themselves. Indirect emotional support might involve acknowledging the normatively distressing nature of the recipient's situation and highlighting how others are coping more poorly or commenting on something positive about the recipient. Assessing whether such indirect support underlies the effects reported here is an important topic for future investigation. It would be interesting to establish whether skillful support providers disguise their support efforts by providing support in indirect ways. Similarly, it would be interesting to determine whether skillful support recipients interpret helpful actions in ways that downplay the recipient's sense of indebtedness or ineptitude.

Our focus in this article has been on supportive acts that providers code as support but recipients do not. However, supportive acts that neither party code as support may most closely approximate what Lieberman (1986) had in mind when he described effective support as support that occurs so smoothly that people may not be aware of it. Clearly, with our current methodology we are unable to identify this type of daily support. We have no way of knowing how common such interactions are or whether they exert a particularly beneficial effect on adjustment. We suspect, however, that they occur frequently, particularly in communal relationships such as marriages (Clark & Reis, 1988) and in companionate relationships, that is, relationships that are sources of pleasurable shared activities (Coyne & Bolger, 1990; Rook, 1987, 1990). To study such support processes it may be necessary to use behavioral observation methods, an approach that is rare in the support literature (see Cutrona & Suhr, 1994; Pasch & Bradbury, 1998, for exceptions).

Future research will also need to establish the generalizability of our findings. It may be that certain types of stressors are more likely to elicit invisible support than others do. It is plausible to expect that emotional support is more likely to be invisible than is instrumental support, but future analyses may show that this is not the case. Moreover, there may be individual differences in the extent to which invisible support is beneficial. For example, although there are important gender differences in stress and support processes (Taylor et al., 2000), our sample of female examinees ($N = 23$) may have been too small to detect them. It is also known that support processes vary as a function of personality (e.g., Nolen-Hoeksema & Davis, 1999), and it will be important to consider this source of heterogeneity in future research.

Caveats and Conclusions

This study has a number of important limitations. First, we have relied on support-provider and support-recipient accounts of support transactions. We have no way of knowing the accuracy of these accounts or whether providers are more or less accurate than recipients. It is likely that both are fallible reporters and that this explains some of the discrepancies between their accounts.

Second, an inherent problem in diary studies is that to reduce time demands on participants, less-than-ideal measures of constructs must be used. In the case of emotional support, this has led us to use a crude single-item measure. Although we have no direct measure of its reliability and validity, it is clear that if it had been completely unreliable we would not have found any effects of our measures of distress. The question of validity is more difficult to answer, except to say that the content of the support item has face validity and the wording is similar to items used in the well-validated Inventory of Socially Supportive Behaviors developed by Barrera and his colleagues (Barrera, Sandler, & Ramsay, 1981).

Third, we have focused on support processes over a relatively short period of time, 32 days, and we have used day-to-day changes in distress as our outcome variable. Thus, we were not able to examine longer term support processes or how these might matter for longer term emotional functioning.

Despite these limitations, we have documented that social support processes are a good deal more complex than previously considered in empirical research on enacted support. In particular, our data suggest that the most effective support transactions may also be the most subtle. This finding poses both methodological and conceptual challenges and raises a wide variety of questions that should be the focus of future investigation.

Abbey, A., Andrews, F. M., & Halman, L. J. (1995). Provision and receipt of social support and disregard: What is their impact on the marital life quality of infertile and fertile couples? *Journal of Personality and Social Psychology, 68,* 455–469.

Aiken, L. S., & West, S. G. (1991). *Multiple regression: Testing and interpreting interactions.* Thousand Oaks, CA: Sage.

Antonucci, T. C, & Israel, B. A. (1986). Veridicality of social support: A comparison of principal and network members' responses. *Journal of Consulting and Clinical Psychology, 54,* 432–437.

Barrera Jr., M. (1986). Distinctions between social support concepts, measures, and models. *American Journal of Community Psychology, 14,* 413–445.

Barrera Jr., M., Sandler, I. N., & Ramsay, T. B. (1981). Preliminary development of a scale of social support: Studies on college students. *American Journal of Community Psychology, 9,* 435–447.

Bolger, N., & Eckenrode, J. (1991). Social relationships, personality, and anxiety during a major stressful event. *Journal of Personality and Social Psychology, 61,* 440–449.

Bolger, N., Foster, M., Vinokur, A. D., & Ng, R. (1996). Close relationships and adjustment to a life crisis: The case of breast cancer. *Journal of Personality and Social Psychology, 70,* 283–294.

Brown, B. B. (1978). Social and psychological correlates of help-seeking behavior among urban adults. *American Journal of Community Psychology, 6,* 425–439.

Brown, P., & Levinson, S. (1987). *Politeness: Some universals in language usage.* New York: Cambridge University Press.

Bryk, A. S., Raudenbush, S. W. (1992). *Hierarchical linear models: Applications and data analysis methods.* Thousand Oaks, CA: Sage.

Clark, M. S., & Reis, H. T. (1988). Interpersonal processes in close relationships. *Annual Review of Psychology, 39,* 609–672.

Cohen, S. (1992). Stress, social support, and disorder. In H. O. F. Veiel & U. Baumann (Eds.), *The meaning and measurement of social support* (pp. 109–124). New York: Hemisphere.

Cohen, S., & Wills, T. A. (1985). Stress, support, and the buffering hypothesis. *Psychological Bulletin, 98,* 310–357.

Coriell, M, & Cohen, S. (1995). Concordance in the face of a stressful event: When do members of a dyad agree that one person supported the other? *Journal of Personality and Social Psychology, 69,* 289–299.

Coyne, J. C, & Bolger, N. (1990). Doing without social support as an explanatory concept. *Journal of Social and Clinical Psychology, 9,* 148–158.

Coyne, J. C, & Smith, D. A. F. (1991). Couples coping with myocardial infarction: A contextual perspective on wives' distress. *Journal of Personality and Social Psychology, 61,* 404–412.

Coyne, J. C, Wortman, C. B., & Lehman, D. R. (1988). The other side of support: Emotional overinvolvement and miscarried helping. In B. H.Gottlieb (Ed.), *Marshaling social support* (pp. 305–330). Thousand Oaks, CA: Sage.

Cutrona, C. E. (1986). Behavioral manifestations of social support: A microanalytic investigation. *Journal of Personality and Social Psychology, 51,* 201–208.

Cutrona, C. E., & Suhr, J. A. (1994). Social support communication in the context of marriage: An analysis of couples' supportive interactions. In B. R. Burleson, T. L. Albrecht, & I. G. Sarason (Eds.), *Communication of social support: Messages, interactions, relationships, and community* (pp. 113–135). Thousand Oaks, CA: Sage.

Dunkel-Schetter, C, & Bennett, T. L. (1990). Differentiating the cognitive and behavioral aspects of social support. In B. R. Sarason, I. G. Sarason, & G. R. Pierce (Eds.), *Social support: An interactional view* (pp. 267–296). New York: Wiley.

Eckenrode, J. (1983). The mobilization of social supports: Some individual constraints. *American Journal of Community Psychology, 11,* 509–528.

Eckenrode, J., & Bolger, N. (1997). Daily and within-day event measurement. In S. Cohen, R. C. Kessler, & L. U. Gordon (Eds.), *Measuring stress: A guide for health and social scientists* (pp. 80–101). New York: Oxford University Press.

Eckenrode, J., & Wethington, E. (1990). The process and outcome of mobilizing social support. In S. W. Duck & R. C. Silver (Eds.), *Personal relationships and social support* (pp. 83–103). Thousand Oaks, CA: Sage.

Fisher, J. D., Nadler, A., & Whitcher-Alagna, S. (1982). Recipient reactions to aid. *Psychological Bulletin, 91,* 27–54.

Goldstein, H. (1995). *Multilevel statistical models* (2nd ed.). New York: Wiley.

Gottlieb, B. H. (1988). Marshaling social support: The state of the art in research and practice. In B. H. Gottlieb (Ed.), *Marshaling social support.* Thousand Oaks, CA: Sage.

Heller, K„ Swindle, R. W., & Dusenbury, L. (1986). Component social support processes: Comments and integration. *Journal of Consulting and Clinical Psychology, 54,* 466–470.

Hobfoll, S. E., & Vaux, A. (1993). Social support: Social resources and social context. In L. Goldberger & S. Breznitz (Eds.), *Handbook of stress* (pp. 685–705). New York: Free Press.

House, J. S., Landis, K. R., & Umberson, D. (1988). Social relationships and health. *Science, 241,* 540–545.

Kenny, D. A., Kashy, D., & Bolger, N. (1998). Data analysis in social psychology. In D. T. Gilbert, S. T. Fiske, & G. Lindzey (Eds.), *Handbook of social psychology* (4th ed.; Vol. 1, pp. 233–265). Boston: McGraw-Hill.

Kessler, R. C, & Greenberg, D. F. (1981). *Linear panel analysis: Models of quantitative change.* New York: Academic Press.

Kreft, I. G. G., & De Leeuw, J. (1998). *Introducing multilevel modeling.* Thousand Oaks, CA: Sage.

Lakey, B., & Cassady, P. B. (1990). Cognitive processes in perceived social support. *Journal of Personality and Social Psychology, 59,* 337— 343.

Lieberman, M. A. (1986). Social supports—me consequences of psychologizing: A commentary. *Journal of Consulting and Clinical Psychology, 54,* 461–465.

Littell, R. C, Milliken, G. A., Stroup, W. W., & Wolfinger, R. D. (1996). *SAS system for mixed models.* Cary, NC: SAS Institute.

Lorr, M., & McNair, D. M. (1971). *The Profile of Mood States manual.* San Diego, CA: Educational and Industrial Testing Service.

Nolen-Hoeksema, S., & Davis, C. G. (1999). "Thanks for sharing that": Ruminators and their social support networks. *Journal of Personality and Social Psychology, 77,* 801–814.

Pasch, L. A., & Bradbury, T. N. (1998). Social support, conflict, and the development of marital dysfunction. *Journal of Consulting and Clinical Psychology, 66,* 219–230.

Reis, H. T. (1984). Social interaction and well-being. In S. Duck (Ed.), *Personal relationships V: Repairing personal relationships.* New York: Academic Press.

Rook, K. S. (1987). Social support versus companionship: Effects on life stress, loneliness, and evaluations by others. *Journal of Personality and Social Psychology, 52,* 1132–1147.

Rook, K. S. (1990). Social relationships as a source of companionship: Implications for older adults' psychological well-being. In B. R. Sara-son, I. G. Sarason, & G. R. Pierce (Eds.), *Social support: An interactional view* (pp. 219–250). New York: Wiley.

Sarason, B. R., Pierce, G. R., & Sarason, I. G. (1990). Social support: The sense of acceptance and the role of relationships. In B. R. Sarason, I. G. Sarason, & G. R. Pierce (Eds.), *Social support: An interactional view* (pp. 97–128). New York: Wiley.

Sarason, B. R., Sarason, I. G., & Gurung, R. A. R. (1997). Close personal relationships and health outcomes: A key to the role of social support. In S. Duck (Ed.), *Handbook of personal relationships* (2nd ed., pp. 547–573). New York: Wiley.

SAS Institute. (1997). *SAS/STAT software: Changes and enhancements through release 6.12.* Cary, NC: Author.

Shapiro, E. G. (1978). Embarrassment and help-seeking. In B. M. DePaulo, A. Nadler, & J. D. Fisher (Eds.), *New directions in helping: Vol. 2. Help-seeking* (pp. 143–164). New York: Academic Press.

Snijders, T. A. B., & Bosker, R. J. (1999). *Multilevel analysis: An introduction to basic and advanced multilevel modeling.* Thousand Oaks, CA: Sage.

Stroebe, W., & Stroebe, M. (1996). The social psychology of social support. In E. T. Higgins & A. W. Kruglanski (Eds.), *Social psychology: Handbook of basic principles* (pp. 597–621). New York: Guilford Press.

Taylor, S. E., Klein, K. C., Lewis, B. P., Gruenewald, T. L., Gurung, R. A. R., & Updegraff, J. A. (2000). Biobehavioral responses to stress in females: Tend-and-befriend, not fight-or-flight. *Psychological Review, 107,* 411–429.

Thompson, A., & Bolger, N. (1999). Emotional transmission in couples under stress. *Journal of Marriage and the Family, 61,* 38–48.

Wethington, E., & Kessler, R. C. (1986). Perceived support, received support, and adjustment to stressful life events. *Journal of Health and Social Behavior, 27,* 78–89.

Wills, T. A. (1990). Social support and interpersonal relationships. In M. S. Clark (Ed.), *Review of personality and social psychology* (Vol. 12, pp. 265–289). Thousand Oaks, CA: Sage.

Niall Bolger, Department of Psychology, New York University; Adam Zuckerman, International Survey Research Corporation, Chicago, Illinois; Ronald C. Kessler, Department of Health Care Policy, Harvard Medical School.

This research was supported in part by National Institute of Mental Health Grant MH60366. We are grateful to David Amarel, Jessica Cameron, James Coyne, Geraldine Downey, Andrew Fuligni, Diane Hughes, Julie Lewis, Edward Seidman, Beth Shinn, and Patrick Shrout for comments on previous drafts of this article.

TIME TO SAY "GOOD-BYE:" DISSOLUTION AND LOSS

Relationship Dissolution

Antecedents, Processes, and Consequences

By Anita L. Vangelisti

Very few people enter marriage and other committed romantic relationships with plans to divorce or break up. Nonetheless, many of their relationships end. Relational dissolution has become a mainstay of popular culture with approximately 50 percent of first-time marriages, and an even higher percentage of remarriages, ending in separation or divorce (Bramlett & Mosher, 2002; Cherlin, 1992). Researchers, theorists, and laypeople, alike, have become increasingly concerned with the effects of relational dissolution on individuals and on society, as about 40 percent of children will experience the divorce of their parents and nearly half of all children will live in a single-parent household at .some point before they reach adulthood (Cherlin, 1992; Click, 1989; see also, Noller, this volume).

The purpose of this chapter is to review the literature associated with the breakdown and termination of marriage and oilier committed romantic relationships. More specifically, the antecedents, processes, and consequences associated with relationship dissolution will be examined. Because the literature covering these issues is vast, the review will necessarily he selective, focusing on major themes and well-established findings. The omission of particular studies or lines of research is not a commentary on their worth, but rather a function of the need to confine the length of the review. It is also important to note that the literature on relationship dissolution does not always provide even-handed

Anita L. Vangelisti; Patricia Noller, Judith A. Feeney, eds., "Relationship Dissolution: Antecedents, Processes, and Consequences," from *Close Relationships: Functions, Forms and Processes*, Pp. 353–374. Published by Routledge, 2006.

coverage of different types of relationships. For example, studies examining the consequences of dissolution focus primarily on the termination of marital relationships, as opposed to the termination of dating or cohabiting relationships. Hence, the current review will include comments, when appropriate, about the types of relationships that were studied.

ANTECEDENTS

Because researchers and theorists, like laypeople, have been concerned with the rate of divorce during the second half of the twentieth century, a great deal of effort has been devoted to understanding the factors that predict relational dissolution (see, e.g., Cate, Levin, & Richmond, 2002; Karney & Bradbury, 1995; Rodrigues, Hall, & Fincham, in press). A review of the literature suggests that these factors can be loosely grouped into three categories: individual, dyadic, and network characteristics. Although most of this literature has focused on the ability of these variables to predict divorce, some research (e.g., on cognitive processes and on the influence of social networks on relational stability') has examined their effects on premarital relationships as well.

Individual Characteristics

A number of researchers have looked at the associations between the characteristics that individual partners bring to marriage and the likelihood that couples will divorce. Many of the characteristics that researchers have examined are relatively stable, sociodemographic variables. For instance, age at marriage is one of the strongest predictors of early divorce (DeMaris & Rao, 1992; Heaton, 2002). People who marry when they are in their teens are the most likely to have unstable unions. There is also evidence that the rate of divorce declines for individuals in their twenties, but increases slightly for those who marry when they are older (Booth, Johnson, White, & Edwards, 1985; Kitson, Barbi, & Roach, 1985), and that discrepancies in partners' ages are positively linked to relational instability (Tzeng, 1992). Race, similarly, is associated with divorce. African American couples are more likely to divorce than are Caucasian couples (Heaton, 2002; White, 1990), even when interpersonal processes such as conflict are controlled for (Orbuch, Veroff, Hassan, & Horrocks, 2002). Further, people in lower-income groups, those with low-status occupations, and those with less education are relatively likely to end their marriages, as are couples in which the husband is unemployed (Kitson et al., 1985; Kurdek, 1993; Tzeng, 1992; White, 1990). A lack of religious participation is another factor that appears to put couples at risk' for divorce: Low religious participation and differences in spouses' religious affiliations are associated with marital dissolution (Heaton, 2002; Kitson el al., 1985).

Researchers have also examined the relationship between variables that reflect family structure and marital stability. For instance, the likelihood that spouses will end their marriage is slightly higher if their parents divorced than if they remained continuously married, and higher for remarriages than for first-time marriages (Amato, 199fi; Glenn & Kramer, 1987). Further, having a child prior to marriage is associated with divorce (Heaton, 2002), but having a child after marriage seems to reduce the risk of divorce (DeMaris & Rao, 1992)—particularly if that child is a boy (Karvez, Warner, & Acock, 1994).

In addition to studying sociodemographic and structural variables, scholars have looked "inside" individuals to assess the influence of personality and cognitive processes on divorce. One of the personality traits most frequently and consistently related to divorce is neuroticism. High levels of neuroticism, defined as a general tendency to experience negative affect, are associated with an increased risk of relational dissolution (e.g., Bouchard, Lussier, & Sabourin, 1999; Kelly & Conley, 1987; Tucker, Kressin, Spiro, & Ruscio, 1998). There is some evidence that other personality variables influence divorce, but the results associated with many of those variables are unclear. For example, Kelly and Conley found that low levels of agreeableness and high levels of extroversion were linked to marital dissolution, but Kurdek (1993) failed to replicate these findings.

Simpson and his colleagues (in press) argue that one of the reasons why researchers do not yet have a clear understanding of the influence of personality on relational outcomes is that they have not put forth models to explain the role of personality in relationships. In response to this gap in the literature, these researchers propose a model that suggests that certain personality traits are indicators of two biologically-based systems: an approach system and an avoidance system. According to Simpson, Winterheld, and Chen, the approach system involves individuals' tendencies to move toward positive stimuli and is evidenced in promotion-focused orientations to relationships, whereas the avoidance system involves tendencies to avoid negative stimuli and is reflected in prevention-focused orientations to relationships. The model put forth by Simpson and his colleagues suggests that certain trait by situation configurations should channel individuals into promotion or prevention-focused states, which in turn should affect interaction patterns, perceptions, and judgments of relationship quality. Thus, for example, neuroticism is likely to move people toward prevention-focused states and to influence their interactions, perceptions, and assessments of their relationships in relatively negative ways.

While Simpson and his coauthors (in press) have focused on explaining the associations between personality and relational outcomes, others have emphasized individuals' perceptions and cognitive processes. Perhaps the most extensive body of research linking cognitive processes to relational outcomes consists of studies on the attributions that individuals make in the context of their marital and romantic relationships (see Bradbury & Fincham, 1990). A number of investigations have indicated that the ways that people perceive their partners interpersonal behavior are associated with relational satisfaction.

Specifically, individuals who interpret their partner's behavior in ways that emphasize the positive aspects of their relationship tend to be satisfied, whereas those who accentuate the negative, distress-maintaining aspects of their partner's behavior are relatively dissatisfied (e.g., Fincham, Beach, & Baucom, 1987; Grigg, Fletcher, & Fitness, 1989; Holtzworth-Munroe & Jacobson, 1985).

Researchers have found not only that distress-maintaining attributions are associated with dissatisfaction and less effective problem-solving behavior (Bradbury & Fincham, 1992), but also that such attributions can cause dissatisfaction over time (Fincham & Bradbury, 1993). Although most studies of attributions in relationships have examined relational satisfaction rather than relational stability, researchers and practitioners tend to agree that maladaptive attributions contribute to the breakdown of happy, committed relationships.

Dyadic Characteristics

When partners come together to form a relationship, their association with each other can be examined not only in terms of their individual characteristics, but also in terms of the characteristics that describe the two of them, as a couple. A number of these dyadic variables have been linked to the breakdown of romantic relationships. For instance, partners who hold dissimilar attitudes are often seen by researchers and clinicians as having a relational liability. Why? Because studies have indicated that attitudinal similarity tends to draw partners together and keep their relationships stable. Research suggests that people are more attracted to potential friends (Newcomb, 1961) and potential romantic partners (Byrne, Ervin, & Lamberth, 1970) who hold attitudes that are similar to their own. Further, attitudinal .similarity is associated with marital satisfaction (Hendrick, 1981). Indeed, Kamey and Bradbury's (1995) meta-analysis of longitudinal studies suggested that spouses who hold similar attitudes are less likely to divorce than those who do not.

One of the most commonly studied dyadic characteristics of romantic relationships is couples' interaction. A relatively large body of literature has demonstrated that individuals who are dissatisfied with their relationship exhibit less positive affect and more negative affect toward each other than do those who are satisfied (Margolin & Wampold, 1981; Noller, 1984; Nolarius & Johnson, 1982; see also Roberts; and Simpson & Trim, this volume). Studies examining both positive and negative behaviors suggest that partners' negative behaviors tend to be more strongly associated with marital satisfaction than are their positive behaviors (Barnett & Nietzel, 1979; Broderick & O'Leary, 1986; Wills, Weiss, & Patterson, 1974). Indeed, researchers have argued that, compared to positive behaviors, negative behaviors are the more sensitive barometer of relational satisfaction (Huston & Vangelisti, 1991). In support of this claim, longitudinal research shows that the expression of negative affect predicts declines in marital satisfaction over time—even when initial levels of satisfaction are controlled for (Gottman & Krokoff, 1989; Levenson & Gottman, 1985).

The general finding that dissatisfied couples engage in more negative and fewer positive behaviors than satisfied couples becomes even more interesting when sequences of partners' behaviors are examined. Studies have demonstrated that two behavioral sequences distinguish dissatisfied couples from those who are satisfied. The first sequence is negative affect reciprocity. Negative affect reciprocity is a pattern in which individuals respond to their partners' negative behavior with more negative behavior. Research suggests that while both satisfied and dissatisfied partners reciprocate each other's positive behaviors, dissatisfied partners also reciprocate each other's negative behaviors (Weiss & Heyman, 1990). There is also some evidence that a sex difference in the reciprocity of negative affect predicts declines in couples' satisfaction. More specifically, decreases in marital satisfaction over time have been associated with more reciprocity of the husband's negative affect by the wife and less reciprocity of the wife's negative affect by the husband (Levenson & Gottman, 1985).

The second behavioral sequence that distinguishes dissatisfied from satisfied couples is the demand-withdraw pattern. This pattern of behavior occurs when, during conflict episodes, one partner communicates in "demanding" ways (e.g., tries to engage the other and/or to address the problem at hand), while the other withdraws (e.g., tries to avoid the problem and/or the interaction). Studies have revealed a consistent positive association between the demand-withdraw pattern and marital dissatisfaction and divorce (e.g., Fogarty, 1976; Heavey, Christensen, & Malamuth, 1995; Noller, Feeney, Bonnell, & Callan, 1994). Also, quite a bit of research has indicated that wives tend to engage in demanding behaviors more frequently than do husbands, and that husbands tend to withdraw more than do wives (e.g., Baucom, Notarius, Burnett, & Haefner, 1990; Christensen & Shenk, 1991; Gottman & Levenson, 1988). It is important to note, however, that this sex difference may be due to differences in the tendency of husbands and wives to desire change in their relationship. A number of theorists (Christensen & Heavey, 1990; Heavey, Layne, & Christensen, 1993; Klinetob & Smith, 1996) have argued that wives are more likely than husbands to desire change in their relationship because wives tend to have less power in their marriage and, as a consequence, tend to be less satisfied with the state of affairs. These theorists suggest that wives' greater desire for change encourages them to complain or demand. In line with this argument, researchers have found that when partners discuss a topic that involves something that husbands want to change more than do wives, the tendency for wives to demand more than husbands disappears (Christensen & Heavey, 1990; Heavey et al,, 1993).

While couples' interaction patterns provide a telling indicator of the quality of their relationship, and the likelihood that it will break down, the quality of their relationship itself is also a potent predictor of relational instability. Not surprisingly, couples who are less satisfied with their relationship are less likely to stay together (Kurdek, 1993; White & Booth, 1991). However, the degree to which spouses' satisfaction contributes to the demise of their relationship appears to vaiy when there is a discrepancy in husbands' and wives' satisfaction. Gager and Sanchez (2003) found that couples were more likely to divorce when husbands were less satisfied than their wives. However, when wives were less satisfied than their husbands, the likelihood of divorce was the same as it was when both spouses were happy. Rusbult and her colleagues (e.g., Drigotas & Rusbult, 1992; Rusbult, 1983) further suggest that relational satisfaction operates in concert with other variables, including partners' investments and the number of attractive alternatives that partners have to the current relationship. For instance, Rusbult (1983) found that dating partners who broke up reported lower satisfaction, less investment, and a greater number of potential alternatives, than did partners who stayed together (also see Fehnlee, Spreeher, & Bassin, 1990).

Network Characteristics

Regardless of their quality, romantic relationships are formed and enacted in the context of other relationships. As noted by Spreeher, Felmlee, Schmeeckle, and Shu (in press), these social networks have a powerful influence on the trajectory of intimate relationships that have reached a developed stage (e.g., dating, cohabiting). In particular, the affective approval of family members and friends decreases the likelihood that a couple breaks up, whereas disapproval enhances the likelihood of a breakup.

Research on dating couples and their social networks suggests that perceptions of approval from a partner's network (Felmlee et al., 1990) and network support (Parks & Adelman, 1983; Parks, Stan, & Eggert, 1983) are positively associated with the stability of relationships over time. The degree to which partners' networks overlap also appears to be linked to relational stability. When network overlap declines, relationships are more likely to dissolve (Milardo, 1982).

It is important to acknowledge that negativity from partners' social networks is not always associated with a decline in satisfaction or with relational dissolution. Indeed, there is some evidence that a "Romeo and Juliet effect" can occur (Driscoll, Davis, & Lipetz, 1972). The "Romeo and Juliet effect" suggests that when partners encounter opposition to their relationship from friends or family members, they become closer or more intimate. Support for this effect, however, is inconsistent (e.g., Leslie, Johnson, & Huston, 1986). One reason for the inconsistency may be that the "Romeo and Juliet effect" only occurs under particular sets of social circumstances. For instance, Driscoll et al. (1972) found that network disapproval did not influence married couples the same way that it did dating couples. Felmlee (2001) further found that disapproval from parents for dating partners' relationships was associated with increased stability only when it was accompanied by approval from close friends.

Whether the focus is on social networks, relationship processes, or individual differences, the factors that predict the breakdown of romantic relationships are complex and multifaceted, and their associations with relational dissolution are similarly so. Research and theory suggest not only that these variables interact with each other to influence relational stability, but also that they shape the processes by which relationships come apart. A marriage between partners who are veiy young, who engage in a great deal of negative communication, and who have networks that disapprove of their relationship is likely to unravel in different ways from one with partners who are older, who have children, who engage in the same sort of negative communication, but who have networks that want them to stay together. Although researchers still know surprisingly little about how individual, dyadic, and network characteristics influence dissolution processes, they have developed a general understanding of the ways relationships come apart. The next section of the present chapter will focus on studies exploring these processes.

PROCESSES

Dissolution processes have been examined from at least two different vantage points. First, scholars have described the steps or stages that partners tend to go through as they terminate their relationships. The descriptions of these stages provide a general picture of the cognitions that partners have and the behaviors that they engage in as their relationships end. Second, researchers have examined the strategies that partners employ in order to break off their relationships with others. Studies looking at disengagement strategies tend to offer a comparatively detailed view of dissolution processes by focusing more narrowly on the components of partners' interactions.

Phases of Dissolution

Several scholars have posited models describing phases experienced by partners as their relationships come apart (see Table 18.1). Among the models most frequently cited are those put forth by Knapp (1978), Duck (1982), Baxter (1984), and Lee (1984). Both Knapp and Duck offer conceptual analyses, whereas the analyses put forth by Baxter and Lee are empirically based.

Although the models described by these four scholars clearly differ, they also have a number of commonalities which, taken together, offer a useful picture of what happens when relationships break down. Table 18.2 lists several of these similarities and notes how they are evidenced across each of the four models. For instance, Duck, Baxter, and Lee all suggest that dissolution processes begin when the partners recognize (either singly or together) that there are problems in the relationship. Duck calls this the intrapsychic phase and suggests that, during this period, individuals focus on their partner's behavior, begin to evaluate their partner, and consider the ramifications of ending the relationship. Baxter notes that the early stages of dissolution involve the onset of relational problems and the decision, on the part of at least one partner, to end the relationship. Lee similarly suggests that the discovery of relationship problems is the first step on the path toward dissolution. While Knapp's model focuses more specifically on the communication patterns that characterize dissolution processes than on their cognitive components, the first two steps in his model, differentiating and circumscribing, both include communication behaviors that might accompany the discovery of relational problems. More specifically, in the differentiating stage, partners begin to engage in communication patterns that show how little they have in common. Joint activities and possessions become individualized and differences in partners' attitudes and interests are highlighted. Circumscribing is characterized by efforts to control and restrict communication; both the number and the range of topics discussed by couples are likely to decline as the partners (either one or both) avoid topics that are threatening or that might create conflict.

TABLE 18.1 Summary of Models Describing Phases of Relationship Dissolution

Knapp (1978)	Duck (1982)	Baxter (1984)	Lee (1984)
Differentiating	Intrapsychic	Onset of relationship problem	Discovery
Circumscribing	Dyadic	The decision to exit the relationship	Exposure
Stagnating	Social	Initiating unilateral dissolution actions	Negotiation
Avoiding	Grave-dressing	The initial reaction of the broken-up with party	Resolution
Terminating		Ambivalence and repair scenarios Initiating bilateral dissolution action Ambivalence and repair scenarios	Transformation

Another common characteristic of the four models is that they all note that at some point partners discuss their relationship problems. These interactions may involve direct negotiations (e.g., confrontations and efforts to repair the relationship), or they may be very indirect (e.g., observations about how much one or both partners have changed). Duck (1982) notes that partners' discussions occur during the dyadic phase, when individuals deal with the dilemmas associated with confronting their partner, engage in negotiation, and evaluate the mutual costs of withdrawal. Baxter's model (1984) suggests that after one partner begins to engage in unilateral dissolution behavior, the other will respond, and one or both partners may experience ambivalence and try to repair the relationship. Individuals' responses to their partner's dissolution behaviors, as well as the efforts on the

	Duck	Baxter	Lee	Knapp
Recognition of problems	Intrapsychic	Onset of relationship problems The decision to exit the relationship	Discovery	Differentiating Circumscribig
Partners discuss problems	Dyadic	Initiating unilateral dissolution actions The initial reaction of the broken-up-with party Ambivalence and repair scenarios	Negotiation	[May occur at any stage; will take different forms at different stages]
Turn to social network	Social	[Implicit: e.g., role of "mutual friend"]	[Implicit: e.g., "extra dyadic interface" for each stage]	[Implicit: e.g., communication with network members may be contrived in the circumscribing stage]
Decision to terminate the relationship	[Implicit: between the social and grave dressing phases]	Initiating unilateral or bilateral dissolution actions	Resolution	[May occur at any stage; more likely as partners move through stagnating and avoiding stages to termination]
Recovery and repair	Grave-dressing	Initiating bilateral dissolution actions Ambivalence and repair scenarios	Transformation	Termination

Table 18.2 Similarities Among Models of Relationship Dissolution

part of one or both partners to repair the relationship, likely involve some form of dyadic interaction, Lee (1984) similarly argues that the dissolution process involves the exposure of relational problems, as well as partners' efforts to engage in negotiations with each other concerning the problems. In Knapp's (1978) model, partners may engage each other in discussions concerning their relationship problems during any of several stages—the key with Knapp's model is that these discussions will look different, depending on the stage. Thus, partners in the differentiating stage will draw attention to their dissimilarities, those who are circumscribing will try to minimize conversations about their problems, and those in the stagnating stage may give up trying to engage their partner because they "already know" what he or she will say.

Each of these models also suggests that partners may turn to their social networks at various points in the dissolution process. People may seek advice or support from network members, and/or they may realize the need to construct an account for those members of what happened with their relationship. In Duck's (1982) model, this process occurs during the social phase, when partners initiate discussions of their impending breakup with network members and create face-saving stories to explain the dissolution of their relationship. Lee (1984) further illustrates the roles that network members may play in the termination of relationships when he describes the "extradyadic interface" for each stage in his model (p. 51). For instance, he notes that when partners begin to negotiate their relationship (and its possible termination), they may consult with network members and evaluate the support that these individuals are likely to provide. Knapp (1978) similarly describes the possible roles of network members in his model. For example, he argues that during the circumscribing stage, communication with members of some social networks may be contrived because partners are trying to hide their relationship problems. In Baxter's (1984) model, the involvement of social networks is less explicitly addressed, but the model does allow for the possibility that partners will engage their social networks as part of the breakup process. For instance, Baxter cites an example describing the role of a "mutual friend" in the initial onset of one participant's relational problems (1984, p. 35).

All four of the models also describe a period during the dissolution process when partners make decisions, and engage in behaviors, to terminate their relationship. In Duck's (1982) model, this period occurs between the social phase and the grave-dressing phase. During this transition, Duck suggests that partners realize that the dissolution of their relationship is inevitable. Lee (1984) similarly notes that in the resolution stage of his model, partners make either unilateral or bilateral decisions to terminate their relationship. Likewise, in Baxter's (1984) model, actions are taken to dissolve the relationship after at least one of the parties makes a decision to end it, and then either one or both engage in (unilateral or bilateral) dissolution behaviors. Knapp (1978) argues that in the avoidance stage of his model, partners engage in communication behaviors that are designed to avert interaction; further, in the termination stage, partners may have one or more conversations that end the relationship or that drastically change the way that they define their association with each other.

A final commonality of the models is that all four acknowledge a time when partners make efforts to "get over" the relationship and move beyond it. Duck (1982) calls this the grave-dressing phase and suggests not only that partners engage in activities to get over their relationship, but also that they reflect on the relationship and begin to distribute an account of the breakup to members of their social networks. Lee (1984) calls this period the transformation stage. He notes that during transformation, actual changes are made in the relationship—partners may change the frequency and duration of their interactions, recover from the affective trauma they have experienced, and/or reconceptualize their relationship. Knapp (1978) discusses partners' efforts to recover from their relationship and reconceptualize it as part of the termination stage. He notes, for example, that this stage is characterized by messages of disassociation—messages that prepare partners for the life they will lead apart from each other. Baxter similarly reported that some of her participants engaged in a "negotiated farewell" when initiating bilateral dissolution action (1984, p. 40). In these conversations, partners appeared to agree that their relationship should end and began to jointly construct a different trajectory for their relationship.

Although dissolution processes are often characterized as a series of steps that partners go through as their relationship ends, the scholars who describe these steps are careful to note that the processes are complex, multifaceted, and sometimes even chaotic. For instance, Knapp states that the notion that relationship dissolution is systematic "does not suggest that the process is linear or that there is a fixed, unchangeable sequence of movement through stages" (1984, p. 50). Lee (1984) similarly notes that while dissolution processes have many regularities, they are also uncertain and uncontrolled (see also Duck & Miell, 1984). Baxter further argues that a "single set of stages or steps does not generalize to all, or even most, relationship dissolutions" (1984, p. 43).

Dissolution Strategies

In addition to examining the phases that many couples experience as their relationships come apart, researchers have studied the strategies that people employ in order to break off their association with a romantic partner. For instance, Cody (1982) asked undergraduate students who had initiated a breakup with a romantic partner to describe what they said or did to terminate the relationship. He found that the strategies reported by the participants fell into five general categories: (1) positive tone (apologizing, expressing regret, trying not to hurt the partner); (2) negative identity management (noting the importance of dating other people, saying that the breakup was the best thing for both partners); (3) justification (explaining dissatisfaction, explaining reasons for the breakup); (4) behavioral de-escalation (avoiding contact, not calling the partner, not returning phone calls); and (5) de-escalation (stating that partners should "call it quits" or "cool off" for a period and that they may "get back together" in the future).

When Cody (1982) examined people's tendencies to report using these strategies in terms of intimacy, he found that individuals who had been involved in relatively intimate relationships were more likely to use justification, de-escalation, and positive tone than were those involved in less intimate relationships. Banks, Altendorf, Greene, and Cody (1987) further found that the nature of partners' social networks influenced the strategies that they reported using. Individuals who said that their network overlapped a great deal with their partners network were relatively likely to use positive tone, de-escalation, and justification strategies. Network overlap, like intimacy, seems to encourage people to employ strategies that are sensitive to their partner's feelings and that demonstrate an effort to account for what has happened.

Baxter (1982) also studied the strategies that partners use to terminate their relationships. She asked people to provide detailed explanations of how they ended a friendship, and generated a list of 35 strategies from these data. Then, she asked different groups of participants to rate the likelihood they would employ the 35 techniques to dissolve friendships or romantic relationships. Baxter found that four factors characterized the strategies that individuals used to end both types of relationships: (1) withdraw/avoidance (efforts to avoid confrontation about the dissolution); (2) manipulatory strategies (intentional manipulation of others to terminate the relationship); (3) positive-tone strategies (concern about the affective response of the other party involved in the disengagement); and (4) open-confrontation strategies (direct confrontation about the disengagement). With the exception of manipulatory strategies, the techniques uncovered by Baxter overlap a great deal with those explored by Cody (1982).

Baxter (1982) suggested that the four types of strategies she found could be characterized by one of two underlying dimensions: direct vs. indirect (open confrontation and withdraw/avoidance) and other vs. self-orientation (positive tone and manipulation). She also found that people who reported that their romantic relationship ended due to external factors were less likely to use withdraw/avoidance than were those who believed their relationship ended because of internal factors. Similarly, those who had relatively close relationships prior to the dissolution were less likely to use withdraw/avoidance. Perhaps people who were involved in relatively close relationships and those who believed the causes of their breakup were due, in part, to internal factors felt more obligated to be open with their partner about the status of their relationship.

The techniques that people use to end their relationships may very well influence the way that they, and their partner, respond to the dissolution. Although researchers have not investigated the association between the use of particular disengagement strategies and the consequences of relational dissolution for individuals and their partners, this would be an interesting association to examine. It is possible that the use of direct, other-oriented strategies would help both parties adjust to the termination process, because these sorts of strategies would enable them to confront the situation and deal with it in a way that attended to the other's feelings. However, there may be situations where the use of direct, other-oriented strategies is detrimental to individuals and/or their partners. For instance, in relationships that are not very close, employing direct strategies (e.g., informing the other person that you do not find them attractive) may be more humiliating for the partner who is being "broken-up with" than using indirect strategies (e.g., not returning phone calls or being "too busy" to go out).

Of course, the effects of relational dissolution on individuals and their partners are influenced by much more than the strategies people use to end their relationships. The following section of this chapter will summarize research on the consequences of relational dissolution as well as some of the variables that influence the way that partners, and any children they might have, adjust to the termination of a relationship. As previously noted, research on the consequences of relational dissolution focuses primarily on divorce and, in line with prior work, the following review will do the same.

CONSEQUENCES OF RELATIONAL DISSOLUTION

Consequences for Partners

Although most people touched by divorce and relational dissolution experience considerable distress, the literature suggests that individuals respond to the breakdown of their relationships in different ways. Amato (2000) argues that two different models are reflected in research on the consequences of divorce. Both models presume a negative association between divorce and individuals' well-being, but the models hold different assumptions about the causal association between these two variables. One of the models, labeled the *divorce-stress-adjustment* perspective, depicts relational dissolution "not as a discrete event but as a process that begins while the couple lives together and ends long after the legal divorce is concluded" (p. 1271). Studies supporting this perspective indicate, for example, that divorce is often associated with a gradual decline in emotional attachment between spouses that can precede the formal termination of the relationship by years (Kayser & Rao-Kelter, in press). Further, the process of dissolution can extend well beyond the date of the formal termination. For instance, a number of scholars argue that women have a particularly difficult time adjusting to divorce after their marriage ends because they tend to face greater economic hardships than do men (e.g., Hanson, McLanahan, & Thomson, 1998).

The second model described by Amato (2000) is the *selection* perspective. This perspective suggests that some people enter marriage with traits that make them particularly vulnerable to marital dissatisfaction, divorce, and problems with postdivorce adjustment. In essence, the selection model assumes that certain individuals are "selected out" of marriage. Evidence supporting this perspective comes from studies indicating that, for example, higher levels of neuroticism (e.g., Karney & Bradbury, 1995) and depression (e.g., Davies, Avison, & McAlpine, 1997) are associated with an increased risk of divorce. Relatively stable characteristics such as neuroticism and depression may not only predate relational dissatisfaction and divorce, but also may continue for an indefinite period following divorce.

Both the divorce-stress-adjustment and the selection perspectives suggest-that, on average, people who are divorced should experience more negative outcomes than those who are married. Indeed, this appears to be the case. Individuals who are divorced tend to report lower levels of well-being than those who are married (e.g. Demo & Acock, 1996; Kitson, 1992; Shapiro, 1996; Umberson & Williams, 1993). They also report being more lonely and socially isolated (Page & Cole, 1991; Pinquart, 2003), having more health problems (Joung, Stronks, van de Mheen, van Poppel, van der Meer, & Mackenbak, 1997), and experiencing more economic difficulties (Ross, 1995) than people who are married (see also Simpson & Trim, this volume).

Of course, comparisons of individuals who are divorced with those who are married do not indicate whether the difficulties experienced by divorced individuals predate the divorce or whether, instead, the divorce predates the difficulties that these individuals tend to experience. As a consequence, these investigations do not provide clear evidence in favor of either the divorce-stress-adjustment perspective or the selection perspective. Longitudinal studies and twin studies have the potential to offer more information about the timing of the onset of difficulties associated with divorce, however the findings of these studies are mixed. On one hand, research indicates that psychological distress tends to rise just before marital separation (Booth & Amato, 1991; Mastekaasa, 1994). The close temporal proximity of distress and marital separation tends to support the divorce-stress-adjustment perspective. On the other hand, studies show that certain individual differences associated with divorce may precede the divorce (Mastekaasa, 1997), and even that the risk of divorce maybe genetically mediated (Jockin, McGue, & Lykken, 1996; McGue & Lykken, 1992). This latter group of studies suggests that people may possess lasting characteristics that make them vulnerable to divorce, thus supporting the selection perspective.

Although both the divorce-stress-adjustment perspective and the selection perspective focus on the negative outcomes of divorce, it is important to acknowledge that a handful of studies suggest that divorce is sometimes associated with positive outcomes. For instance, Marks (1996) found that while people who were separated or divorced reported being more distressed that those who were married, those who were separated or divorced also reported greater autonomy—a characteristic that is considered an important criterion of adult development (p. 927). Marks also found that women who were separated or divorced reported more personal growth than those who were married. The generally negative outcomes of divorce, thus, may be qualified by positive outcomes for particular individuals under particular circumstances.

Consequences for Children

As a group, children whose parents have divorced fare more poorly on a number of different outcome measures than those whose parents remain continually married. Children with divorced parents tend to have poorer psychological adjustment, lower academic achievement, and more behavioral problems than those with parents who have not divorced (Doherty & Needle, 1991; Grych & Fincham, 1992; Hetherington, Cox, & Cox, 1982; Kurdek, Fine, & Sinclair, 1994; Stolberg & Anker, 1984).

Although the literature suggests that divorce generally has a negative influence on children, two qualifications are in order. First, the differences between children with divorced parents and those with continually married parents are relatively small. A meta-analysis of 92 studies indicated that the differences between these two groups are modest (Amato & Keith, 1991). Second, research suggests that children, like their parents, respond to divorce in a variety of ways. Most, if not all, children experience the divorce of their parents as extremely stressful, but some emerge from the experience with long-term behavioral and emotional problems while others emerge relatively unscathed (Hetherington, Stanley-Hagan, & Anderson, 1989).

The diversity in children's responses to marital dissolution has been studied both in terms of the individual differences of children who experience divorce and in terms of the economic and social conditions that precede and follow divorce. For instance, children's understanding of marital dissolution is affected by their age. Due to their limited social and cognitive capacities, younger children (e.g., preschoolers) are less able to accurately evaluate their parents' divorce, are more likely to blame themselves for the breakdown of their parents' relationship, and are more likely to fear abandonment following the divorce than are older children (Wallerstein, Corbin, & Lewis, 1988). Boys who live in single-parent families with their mothers following a divorce tend to have more behavioral and social problems than do girls living in the same situation (Hetherington et al, 1982; Hetherington, Cox, & Cox, 1985). Further, children who are temperamentally difficult are more often the target of their parents' criticism and anger and, perhaps as a consequence, have more difficulty adjusting to divorce than do other children (Hetherington, 1989).

While individual differences such as age, sex, and temperament certainly affect the resources that are available for children to use in coping with divorce, the influence of those differences on children's adjustment cannot be accurately interpreted apart from their economic and social contexts. For example, research suggests that children whose parents experience economic difficulties after divorcing are more likely to be negatively influenced by divorce than those whose parents do not experience such difficulties (McLanahan & Sandefur, 1994). Similarly, those with fathers who pay child support fare better in school than do children with fathers who do not pay support (King, 1994). Although parents' economic situation clearly influences children's adjustment, there is also evidence suggesting drat the stability of parents' income following divorce can play as much, or more, of a role in predicting children's well-being (Goldberg, Greenberger, Hamill, & O'Neil, 1992).

This latter finding is very likely due to the fact that declines in parents' income are associated with other changes that are stressful to children (e.g., changes in housing, maternal employment, childcare, and educational aspirations). Unfortunately, research also suggests that parents with low and unstable incomes are more likely to divorce than those who have higher and relatively stable incomes (Hernandez, 1988), so there is a greater likelihood that children from divorced families will experience economic hardship.

Of course, the association between economic and marital difficulties may be bidirectional (but see Conger, Rueter, & Elder, 1999). On the one hand, economic hardship may set the stage for divorce by creating marital stress (e.g., when couples fight over finances), whereas, on the other, stress in the marital relationship may set the stage for economic difficulties (e.g., when a father distances himself from the family prior to divorce and, as a consequence, does not pay child support).

In either case, the social and relational contexts in which children live affect their well-being. For instance, research has repeatedly demonstrated that inter-parental conflict is associated with the, ability of children to adjust to divorce, In fact, a number of studies suggest that the conflict associated with divorce, rather than the divorce itself, accounts for the difficulties experienced by many children from divorced families (Amato, 1993; Gano-Phillips & Fincham, 1995). Interparental conflict is particularly harmful to children when it is intense, prolonged, remains unresolved, and directly involves the children (Davies & Cummings, 1994; Grych & Fincham, 1990). Indeed, there is evidence suggesting that children with parents who engage in chronic, intense conflict are more well adjusted if their parents divorce than if they stay married (Amato & Booth, 1997). It is important to note, however, that divorce does not always end conflict between parents. Parents who are divorced can continue to engage in intense, regular, and frequent conflict. Not surprisingly, conflict between parents following divorce—like conflict prior to divorce—is negatively associated with children's well-being (Buchanan, Maccoby, & Dombusch, 1996; Emery, 1999; Vanderwater & Lansford, 1998).

CONCLUSIONS

The prevalence of divorce and relational dissolution has stimulated a great deal of empirical and theoretical study. Scholars have examined the antecedents of relational disengagement, exploring the influence of individual, dyadic, and network variables. They have looked at the processes associated with relational dissolution, have put forth models to describe those processes, and have studied the strategies that people use to end their romantic relationships. Researchers have also analyzed the consequences of relational disengagement—both for adult partners and for children whose parents divorce.

In spite of the, time and attention that scholars have devoted to the study of relational dissolution, the literature is surprisingly fragmented. Bringing together the fragmented parts of the current literature to form a clear, coherent picture of disengagement will not be an easy task. It will require researchers to face a number of complex theoretical and methodological challenges. For instance, Karney and Bradbury (1995) note that the vast majority of the studies they examined in their review of longitudinal research on marital stability looked at direct, linear associations between predictors and outcomes when, in reality, it is veiy possible that some of the presumed direct effects are actually mediated by other variables. Researchers who study the consequences of divorce for partners and their children have begun to identify possible mediators and moderators that influence individuals' adjustment, but a great deal remains to be done before scholars will be able to generate integrative frameworks describing the predictors, processes, and consequences of relational disengagement.

In their call to researchers to focus on developing integrative models of relational dissolution, Rodrigues et al. (in press) argue for the importance of examining the various associations between intrapersonal and interpersonal variables. Rodrigues and her colleagues suggest that the current disconnect between intrapersonal and interpersonal levels of analysis is evidenced by some investigators focusing their attention on the demographic predictors of divorce, and others treating the same (demographic) variables "as nuisance factors that need to be controlled." If researchers and theorists are to develop comprehensive models of relational disengagement, they will need to move beyond treating particular groups of variables as nuisance factors or as error variance and will need, instead, to consider carefully the role of those variables in shaping dissolution processes. More broadly, scholars who study relational disengagement will need to look across various levels of analysis (e.g., individual, dyadic, and network levels) to explore how the factors at each level operate together.

Cate and his colleagues (2002) make another observation relevant to the challenges faced by those who study relational breakdown. These researchers note that the bulk of the literature on relational stability is consistent with a model that Surra (1990) labeled *early determinism*—a model that assumes "that early relationship features work throughout the course of the relationship to determine stability or other relationship states" (Cate et al., 2002, p. 280). Although Cate et al. s assessment focuses on studies of premarital relationships, it pertains to research on marital relationships as well. The case put forth by Cate and his colleagues is that relationship development and deterioration involve much more than simple, linear associations between a set of predictors and relationship outcomes. As noted by Surra, relationships are characterized both by periods of stability and periods of turmoil. Relational disengagement, thus, is likely to occur in a nonlinear fashion and to be influenced, at different points in time, by different variables. Inasmuch as this is the case, understanding dissolution processes will require longitudinal studies that assess relationship variables at multiple points in time.

Amato, P. R. (1993). Children's adjustment to divorce: Theories, hypotheses, and empirical support. *Journal of Marriage and the Family,* 55, 23–38.

Amato, P. R. (1996). Explaining the intergenerational transmission of divorce. *Journal of Marriage and the Family, 58,* 628–640.

Amato, P. R. (2000). The consequences of divorce for adults and children. *Journal of Marriage and the Family, 62,*1269–1287.

Amato, P. R., & Booth, A, (1997). *A generation at risk: Growing up in an era of family upheaval.* Cambridge, MA: Harvard University Press.

Amato, P. R., & Keith, B, (1991), Consequences of parental divorce for children's well-being-. A meta-analysis. *Psychological Bulletin, 110,* 26–46.

Banks, S. P., Altendorf, D. M, Greene, J. O., & Cody, M. J. (1987). An examination of relationship disengagement. Perceptions, breakup strategies, and outcomes. *Western Journal of Speech Communication, 51,*19–41.

Barnett, L. R., & Nietzel, M. T. (1979). Relationship of instrumental and affectional behaviors and self-esteem to marital satisfaction in distressed and non distressed couples. *Journal of Consulting and Clinical Psychology, 47,* 946–957.

Baucom, D. H., Notarius, C. I., Burnett, C. K., & Haefner, P. (1990). Gender differences and sex-role identity in marriage. In F. D. Fincham & T. N. Bradbury (Eds.), *The psychology of marriage* (pp. 150–171). New York, NY: Guilford Press.

Baxter, L. A. (1982). Strategies for ending relationships: Two studies. *Western Journal of Speech Communication, 46,* 223–241.

Baxter, L. A. (1984). Trajectories of relationship disengagement. *Journal of Social and Personal Relationships, 1,* 29–48.

Booth, A., & Amato, P. R. (1991). Divorce and psychological stress. *Journal of Health and Social Behavior,* 32, 396–407.

Booth, A., Johnson, D. R., White, L, K., & Edwards, J. N. (1985). Predicting divorce and permanent separation. *Journal of Family Issues, 6,* 331–346.

Bradbury, T. N., & Fincham, F. D. (1990). Attributions in marriage: Review and critique. *Psychological Bulletin, 107,* 3–33.

Bradbury, T. N., & Fincham, F. D. (1992). Attributions and behavior in marital interaction. *Journal of Personality and Social Psychology, 63,* 613–628.

Bramlett, M. D., & Mosher, W. D. (2002). *Cohabitation, marriage, divorce, and remarriage in the United States. Vital health statistics, Series 23, Number 2.* Hyattsville, MD: National Center for Health Statistics.

Broderick, J. E,, & O'Leary, K. D. (1986). Contributions of affect, attitudes, and behavior to marital satisfaction. *Journal of Consulting and Clinical Psychology, 54,*514–517.

Buchanan, C. M,, Maccoby, E. E., & Dornbusch, S. M. (1996). *Adolescents after divorce.* Cambridge, MA: Harvard University Press.

Bouchard, G„ Lussier, Y„ & Sabourin, S. (1999). Personality and marital adjustment: Utility of the five-factor model of personality. *Journal of Marriage and the Family, 61,* 651–660.

Byrne, D., Ervin, C. E„ & Lamberth, J. (1970). Continuity between the experimental study of attraction and real-life computer dating. *Journal of Personality and Social Psychology, 16,* 157–165.

Cate, R. M., Levin, L. A., & Richmond, L. S. (2002). Premarital relationship stability: A review of recent research. *Journal of Social and Personal Relationships, 19,*261–284.

Cherlin, A. J. (1992), *Marriage, divorce, remarriage* (2nd ed.). Cambridge, MA: Harvard University Press.

Christensen, A., & Heavey, C. L. (1990), Gender and social structure in the demand-withdraw pattern of marital conflict. *Journal of Personality and Social Psychology,* 5.9, 73-fll.

Christensen, A., & Shenk, J. L. (1991). Communication, conflict, and psychological distance in non distressed, clinic, and divorcing couples. *Journal of Consulting and Clinical Psychology, 59,* 458–463.

Cody, M. J. (1982). A typology of disengagement strategies and an examination of the role intimacy, reactions to inequity, and relational problems play in strategy selection. *Communication Monographs, 49,* 148–170.

Conger, R. D., Rueter, M. A., & Elder, G. H. (1999). Couple resilience to economic pressure. *Journal of Personality and Social Psychology, 76,* 54–71.

Davies, L., Avison, W. R., & McAlpine, D. D. (1997). Significant life experiences and depression among single and married mothers. *Journal of Marriage and the Family,* 59, 294–308.

Davies, P. T., & Cummings, E. M. (1994). Marital conflict and child adjustment: An emotional security hypothesis. *Psychological Bulletin, 116,* 387–411.

DeMaris, A., & Rao, K. V. (1992). Premarital cohabitation and subsequent marital stability in the United States: A reassessment. *Journal of Marriage and the Family, 54,* 178–190.

Demo, D. H., & Acock, A. C. (1996). Motherhood, marriage, and remarriage: The effects of family structure and family relationships on mothers' well-being. *Journal of Family Issues, 17,* 388–407.

Doherty, W. J., & Needle, R. H. (1991). Psychological adjustment and substance use among adolescents before and after a parental divorce. *Child Development, 62, 328–337,*

Driscoll, R., Davis, K. E., & Lipetz, M. E. (1972). Parental interference and romantic love: The Romeo and Juliet effect, *journal of Personality and Social Psychology, 24,* 1–10.

Drigotas, S. M., & Rusbult, C. E. (1992). Should I stay or should I go? A dependence model of breakups. *Journal of Personality and Social Psychology, 62,* 62–87.

Duck, S. (1982). A topography of relationship disengagement and dissolution. In S. Duck (Ed.), *Personal relationships 4: Dissolving personal relationships* (pp. 1–30). New York, NY: Academic Press.

Duck, S., & Midi, D. E. (1984). Towards an understanding of friendship development and breakdown. In H. Tajfel, C. Eraser, & J. Jaspars (Eds.), *The social dimension: European perspectives on social psychology.* Cambridge, UK: Cambridge University Press.

Emery, R. E, (1999). Post divorce family life for children: An overview of research and some implications for policy. In R. A. Thompson & P. R. Avnato (Eds.), *The post divorce family: Children, parenting, and society* (pp. 3–27). Thousand Oaks, CA: Sage.

Felmlee, D. (2001). No couple is an island: A social network perspective on dyadic stability. *Social Forces, 4,* 1259–1287.

Felmlee, D., Sprecher, S., & Bassin, E. (1990). The dissolution of intimate relationships: A hazard model. *Social Psychology Quarterly, 53,* 13–30.

Fincham, F. D., Beach, S. R., & Baucom, D. II. (1987). Attribution processes in distressed and non distressed couples: 4. Self-partner attribution differences. *Journal of Personality and Social Psychology, 52,* 739–748.

Fincham, F. D., & Bradbury, T. N. (1993). Marital satisfaction, depression, and attributions: A longitudinal analysis. *Journal of Personality and Social Psychology, 64,* 442–452.

Fogarty, T. F. (1976). Marital crisis. In P. J. Guerin (Ed.), *Family therapy: Theory and practice* (pp. 325–334). New York, NY: Gardner.

Gager, C. T„ & Sanchez, L. (2003). Two as one? Couples' perceptions of time spent together, marital quality, and the risk of divorce. *Journal of Family Issues, 24,* 21–50.

Gano-Phillips, S., & Finchain, F. D. (1995). Family conflict, divorce, and children's adjustment. In M. A. Fitzpatrick & A. L. Vangelisti (Eds.), *Explaining family interactions* (pp. 206–231). Thousand Oaks, CA: Sage.

Glenn, N. D., & Kramer, K. B. (1987). The marriages and divorces of the children of divorce. *Journal of Marriage and the Family, 49,* 811—825.

Glick, P. C. (1989). Remarried families, stepfamilies, and stepchildren: A brief demographic profile. *Family Relations, 38,* 24–27.

Goldberg, W. A., GreenbergenE., Hamill, S., & O'Neil, R. (1992). Role demands in the lives of employed single mothers with preschoolers. *Journal of Family Issues, 13,* 312–333.

Gottman, J. M„ & Krokoff, L. J. (1989). Marital interaction and satisfaction: A longitudinal view. *Journal of Consulting and Clinical Psychology, 57,* 47–52.

Gottman, J. M., & Levenson, R. W. (1988). The social psychophysiology of marriage. In P. Noller & M. A. Fitzpatrick (Eds.), *Perspectives on marital interaction* (pp. 182–200). Philadelphia, PA: Multilingual Matters.

Grigg, F„ Fletcher, G. J. 0„ & Fitness, J. (1989). Spontaneous attributions in happy and unhappy dating relationships. *Journal of Social and Personal Relationships, 6,* 61–68.

Grych, J. I-L, & Fincham, F. D. (1990). Marital conflict and children's adjustment: A cognitive-contextual framework. *Psychological Bulletin, 108,* 267–290.

Grych, J. H., & Fincham, F. D. (1992). Marital dissolution and family adjustment: An attributional analysis. In T. L. Orbuch (Ed.), *Close relationship loss: Theoretical approaches* (pp. 157–173). New York, NY: Springer-Verlag.

Hanson, T. L., McLanahun, S. S„ & Thomson, E. (1998). Windows on divorce: Before and after. *Social Science Review, 27,* 329–349.

Heaton, T. B. (2002). Factors contributing to increasing stability in the United States. *Journal of Family Issues, 23,* 392–409.

Heavey, C. L,, Christensen, A., & Malamuth, N. M. (1995). The longitudinal impact of demand and withdrawal during marital conflict. *Journal of Consulting and Clinical Psychology,* 63, 797–801.

Heavey, C. L., Layne, C, & Christensen, A. (1993). Gender and conflict structure in marital interaction: A replication and extension. *Journal of Consulting and Clinical Psychology, 61,16–27.*

Hendrick, S. S. (1981). Self-disclosure and marital satisfaction. *Journal of Personality and Social Psychology, 40,* 1150–1159.

Hernandez, D. J. (1988). Demographic trends and the living arrangements of children. In E. M. Hetherington & J. D. Arasteh (Eds.), *Impact of divorce, single-parenting, and slepparenting on children* (pp. 3–22) Hillsdale, NJ: Lawrence Erlbaum Associates, Inc.

Hetherington, E. M. (1989). Coping with family transitions: Winners, losers, and survivors. *Child Development, 60,*1–14.

Hetherington, E. M., Cox, M,, & Cox., R. (1982). Effects of divorce on parents and children. In M. Lamb (Ed.), *Nontraditional families* (pp. 233–288). Hillsdale, NJ: Lawrence Erlbaum Associates, Inc.

Hetherington, E. M., Cox, M., & Cox, R. (1985). Long-term effects of divorce and remarriage on the adjustment of children. *Journal of the American Academy of Psychiatry, 24,* 518–530.

Hetherington, E. M., Stanley-Hagan, M., & Anderson, E. R. (1989). Marital transitions: A child's perspective. *American Psychologist, 44,* 303–312.

Holtzworth-Munroe, A., & Jacobson, N. S. (1985). Causal attributions of married couples: When do they search for causes? What do they conclude when they do? *Journal of Personality and Social Psychology, 48,* 1398–1412.

Huston, T. L,, & Vangelisti, A. L. (1991). Socioemotional behavior and satisfaction in marital relationships. *Journal of Personality and Social Psychology, 61,* 721–733.

Jockin, V, McGue, M., & Lykken, D. T. (1996). Personality and divorce. *Journal of Personality and Social Psychology, 71,* 288–299.

Joung, I. M. A., Stronks, K., van de Mheen, IT., van Poppel, F. W. A., van der Meer, J. B. W.,, & Maekenback, J. P. (1997). The contribution of intermediary factors to marital status differences in self-reported health. *Journal of Marriage and the Family,* 59, 476–490.

Kamey, B. R,, & Bradbury, T. N. (1995). The longitudinal course of martial quality and stability: A review of theory, methods, and research. *Psychological Bulletin, 118,*3–34.

Katvez, A. R., Warner, R. L., & Acock, A. C. (1994). Girls or boys? The relationship of child gender to marital instability. *Journal of Marriage and the Family, 56,* 89–100.

Kayser, K., & Rao-Kelter, S. (in press). The process of disaffection in relationship breakdown. In M. A. Fine & J. H. Harvey (Eds.), *Handbook of divorce and relationship dissolution,* Mahwah, NJ: Lawrence Erlbaum Associates, Inc.

Kelly, E. L., & Conley, J. J. (1987). Personality and compatibility: A prospective analysis of marital stability and marital satisfaction. *Journal of Personality and Social Psychology, 52,* 27–40.

King, V. (1994). Nonresident father involvement and child well-being: Can dads make a difference? *Journal of Family Issues, 15,* 78–96.

Kitson, G. C. (1992). *Portrait of divorce: Adjustment to marital break down.* New York, NY: Guilford Press.

Kitson, G. C., Barbi, K. B., & Roach, M. J. (1985). Who divorces and why?: A review. *Journal of Family Issues, 6,* 255–293.

Klinetob, N. A., & Smith, D. A. (1996). Demand-withdraw communication in marital interaction: Tests of interspousal contingency and gender role hypotheses. *Journal of Marriage and the Family, 58,* 945–958.

Knapp, M. L. (1978). *Social intercourse: From greeting to goodbye.* Boston, MA: Allyn & Bacon.

Kurdek, L. A. (1993). Predicting marital dissolution: A 5-year prospective longitudinal study of newlywed couples. *Journal of Personality and. Social Psychology, 64,* 221–242.

Kurdek, L. A., Fine, M. A., & Sinclair, R. J. (1994). The relation between parenting transitions and adjustment in young adolescents. *Journal of Early Adolescence, 14,* 412–432.

Lee, L. (1984). Sequences in separation: A framework for investigating endings of the personal (romantic) relationship. *Journal of Social and Personal Relationships, 1,* 49–73.

Leslie, L. A., Johnson, M. P., & Huston, T. L. (1986). Parental reactions to dating relationships: Do they make a difference? *Journal of Marriage and the Family, 48,* 57–66.

Levenson, R. W, & Gottman, J. M. (1985). Physiological and affective predictors of change in relationship satisfaction. *Journal of Personality and Social Psychology, 49,* 85–94.

Margolin, G., & Wampold, B. (1981). Sequential analysis of conflict and accord in distressed and non distressed marital partners. *Journal of Consulting and Clinical Psychology, 49,* 554–567.

Marks, N. E (1996). Flying solo at midlife; Gender, marital status, and psychological well-being. *Journal of Marriage and the Family, 58,* 917–932.

Mastekaasa, A. (1994). Psychological well-being and marital dissolution. *Journal of Family Issues, 15,* 208–228.

Mastekaasa, A. (1997). Marital dissolution as a stressor: Some evidence on psychological, physical, and behavioural changes during the preseparation period. *Journal of Divorce and. Remarriage, 26,* 155–183.

McGue, M., & Lykken, D. T. (1992). Genetic influence on risk of divorce. *Psychological Science, 3,* 368–373.

McLanahan, S. S., & Sandefur, G. (1994). *Growing up with a single parent: What hurts, what helps.* Cambridge, MA: Harvard University Press.

Milardo, R. M. (1982). Friendship networks in developing relationships: Converging and diverging social environment. *Social Psychology Quarterly, 45,* 162–172.

Newcomb, T. M. (1961). *The acquaintance process.* New York, NY: Holt, Rinehart, & Winston.

Noller, P. (1984). *Nonverbal communication and. marital interaction.* Oxford, UK: Pergamon.

Noller, P., Feeney, J. A., Bormell, D., & Callan, V. (1994). A longitudinal study of conflict in early marriage. *Journal of Social and Personal Relationships, 11,* 233–252.

Notarius, C. I., & Johnson, J. S. (1982). Emotional expression in husbands and wives. *Journal of Marriage and the Family, 45,* 483–489.

Orbuch, T. L„ Veroff, J., Hassan, H„ & Horrocks, J. (2002). Who will divorce: A 14-year longitudinal study of black and white couples. *Journal of Social and Personal Relationships, 19,* 179–202.

Page, R. M, & Cole, G. E. (1991). Demographic predictors of self-reported loneliness in adults. *Psychological Reports, 68,* 939–945.

Parks, M. R., & Adelman, M. B. (1983). Communication networks and the development of romantic relationships: An expansion of uncertainty reduction theory. *Human Communication research, 10,* 55–79.

Parks, M. R., Stan, C, & Eggert, L. (1983). Romantic involvement and social network involvement. *Social Psychology Quarterly, 46,* 116–130.

Pinquart, M. (2003). Loneliness in married, widowed, divorced, and never-married older adults. *Journal of Social and Personal Relationships, 20,* 31–53.

Rodrigues, A. E., Hall, J. II., & Fine-ham, F. D. (in press). What predicts divorce and relationship satisfaction? In M. A. Fine & J. H. Harvey (Eds.), *Handbook of tliwrcc and relationship dissolution.* Mahwah, NJ: Lawrence Erlbaum Associates, Inc.

Ross, C. E. (1995), Reconceptualizing marital status as a continuum of social attachment. *Journal of Marriage and the Family,* 57, 129–140.

Rusbult, C. E. (1983). A longitudinal test of the investment model: The development (and deterioration) of satisfaction and commitment in heterosexual involvements. *Journal of Personality and Social Psychology, 45,* 101–117.

Shapiro, A. M. (1996). Explaining psychological distress in a sample of remarried and divorced persons. *Journal of Family Issues, 17,* 186–203.

Simpson, J. A., Winterheld, H. A., & Chen, J. Y. (in press). Personality and relationships: A temperament perspective. In A. L. Vangelisti & D. Perlman (Eds.), *The Cambridge handbook of personal relationships.* New York, NY: Cambridge University Press.

Sprechei, S., Felmlee, D„ Schmeeckle, M., & Shu, X. (in press). No breakup occurs on an island: Social networks and relationship dissolution. In M. A. Fine & J. II. Harvey (Eds.), *Handbook of divorce and relationship dissolution.* Mahwah, NJ: Lawrence Erlbaum Associates, Inc.

Stolberg, A. L., & Anker, J. M. (.1984). Cognitive and behavioral changes in children resulting from parental divorce and consequence environmental changes. *Journal of Divorce, 8,* 184–197.

Surra, C. A. (1990). Research and theory on mate selection and premarital relationships in the 1980s./mow// *of Marriage and the Family,* 52, 844–865.

Tucker, J. S., Kressin, N. R., Spiro, A., Ill, & Ruscio, J. (1998). Intrapersonal characteristics and the timing of divorce: A prospective investigation. *Journal of Social and Personal Relationships, 15,* 211–225.

Tzeng, M. (1992). The effects of socioeconomic heterogamy and changes on marital dissolution for first marriages. *Journal of Marriage and the Family, 54,* 609–619.

Umberson, D., & Williams, C. L. (1993). Divorced fathers: Parental role strain and psychological distress. *Journal of Family Issues, 14,* 378–400.

Vanderwater, E. A., & Lansford, J. E. (1998). Influences of family structure and parental conflict on children's well-being. *Family Relations, 47,* 323–330.

Wallerstein, J., Corbin, S. B,, & Lewis, J. M. (1988). Children of divorce: A ten-year study. In E. M. Hetherington & J. Arasteh (Eds.), *Impact of divorce, single-parenting, and stepparenting on children* (pp. 198–214). Hillsdale, NJ: Lawrence Erlbaum Associates, Inc.

Weiss, R. L., & Heyman, R. E. (1990). Observation of marital interaction. In F. D. Fincham & T. N, Bradbury (Eds.), *The psychology of marriage: Basic issues and applications* (pp. 87–117). New York, NY: Guilford' Press.

White, L. K. (1990). Determinants of divorce: A review of research in the eighties. *Journal of Marriage and the Family,* 52, 904–912.

White, L. K., & Booth, A. (1991). Divorce over the life course: The role of marital happiness. *Journal of Family Issues, 12,* 5–21.

Wills, T. A., Weiss, R. L., & Patterson, G. R. (1974). A behavioral analysis of the determinants of marital satisfaction. *Journal of Consulting and Clinical Psychology, 42,* 802–811.

Broken Attachments

Relationship Loss From the Perspective of Attachment Theory

By Cindy Hazan and Phillip R. Shaver

Loss is an integral part of close relationships. Death, estrangement, and geographical distance often separate us from those with whom we are close. Relationships are continually being constituted and dissolved. If we are truly to understand close relationships, we must not limit ourselves to studying them only during their constitutive phase but also throughout their natural cycle. As there is much to learn from studying attraction and relationship formation (e.g., Berscheid & Peplau, 1983; Berscheid & Walster, 1978), so there is much to learn from studying relationship dissolution (e.g., Duck, 1982; Hill, Rubin, & Peplau, 1976; Levinger, 1976; Weiss, 1975). As Lewin observed, it is when an entity is moving and changing that its dynamics reveal themselves most clearly (cited in Deutsch, 1954). And as Bowlby (1979) suggests in the title of one of his books, to understand human relationships we must examine both "the making and [the] breaking of affectional bonds."

In this chapter, we examine relationship loss from the perspective of attachment theory (Bowlby, 1969, 1973, 1980), as it applies to infants and young children (e.g., Ainsworth, Blehar, Waters, & Wall, 1978; Bretherton & Waters, 1985; Main & Cassidy, 1988; Sroufe, 1983; Waters & Deane, 1985) and as it applies to adolescents and adults (e.g., Hazan & Shaver, 1987, 1990; Kobak & Sceery, 1988; Main & Goldwyn, 1984; Ricks, 1985; Weiss, 1982). Although many relationships qualify as close, we limit our discussion to *attachment* relationships (described more fully later)—the central and most profound class of close relationships, such as those between parents and children and between adult partners.

Cindy Hazan, Phillip R. Shaver; Terri L. Orbuch, ed., "Broken Attachments: Relationship Loss from the Perspective of Attachment Theory," from *Close Relationship Loss: Theoretical Approches*, Pp. 90–108. Published by Springer, 1992. Copyright by Springer Science + Business Media. Permission to reprint granted by the rights holder.

Attachment theory emphasizes the full cycle of relationships—their formation, maintenance, and dissolution—and the defining features of an attachment relationship include reactions to both the presence and absence of an attachment figure. In fact, it is difficult to discuss the function or dynamics of attachment without considering loss. The behavioral system that regulates attachment feelings and behaviors includes "built-in" responses to loss, and the primary motive for creating attachment theory in the first place was to explain children's reactions to separation from their mothers (Bowlby, 1958, 1969).

The process of mourning a loss is something that most of us take for granted. We are not shocked by a mourner's rage and desperation at the sudden death of a beloved. We anticipate the sadness and despair of the recently widowed. We are not surprised when a newly separated friend has difficulty sleeping or concentrating. To understand loss, however, we must look beneath the surface, see beyond what most of us take for granted. What explains the way we respond?

Our goal in this chapter is to answer this question. We begin with a definition of attachment and an overview of attachment theory, followed by a description of childhood responses to separation and loss. This was attachment theory's major purview in the beginning, and there is still more known about children from an attachment point of view than is known about adults. Next, we consider responses to loss in adulthood, focusing on both bereavement and estrangement, which bear striking similarities to childhood reactions. Following the discussion of normative responses to loss, we describe the major individual differences. This is where some of the most recent research has been done and where a host of answerable questions have yet to be addressed. Finally, we briefly consider loneliness as the natural consequence of relationship loss. Throughout the chapter, we illustrate our argument with excerpts from interviews and various works of literature. Loss has inspired not only grieving but art as well.

Attachment Relationships

According to attachment theory, humans are innately predisposed to form close relationships, and behavior in such relationships is regulated in part by a set of innate behavioral systems. The primary job of the attachment system, at least in infancy, is to regulate proximity to the attachment figure. Using concepts borrowed from control systems theory (e.g., G. A. Miller, Galanter, & Pribram, 1960; Young, 1964), it can be said that the attachment system includes a "set-goal" for proximity. The set-goal functions somewhat like a thermostat: When the room temperature drops below a set temperature, the heat comes on; once the set temperature is reached, the heat goes off. The attachment system is activated whenever distance from the attachment figure exceeds the set-goal for proximity, such as when the attachment figure changes location or disappears from sight, or when environmental conditions change in an unexpected and/or threatening way. Once activated, the system triggers a series of behaviors (e.g., calling, crawling, clinging) that serve to reestablish proximity. Bowlby (1973) refers to these attachment behaviors as "separation protest," and such behavior distinguishes attachments from other kinds of close relationships. As long as an infant is within the set range of the attachment figure, there is no special effort exerted to increase proximity, and attention can be directed elsewhere.

In addition to the separation-protest feature, attachment relationships are functionally distinct from other close relationships. Attachments serve two functions: They provide a "safe haven" to which to retreat (Bowlby, 1969) and a "secure base" from which to engage in activity (Ainsworth, 1967; Ainsworth et al., 1978). A central tenet of attachment theory is that the features and functions of attachment relationships are essentially the same "from the cradle to the grave" (Bowlby, 1977). Other aspects of attachment change dramatically with physical and psychological development. For example, the distance from the attachment figure that can be comfortably tolerated (i.e., the set-goal for proximity) increases steadily from infancy through childhood and adolescence. In addition, psychological closeness takes on increasing importance relative to physical closeness (Main, Kaplan, & Cassidy, 1985), although the need for physical closeness never disappears entirely.

Perhaps the most significant change in attachment between infancy and adulthood is a structural one. Infants and children are attached to their care givers; that is, they use their care givers as havens of safety and secure bases for exploration and protest separation from them. Care givers, however, are not normally attached, in the technical sense, to their infants or children. The relationship is complementary, with attachment figures providing, but generally not receiving, care. In adulthood, attachment relationships are usually more reciprocal, with the partners serving as care givers for, and seeking care from (i.e., being attached to), each other, and also typically involve sex. The prototypical adult attachment relationship is thus structurally more complex, involving the integration of at least three behavioral systems: attachment, care giving, and sexual mating (Shaver, Hazan, & Bradshaw, 1988).

Within an attachment theoretical framework, *love* refers to a relationship that involves one or more of these behavioral systems. Love of parent implicates the attachment system; love of offspring, the care-giving system; and being passionately "in love," the sexual mating system. In other words, attachment, care giving, and sexual mating may be conceptualized as three different *types* of love, or as the *components* of the prototypical adult love relationship. (See Sternberg, 1986, for a similar componential approach.)

In infancy and childhood, the primary attachment figure is usually a parent, most often the mother. By late adolescence or early adulthood, the attachment figure of infancy and childhood is replaced by a peer (Hazan & Hutt, 1990; Weiss, 1982). This does not mean that parents are relinquished as attachment figures. Rather, their position in the hierarchy of attachment figures changes.

The process of becoming attached is strikingly similar for individuals of all ages. First, a potential attachment figure is targeted. Though the characteristics of the target person no doubt vary tremendously across individuals and available partners, attachment theory suggests that this person will be perceived as potentially available, responsive, and "wiser." For infants, this could include any older child or adult, whereas for adults it may include anyone who possesses a valued quality or skill. Efforts are then directed toward maintaining proximity to, and attracting the attention of, that individual (Bowlby, 1979). In infancy and childhood, proximity seeking results mostly from fear, while in adulthood it is primarily motivated by sexual attraction.

Whether the relationship involves an infant-care-giver pair or an adult couple, responsiveness is critically important. It is the primary determinant of the quality of attachment between infants and care givers (Ainsworth et al., 1978) and an important feature of interpersonal attraction among adults (Aron, Dutton, Aron, & Iverson, 1989; Berscheid & Walster, 1978; Rubin, 1973). Responsiveness of the target person usually evokes feelings of joy, security, and confidence; unresponsiveness commonly results in anxiety and obsessive preoccupation (Tennov, 1979). Interactions between individuals who are becoming attached are also similar in infancy and adulthood in that they typically involve extended mutual gazing and unique physical closeness (Robson, 1967; Rubin, 1974; Sroufe, 1983). (See Shaver et al., 1988, for a more complete list of similarities.)

The attached individual gradually contructs a mental representation or "internal working model" of the target person or attachment figure through a process analogous to imprinting. (This may be the purpose of all that mutual gazing and intimate personal storytelling.) This working model includes information about how likely it is that an attachment figure will be accessible and responsive. It is jointly determined by the innate predisposition to form attachments and the experiences one has actually had in attachment relationships (Bretherton, 1987; Main et al., 1985). Bowlby (1973) calls the models "tolerably accurate reflections" of actual experience. Any continuity in the quality of attachments that an individual forms at different ages is assumed to be mediated by these models as they influence social information processing, emotional regulation, and behavior in close relationships.

Responses to Loss During Childhood

When the attachment system is activated and attachment behaviors are triggered, they continue to be engaged until sufficient proximity to an attachment figure has been established. For an average infant on an average day, this can usually be accomplished simply by calling out, crying briefly, or crawling to the care giver. But how does the system respond when the care giver is unavailable for an extended period of time, perhaps indefinitely? It was while observing children in just such situations that Bowlby in the late 1940s and early 1950s first began to formulate his theory.

Much of the early theorizing about childhood grief came from clinical cases of young children housed in residential nurseries in London (Bowlby, 1953; Heinicke, 1956; Robertson, 1953; Spitz, 1953). Many observers were struck by the intensity of the children's initial reactions to separation and were surprised by its lasting effects. In addition, they were impressed by the strong similarity of response across children, which seemed to follow an invariant sequence.

First, there was an initial *protest* response, characterized by anxiety and anger, and a preoccupation with and search for the care giver—behaviors that, under different circumstances, would probably have the desired effect of locating mother or attracting her attention. Despite the fact that the nursery staff was generally competent and willing to provide care, the children were inconsolable. Those who were reunited with their mothers during this phase showed prolonged effects of the separation. For at least several months afterward, the children were unusually anxious and clingy. They sought constant and close proximity to their care givers and were difficult to reassure. Here is an example of a 16-month-old girl, Dawn, who had spent 15 days in a residential nursery:

During the first day Dawn was active and fairly cheerful, apparently unaware of the situation. Next morning, however, she cried desperately for "Mummy, Daddy." For long periods she stood by the door through which her father had disappeared. Attempts by staff to comfort her were to no avail. During the next three days she continued to fret inconsolably and was to be seen much of the time standing near the door. (Bowlby, 1980, p. 421)

Even the *threat* of loss can provoke clingy protest behavior. The following example appears in Bowlby's (1973) volume on separation:

A mother denies using threats and then corrects herself: "No—oh, I tell a lie, I once did—and upset her that much that I've never said it any more." (What did you say?) "Well, she was having an argument with me, and she says to me, 'You don't live here. Hop it!' So I says, 'Oh, well, I can do that! Where's my coat? I'm moving!' So I got my coat from the back, and I was gone. I just stood outside the door, and she cried so bitter, she did. As soon as I came in, she got hold of my leg and wouldn't let go, sort of thing. I'll *never* say it no more." (p. 228)

For the children who were not reunited with care givers, the protest behavior eventually subsided, either from fatigue or from the realization that the behavior was futile. The intense activity eventually gave way to *despair,* a phase characterized by withdrawal, passivity, and depression. Bowlby borrowed from Anna Freud and Dorothy Burlingham (1943) an example of 3-year-old Patrick, a boy who had been taken from his mother on previous occasions and sent to a foster-home, and into a hospital (with measles). At the time of Freud and Burlingham's observations, he was in a residential nursery and separated from his mother, who was physically ill. At first, he insisted vigorously that his mother would come and pick him up, put on his coat, and take him home. Gradually, he substituted highly visible dressing gestures for words. Still later,

> what showed as an expressive movement one day was reduced the next to a mere abortive flicker of his fingers. While the other children were mostly busy with their toys, playing games, making music, etc., Patrick, totally uninterested, would stand somewhere in a corner, moving his hands and lips with an absolutely tragic expression on his face. (Bowlby, 1980, p. 12)

If left alone for an extended period of time, most children in the nursery began to come out of depression and despair, began to eat and sleep normally again, and appeared to have recovered. It was only when some of the "recovered" children returned home that this interpretation was called into question. What had looked like adaptation was actually something more like emotional distancing. The children who appeared to have recovered from the separation avoided contact with their care givers. They had entered a psychologically defensive phase which Bowlby called *detachment*.

Owen was aged 2 years and 2 months at the start of what proved to be an 11-week separation. Both during the journey home with his father and after he had entered the house and met mother he remained characteristically numb, silent, and unresponsive. … Then, and during the next couple of days, he began sometimes to turn to his father; but his mother he continued to ignore. During his second day home he bumped his knee and, when he seemed about to cry, mother at once offered comfort. Owen however passed her by and went to father instead. (Heinicke & Westheimer, 1966, quoted in Bowlby, 1980, p. 21)

Responses to Loss in Adulthood

Although attachment theory is explicitly a life-span theory, for many years, empirical studies of attachment were limited to infants and mothers. This is likely due to Bowlby's emphasis on the importance of the first attachment relationship for the formation of lasting internal working models. His initial formulation of the theory appeared under the title, "The Nature of the Child's Tie to His Mother" (Bowlby, 1958). The exclusive focus on infancy was additionally facilitated by the development of a paradigm for assessing infant attachment (Ainsworth et al., 1978) and the lack of procedures for assessing attachment beyond infancy.

The first efforts to test the life-span implications of attachment theory were made by Parkes (1972) and Weiss (1975). They, like Bowlby, started with loss. Weiss primarily investigated loss due to divorce; Parkes studied bereavement in widows and widowers. Later, Shaver and Rubenstein (1980) demonstrated a link between childhood experiences of loss and subsequent adult loneliness.

Loss That Is Due to Death

Although there is tremendous cultural variation in the rituals and customs surrounding death, the human response to the demise of an attachment figure hardly varies (Gorer, 1973; Marris, 1958; S. I. Miller & Schoenfeld, 1973; Palgi, 1973). The contemporary anthropologist Renato Rosaldo (1989), known generally for talking about cultural differences in emotional reactions, learned about the power and uniformity of grief reactions when his wife unexpectedly died in an accident while they were engaged in fieldwork:

> Immediately upon finding her body I became enraged. How could she abandon me? How could she have been so stupid as to fall? ... Powerful visceral emotional states swept over me, at times separately and at other times together. I experienced the deep cutting pain of sorrow almost beyond endurance, the cadaverous cold of realizing the finality of death ... the mournful keening that started without my willing, and frequent tearful sobbing, (p. 9)

The way in which adults respond to loss of an attachment figure is not essentially different from the way children, the world over, respond (Bowlby, 1980; Heinecke & Westheimer, 1966; Parkes & Weiss, 1983). After a brief period of numbness in cases of unexpected death, adults normally enter a phase of intense protest behavior. Individuals report feeling agitated, anxious, and preoccupied with thoughts of the lost partner, coupled with a compulsion to search for him or her, as though trying to undo the loss even when it is obviously irreversible. It is not uncommon for individuals to be drawn to places where the partner used to go or even to the partner's gravesite. Lindemann (1944) observed in the widows he studied a marked "restlessness, inability to sit still, moving about in an aimless fashion, continually searching for something to do. There is, however, at the same time, a painful lack of capacity to initiate and maintain normal patterns of activity" (p. 148). Parkes (1972) studied London widows and found them

> drawn to places associated with their husband ... most were reluctant to leave the home where he had lived; they treasured possessions and parts of the house that were especially "his," and tended to return repeatedly to them. ... One of these terminated a visit to her sister prematurely because she felt that she had left her husband too long. (p. 50)

Widowed partners often find it difficult to inhibit care-giving impulses. Parkes (1972) reported that, "One widow felt concern for her deceased husband whenever the weather was inclement. 'It's terrible if it's raining. It's as if I want to pick him up and bring him home'" (p. 51).

Occasionally, the normal but generally inarticulate yearnings of the bereaved can be expressed in art. In "The Going," written in the months following the death of his wife, Thomas Hardy describes his experiences of searching:

> Why do you make me leave the house
> And think for a breath it is you I see At the end
> of the alley of bending boughs Where so
> often at dusk you used to be;
>
> Till in the darkening dankness
>
> The yawning blankness Of
> the perspective sickens me!

In a letter written by D. H. Lawrence 5 days after the death of his mother, with whom he had had a very close and somewhat disturbed relationship, he says:

> I am so miserable without my "matouchka." When I am not in good health my mind repeatedly presents me a picture: no matter what my thoughts are, or what I am doing, the image of a memory floats up. This afternoon, it is just the winsome, wavy grey hairs at my mother's temple, and her hand under her cheek as she lay. (Lawrence quoted in Aberbach, 1989, p. 40)

For most mourners, realization that the loss cannot be recovered results in deep sadness and despair. The intense activity and rumination of the protest phase give way to lethargy and depression. Many widows and widowers report being incapable of getting out of bed, unconcerned about responsibilities or personal appearance, and a general lack of interest in life and other people (Parkes, 1972). The despair lasts an average of a few weeks or months before the process of recovery begins.

From an attachment-theoretical perspective, the goal of healthy mourning is to achieve an adaptive degree of "detachment" from the lost partner and a return to ordinary living. Weiss (1988) argues that the process of recovery from the loss of an attachment figure actually involves three separate processes. First, individuals grieving a lost attachment figure are highly motivated to develop a causal explanation of the loss, the outcome of a process of *cognitive acceptance.* The absence of a satisfactory account of how and why (maybe even whether, as in the case of the wives of soldiers "missing in action") the loss occurred may inhibit further recovery. (For more on the nature and value of accounts of traumatic experiences, see Harvey, Orbuch, & Weber, 1990, and Chapter 10 in this volume.)

If the loss can be understood and accepted cognitively, the groundwork is laid for the process of *emotional acceptance.* For the loss to be emotionally accepted, memories of the partner must be "neutralized" (Weiss, 1988), or "decathected," as S. Freud (1917–1955) put it. Neutralization can be facilitated by recalling memories one by one until habituation to each is achieved or until the memories are no longer paralyzingly painful. The process of neutralization may require many months or years, and vulnerability to momentary remorse or distress may last almost indefinitely. As widows and widowers sometimes say, "You never get over it, you just get used to it" (Weiss, 1988). Anniversaries tend to serve as reminders that the pain may never disappear completely.

Finally, individuals must undergo some degree of *identity change.* This involves developing a new image of the self that reflects the reality of the changed circumstances. To the extent that a person understands and accepts both the loss and its myriad implications, recovery has occurred. It is evidenced in a certain degree of freedom from distress, the ability to attend to the business of life, and a capacity for joy and hopefulness, perhaps even a new relationship. According to one estimate, return to preloss functioning takes, on average, 3 or 4 years (Glick, Weiss, & Parkes, 1974).

Loss That Is Due to Estrangement

When the loss of an attachment relationship results from estrangement rather than death, the sequence of response is very similar, presumably because the unavailability of the partner, for whatever reason, activates the attachment system. Still, responses to estrangement differ in important ways from responses to death.

Unlike death, estrangement is typically a voluntary loss, at least for the "leaver" as opposed to the "left." The process of detachment on the part of the leaver commonly begins in secret (Vaughan, 1986). This allows for a very gradual breaking away, which is undoubtedly less painful than sudden loss. As they contemplate ending the relationship, leavers experience the kind of anxiety that characterizes attachment-system activation. Most report alternating frequently between wanting to separate from the partner and panicking at the thought of losing the relationship. A 30-year-old woman told Weiss (1975, p. 25): When the idea occurred to me that I could live without Dave and be happier, my immediate next feeling was just gut fear. It's really hard to explain. It was just terror. I would think that you would start feeling happy if you would feel you could maybe make a better life without somebody. But my whole instinct was just fear.
Such vacillation can continue all the way to, and through, the separation. Here is a painfully humorous example from Weiss's study (1975, p. 46):

> Wednesday afternoon I had the second of two conferences with my husband and his lawyer and my lawyer and myself. At the end of the second one I told my lawyer that I was not going to do that any more. In preparation for seeing him I had gotten myself as beautiful as I could. And I felt that as long as my husband was in the room, I felt protected, and that it was just the two of us,

> not the lawyers. And, midnight, I was sitting in bed, eating vegetable soup, my first meal of the day, and I wanted to call him and say, "What a colossal mistake we've made. I only feel together when I'm with you."

Eventually, the panic causes either a revaluing of the relationship and a resolution to stay with the partner, or it gives way to sadness over the realization that the relationship cannot be saved. When loss seems inevitable, the leaver can begin the process of detachment even before the actual separation occurs. Recovery, in this case, also requires both emotional and cognitive acceptance, as well as a change in identity (or working models) to reflect the impending change in relationship status. Identity change can be accomplished by, for example, forming new friendships that exclude the partner, participating in recreational activities that are unlikely to interest the partner, or more subtly, using "I" rather than "we" language (Vaughan, 1986).

The eventual separation often comes as a surprise to the partner. Although the *sequence* of responses is typically similar to what has been experienced by the leaver, it is likely to be much more intense (Vaughan, 1986). The partner who is left behind does not have the same options to "try out" separation or to work on developing a new identity before it is needed.

Another important difference compared with death-related loss is that, in the case of estrangement, the lost attachment is potentially recoverable. When the attachment system is activated, the natural response is to seek proximity to the attachment figure, and this seems to happen whether establishing proximity is possible or not. The fact that an estranged partner may still be attainable can foster not only hope but protracted protest (Weiss, 1975, 1988). Movement toward recovery may thus be hindered. In some cases, chronic activation of the attachment system in the absence of the former partner may result in premature attachment to another person. A likely candidate would be an individual providing support and care during a difficult time.

Recently separated individuals report occasional intense, though shortlived, feelings of euphoria (Bowlby, 1980; Weiss, 1988). For the partner who has been left, this somewhat mysterious deviation from negative emotions tends to follow relatively trivial but successful coping experiences. One man recalled waking at 4:00 in the morning and thinking about his estranged wife:

> I couldn't get back to sleep. I got out of bed and made myself follow my morning routine. I straightened out the apartment and washed the dishes. I got dressed and went out. It was still early so I started to walk, instead of taking the bus. It was a brisk, snowy morning, just after dawn. I suddenly felt happy. I had gotten myself through the night. I was going to see people during the day. I was all right. It was a fine world. (Weiss, 1975, p. 54)

For the partner who initiated the separation, euphoria also results from feeling that the self is competent to face the challenges of life alone and from fantasizing about the wonderful life and exciting new relationships that lie ahead.

By the time a couple decides to separate, all former fondness and affection may have eroded. For this reason many newly separated individuals, especially those who initiated the separation, are surprised when they begin to experience intense anxiety and a compulsion to be near the former partner. One of Weiss's subjects traveled across the continent from his estranged wife to see a former girlfriend: "Here I was, three days with someone of the opposite sex, trying to start rebuilding, and I just got overwhelmed with panic at being three thousand miles from Laura" (Weiss, 1975, p. 49). Weiss argues that this very common feeling is due to the persistence of attachment and suggests that an attachment bond can be broken only by an extended period of psychological and/or physical distance.

Psychological Loss and Individual Differences in Attachment

When Bowlby identified the protest-despair-detachment response to loss, he was observing the behavior of children who had been *physically* separated from their mothers. In the first laboratory tests of attachment theory, Ainsworth and her colleagues (1978) discovered that the effects of *psychological* distance are similar.

In studying the quality of attachment between infants and their mothers, Ainsworth identified three primary patterns, one *secure* and two insecure patterns: *insecure-resistant* and *insecure-avoidant.* These patterns were revealed in the infants' behavior in a laboratory "strange situation," where many aspects of attachment were noted, especially the behavior the infants displayed in response to brief separations from mother. Securely attached infants were distressed by the brief separations; they typically abandoned any exploratory activity and cried. When mother returned, however, the securely attached infants were easily comforted and quickly resumed exploration. Insecure-resistant infants showed signs of distress even before separation and on reunion appeared alternately angry and afraid. The typical insecure-resistant infant was too preoccupied with mother to spend much if any time exploring. Infants exhibiting the insecure-avoidant pattern did not appear distressed by the separation and did not seek proximity to mother on reunion. Instead, they focused their attention on the available toys (Ainsworth et al., 1978).

It was possible to explain the three observed patterns of attachment in terms of experience. Before their visit to the laboratory when the infants. were 12 months of age, the infant-mother dyads had been naturalistically observed at home on a regular basis. Infants who appeared securely attached in the laboratory had experienced consistent responsiveness from their mothers. In contrast, the insecurely attached infants had not received such consistent or responsive care. Mothers of the insecure-resistant infants had been inconsistent in their responses, sometimes ignoring their infants' bids for closeness, sometimes responding effectively, and sometimes intrusively imposing affection when the infants were engaged in play. Mothers of the insecure-avoidant infants were consistently unresponsive and appeared to find physical contact with their infants aversive.

In terms of attachment theory, the infants' experiences with their attachment figures had taught them what to expect whenever they sought proximity. Such expectations form the basis of internal working models. There is considerable evidence that working models of attachment, like any well-rehearsed cognitive schema, tend to be stable (Erikson, Sroufe, & Egeland, 1985; Hazan & Hutt, 1989; Main et al., 1985; Waters, Wippman, & Sroufe, 1979). Recent research by Main et al. (1985), Kobak and Sceery (1988), and us (e.g., Hazan & Shaver, 1987, 1990) indicates that the same three patterns of attachment also characterize relationship functioning in adolescence and adulthood.

In the case of secure attachment, working models are organized around the expectation that attachment figures will be reliably available and responsive. In the case of insecure attachment, working models are organized around the expectation that attachment figures may *not* be available and responsive; in other words, they are organized around the *anticipation of loss.* The three patterns of attachment reflect the functioning of the attachment behavioral system, as summarized in Figure 5.1. Insecure-resistant, or anxious-ambivalent, infants can be thought of as stuck in a state of attachment system activation, a chronic panic and protest loop. The attachment figure's unpredictable availability keeps the infants hopeful and persistent. In contrast, the behavior of the insecure-avoidant infants is functionally equivalent to defensive detachment. Their primary care givers have been, for all intents and purposes, psychologically absent.

Individual Differences in Response to Loss

Some individuals fail to recover from the loss of an attachment relationship, especially those who are insecurely attached (Bowlby, 1980, 1988). For example, Bowlby (1980) described two forms of "disordered mourning": chronic mourning and the absence of conscious grieving. Chronic mourning is essentially persistent protest accompanied by feelings of anxiety and anger or an inability to overcome depression and despair. It seems likely that anxious-ambivalent adults would be most vulnerable to such chronic mourning. This notion is supported by M. Main's (personal communication, 1988) finding that unresolved grief is associated with anxious-resistant or "preoccupied" attachment. The absence of conscious grieving is essentially a premature movement to the detachment phase characterized by pathological self-sufficiency and flat affect. Results from a recent study of the breakup of dating relationships (Simpson, 1990) suggest that avoidant individuals are most prone to premature detachment.

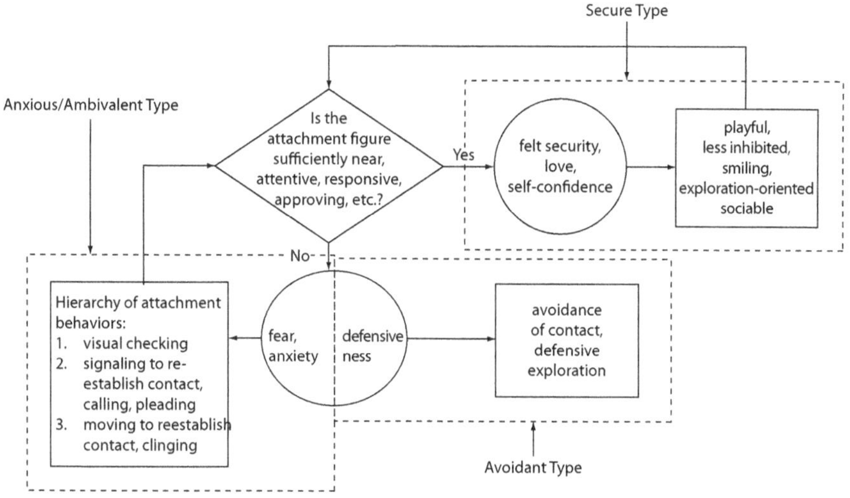

Figure 5.1. *Dynamics of attachment.*

The Probability of Loss

As mentioned, insecure attachment involves the anticipation (and fear) of loss, and ironically it is insecure individuals who are more prone to *experience* relationship losses. Insecurely attached infants experience more rejection from their primary care givers (Ainsworth et al., 1978; Main & Stadtman, 1981), and insecurely attached preschoolers are more likely to be rejected by their peers (Main & Weston, 1981; Sroufe, 1983). Insecure attachment in adulthood is associated with a higher rate of divorce and shorter lived romantic relationships (Hazan & Shaver, 1987). In addition, insecurely attached adults are less competent in providing care to their partners (Kobak & Hazan, 1990), which contributes to relationship dissatisfaction and dissolution.

Just as some people are especially susceptible to broken attachments, breakups are probably more likely to occur at certain junctures in a relationship. It is well-documented that the intense passion that typifies new romantic pairings eventually wanes (Reedy, Birren, & Schaie, 1981; Shaver & Hazan, 1988; Sternberg, 1986). This early passionate phase is what is generally refered to as being "in love" or, as Tennov (1979) calls it, "limerent." Once the passion has faded or subsided, a couple must have something else to keep them together, such as an attachment bond. One might predict that separations would be more likely to occur at the point in the relationship when passion begins to wane. Best estimates are that the passionate phase lasts at most 2 or 3 years (Tennov, 1979), though it must certainly pass more quickly in the case of adolescents, whose average romantic relationship endures a few weeks or months (Hill etal., 1976).

It is interesting to note that while the rate of divorce in Western countries has increased dramatically in recent decades (Burgess, 1981; Norton & Glick, 1979), the profile of divorce has hardly changed at all. There is still a global peak in relationship breakups at 4 years, a phenomenon only half-facetiously labeled the "4 year itch" (Fisher, 1987). It takes 2 to 3 years for passion to fade, and it may take about that long for an attachment bond to be fully formed. In children there is a marked shift in attention away from mother and toward peers at around 3 years of age (Bowlby, 1969). Moreover, Parkes and Weiss (1983) found that divorced individuals who had been married for 2 years or less showed a relative lack of suffering, perhaps an indication that an attachment had not yet been formed.

Loneliness as Protest Without an Object

Weiss (1973) identified two types of loneliness. One type, which he calls social isolation, is the kind of loneliness felt in the absence of a social network or community involvement. The symptoms of social isolation are similar to what children experience when they are without playmates, feelings Rubenstein and Shaver (1982) called "impatient boredom." Weiss calls the other type of loneliness emotional isolation, a feeling one experiences in the absence of an attachment relationship. Its symptoms closely resemble the symptoms of attachment system activation, including anxiety and fear. Loneliness that is due to the absence of an attachment relationship is like protest without an object. Weiss (1973) has pointed out that trying to cure loneliness of the social isolation type with an attachment relationship, or to sooth the loneliness of emotional isolation with new friendships, rarely works. This suggests that recovery from loss, as accomplished by emotional detachment from a lost partner, may serve simply to land one back where one started—in protest, only this time without a specific person toward whom to direct attachment behaviors.

Conclusion

The breaking of an attachment bond evokes distinct feelings and behaviors that vary little across age and culture. The first response is one of panic and often irrational attempts to reestablish contact. When this is not possible, most individuals sadly withdraw and, with time and distance, adjust to the loss and perhaps establish new attachments. The universal nature of human response to close relationship loss is suggestive of inborn predispositions, and one of the pieces of evidence that Bowlby (1980) used to support his claim that attachment is regulated by an innate behavioral system.

It is easy to imagine how the protest-despair-detachment sequence of response to loss would be adaptive. When our basic sense of safety and security is in any way threatened, it makes good sense to drop whatever we are doing and work to reestablish it. But it also makes sense to give up at some point, not to persist to the point of dropping dead from exhaustion but instead to seek comfort and protection elsewhere.

There seems little doubt that close relationships are important for healthy development and adjustment. Unattached individuals are more susceptible to everything from automobile accidents to alcohol abuse (Bloom, Asher, & White, 1978), from dissatisfaction with life (Campbell, 1981) to death from cancer (Goodwin, Hurt, Key, & Sarret, 1987). The grieving and lonely are vulnerable to disease and deterioration, as studies of their hearts and immune systems demonstrate (e.g., Kiecolt-Glaser, Garner, et al., 1984; Kiecolt-Glaser, Ricker, et al., 1984; Lynch, 1977). All this suggests that close relationships satisfy basic human needs, not tremendously different in importance from the need for food and water.

If the function of mourning is detachment, then one can see that loneliness is a useful response. When lonely, we are reminded of our social needs, and we remain somewhat distressed and uncomfortable until we take action to establish a new relationship. Such is the natural cycle of the making and breaking of affectional bonds—a dynamic equilibrium maintained by a behavioral system designed to strike a balance between the costs and benefits of being attached.

Acknowledgment.

Preparation of this chapter was facilitated by National Science Foundation grant BSN-8808736.

References

Aberbach, D. (1989). *Surviving trauma: Loss, literature, and psychoanalysis.* New Haven, CT: Yale University Press.

Ainsworth, M. D. (1967). *Infancy in Uganda: Infant care and the growth of love.* Baltimore, MD: Johns Hopkins University Press.

Ainsworth, M. D. S., Blehar, M. C, Waters, E., & Wall, S. (1978). *Patterns of attachment: Assessed in the strange situation and at home.* Hillsdale, NJ: Lawrence Erlbaum. Aron, A., Dutton, D. G.,

Aron, E. R., & Iverson, A. (1989). Experiences of falling in love. *Journal of Social and Personal Relationships, 6,* 243–257.

Berscheid, E., & Peplau, L. A. (1983). The emerging science of relationships. In H. H. Kelley, E. Berscheid, A. Christensen, J. H. Harvey, T. L. Huston, G. Levinger, E. McClintock, L. A. Peplau, & D. R. Peterson (Eds.), *Close relationships* (pp. 1–19). New York: Freeman.

Berscheid, E., & Walster, E. (1978). *Interpersonal attraction.* Reading, MA: Addison-Wesley.

Bloom, B., Asher, S. J., & White, S. W. (1978). Marital disruption as a stressor: A review and analysis. *Psychological Bulletin, 85,* 867–894.

Bowlby, J. (1953). Some pathological processes set in train by early mother-child separation. *Journal of Mental Science, 99,* 265–272.

Bowlby, J. (1958). The nature of the child's tie to his mother. *International Journal of Psychoanalysis, 39,* 350–373.

Bowlby, J. (1969). *Attachment and loss: Vol. 1. Attachment.* New York: Basic Books.

Bowlby, J. (1973). *Attachment and loss: Vol. 2. Separation: Anxiety and anger.* New York: Basic Books.

Bowlby, J. (1977). The making and breaking of affectional bonds. *British Journal of Psychiatry, 130,* 201–210, 421–431.

Bowlby, J. (1979). *The making and breaking of affectional bonds.* London: Tavistock.

Bowlby, J. (1980). *Attachment and loss: Vol. 3. Loss: Sadness and depression.* New York: Basic Books.

Bowlby, J. (1988). *A secure base: Parent-child attachment and healthy human development.* New York: Basic Books.

Bretherton, I. (1987). New perspective on attachment relations: Security, Communication, and internal working models. In J. Osofsky (Ed.), *Handbook on infant development.* (2nd ed.) (pp. 1061–1100). New York: John Wiley & Sons.

Bretherton, I., & Waters, E. (Eds.). (1985). Growing points of attachment theory and research. *Monographs of the Society for Research in Child Development,* 50(1–2), v-xi.

Burgess, R. L., (1981). Relationships in marriage and the family. In S. Duck & R. Gilmour (Eds.), *Personal relationships 1. Studying personal relationships* (pp. 179–196). New York: Academic Press.

Campbell, A. (1981). *The sense of well being in America: Patterns and trends.* New York: McGraw-Hill.

Deutsch, M. (1954). Field theory in social psychology. In G. Lindzey (Ed.), *Handbook of social psychology.* Reading, MA: Addison-Wesley.

Duck, S. (Ed.) (1982). *Personal relationships 4: Dissolving personal relationships.* London: Academic Press.

Erickson, M. F., Sroufe, L. A., & Egeland, B. (1985). The relationship between quality of attachment and behavior problems in preschool in a high-risk sample. *Monographs of the Society for Research in Child Development,* 50(1–2), 147- 166.

Fisher, H. E. (1987). The four-year itch: Do divorce patterns reflect our evolutionary heritage? *Natural History, 10,* 22–25.

Freud, A., & Burlingham, D. (1943). *War and children.* New York: International Universities Press.

Freud, S. (1917/1919). Mourning and melancholia. In J. Strachey (1955) (Ed. And Trans.), *The standard edition of the complete psychological works of Sigmund Freud* (Vol. 18, pp. 67–143). London: Hogarth Press. (Original work published 1917)

Glick, I., Weiss, R. S., & Parkes, C. M. (1974). *The first year of bereavement.* New York: Wiley-Interscience.

Goodwin, J. S., Hurt, W. C, Key, C. R., & Sarret, J. M. (1987). The effect of marital status on stage, treatment and survival of cancer patients. *Journal of the American Medical Association, 258,* 3125–3130.

Gorer, G. (1973). Death, grief and mourning in Britain. In E. J. Anthony & C. Koupernik (Eds.). *The child in his family: The impact of disease and death,* New York: Wiley.

Hardy, T. (1912–1913). The going. In J. Gibson (Ed.), *The complete poems of Thomas Hardy.* (1976) London, England: Macmillan.

Harvey, J. H., Orbuch, T. L., & Weber, A. L. (1990). A social psychological model of account-making in response to severe stress. *Journal of Language and Social Psychology, 9,* 191–207.

Hazan, C, & Hutt, M. J. (1989, October). *Continuity and change in inner working models of attachment.* Paper presented at the meeting of the Society for Experimental Social Psychology, Santa Monica, CA.

Hazan, C, & Hutt, M. J. (1990). *From parent to peer: Transition in attachment.* Unpublished manuscript.

Hazan, C, & Shaver, P. R. (1987). Romantic love conceptualized as an attachment process. *Journal of Personality and Social Psychology, 52,* 511–524.

Hazan, C, & Shaver, P. R. (1990). Love and work: An attachment-theoretical perspective. *Journal of Personality and Social Psychology, 59,* 270–280.

Heinicke, C. M. (1956). Some effects of separating two-year-old children from their parents: A comparative study. *Human Relations, 9,* 105–176.

Heinicke, C. M., & Westheimer, I. (1966). *Brief separations.* New York: International Universities Press.

Hill, C. T., Rubin, Z., & Peplau, L. A. (1976). Breakups before marriage: The end of 103 affairs. *Journal of Social Issues, 32,* 147–168.

Kiecolt-Glaser, J. K., Garner, W., Speicher, C, Penn, G. M., Holliday, J., & Glaser, R. (1984, January-February). Psychological modifiers of immunocompetence in medical students. *Psychosomatic Medicine, 46,* 7–14.

Kiecolt-Glaser, J. K., Ricker, D., George, J., Messick, G., Speicher, G. E., Garner, W., & Glaser, R. (1984, January-February). Urinary Cortisol levels, cellular immunocompetence, and loneliness in psychiatric inpatients. *Psychosomatic Medicine, 46,* 15–23.

Kobak, R. R., & Hazan, C. (1990). *Working models in marital relationships: The role of attachment in communication and relationship satisfaction.* Unpublished manuscript.

Kobak, R. R., & Sceery, A. (1988). The transition to college: Working models of attachment, affect regulation, and perceptions of self and others. *Child Development, 88,* 135–146.

Levinger, G. (1976). A social psychological perspective on marital dissolution. *Journal of Social Issues, 32,* 21–47.

Lindemann, E. (1944). Symptomatology and management of acute grief. *American Journal of Psychiatry, 101,* 141–149.

Lynch, J. J. (1977). *The broken heart: The medical consequences of loneliness.* New York: Basic Books.

Main, M., & Cassidy, J. (1988). Categories of response to reunion with the parent at age 6: Predictable from infant attachment classifications and stable over a 1-month period. *Developmental Psychology, 24,* 1–12.

Main, M., & Goldwyn, R. (1984). Predicting rejection of her infant from mother's representation of her own experience: Implications for the abused- abusing intergenerational cycle. *Child Abuse and Neglect, 8,* 203–217.

Main, M., Kaplan, N., & Cassidy, J. (1985). Security in infancy, childhood, and adulthood: A move to the level of representation. *Monographs of the Society for Research in Child Development,* 50(1–2), 66–104.

Main, M., & Stadtman, J. (1981). Infant response to rejection of physical contact by the mother: Aggression, avoidance, and conflict. *Journal of the American Academy of Child Psychiatry, 20,* 292–307.

Main, M., & Weston, D. (1981). The quality of the toddler's relationship to mother and father: Related to conflict behavior and the readiness to establish new relationships. *Child Development, 52,* 932–940.

Marris, P. (1958). *Widows and their families.* London: Routledge & Kegan Paul.

Miller, G. A., Galanter, E., & Pribram, K. H. (1960). *Plans and the structure of behavior.* New York: Holt, Rinehart & Winston.

Miller, S. I., & Schoenfeld, L. (1973). Grief in the Navajo: Psychodynamics and culture. *International Journal of Psychiatry, 19,* 187–191.

Norton, A. J., & Glick, P. C. (1979). Marital instability in America: Past, present, and future. In G. Levinger & O. C. Moles (Eds.), *Divorce and separation.* New York: Basic Books.

Palgi, P. (1973). The socio-cultural expressions and implications of death, mourning and bereavement arising out of the war situation in Israel. *Israel Annals of Psychiatry, 11,* 301–329.

Parkes, C. M. (1972). *Bereavement.* New York: International Universities Press. Parkes, C. M., & Weiss, R. S. (1983). *Recovery from bereavement.* New York: Basic Books.

Reedy, M. N., Birren, J. E., & Schaie, K. W. (1981). Age and sex differences in satisfying love relationships across the adult life span. *Human Development, 24,* 52–66.

Ricks, M. H. (1985). The social transmission of parental behavior: Attachment across generations. *Monographs of the Society for Research in Child Development,* 50(1–2), 211–227.

Robertson, J. (1953). Some responses of young children to loss of maternal care. *Nursing Times, 49,* 382–386.

Robson, K. S. (1967). The role of eye-to-eye contact in maternal-infant attachment. *Journal of Child Psychology and Psychiatry, 8,* 13–25.

Rosaldo, R. (1989). *Culture and truth: The remaking of social analysis.* Boston: Beacon Press.

Rubenstein, C, & Shaver, P. (1982). *In search of intimacy.* New York: Delacorte.

Rubin, Z. (1973). *Liking and loving.* New York: Holt, Rinehart & Winston.

Rubin, Z. (1974). Lovers and other strangers: The development of intimacy in encounters and relationships. *American Scientist, 62,* 182–190.

Shaver, P. R., & Hazan, C. (1988). A biased overview of the study of love. *Journal of Social and Personal Relationships,* 5, 473–501.

Shaver, P. R., Hazan, C. & Bradshaw, D. (1988). Love as attachment: The integration of three behavioral systems. In R. J. Sternberg & M. L. Barnes (Eds.), *The psychology of love* (pp. 68–99). New Haven, CT: Yale University Press.

Shaver, P. R., & Rubenstein, C. (1980). Childhood attachment experience and adult loneliness. In L. Wheeler (Ed.), *Review of personality and social psychology* (Vol. 1, pp. 42–73). Beverly Hills, CA: Sage.

Simpson, J. (1990). The influence of attachment styles on romantic relationships. *Journal of Personality and Social Psychology, 59,* 971–980.

Spitz, R. A. (1953). Aggression: Its role in the establishment of object relations. In R. M. Loewenstein (Ed.), *Drives, affects and behaviour.* New York: International Universities Press.

Sroufe, L. A. (1983). Infant-caregiver attachment and patterns of adaptation in preschool: The roots of maladaptation and competence. In M. Perlmutter (Ed.), *Minnesota symposium on child psychology* (Vol. 16, pp. 41–83). Hillsdale, NJ: Lawrence Erlbaum.

Sternberg, R. J. (1986). A triangular theory of love. *Psychological Review, 93,* 119–135.

Tennov, D. (1979). *Love and limerence: The experience of being in love.* New York: Stein & Day.

Vaughan, D. (1986). *Uncoupling: How relationships come apart.* Oxford: Oxford University Press.

Waters, E., & Deane, K. E. (1985). Defining and assessing individual differences in attachment relationships: Q-methodology and the organization of behavior in infancy and early childhood. *Monographs of the Society for Research in Child Development,* 50(1–2), 41–65.

Waters, E., Wippman, J., & Sroufe, A. (1979). Attachment, positive affect, and competence in the peer group: Two studies in construct validation. *Child Development, 50,* 821–829.

Weiss, R. S. (1973). *Loneliness: The experience of emotional and social isolation.* Cambridge, MA: MIT Press. Weiss, R. S. (1975). *Marital separation.* New York: Basic Books.

Weiss, R. S. (1982). Attachment in adults. In C. M. Parkes & J. Stevenson-Hinde (Eds.), *The place of attachment in human behavior* (pp. 171–184). New York: Basic Books.

Weiss, R. S. (1988). Loss and recovery. *Journal of Social Issues, 44,* 37–52.

Young, J. Z. (1964). *A model of the brain.* London, England: Oxford University Pres

Relationships as Regulators

A Psychobiologic Perspective on Bereavement

By Myron A. Hofer, MD

In the spirit of adventure that has been characteristic of our Society, I am going to ask you to join me in a mental journey. The purpose is to try to look at something familiar in a new way. We are going to be looking at bereavement—something you all know a lot about—and I am going to try to get a different perspective on it by using information gathered in very different contexts and by trying to imagine what it is that experiments on infant separation in animals might be telling us about adult human bereavement.

First, I would like to persuade you that there is still a mystery concerning bereavement. Actually it puzzles us on many accounts: is it a disease or a natural function, a temporary insanity or a mobilization of creative energy? The mystery I would like to examine, however, is its place in natural history, its biologic basis, particularly how the experience comes to produce biologic changes in bereaved people.

George Engel asked us, in his presidential address more than 20 years ago (1), is grief a disease? However, medicine at large and even psychosomatic research has been reluctant to intrude on an event that has been embedded in cultural practices and in the intimacy of family traditions since the beginnings of historic time. Nonetheless, new evidence of biologic changes after major loss and of the health consequences of bereavement are beginning to persuade us differently.

We know something about the cultural history of bereavement and a good deal about its psychology, but relatively little of its biology or natural history. One of John Bowlby's great

Myron A. Hofer, "Relationships as Regulators: A Psychobiologic Perspective on Bereavement," from *Psychosomatic Medicine*, Vol. 46, No. 3; May/June 1984, Pp. 183–197.

contributions has been to place attachment and loss in the perspectives of development and evolution (2). This perspective was foreseen by Darwin in his marvelous book, *The Expression of the Emotions in Man and Animals* (3). Darwin suggested that the emotions of adult human grief had much in common with the separation response of children and with the forms of grief existing in other species of animals. However, despite the insight provided by these men, at present we can only see the dim outlines of what the biology of bereavement may turn out to be.

ADULT BEREAVEMENT

In Table 1, drawing from the work of Eric Lindemann (4), Colin Murray Parkes (5), and Paula Clayton (6), the major known features of the human adult response to bereavement are summarized. I have emphasized something that Eric Lindemann pointed out 40 years ago, that there are really two forms of disturbance: the acute, recurrent waves of distress, which last only minutes, and the chronic, more slowly developing background disturbance, which is measured in weeks and months. Table 1 summarizes the symptoms characterizing these two forms of response, with the behavioral and psychologic symptoms listed on the left and the physiologic symptoms on the right. I would particularly call your attention to the cognitive and perceptual disturbance caused by bereavement, with its impairments of concentration, memory, judgment, and decisiveness, including illusions and even hallucinations of the lost person in 12—40% of cases (7). This disorganization of ego functioning contributes to a sense of impending loss of control. We know very little about the physiologic changes. The sleep disturbance has not been characterized in any detail and the evidence for cardiovascular changes is based on epidemiologic data (8). Psychoendocrine research is currently being carried out by John Mason's group at Yale, a continuation of work we began together many years ago in Washington (9). Two papers have described reduced lymphocyte response in the bereaved (10,11).

It is generally assumed that the acute and chronic symptoms are both parts of the same process, but it is possible that we are wrong in taking this for granted. In this paper I will focus on the chronic background disturbance during which most of the severe biologic changes occur.

TABLE 1. Bereavement in the Human Adult

Behavior	*Physiology*
Acute: Waves of Distress, La	sting Minutes
Agitation	Tears
Crying	Sighing respiration
Aimless activity—inactivity	Muscular weakness
Preoccupation with image of deceased	
Chronic: Background Disturbance, La	sting Weeks to Months
Social withdrawal	Decreased body weight
Decreased concentration, attention	Steep disturbance
Restlessness, anxiety	Muscular weakness
Decreased or variable food intake	Cardiovascular changes
Postures and facial expressions of sadness	Endocrine changes
Illusions, hallucinations	Immunologic changes
Depressed mood	

INFANT RESPONSES TO SEPARATION

Table 2 is a summary of infant responses to separation from the mother, taken from studies of several animal species as well as of human infants. Comparison of Tables 1 and 2 will show how prescient Darwin really was. The infant responses to maternal separation closely resemble adult responses to bereavement. Species differences and individual variability (16) do occur, but the broad outline and even some of the details are surprisingly similar for different species. For example, decreased body temperature, low heart rates, and a similar pattern of sleep disturbance are found in both infant rats (28,34] and monkeys (29). In the infant, however, the acute distress does not occur in waves as in the adult, but precedes the more slowly developing chronic changes.

TABLE 2. Infant Separation Responses

Behavior	*Physiology*
Acute: "Protest" Phase,	Lasting Minutes to Hours
Agitation (12–18)	Increased heart rate (19,20)
Vocalization (12–18)	Increased Cortisol (21)
Searching, inactivity (12–18)	Increased catecholamines (22)
Chronic: Slow-Developing "Despair*	Phase, Lasting Hours to Days
Decreased social interaction, play (13,14,18,23)	Decreased body weight (18,25)
Mouthing, rocking (12)	Sleep disturbance
Hyporesponsiveness or hyperresponsiveness	Decreased rapid eye movement, increased arousals
(14,23,27)	(28,29)
Decreased or variable food intake (18,25,26,30)	Metabolic
Postures and facial expressions of sadness (1 3,14)	Decreased core temperature (19,27) Decreased oxygen consumption (31) Cardiovascular Decreased cardiac rate (19,27), increased vascular resistance (32) Increased ectopic beats (20) Endocrine Decreased growth hormone (33) Immunologic Decreased T-cell activity (69,70)

Here again, it has been assumed that the acute and the slow-developing changes are part of the same process. In an attempt to determine why this set of behavioral responses evolved, Bowlby (2) and others (14,18) have proposed that both the "protest" and "despair" phases are strategies selected during evolution because of their adaptive value. The arousal of the protest stage tends to result in the mother finding the infant or returning to it, and the inhibition of the despair phase results in safe hiding from predators and metabolic conservation until reunion with the mother becomes possible. In this view, all of the physiologic changes are thought to be correlates of the affective response to the perception and recognition of the loss, just as in adult bereavement.

TWO KINDS OF SEPARATION RESPONSE

Our experiments have caused us to question the tidy view outlined previously. We found that the protest phase in the 2-week-old rat pup, complete with ultrasonic vocalizations, could be readily prevented with a familiar littermate, a surrogate, if it smelled and felt like a littermate, or with the mother, even if she were anesthetized and therefore unresponsive (35). So far this response is like that of young infants of other species (36,37). However, we were observing the slow-developing biologic changes in particular, which to our great surprise continued to occur even when the protest phase was completely prevented by the presence of effective surrogates (25,27,28,31,38). We were forced to conclude that the slow-developing changes were independent of the acute isolation distress and that the two phases might be caused by different processes (39).

What could produce slow-developing biologic changes without eliciting isolation distress? The clue we found lay in the differences between an active functioning and an unresponsive anesthetized mother. At first, we thought that this effect would be mediated by the infant's perception that something was wrong with the unresponsive mother, which would in turn elicit an affective response that would produce all of the slow-developing biologic changes as an integrated psychophysiologic response. This sequence of events, however, is not what we found. Instead, it was discovered that a single aspect of the mother—infant relationship could entirely prevent one of the physiologic changes without affecting any of the others. Thus, the pattern of slow-developing changes was in reality a composite or assemblage of separate independent processes, each operating over a different pathway. The only reason that all of these changes occurred as a pattern in the separated infant was because all of the individual processes were activated at once by the *withdrawal* of all active aspects of the mother-infant relationship simultaneously.

This idea prompted us to perform several analytic experiments to try to identify and understand the individual processes within the relationship that were withdrawn by the separation. Our group has presented the findings of these experiments from time to time to this Society over the past 10 years.

HIDDEN REGULATORS

In Table 3,1 have summarized the work done in our laboratory and in some others that allows us to see what these individual processes may be. This work owes much to my colleagues Herbert Weiner, Sigurd Ackerman, Stephen Brake, and Harry Shair. On the left, the biologic and behavioral systems of the 2-week-old infant rat that show the slow-developing changes after separation are listed: on the right, opposite each functional change, the specific aspects of the mother—infant interaction that ordinarily maintain normal levels of that function are shown. The infant's homeo-static system appears to be relatively "open"; thus, biologic regulation is delegated in part to the mother, even in the 2-week-old pup, which is beginning to eat solid food and can survive on its own (25).

Each of these regulators within the normal mother—infant interaction has its own dynamics and its own transduction mechanisms, about which we are beginning to explore. Some Interactions with the mother serve to maintain levels of functions in their systems at a relatively high level during normal conditions (for example, heart rate and oxygen consumption); others normally down-regulate their systems (for example, those underlying behavioral reactivity, arousals during sleep, and sucking). Stephen Brake has shown the degree of'., specificity that can exist with these regulators: even within one system, that regulating sucking, intraoral stimulation by the mother's teat governs nonnutritive sucking levels, whereas gastric fill from the milk she has supplied regulates the intensity of the pups sucking in response *to milk.*

A great deal more must be learned about the way in which these regulators work and how the infant adapts to their withdrawal. However, the realization that they exist has already had implications for the understanding of developmental processes (45). These biologic regulators may constitute an early stage in the development of what we believe to be psychologic regulators within early social interactions, as infants get older and as species evolve. Doctoral dissertation research by Edward Plimpton in Leonard Rosenblum's laboratory (30) has shown that in the monkey (as well as in the rat) the acute and chronic phases of the reaction to early maternal separation can be affected differentially and may be independent processes. Bonnet macaque infants were raised under conditions in which the mother was required to forage for their food, as well as under standard laboratory feeding ad libitum. The situation in which the demand for foraging was high altered the mother-infant interaction in those dyads, creating more evidence of tension, more maternal rejections of infant approaches, and earlier infant independence. When separated from their mothers, these infants showed the same level of protest behavior as those reared under standard conditions. but differed markedly in the more slowly developing "despair"-type behavior, becoming much more depressed and engaging in less complex behaviors during the second week of separation. These findings reveal that differences in the nature and quality of behavioral interaction within the dyad can have marked effects on the infant's response after separation and suggest the presence of regulators within the interaction that determine the form of the response after withdrawal by separation. It remains for future work to unravel the psychobiologic processes at work in these interesting effects that so closely parallel and complement our results in laboratory rats.

TABLE 3. Regulators Hidden Within the Mother-Infant Interaction

Infant systems	Direction	Maternal regulators
	Behavioral	
Activity level	Increased Decreased	Body warmth (25,27,31) Tactile and olfactory (38,40)
3UCK!ng Nutritive Nonnutritive	Decreased Decreased	Milk (distention) (41) Tactile (perioral) (41)
	Neurochemical (Central Nervous System)	
NE, DA ODC	Increased Increased	Body warmth (31) Tactile (dorsal) (42)
	Metabolic	
Oxygen consumption	Increased	Milk (sugar) (43)
	Sleep—Wake	States
REM sleep Arousals	Increased Decreased	Periodicity, milk and tactile (34) Periodicity, milk and tactile (34)
	Cardiovascular	
Heart rate (ß-adrenergic) (α-adrenergic)	Increased Resistance Decreased	Milk (interoreceptors) (24,44) Milk (interoreceptors) (32)
	Endocrine	
Growth hormone	Increased	Tactile (dorsal) (33,42)

IMPLICATIONS

Is there anything in this unexpected story about separated infant animals that might help us to look at human adult bereavement in a new way? We must be very careful when we try to generalize across such a vast phylogenetic distance; nonetheless, we know that evolution is conservative, tending to use what is available and adding new features in new species, but retaining much of the old.

It is necessary to try to see what the results in these other species are telling us that might get us to look at human questions in a new way, I have been trying to do so and would like to share some of my speculative thoughts.

We know that in adult animals and humans, homeostatic regulatory systems remain under environmental control to a certain degree. For example, young women that live together for a period of time develop synchrony in their menstrual cycles (46). The sensory receptors for this social regulating influence are not known for the human, but for other species showing the same phenomenon are known to be olfactory mediated (47).

Thus, it may not be too far-fetched to ask whether it is possible that some of the changes following human bereavement might not result from withdrawal of specific sensorimotor regulators hidden within the many complex interactions of the relationship that has ended.

Are there any studies that might provide some evidence in answer to this question? Two lines of work have occurred to me, the studies done in the late 1950s and early 1960s on sensory deprivation and more recent work in the field of chronobiology. In both types of experiments, subjects are not bereaved in the usual sense of the word, but social interaction is either withdrawn or altered in its schedule over a period of hours or days. If there is any validity to our notion, subjects in these experiments should show some of the slow-developing, more chronic symptoms of adult human bereavement, without, of course, any of the acute grief responses.

SENSORY DEPRIVATION

Based on centuries of observations by explorers, mystics, shipwrecked sailors, and prisoners in solitary confinement and spurred on by the success of Russian and Chinese brainwashing techniques in the early 1950s, a number of groups began to study the acute effects of reduced environmental stimulation on human subjects. These lines of research were brought together in a symposium on sensory deprivation, held in 1958 at Harvard Medical School (48). Subjects were generally confined in dark, lightproof, soundproof single cubicles, often with a portable refrigerator, toilet, and urine collection bottles, and monitored electrophysiologically. Gauntlet-type gloves were worn to reduce hand sensation and associated activity and noise. Subjects remained in these cubicles for periods as long as 4 days in some studies and as short as 4 hr in others.

Table 4 summarizes the changes reported in these studies. These changes are strikingly similar to the chronic "background" symptoms reported in the classic studies on bereavement by Lindemann (4), Parkes (5), and Clayton (6) (Table 1). The acute episodes of grief are missing, as is depressed mood, but the cognitive and perceptual disturbance has much in common with that seen in the bereaved: diminished concentration and memory, difficulty in ordering thoughts and making decisions, diminished confidence in personal judgment, recurrence of "unbidden images," and illusions, particularly hallucinations—all resulting in fears of loss of control. Of course, in bereavement the mental content and the nature of the illusory perceptions are primarily related to the lost person, whereas in sensory deprivation the material has a highly variable and primitive, "primary process" quality.

Hallucinations occurred in as many as 25 of 29 subjects in one sensory deprivation study (49), reminding one of the clinical reports of hallucinations in nonpsychotic elderly people who rapidly develop cataracts (50). In the latter patients, increasing the level of light caused the abnormal perceptions to subside temporarily, and cataract removal was curative. Hallucinations were more frequent during sensory deprivation, the greater the degree of enforced inactivity, suggesting an element (regulator) that might be specifically related to a particular symptom. The anorexia and weight loss of sensory deprivation are also worth noting. There was loss of interest in the abundant and palatable food and in one study, subjects lost weight at an average rate of 2.03 kg in 3 days (51).

TABLE 4. Symptoms after Sensory Deprivation

Fluctuating concentration and attention Restlessness, anxiety	Decreased body weight
Difficulty ordering thoughts	Steep disturbance
illusions, hallucinations	Muscular weakness Decreased food intake

What these studies certainly tell us is how dependent we are on everyday environmental stimuli for the proper functioning of our minds. The loss of customary environmental stimulation seems to reproduce several of the cardinal symptoms of the bereaved. Of course, the bereaved are not deprived of nearly as many sources of sensory stimulation as the subjects in this study. However, when one person becomes enormously important to another, unrelated events and interactions have relatively little impact; thus, the loss of this one source may actually constitute a massive deprivation of relevant environmental input. In addition, the social withdrawal and self-enforced inactivity of the bereaved may contribute to the sensory deficit and may intensify the symptoms.

SOCIAL ENTRAINMENT OF BIOLOGIC RHYTHMS

The second set of studies do not entail such extensive sensory deprivation, but rather a specific sort of hidden regulatory process involved in controlling circadian and other rhythms. As you know, all of our biologic systems have a 24-hr functional rhythm, as do psychologic functions such as attention, memory, and even tolerance to pain (52). These rhythms are organized in a complicated web of cycles that overlap to various degrees, creating a fabric of interweaving functional waveforms. Recent chronobiologic research, as reviewed by Moore-Ede et al. (53), has revealed that the pattern of this fabric is maintained by a hierarchic system of oscillators that culminates in two separate circadian pacemakers in the hypothalamus. These biologic clocks organize the functional rhythms under their control, but the pacemakers require daily synchronization to match their rhythms to our schedule. The environmental events that can synchronize or entrain rhythms, vary somewhat from species to species, and were given the name Zeitgebers by Aschoff in the early 1950s.

Under conditions of absent or insufficient Zeitgebers, two things happen. First, the major pacemakers run free at a period of about 25 hr, thus disengaging biologic rhythms from the 24-hr daily cycle. Second, after a period of days, the two major oscillators desynchronize from each other and major rhythmic biologic functions lose their constant phase relationships to each other. There is growing evidence that this internal desynchronization is harmful to homeostatic and adaptive functioning (54).

Thus, the nature of environmental events that can entrain our biologic clocks is obviously of considerable importance. Recent evidence shows that light-dark and ambient temperature cycles are the primary Zeitgebers for insects; for mammals, particularly primates, periodic and regularly occurring social interactions may be the relevant daily cues (55).

What might all of these findings have to do with bereavement? It seems possible that one of the important regulators that may be withdrawn by bereavement are the events that served to entrain and synchronize the biologic clocks of the survivor. If the synchrony of the rhythmic cycles of all of our internal systems is dependent upon environmental events that include interactions with another person, loss of these interactions may lead to desynchronization.

If this line of thought has any validity, we should be able to find two kinds of supporting evidence: 1) that social interactions are indeed capable of synchronizing biologic rhythms in the human; and 2) that lack of synchrony is in fact associated with some of the chronic symptoms seen in the bereaved.

What reasons do we have to believe that social interactions can function as Zeitgebers for humans? First, recent experiments (56) show that when individuals are isolated from daily cues in special environments and housed together in groups, each group develops its own circadian period to which all members of the group become entrained. If one subject is moved between groups, he gradually resynchronizes his biologic rhythms to the new group's period. Second, in another experiment done by Wever (57,58), singly housed subjects were studied in rooms insulated from the everyday world around them, except for the lighting system, which was on an automatic 24-hr cycle. A system of bells was used to signal the time at which urine samples would be picked up for metabolic studies. These bells were the subject's one remaining link to the people outside his apartment. Initially it appeared that the morning "lights-on" signal was sufficient to entrain the subject's rhythms to 24 hr. However, when the bells were discontinued as a control procedure, the subject's circadian rhythms slipped away from a 24-hr rhythm, despite the morning "lights-on" signal, and ran free at close to 25 hr. These experiments led Wever to infer that even symbolic events, such as the bells, that stand for social interactions may be sufficient for social entrainment in humans.

Next, we may consider the symptoms reported to occur in situations that involve loss of synchrony between circadian rhythms and the 24-hr day, jet travel across time zones and a change in work shift. Again we find the appearance of many of the major chronic symptoms of bereavement (Table 5). In one study (59) individuals required to remain in their hotel rooms after flying across six time zones were found to take longer to recover than those required to leave their hotel rooms and interact with the people of the new location, thus suggesting the importance of social entrainment processes for adjustment to a new environmental time schedule.

WITHDRAWAL OF SENSORIMOTOR STIMULATION

Evidence from the studies on sensory deprivation and chronobiology indicate that we are surprisingly dependent on the levels and patterns of stimulation in our everyday lives for maintaining and regulating the complex organization of our mental and physical functioning. We are not directly aware of the role that this stimulation plays until it becomes insufficient or its patterning is radically changed, Then, we notice that our concentration and attention are impaired, our perception is somewhat distorted, we do not sleep well, our appetite is reduced or subject to sudden cravings, and we are periodically overcome with fatigue. In its extreme form, we feel that we are falling apart mentally. We see and hear things that are not there.

TABLE 5. Symptoms Accompanying Loss of Synchrony between Circadian Rhythms and 24-hr Day

Symptoms after Jet Travel across Time Zones
Decreased vigilance, attention span
Decreased appetite Sleep disturbance
Malaise, fatigue
Symptoms after Change in Work Shift
Decreased vigilance
Cognitive impairment
insomnia
Weakness, fatigability
Depression, hostility

The similarities between these symptoms and the chronic background symptoms of bereavement are striking. The interpretation of the results of these studies is that the subjects are suffering from withdrawal of patterns of sensorimotor stimulation that had been exerting an imperceptible regulating action on the subjects' minds and on their internal biologic systems.

Might these same sorts of regulating actions be going on in close human social relationships such that bereavement also produces a set of withdrawal responses? This reaction could be possible when one of two persons who have been living very closely together dies. However, what about the situation in which the two grew up together, but now see each other only occasionally, living many hundreds of miles apart, and the death is announced over the telephone? Do the chronic background symptoms of bereavement occur to the same degree in this case, in which the loss is not one of actual interaction but of hopes, expectations, and memories? I know of no studies on this question, but it would certainly be interesting if the acute waves of distress occurred to the same degree in this situation of "bereavement at a distance" but the chronic background symptoms were much less pronounced. Evidence on this point would give us an idea of the relative importance of the withdrawal of sensorimotor aspects of a relationship in the acute and to the chronic symptoms of bereavement.

INTERNAL REPRESENTATIONS

Human relationships are conducted at the mental or symbolic as well as at the sensorimotor levels. Our lives are lived as much within the internal world of mental representations as among the actual people themselves. This enables us to endure temporary separations without full-scale bereavement responses. Therefore, the inner experience of our relationship with another person, the memories, the expectations, and the way we bring our perception of their reactions and responses into our everyday lives through fantasy, are at least as important to consider as the actual interpersonal interactions themselves.

Could these elements of our inner life come to serve as biologic regulators, much the way the actual sensorimotor interactions with the mother function for the infant animal in our experiments? And could this link internal object relations to biologic systems? I think this may be possible. Certainly, associative or Pavlovian conditioning is a well-known mechanism by which symbolic cues and even internal time sense can come to control physiologic responses (60).

Thus, it seems possible that the regulating action of important human relationships upon biologic systems may be transduced, not only by sensorimotor and

temporal patterning of the actual interactions, but also by the internal experiences of the relationship as it is carried out in the mind of the person involved. A loss that is believed to be permanent is sustained at both levels of organization, so that both representational and actual interactions are affected by the event.

People whom we have known for a long time are represented in our minds by a multitude of memories and expectancies, running the whole range of sensory imagery and involving cognitive, emotional, and action derivatives. These representations appear to be laid down in memory during social interactions as distillates of actions performed and experienced, imbued with the dominant motivational setting and with preexisting fantasies. These individual units of experience are integrated into something like a network of attributes and invested with affect, resulting in the formation of an "internal object representation." Ordinarily the whole network is reexperienced as a unified entity when only one attribute is elicited, but it can be temporarily broken down into constituent units (for example, during psychotherapy). In bereavement, once the reality of the loss is accepted, the integration begins to loosen and individual representational units recover their separate existence in the mind of the survivor, so that, as Freud described it, "the work of mourning is carried out piecemeal" (61). Proust, however, gave us the clearest view of this process when he wrote in this famous passage about his own inner experience following the death of his lover, Albertine (62):

> If all of a sudden I thought of her room ... her piano, her motorcar ... (every) one of the things which she had used, seemed to be giving me a fresh translation, a different version, to announce to me for a second time the news of her departure ... it was not one, it was innumerable Albertines that I must ... forget.

Thus, evidence from the psychology of grief supports the idea that multiple representations of the lost person exist, and in grief, unlike normal states, they tend to fragment and are dealt with separately by the bereaved individual. It is possible that each of these individual units of representation may be related to particular biologic responses, much the way certain memories make us blush.

In older children and adults, these internal representations may serve as active but symbolic surrogates that prevent the release of withdrawal responses after separation through their associative connections with biologic systems. This may be what allows some people to survive relatively long periods of isolation from others. The tendency to rely on sensorimotor pathways is strong, however, and reemerges with more prolonged separation. I have heard that for "solo" sailors on long voyages, the boat becomes personified in their minds and they find themselves attuned to her every movement, as if her sensorimotor stimulation had replaced that of social interactions.

When we are convinced that we have experienced a permanent loss and not simply a separation, however, one aspect of our interaction with our internal representations is irrevocably changed: our expectations. We cannot anticipate doing things with the person ever again, or even hearing what he thinks or feels about anything. Certainly he will not return at a certain time of day. It is the experiencing of these multiple expectancies that elicits the repeated waves of distress that constitute the acute form of the bereavement response outlined in Table 1, We may also suppose that it is in these expectancies that the regulator functions of the internal object relationship reside.

Mourning involves the repeated experiencing of these expectancies and their painful revision according to the "command of reality" (61). Is it possible that this revision includes or results in the dissolution of their associative link to biologic systems, so that the internal representation gradually ceases to be an effective regulator? This idea would fit well with the disorganization so characteristic of the mourning period and with the reorganization that ensues when the person successfully turns to new people and new pursuits as he emerges from his grief.

PHYSIOLOGIC EFFECTS OF SOCIAL RELATIONSHIPS

If we are on the right track at this point, we should be able to find evidence that the *presence* of human social relationships can modify physiologic responses in the participants and have important effects on health outcome. Here we are on firmer ground, thanks to members of this Society such as Sidney Cobb (63), Bill Greene (64), Margaret Singer (65), and others, because these researchers have documented the prime importance of social support for health and delineated specific aspects of social transactions, such as the intensity of "engagement—involvement," as important modifiers of physiologic responses. We now know that variations in the doctor—patient relationship and even the experimenter—subject interaction can have more intense effects on physiologic responses than the medications given by the doctor or the experimental variables introduced by the researcher.

This work has prompted another set of questions, which ask more specifically *how* social relationships may exert these effects. For infant animals sensorimotor systems predominate; for human adults, however, the elements of meaning and motivation are surely crucial, as well as other abstract elements such as predictability and the degree of control exercised by the participants.

Many people who have tried to approach this problem have been impressed with the importance of seemingly minor aspects of social interaction (66). The nonverbal signals, mannerisms, tones of voices, gestures, facial expressions, brief touches, and even the timing of events and pauses between words may have physiologic consequences—often outside the awareness of the participants. I am reminded of John Mason's study (67) of B-52 bomber crews, whose individual members all tended to show similar levels of adrenal cortical output while they worked closely together. How can such a hormonal regulatory effect be transmitted? This question is a challenge for the future.

CONCLUSION

Finally, I would like to return to the experiments with infant animals, not because they can ever answer basic questions about human nature, but because they may have given us a new perspective on the problem of human bereavement and alerted us to possibilities that we might not otherwise have imagined. First, they suggest that in response to loss, several different processes may be at work having different biologic mechanisms. In particular, the acute affective responses may be distinguished from more slowly developing disturbances of biologic and psychologic organization. Second, they suggest that we look carefully at the relationship *before* the loss took place and try to understand more precisely who and what has been lost, rather than beginning our investigation with the disruption of the emotional tie or bond between the two individuals, as if bereavement were simply a stress that was suddenly imposed. Third, the studies on infant animals show us that complete homeostasis is a later development than we had thought and suggest that independent self-regulation may not exist, even in adulthood. Social interactions may continue to play an important role in the everyday regulation of internal biologic systems throughout life. Finally, they make us consider the possibility that some of the changes following bereavement, particularly the chronic biologic changes, may be caused by withdrawal of the multiple regulators woven into the fabric of the relationship before the loss.

I would *like to acknowledge the* support *of the* Research Scientist Development Program and *of project* grants *from the National* Institute *of Mental Health.* I *am grateful to* Sigurd Ackerman, Daniel Stern, Herbert Werner, *Eliot* Weitzman, Robert Michels, and John *Bowlby, who contributed in different ways to this paper,*

REFERENCES

Engel G: Is grief a disease? A challenge for medical research. Psychosom Med 23:18—22, 1961

Bowlby J: Attachment and Loss, Vol 1: Attachment. Basic Books, 1969

Darwin C: The Expression of the Emotions in Man and Animals, Chicago, University of Chicago Press, 1965

Lindemann E: The symptomatology and management of acute grief. Am J Psychiatry 101:141—148,1944

Parkes M: Bereavement Studies of Grief in Adult Life, New York, International Universities Press, 1972

Clayton PJ: Mortality and morbidity in the first year of widowhood. Arch Gen Psychiatry 30:747–750, 1974

Rees WD: The bereaved and their hallucinations, in Bereavement, Its Psychosocial Aspects. New York, Columbia University Press, 1975, pp 66–71

Parkes CM, Benjamin B, Fitzgerald RG: Broken heart: a statistical study of increased mortality among widowers. Br Med J 1:740–743, 1969

Hofer MA, Wolff CT, Friedman SB, Mason JW: A psychoendocrine study of bereavement. Parts 1 and 2. Psychosom Med 34:481–507, 1972

Bartrop RW, Lazarus L, Luckhurst E, Kilch LG, Penny R: Depressed lymphocyte function after bereavement. Lancet 834–836, 1977

Schleifer SJ, Keller SE, Camerino M, Thornton JC, Stein M: Suppression of lymphocyte stimulation following bereavement. JAMA, in press

Shirley M, Poyntz L: Influences of separation from mother on children's emotional responses. J Psychol 12:251–282, 1941

Robertson J: Some responses of young children to loss of maternal care. Nurs Times 49:382—389, 1953

Kaufman IC, Rosenblum LA: Effects of separation from mother on the emotional behavior of infant monkeys. Ann NY Acad Sci 159:681–695, 1969

Brown KA, Buchwald JS, Johnson J, Mikolich: Vocalization in the cat and kitten. Dev Psychobiol 11:559–570, 1978

Lewis JK, McKinney WT, Young LD, Kraemer GW: Mother-infant separation in rhesus monkeys as a model of human depression—a reconsideration. Arch Gen Psychiatry 33:699—705, 1976

Kaplan J: The effects of separation and reunion on the behavior of mother and infant squirrel monkeys. Dev Psychobiol 3:43–52, 1970

Scott JP, Stewart JM, DeGhet VJ: Separation in infant dogs, in Separation and Depression: Clinical and Research Aspects. Publication No. 94. Edited by JP Scott, EC Senry. Washington, DC, American Association for the Advancement of Science, 1973, pp 3—32

Reite M, Kaufman IC, Pauley JD, Stynes AJ: Depression in infant monkeys: physiological correlates. Psychosom Med 36:363–367, 1974

Seiler C, Cullen JS, Zimmerman J, Reite M; Cardiac arrhythmias in infant pigtail monkeys following maternal separation. Psychophysiology 16:130–135, 1979

Smotherman WP, Hunt LE, McGinnis LM, Levine S: Mother-infant separation in group living rhesus macaques: a hormonal analysis. Dev Psychobiol 12:211–217, 1979

Breese GR, Smith RD, Mueller RA, Howard JL, Prange AJ, Lipton MA, Young LD, McKinney WT, Lewis JK; Induction of adrenal catecholamine synthesizing enzymes following mother—infant separation. Nature 246:94–96, 1977

Hinde RA, Spencer-Booth Y: Effects of brief separation from mother on rhesus monkeys. Science 173:111–118, 1971

Hofer MA: The role of nutrition in the physiological and behavioral effects of early maternal separation in infant rats. Psychosom Med 35:350–359, 1973

Hofer MA: Survival and recovery of physiologic functions after early maternal separation in infant rats. Psychosom Med 15:475–480, 1975

Butler SR, Suskind MR, Schanberg S: Maternal behavior as a regulator of polyamine biosynthesis in brain and heart of the developing rat pup. Science 199:445—447, 1978

Hofer MA: The effects of brief maternal separations on behavior and heart rate of 2 week old rat pups. Physiol Behav 10:423–427, 1973

Hofer MA: The organization of sleep and wakefulness after maternal separation in young rats. Dev Psychobiol 9:189–206, 1976

Reite M, Short RA: Nocturnal sleep in separated monkey infants. Arch Gen Psychiatry 35:1247—1253, 1978

Plimpton E: Environmental variables and the response to maternal loss. Doctoral dissertation, School of Graduate Studies, Downstate Medical Center, Brooklyn, NY, 1981

Stone E, Bonnet K, Hofer MA: Survival and development of maternally deprived rats: role of body temperature. Psychosom Med 38:242–249, 1976

Shear KM, Brunelii SA, Hofer MA: The effects of maternal deprivation and of refeeding on the blood pressure of infant rats. Psychosom Med 45:3—9, 1983

Kuhn CM, Butler SR, Schanberg SM: Selective depression of growth hormone during maternal deprivation in rat pups. Science 201:1034–1036, 1978

Hofer MA, Shair H: Control of sleep wake states in the infant rat by features of the mother infant relationship. Dev Psychobiol 15:229–244, 1982

Hofer MA, Shair H: Sensory processes in the control of isolation-induced ultrasonic vocalization by 2 week old rats. J Comp Physiol Psychol 94:271–279, 1980

Igel GJ, Calvin AD: The development of affectional responses in infant dogs, j Comp Physiol Psychol 53:302–305, 1960

Mason WM, Kenney MD: Redirection of filial attachments in rhesus monkeys: dogs as mother surrogates, Science 183:1209–1211, 1974

Hofer MA: Studies on how early maternal separation produces behavioral change in young rats. Psychosom Med 37:245–264, 1975

Hofer MA: On the relationship between attachment and separation processes in infancy, in Emotion: Theory Research and Experience, Vol 2: Early Development. Edited by R Plutchik. New York, Academic Press, 1983, pp 199–219

Hofer MA: Effects of reserpine and amphetamine on the development of hyperactivity in maternally deprived rat pups. Psychosom Med 42:513–520, 1980

Brake S, Sager DJ, Sullivan R, Hofer MA: The role of intraoral and gastrointestinal cues in the control of sucking and milk consumption in rat pups. Dev Psychobiol 15:529—541,1982

Evoniuk GE, Kuhn CM, Schanberg SM: The effect of tactile stimulation on serum growth hormone and tissue ornithine decarboxylase activity during maternal deprivation in rat pups, Commun Psycho-pharmacol 3:363–370, 1979

Bignall KE, Palmer JE, Heggeness FW: Sympathetic inhibition of thermogenesis in the infant rat. Am J Physiol 233:R23–29, 1977

Hofer MA, Weiner H: Physiological mechanisms for cardiac control by nutritional intake after early maternal separation in the young rat. Psychosom Med 37:8—24, 1975

Hofer MA: Parental contributions to the development of their offspring, in Parental Care in Mammals. Edited by DJ Gubernick, PD Klopfer. New York, Plenum, 1981, pp 77–115

McClintock MK: Menstrual synchrony and suppression. Nature 229:244–245, 1971

McClintock MK: Estxous synchrony and its mediation by airborne chemical communication (Rattus norvegicus). Horm Behav 10:264–276, 1978

Solomon P, Kubzansky PE, Leiderman PD, Mendeison JH, Trumbull R, Wexler D (eds): Sensory Deprivation. Cambridge, MA, Harvard University Press, 1961

Heron W: Cognitive and physiological effects of perceptual isolation, in Sensory Deprivation. Edited by P Solomon et al. Cambridge MA, Harvard University Press, 1961, pp 6–33

Bartiett JEA: A case of organized visual hallucinations in an old man with cataract. Brain 74:363—373, 1951

Vernon JA, McGill TE, Gulick WL, Candland DK: The effects of human isolation upon some perceptual and motor skills, in Sensory Deprivation. Edited by P Solomon et al. Cambridge, MA, Harvard University Press, 1961, pp 41–57

Luce GG: Biological Rhythms in Psychiatry and Medicine. Public Health Service Publication No. 2088, Washington, DC, 1970

Moore-Ede MC, Sulzman FM, Fuller CA: The Clocks that Time Us. Cambridge, MA, Harvard University Press, 1982

Moore-Ede MC, Sulzman FM, Fuller CA: The Clocks that Time Us. Cambridge, MA, Harvard University Press, 1982, pp 341–343

Moore-Ede MC, Sulzman FM, Fuller CA: The Clocks that Time Us. Cambridge, MA, Harvard University Press, 1982, pp 68–71

Vernikos - Danellis J, Winget CM: The importance of light, postural and social cues in the regulation of the plasma cortical rhythms in man, in Chronopharmacology, Edited by A Reinberg, F Halbert. New York, Pergamon, 1979, pp 101–106

Wever R: Zur zeitgeber-Starkke eines licht-dunkelwechsels fur die circadiane periodik des menschen. Pfleugers Arch 321:133–142, 1970

Wever R: Influence of light on human citcadian rhythms. Nord Counc Arct Med Res Rep 10:33—47, 1974

Klein KE, Wegmann HM: The resynchronization of human circadian rhythms after transmeridian flights as a result of flight direction and mode of activity, in Chronobiology. Edited by LE Scheving, F Halberg, JE Pauly. Tokyo, Igaku, 1974, pp 564–570

Black AH, Prokasy NF (eds): Classical Conditioning II: Current Research and Theory. New York, Appleton-Century-Crofts, 1972

Freud S: Mourning and Melancholia. The Standard Edition of the Complete Psychological Works of Sigmund Freud, Vol. 14. London, Hogarth, 1957

Proust M: Remembrance of Things Past, Vol 2: The Sweet Cheat Gone. New York, Random House, 1934

Cobb S: Social support as a moderator of life stress. Psychosom Med 38:300–314, 1976

Greene WA, Conron G, Schlash DS, Schreiner BF: Psychologic correlates of growth hormone and adrenal secretory responses of patients undergoing cardiac catheterization. Psychosom Med 32:599–614,1970

Singer MT: Engagement—involvement: a central phenomenon in psychophysiological research. Psychosom Med 36:1–17, 1974

Weiner H, Singer MT, Reiser MF: Cardiovascular responses and their psychological correlates: a study in healthy young adults and patients with peptic ulcer and hypertension. Psychosom Med 24:477–498, 1962

Mason J: Psychological influences on the pituitary adrenal-cortical system. Recent Prog Horm Res 15:345–389, 1959

Hofer MA, Shair H: Ultrasonic vocalization during social interaction and isolation in 2 week old rats. Dev Psychobiol 11:495–504, 1978

Laudenslager ML, Reite M, Harbeck RJ: Suppressed immune response in infant monkeys associated with paternal separation. Behav Neurobio 36:40–48, 1982

Keller SE, Ackerman SH, Schleifer SJ, Shindledecker RD, Camerino MS, Hofer MA, Weiner H, Stein M: Effect of premature weaning on lymphocyte stimulation in the rat. Psychosom Med 45:75,1983

**Presented at the Annual Meeting of the American Psychosomatic Society, March 26, 1983.*

IMPROVING OUR RELATIONSHIPS: WHAT WORKS AND WHY

Finding and Fostering the Positive in Relationships

Positive Interventions in Couples Therapy

By Carol Kauffman
Harvard Medical School
Jordan Silberman
University of Rochester, School of Medicine and Dentistry

Research of positive psychology interventions (PPIs) has expanded dramatically in recent years, and many novel PPIs may be useful in couples therapy. The present work identifies, summarizes, and suggests adaptations of PPIs that may improve couples therapy outcomes. Each intervention is presented as part of a larger organizational framework that may help couples therapists determine how and when each intervention can be effectively applied. Finally, a case illustration demonstrates how these methods can complement traditional therapeutic approaches.

Keywords: positive psychology; psychotherapy; relationships couples; strengths

Research of positive psychology interventions (PPIs) has expanded dramatically in recent years, giving rise to a large and growing body of literature that may be applicable to couples psychotherapy. Couples therapists may feel overwhelmed by this multitude of riches; it is difficult to extract the specific methods that are applicable to couples therapy from the growing positive psychology (PP) literature. Equally challenging

Carol Kauffman, Jordan Silberman, "Finding and Fostering the Positive in Relationships: Positive Interventions in Couples Therapy," from *Journal of Clinical Psychology*, Vol. 65, No. 5, Pp. 520–531.

is the task of combining PP-based methods into a coherent strategy. In this article, we identify, summarize, and suggest adaptations of PPIs that may improve couples therapy outcomes. Interventions are presented as part of a three-step organizational framework, which may help couples therapists determine how and when specific interventions can be most effectively applied.

The first step of the organizational framework involves balancing the focus— learning to complement our usual focus on pathologies and problems with an emphasis on relationship strengths and goals. Step two examines interventions that can increase a couple's reservoir of positive emotion. In the final step, we build a lexicon of strengths, and we discuss strategies that can help partners cultivate awareness of each others' greatest qualities.

We emphasize from the outset that these PP methods are a supplement—but by no means a replacement—to essential pathology-focused intervention. Contrary to misperceptions, positive psychologists do not endorse unbridled or unbalanced focus on the positive. We do not espouse that all individuals are paragons of mental health, nor do we discount the importance of openly addressing problems. Positive psychologists simply believe that clients will benefit more from therapy if clinicians help people metabolize the full range of life experiences: the comfort and joy, as well as the pain and grief.

Complementing efforts to fix problems with efforts to cultivate the positive in relationships is not proposed solely on the basis of ideology; there is a growing body of research suggesting that a balance between these two fundamental approaches gives rise to better treatment outcomes than either approach individually. Studies suggest, for example, that a 5:1 ratio of positive to negative comments predicts long-term marriage stability, while a ratio of 0.8:1 or lower predicts divorce (Gottman, 2004). Achieving healthier ratios of positivity to negativity is, of course, far more achievable if both sides of the equation are addressed. Many other findings suggest that bolstering positive aspects of relationships can produce substantial and long-term benefits (e.g. Gable, Gonzaga, & Strachman, 2006; Gable, Reis, Impett, & Asher, 2004; Gottman & Levenson, 2000). Perhaps the most convincing evidence in support of this claim comes from a recent meta-analysis of more than 200 studies. After scrutinizing four decades of research, study authors found that frequent positive affect precedes—and is likely to promote—outcomes including greater sociability, more and better friendships, improved skill in conflict resolution, and enhanced marital satisfaction (Lyubomirsky, King, & Diener, 2005).

Three PP Steps in Couples Therapy

Step 1: Balancing the Focus

For our cave-dwelling ancestors, a negative focus was essential for survival; those who were most keenly aware of threats from predators were most likely to survive and bequeath their negativity-inducing genes to progeny. The genes that kept our ancestors focused on threats persist in the gene pool today, and may partially explain a phenomenon that has been described simply as "bad is stronger than good" (Baumeister, Bratslavsky, Vohs, & Finkenauer, 2001). This phenomenon involves a tendency to experience a wide range of negative events more powerfully than positive events. For most individuals, negative information and negative emotion have greater psychological impact than positive information and positive emotion of comparable magnitude.

As a result of this negativity bias, as well as influence of the medical model, we have well-developed ideas regarding relationship dysfunction but less well-defined ideas regarding healthy relationships. Our negativity bias may also be one of the factors that motivates therapists to focus far more on pathology than on positive issues. It may be helpful for psychotherapists to gain familiarity with positive relationship models and to supplement their efforts to palliate pathology with efforts to promote positive aspects of relationships.

To paint a clearer picture of a positive relationship, we draw upon the seminal work of psychiatrist Jean Baker Miller (1986), who describes five characteristics of "growth-fostering relationships." She suggests that such relationships are marked by zest, empowerment, knowledge, self-worth, and connection. Growth-fostering relationships empower people to undertake novel actions and challenges both within and beyond the relationship context. They are also conducive to a pattern of growth in which individuals often gain new knowledge about themselves as well as their partners. A sense of self-worth arises from growth-fostering relationships when one partner validates the other's experiences and emotions. Finally, partners in growth-fostering relationships develop a desire to forge new connections with people outside of the relationship and to strengthen connections in existing relationships.

Therapists can keep these qualities in mind as their work proceeds, using this relationship model in order to gauge a couple's progress toward more positive functioning. The therapist can consider questions such as: "How much zest is in this relationship? Are any elements of growth-fostering relationships sorely lacking?" Components of this relationship model can also be assessed formally with the Relationship Health Index (Liang et al., 2002), a psychometrically sound instrument.

Enhancing therapists' awareness of the positive may be invaluable, but this is only part of the equation; it is also important that clients develop a more balanced focus. Couples often get entangled in a cycle of negativity that is difficult to disrupt. In accordance with the negativity bias, individuals ruminate on negative aspects of their relationships, while devoting little attention to the positive. Partners' past mistakes loom large, while memories of joy and caring are often obscured.

How can we help couples to balance their perspectives? We might begin, as many couples therapists already do, by acknowledging clients' challenges and reminding them that the relationship also has assets that can provide a foundation for growth. Many evidence-based PPIs are now available that may help couples capitalize on these relationship assets.

One of the most well-researched PPIs is the "gratitude visit," a simple exercise that has been shown to enhance well-being and decrease depression for at least 6 months (e.g. Seligman, Steen, Park, & Peterson, 2005). Instructions for this exercise are as follows. Think of a person you feel gratitude towards, for something he or she has done in the past. Draft a concrete and well-written letter to this individual, describing what the person did, and how your life today is better as a result. Call this individual, and arrange to meet with him or her. Do not mention the purpose of your meeting. When you meet with your "gratitude recipient," read your letter aloud, with passion. In couples work, one may weave a variation of this exercise into the ongoing process or assign it to each member of the couple as homework.

Learning to forgive transgressors often presents a greater challenge (e.g. Lyubomirsky, 2008). Although forgiveness can be difficult, it can also be essential for long-term relationship stability. Rather than initially delving into the forgiveness of egregious transgressions, an introductory forgiveness exercise may be beneficial (Lyubomirsky). In this exercise, clients revisit experiences with one another in which the roles were reversed—a time when the current forgiver endured the role of "forgivee." Revisiting such experiences may help people empathize with the shame and turmoil of being a transgressor, and open people to the possibility of forgiveness.

The Letting Go of Grudges exercise (K. Reivich, personal communication, February, 2009) may also help couples cultivate the ability to forgive. In this exercise, each partner thinks of a grudge they harbor regarding their significant other, and writes a description of the grudge in the center of a circle on an otherwise blank sheet of paper. Each person then draws 15 additional circles around the central "grudge circle," and fills these peripheral circles with a word or phrase that captures something they appreciate about their partner. Peripheral circles can enclose a positive characteristic or a positive memory of the partner. The purpose is not to dismiss negative issues. Rather, the purpose is simply to expand the focus, to help people pay attention to positive aspects of their partners and relationships.

Couples may benefit from healthy responses to not only transgressions but also positive events. The manner in which one partner responds when the other shares positive news, in fact, is a better predictor of relationship well-being and break-up than partners' responses to negative events (Gable et al., 2006). Therefore, learning to respond effectively to positive news may be a key skill for couples to develop.

When an individual describes a positive event to his or her partner, the partner can respond in several ways. Some responses are enthusiastic, while others are understated. While some responses are positive in nature, others are dismissive, demeaning, or otherwise negative. These response types can be categorized as active versus passive, and constructive versus destructive. A two-by-two table can be constructed displaying all possible combinations of these response types (see Table 1). At the bottom of this typology is the passive negative response: a curmudgeonly, unenthusiastic, dismissive acknowledgment of another person's good news. Active constructive responding (ACR) lies at the opposite end of the spectrum. Responses that are active and constructive are marked by energy, vitality, and positivity.

This typology of responses is not merely an intellectual exercise; the model describes patterns of behavior that predict important relationship outcomes (Gable et al., 2006, 2004) and that are modifiable through relatively simple intervention (e.g. Seligman, Rashid, & Parks, 2006). The four basic response types can be easily explained, and couples can be encouraged to respond in an active constructive manner. One recent study found success in encouraging people to respond actively and constructively at least once per day for one week when interacting with a partner or other individual (Seligman et al., 2006). In relationships marked by ACR, partners may feel more understood, validated, cared for, and satisfied with their relationships (Gable et al., 2006).

It is striking that, of the four possible response types, only the active constructive response appears to enhance relationships. Evidence suggests that the other three response types all predict far poorer relationship outcomes. Destructive responses are obviously dysfunctional, and counterintuitive findings suggest that the passive-constructive response is just as unhelpful as destructive response patterns (Gable et al., 2006).

Table 1 Typology of Responses to Positive Disclosures

	Constructive response	Destructive response
Active response	Active constructive: Partner 1: I got a raise at work today! Partner 2: "That's so great! I'm proud of you! How shall we celebrate?"	Active destructive: Partner 1: I got a raise at work today! Partner 2: "Do you think you can handle it responsibility? Managing this money is just going to be another chore."
Passive response	Passive constructive: Partner 1: I got a raise at work today! Partner 2: "That's nice." (stated without	Passive destructive: Partner 1: I got a raise at work today! Partner 2: "It's not enough to pay the enthusiasm or eye contact) bills."(stated without enthusiasm or eye .. contact

Step 2: Enhancing Positive Emotions

In addition to its intrinsic value, positive emotion may also give rise to a variety of benefits that are important in the context of couples therapy. Evidence suggests, for example, that positive affect encourages interpersonal openness (Fredrickson Cohn, Coffey, Pek, &

Finkel, in press), which may be beneficial for the relationship and the therapeutic process. Positive emotion can also promote "big picture thinking" (e.g. Fredrickson & Branigan, 2005) and may, therefore, help couples transcend their focus on grievances.

To help couples access more positive affect, it is important to first acknowledge that positive affect can be enhanced in many ways and that different approaches work best for different people (e.g. Lyubomirsky, 2008). Some find a present-focused experience more fulfilling, while others are energized by focusing on the past or the future. Couples can learn to appreciate their differences in this regard, rather than allowing each partner to assume that his or her own path to positive affect is also ideal for the other. When selecting PPIs, one takes into account clients' strengths and unique lifestyles. A formal "person-activity fit diagnostic" is also available; this may help individuals select PPIs in a more structured and evidence-based manner (Lyubomirsky).

One well-studied technique for enhancing positive emotion is the Three Good Things exercise. Instructions for this exercise are as follows. Each night, just before going to sleep, write down three things that you are grateful for or that went well during the preceding day. Items can be small in scope, such as "my husband took my place in the carpool." For each item, also answer the following question: What did I do to help make the good thing happen? This question can help you appreciate your own role in positive events. You might write something like: "I mentioned to my husband that I have a busy week." This deceptively simple exercise has been shown to increase happiness and decrease depressive symptoms for at least six months (Seligman et al., 2005). To modify this intervention for couples, the therapist might ask clients to identify one good thing that their partner did each day, for one week. After identifying a partner's positive behavior, each individual might be asked to consider what they did to encourage this behavior. In therapy it is often nearly automatic to explore each partner's contribution to negative dynamics. We suggest that couples therapists can harness a more balanced perspective to begin brining equal attention and rigor to positive relationship dynamics.

In addition to focusing on positive events that have occurred in the recent past, one can also enhance positive emotion by considering positive events that may take place in the future. The Best Possible Future Self exercise (Sheldon & Lyubomirsky, 2006) may be helpful to this end. Clients are asked to imagine themselves in the future and to assume that everything has gone as well as it possibly could. They have worked hard and accomplished all of their goals and dreams. In couples therapy, it may be helpful to modify this exercise by asking couples to describe their relationship five years in the future, again assuming that everything has gone as well as it possibly could. In addition to promoting positive affect, this may help the couple clarify relationship goals, and prompt each partner to assume his or her share of the responsibility for bringing their ideal future to fruition. In the midst of relationship strife, it is easy for couples to imagine the future as a downward spiral ending in divorce. This exercise can help couples clearly visualize an upward spiral, and may help foster optimism.

Having discussed PPIs that address the past (Three Good Things) and the future (Best Possible Future Self), we turn our attention to an exercise that focuses on the present. An alternate path to positive emotion is through savoring life's pleasures, both those that are subtle and those that are spectacular (Bryant & Veroff, 2007). Couples can be encouraged to set aside a period of time—which can be as short as 30 minutes per week—and to devote this time to focusing mindfully on pleasurable activities. It is not important which activities are chosen, but it is essential that individuals savor in the present moment. When savoring, one cannot rush through experiences in the same way that many people rush through their day-to-day lives. Savoring involves slowing down, doing just one activity at a time, and focusing attention fully on the joys that can be found in the present moment. This technique might be considered a specific type of mindfulness skill, and it is an excellent way to help busy people manage stress.

Step 3: Building on Strengths

A large body of research suggests that the tendency to see strengths in a partner is one of the most powerful predictors of relationship longevity. Those who are highly aware of positive qualities in their partners—even qualities that others fail to notice—are far more likely to be happy in their relationships and far less likely to break up or divorce (e.g. Murray, 2005; Murray, Holmes, Dolderman, & Griffin, 2000). It may be crucial to guide individuals through the process of identifying and focusing on partners' strengths.

Perhaps the best tool available for developing a focus on partners' qualities is the Values in Action Institute Survey of Character (VIA-IS; Mayerson Foundation, 2007). The VIA project was a massive effort to identify the strengths of character that are valued by the majority of the world's cultures. The product was a typology of 24 character strengths, such as kindness, curiosity, and courage. A psychometrically sound inventory for assessing these strengths is available for free online (Mayerson Foundation, 2007).

The original purpose of the VIA was assessment. However, the VIA also suggests avenues for couples to learn a positive language and to appreciate and build strengths within the relationship. Therapists might request that couples complete the measure before a session or as part of an intake packet. After completing the inventory, therapists might review VIA feedback with clients. It may be useful to identify complementarities in couples' strengths profiles, to consider how strengths of one partner relate to strengths of the other partner, and to ask that each individual reflect on ways in which their partner's strengths arise in day-to-day life. Clients might be encouraged to identify specific actions in their partners that exemplify use of partners' signature strengths.

It may be helpful for couples to intentionally apply their strengths in new ways within the relationship. This may provide additional pathways for couples to build their capacity to connect with one another. For example, one might apply the strengths of kindness and social intelligence by finding a new way to make one's partner smile. Clients might be asked to apply their strengths in a new way every day for one week. This approach has been shown to enhance psychological well-being and reduce depression for at least six months (e.g. Seligman et al., 2005).

Finding and focusing on strengths may generate useful questions that therapists can pose to their clients. At moments of conflict or distress, the therapist can help the couple explore questions like: "How can you use your strength of curiosity (or creativity, or authenticity) to help resolve this issue?" If this is effective in the context of a therapy session, the partner can be encouraged to replicate this strengths-based approach outside of the office.

A strengths-based approach can also be useful for "fanning the embers of fondness" for one's partner (Seligman, 2002, p. 198). In this strengths-based exercise, each individual is asked to identify the three VIA strengths that characterize their partner's best qualities. Clients write down examples of recent behaviors that illustrate their partners' strengths. The couple then trades descriptions of each others' strengths and specific examples of how strengths have come to fruition. This exercise may help each partner feel validated by the other partner's recognition, and it may motivate a partner to live up to descriptions of himself or herself as a loving, fair, or forgiving individual (Seligman, 2002).

Case Illustration

Client Description and Presenting Problem

John and Jane were in their early forties, and had been married for 10 years. Both were deeply unhappy with their relationship. The two often merely tolerated each other, and they led largely separate lives. Connection felt impossible. Each partner blamed the other for the distance between them, and both partners felt hurt and rejected. Although John and Jane had both contemplated divorce, they were committed to making their relationship work for the sake of their sons, who were six and nine years of age. Moreover, despite their marital challenges, John and Jane did still love each other.

John felt that he was responsible for everything, that Jane was "out of it" much of the time, and that she could never handle minor criticism. Professionally, Jane was highly competent. At home, however, John felt that she reverted to "little girl mode," and that he had to "run the show." John did not want to leave the marriage, but felt that he was getting very little for himself.

Although his marital difficulties had been ongoing for some time, John felt that he and Jane should be able to work things out on their own; he did not present for therapy until Jane demanded that he do so. John felt lonely, poorly understood, emotionally abandoned, and pessimistic regarding potential for improvement in the marriage. He did not expect therapy to help. Although John was on the depressive continuum, he did not meet diagnostic criteria for a mental disorder. Despite feeling dysthymic at times, his level of functioning was generally high. He exercised regularly, and he felt that other aspects of his life were good.

Jane, on the other hand, felt that John was devaluing her—that he overlooked the substantial contributions she made at home, as well as her efforts to improve their marriage. She acknowledged being "fuzzy-headed" at times, but also felt that John's oversensitivity to her moods created many of the problems that he then blamed on her. Both agreed that their marriage felt acceptable for just two months of the year, and that the rest of their time was chronically painful. Jane also came from an incestuous family, though she had not been directly abused. She had been in individual therapy for many years, and her therapist felt that she had made significant progress.

In contrast to the marital relationship, the couple's co-parenting relationship was unproblematic and effective. Each felt personally gratified as a parent, and each felt that the other was an excellent parent. Very few of their impasses involved their well-adjusted children.

Case Formulations and Course of Treatment: Traditional Approaches

In accordance with our belief that PP should supplement (but not replace) traditional methods, we first approach the case from cognitive and dynamic perspectives. We then describe how PPIs served as productive adjunct therapies. Couples work based on the cognitive and dynamic case formulations helped Jane and John progress to a significantly less destructive relationship. The therapy helped them progress from a "negative seven to a zero." Their methods of relating improved significantly, but their marriage was by no means vibrant.

Interpreting the case from a cognitive perspective, it was clear that John and Jane had numerous distorted thoughts. These distortions incited each partner to conceptualize the other as the cause of their mutual distress. Both partners showed significant personalization, catastrophization, overgeneralization, and black and white thinking.

Addressing destructive cognitions led to improvement in the couple's patterns of behavior. Each partner took more responsibility for automatic thoughts, reflected upon these thoughts, and disputed their own faulty assumptions. This led John and Jane to interpret events in their marriage in a way that brought them closer to neutral, and it helped to slow their descent into conflict. However, with only rare exception, cognitive intervention alone did not prevent them from re-entering their negative cycle.

A psychodynamic perspective suggested that John and Jane were a "perfect" match; their negative dynamics were nearly symmetrical. Each partner triggered a powerful maternal transference in the other. John experienced that Jane would feel and behave as John's mother would have, and vice-versa. For John, Jane's withdrawal activated memories of his depressed, often unavailable, borderline mother. This triggered a downward spiral that led John to act in a critical and angry manner and to become unduly pessimistic and withdrawn. His behavior, in turn, happened to be a near-perfect imitation of Jane's mother. Jane felt threatened by this way of relating. She became angry but could not communicate her experience or its origin. Instead, she withdrew, became disconnected from her husband, and felt helpless. Jane's lack of availability intensified John's pessimism, hostility, and certainty that they were doomed to lead separate lives in the same house. Contrary to the therapist's original hypothesis, issues relating to Jane's paternal relationship were not the core of the marital dysfunction. Exploration of intra- and interpersonal dynamics helped the couple become aware of how their behavioral patterns were fueled by past familial experiences. A better understanding of these phenomena helped each partner become more empathic to the experience of the other, which helped them to choose to connect.

Case Formulations and Course of Treatment: Positive Psychology

Approaching the case from a PP perspective, the couple appeared to be chronically deprived of positive experiences with each other. Using the above interventions, the couple was able to ameliorate a substantial amount of relationship dysfunction. PPIs were a useful supplement to the therapy; these interventions helped the couple transition to the positive side of the scale.

A positive psychological assessment of the couple utilized measures including the Approaches to Happiness Questionnaire (Peterson, Park, & Seligman, 2005) and the aforementioned VIA-IS. Jane was high in both positive and negative affect, while John was high in negative affect and lower in positive affect. The Approaches to Happiness measure—which assesses the prominence of hedonism, engagement, and meaning in an individual's life—suggested that Jane was low in the hedonic approach to happiness, extremely high in engagement, and moderate in purpose. John was moderate in the hedonic path, low in engagement, and moderate in purpose. The VIA-IS reported the following top character strengths for Jane: curiosity, capacity to love and be loved, and zest. John's top strengths were authenticity, prudence, and judgment.

John and Jane found several PPIs that helped them appreciate what each partner brought to the marriage. The Three Good Things exercise was modified for couples therapy by asking each partner what the other did that was positive when things went wrong. Over time, this evolved into a more direct exploration of what they felt the other did well, and they eventually attempted the exercise for themselves on a daily basis for one week. Doing so helped them notice the myriad of day-to-day tasks that each partner did to help the other, such as cooking meals, organizing children's schedules, and helping to put their children to bed. The partners' appreciation for each other gradually increased as they integrated their new awareness of each others' contributions into the ways they thought about one another.

Jane found the Letting Go of Grudges exercise to be surprisingly useful. She was initially averse to the idea of forgiveness. However, she quickly understood that the exercise was not aimed at forcing her to give up negative feelings, but rather to see if other experiences could balance out these feelings. Once she understood this, her curiosity took over and she tried it. As she did the exercise for the first time, she realized that she could feel positively and negatively about her husband at the same time. "Now when I see John starting to react negatively," Jane explained, "I think 'Oh God, not again. I hate when he does this.' I can then visualize a circle with what I dislike in it, and try to remind myself why I married him—that's what fits in the other circles. I remember my respect for his unique way of seeing things, his incredible reliability and parenting, and all of the helpful things he does every day. I feel able to hang on to what's good about him and us, and I can stay more constructive and present." John described his experience with this exercise quite differently. "I've never filled out the form, but I do remind myself of the Jane I love, not the one that's in front of me at that moment."

For John and Jane, the reversal exercises helped them access more positive emotion regarding each other, which, at times, helped to create more positive interactions and a positive upward spiral. Therapy never included the Best Possible Future Self exercise explicitly, but they did respond to focused questions that asked what their relationship would look like if they were able to be at their best with one another. They found this exercise mildly useful, but, for both partners, focusing on the present felt more appropriate.

In that light, they invested more time in savoring positive experiences with one another. Bearing in mind that their approaches to happiness were not identical, the couple planned some activities that John would appreciate most and some that were more appealing to Jane. John was more interested in physical and sexual sources of connection, while Jane found a stronger source of connection in talking and being involved together in activities. Over time, they developed greater generosity toward each other. Their sex life improved as Jane began to see this as part of a larger effort for marital closeness, and she found that she could apply savoring techniques to this aspect of her life. Jane also joined him more often on trips to the gym. John was willing to go to the theater more frequently and to watch movies that Jane loved. Both realized that infusing the relationship with more fun was a necessity, not a luxury.

Applying a strengths-based model, John and Jane were able to cultivate greater appreciation for each other's unique qualities. Jane found it particularly useful to clearly identify John's strengths of authenticity, prudence, and judgment and to see these strengths in a new light. When John launched into a discourse about Jane's faults, she saw this as part of his capacity for authenticity and judgment, which were characteristics she valued highly in other contexts. She used a similar strategy with regard to John's strength of prudence. Jane had previously been frustrated by John's need to plan; she experienced this behavior as controlling and compulsive. However, she was able to begin appreciating John's keen awareness of strategy and time sense and "borrow" these skills by requesting his advice when this strength could be constructively applied to Jane's own problems. John was able to appreciate Jane's capacity to love and be loved, to understand how helpful this strength was as a mother, and to see how hard Jane was working to improve their relationship.

In addition to nurturing appreciation of each others' strengths, the VIA-IS assessment also allowed the partners to better harness their own strengths. For example, Jane utilized her strength of curiosity to resolve recurrent conflicts. John often felt that she was "tuning him out," while Jane thought that he was often overly critical. When heated discussions about these feelings arose, Jane would ask herself: "How can I use my curiosity to get through this conversation?" Just having this question in mind shifted her experience of the encounter, and it helped her stay connected to her husband's emotions. Mustering all the curiosity she could, she often found herself wondering what caused John to erupt in some cases but not in others. This led her to better understand John's concerns, and John felt more validated. More generally, the strengths orientation helped them develop a positive language to appreciate each other's preferences, rather than giving in to the temptation to devalue each other.

By the end of their therapy—which lasted for two years at a frequency of three sessions per month—the couple felt that their marriage was acceptable and comfortable for 10 months of the year and that the other two months remained difficult. They did feel that negative spirals could now often be "fixed" within a day, whereas negative spirals that occurred prior to therapy generally led to months of marital discord.

Prognosis and Outcome

The couple's relationship was significantly improved, although it was still fragile at times. Conflicts arose that threatened to propel the marriage into negative spirals, but recovery from these crashes was quicker and occurred far less often. Their positive focus and language created more connection, positive emotion, and interpersonal openness. John and Jane now use multiple methods—from cognitive, psychodynamic, and PP traditions—to prevent descent into negative spirals. These methods have helped them to stabilize their relationship and to cultivate the positive spiral that they now frequently enjoy.

Clinical Issues and Summary

The present article may begin to provide a blueprint for incorporating PPIs into couples therapy. We have described PP-based methods that may help couples therapists to integrate and apply the findings of positive psychological science in clinical practice. These methods can help couples attend to positive issues, enhance positive emotion, and develop awareness of their partners' strengths. It is our hope that these PP methods will help individuals resolve relationship conflict and achieve more fulfilling and lasting relationships.

Baumeister, R.F., Bratslavsky, E., Finkenauer, C., & Vohs, K.D. (2001). Bad is stronger than good. Review of General Psychology, 5(4), 323–370.

Bryant, F.B., & Veroff, J. (2007). Savoring: A new model of positive experiences. Mahwah, NJ: Lawrence Erlbaum.

Cheavens, J., Feldman, D., Gum, A., Michael, S., & Snyder, C.R. (2006). Hope therapy in a community sample: A pilot investigation. Social Indicators Research, 77, 61–78.

Gable, S.L., Gonzaga, G., & Strachman, A. (2006). Will you be there for me when things go right? Supportive responses to positive event disclosures. Journal of Personality and Social Psychology, 91(5), 904–917.

Gable, S.L., Reis, H.T., Asher, E.R., & Impett, E.A. (2004). What do you do when things go right? The intrapersonal and interpersonal benefits of sharing positive events. Journal of Personality and Social Psychology, 87(2), 228–245.

Gottman, J.M. (2004). What predicts divorce? The relationship between marital processes and marital outcomes. Hillsdale, NJ: Erlbaum.

Gottman, J.M., & Levenson, R.W. (2000). The timing of divorce: Predicting when a couple will divorce over a 14-year period. Journal of Marriage & the Family, 62(3), 737–745. Fredrickson, B.L., & Branigan, C.A. (2005). Positive emotions broaden the scope of attention and thought–action repertoires. Cognition and Emotion, 19(3), 313–332.

Fredrickson, B.L., Cohn, M.A., Coffey, K.A., Pek, J., & Finkel, S.M. (in press). Open hearts build lives: Positive emotions, induced through loving-kindness meditation, build consequential personal resources. Journal of Personality and Social Psychology.

Liang, B., Tracy, A., Taylor, C., Williams, L., Jordan, J., & Miller, J.B. (2002). The relational health indices. Psychology of Women Quarterly, 26(1), 25–35.

Lyubomirsky, S. (2008). The how of happiness. A scientific approach to getting the life you want. New York: Penguin Press.

Lyubomirsky, S., King, L., & Diener, E. (2005). The benefits of frequent positive affect: Does happiness lead to success? Psychological Bulleting, 131(6), 803–855.

Mayerson Foundation. (2007). Take the VIA survey. Retrieved February 4, 2009, from http://viastrengths.org/VIASurvey/tabid/55/Default.aspx

Miller, J.B. (1986). What do we mean by relationships? Wellesley, MA: Stone Center Working Paper Series.

Murray, S.L. (2005). Regulating the risks of closeness: A relationship-specific sense of felt security. Current Directions in Psychological Science, 14, 74–78.

Murray, S.L., Holmes, J.G., Dolderman, D., & Griffin, D.W. (2000). What the motivated mind sees: Comparing friends' perspectives to married partners' views of each other. Journal of Experimental Social Psychology, 36(6), 600–620.

Peterson, C., Park, N, & Seligman, M.E.P. (2005). Orientations to happiness and life satisfaction: The full life versus the empty life. Journal of Happiness Studies, 6(1), 25–41. Seligman, M.E.P. (2002). Authentic happiness. New York: Free Press.

Seligman, M.E.P., Rashid, T., & Parks, A. (2006). Positive psychotherapy. American Psychologist, 61(8), 774–788.

Seligman, M.E.P., Steen, T., Park, N., & Peterson, C. (2005). Positive psychology progress: Empirical validation of interventions. American Psychologist, 60(5), 410–421.

Sheldon, K.M., & Lyubomirsky, S. (2006). How to increase and sustain positive emotion: The effects of expressing gratitude and visualizing best possible selves. Journal of Positive Psychology, 1, 73–82.

We are grateful to the Institute of Coaching at McLean Hospital, Harvard Medical School, for supporting this work. We also wish to thank Tayyab Rashid for his encouragement and helpful feedback.

Learning Sobriety Together

Behavioural Couples Therapy For Alcoholism and Drug Abuse

By William Fals-Stewart, Wendy (K.K.) Lam, and
Michelle L. Kelley

Among the various types of partner- and family-involved interventions used to treat adults with substance use disorders, Behavioural Couples Therapy (BCT) has garnered the strongest empirical support for its efficacy. During the past thirty years, multiple studies have consistently found married or cohabiting substance-abusing patients who engage in BCT, compared to traditional individual-based counselling or partner-involved attention control treatments, report significantly greater (1) reductions in substance use, (2) levels of relationship satisfaction, and (3) greater improvements in other areas of relationship and family adjustment (e.g. reductions in partner violence, improvements in custodial children's adjustment). In addition to discussing the theoretical rationale for BCT as a treatment of substance abuse, this article describes specific therapeutic techniques used as part of this intervention and summarizes the relevant evaluative empirical literature.

Traditionally, alcoholism and other substance use disorders have been viewed by the majority of treatment providers, as well as by the public at large, as individual problems that were thus most effectively treated by focusing largely or exclusively on the individual. During the past three decades, this narrow individual-focused

William Fals-Stewart, Wendy Lam, Michelle Kelley, "Learning Sobriety Together: Behavioural Couples Therapy for Alcoholism and Drug Abuse," from *Journal of Family Therapy*, Vol. 31, No. 2; May 2009, Pp. 115–125. Published by Blackwell Publishing, 2009.

conceptualization has slowly given way to an increased awareness and acceptance of family members' potentially crucial roles in the etiology, maintenance and long-term course in addictive behaviour. As understanding of how spouse and family member interaction influences substance use and abuse has evolved, treatment providers and researchers alike have placed greater emphasis on understanding drinking and drug use from a systemic perspective and, in turn, on using partner- and family-involved interventions to address individuals' substance abuse.

By the mid-1970s, there were calls from providers, treatment agencies and the federal government to examine the potential efficacy of couple and family therapies that appeared to hold such great promise as interventions for substance use disorders (e.g. Keller, 1974). Since that time, research on partner- and family-involved therapies gradually moved from case studies to small-scale pilot trials and, as evidence of efficacy accumulated, to large-scale randomized clinical trials. Reviews of this accumulated extant empirical literature indicate the early promise of marital and family therapy as an intervention for substance abuse has been, by and large, realized. As a case in point, meta-analytic reviews of randomized clinical trials have concluded that, compared to individual-based interventions that focus exclusively on the substance-abusing patient, family-involved treatments result in higher levels of abstinence, for both alcoholism (O'Farrell and Fals-Stewart, 2001) and drug abuse (Stanton and Shadish, 1997).

Although investigators have examined the effectiveness of many different types of family therapy with substance-abusing patients and their family members, three theoretical perspectives have come to dominate family-based conceptualizations of substance use. These perspectives provide the foundation for the treatment strategies most often used with substance users (for a review, see Fals-Stewart et al., 2003). The best known of these is the family disease approach, which views alcoholism and other drug abuse as an illness of the family, suffered not only by the substance user but also by family members (who are viewed as suffering from co-dependence). Treatment involves the substance-abusing patient and his or her family members addressing their respective disease processes individually; formal family treatment is largely de-emphasized in this model. The family systems approach applies general systems theory to families, with particular attention paid to ways in which families maintain a dynamic balance between substance use and family functioning; interactional behaviour is viewed as being organized around alcohol or drug use. As such, family therapy is used to understand the functional role of substance use in the family system, with the goal of modifying family dynamics and interactions to support the substance-abusing patient's abstinence rather than his or her drinking or drug use. Behavioural approaches assume that family members' interactions serve to reinforce alcohol- and drug-using behaviour. The goal of family therapy from this perspective is to eliminate reinforcement for substance use and to promote reinforcement of behaviour conducive to abstinence.

Derived from a general behavioural conceptualization of substance abuse, Behavioral Couples Therapy (BCT) is a type of family therapy for substance abuse that has, to date, very strong empirical support for its overall effectiveness across multiple areas of functioning. For example, a meta-analysis of twelve controlled studies showed a medium effect size favouring BCT over individual treatment (Powers et al., in press). BCT has also been listed in the Substance Abuse and Mental Health Services Administration National Registry of Evidence-based Programs and Practices. In the United Kingdom, BCT was one of only two therapeutic interventions which the National Institute of Clinical Excellence (NICE, the main UK body reviewing treatments that should be provided as part of the National Health Service) recommended for use in drug treatment services. In this review, we (1) provide a conceptual rationale as to why partner-involved therapies for substance-abusing patients may be particularly appealing compared to more traditional individual-based approaches; (2) describe elements of BCT when used with substance-abusing patients and their partners; (3) examine available evidence supporting the efficacy of BCT with alcoholic and drug-abusing patients; and (4) discuss future directions with respect to BCT and partner-involved therapies more broadly with these patients.

The use of couple therapy to treat substance use disorders: conceptual and practical considerations

Theoretical rationale

The relationship between substance use and couple dysfunction is a dynamic one and appears to constitute a type of 'reciprocal causality'. For example, compared to well-functioning dyads, couples in which one of the partners abuses drugs or alcohol usually have extensive relationship problems, often characterized by comparatively high levels of relationship dissatisfaction, instability (i.e. partners taking significant steps towards separation or divorce), high prevalence and frequency of verbal and physical aggression (e.g. Fals-Stewart et al., 1999), significant sexual problems (O'Farrell et al., 1997), and often significant levels of psychological distress in both partners and other family members, such as children (Kelley and Fals-Stewart, 2002).

Conversely, while chronic substance use and concomitant behaviour appears to be corrosive to relationship satisfaction for both partners, relationship dysfunction very likely creates a dyadic and familial context that increases the likelihood of problematic substance use and relapse among alcoholics and drug abusers following treatment (e.g. Maisto et al., 1988). Indeed, there are several relationship-based antecedent conditions and reinforcing consequences of substance use. Marital and family problems (e.g. poor communication and problem-solving, arguing, financial stressors) often serve as precursors to excessive drinking or drug use and, unfortunately, resulting family interactions can inadvertently help to facilitate continued drinking or drug use once these behaviours have developed. For example, substance abuse often provides more subtle adaptive consequences for the couple, such as facilitating the expression of emotion and affection (e.g. caretaking when a partner is suffering from a hangover). Finally, even when recovery from the alcohol or drug problem has begun, marital and family conflicts can, and very often do, precipitate relapses. Thus, the association between substance use and relationship problems does not evolve from a unidirectional causality, but rather each can serve as a precursor to the other, creating a 'vicious cycle' from which couples that include a partner who abuses drugs or alcohol often have difficulty escaping.

Taken as a whole, the strong interrelationship between substance use and family interaction would suggest that interventions addressing the behaviour of only one member of the family, in isolation from the family system, would be less than optimal. However, traditional treatments for substance abuse, which focus largely on the individual substance-abusing patient, usually do just that. In contrast, BCT (and, for that matter, family-based treatments for substance abuse in general) have two primary objectives that are founded upon the recognition of the interrelationship between substance use and family interaction: (1) eliminate abusive drinking and drug use and harness the support of the dyadic system to support positively the patients' efforts to change and, relatedly, (2) alter dyadic and family interaction patterns to promote a family environment that is more conducive to long-term stable abstinence. As depicted in Figure 1, the goal of BCT is to create a 'virtuous cycle' between substance use recovery and relationship functioning by using interventions designed to address both issues concurrently.

Therapeutic techniques used in BCT for substance abuse

BCT treats the alcoholic or drug-abusing patient together with a spouse or partner to build support for abstinence and to improve relationship functioning. BCT assumes partners can reward abstinence and that alcoholics from happier, more cohesive relationships have a lower risk of relapse. BCT has two main components. Substance-focused interventions to directly build support for abstinence include (1) a recovery contract with a calendar to record self-help meetings attended (e.g. Alcoholics Anonymous, Al-Anon), drug urine screen results, and completion of a daily 'trust discussion' in which the patient states an intent to stay abstinent that day and the partner expresses support for the patient's efforts; (2) teaching partners to decrease behaviours that may trigger or enable substance use; and (3) helping the couple decrease the patient's exposure to alcohol and drugs by removing these from the home and avoiding or managing family and social gatherings that may include drinking or drug use. Relationship-focused interventions increase positive feelings, shared activities and constructive communication. For those couples with poor dyadic adjustment, the focus tends to be on improving the relationship initially and then gradually moving towards abstinence maintenance. Couples who start treatment with

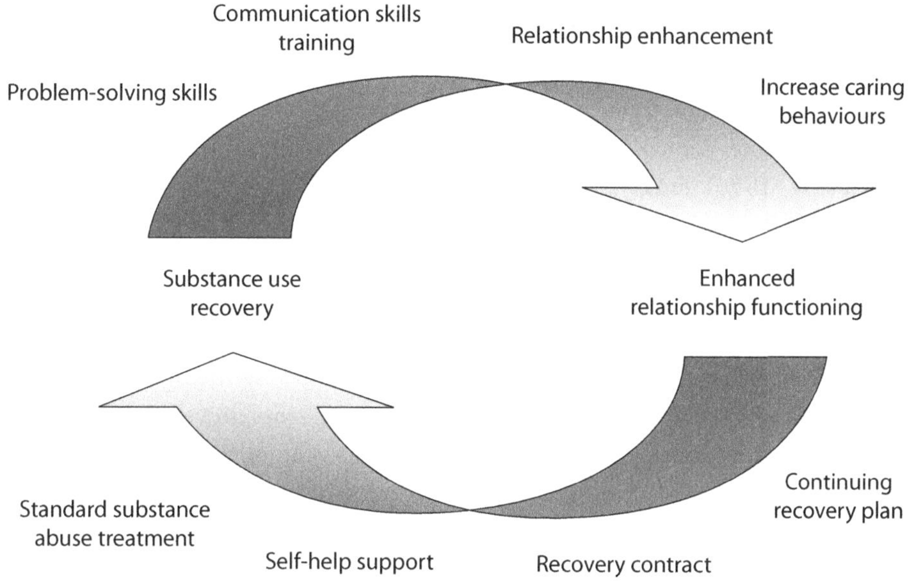

Figure1. *Virtuous cycle illustrating concurrent treatment for substance use and relationship functioning.*

higher relationship satisfaction move more swiftly through the relationship enhancement aspects of BCT and on to abstinence maintenance. Traditionally, the substance-abusing patient and his or her partner are seen together in BCT, typically for between fifteen and twenty outpatient couple sessions over five to six months. However, abbreviated versions of BCTand multi-couple group BCT have also been developed and are available. A recent book fully describes the therapeutic elements of BCT, as well as variations in delivery format (O'Farrell and Fals-Stewart, 2006).

Empirical support

BCT as a treatment for alcoholism

A series of studies has compared drinking and relationship outcomes for alcoholic clients treated with BCT versus those participants who received individual alcoholism counselling. Outcomes have been measured at six-month follow-up in earlier studies and at eighteen to twenty-four months after treatment in more recent trials. The studies show a fairly consistent pattern of more abstinence and fewer alcohol-related problems, happier relationships, and lower risk of marital separation for alcoholic clients who receive BCT than for clients who receive only individual treatment (McCrady et al.,1991; O'Farrell et al., 1992). Intimate partner violence, with more than 60 per cent prevalence among alcoholic couples before entering BCT, decreased significantly in the two years after BCT and was nearly eliminated with abstinence (e.g. O'Farrell and Murphy, 1995). Cost outcomes in small-scale studies show that reduced hospital and gaol days following BCT save more than five times the cost of delivering BCT for alcoholic clients and their partners (O'Farrell et al., 1996). Finally, for male alcoholic clients, BCT improves the psychosocial adjustment of couples' children more than does individual-based treatment (Kelley and Fals-Stewart, 2002), even though children are not directly treated in either intervention. Thus, there may be a 'trickle-down' effect of the communication skills training used as part of BCT, with improved methods of interacting permeating the entire family system. An abbreviated form of BCT (which requires approximately half the number of sessions and places proportionally more emphasis on substance use reduction than standard BCT) appears to be as effective as the standard variant across a number of important areas of adjustment (e.g. drinking behaviour, relationship satisfaction), but is far less costly to deliver (Fals-Stewart et al., 2005). Finally, although most studies of BCT for alcoholism have focused on male patients, results of a recent trial revealed that BCT was more effective than other alternatives for female alcoholic patients (Fals-Stewart et al., 2006).

Research on BCT as a treatment for drug abuse

Although research on BCT for alcoholism has been ongoing for several decades, the past ten years have seen several studies of BCT with drug-abusing patients and their partners appear in the empirical literature. Fals-Stewart et al. (1996) conducted the first randomized study of BCT with drug-abusing clients, comparing BCT plus individual treatment to an equally intensive individual-based treatment. Clinical outcomes in the year following treatment favoured the group that received BCT on both drug use and relationship outcomes. Compared to those who participated in individual-based treatment only (i.e. twelve-step facilitation, cognitive-behavioural treatment, depending on the study), BCT participants had significantly fewer cases that relapsed, fewer days of drug use, fewer drug-related arrests and hospitalizations, and longer time to relapse. Couples in BCT also had more positive relationship adjustment on multiple measures and fewer days separated due to relationship discord than couples whose partners received individual-based treatment only. Cost benefit and cost effectiveness in this study also favour BCT over individual treatment (Fals-Stewart et al., 1997). Finally, domestic violence outcomes in this same study also favoured BCT (Fals-Stewart et al., 2002b). Although nearly half of the couples reported male-to-female violence in the year before treatment, the number reporting violence in the year after treatment was significantly lower for BCT (17 per cent) than for individual treatment (42 per cent).

In another randomized study of BCT with drug-abusing clients (Fals-Stewart et al., 2001), thirty married or cohabiting male clients in a methadone maintenance programme were randomly assigned to individual treatment only or to BCT plus individual treatment.

The individual treatment was standard outpatient drug abuse counselling for the drug-abusing partner. Results during the six months of treatment favoured the group that received BCT on both drug use and relationship outcomes. Fals-Stewart and O'Farrell (2003) conducted a clinical trial in which eighty married or cohabiting men with opioid addiction were randomly assigned to equally intensive naltrexone involved treatments: (1) BCT plus individual treatment (i.e. the client had both individual and couple sessions and took naltrexone daily in the presence of his spouse) or (2) individual treatment only (i.e. the counsellor asked the client about naltrexone compliance but there was no spouse involvement or compliance contract). In the year following treatment, those who received BCT had significantly more days abstinent from opioids and other drugs, longer time before relapse, and fewer drug-related legal and family problems than those who received individual treatment.

As with alcoholism, nearly all studies of BCT for drug abuse have focused on male patients. However, a randomized clinical trial of BCT with drug-abusing female patients revealed it to be more effective than individual-based treatment in terms of substance use reduction and other outcomes of interest (Winters et al., 2002).

Conclusions and future directions

Given the very broad positive effects observed for substance-abusing patients who participate in BCT, one could cogently argue that BCT is the most efficacious treatment available for alcoholism and drug abuse. The size and scope of the empirical literature exploring the efficacy of BCT leaves little doubt as to its positive effects on those patients and their partners who participate, not only in terms of reducing drinking and drug use, but also in other areas of clear public health significance (e.g. intimate partner violence, children's adjustment).

Although BCT is efficacious, very little research has been conducted to determine how it works. In other words, what are the mechanisms of action that make BCT curative? If these factors can be identified, then BCT can be modified to maximize its efficiency and effectiveness. BCT has also been used almost exclusively with couples in which only one partner abuses alcohol or other drugs; future studies need to examine how BCT can be modified and adapted to meet the unique needs of dual substance-abusing couples.

Despite the very strong research support for its efficacy, BCT is not yet widely used in community-based alcoholism and drug abuse treatment settings. Fals-Stewart and Birchler (2001) conducted a national survey of 398 randomly selected US substance abuse treatment programmes. In general, BCT was viewed as too costly to deliver and requiring too many sessions in its standard form. In addition, most BCT studies used Master's-level therapists as treatment providers, but most community-based substance abuse treatment programmes employ counsellors with less formal education or clinical training. A series of more recently completed studies addressed each of these concerns. First, Fals-Stewart et al. (2005a) evaluated the efficacy of an abbreviated version of BCT and found it to be as effective as the standard version, in terms of reductions in drinking and improvements in dyadic adjustment of participants. Second, Fals-Stewart et al. (2002a) demonstrated that combined with twelve sessions of group drug counselling for the substance abuser, BCT delivered in a twelve-session small group format versus the standard twelve-session individual couple format was equally effective and, again, more effective than twenty-four sessions of group drug counseling (GDC) for the substance abuser alone in reducing substance use and improving relationship outcomes during a twelve-month post-treatment follow-up period. Third, Fals-Stewart and Birchler (2002) examined the differential effect of BCT based on counsellors' educational background, comparing outcomes of couples that received BCT who were randomly assigned to either a Bachelor's- or Master's-level counsellor. Results showed that, in comparison to those treated by Master's-level counsellors, those treated by Bachelor's-level counsellors obtained equivalent positive outcomes.

Because BCT has been shown to be efficacious across a number of different formats (e.g. abbreviated form ats, multi-couple group therapy, standard conjoint format), BCT is an intervention that may be a strong candidate for a stepped care approach (e.g. Sobell and Sobell, 2000), moving from least to most intensive as treatment response dictates. There is some suggestion that such an approach may be the most acceptable to providers and patients (Fals-Stewart et al., 2004). It is critical, however, to find ways to put BCT into community practice so that patients entering treatment for substance abuse in these settings have access to this very effective intervention.

References

Fals-Stewart, W. and Birchler, G. R. (2001) A national survey of the use of couples therapy in substance abuse treatment. Journal of Substance Abuse Treatment, 20: 277–283.

Fals-Stewart, W. and Birchler, G. R. (2002) Behavioral couples therapy for alcoholic men and their intimate partners: the comparative effectiveness of Master's- and Bachelor's-level counselors. Behavior Therapy, 33: 123–147.

Fals-Stewart, W. and O'Farrell, T. J. (2003) Behavioral family counseling and naltrexone for male opioid-dependent patients. Journal of Consulting and Clinical Psychology, 71: 432–442.

Fals-Stewart, W., Birchler, G.R and Kelley, M. L. (2006) Learning sobriety together: a randomized clinical trial examining behavioral couples therapy with female alcoholic patients. Journal of Consulting and Clinical Psychology, 74: 579–591.

Fals-Stewart, W., Birchler, G. R. and O'Farrell, T. J. (1996) Behavioral couples therapy for male substance-abusing patients: effects on relationship adjustment and drug-using behavior. Journal of Consulting and Clinical Psychology, 64: 959–972.

Fals-Stewart, W., Birchler, G. R. and O'Farrell, T. J. (1999) Drug-abusing patients and their partners: dyadic adjustment, relationship stability and substance use. Journal of Abnormal Psychology, 108: 11–23.

Fals-Stewart, W., Birchler, G. R. and O'Farrell, T. J. (2002a) Behavioral couples therapy for drug-abusing men and their intimate partners: group therapy versus conjoint therapy formats. In D. C. Atkins (Chair), Affairs, Abuse, Drugs, and Depression: The Promises and Pitfalls of Couple Therapy. Symposium

conducted at the 36th Annual Meeting of the Association for the Advancement of Behavior Therapy, Reno, NV.

Fals-Stewart, W., Logsdon, T. and Birchler, G. R. (2004) Diffusion of an empirically supported treatment for substance abuse: an organization autopsy of technology transfer success and failure. Clinical Psychology: Science and Practice, 11: 177–182.

Fals-Stewart, W., O'Farrell, T. J. and Birchler, G. R. (1997) Behavioral couples therapy for male substance-abusing patients: a cost outcomes analysis. Journal of Consulting and Clinical Psychology, 65: 789–802.

Fals-Stewart, W., O'Farrell, T. J. and Birchler, G. R. (2001) Behavioral couples therapy for male methadone maintenance patients: effects on drug-using-behavior and relationship adjustment. Behavior Therapy, 32: 391–411.

Fals-Stewart, W., O'Farrell, T. J. and Birchler, G. R. (2003) Family therapy techniques. In F. Rotgers, J. Morgenstern and S. T. Walters (eds), Treating Substance Abuse: Theory and Technique (pp. 140–165). New York: Guilford Press.

Fals-Stewart, W., Kashdan, T. B., O'Farrell, T. J. and Birchler, G. R. (2002b) Behavioral couples therapy for drug-abusing patients: effects on partner violence. Journal of Substance Abuse Treatment, 22: 87–96.

Fals-Stewart, W., Yates, B., Klostermann, K., O'Farrell, T. J. and Birchler, G. R. (2005) Brief relationship therapy for alcoholism: clinical and cost outcomes. Psychology of Addictive Behaviors, 19: 363–371.

Keller, M. (1974) Trends in treatment of alcoholism. In Second Special Report to the U.S. Congress on Alcohol and Health (pp. 145–167). Washington, DC: Department of Health, Education, and Welfare.

Kelley, M. L. and Fals-Stewart, W. (2002) Couples- versus individual-based therapy for alcoholism and drug abuse: effects on children's psychosocial functioning. Journal of Consulting and Clinical Psychology, 70: 417–427.

Maisto, S. A., O'Farrell, T. J., McKay, J., Connors, G. J. and Pelcovitz, M. A. (1988) Alcoholics' attributions of factors affecting their relapse to drinking and reasons for terminating relapse events. Addictive Behaviors, 13: 79–82.

McCrady, B., Stout, R., Noel, N., Abrams, D. and Nelson, H. (1991) Comparative effectiveness of three types of spouse involved alcohol treatment: outcomes 18 months after treatment. British Journal of Addiction, 86: 1415–1424.

O'Farrell, T. J. and Fals-Stewart, W. (2001) Family-involved alcoholism treatment: an update. In M. Galanter (ed.), Recent Developments in Alcoholism, Volume 15: Services Research in the Era of Managed Care (pp. 329–356). New York: Plenum Press.

O'Farrell, T. J. and Fals-Stewart, W. (2006) Behavioral Couples Therapy for Alcoholism and Drug Abuse. New York: Guilford Press.

O'Farrell, T. J. and Murphy, C. M. (1995) Marital violence before and after alcoholism treatment. Journal of Consulting and Clinical Psychology, 63: 256–262.

O'Farrell, T. J., Choquette, K. A., Cutter, H. S. G. and Birchler, G. R. (1997) Sexual satisfaction and dysfunction in marriages of male alcoholics: comparison with nonalcoholic maritally conflicted and nonconflicted couples. Journal of Studies on Alcohol, 58: 91–99.

O'Farrell, T. J., Cutter, H. S. G., Choquette, K. A., Floyd, F. J. and Bayog, R. D. (1992) Behavioral marital therapy for male alcoholics: marital and drinking adjustment during the two years after treatment. Behavior Therapy, 23: 529–549.

O'Farrell, T. J., Choquette, K. A., Cutter, H. S. G., Floyd, F. J., Bayog, R. D., Brown, E. D., Lowe, J., Chan, A. and Deneault, P. (1996) Cost-benefit and cost-effectiveness analyses of behavioral marital therapy as an addition to outpatient alcoholism treatment. Journal of Substance Abuse, 8: 145–166.

Powers, M. B., Vedel, E. and Emmelkamp, P. M. G. (in press) Behavioral couples therapy (BCT) for alcohol and drug use disorders: a meta-analysis. Clinical Psychology Review.

Sobell, M. B. and Sobell, L. C. (2000) Stepped care as a heuristic approach to the treatment of alcohol problems. Journal of Consulting and Clinical Psychology, 68: 573–579.

Stanton, M. D. and Shadish, W. R. (1997) Outcome, attrition, and family-couples treatment for drug abuse: a meta-analysis and review of the controlled, comparative studies. Psychological Bulletin, 122: 170–191.

Winters, J., Fals-Stewart, W., O'Farrell, T. J., Birchler, G. R. and Kelley, M. L. (2002) Behavioral couples therapy for female substance-abusing patients: effects on substance use and relationship adjustment. Journal of Consulting and Clinical Psychology, 70: 344–355.

CPSIA information can be obtained at www.ICGtesting.com
Printed in the USA
LVOW02s0838260814

400841LV00009B/49/P

9 781609 277741